PHILIP'S

MODERN SCHOOL ·ATLAS·

CONTENTS

Published in Great Britain in 1996
by George Philip Limited,
an imprint of Reed Books,
Michelin House, 81 Fulham Road, London SW3 6RB,
and Auckland, Melbourne, Singapore and Toronto

Cartography by Philip's

Ninety-first edition

Copyright © 1996 Reed International Books Limited

ISBN 0–540–06348–7 Paperback edition
ISBN 0–540–06349–5 Hardback edition

BRITISH ISLES MAPS

A separate map key is provided on the first page of the World Maps section.

SETTLEMENTS

■ **LONDON**   ■ **GLASGOW**   ▣ **BRADFORD**   ▢ **Brighton**   ◉ Gateshead

◉ Aylesbury   ◎ Sligo   ⊙ Selkirk   ○ Burford   ○ Lampeter

Settlement symbols and type styles vary according to the population and importance of towns

Built up areas   □ London Boroughs

ADMINISTRATION

▬▬▬	International boundaries	**W A L E S**	Country names
─────	National boundaries	KENT	Administrative area names
─·─·─·	Administrative boundaries	*EXMOOR*	National park names

COMMUNICATIONS

Motorways	Main passenger railways
under construction	*under construction*
	in tunnels
Major roads	
under construction	Other passenger railways
in tunnels	*under construction*
	in tunnels
Other important roads	
under construction	Canals
in tunnels	*in tunnels*

⊕ Major airports   ⊕ Other airports

PHYSICAL FEATURES

	Perennial rivers	▲ 444	Elevations in metres
	Tidal flats	△ 1342	Elevations-highest in county (or administrative area) in metres
	Lakes or reservoirs		
	Reservoirs under construction	▾ 38	Depths below sea level in metres

ELEVATION AND DEPTH TINTS

Height of Land above Sea Level	Land below Sea Level	Depth of Sea

in metres	1000	750	500	400	200	100	0							
								150	300	600	1500	3000	6000	in feet
in feet	3000	2250	1500	1200	600	300								
							0	20	50	100	200	500	1000	2000	in metres

2

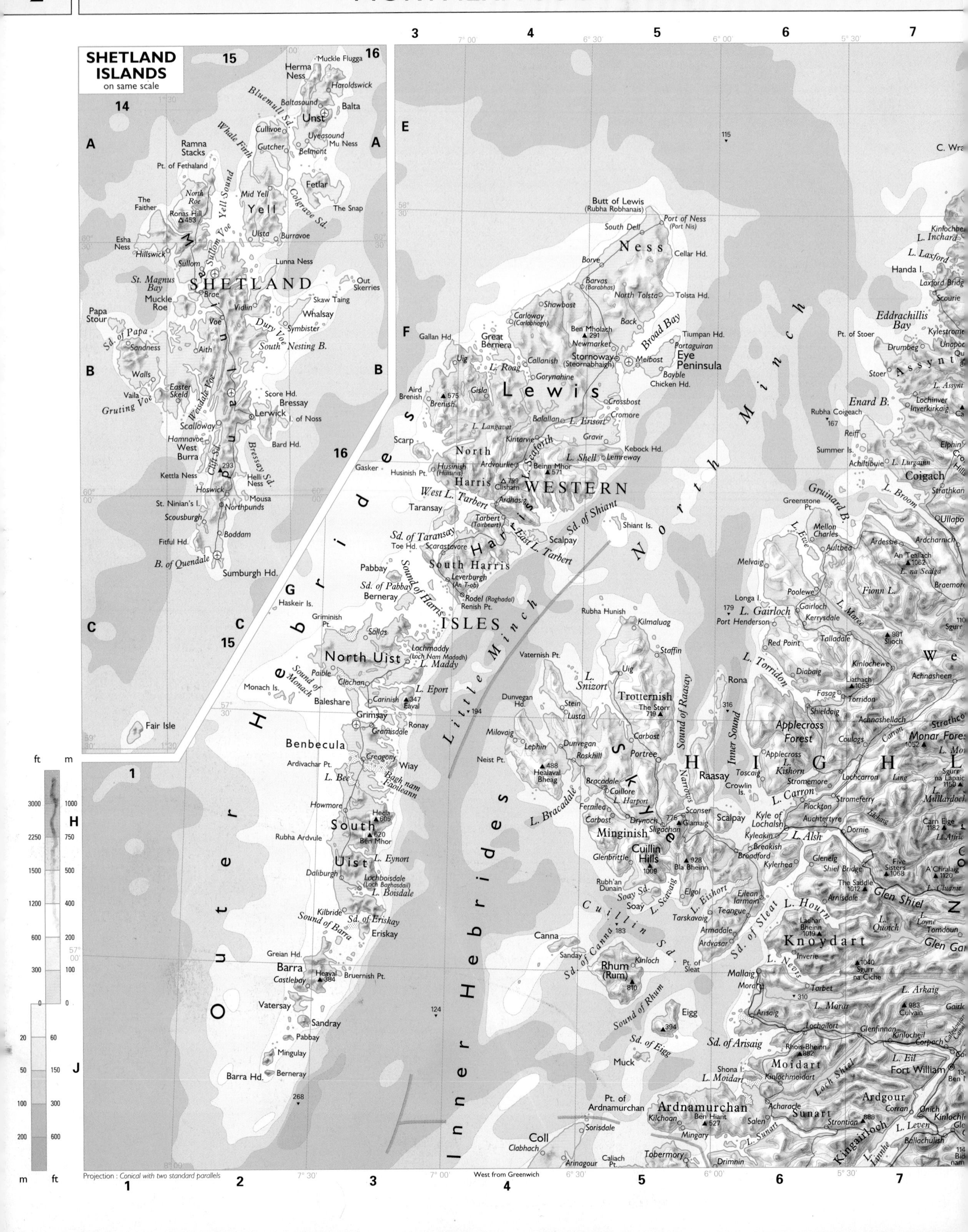

SHETLAND ISLANDS on same scale

15   16

14

A

Muckle Flugga
Herma Ness
Haroldswick
Baltasound   Balta
Bluemull Sd.
Whale Firth   **Unst**
Ramna Stacks   Cullivoe
Pt. of Fethaland   Gutcher   Belmont
Uyeasound
Mu Ness
Fetlar
North Roe   Mid Yell   The Snap
The Faither   Ronas Hill △453
Yell
Esha Ness   Ulsta   Burravoe
Hillswick   Sullom   Lunna Ness
St. Magnus Bay   Brae   Out Skerries
SHETLAND
Papa Stour   Muckle Roe   Vidlin
Voe   Skaw Taing
Sd. of Papa   Sandness   Aith   **Whalsay**
Symbister
Walls   South Nesting B.
Vaila   Easter Skeld   Score Hd.   **Bressay**
Gruting Voe   Scalloway   Lerwick
Hamnavoe   I. of Noss
West Burra   293   Bard Hd.
Kettla Ness   Helli Ness   Mousa
Hoswick
St. Ninian's I.   Northpunds
Scousburgh   Boddam
Fitful Hd.
B. of Quendale   Sumburgh Hd.

B

C

16

15

Fair Isle

1

2

ft   m
3000   1000
2250   750
1500   500
1200   400
600   200
300   100
0   0
20   60
50   150
100   300
200   600
m   ft

H

J

3   **4**   **5**   **6**   **7**

7° 00   6° 30   6° 00   5° 30

E

C. Wra

115

Butt of Lewis (Rubha Robhanais)
Port of Ness (Port Nis)
Kinlochbe
South Dell
Ness   Cellar Hd.   L. Inchard
Borve   L. Laxford
Barvas (Barabhas)   North Tolsta   Tolsta Hd.   Handa I.
Shawbost   Back   Laxford Bridg
Carloway (Carlabhagh)   Ben Mholach ▲291   Broad Bay   Scourie
Gallan Hd.   Tiumpan Hd.   Eddrachillis Bay
Uig   Great Bernera   Newmarket   Portaguiran   Pt. of Stoer   Kylestrome
F   Callanish   Stornoway (Steornabhaigh)   **Eye Peninsula**   Drumbeg   Unapoo
L. Roag   Melbost   Eye   Assynt
Aird   Gisla   **Lewis**   Bayble   Stoer
Brenish   Brenish ▲575   Chicken Hd.   Rubha Coigeach   Enard B.
L. Langavat   Crossbost   167   Lochinver Inverkirkaig
Scarp   Balallan   Cromore   Reiff
Kintarvie   L. Erisort   L. Assynt
Gasker   Husinish Pt.   **North**   Scaforth   Gravir   Summer Is.   L. Lurgainn
Husinish (Husinis)   Beinn Mhor ▲571   L. Shell   Lemreway   Achiltibuie   Coigach
Harris   Clisham ▲799   **WESTERN**   Kebock Hd.   Gruinard B.
West L. Tarbert   Ardhasig   Greenstone Pt.   Strathcan
Taransay   Ardvourlie   Mellon Charles   L. Broom   Ullapo
Tarbert (Tairbeart)   Sd. of Shiant   Aultbea   Ardessie   Ardcharnich
Sd. of Taransay   Shiant Is.   An Teallach ▲1062   Braemo
Toe Hd.   Scarastavore   East L. Tarbert   Scalpay   Melvaig   L. na Sealga
Pabbay   **South Harris**   Fionn L.
Sd. of Pabbay   Leverburgh (An T-ob)   Longa I.   Poolewe
Berneray   Rodel (Roghadal)   L. Gairloch   Gairloch   Kerrysdale
Haskeir Is.   Renish Pt.   Rubha Hunish   179   Port Henderson   Kinlochewe
G   Griminish Pt.   Kilmaluag   Red Point   Talladale   Slioch ▲981
Sollas   Vaternish Pt.   Staffin   Diabaig   Liathach ▲1053   **We**
ISLES   **Trotternish**   Rona   Fasag   Achnasheen
Lochmaddy (Loch Nam Madadh)   Uig   The Storr 719   316   Torridon   Shieldaig   Achnashellach
North Uist   L. Maddy   Dunvegan Hd.   Stein   Sound of Raasay   **Applecross Forest**   Coulags   Monar Fores
Paible   Clachan   Lusta   L. Snizort   Carbost   1052   L. Mo
Monach Is.   L. Eport   347   Milovaig   Portree   Applecross   Stromemore   Sgurr na Lapaich
Carinish   Eaval   Lephin   Dunvegan   Toscaig   Kishorn   1150
Sound of Monach   Baleshare   194   Neist Pt.   Roskhill   Raasay   Lochcarron   Lang
Grimsay   Ronay   Healaval Bheag ▲488   **Skye**   Crowlin Is.   Stromeferry   Carn Eige ▲1182
Gramisdale   Bracadale   Coillore   Sconser   Plockton   L. Millardoch
Benbecula   Wiay   L. Harport   Carbost   Kyle of Lochalsh   Dornie
Ardivachar Pt.   Creagory   Bracadale   Drynoch   726   Glamaig   Scalpay   Auchtertyre   A'Chralaig ▲1120
L. Bee   Bagh nam Faoileann   **Minginish**   Kyleakin   L. Alsh   Five Sisters 1068
Howmore   Hecla ▲605   Glenbrittle   **Cuillin Hills** 1009   Bla Bheinn ▲928   Breakish   Kylerhea   Glenelg   Shiel Bridge   The Saddle 1012   L. Cluanie
Rubha Ardvule   Ben Mhor ▲620   Rubh'an Dunain   Elgol   Broadford   Arnisdale   Glen Shiel
South Uist   L. Eynort   Soay Sd.   L. Eishort   Eilean Iarmain   Ladhar Bheinn ▲1019   L. Quoich
Daliburgh   Soay   Teangue   Glen Ga
Lochboisdale (Loch Boghasdail)   Cuillin Sd.   L. Scavaig   Tarskavaig   **Knoydart**   1040   Glen Garr
L. Boisdale   Armadale   L. Hourn   Sgurr na Ciche
Kilbride   Canna   183   Ardvasar   Inverie
Sd. of Eriskay   Sanday   Pt. of Sleat   Mallaig   L. Arkaig
Sound of Barra   Eriskay   **Rhum (Rum)**   Kinloch   Morar   Culvain ▲983
Greian Hd.   810   310   Tarbet   L. Morar   Gaitle
Barra   Castlebay   Heaval ▲384   Bruernish Pt.   Arisaig   Lochailort   Glenfinnan
Vatersay   Eigg   Kinlocheil   Kinlocheil Corpach
Sandray   Sd. of Eigg   Rhois-Bheinn ▲882   L. Eil
Pabbay   Sd. of Rhum   394   **Moidart**   Kinlochmoidart   Fort William
Mingulay   Berneray   Sd. of Arisaig   Shona I.   L. Moidart
Barra Hd.   Muck   **Ardgour**   Ben
124   268   Pt. of Ardnamurchan   **Ardnamurchan**   Acharacle   Corran   Onich
Ben Hiant ▲527   Salen   **Sunart**   Strontian   888   Kinlochleven
Kilchoan   L. Sunart   L. Leven   Gle
Sorisdale   Mingary   Kingairloch   Ballachulish
Coll   Drimnin   L. Lannhe   Bid
Clabbach   Tobermory   L
Arinagour   Caliach Pt.

Inner Hebrides   **Little Minch**   **North Minch**   **Outer Hebrides**

West from Greenwich

1   **2**   **3**   **4**   **5**   **6**   **7**

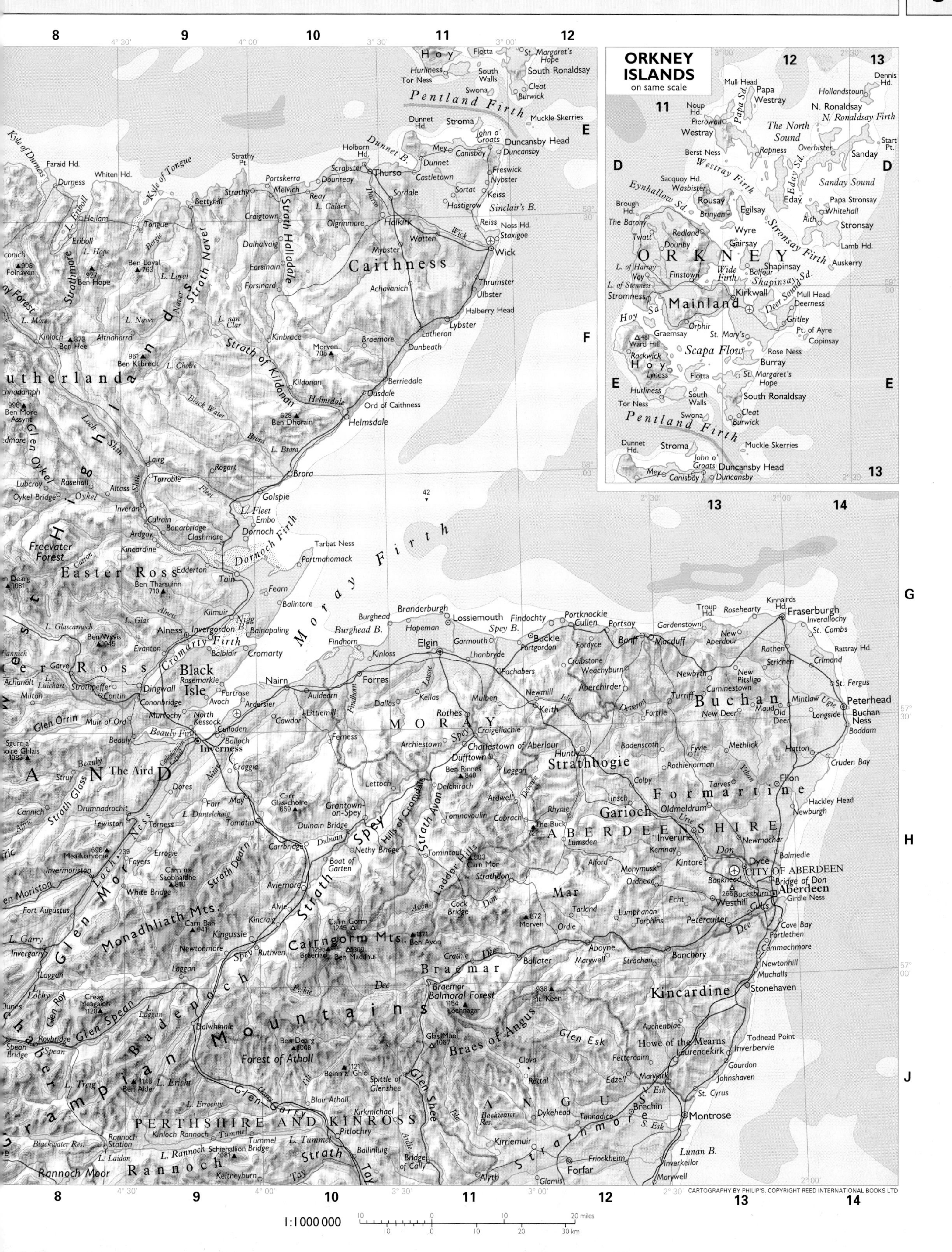

ORKNEY ISLANDS
on same scale

CARTOGRAPHY BY PHILIP'S. COPYRIGHT REED INTERNATIONAL BOOKS LTD

1:1 000 000

20 miles

30 km

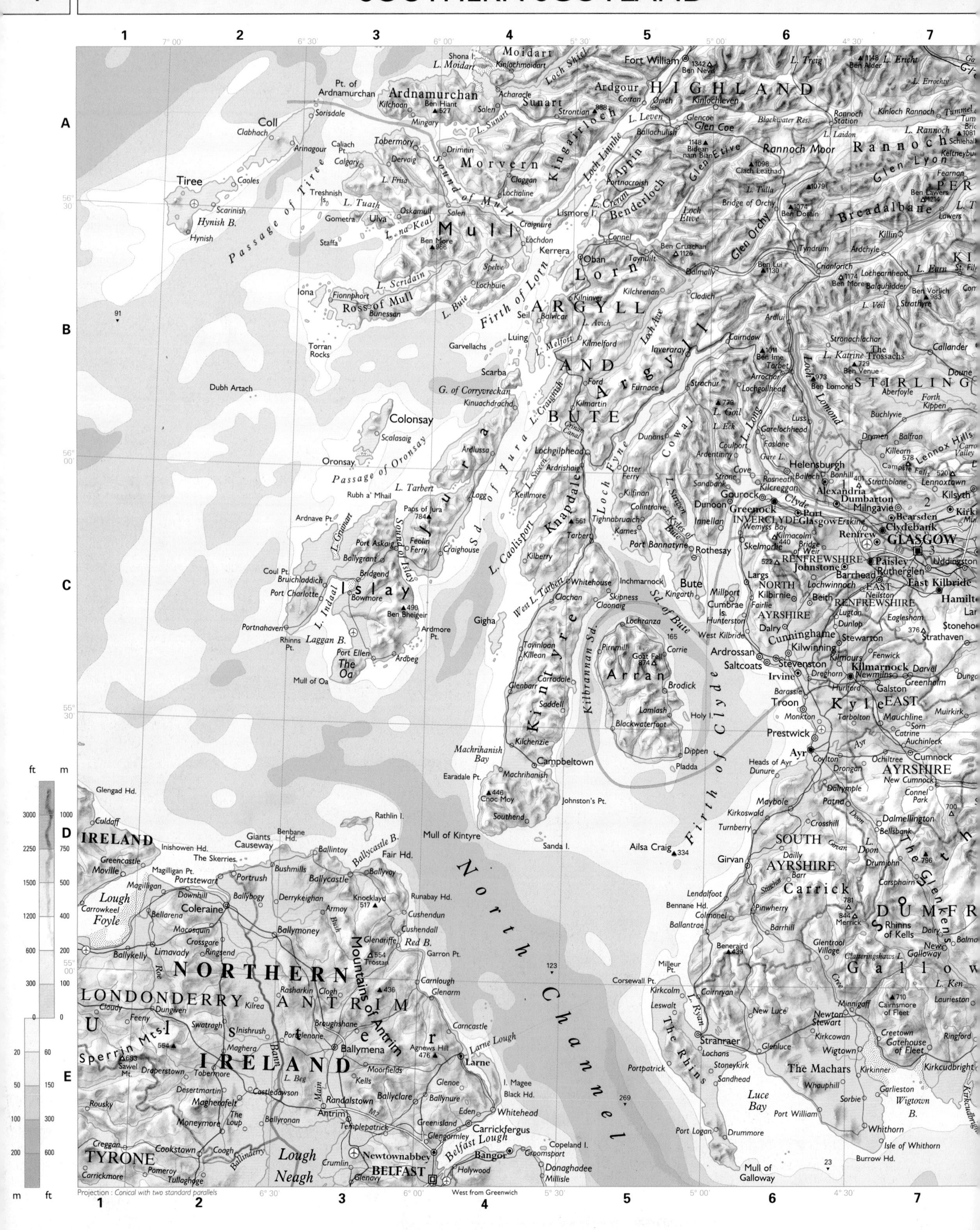

1
2
3
4
5
6
7
A
B
C
D
E
7° 00'
6° 30'
6° 00'
5° 30'
5° 00'
4° 30'
56° 30'
56° 00'
55° 30'
55° 00'
Moidart
Shona I.
L. Moidart
Kinlochmoidart
Loch Shiel
Fort William
Ben Nevis
1342
L. Treig
Ben Alder
1148
L. Ericht
L. Errochty
Pt. of Ardnamurchan
Ardnamurchan
Kilchoan
Ben Hiant
527
Acharacle
Sunart
Ardgour
HIGHLAND
Corran
Onich
Kinlochleven
Strontian
888
Salen
L. Sunart
Mingary
Kingairloch
L. Leven
Glencoe
Glen Coe
Blackwater Res.
Rannoch Station
Kinloch Rannoch
Tummel
L. Laidon
L. Rannoch
1081
Schiehallion
Coll
Sorisdale
Clabhach
Arinagour
Caliach Pt.
Tobermory
Drimnin
Calgary
Dervaig
Morvern
Loch Linnhe
Ballachulish
Appin
1148
Bidean nam Bian
Glen Etive
Rannoch Moor
Rannoch
Glen Lyon
Tiree
Caoles
Passage of Tiree
Treshnish Is.
L. Frisa
Sound of Mull
Claggan
Portnacroish
1098
Clach Leathad
L. Tulla
1079
Fearnan
Ben Lawers
1214
Scarinish
Hynish B.
Hynish
L. Tuath
Gometra
Ulva
Oskamull
Salen
Lochaline
Lismore I.
L. Creran
Benderloch
Loch Etive
Bridge of Orchy
1074
Ben Dorain
Breadalbane
Lawers
Staffa
L. na Keal
Mull
Craignure
Ben More
966
Lochdon
Kerrera
Connel
Ben Cruachan
1126
Glen Orchy
Tyndrum
Killin
Ardchyle
Oban
Taynuilt
L. Spelve
Lorn
Dalmally
Ben Lui
1130
Crianlarich
Lochearnhead
L. Earn
L. Scridain
Lochbuie
Kilchrenan
Ben More
1174
Balquhidder
Ben Vorlich
983
Iona
Fionnphort
Ross of Mull
Bunessan
L. Buie
Firth of Lorn
Kilninver
Cladich
L. Voil
Strathyre
91
Seil
Balvicar
ARGYLL
L. Avich
Ardlui
Luing
Garvellachs
L. Melfort
Kilmelford
Loch Awe
Cairndow
Stronachlachar
The Trossachs
Callander
Torran Rocks
Inveraray
1011
Ben Ime
Tarbet
Loch Lomond
L. Katrine
729
Ben Venue
Doune
AND
Scarba
Ford
Argyll
Arrochar
973
Ben Lomond
STIRLING
Dubh Artach
G. of Corryvreckan
Kinuachdrachd
Kilmartin
Furnace
Strachur
Lochgoilhead
Aberfoyle
Forth
Kippen
779
L. Goil
Colonsay
BUTE
Crinan Canal
L. Eck
L. Long
Buchlyvie
Scalasaig
Ardlussa
Jura
Dunans
Cowal
Luss
Garelochhead
Drymen
Balfron
Faslane
Killearn
Lennox Hills
Oronsay
Passage of Oronsay
Lochgilphead
Coulport
Ardentinny
Gare L.
Helensburgh
578
Campsie Fells
520
Ardrishaig
Otter Ferry
Cove
Strone
Sandbank
Rosneath
Balloch
Bonhill
401
Strathblane
Lennoxtown
Passage of Oronsay
L. Tarbert
Lagg
Keillmore
Knapdale
Loch Fyne
Kilfinan
L. Striven
Kilcreggan
Alexandria
Dumbarton
Kilsyth
Rubh a' Mhail
Sd. of Jura
L. Sween
Colintraive
Dunoon
Gourock
Clyde
Milngavie
Bearsden
Paps of Jura
784
Greenock
Port Glasgow
Erskine
Clydebank
Ardnave Pt.
L. Gruinart
Sound of Islay
561
Tighnabruaich
Kyles of Bute
Innellan
INVERCLYDE
Wemyss Bay
Renfrew
GLASGOW
Port Askaig
Feolin Ferry
Craighouse
L. Caolisport
Tarbert
Kames
Port Bannatyne
Rothesay
Skelmorlie
440
Kilmacolm
Bridge of Weir
Ballygrant
Kilberry
522
RENFREWSHIRE
Paisley
Uddingston
Coul Pt.
Bruichladdich
Bridgend
Johnstone
Barrhead
Rutherglen
Islay
Whitehouse
Inchmarnock
Bute
Largs
NORTH
Lochwinnoch
EAST
East Kilbride
Port Charlotte
Bowmore
Clachan
Kingarth
Millport
Kilbirnie
Beith
Neilston
RENFREWSHIRE
Hamilton
L. Indaal
490
Ben Bheigeir
West L. Tarbert
Skipness
Claonaig
Sd. of Bute
Cumbrae Is.
Fairlie
AYRSHIRE
Lugton
Eaglesham
Portnahaven
Ardmore Pt.
Gigha
Lochranza
Hunterston
Dalry
Dunlop
376
Strathaven
Rhinns Pt.
Laggan B.
Kintyre
165
Pirnmill
Corrie
West Kilbride
Cunninghame
Stewarton
Port Ellen
Tayinloan
Killean
Goat Fell
874
Ardrossan
Kilwinning
Fenwick
The Oa
Ardbeg
Kilbrannan Sd.
Saltcoats
Stevenston
Kilmaurs
Kilmarnock
Darvel
Carradale
Arran
Brodick
Irvine
Dreghorn
Newmilns
Greenholm
Mull of Oa
Glenbarr
Hurlford
Galston
Barassie
EAST
Saddell
Lamlash
Troon
Kyle
Muirkirk
Holy I.
Monkton
Tarbolton
Mauchline
Sorn
Blackwaterfoot
Prestwick
Catrine
Auchinleck
Kilchenzie
Dippen
Ayr
Ayr
Machrihanish Bay
Campbeltown
Pladda
Firth of Clyde
Coylton
Ochiltree
Cumnock
Heads of Ayr
Dunure
Drongan
AYRSHIRE
Eradale Pt.
Machrihanish
New Cumnock
Dalrymple
Connel Park
446
Cnoc Moy
Johnston's Pt.
Maybole
Patna
Glengad Hd.
Southend
Kirkoswald
Doon
Dalmellington
Culdaff
Rathlin I.
Crosshill
Bellsbank
IRELAND
Giants Causeway
Benbane Hd.
Mull of Kintyre
Sanda I.
Ailsa Craig
334
Turnberry
SOUTH
L. Doon
Inishowen Hd.
Ballintoy
Ballycastle B.
Fair Hd.
Girvan
Dailly
AYRSHIRE
Dalmellington
796
Greencastle
The Skerries
Bushmills
Ballycastle
Ballyvoy
Barr
Drumjohn
The Glenkens
Moville
Magilligan Pt.
Portstewart
Portrush
North Channel
Carrick
Carsphairn
Lough Foyle
Magilligan
Downhill
Ballybogy
Derrykeighan
Knocklayd
517
Runabay Hd.
Lendalfoot
781
Carrowkeel
Bellarena
Coleraine
Armoy
Cushendun
Bennane Hd.
Colmonel
Pinwherry
844
Merrick
DUMFR
Macosquin
Ballymoney
Bush
Cushendall
Ballantrae
Barrhill
Rhinns of Kells
Dalry
Crossgare
Ringsend
Glenariff
Red B.
Beneraird
439
Glentrool Village
New Galloway
Balmaclellan
Ballykelly
Limavady
554
Trostan
Garron Pt.
Milleur Pt.
Clatteringshaws L.
NORTHERN
Mountains of Antrim
123
Corsewall Pt.
Galloway
Roe
Carnlough
Glenarm
Kirkcolm
Cairnryan
Cree
L. Ken
LONDONDERRY
Kilrea
Rasharkin
Clogh
436
ANTRIM
Leswalt
L. Ryan
New Luce
Minnigaff
710
Cairnsmore of Fleet
Laurieston
Claudy
Dungiven
Feeny
Swatragh
Broughshane
Carncastle
The Rhins
Newton Stewart
Creetown
Ulster
Sperrin Mts.
Inishrush
Portglenone
Larne Lough
Stranraer
Glenluce
Kirkcowan
Gatehouse of Fleet
Ringford
584
Maghera
Ballymena
Agnews Hill
476
Larne
Lochans
Wigtown
Kirkcudbright
683
Sawel Mt.
Draperstown
Tobermore
IRELAND
L. Beg
Moorfields
Stoneykirk
The Machars
Kirkinner
Bann
Kells
Glenoe
I. Magee
Portpatrick
Sandhead
Whauphill
Garlieston
Desertmartin
Castledawson
Main
Ballynure
Black Hd.
Luce Bay
Sorbie
Wigtown B.
Rousky
Magherafelt
Randalstown
Ballyclare
269
Port William
Moneymore
The Loup
Antrim
Eden
Whitehead
Ballyronan
Templepatrick
Greenisland
Carrickfergus
Port Logan
Drummore
Whithorn
Creggan
Glengormley
Belfast Lough
Copeland I.
Isle of Whithorn
Cookstown
Coagh
Ballinderry
Lough Neagh
Crumlin
Newtownabbey
Bangor
Groomsport
23
Burrow Hd.
TYRONE
Pomeroy
Donaghadee
Mull of Galloway
Carrickmore
Tullaghoge
Glenavy
BELFAST
Holywood
Millisle
M2
ft
m
3000
2250
1500
1200
600
300
0
1000
750
500
400
200
100
0
20
50
100
200
60
150
300
600
m
ft
Projection : Conical with two standard parallels
West from Greenwich

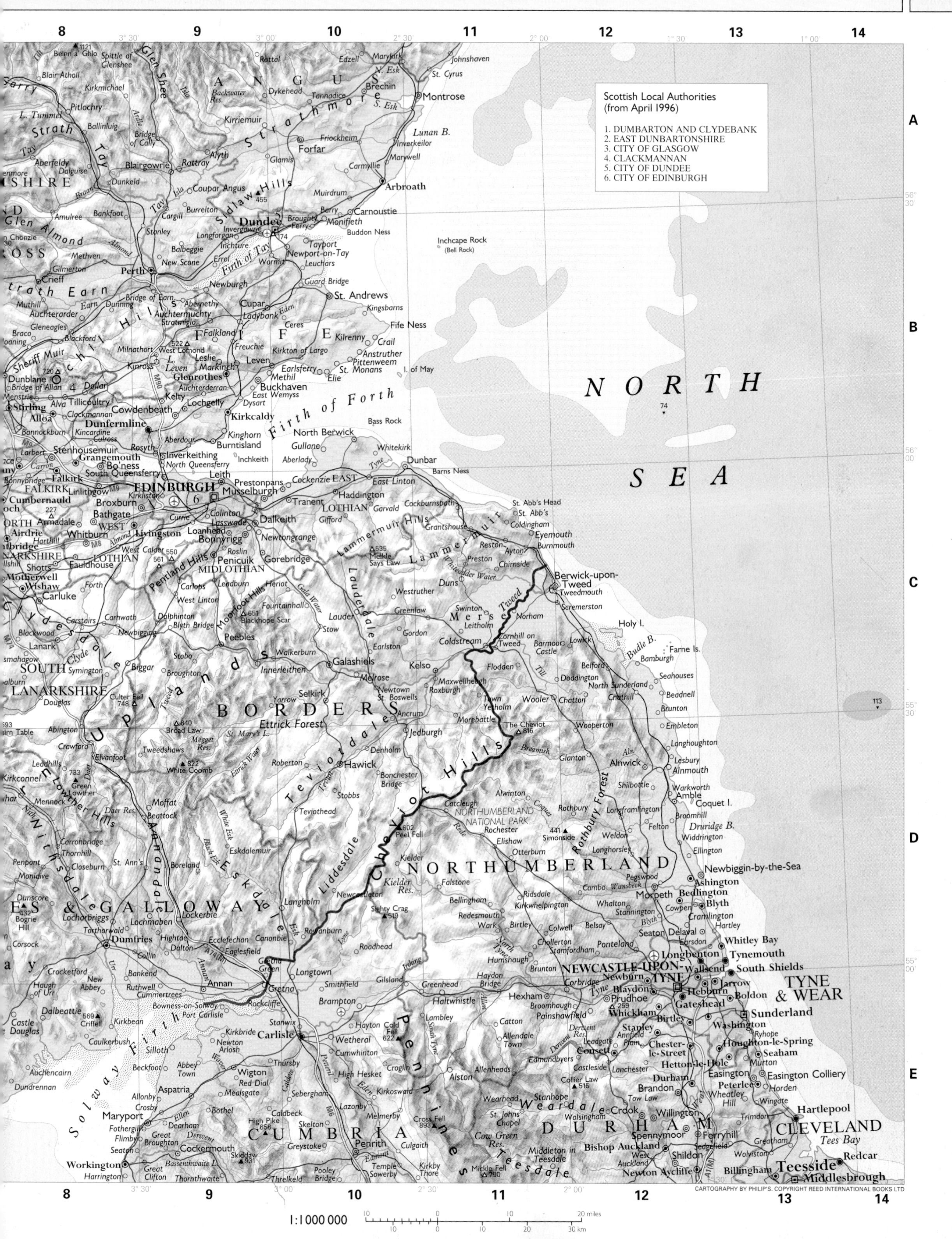
Scottish Local Authorities
(from April 1996)
1. DUMBARTON AND CLYDEBANK
2. EAST DUNBARTONSHIRE
3. CITY OF GLASGOW
4. CLACKMANNAN
5. CITY OF DUNDEE
6. CITY OF EDINBURGH
NORTH SEA
ANGUS
FIFE
BORDERS
NORTHUMBERLAND
DURHAM
CUMBRIA
CLEVELAND
TYNE & WEAR
EDINBURGH
NEWCASTLE-UPON-TYNE
Firth of Forth
Firth of Tay
Solway Firth
Cheviot Hills
Pennines
1:1 000 000
CARTOGRAPHY BY PHILIP'S. COPYRIGHT REED INTERNATIONAL BOOKS LTD

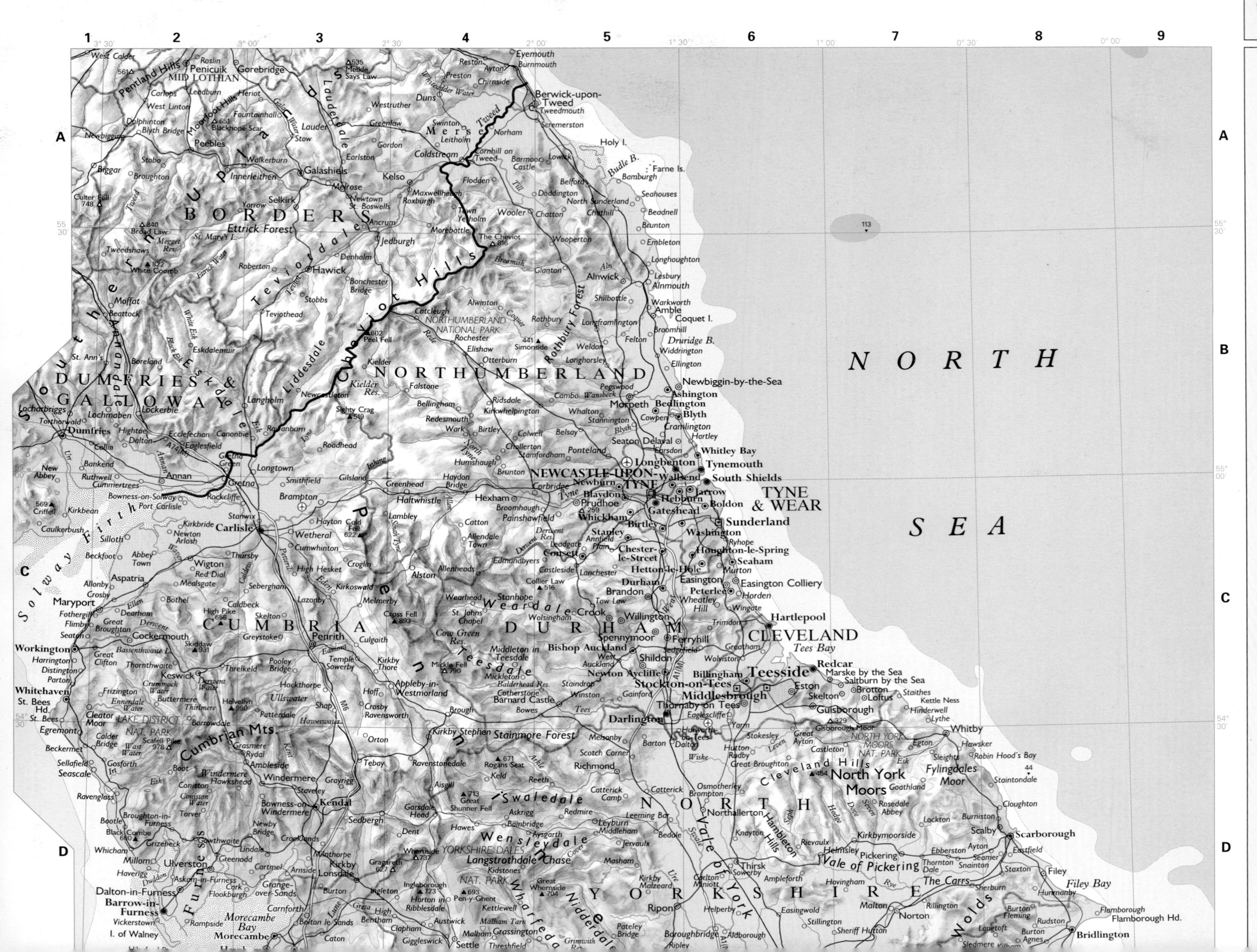
NORTH SEA
NORTHUMBERLAND
TYNE & WEAR
DURHAM
CLEVELAND
CUMBRIA
NORTH YORKSHIRE
BORDERS
DUMFRIES & GALLOWAY
MID LOTHIAN
Southern Uplands
Pennines
Solway Firth
Cheviot Hills
Cumbrian Mts
North York Moors
Cleveland Hills
Hambleton Hills
Vale of York
Vale of Pickering
Wolds
Morecambe Bay
NEWCASTLE-UPON-TYNE
Sunderland
Middlesbrough
Teesside
Hartlepool
Darlington
Carlisle
Scarborough
Berwick-upon-Tweed
Dumfries
Kendal
Whitby
Bridlington
Flamborough Hd.
Filey Bay
Tees Bay
Teesdale
Weardale
Swaledale
Wensleydale
Wharfedale
Nidderdale
Liddesdale
Teviotdale
Lauderdale
Eskdale
Kielder Res.
Holy I.
Farne Is.
Coquet I.
Rothbury Forest
Ettrick Forest
Stainmore Forest
Langstrothdale Chase
Fylingdales Moor
The Carrs
NORTHUMBERLAND NATIONAL PARK
YORKSHIRE DALES NAT. PARK
LAKE DISTRICT NAT. PARK
NORTH YORK MOORS NAT. PARK
M6
A
B
C
D
1
2
3
4
5
6
7
8
9

1:1 000 000

Projection : Conical with two standard parallels

West from Greenwich

CARTOGRAPHY BY PHILIP'S. COPYRIGHT REED INTERNATIONAL BOOKS LTD.

See page 10 for key to Welsh Unitary Authorities.

Projection : Conical with two standard parallels   West from Greenwich

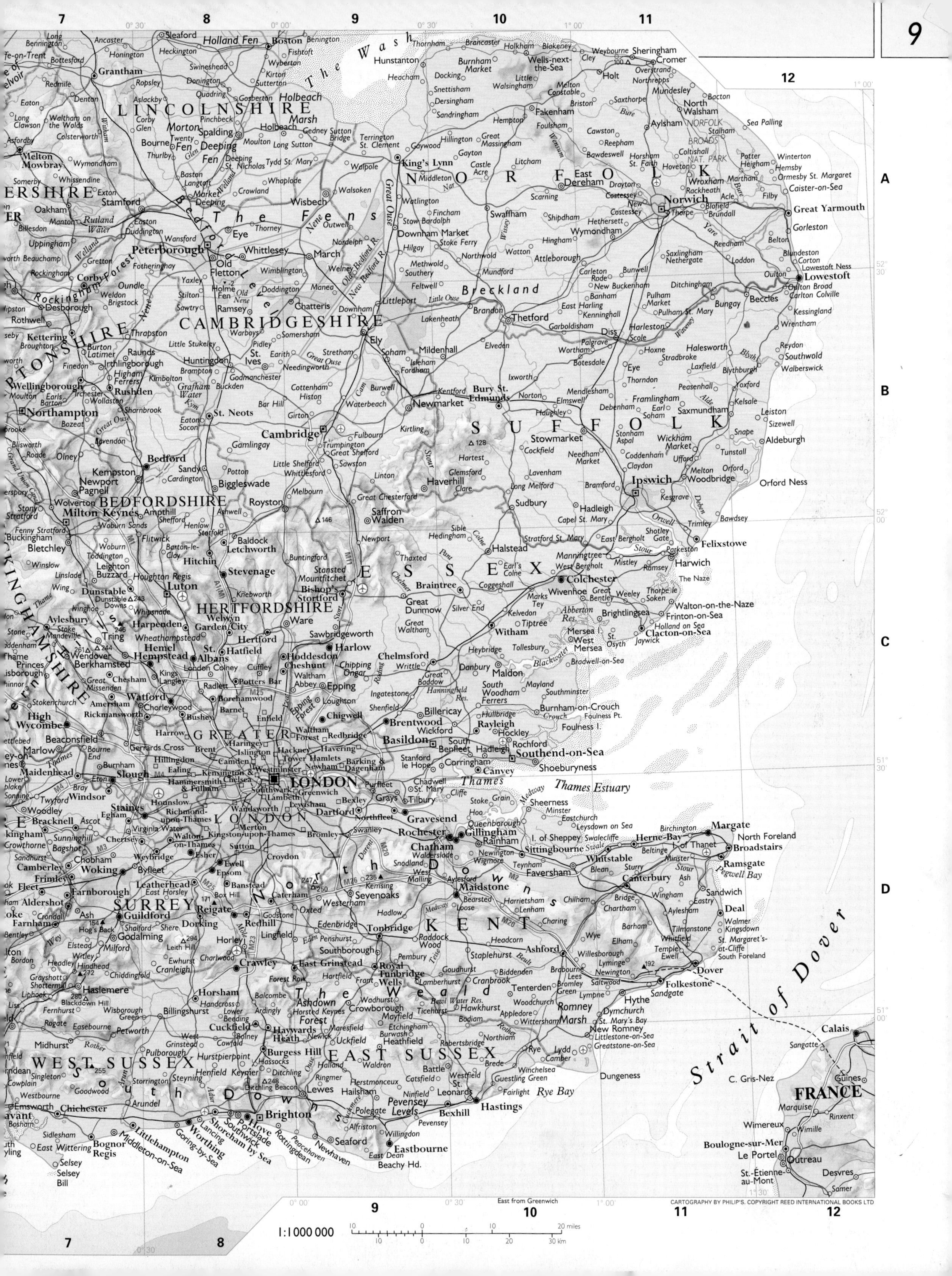
7
8
9
10
11
12
0° 30'
0° 00'
1° 00'
52° 30'
52° 00'
51° 30'
51° 00'
1° 30'
A
B
C
D
The Wash
Holland Fen
Boston
Grantham
LINCOLNSHIRE
Holbeach Marsh
Spalding
Sheringham
Cromer
Hunstanton
Burnham Market
Wells-next-the-Sea
Holt
North Walsham
Fakenham
Aylsham
NORFOLK BROADS NAT. PARK
King's Lynn
NORFOLK
East Dereham
Norwich
Great Yarmouth
Gorleston
Swaffham
Wymondham
Downham Market
Lowestoft
Beccles
Thetford
Breckland
Diss
Southwold
Stamford
Oakham
Rutland Water
Peterborough
The Fens
Whittlesey
March
Wisbech
Ely
CAMBRIDGESHIRE
Huntingdon
St. Ives
Newmarket
Bury St. Edmunds
SUFFOLK
Stowmarket
Ipswich
Woodbridge
Aldeburgh
Orford Ness
Felixstowe
Harwich
Cambridge
Haverhill
Sudbury
Bedford
Northampton
Kettering
Wellingborough
Corby
St. Neots
BEDFORDSHIRE
Milton Keynes
Luton
Stevenage
Hitchin
Royston
Saffron Walden
ESSEX
Colchester
Braintree
Chelmsford
Clacton-on-Sea
Walton-on-the-Naze
Maldon
HERTFORDSHIRE
Hertford
St. Albans
Harlow
Watford
Aylesbury
High Wycombe
Southend-on-Sea
Basildon
Brentwood
GREATER LONDON
LONDON
Thames
Thames Estuary
Slough
Windsor
Maidenhead
Reading
Gravesend
Dartford
Rochester
Chatham
Gillingham
Sheerness
Margate
Broadstairs
Ramsgate
Canterbury
Whitstable
Herne Bay
North Foreland
Sandwich
Deal
Dover
Folkestone
Maidstone
North Downs
Sevenoaks
Tonbridge
KENT
Ashford
Royal Tunbridge Wells
The Weald
Guildford
SURREY
Woking
Reigate
Crawley
Horsham
East Grinstead
Ashdown Forest
WEST SUSSEX
EAST SUSSEX
South Downs
Chichester
Worthing
Brighton
Lewes
Eastbourne
Beachy Hd.
Hastings
Bexhill
Rye
Rye Bay
Romney Marsh
Dungeness
Strait of Dover
Calais
C. Gris-Nez
FRANCE
Boulogne-sur-Mer
East from Greenwich
CARTOGRAPHY BY PHILIP'S. COPYRIGHT REED INTERNATIONAL BOOKS LTD
1:1 000 000
20 miles
30 km

Welsh Unitary Authorities
(from April 1996)

1. MERTHYR TYDFIL
2. BLAENAU GWENT
3. CARDIFF
4. NEWPORT
5. TORFAEN

CHANNEL ISLANDS
on same scale

FRANCE

Passage de la Déroute

Alderney · St. Anne
C. de la Hague
Les Pieux
Barneville-Carteret
Carteret
Grosnez Pt.
St. Ouens Bay
St. Brelade
Jersey
Trinity
Rozel
St. Martin
Gorey
la Rocque Pt.
St. Peter
St. Helier
St. Sampson
St. Peter Port
St. Martin
Guernsey
Herm
Sark
Torteval

CARTOGRAPHY BY PHILIP'S. COPYRIGHT REED INTERNATIONAL BOOKS LTD

SCILLY ISLES
on same scale

Isles of Scilly
Tresco · St. Martin's
Bryher
Hugh Town · St. Mary's
Broad Sd. · St. Mary's Sd.
Crow Sound
St. Agnes

Gurnard's Hd. · Pendeen · 252 · Penzance
C. Cornwall · St. Just · Newlyn · St. Buryan
Sennen · Land's End · St. Levan
Wolf Rock

AVON
SOMERSET
DORSET
DEVON
CORNWALL
GLAMORGAN

Bristol Channel

Bristol Channel

Barnstaple or Bideford Bay

Lyme Bay

Bridgwater Bay

EXMOOR NATIONAL PARK

DARTMOOR NATIONAL PARK

BRISTOL
CARDIFF
NEWPORT
Bath
Keynsham
Weston-super-Mare
Bridgwater
Taunton
Yeovil
Dorchester
Weymouth
Exeter
Barnstaple
Bideford
Plymouth
Torquay · Torbay · Paignton · Brixham
Newton Abbot
Dawlish
Teignmouth
Exmouth
Sidmouth
Honiton
Bridport
Truro
Falmouth
Helston
Penzance
Newquay
St. Austell
Bodmin
Launceston
Bude
Redruth · Camborne
St. Ives
Land's End
Lizard Pt.

Mendip Hills
Quantock Hills
Blackdown Hills
Brendon Hills
Polden Hills
North Dorset Downs
South Dorset Downs
Blackmoor Vale
Dunkery Beacon 520
High Willhays 621
Yes Tor 619

Portland Bill
I. of Portland

West from Greenwich

Projection: Conical with two standard parallels

1:1 000 000

20 miles
30 km

m / ft elevation scale: 3000 2250 1500 1200 900 600 300 0 / 1000 750 500 400 300 200 100 0

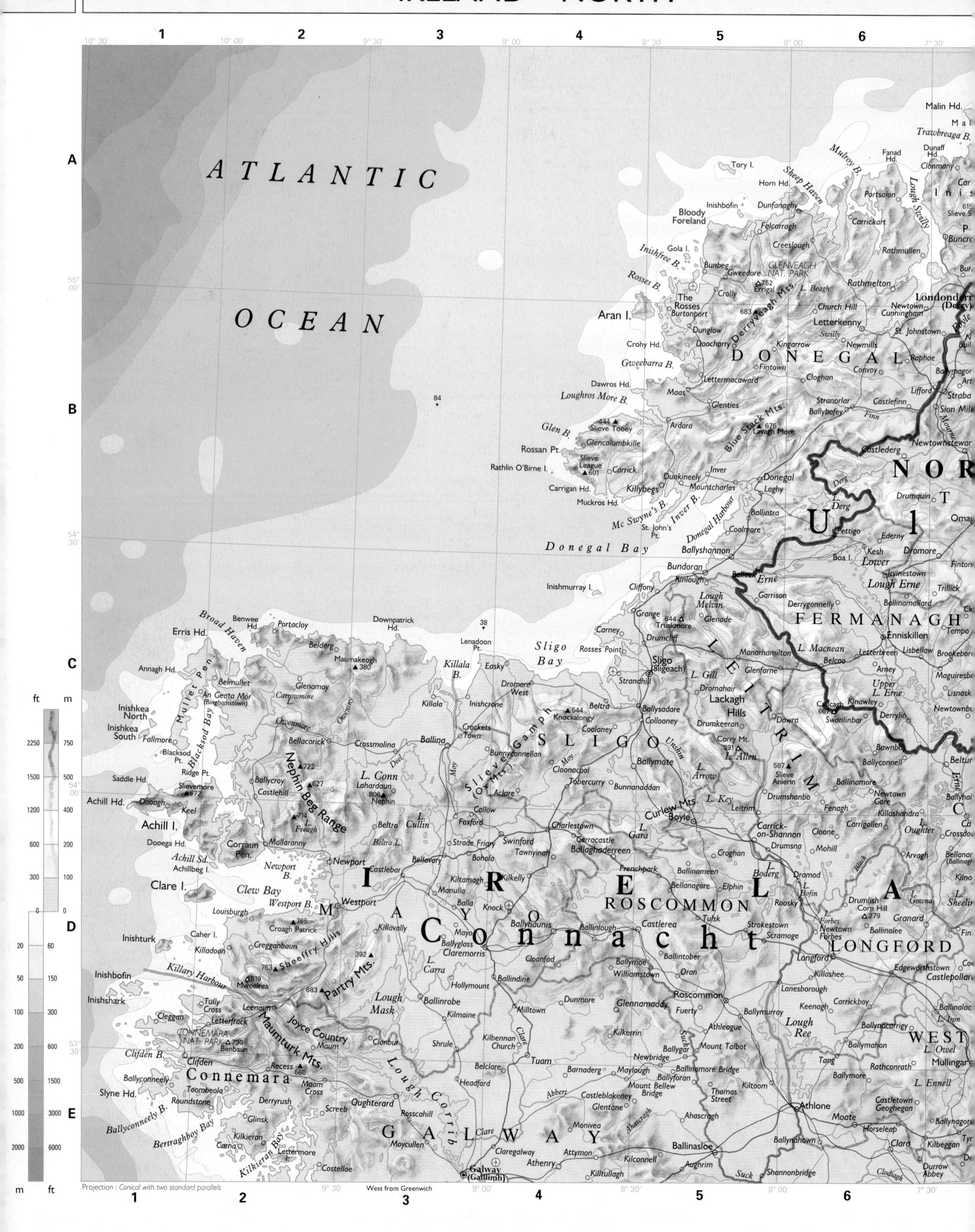
ATLANTIC OCEAN
Donegal Bay
DONEGAL
SLIGO
LEITRIM
FERMANAGH
ROSCOMMON
LONGFORD
MAYO
GALWAY
IRELAND
Connacht
Connemara
Sligo Bay
Clew Bay
Lough Mask
Lough Corrib
Achill I.
Clare I.
Aran I.
Projection : Conical with two standard parallels
West from Greenwich

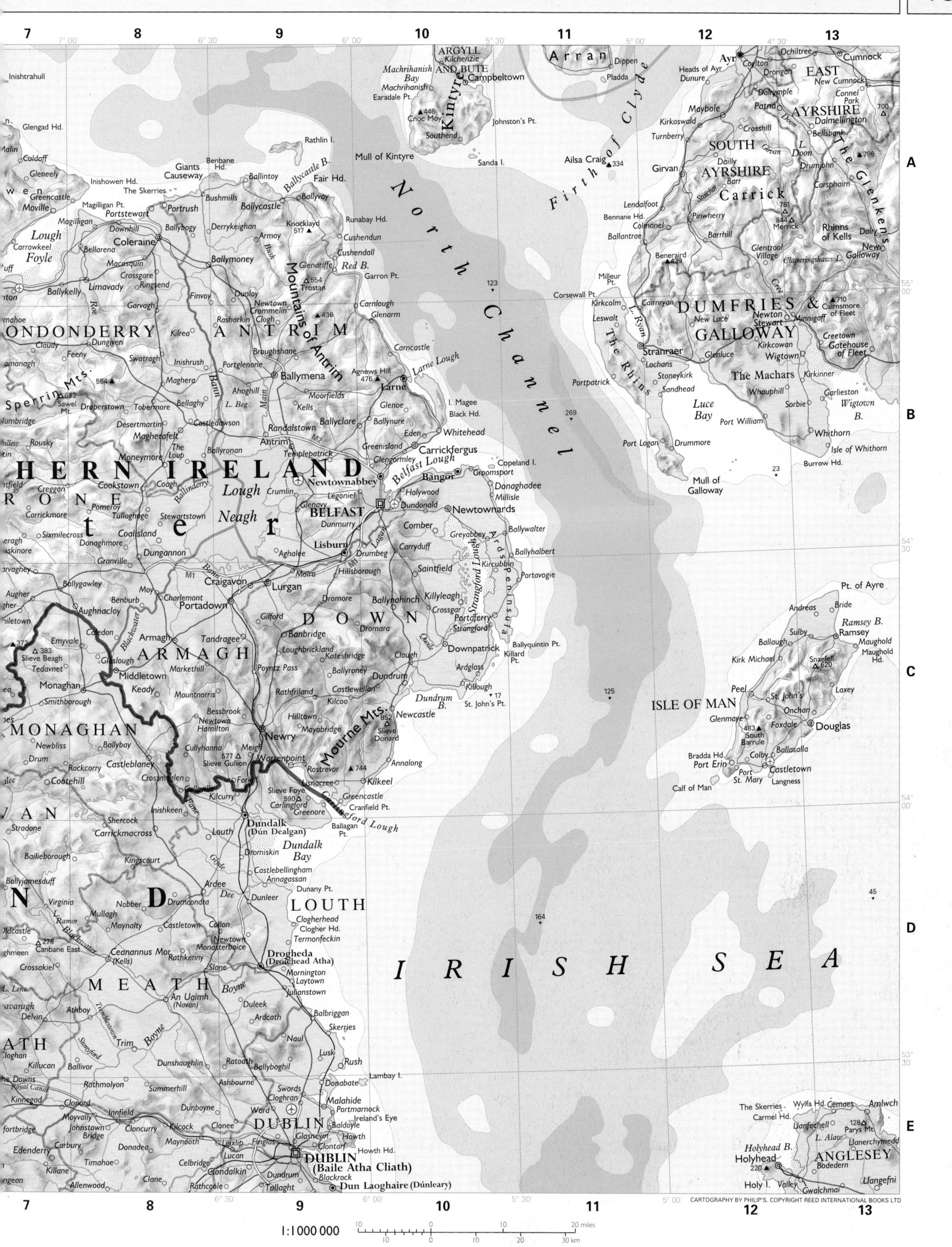

NORTHERN IRELAND
Ulster
ANTRIM
LONDONDERRY
TYRONE
ARMAGH
DOWN
MONAGHAN
LOUTH
MEATH
ARGYLL AND BUTE
EAST AYRSHIRE
SOUTH AYRSHIRE
DUMFRIES & GALLOWAY
ISLE OF MAN
ANGLESEY
North Channel
IRISH SEA
Firth of Clyde
Kintyre
Arran
Carrick
The Machars
The Rhins
Mountains of Antrim
Mourne Mts.
Sperrin Mts.
Ards Peninsula
Lough Neagh
Lough Foyle
Strangford Lough
Belfast Lough
Larne Lough
Carlingford Lough
Dundalk Bay
Luce Bay
Wigtown B.
Ballycastle B.
Red B.
Dundrum B.
Holyhead B.
Ramsey B.
Inishtrahull
Glengad Hd.
Culdaff
Gleneely
Inishowen Hd.
Greencastle
Moville
Magilligan Pt.
Magilligan
Portstewart
Portrush
Giants Causeway
Benbane Hd.
The Skerries
Bushmills
Ballintoy
Ballycastle
Fair Hd.
Ballyvoy
Rathlin I.
Mull of Kintyre
Knocklayd
Runabay Hd.
Cushendun
Cushendall
Glenariffe
Trostan
Garron Pt.
Carnlough
Glenarm
Carncastle
Coleraine
Downhill
Bellarena
Carrowkeel
Macosquin
Ballymoney
Ballybogy
Derrykeighan
Armoy
Limavady
Ballykelly
Crossgare
Ringsend
Garvagh
Finvoy
Dunloy
Newtown Crommelin
Clogh
Rasharkin
Kilrea
Claudy
Dungiven
Feeny
Swatragh
Inishrush
Portglenone
Broughshane
Ballymena
Agnews Hill
Larne
Maghera
Ahoghill
Sawel Mt.
Draperstown
Tobermore
Bellaghy
L. Beg
Kells
Moorfields
Glenoe
Ballynure
Ballyclare
Desertmartin
Magherafelt
Castledawson
Randalstown
Antrim
Templepatrick
Eden
Whitehead
I. Magee
Black Hd.
Greenisland
Carrickfergus
Glengormley
Newtownabbey
Moneymore
The Loup
Ballyronan
Cookstown
Coagh
Crumlin
Copeland I.
Groomsport
Bangor
Donaghadee
Millisle
Holywood
Dundonald
Newtownards
BELFAST
Dunmurry
Comber
Greyabbey
Ballywalter
Ballyhalbert
Kircubbin
Portavogie
Lisburn
Drumbeg
Carryduff
Aghalee
Moira
Hillsborough
Saintfield
Creggan
Pomeroy
Carrickmore
Tullaghoge
Stewartstown
Sixmilecross
Coalisland
Donaghmore
Dungannon
Granville
Ballygawley
Augher
Aughnacloy
Moy
Benburb
Charlemont
Craigavon
Portadown
Lurgan
Dromore
Ballynahinch
Killyleagh
Crossgar
Portaferry
Strangford
Gilford
Banbridge
Dromara
Loughbrickland
Katesbridge
Downpatrick
Ballyquintin Pt.
Killard Pt.
Caledon
Emyvale
Slieve Beagh
Tedavnet
Armagh
Tandragee
Glaslough
Middletown
Markethill
Poyntz Pass
Clough
Ballyroney
Dundrum
Ardglass
Killough
St. John's Pt.
Monaghan
Keady
Smithborough
Mountnorris
Rathfriland
Castlewellan
Kilcoo
Bessbrook
Newtown Hamilton
Hilltown
Mayobridge
Newcastle
Slieve Donard
Newry
Meigh
Warrenpoint
Rostrevor
Annalong
Kilkeel
Newbliss
Ballybay
Drum
Rockcorry
Castleblaney
Cullyhanna
Slieve Gullion
Crossmaglen
Cullaville
Forkhill
Kilcurry
Slieve Foye
Carlingford
Greenore
Greencastle
Cranfield Pt.
Cootehill
Inishkeen
Dundalk (Dún Dealgan)
Ballagan Pt.
Shercock
Carrickmacross
Stradone
Louth
Bailieborough
Kingscourt
Dromiskin
Castlebellingham
Annagassan
Dunany Pt.
Ballyjamesduff
Ardee
Dunleer
Virginia
Nobber
Drumconrath
Mullagh
Moynalty
Castletown
Collon
Clogherhead
Clogher Hd.
Termonfeckin
Newtown Monasterboice
Canbane East
Ceanannus Mor (Kells)
Rathkenny
Drogheda (Droichead Atha)
Slane
Mornington
Laytown
Julianstown
Crossakiel
An Uaimh (Navan)
Duleek
Ardcath
Athboy
Delvin
Balbriggan
Skerries
Trim
Naul
Lusk
Rush
Killucan
Ballivor
Dunshaughlin
Ratoath
Ballyboghil
Lambay I.
Rathmolyon
Summerhill
Ashbourne
Swords
Donabate
Kinnegad
Clonard
Dunboyne
Cloghran
Malahide
Portmarnock
Ireland's Eye
Moyvally
Innfield
Clonee
Ward
Johnstown Bridge
Kilcock
Clonclurry
DUBLIN
Baldoyle
Howth
Glasnevin
Clontarf
Maynooth
Leixlip
Finglas
Howth Hd.
Edenderry
Carbury
Donadea
Lucan
DUBLIN (Baile Atha Cliath)
Timahoe
Celbridge
Clondalkin
Dundrum
Blackrock
Killane
Allenwood
Clane
Rathcoole
Tallaght
Dun Laoghaire (Dúnleary)
Kilchenzie
Machrihanish Bay
Machrihanish
Campbeltown
Earadale Pt.
Cnoc Moy
Southend
Johnston's Pt.
Sanda I.
Dippen
Pladda
Ailsa Craig
Ayr
Coylton
Ochiltree
Cumnock
Heads of Ayr
Dunure
Drongan
New Cumnock
Dalrymple
Connel Park
Maybole
Patna
Dalmellington
Kirkoswald
Crosshill
Bellsbank
Turnberry
Girvan
Doon
L. Doon
Drumjohn
The Glenkens
Dailly
Barr
Carsphairn
Lendalfoot
Bennane Hd.
Pinwherry
Merrick
Colmonel
Ballantrae
Barrhill
Rhinns of Kells
Dalry
Glentrool Village
New Galloway
Clatteringshaws L.
Benerairrd
Milleur Pt.
Corsewall Pt.
Kirkcolm
Cairnryan
L. Ryan
Cairnsmore of Fleet
Leswalt
New Luce
Newton Stewart
Minnigaff
Stranraer
Glenluce
Kirkcowan
Creetown
Gatehouse of Fleet
Lochans
Wigtown
Portpatrick
Stoneykirk
Sandhead
Kirkinner
Whauphill
Garlieston
Sorbie
Port William
Whithorn
Port Logan
Drummore
Isle of Whithorn
Burrow Hd.
Mull of Galloway
Pt. of Ayre
Andreas
Bride
Ramsey
Sulby
Maughold
Maughold Hd.
Ballaugh
Kirk Michael
Snaefell
Peel
St. John's
Laxey
Onchan
Glenmaye
South Barrule
Foxdale
Douglas
Bradda Hd.
Port Erin
Colby
Ballasalla
Port St. Mary
Castletown
Calf of Man
Langness
The Skerries
Wylfa Hd.
Cemaes
Amlwch
Carmel Hd.
Llanfechell
Parys Mt.
L. Alaw
Llanerchymedd
Holyhead
Bodedern
Holy I.
Valley
Gwalchmai
Llangefni
M1
M2
7
8
9
10
11
12
13
A
B
C
D
E
7° 00′
6° 30′
6° 00′
5° 30′
5° 00′
4° 30′
55° 00′
54° 30′
54° 00′
53° 30′
1:1 000 000
20 miles
30 km

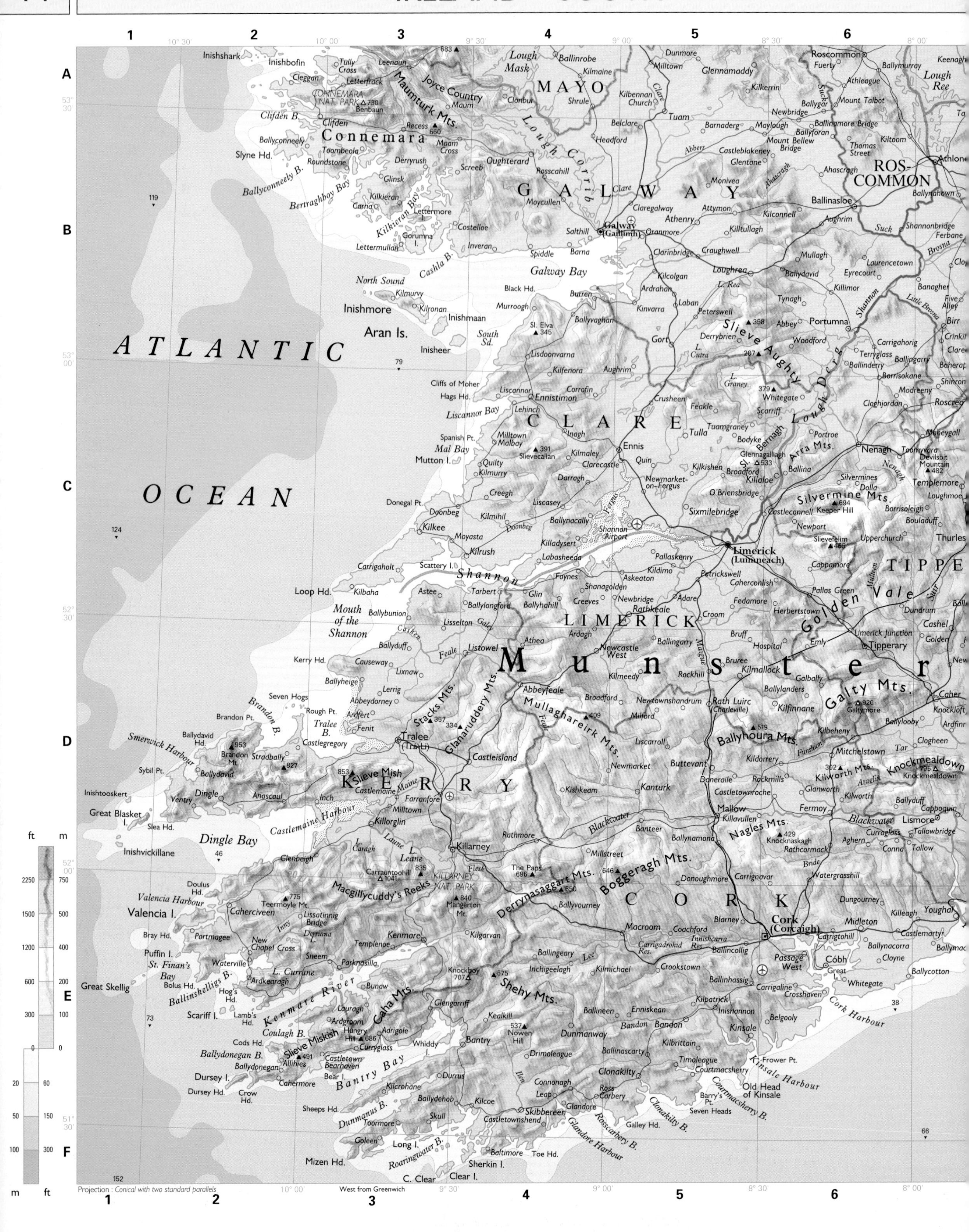
ATLANTIC
OCEAN
Munster
MAYO
GALWAY
ROS-
COMMON
CLARE
LIMERICK
KERRY
CORK
TIPPE
Connemara
Joyce Country
Maumturk Mts.
Lough Corrib
Lough Mask
Lough Ree
Lough Derg
Galway Bay
Aran Is.
Inishmore
Inishmaan
Inisheer
North Sound
South Sd.
Slieve Aughty
Silvermine Mts.
Golden Vale
Galty Mts.
Ballyhoura Mts.
Mullaghareirk Mts.
Glanaruddery Mts.
Stacks Mts.
Slieve Mish
Macgillycuddy's Reeks
Derrynasaggart Mts.
Boggeragh Mts.
Nagles Mts.
Knockmealdown
Shehy Mts.
Caha Mts.
Slieve Miskish
Kilworth Mts.
Arra Mts.
Shannon
Mouth of the Shannon
Blackwater
Kenmare River
Bantry Bay
Dingle Bay
Castlemaine Harbour
Tralee B.
Brandon B.
Smerwick Harbour
Valencia Harbour
Ballinskelligs B.
Dunmanus B.
Roaringwater B.
Clonakilty B.
Rosscarbery B.
Glandore Harbour
Courtmacsherry B.
Kinsale Harbour
Cork Harbour
Liscannor Bay
Mal Bay
Limerick (Luimneach)
Galway (Gaillimh)
Cork (Corcaigh)
Tralee (Trá Lí)
Shannon Airport
Ennis
Killarney
Tipperary
Mallow
Bantry
Kinsale
Youghal
Clonakilty
Skibbereen
Dingle
Kenmare
Listowel
Newcastle West
Nenagh
Thurles
Athlone
Tuam
Athenry
Loughrea
Ballinasloe
Roscommon
Kilrush
Kilkee
Fermoy
Mitchelstown
Macroom
Dunmanway
Cobh
Midleton
Charleville
Great Skellig
Valencia I.
Great Blasket I.
Mizen Hd.
Cape Clear
Sherkin I.
Clear I.
Dursey I.
Loop Hd.
Kerry Hd.
Cliffs of Moher
Old Head of Kinsale
Slyne Hd.
Projection : Conical with two standard parallels
West from Greenwich
10° 30'
10° 00'
9° 30'
9° 00'
8° 30'
8° 00'
53° 30'
53° 00'
52° 30'
52° 00'
51° 30'
ft
m
2250
750
1500
500
1200
400
600
200
300
100
0
20
60
50
150
100
300

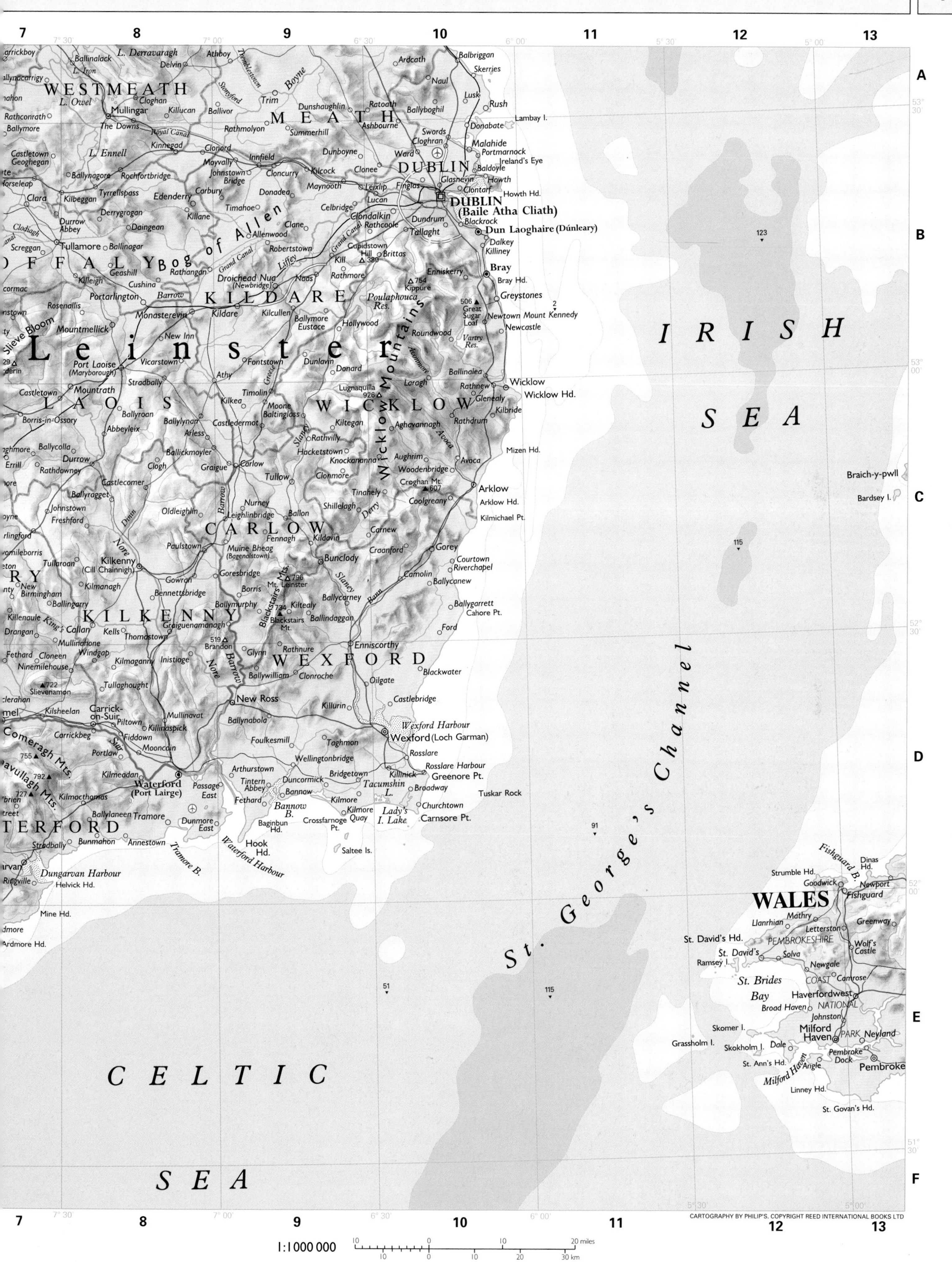

1:1 000 000

10   0   10   20 miles
10   0   10   20   30 km

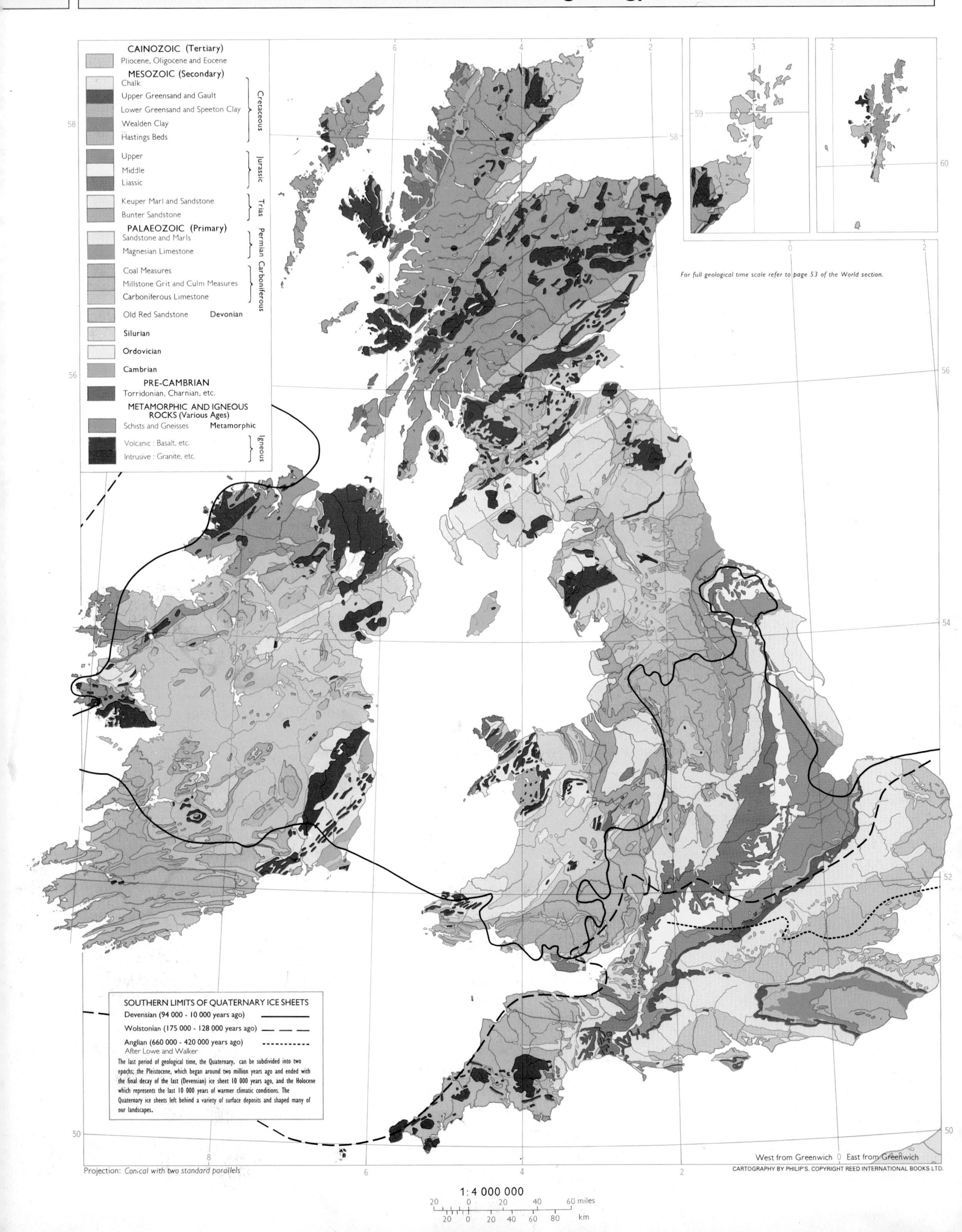

CAINOZOIC (Tertiary)
Pliocene, Oligocene and Eocene

MESOZOIC (Secondary)

Cretaceous
- Chalk
- Upper Greensand and Gault
- Lower Greensand and Speeton Clay
- Wealden Clay
- Hastings Beds

Jurassic
- Upper
- Middle
- Liassic

Trias
- Keuper Marl and Sandstone
- Bunter Sandstone

PALAEOZOIC (Primary)

Permian
- Sandstone and Marls
- Magnesian Limestone

Carboniferous
- Coal Measures
- Millstone Grit and Culm Measures
- Carboniferous Limestone

- Old Red Sandstone   Devonian
- Silurian
- Ordovician
- Cambrian

PRE-CAMBRIAN
Torridonian, Charnian, etc.

METAMORPHIC AND IGNEOUS ROCKS (Various Ages)
- Schists and Gneisses   Metamorphic

Igneous
- Volcanic : Basalt, etc.
- Intrusive : Granite, etc.

For full geological time scale refer to page 53 of the World section.

SOUTHERN LIMITS OF QUATERNARY ICE SHEETS
Devensian (94 000 - 10 000 years ago)

Wolstonian (175 000 - 128 000 years ago) — — —

Anglian (660 000 - 420 000 years ago) - - - - - -
After Lowe and Walker

The last period of geological time, the Quaternary, can be subdivided into two epochs; the Pleistocene, which began around two million years ago and ended with the final decay of the last (Devensian) ice sheet 10 000 years ago, and the Holocene which represents the last 10 000 years of warmer climatic conditions. The Quaternary ice sheets left behind a variety of surface deposits and shaped many of our landscapes.

West from Greenwich 0 East from Greenwich

Projection: *Conical with two standard parallels*

CARTOGRAPHY BY PHILIP'S. COPYRIGHT REED INTERNATIONAL BOOKS LTD.

1 : 4 000 000

20   0   20   40   60 miles

20 0 20 40 60 80 km

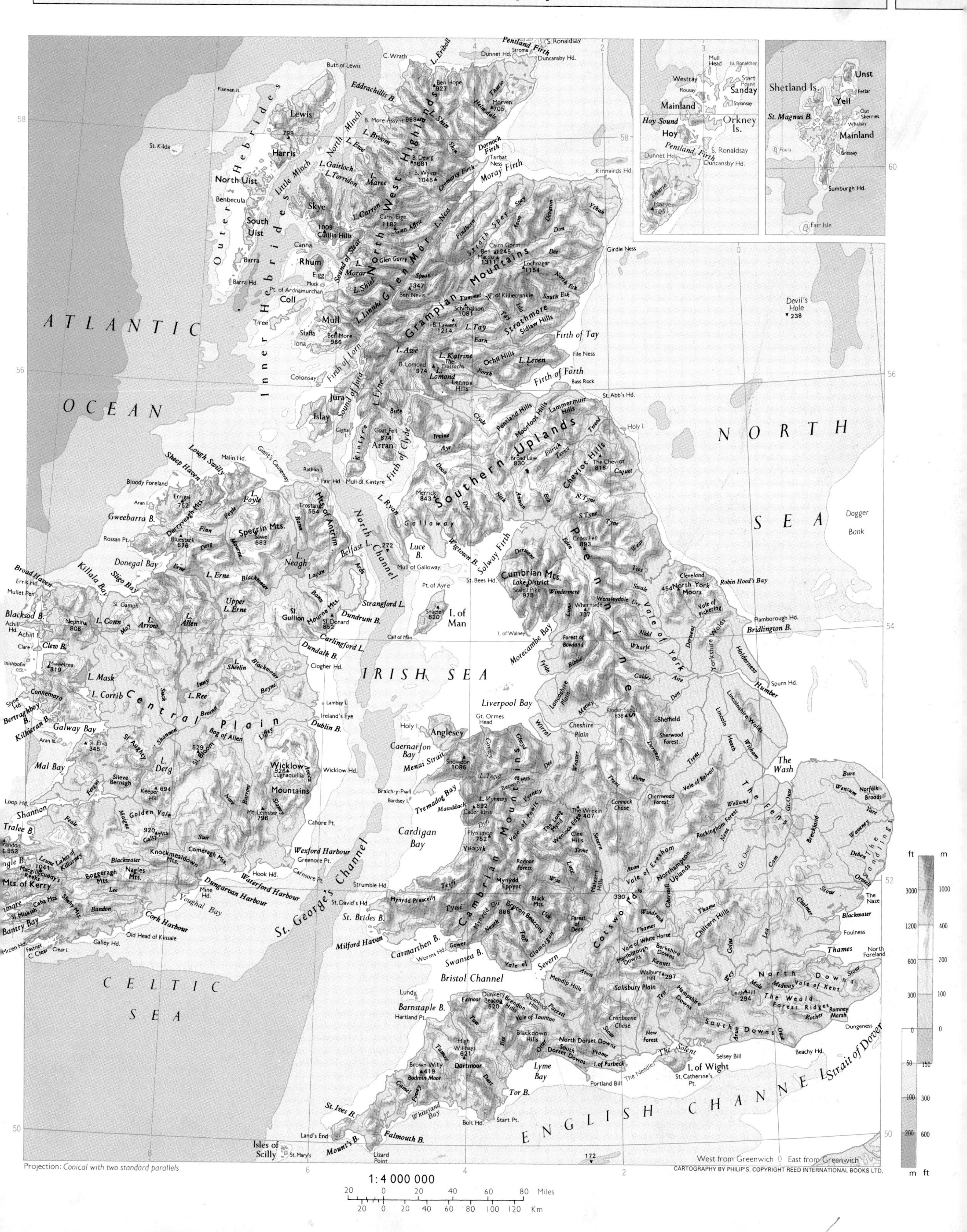

Projection: Conical with two standard parallels

1 : 4 000 000

West from Greenwich 0 East from Greenwich
CARTOGRAPHY BY PHILIP'S. COPYRIGHT REED INTERNATIONAL BOOKS LTD.

JANUARY TEMPERATURE
Actual surface temperature

°C
7
6
5
4
3
2
1
0

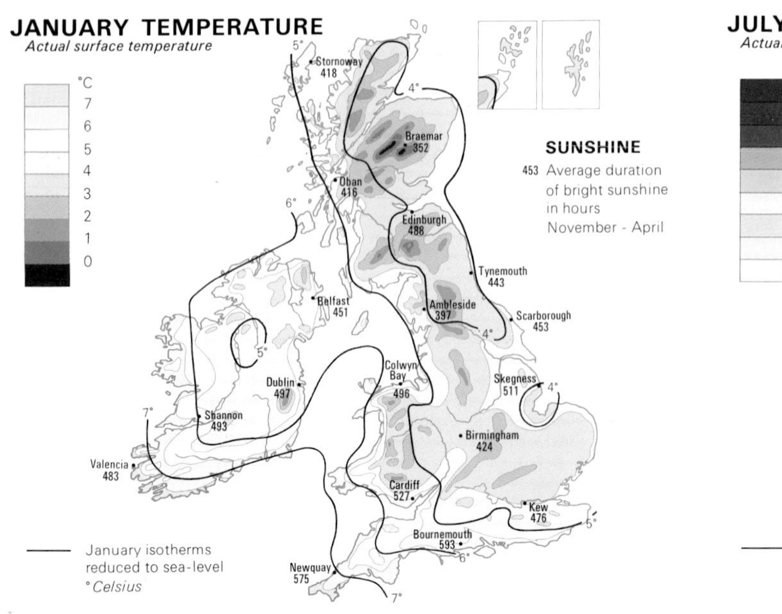

SUNSHINE

453 Average duration
of bright sunshine
in hours
November - April

— January isotherms
reduced to sea-level
°Celsius

Stornoway 418
Braemar 352
Oban 416
Edinburgh 488
Tynemouth 443
Belfast 451
Ambleside 397
Scarborough 453
Dublin 497
Colwyn Bay 496
Skegness 511
Shannon 493
Birmingham 424
Valencia 483
Cardiff 527
Kew 476
Bournemouth 593
Newquay 575

JULY TEMPERATURE
Actual surface temperature

°C
17
16
15
14
13
12
11
10

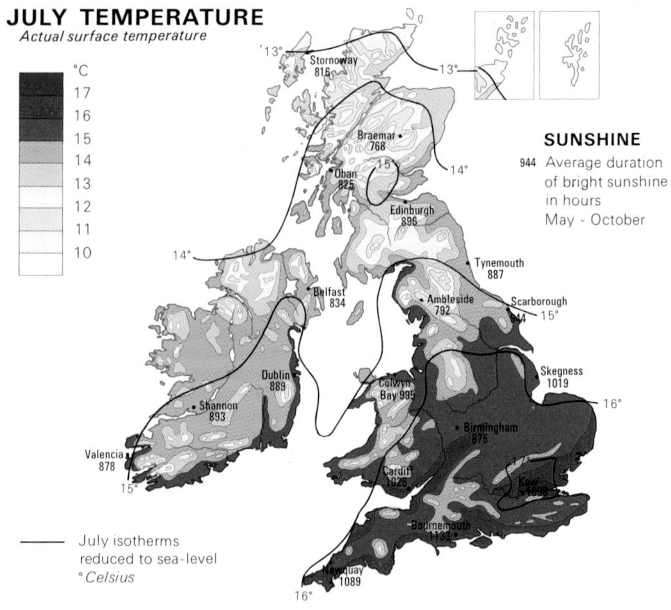

SUNSHINE

944 Average duration
of bright sunshine
in hours
May - October

— July isotherms
reduced to sea-level
°Celsius

Stornoway 816
Braemar 768
Oban 825
Edinburgh 896
Tynemouth 887
Belfast 834
Ambleside 792
Scarborough 944
Dublin 889
Colwyn Bay 995
Skegness 1019
Shannon 893
Birmingham 875
Valencia 878
Cardiff 1026
Kew
Bournemouth 1133
Newquay 1089

ANNUAL RAINFALL

mm
2500
2000
1500
1000
750
625

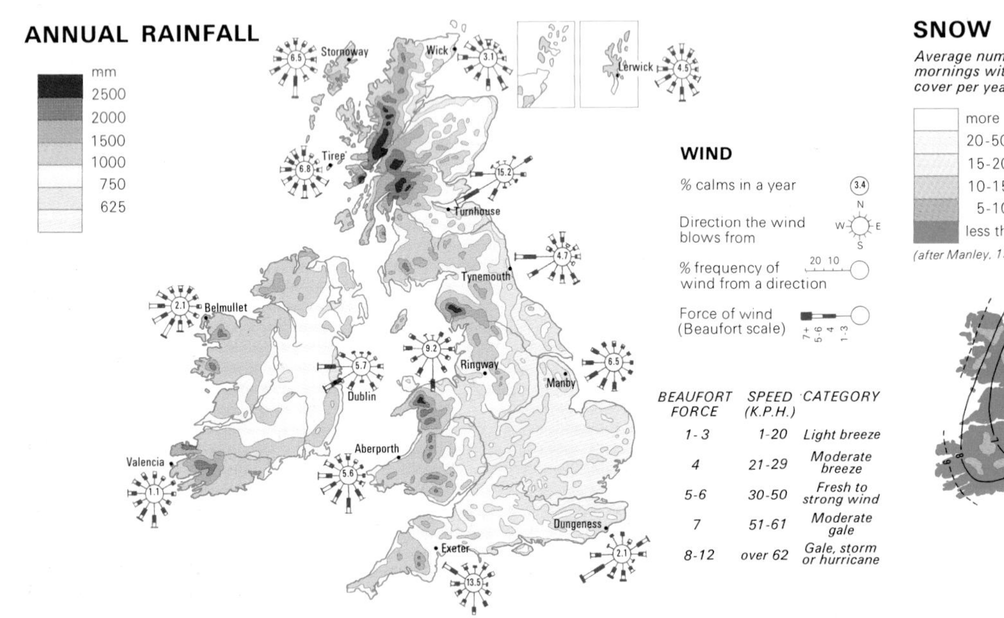

WIND

% calms in a year (3.4)

Direction the wind
blows from

% frequency of
wind from a direction 20 10

Force of wind
(Beaufort scale) 7+ 5-6 1-3

BEAUFORT FORCE	SPEED (K.P.H.)	CATEGORY
1- 3	1-20	Light breeze
4	21-29	Moderate breeze
5-6	30-50	Fresh to strong wind
7	51-61	Moderate gale
8-12	over 62	Gale, storm or hurricane

Stornoway · Wick · Lerwick 4.5 · 3.1
Tiree 6.8
Turnhouse 15.2
Belmullet 2.1
Tynemouth 4.7
Dublin 5.7 · Ringway 9.2 · Manby · 6.5
Valencia 1.1
Aberporth 5.6
Dungeness 2.1
Exeter 13.5

SNOW

*Average number of
mornings with snow
cover per year*

more than 50
20-50
15-20
10-15
5-10
less than 5

(after Manley, 1970)

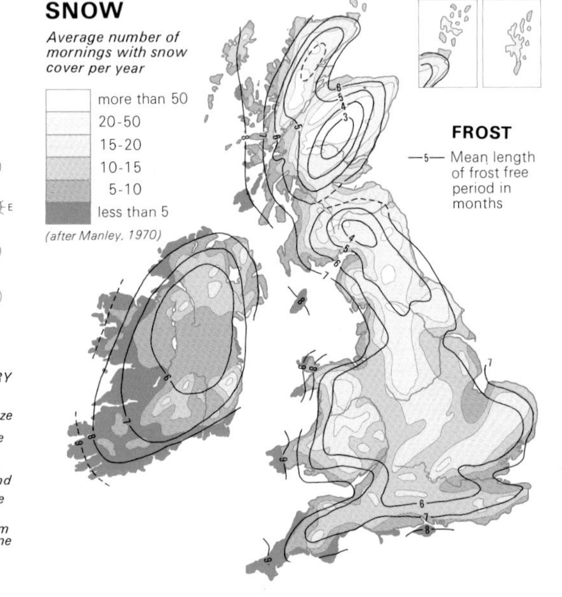

FROST

—5— Mean length
of frost free
period in
months

VARIABILITY OF RAIN

The percentage frequency with
which rainfall varies from the
normal rainfall regime in an area:
the higher the percentage figure,
the more variable the rainfall.

over 20%
18-20%
16-18%
14-16%
12-14%
10-12%
under 10%

(after Gregory, 1955)

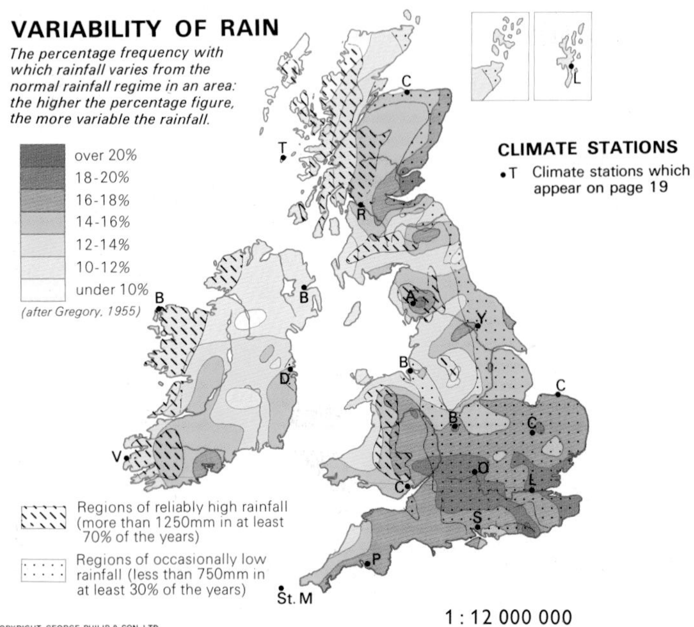

CLIMATE STATIONS

•T Climate stations which
appear on page 19

Regions of reliably high rainfall
(more than 1250mm in at least
70% of the years)

Regions of occasionally low
rainfall (less than 750mm in
at least 30% of the years)

1 : 12 000 000

COPYRIGHT: GEORGE PHILIP & SON LTD.

SYNOPTIC CHART FOR A TYPICAL WINTER DEPRESSION
21st January 1971

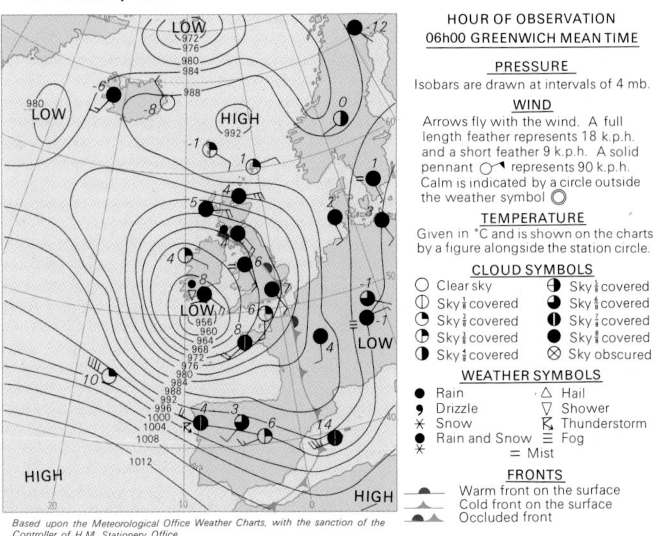

HOUR OF OBSERVATION
06h00 GREENWICH MEAN TIME

PRESSURE
Isobars are drawn at intervals of 4 mb.

WIND
Arrows fly with the wind. A full
length feather represents 18 k.p.h.
and a short feather 9 k.p.h. A solid
pennant represents 90 k.p.h.
Calm is indicated by a circle outside
the weather symbol ◯

TEMPERATURE
Given in °C and is shown on the charts
by a figure alongside the station circle.

CLOUD SYMBOLS
○ Clear sky   ◑ Sky ½ covered
◔ Sky ⅒ covered   ◕ Sky ⅝ covered
◔ Sky ¼ covered   ◕ Sky ¾ covered
◑ Sky ⅜ covered   ● Sky ⅞ covered
◑ Sky ½ covered   ⊗ Sky obscured

WEATHER SYMBOLS
● Rain   △ Hail
, Drizzle   ▽ Shower
✳ Snow   ⚡ Thunderstorm
✶ Rain and Snow   ≡ Fog
                  = Mist

FRONTS
▲ Warm front on the surface
▲ Cold front on the surface
▲ Occluded front

*Based upon the Meteorological Office Weather Charts, with the sanction of the
Controller of H.M. Stationery Office*

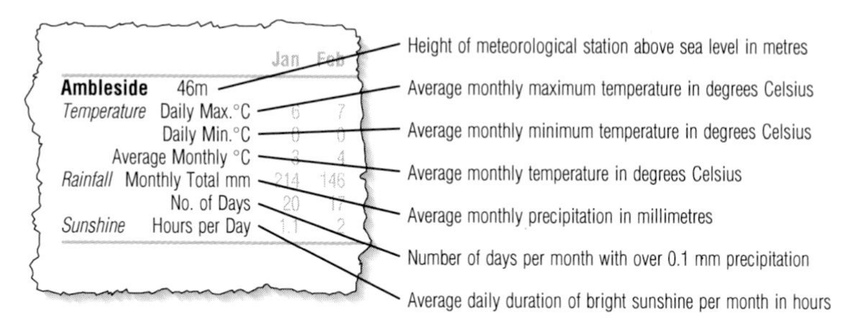

Height of meteorological station above sea level in metres — Average monthly maximum temperature in degrees Celsius — Average monthly minimum temperature in degrees Celsius — Average monthly temperature in degrees Celsius — Average monthly precipitation in millimetres — Number of days per month with over 0.1 mm precipitation — Average daily duration of bright sunshine per month in hours

Ambleside 46m

		Jan	Feb	Mar	Apr	May	June	July	Aug	Sep	Oct	Nov	Dec	Year
Temperature	Daily Max.°C	6	7	9	12	16	19	20	19	17	13	9	7	13
	Daily Min.°C	0	0	2	4	6	9	11	11	9	6	3	1	5
	Average Monthly °C	3	4	6	8	11	14	15	15	13	10	6	4	9
Rainfall	Monthly Total mm	214	146	112	101	90	111	134	139	184	196	209	215	1851
	No. of Days	20	17	15	15	14	15	18	17	18	19	19	21	208
Sunshine	Hours per Day	1.1	2	3.2	4.5	6	5.7	4.5	4.2	3.3	2.2	1.4	1	3.3

Belfast 4m

		Jan	Feb	Mar	Apr	May	June	July	Aug	Sep	Oct	Nov	Dec	Year
Temperature	Daily Max.°C	6	7	9	12	15	18	18	18	16	13	9	7	12
	Daily Min.°C	2	2	3	4	6	9	11	11	9	7	4	3	6
	Average Monthly °C	4	4	6	8	11	13	15	15	13	10	7	5	9
Rainfall	Monthly Total mm	80	52	50	48	52	68	94	77	80	83	72	90	845
	No. of Days	20	17	16	16	15	16	19	17	18	19	19	21	213
Sunshine	Hours per Day	1.5	2.3	3.4	5	6.3	6	4.4	4.4	3.6	2.6	1.8	1.1	3.5

Belmullet 9m

		Jan	Feb	Mar	Apr	May	June	July	Aug	Sep	Oct	Nov	Dec	Year
Temperature	Daily Max.°C	8	9	10	12	14	16	17	17	16	14	10	9	12
	Daily Min.°C	3	4	4	6	8	10	11	11	10	8	5	4	7
	Average Monthly °C	5	6	7	9	11	13	14	14	13	11	8	6	10
Rainfall	Monthly Total mm	108	64	82	70	75	80	76	95	108	116	127	131	1132
	No. of Days	18	13	16	15	14	12	14	17	16	18	20	22	195
Sunshine	Hours per Day	1.9	2.5	3.4	5.2	7	6	4.6	5.1	3.9	2.9	1.9	1.3	3.8

Birkenhead 60m

		Jan	Feb	Mar	Apr	May	June	July	Aug	Sep	Oct	Nov	Dec	Year
Temperature	Daily Max.°C	6	6	9	11	15	17	19	19	16	13	9	7	12
	Daily Min.°C	2	2	3	5	8	11	13	13	11	8	5	3	7
	Average Monthly °C	4	4	6	8	11	14	16	16	14	10	7	5	10
Rainfall	Monthly Total mm	64	46	40	41	55	55	67	80	66	71	76	65	726
	No. of Days	18	13	13	13	13	13	15	15	15	17	17	19	181
Sunshine	Hours per Day	1.6	2.4	3.5	5.3	6.3	6.7	5.7	5.4	4.2	2.9	1.8	1.3	3.9

Birmingham 163m

		Jan	Feb	Mar	Apr	May	June	July	Aug	Sep	Oct	Nov	Dec	Year
Temperature	Daily Max.°C	5	6	9	12	16	19	20	20	17	13	9	6	13
	Daily Min.°C	2	2	3	5	7	10	12	12	10	7	5	3	7
	Average Monthly °C	3	4	6	8	11	15	16	16	14	10	7	5	10
Rainfall	Monthly Total mm	74	54	50	53	64	50	69	69	61	69	84	67	764
	No. of Days	17	15	13	13	14	13	14	14	14	15	17	18	178
Sunshine	Hours per Day	1.4	2.1	3.2	4.6	5.4	6	5.4	5.1	3.9	2.8	1.6	1.2	3.6

Cambridge 12m

		Jan	Feb	Mar	Apr	May	June	July	Aug	Sep	Oct	Nov	Dec	Year
Temperature	Daily Max.°C	6	7	11	14	17	21	22	22	19	15	10	7	14
	Daily Min.°C	1	1	2	4	7	10	12	12	10	6	4	2	6
	Average Monthly °C	3	4	6	9	12	15	17	17	14	10	7	5	10
Rainfall	Monthly Total mm	49	35	36	37	45	45	58	55	51	51	54	41	558
	No. of Days	15	13	10	11	11	11	12	12	11	13	14	14	147
Sunshine	Hours per Day	1.7	2.5	3.8	5.1	6.2	6.7	6	5.7	4.6	3.4	1.9	1.4	4.1

Cardiff 62m

		Jan	Feb	Mar	Apr	May	June	July	Aug	Sep	Oct	Nov	Dec	Year
Temperature	Daily Max.°C	7	7	10	13	16	19	20	21	18	14	10	8	14
	Daily Min.°C	2	2	3	5	8	11	12	13	11	8	5	3	7
	Average Monthly °C	4	5	7	9	12	15	16	17	14	11	8	6	10
Rainfall	Monthly Total mm	108	72	63	65	76	63	89	97	99	109	116	108	1065
	No. of Days	18	14	13	13	13	13	14	15	16	16	17	18	180
Sunshine	Hours per Day	1.7	2.7	4	5.6	6.4	6.9	6.2	6	4.7	3.4	1.9	1.5	4.3

Craibstone 91m

		Jan	Feb	Mar	Apr	May	June	July	Aug	Sep	Oct	Nov	Dec	Year
Temperature	Daily Max.°C	5	6	8	10	13	16	18	17	15	12	8	6	11
	Daily Min.°C	0	0	2	3	5	8	10	10	8	6	3	1	5
	Average Monthly °C	3	3	5	7	9	12	14	13	12	9	6	4	8
Rainfall	Monthly Total mm	78	55	53	51	63	54	95	75	67	92	93	80	856
	No. of Days	19	16	15	15	14	14	18	15	16	18	19	18	197
Sunshine	Hours per Day	1.8	2.9	3.5	4.9	5.9	6.1	5.1	4.8	4.3	3.1	2	1.5	3.8

Cromer 54m

		Jan	Feb	Mar	Apr	May	June	July	Aug	Sep	Oct	Nov	Dec	Year
Temperature	Daily Max.°C	6	7	9	12	15	18	21	20	18	14	10	8	13
	Daily Min.°C	1	1	3	5	7	10	12	13	11	8	5	3	7
	Average Monthly °C	4	4	6	8	11	14	16	16	15	11	7	5	10
Rainfall	Monthly Total mm	58	46	37	39	48	39	63	56	54	61	64	53	618
	No. of Days	18	16	13	13	11	11	13	12	14	16	18	18	173
Sunshine	Hours per Day	1.8	2.6	4	5.4	6.4	6.8	6.3	5.8	5	3.6	2	1.9	4.3

Dublin 47m

		Jan	Feb	Mar	Apr	May	June	July	Aug	Sep	Oct	Nov	Dec	Year
Temperature	Daily Max.°C	8	8	10	13	15	18	20	19	17	14	10	8	14
	Daily Min.°C	1	2	3	4	6	9	11	11	9	6	4	3	6
	Average Monthly °C	4	5	7	8	11	14	15	15	13	10	7	5	10
Rainfall	Monthly Total mm	67	55	51	45	60	57	70	74	72	70	67	74	762
	No. of Days	13	10	10	11	10	11	13	12	12	11	12	14	139
Sunshine	Hours per Day	1.9	2.5	3.4	5	6.2	6	4.8	4.9	3.9	3.2	2.1	1.6	3.8

Durham 102m

		Jan	Feb	Mar	Apr	May	June	July	Aug	Sep	Oct	Nov	Dec	Year
Temperature	Daily Max.°C	6	6	9	12	15	18	20	19	17	13	9	7	13
	Daily Min.°C	0	0	1	3	6	9	11	10	9	6	3	2	5
	Average Monthly °C	3	3	5	7	10	13	15	15	13	9	6	4	9
Rainfall	Monthly Total mm	59	51	38	38	51	49	61	67	60	63	66	55	658
	No. of Days	17	15	14	13	13	14	15	14	14	16	17	17	179
Sunshine	Hours per Day	1.7	2.5	3.3	4.6	5.4	6	5.1	4.8	4.1	3	1.9	1.4	3.6

Lerwick 82m

		Jan	Feb	Mar	Apr	May	June	July	Aug	Sep	Oct	Nov	Dec	Year
Temperature	Daily Max.°C	5	5	6	8	11	13	14	14	13	10	8	6	9
	Daily Min.°C	1	1	2	3	5	7	10	10	8	6	4	3	5
	Average Monthly °C	3	3	4	5	8	10	12	12	11	8	6	4	7
Rainfall	Monthly Total mm	109	87	69	68	52	55	72	71	87	104	111	118	1003
	No. of Days	25	22	20	21	15	15	17	17	19	23	24	25	243
Sunshine	Hours per Day	0.8	1.8	2.9	4.4	5.3	5.3	4	3.8	3.5	2.2	2.2	0.5	3

London (Kew) 5m

		Jan	Feb	Mar	Apr	May	June	July	Aug	Sep	Oct	Nov	Dec	Year
Temperature	Daily Max.°C	6	7	10	13	17	20	22	21	19	14	10	7	14
	Daily Min.°C	2	2	3	6	8	12	14	13	11	8	5	4	7
	Average Monthly °C	4	5	7	9	12	16	18	17	15	11	8	5	11
Rainfall	Monthly Total mm	54	40	37	37	46	45	57	59	49	57	64	48	593
	No. of Days	15	13	11	12	12	11	12	11	13	13	15	15	153
Sunshine	Hours per Day	1.5	2.3	3.6	5.3	6.4	7.1	6.4	6.1	4.7	3.2	1.8	1.3	4.1

Oxford 63m

		Jan	Feb	Mar	Apr	May	June	July	Aug	Sep	Oct	Nov	Dec	Year
Temperature	Daily Max.°C	7	7	11	14	17	20	22	22	19	14	10	8	14
	Daily Min.°C	1	1	2	5	7	10	12	12	10	7	4	2	6
	Average Monthly °C	4	4	6	9	12	15	17	17	14	11	7	5	10
Rainfall	Monthly Total mm	61	44	43	41	55	52	55	60	59	64	69	57	660
	No. of Days	13	10	9	9	10	9	10	10	10	11	12	13	126
Sunshine	Hours per Day	1.7	2.6	3.9	5.3	6.1	6.6	5.9	5.7	4.4	3.2	2.1	1.6	4.1

Plymouth 27m

		Jan	Feb	Mar	Apr	May	June	July	Aug	Sep	Oct	Nov	Dec	Year
Temperature	Daily Max.°C	8	8	10	12	15	18	19	19	18	15	11	9	14
	Daily Min.°C	4	4	5	6	8	11	13	13	12	9	7	5	8
	Average Monthly °C	6	6	7	9	12	15	16	16	15	12	9	7	11
Rainfall	Monthly Total mm	99	74	69	53	63	53	70	77	78	91	113	110	950
	No. of Days	19	15	14	12	12	12	14	14	15	16	17	18	178
Sunshine	Hours per Day	1.9	2.9	4.3	6.1	7.1	7.4	6.2	6.4	6.4	5.1	3.7	2.2	1.7	4.6

Renfrew 6m

		Jan	Feb	Mar	Apr	May	June	July	Aug	Sep	Oct	Nov	Dec	Year
Temperature	Daily Max.°C	5	7	9	12	15	18	19	19	16	13	9	7	12
	Daily Min.°C	1	1	2	4	6	9	11	11	9	6	4	2	6
	Average Monthly °C	3	4	6	8	11	14	15	15	13	9	7	4	9
Rainfall	Monthly Total mm	111	85	69	67	63	70	97	93	102	119	106	127	1109
	No. of Days	19	16	15	15	14	15	17	17	17	18	18	20	201
Sunshine	Hours per Day	1.1	2.1	2.9	4.7	6	6.1	5.1	4.4	3.7	2.3	1.4	0.8	3.4

St Helier 9m

		Jan	Feb	Mar	Apr	May	June	July	Aug	Sep	Oct	Nov	Dec	Year
Temperature	Daily Max.°C	9	8	11	13	16	19	21	21	19	16	12	10	15
	Daily Min.°C	5	4	6	7	10	13	15	15	14	11	8	6	9
	Average Monthly °C	7	6	8	10	13	16	18	18	17	13	10	8	12
Rainfall	Monthly Total mm	89	68	57	43	44	39	48	67	69	77	101	99	801
	No. of Days	19	15	13	12	11	10	11	12	15	15	17	19	169
Sunshine	Hours per Day	2.3	3.1	5	6.7	7.8	8.5	7.8	7.6	5.6	4.1	2.5	1.8	5.3

St Mary's 50m

		Jan	Feb	Mar	Apr	May	June	July	Aug	Sep	Oct	Nov	Dec	Year
Temperature	Daily Max.°C	9	9	11	12	14	17	19	19	18	15	12	10	14
	Daily Min.°C	6	6	7	7	9	12	13	14	13	11	9	7	9
	Average Monthly °C	8	7	9	10	12	14	16	16	15	13	10	9	12
Rainfall	Monthly Total mm	91	71	69	46	56	49	61	64	67	80	96	94	844
	No. of Days	22	17	16	13	14	14	16	15	16	17	19	21	200
Sunshine	Hours per Day	2	2.9	4.2	6.4	7.6	7.6	6.7	6.7	5.2	3.9	2.5	1.8	4.8

Southampton 20m

		Jan	Feb	Mar	Apr	May	June	July	Aug	Sep	Oct	Nov	Dec	Year
Temperature	Daily Max.°C	7	8	11	14	17	20	22	22	19	15	11	8	15
	Daily Min.°C	2	2	3	5	8	11	13	13	11	7	5	3	7
	Average Monthly °C	5	5	7	10	13	16	17	17	15	11	8	6	11
Rainfall	Monthly Total mm	83	56	52	45	56	49	60	69	70	86	94	84	804
	No. of Days	17	13	13	12	12	13	13	14	14	16	17	166
Sunshine	Hours per Day	1.8	2.6	4	5.7	6.7	7.2	6.5	6.4	4.9	3.6	2.2	1.6	4.5

Tiree 9m

		Jan	Feb	Mar	Apr	May	June	July	Aug	Sep	Oct	Nov	Dec	Year
Temperature	Daily Max.°C	7	7	9	10	13	15	16	16	15	12	10	8	12
	Daily Min.°C	4	4	4	7	10	11	11	10	8	6	5	7
	Average Monthly °C	5	5	6	8	10	12	14	14	13	10	8	6	9
Rainfall	Monthly Total mm	117	77	67	64	55	70	91	90	118	129	122	128	1128
	No. of Days	23	19	17	17	15	16	20	18	20	23	22	24	234
Sunshine	Hours per Day	1.3	2.6	3.7	5.7	7.5	6.8	5.2	5.3	4.2	2.6	1.6	0.9	4

Valencia 9m

		Jan	Feb	Mar	Apr	May	June	July	Aug	Sep	Oct	Nov	Dec	Year
Temperature	Daily Max.°C	9	9	11	13	15	17	18	18	17	14	12	10	14
	Daily Min.°C	5	4	5	6	8	11	12	13	11	9	7	6	8
	Average Monthly °C	7	7	8	9	11	0	15	15	14	12	9	8	11
Rainfall	Monthly Total mm	165	107	103	75	86	81	107	95	122	140	151	168	1400
	No. of Days	20	15	14	13	13	13	15	15	16	17	18	21	190
Sunshine	Hours per Day	1.6	2.5	3.5	5.2	6.5	5.9	4.7	4.9	3.8	2.8	2	1.3	3.7

York 17m

		Jan	Feb	Mar	Apr	May	June	July	Aug	Sep	Oct	Nov	Dec	Year
Temperature	Daily Max.°C	6	7	10	13	16	19	21	21	18	14	10	7	13
	Daily Min.°C	1	1	2	4	7	10	12	12	10	7	4	2	6
	Average Monthly °C	3	4	6	9	12	15	17	16	14	10	7	5	10
Rainfall	Monthly Total mm	59	46	37	41	50	50	62	68	55	56	65	50	639
	No. of Days	17	15	13	13	13	14	15	14	14	15	17	17	177
Sunshine	Hours per Day	1.3	2.1	3.2	4.7	6.1	6.4	5.6	5.1	4.1	2.8	1.6	1.1	3.7

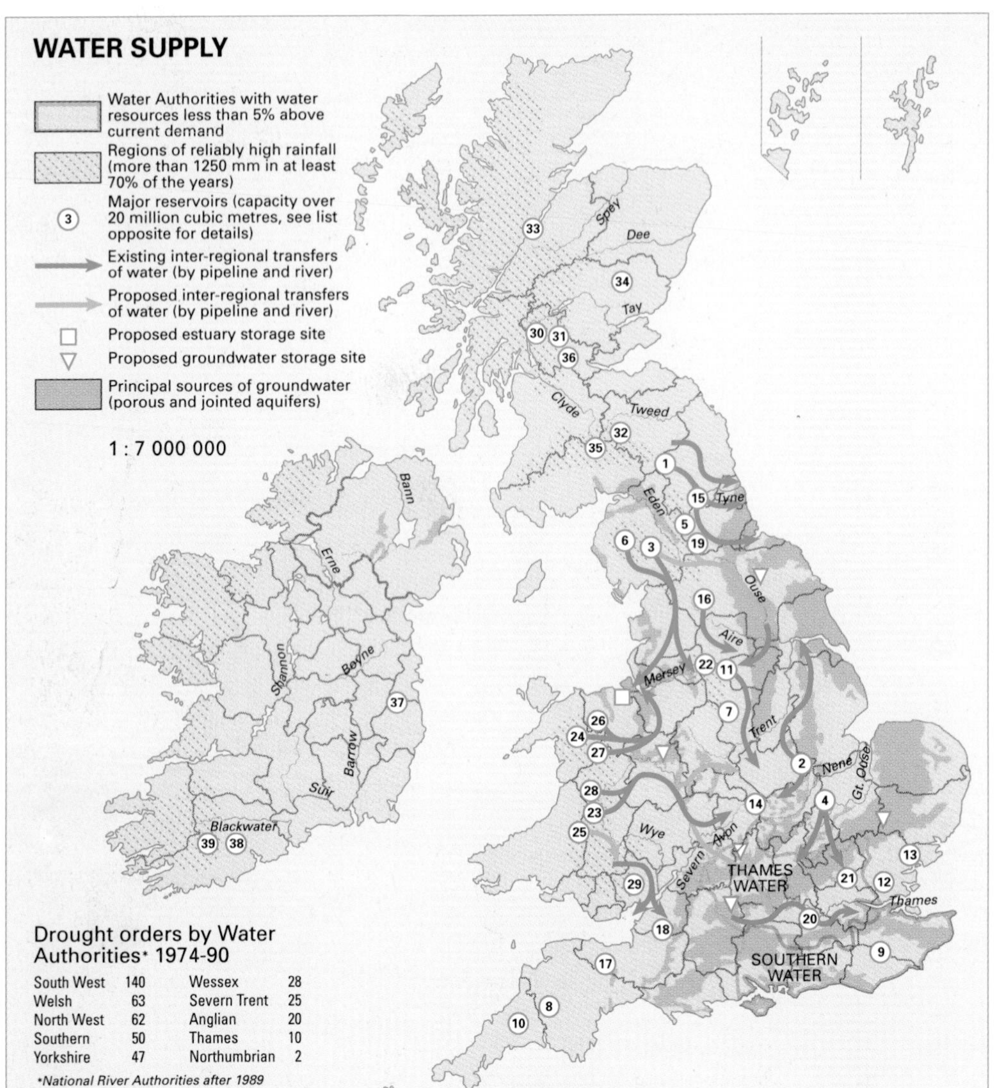

WATER SUPPLY

Water Authorities with water resources less than 5% above current demand

Regions of reliably high rainfall (more than 1250 mm in at least 70% of the years)

③ Major reservoirs (capacity over 20 million cubic metres, see list opposite for details)

→ Existing inter-regional transfers of water (by pipeline and river)

→ Proposed inter-regional transfers of water (by pipeline and river)

□ Proposed estuary storage site

▽ Proposed groundwater storage site

Principal sources of groundwater (porous and jointed aquifers)

1 : 7 000 000

Drought orders by Water Authorities* 1974-90

South West	140	Wessex	28
Welsh	63	Severn Trent	25
North West	62	Anglian	20
Southern	50	Thames	10
Yorkshire	47	Northumbrian	2

*National River Authorities after 1989

Major reservoirs (with capacity in million m³)

England		Wales	
1 Kielder Res.	198	23 Elan Valley	99
2 Rutland Water	123	24 Llyn Celyn	74
3 Haweswater	85	25 Llyn Brianne	62
4 Grafham Water	59	26 Llyn Brenig	60
5 Cow Green Res.	41	27 Llyn Vyrnwy	60
6 Thirlmere	41	28 Llyn Clywedog	48
7 Carsington Res.	36	29 Llandegfedd Res.	22
8 Roadford Res.	35		
9 Bewl Water Res.	31	**Scotland**	
10 Colliford Lake	29	30 Loch Lomond	86
11 Ladybower Res.	28	31 Loch Katrine	64
12 Hanningfield Res.	27	32 Megget Res.	64
13 Abberton Res.	25	33 Loch Ness	26
14 Draycote Water	23	34 Backwater Res.	25
15 Derwent Res.	22	35 Daer Res.	23
16 Grimwith Res.	22	36 Carron Valley Res.	21
17 Wimbleball Lake	21		
18 Chew Valley Lake	20	**Ireland**	
19 Balderhead Res.	20	37 Poulaphouca Res.	168
20 Thames Valley (linked reservoirs)		38 Inishcarra Res.	57
21 Lea Valley (linked reservoirs)		39 Carrigadrohid Res.	33
22 Longdendale (linked reservoirs)			

Average daily domestic water use in England and Wales (1990)

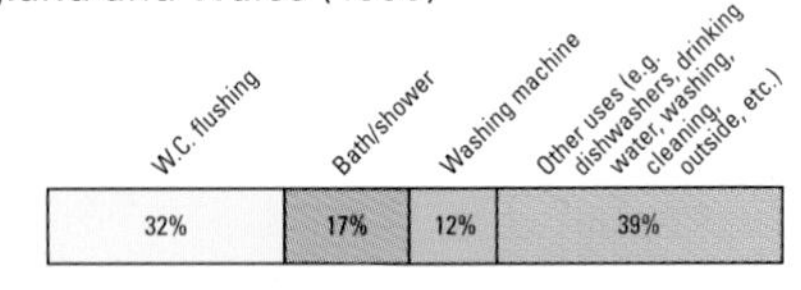

W.C. flushing	Bath/shower	Washing machine	Other uses (e.g. dishwashers, drinking water, washing, cleaning, outside, etc.)
32%	17%	12%	39%

Water abstractions in England and Wales (1990) 35 249 megalitres per day* of which:

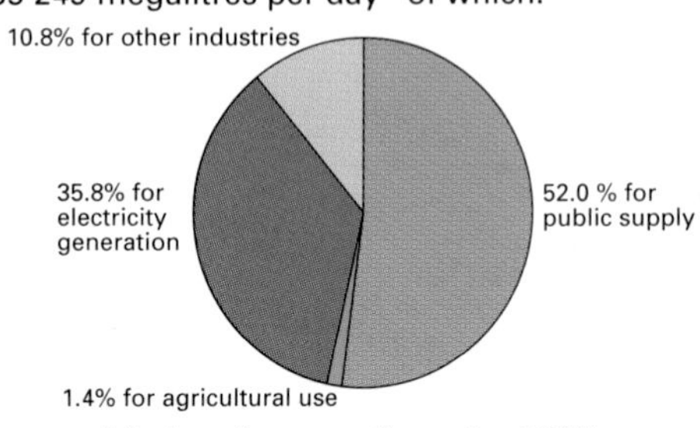

10.8% for other industries

35.8% for electricity generation

52.0 % for public supply

1.4% for agricultural use

*average daily domestic consumption per head 136 litres.

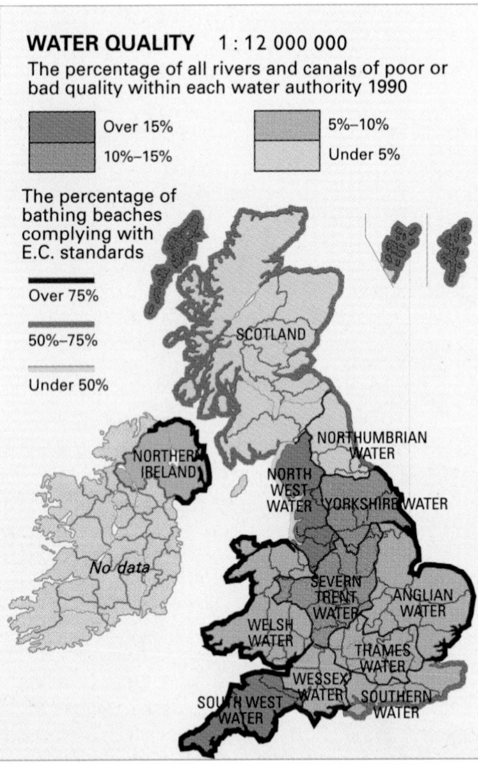

WATER ABSTRACTIONS   1 : 12 000 000

THAMES WATER   Water authority

6.8   Number of households supplied (in millions)

1883 (16%)   Water supply* in megalitres per day (with percentage of total abstraction from groundwater in brackets)

*Piped mains water, excluding water abstracted for agricultural and industrial use

SCOTLAND
5.1 | 2248 (0%)

N. IRELAND
1.6 | 666 (0%)

NORTHUMBRIAN WATER
1.3 | 1060 (9%)

NORTH WEST WATER
6.8 | 1883 (16%)

YORKSHIRE WATER
4.0 | 1498 (13%)

SEVERN TRENT WATER
6.8 | 2421 (20%)

ANGLIAN WATER
3.8 | 1928 (43%)

WELSH WATER
2.7 | 2671 (1%)

THAMES WATER
7.0 | 3827 (39%)

WESSEX WATER
1.1 | 798 (51%)

SOUTHERN WATER
2.0 | 1621 (50%)

SOUTH WEST WATER
1.4 | 630 (9%)

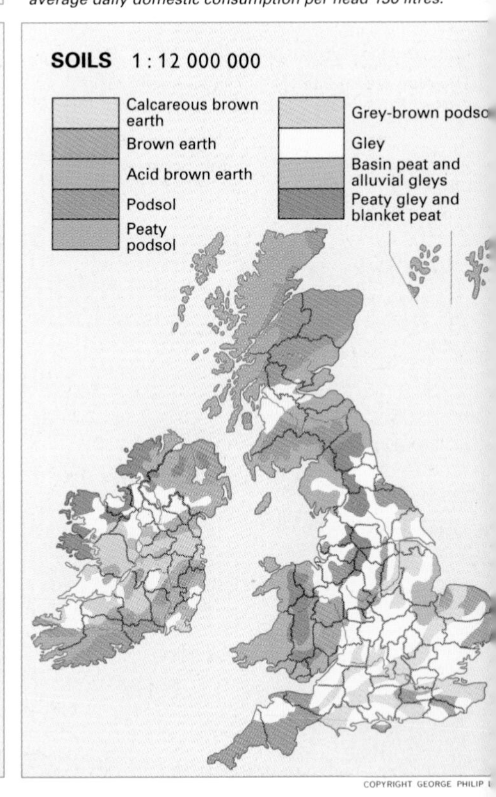

WATER QUALITY   1 : 12 000 000

The percentage of all rivers and canals of poor or bad quality within each water authority 1990

Over 15%
10%–15%
5%–10%
Under 5%

The percentage of bathing beaches complying with E.C. standards

Over 75%
50%–75%
Under 50%

SCOTLAND

NORTHERN IRELAND

No data

NORTHUMBRIAN WATER

NORTH WEST WATER

YORKSHIRE WATER

SEVERN TRENT WATER

ANGLIAN WATER

WELSH WATER

THAMES WATER

WESSEX WATER

SOUTHERN WATER

SOUTH WEST WATER

SOILS   1 : 12 000 000

Calcareous brown earth
Brown earth
Acid brown earth
Podsol
Peaty podsol
Grey-brown podsol
Gley
Basin peat and alluvial gleys
Peaty gley and blanket peat

AIR QUALITY : Emissions in thousand tonnes

	Sulphur dioxide			Nitrogen oxides		
	1975	1981	1987	1975	1981	1987
Belgium	–	856	610	–	317	271
Denmark	418	363	248	182	212	266
France	3 329	2 735	1 517	1 608	1 779	1 652
Germany	3 325	3 034	2 223	2 532	2 851	2 969
Greece	–	546	–	–	217	–
Irish Republic	186	189	138	60	68	68
Italy	3 250	3 211	2 075	1 499	1 585	1 570
Luxembourg	–	24	13	–	23	22
Netherlands	386	445	274	447	547	560
Portugal	178	266	286	104	166	303
Spain	–	2 543	–	–	937	–
United Kingdom	5 310	4 387	3 863	2 365	2 328	2 429

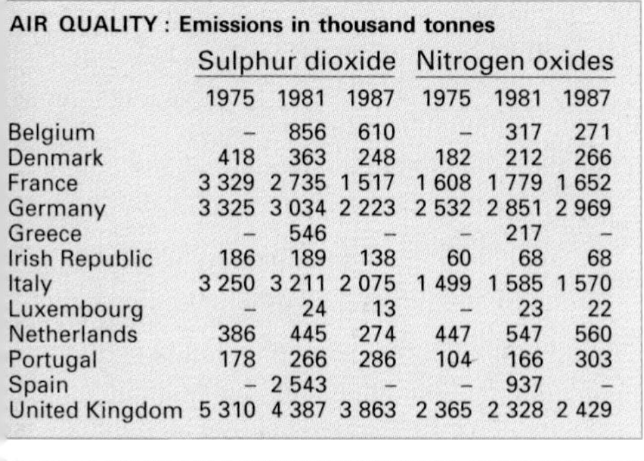

FORESTRY   1 : 12 000 000

The percentage of the total area covered by woodland and forest

- Over 20%
- 15%-20%
- 10%-15%
- 5%-10%
- Under 5%

△ 50%-80% coniferous
△ Over 80% coniferous

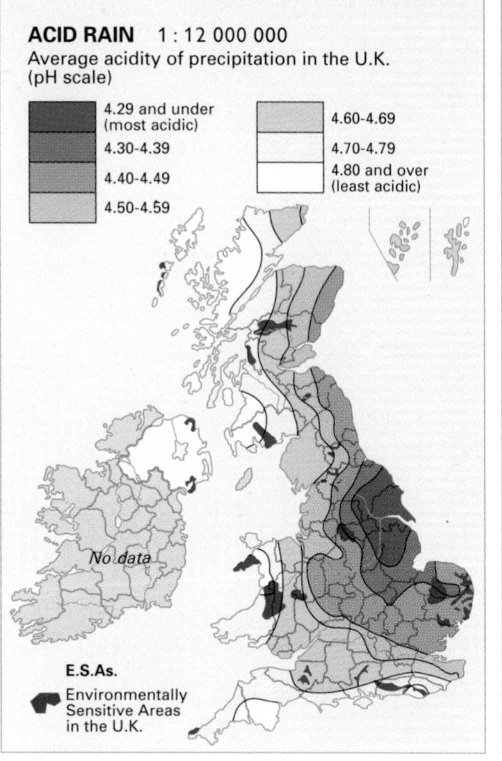

NATURAL VEGETATION   1 : 12 000 000

The plant cover associated with a particular environment if it is unaffected by human activity

- Oak
- Beech and Oak
- Ash and Oak
- Birch and Oakwood
- Scots Pine
- Heath, moorland, water meadows, fen, bog and marsh

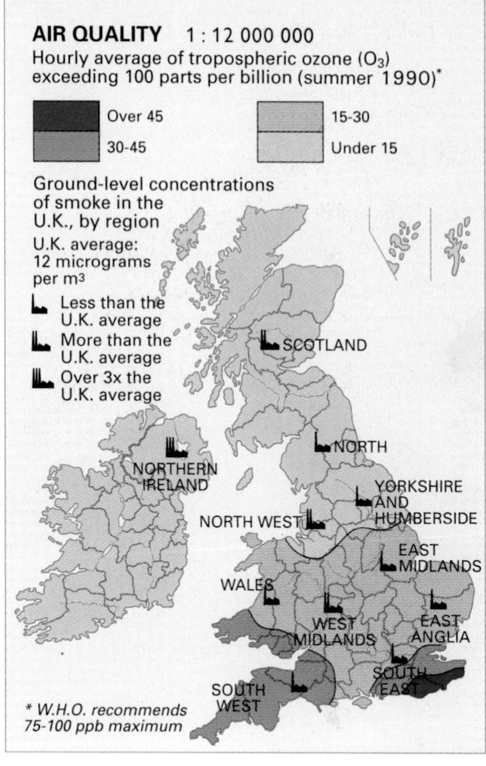

ACID RAIN   1 : 12 000 000

Average acidity of precipitation in the U.K. (pH scale)

- 4.29 and under (most acidic)
- 4.30-4.39
- 4.40-4.49
- 4.50-4.59
- 4.60-4.69
- 4.70-4.79
- 4.80 and over (least acidic)

No data

E.S.As.
Environmentally Sensitive Areas in the U.K.

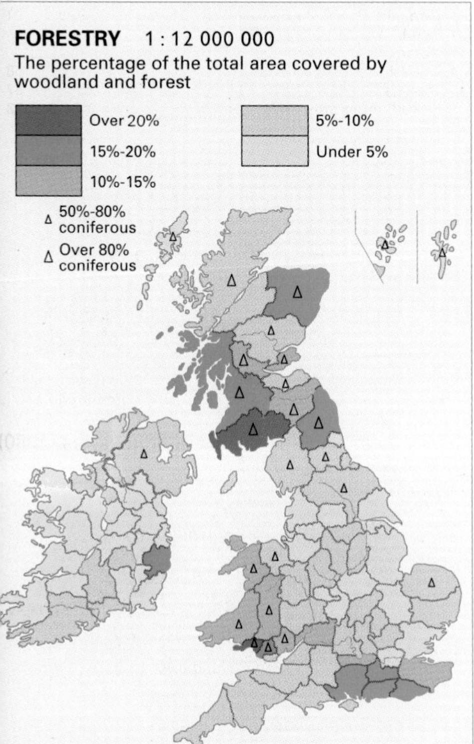

AIR QUALITY   1 : 12 000 000

Hourly average of tropospheric ozone (O_3) exceeding 100 parts per billion (summer 1990)*

- Over 45
- 30-45
- 15-30
- Under 15

Ground-level concentrations of smoke in the U.K., by region
U.K. average: 12 micrograms per m^3

- Less than the U.K. average
- More than the U.K. average
- Over 3x the U.K. average

SCOTLAND
NORTHERN IRELAND
NORTH
YORKSHIRE AND HUMBERSIDE
NORTH WEST
EAST MIDLANDS
WALES
WEST MIDLANDS
EAST ANGLIA
SOUTH WEST
SOUTH EAST

* W.H.O. recommends 75-100 ppb maximum

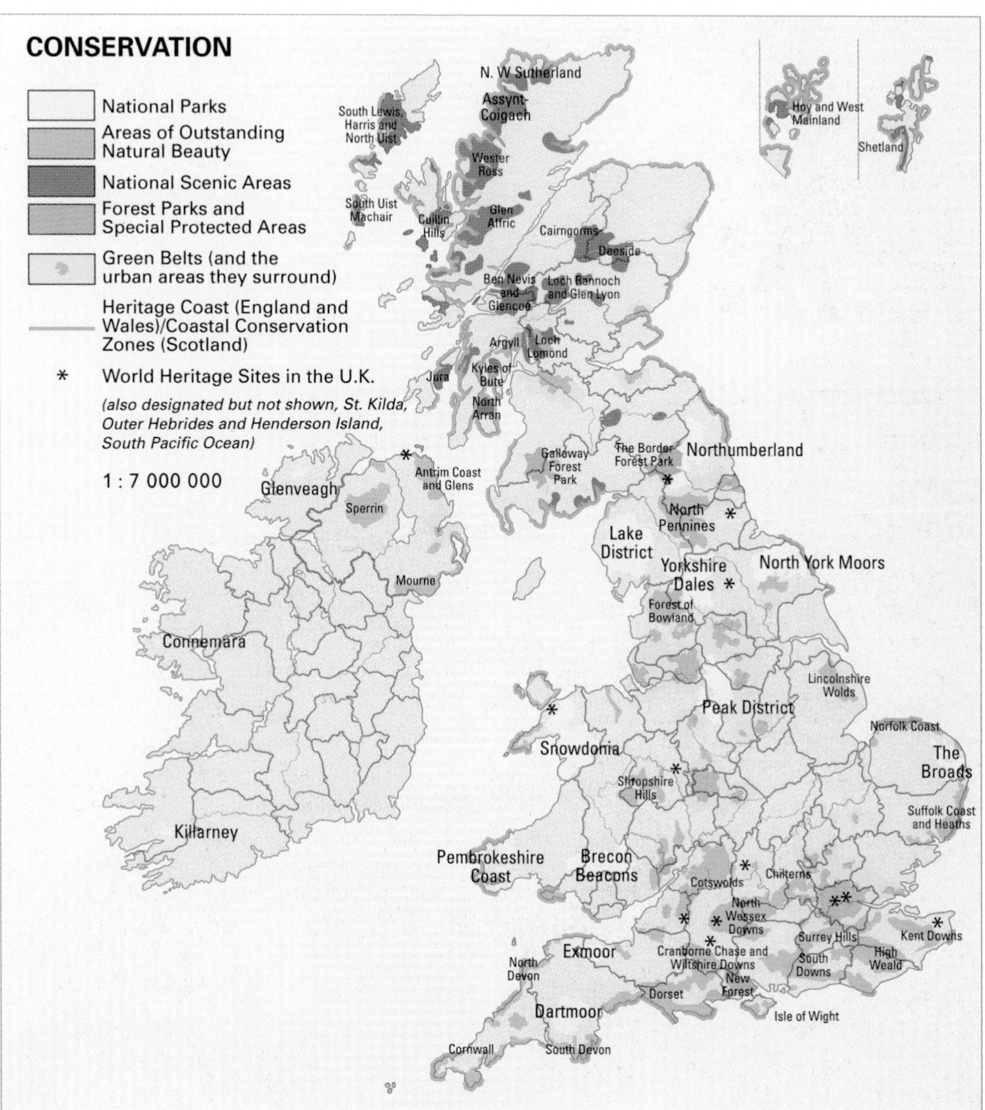

CONSERVATION

- National Parks
- Areas of Outstanding Natural Beauty
- National Scenic Areas
- Forest Parks and Special Protected Areas
- Green Belts (and the urban areas they surround)
- — Heritage Coast (England and Wales)/Coastal Conservation Zones (Scotland)
- * World Heritage Sites in the U.K.

(also designated but not shown, St. Kilda, Outer Hebrides and Henderson Island, South Pacific Ocean)

1 : 7 000 000

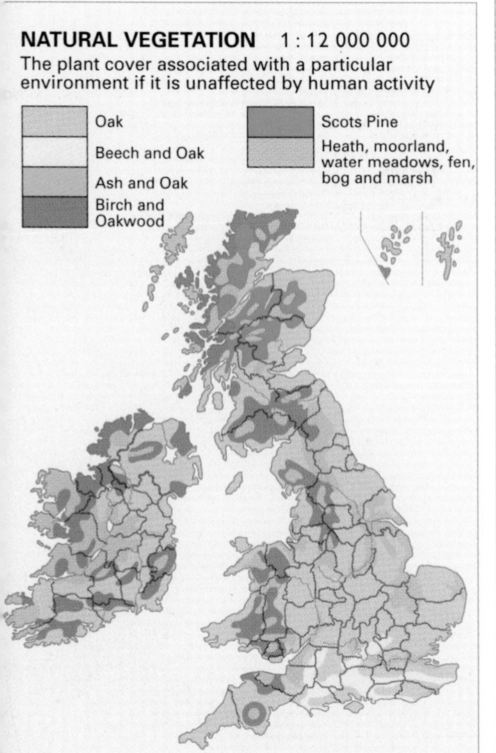

TYPES OF FARM

Dairy cattle

Beef cattle

Sheep

● Pigs and/or Poultry

Mixed farming

Market gardening
(fruit and vegetables)

Cereals

Other crops (mainly
potatoes, sugar beet)

Northern limit of
9 month growing season

Forests

Built-up areas

1 : 7 000 000

Areas with over 1000mm
rainfall per year

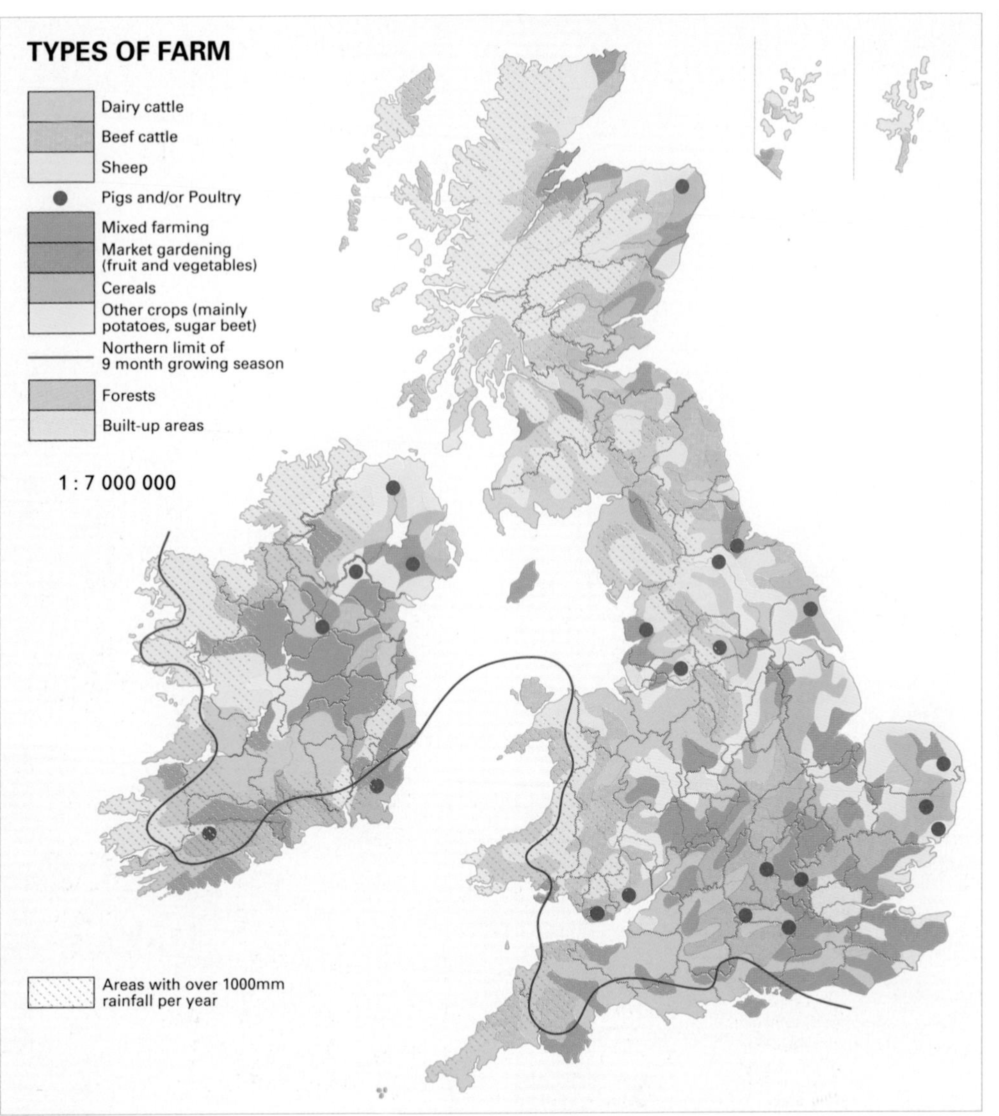

LAND UNDER AGRICULTURE   1 : 12 000 000

The percentage of the total land area
used for farming

Over 80%

60%-80%

40%-60%

20%-40%

0-20%

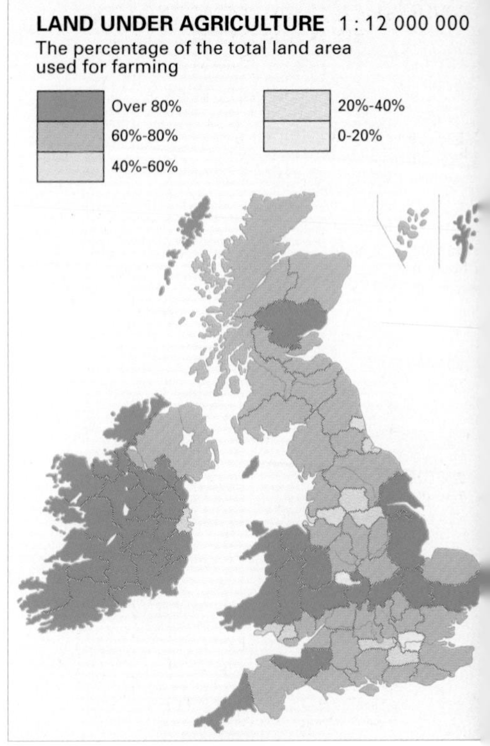

AGRICULTURAL LAND USE 1990 (U.K. only)

Other agricultural land 4.7%

Wheat 11.6%

Barley 8.8%

Oats 0.6%

Potatoes 1.0%

Sugar beet 1.1%

Fodder crops 2.0%

Rape 2.3%

Horticultural 1.2%

Rough grazing 27.2%

Pasture 39.5%

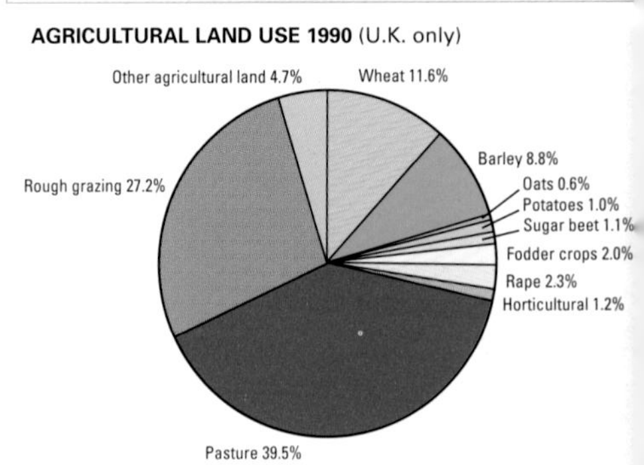

WHEAT   1 : 12 000 000

The percentage of the total farmland used
for growing wheat

Over 40%

30%-40%

20%-30%

10%-20%

0-10%

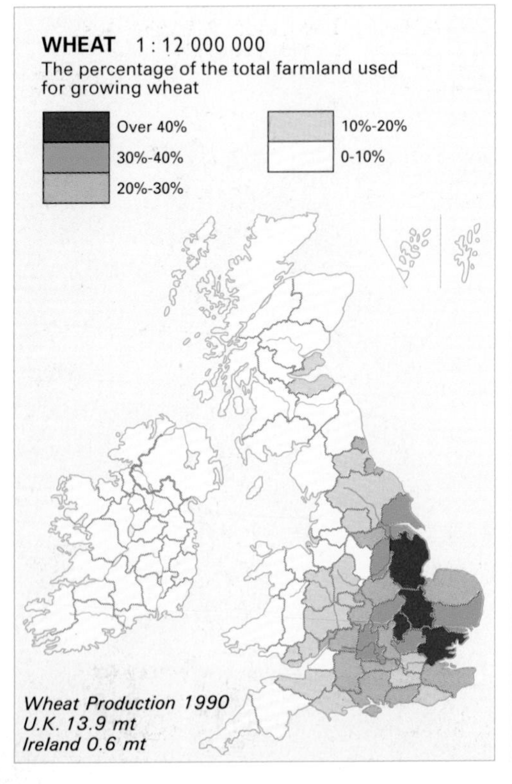

Wheat Production 1990
U.K. 13.9 mt
Ireland 0.6 mt

BARLEY   1 : 12 000 000

The percentage of the total farmland used
for growing barley

Over 20%

10%-20%

0-10%

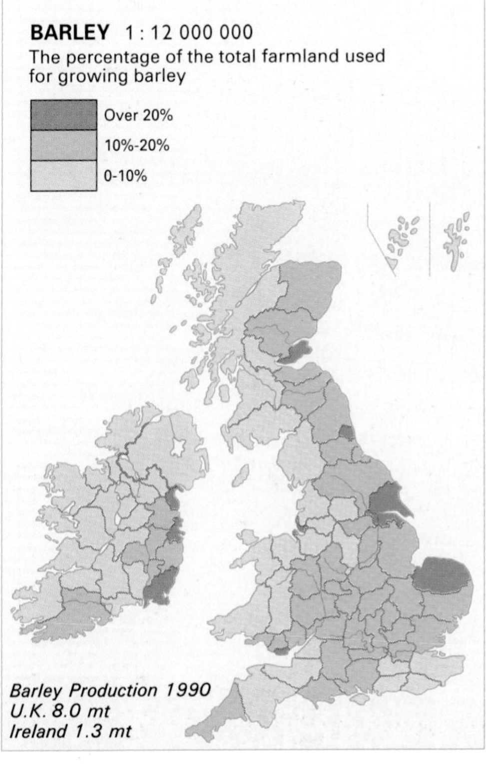

Barley Production 1990
U.K. 8.0 mt
Ireland 1.3 mt

PASTURE   1 : 12 000 000

The percentage of the total farmland used
for grazing livestock

80%-100%

60%-80%

40%-60%

20%-40%

0-20%

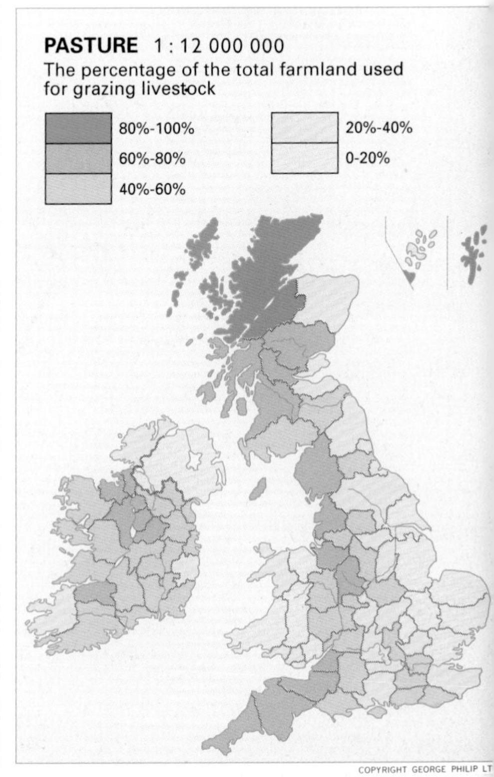

NUMBER AND SIZE OF AGRICULTURAL HOLDINGS IN THE U.K.

Average size of holdings (hectares)

	1940	1980	1989
England & Wales	33.8	60.2	57.9
Scotland	81.8	96.2	195.9
Northern Ireland	13.7	24.2	25.2

Over 100 hectares
50-100 hectares
40-50 hectares
20-40 hectares
5-20 hectares
2-5 hectares
Under 2 hectares

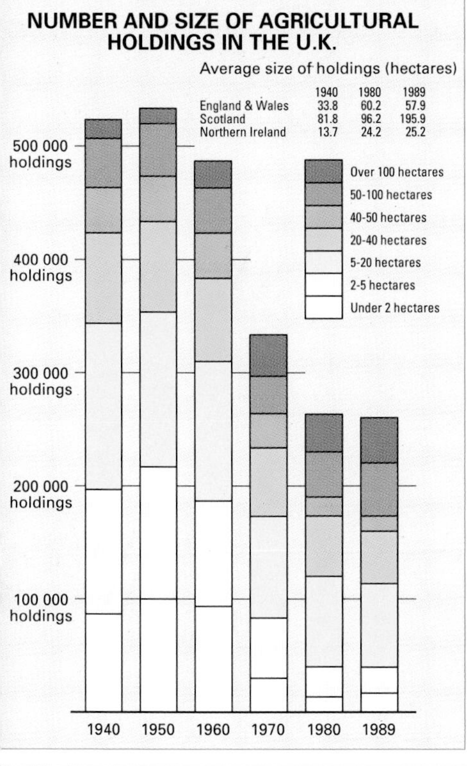

POTATOES   1 : 12 000 000
The percentage of the total farmland used for growing potatoes

Over 3%
2%-3%
1%-2%
Under 1%

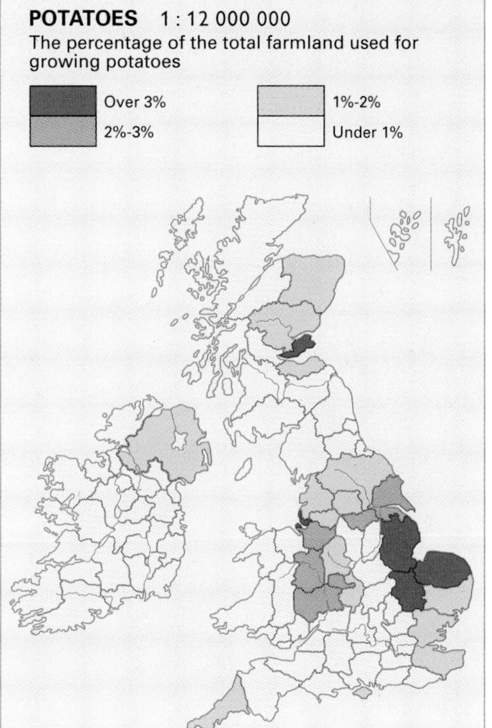

MARKET GARDENING   1 : 12 000 000
The percentage of the total farmland used for market gardening

Over 5%
2.5%-5%
1.0%-2.5%
Under 1%

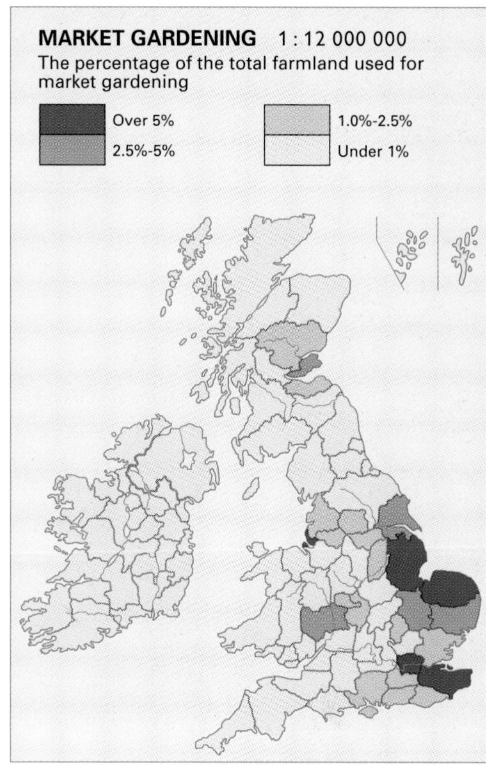

FISHING

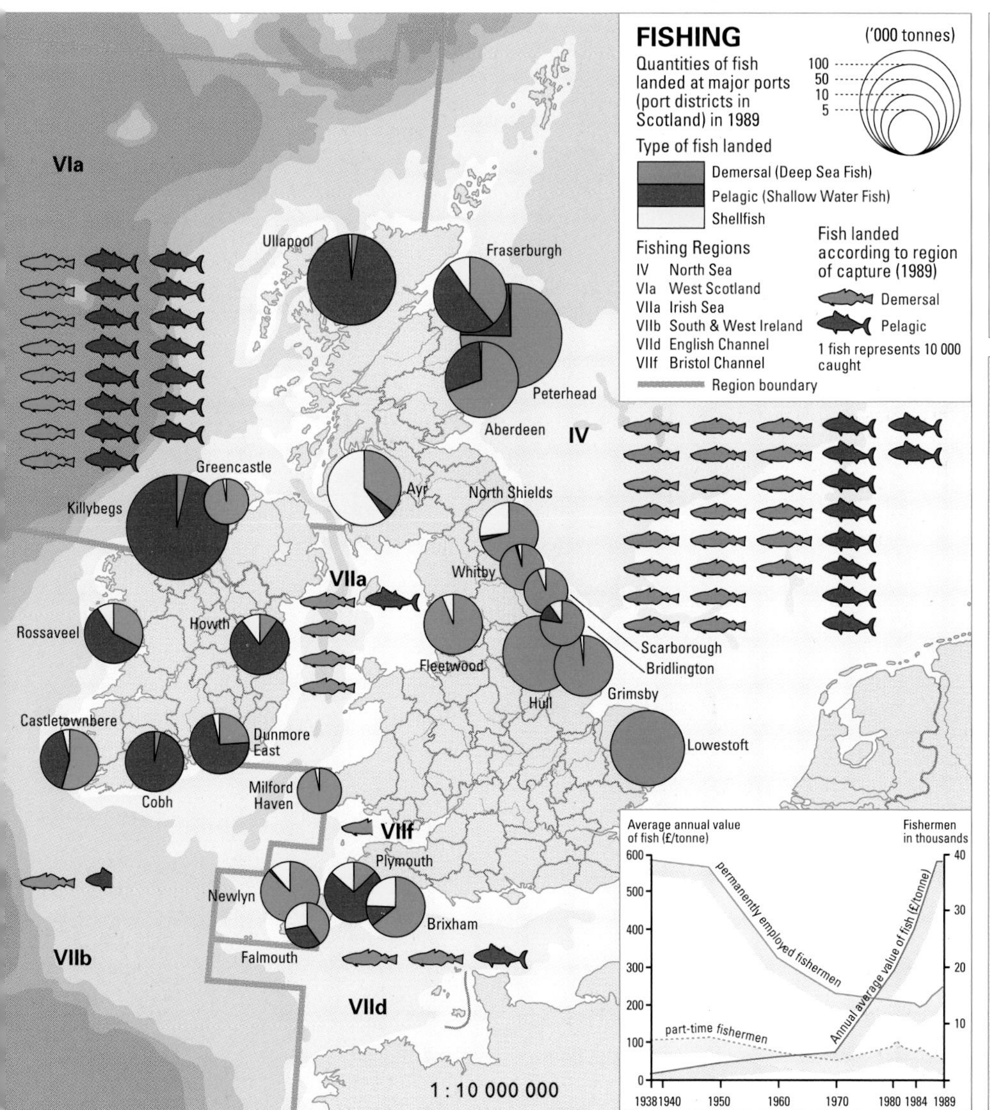

('000 tonnes)

Quantities of fish landed at major ports (port districts in Scotland) in 1989

Type of fish landed
Demersal (Deep Sea Fish)
Pelagic (Shallow Water Fish)
Shellfish

Fishing Regions
IV North Sea
VIa West Scotland
VIIa Irish Sea
VIIb South & West Ireland
VIId English Channel
VIIf Bristol Channel

Fish landed according to region of capture (1989)
Demersal
Pelagic
1 fish represents 10 000 caught
Region boundary

1 : 10 000 000

Average annual value of fish (£/tonne)
permanently employed fishermen
part-time fishermen
Annual average value of fish (£/tonne)
Fishermen in thousands

1000 500 200 100 50 m

VALUE OF AGRICULTURAL OUTPUT (U.K. only)

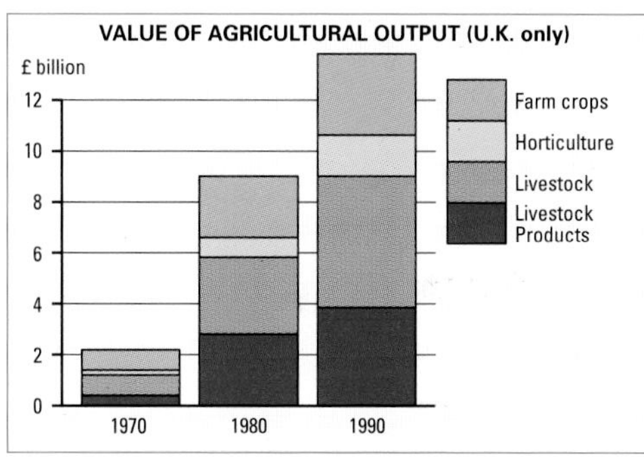

£ billion
Farm crops
Horticulture
Livestock
Livestock Products

AGRICULTURAL LAND & LIVESTOCK, 1970-90 (U.K. only)

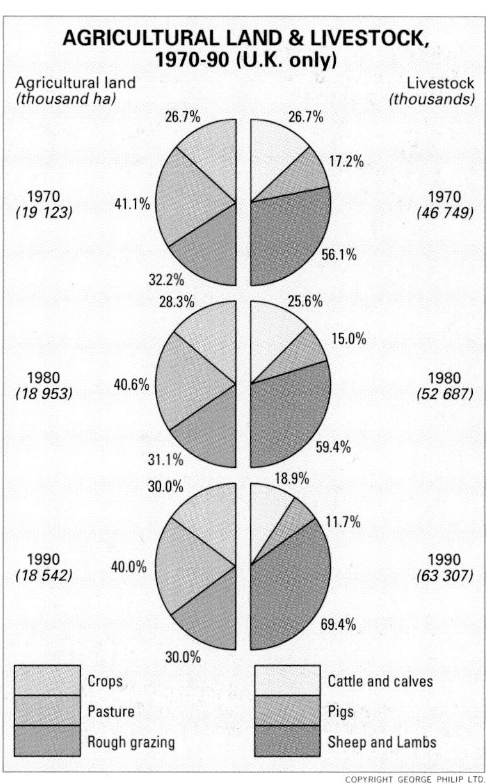

Agricultural land (thousand ha)
Livestock (thousands)

Crops
Pasture
Rough grazing
Cattle and calves
Pigs
Sheep and Lambs

COPYRIGHT GEORGE PHILIP LTD.

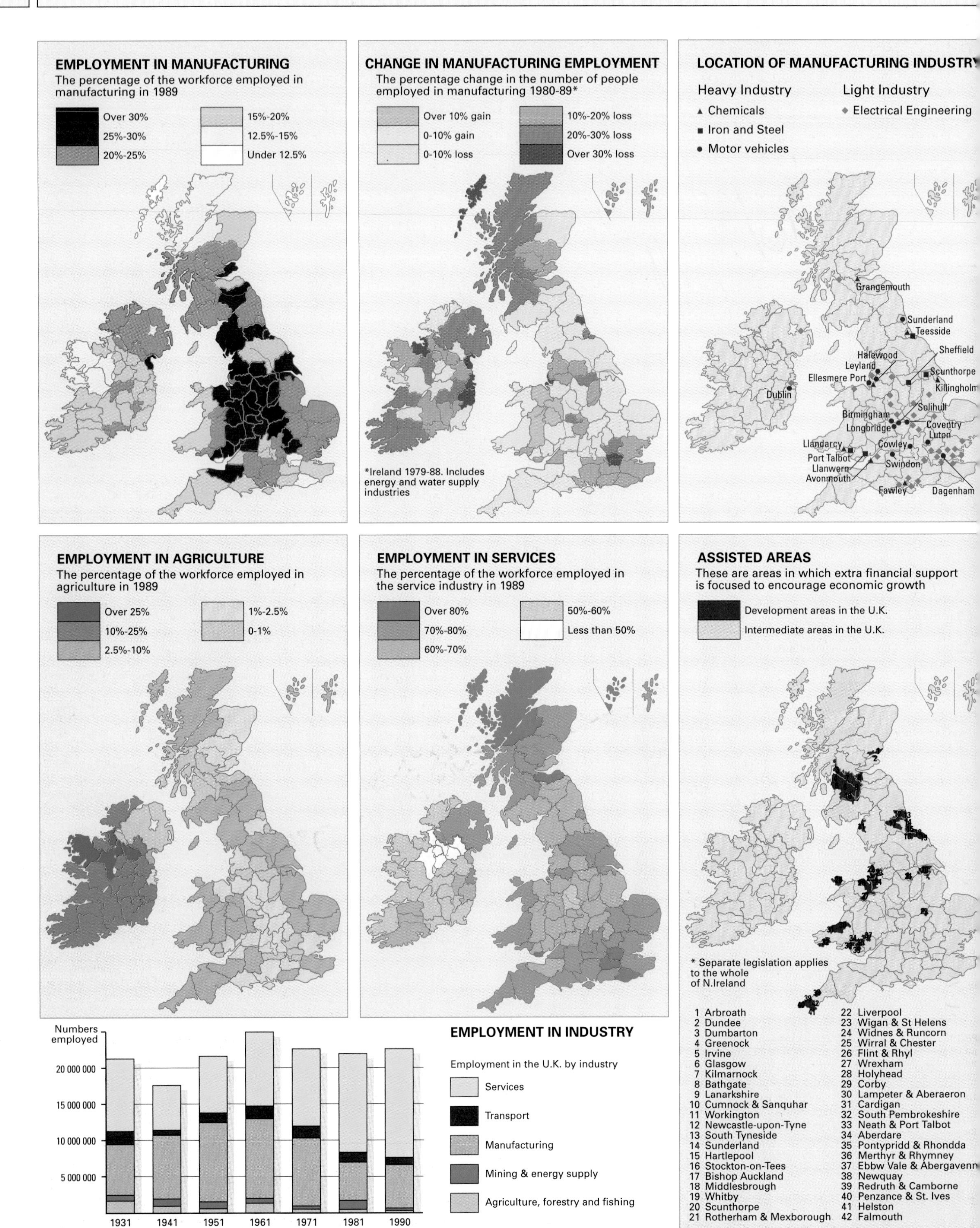

EMPLOYMENT IN MANUFACTURING
The percentage of the workforce employed in manufacturing in 1989

- Over 30%
- 25%-30%
- 20%-25%
- 15%-20%
- 12.5%-15%
- Under 12.5%

CHANGE IN MANUFACTURING EMPLOYMENT
The percentage change in the number of people employed in manufacturing 1980-89*

- Over 10% gain
- 0-10% gain
- 0-10% loss
- 10%-20% loss
- 20%-30% loss
- Over 30% loss

*Ireland 1979-88. Includes energy and water supply industries

LOCATION OF MANUFACTURING INDUSTRY

Heavy Industry
- ▲ Chemicals
- ■ Iron and Steel
- ● Motor vehicles

Light Industry
- ◆ Electrical Engineering

Grangemouth
Sunderland
Teesside
Sheffield
Halewood
Leyland
Ellesmere Port
Scunthorpe
Killingholm
Dublin
Solihull
Birmingham
Longbridge
Coventry
Luton
Llandarcy
Cowley
Port Talbot
Llanwern
Swindon
Avonmouth
Fawley
Dagenham

EMPLOYMENT IN AGRICULTURE
The percentage of the workforce employed in agriculture in 1989

- Over 25%
- 10%-25%
- 2.5%-10%
- 1%-2.5%
- 0-1%

EMPLOYMENT IN SERVICES
The percentage of the workforce employed in the service industry in 1989

- Over 80%
- 70%-80%
- 60%-70%
- 50%-60%
- Less than 50%

ASSISTED AREAS
These are areas in which extra financial support is focused to encourage economic growth

- Development areas in the U.K.
- Intermediate areas in the U.K.

* Separate legislation applies to the whole of N.Ireland

1 Arbroath
2 Dundee
3 Dumbarton
4 Greenock
5 Irvine
6 Glasgow
7 Kilmarnock
8 Bathgate
9 Lanarkshire
10 Cumnock & Sanquhar
11 Workington
12 Newcastle-upon-Tyne
13 South Tyneside
14 Sunderland
15 Hartlepool
16 Stockton-on-Tees
17 Bishop Auckland
18 Middlesbrough
19 Whitby
20 Scunthorpe
21 Rotherham & Mexborough
22 Liverpool
23 Wigan & St Helens
24 Widnes & Runcorn
25 Wirral & Chester
26 Flint & Rhyl
27 Wrexham
28 Holyhead
29 Corby
30 Lampeter & Aberaeron
31 Cardigan
32 South Pembrokeshire
33 Neath & Port Talbot
34 Aberdare
35 Pontypridd & Rhondda
36 Merthyr & Rhymney
37 Ebbw Vale & Abergavenny
38 Newquay
39 Redruth & Camborne
40 Penzance & St. Ives
41 Helston
42 Falmouth

EMPLOYMENT IN INDUSTRY

Numbers employed

Employment in the U.K. by industry

- Services
- Transport
- Manufacturing
- Mining & energy supply
- Agriculture, forestry and fishing

1931 1941 1951 1961 1971 1981 1990

1 : 12 000 000

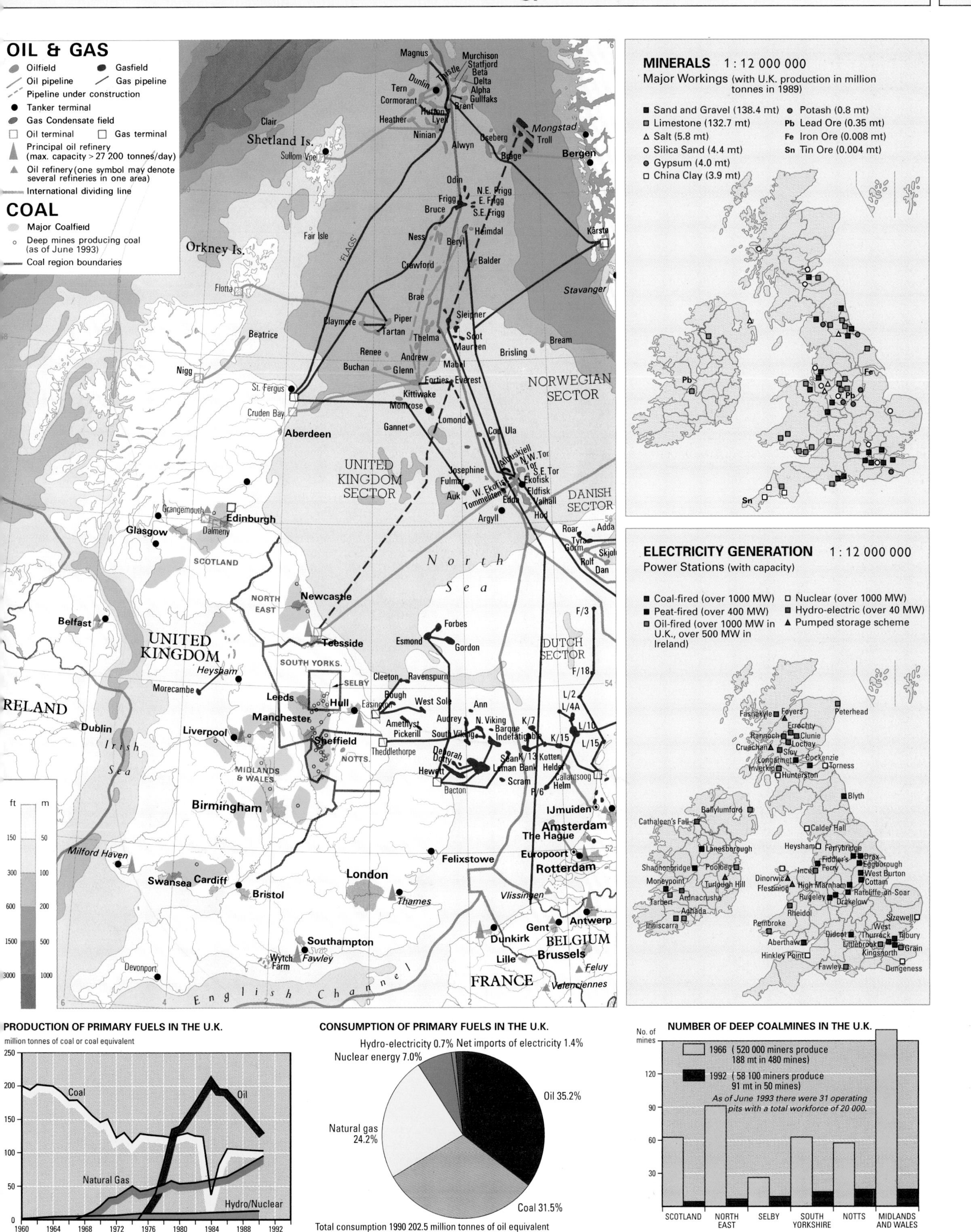

OIL & GAS

- Oilfield
- Gasfield
- Oil pipeline
- Gas pipeline
- Pipeline under construction
- Tanker terminal
- Gas Condensate field
- Oil terminal
- Gas terminal
- Principal oil refinery (max. capacity > 27 200 tonnes/day)
- Oil refinery (one symbol may denote several refineries in one area)
- International dividing line

COAL

- Major Coalfield
- Deep mines producing coal (as of June 1993)
- Coal region boundaries

MINERALS   1 : 12 000 000

Major Workings (with U.K. production in million tonnes in 1989)

- Sand and Gravel (138.4 mt)
- Limestone (132.7 mt)
- Salt (5.8 mt)
- Silica Sand (4.4 mt)
- Gypsum (4.0 mt)
- China Clay (3.9 mt)
- Potash (0.8 mt)
- Pb Lead Ore (0.35 mt)
- Fe Iron Ore (0.008 mt)
- Sn Tin Ore (0.004 mt)

ELECTRICITY GENERATION   1 : 12 000 000

Power Stations (with capacity)

- Coal-fired (over 1000 MW)
- Peat-fired (over 400 MW)
- Oil-fired (over 1000 MW in U.K., over 500 MW in Ireland)
- Nuclear (over 1000 MW)
- Hydro-electric (over 40 MW)
- Pumped storage scheme

PRODUCTION OF PRIMARY FUELS IN THE U.K.

million tonnes of coal or coal equivalent

CONSUMPTION OF PRIMARY FUELS IN THE U.K.

Hydro-electricity 0.7%   Net imports of electricity 1.4%
Nuclear energy 7.0%
Oil 35.2%
Natural gas 24.2%
Coal 31.5%

Total consumption 1990 202.5 million tonnes of oil equivalent

NUMBER OF DEEP COALMINES IN THE U.K.

No. of mines

1966 (520 000 miners produce 188 mt in 480 mines)
1992 (58 100 miners produce 91 mt in 50 mines)

As of June 1993 there were 31 operating pits with a total workforce of 20 000.

SCOTLAND   NORTH EAST   SELBY   SOUTH YORKSHIRE   NOTTS   MIDLANDS AND WALES

COPYRIGHT GEORGE PHILIP LTD.

ROADS AND FERRIES

- M6 Motorways
- Main primary routes

(56) Average 24 hour flow of vehicles at a selected point on a motorway. Figures are given in thousands

- - - - - Principal ferry routes
- -Oslo- Long haul sea ferry destinations

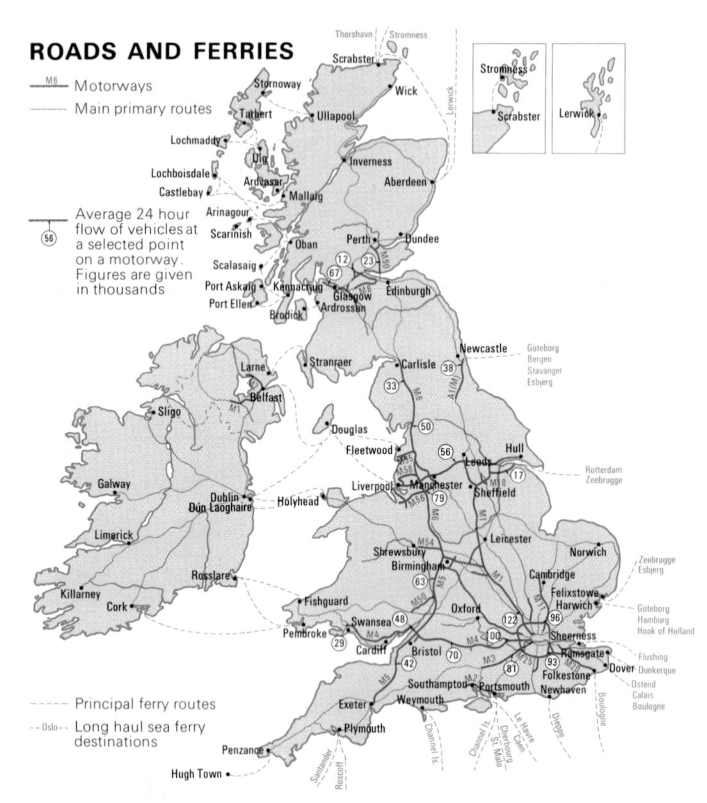

RAILWAYS

- Electrified lines
- Other main lines

Furthest distances from London reached within a journey time of
3 hours 6 hours
1950 ▲ ●
1990 ▲ ●

Channel Tunnel
- - - - Channel Tunnel
- Proposed high speed rail link

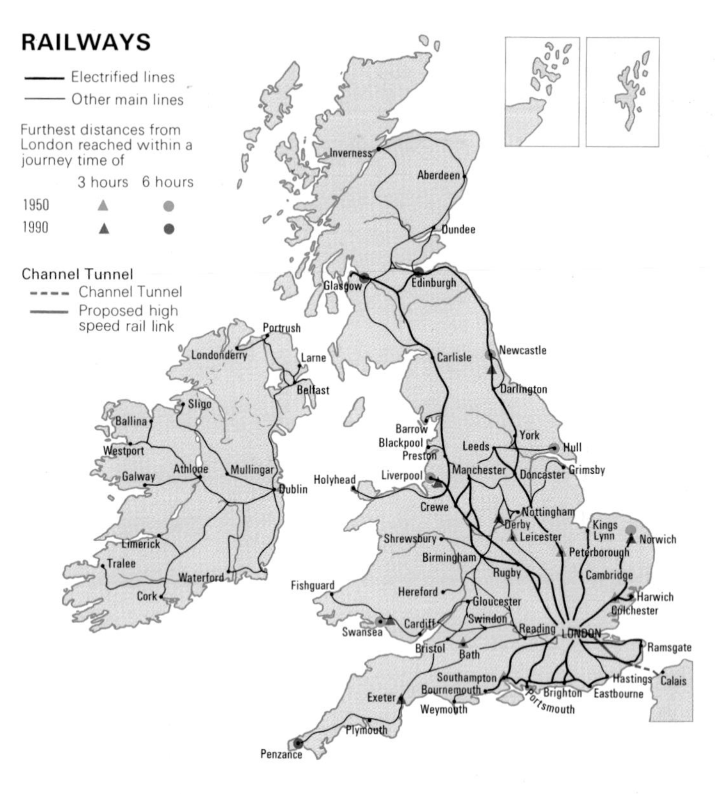

CHANNEL TUNNEL

Estimated journey times between London-Brussels and London-Paris

Hours

	1990/1	Best time achievable using existing networks
	1994	Opening of Channel Tunnel
	1996	Estimated completion date of new line in Belgium
	2000	Estimated completion date of high speed rail link

London – Brussels   London – Paris

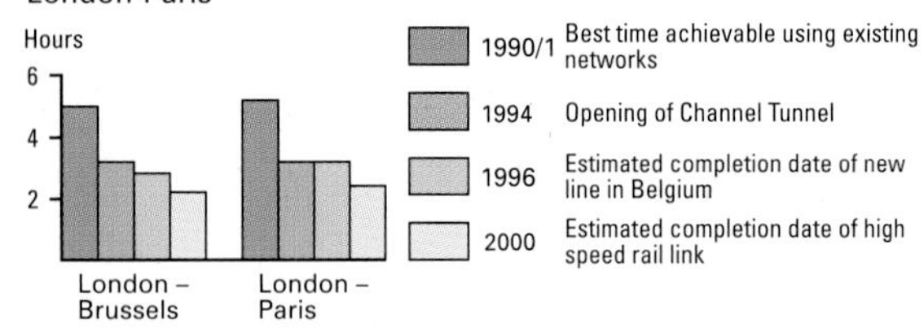

MEANS OF TRANSPORTATION WITHIN THE U.K.

'000 million tonne km 200 175 150 125 100 75 50 25 0

GOODS

0 100 200 300 400 500 600 700 '000 million passenger km

PASSENGERS

1975
1980
1985
1990

- Road
- Water
- Rail
- Pipelines
- Private Transport
- Public Transport
- Rail

Air transport accounted for only 2200 million passengers in 1975, 3000 million in 1980, 4000 million in 1985 and 50 million in 1990.

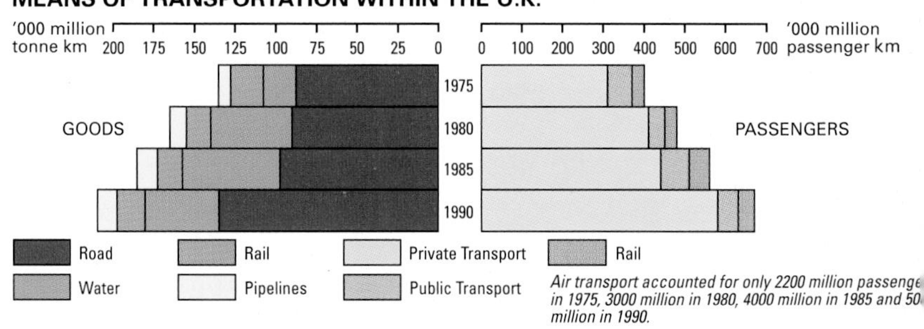

PORTS

Goods traffic by port group
Foreign and domestic traffic million tonnes
100 75 50 25 Fuel
Other goods

Ports handling over 1 million tonnes of goods traffic million tonnes
- ■ 50-60
- □ 40-50
- ◉ 30-40
- ◎ 20-30
- • 10-20
- · 1-10

- ● Ports where fuel represents over 75% of all goods handled
- *Hull* Ports handling over 1 million tonnes of unitized traffic
- Port group boundaries

The total figure for the Irish Rep. does not include domestic traffic

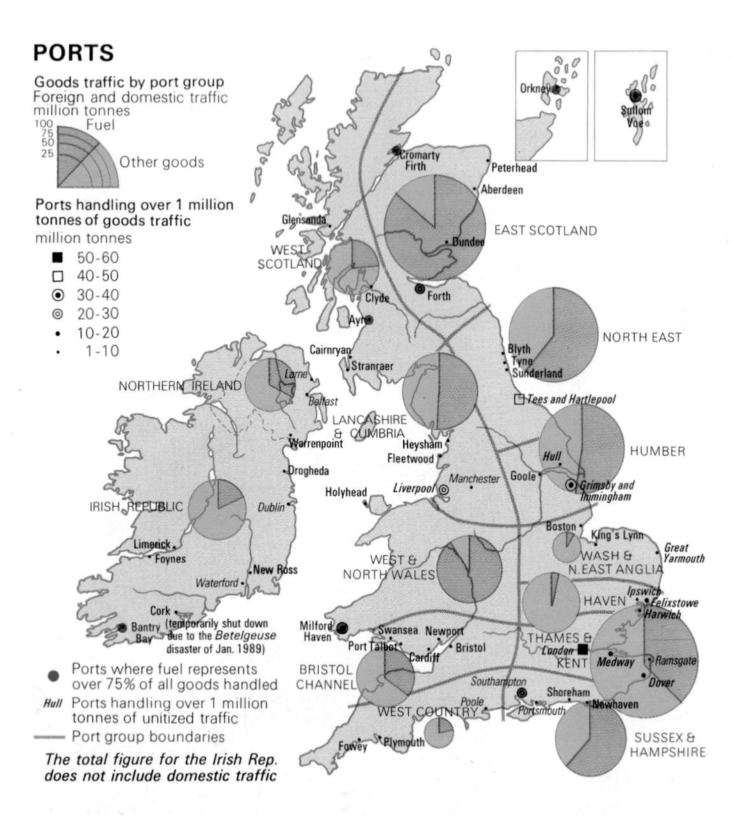

AIRPORTS

Passenger traffic
'000 passengers
50 000
International
5000
1000
250
Domestic

- Selected airports with less than 200 000 passengers

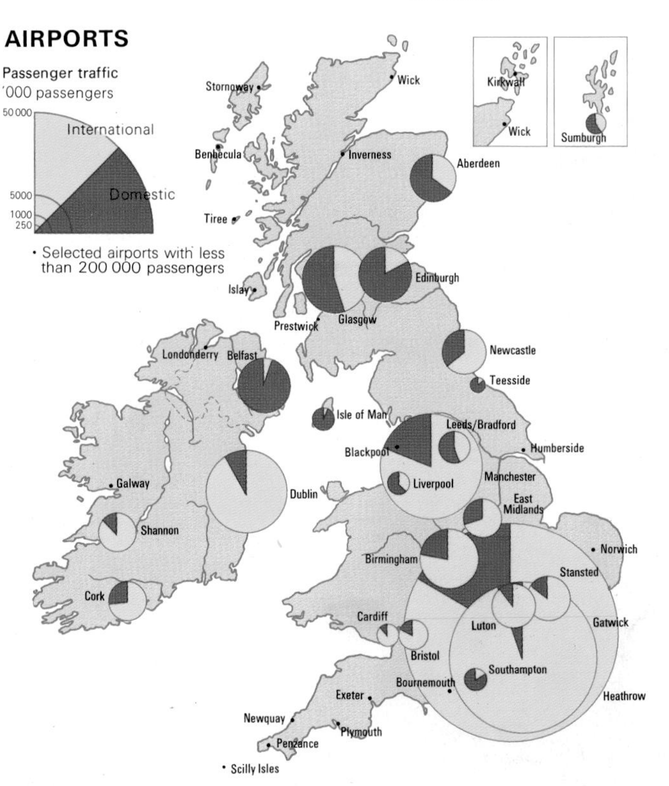

1 : 10 000 000

COPYRIGHT. GEORGE PHILIP & SON. LTD.

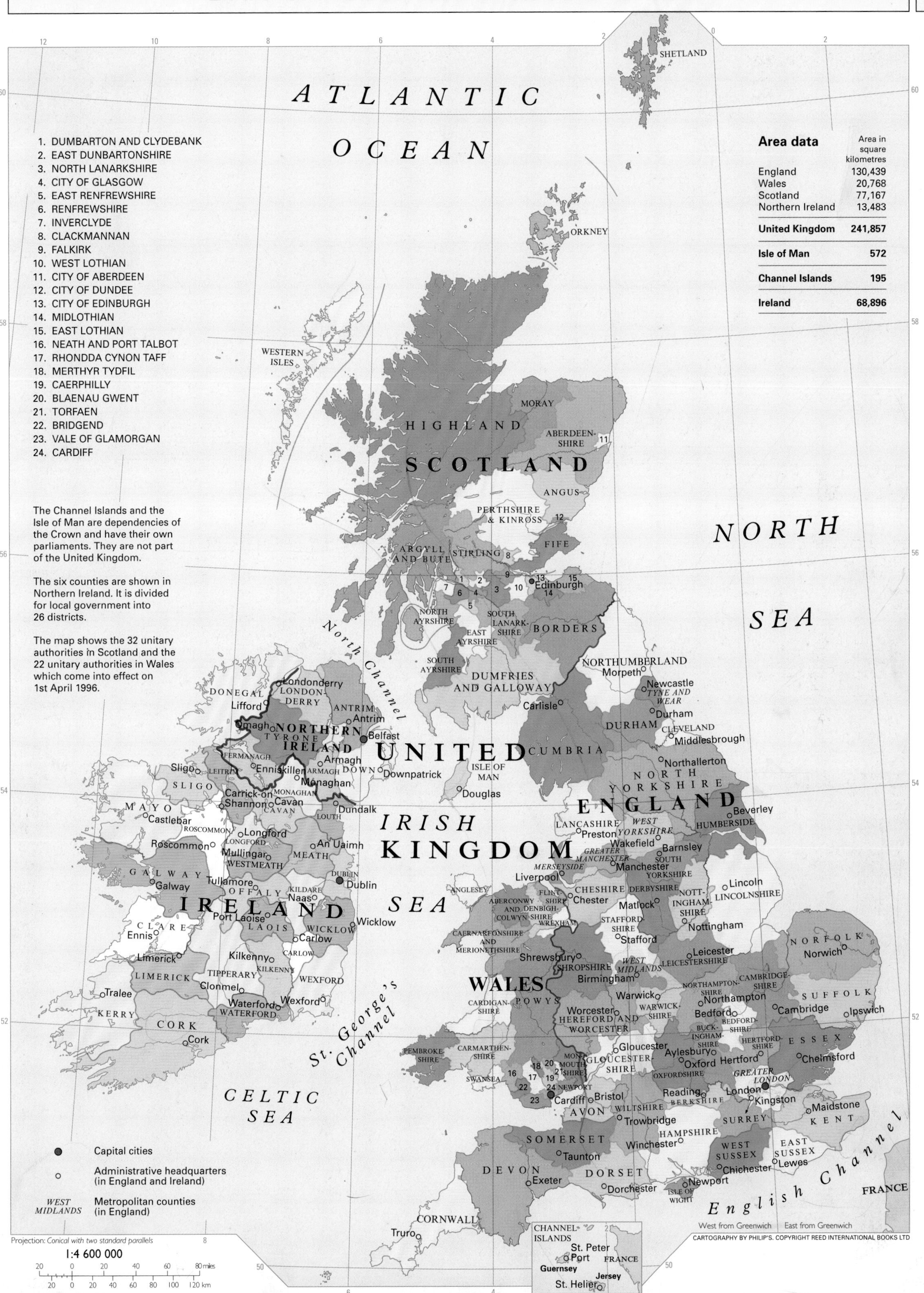

1. DUMBARTON AND CLYDEBANK
2. EAST DUNBARTONSHIRE
3. NORTH LANARKSHIRE
4. CITY OF GLASGOW
5. EAST RENFREWSHIRE
6. RENFREWSHIRE
7. INVERCLYDE
8. CLACKMANNAN
9. FALKIRK
10. WEST LOTHIAN
11. CITY OF ABERDEEN
12. CITY OF DUNDEE
13. CITY OF EDINBURGH
14. MIDLOTHIAN
15. EAST LOTHIAN
16. NEATH AND PORT TALBOT
17. RHONDDA CYNON TAFF
18. MERTHYR TYDFIL
19. CAERPHILLY
20. BLAENAU GWENT
21. TORFAEN
22. BRIDGEND
23. VALE OF GLAMORGAN
24. CARDIFF

The Channel Islands and the Isle of Man are dependencies of the Crown and have their own parliaments. They are not part of the United Kingdom.

The six counties are shown in Northern Ireland. It is divided for local government into 26 districts.

The map shows the 32 unitary authorities in Scotland and the 22 unitary authorities in Wales which come into effect on 1st April 1996.

Area data

	Area in square kilometres
England	130,439
Wales	20,768
Scotland	77,167
Northern Ireland	13,483
United Kingdom	**241,857**
Isle of Man	**572**
Channel Islands	**195**
Ireland	**68,896**

● Capital cities

○ Administrative headquarters (in England and Ireland)

WEST MIDLANDS Metropolitan counties (in England)

Projection: Conical with two standard parallels

1:4 600 000

CARTOGRAPHY BY PHILIP'S. COPYRIGHT REED INTERNATIONAL BOOKS LTD

POPULATION DENSITY 1891 1:12 000 000
See map at right for reference to colours

Density in 1891 by country:
U.K. 142 people per km²
Ireland 49 people per km²

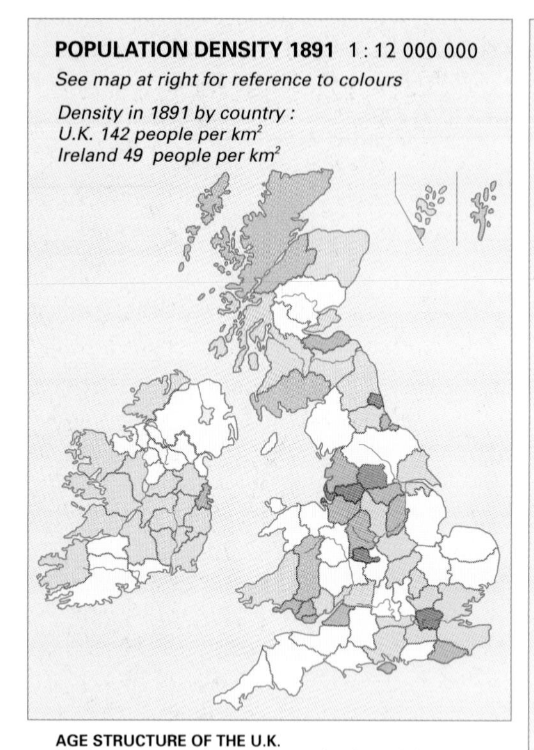

POPULATION DENSITY 1991
Persons per km²

	Over 1000
	500–1000
	200–500
	100–200
	50–100
	25–50
	Under 25

The density for the whole of the U.K. is 223 people per km², the density for Ireland is 51.

1:7 000 000

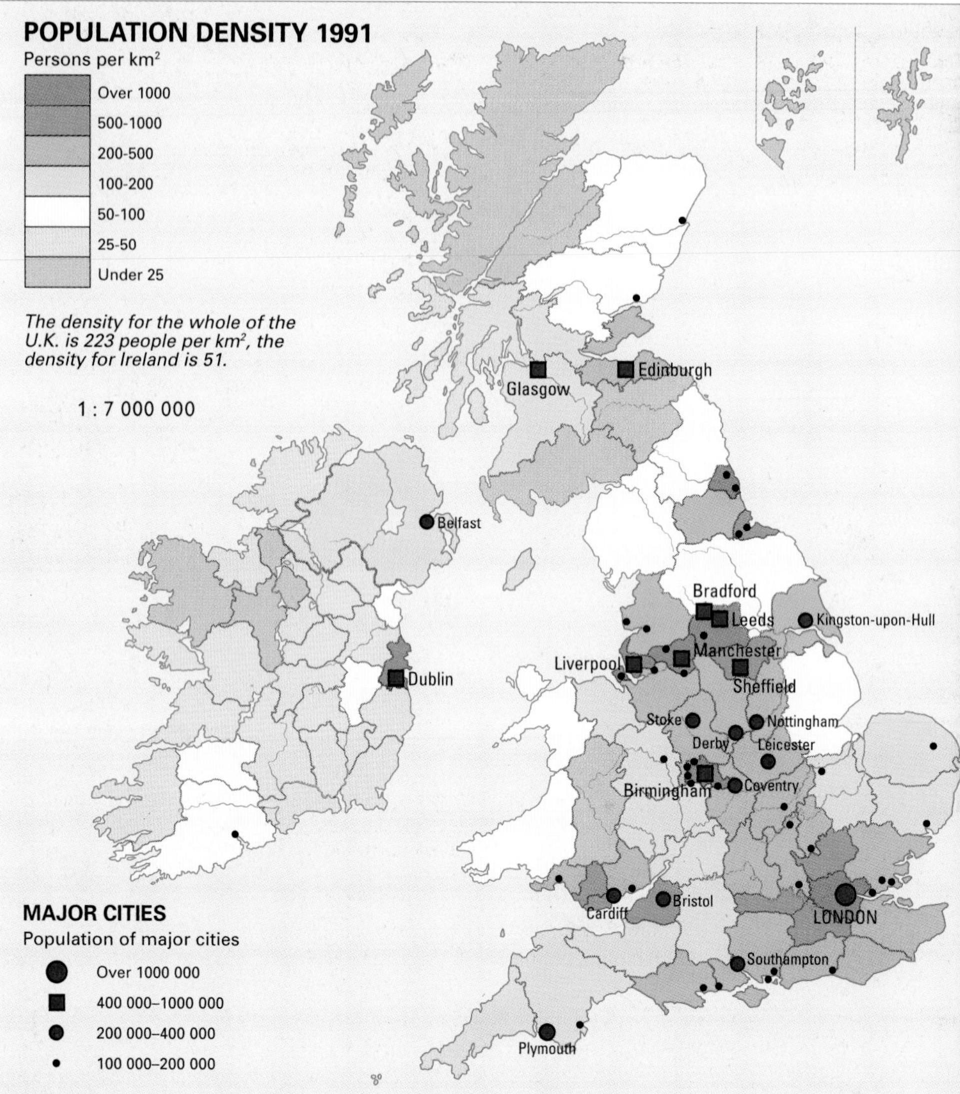

MAJOR CITIES
Population of major cities

⬤	Over 1 000 000
◼	400 000–1 000 000
●	200 000–400 000
•	100 000–200 000

AGE STRUCTURE OF THE U.K.
The bars represent the percentage of males and the percentage of females in the age group shown

| 1901 | 1990 | — Projected 2150 |

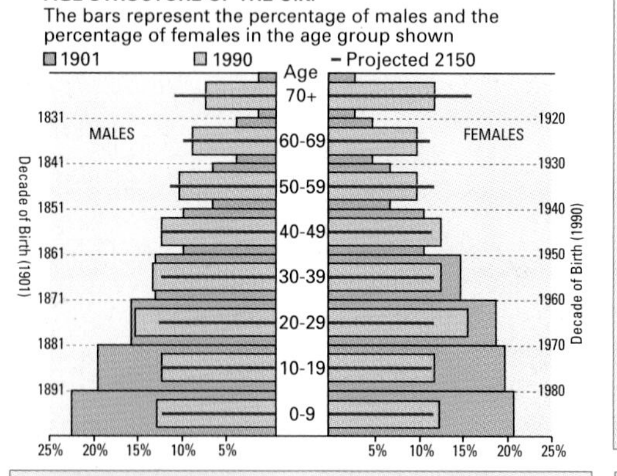

YOUNG PEOPLE 1:12 000 000
The percentage of the population under 15 years old in 1990 (Ireland 1986)

	Over 30%		19%–20%
	25%–30%		18%–19%
	20%–25%		Under 18%

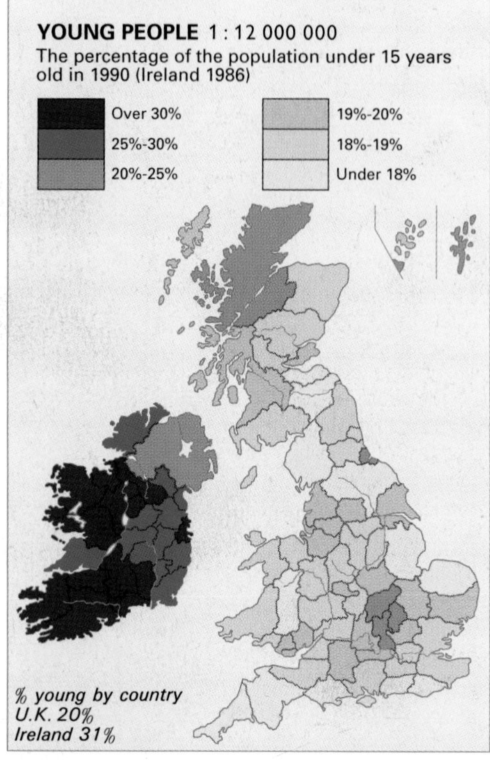

% young by country
U.K. 20%
Ireland 31%

OLD PEOPLE 1:12 000 000
The percentage of the population over pensionable age* in 1989

	Over 20%		12.5%–15%
	17.5%–20%		10%–12.5%
	15%–17.5%		Under 10%

* *Pensionable age is 65 for males, 60 for females*

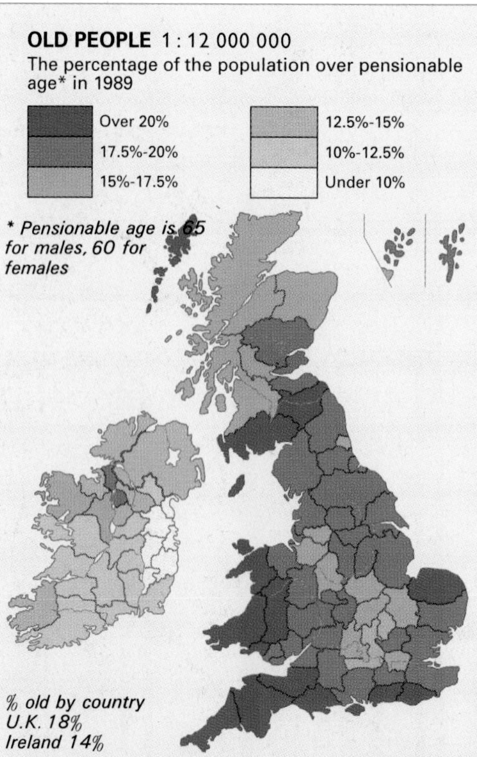

% old by country
U.K. 18%
Ireland 14%

URBANIZATION 1:12 000 000
The percentage of the population living in towns and cities (latest available year)

	Over 90%		60%–70%
	80%–90%		50%–60%
	70%–80%		Under 50%

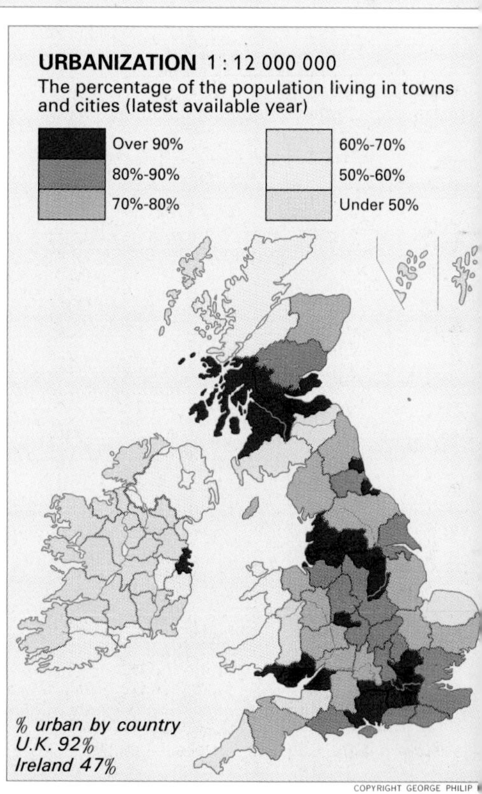

% urban by country
U.K. 92%
Ireland 47%

NATURAL POPULATION CHANGE

The difference between the number of births and the number of deaths per thousand inhabitants in 1990

- Over 10 more births
- 5-10 more births
- 2.5-5 more births
- 0-2.5 more births
- 0-2.5 more deaths
- Over 2.5 more deaths

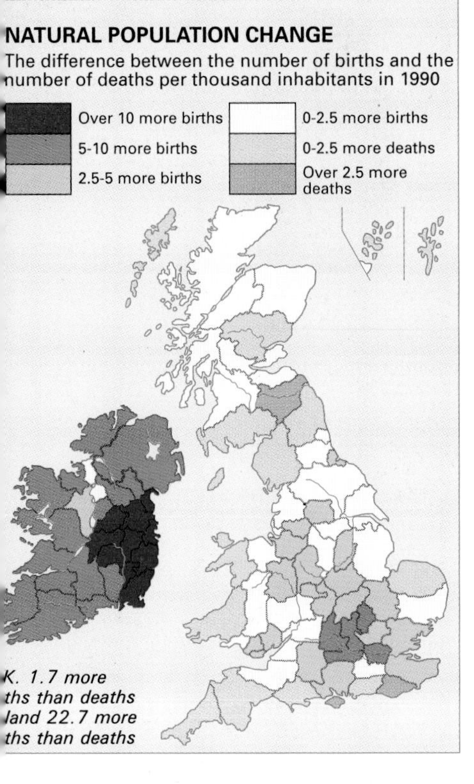

K. 1.7 more
ths than deaths
land 22.7 more
ths than deaths

ETHNIC GROUP

Ethnic minority groups

Thousands
500
100
50

Other — Indian/ Pakistani/ Bangladeshi
W. Indian/ African

Ethnic minorities as a % of total population in each region named
- Over 6%
- 4%-6%
- 2%-4%
- 0-2%

No available data for Ireland or Northern Ireland

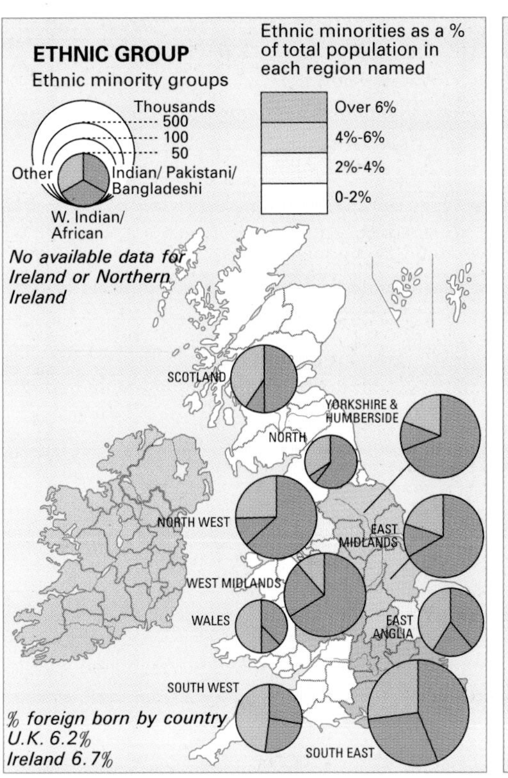

% foreign born by country
U.K. 6.2%
Ireland 6.7%

MIGRATION 1 : 12 000 000

The difference between the number moving in and the number moving away (per 1000 inhabitants)*

- Over 15 moved in
- 10-15 moved in
- 5-10 moved in
- 0-5 moved in
- 0-5 moved away
- 5-10 moved away

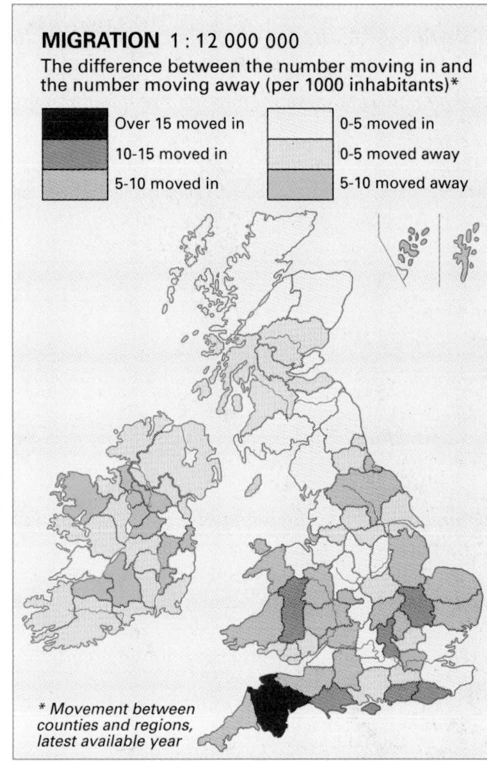

* Movement between counties and regions, latest available year

U.K. VITAL STATISTICS 1900-2000

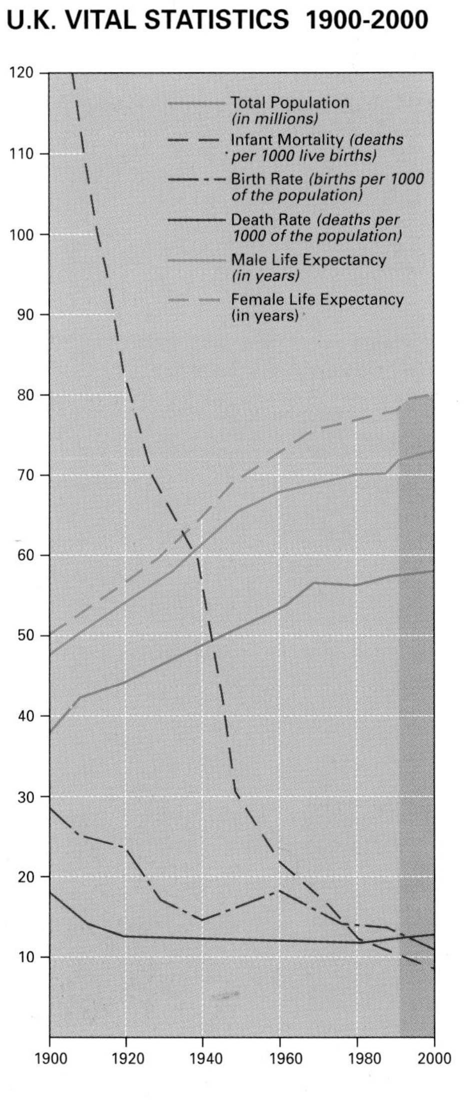

Legend:
- Total Population (in millions)
- Infant Mortality (deaths per 1000 live births)
- Birth Rate (births per 1000 of the population)
- Death Rate (deaths per 1000 of the population)
- Male Life Expectancy (in years)
- Female Life Expectancy (in years)

POPULATION CHANGE 1961-1991

The percentage change in the number of people between 1961 and 1991

- Over 30% gain
- 25%-30% gain
- 20%-25% gain
- 15%-20% gain
- 10%-15% gain
- 5%-10% gain
- 0-5% gain
- 0-5% loss
- 5%-10% loss
- Over 10% loss

1 : 7 000 000

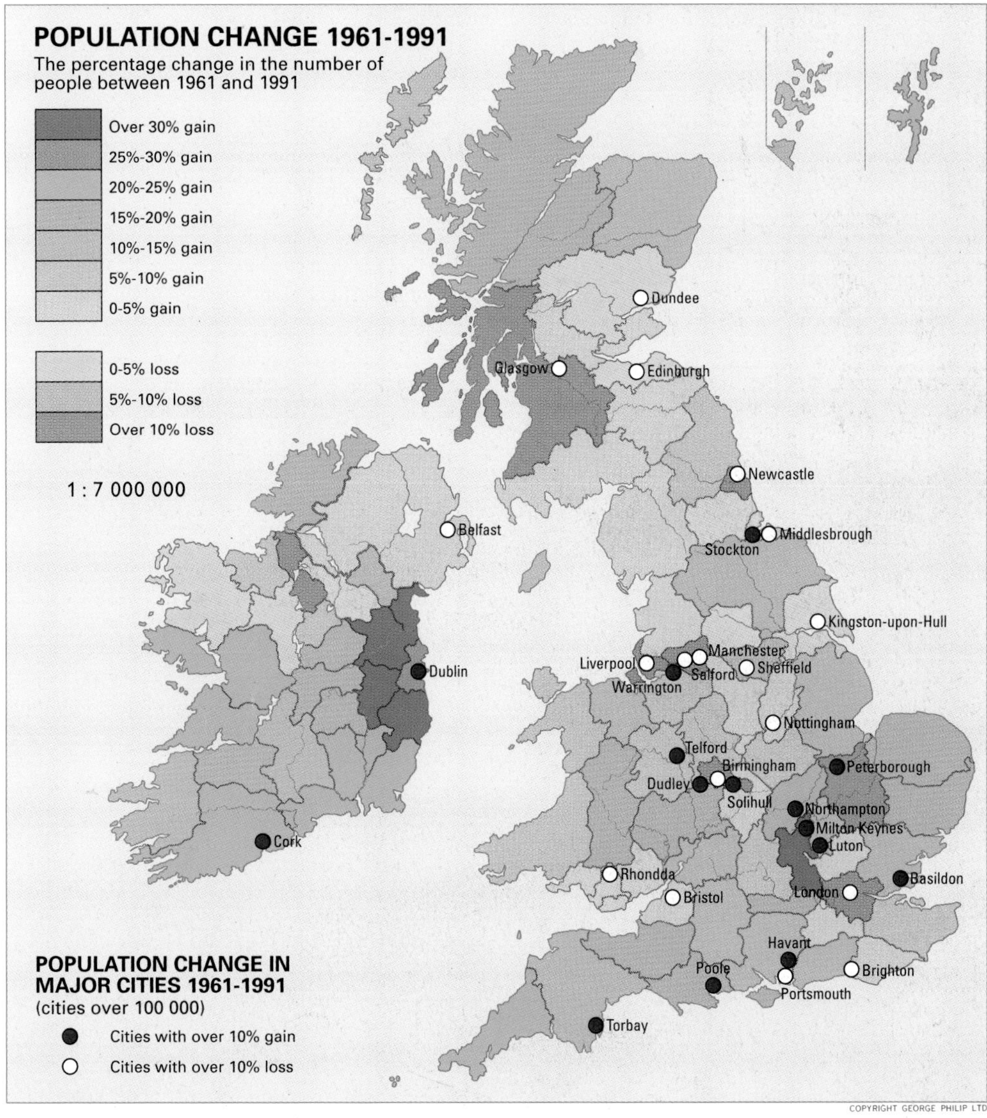

POPULATION CHANGE IN MAJOR CITIES 1961-1991
(cities over 100 000)

- ● Cities with over 10% gain
- ○ Cities with over 10% loss

HOUSE OWNERSHIP 1 : 12 000 000

The percentage of dwellings which are owner-occupied in 1990 (Ireland 1985)

- Over 80%
- 70%-80%
- 60%-70%
- 50%-60%
- Under 50%

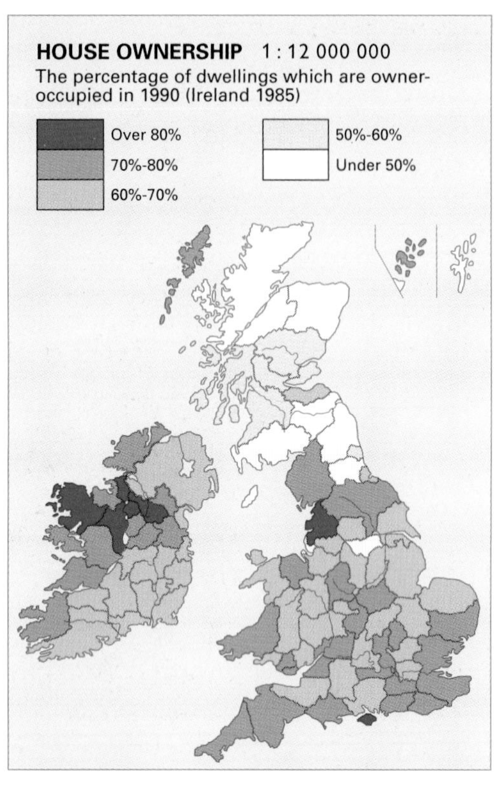

CAR OWNERSHIP 1 : 12 000 000

The number of new* cars per thousand people in 1990

- Over 50
- 40-50
- 30-40
- 20-30
- 10-20

No data

*First year of registration

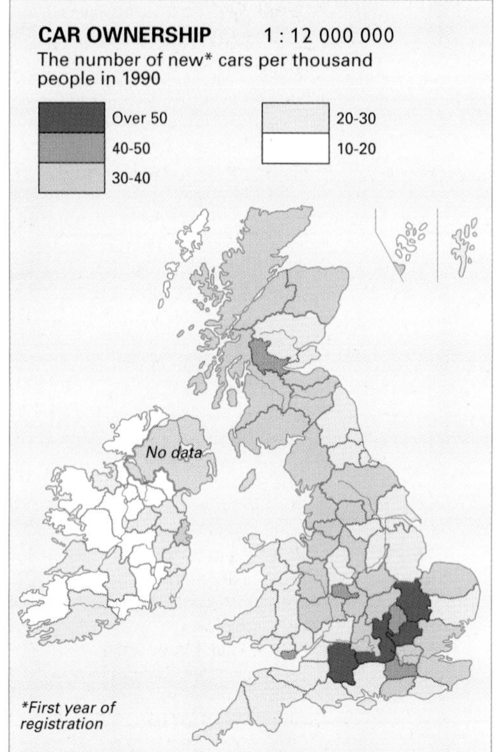

INCOME 1 : 12 000 000

The average gross weekly earnings of males in full employment in 1991 (U.K. only)*

- Over £375
- £350-£375
- £325-£350
- £300-£325
- £275-£300
- Under £275

*No data available for Ireland, Borders or Islands

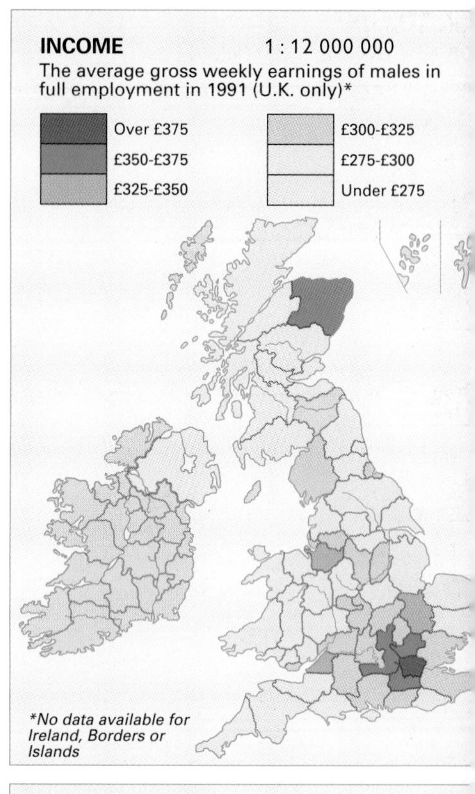

HEALTH 1 : 12 000 000

The number of doctors per 100 000 people (by health authority, latest available year)

- Over 90
- 80-90
- 70-80
- 60-70
- 50-60
- Under 50

Regional health authority boundaries

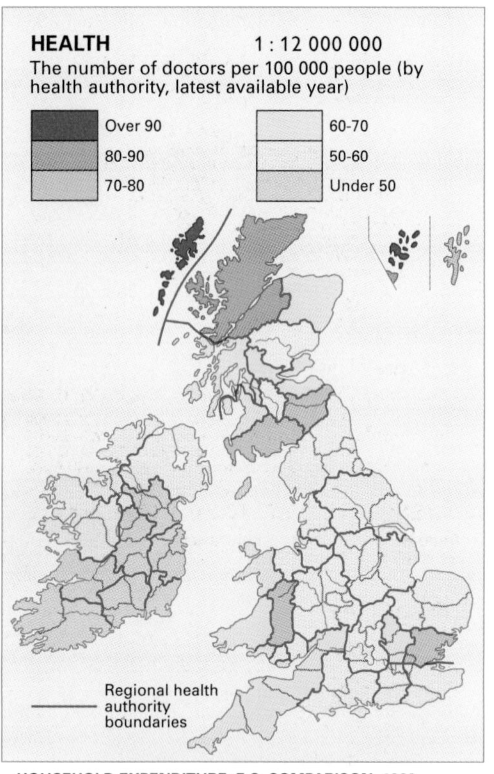

EDUCATION 1 : 12 000 000

The percentage of pupils aged 16 staying on in education in 1989 (U.K. only)

- Over 85%
- 80%-85%
- 75%-80%
- 70%-75%
- 65%-70%
- Under 65%

No comparable data

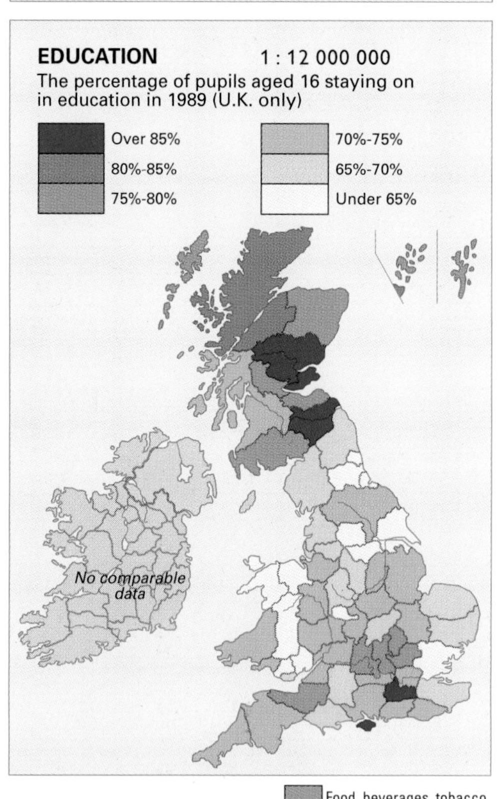

UNEMPLOYMENT 1 : 12 000 000

The percentage of the workforce unemployed in 1992

- Over 17.5%
- 15%-17.5%
- 12.5%-15%
- 10%-12.5%
- 7.5%-10%
- Under 7.5%

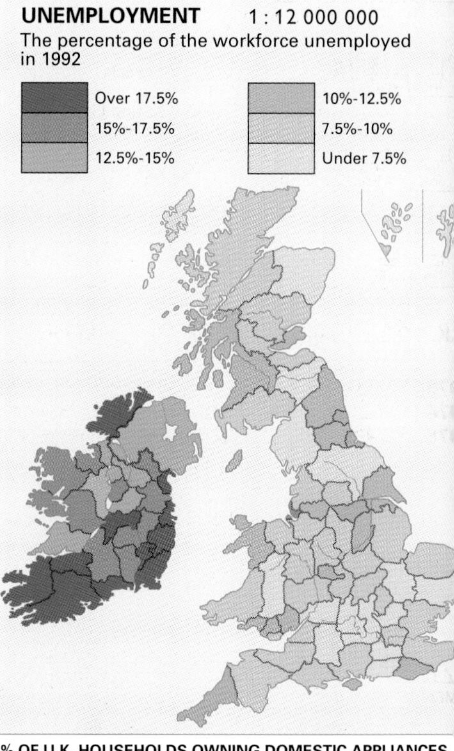

HOUSEHOLD EXPENDITURE: E.C. COMPARISON 1989

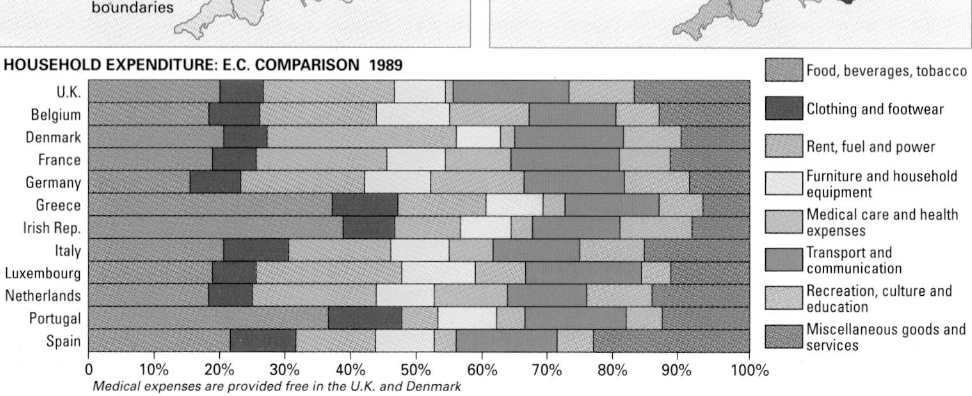

- Food, beverages, tobacco
- Clothing and footwear
- Rent, fuel and power
- Furniture and household equipment
- Medical care and health expenses
- Transport and communication
- Recreation, culture and education
- Miscellaneous goods and services

U.K.
Belgium
Denmark
France
Germany
Greece
Irish Rep.
Italy
Luxembourg
Netherlands
Portugal
Spain

0 10% 20% 30% 40% 50% 60% 70% 80% 90% 100%

Medical expenses are provided free in the U.K. and Denmark

% OF U.K. HOUSEHOLDS OWNING DOMESTIC APPLIANCES

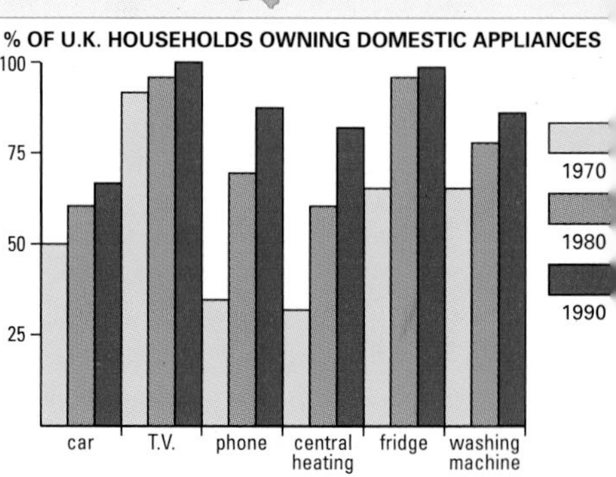

100
75
50
25

car T.V. phone central heating fridge washing machine

1970
1980
1990

U.K. TRADE
TOP TEN TRADING PARTNERS 1990

One container represents 1% of the total value of imports or 1% of the total value of exports

IMPORTS

- Germany £19.9b
- U.S.A. £14.4b
- France £11.7b
- Netherlands £10.5b
- Japan £6.7b
- Italy £6.7b
- Belgium/Lux. £5.7b
- Irish Republic £4.5b
- Switzerland £4.2b
- Norway £4.2b

Total Imports 1990 £126billion
Total Exports 1990 £104billion

EXPORTS

- Germany £13.1b
- U.S.A. £13.0b
- France £10.9b
- Netherlands £7.5b
- Belgium/Lux. £5.6b
- Italy £5.6b
- Irish Republic £5.3b
- Spain £3.7b
- Sweden £2.7b
- Japan £2.6b

TYPE OF GOODS
- Machinery and Transport Equipment
- • Road Vehicles
- Other manufactured Goods
- Chemicals
- Food and Live Animals
- Mineral fuels, Lubricants, etc.
- Other Goods

U.K. TOTAL FOREIGN TRADE 1970-1990 (£ million)

	Imports	Exports		Imports	Exports
1970	£9 051m	£8 063m	**1982**	£56 940m	£55 538m
1974	£23 117m	£16 494m	**1986**	£84 790m	£78 331m
1978	£40 969m	£37 368m	**1990**	£126 165m	£103 91m

TOURISM
TOP 20 TOURIST ATTRACTIONS (U.K. 1991)

- ● Theme Park
- ◐ Museum
- ○ Country Park
- ◑ Historic Property

	Visitors
● Blackpool Pleasure Beach	6 500 000
◐ British Museum, London	5 061 287
◐ National Gallery, London	4 280 139
○ Strathclyde Country Park	4 220 000
● Palace Pier, Brighton	3 500 000
● Pleasure Beach, Gt. Yarmouth	2 500 000
◐ Madame Tussauds, London	2 248 956
● Eastbourne Pier	2 200 000
● Alton Towers, Staffs.	1 968 000
◑ Tower of London	1 923 520
◐ Tate Gallery, London	1 816 421
● Pleasureland, Southport	1 750 000
◐ Natural History Museum, London	1 571 681
◑ St. Pauls Cathedral, London	1 500 000
● Chessington World of Adventures, Surrey	1 410 000
◐ Science Museum, London	1 327 503
○ Bradgate Park, Leics.	1 300 000
● Blackpool Tower	1 300 000
● Frontierland, Morecambe	1 300 000
○ Sandwell Valley Country Park	1 250 000

FOREIGN VISITORS TO THE U.K.

Nature of visit
- Business
- Leisure

Country of origin
- North America
- Western Europe
- Other

No. of visits (millions)

1970   1980   1990

INCOME FROM TOURISM

SCOTLAND
NORTHERN IRELAND
NORTHUMBRIA
CUMBRIA
YORKSHIRE AND HUMBERSIDE
NORTH WEST
EAST MIDLANDS
HEART OF ENGLAND
EAST ANGLIA
WALES
THAMES AND CHILTERNS
LONDON
WEST COUNTRY
SOUTH EAST
SOUTHERN

The percentage of total U.K. income from tourism by region in 1990

- Over 25%
- 10%-25%
- 5%-10%
- 2.5%-5%
- 0-2.5%

Total income from tourism
U.K. 1990   £10.2 billion
Ireland 1990   £7.7 billion

VISITS ABROAD BY U.K. RESIDENTS

Top 10 destinations visited, 1990

No. of U.K. visitors ('000)
0 1000 2000 3000 4000 5000 6000 7000

- France
- Spain
- Irish Rep.
- U.S.A.
- Germany
- Greece
- Netherlands
- Italy
- Portugal
- Belgium

Total visits by area, 1990

North America	2 349 000
Western Europe E.C.	22 032 000
Western Europe non E.C.	3 786 000
Rest of World	3 016 000

DEPENDENCE ON TRADE WITH THE U.K.

Trade with the U.K. as a percentage of each country's total trade

- Over 10%
- 7.5%-10%
- 5.0%-7.5%
- 2.5%-5.0%
- 1.0%-2.5%
- Under 1.0%

CHANGES IN TRADE WITH THE U.K.

Percentage change in exports and imports for selected countries 1985-1990

Change
- 1000%
- 500%
- 100%
- 50%

Increase 1985-1990
Exports to U.K.   Imports from U.K.
Decrease 1985-1990

CANADA
NORWAY
Former U.S.S.R.
U.S.A.
JAPAN
MEXICO
ALGERIA
IRAN
JAMAICA
NIGERIA
INDIA
SINGAPORE
SAUDI ARABIA
ECUADOR
KENYA
INDONESIA
MALAYSIA
SOUTH AFRICA
AUSTRALIA
ARGENTINA

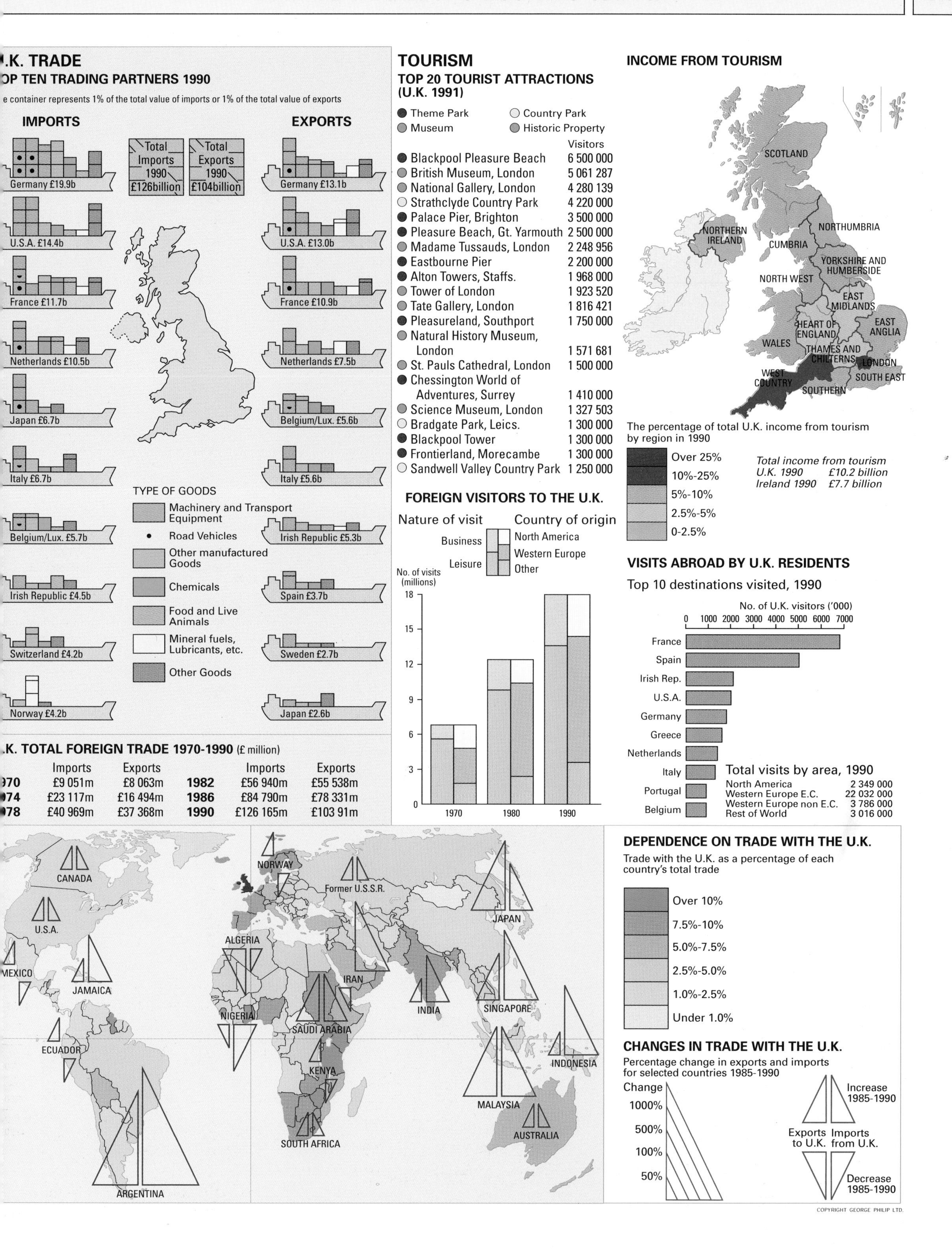

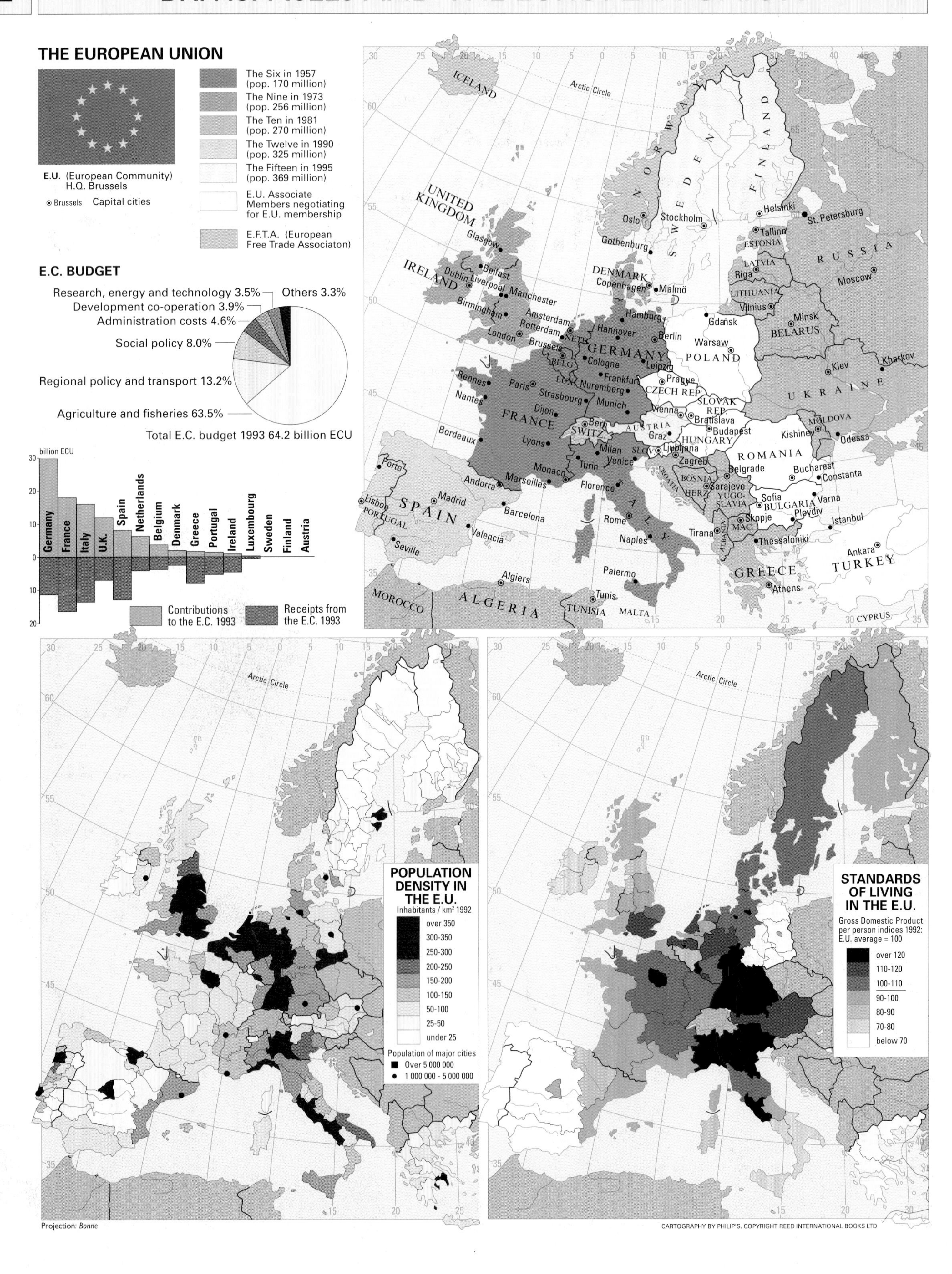

THE EUROPEAN UNION

E.U. (European Community) H.Q. Brussels

⊙ Brussels   Capital cities

The Six in 1957 (pop. 170 million)
The Nine in 1973 (pop. 256 million)
The Ten in 1981 (pop. 270 million)
The Twelve in 1990 (pop. 325 million)
The Fifteen in 1995 (pop. 369 million)
E.U. Associate Members negotiating for E.U. membership
E.F.T.A. (European Free Trade Associaton)

E.C. BUDGET

Research, energy and technology 3.5%
Development co-operation 3.9%
Administration costs 4.6%
Social policy 8.0%
Regional policy and transport 13.2%
Agriculture and fisheries 63.5%
Others 3.3%

Total E.C. budget 1993 64.2 billion ECU

billion ECU

Germany, France, Italy, U.K., Spain, Netherlands, Belgium, Denmark, Greece, Portugal, Ireland, Luxembourg, Sweden, Finland, Austria

Contributions to the E.C. 1993
Receipts from the E.C. 1993

POPULATION DENSITY IN THE E.U.

Inhabitants / km² 1992

over 350
300–350
250–300
200–250
150–200
100–150
50–100
25–50
under 25

Population of major cities
■ Over 5 000 000
• 1 000 000 – 5 000 000

STANDARDS OF LIVING IN THE E.U.

Gross Domestic Product per person indices 1992: E.U. average = 100

over 120
110–120
100–110
90–100
80–90
70–80
below 70

Projection: *Bonne*

INDEX TO
BRITISH ISLES MAPS

This index lists the major placenames which appear on the large-scale maps of the British Isles (pages *2–15* with the yellow band). Placenames for the rest of the world can be found in the World Index, with the turquoise band.

The first number beside each name in the index gives the map page on which that feature or place will be found. The letter and figure immediately after the page number give the grid square within which the feature is situated. The letter represents the latitude and the figure the longitude. In some cases the feature may fall within the specified square, while the name is outside. This is usually the case only with very large features. Rivers are indexed to their mouths or confluence.

The 'geographical co-ordinates' which follow the letter-figure references give the latitude and longitude of each place. The first co-ordinate indicates latitude – the distance north of the Equator. The second co-ordinate indicates longitude – the distance east or west of the Greenwich Meridian. Both latitude and longitude are measured in degrees and minutes (there are 60 minutes in a degree).

Thus the entry in the index for Runcorn reads:

Runcorn **7 F3**   53 20N   2 44W

This indicates that Runcorn appears on map page 7 in grid square F3 at latitude 53 degrees, 20 minutes north and at longitude 2 degrees, 44 minutes west. To find Runcorn by using the geographical co-ordinates, look at the edges of the map. The degrees of latitude are indicated by blue figures on the left-hand edge of the map and the degrees of longitude are marked on the bottom edge of the map. Runcorn will be found where lines extended from the two points on the map edge would cross on the map.

An open square □ indicates that the name refers to an administrative unit such as a county or region; rivers are indicated by an arrow �542. Names composed of a proper name (Wight) and a description (Isle of) are positioned alphabetically by the proper name. All names beginning St. are alphabetized under Saint. A list of abbreviations used can be found in the World Index at the end of the atlas.

A

Abberton Res. . . .	9 C10	51 50N	0 52 E
Abbeyfeale	14 D4	52 23N	9 20W
Aberaeron	10 C5	52 15N	4 16W
Aberayron =			
Aberaeron	10 C5	52 15N	4 16W
Abercarn	10 D7	51 39N	3 9W
Aberchirder	3 G12	57 34N	2 40W
Aberconwy &			
Colwyn	10 A6	53 10N	3 44W
Aberdare	10 D7	51 43N	3 27W
Aberdeen	3 H13	57 9N	2 6W
Aberdeenshire □ .	3 H12	57 17N	2 36W
Aberdovey =			
Aberdyfi	10 B5	52 33N	4 3W
Aberdyfi	10 B5	52 33N	4 3W
Aberfeldy	5 A8	56 37N	3 50W
Abergavenny	10 D7	51 49N	3 1W
Abergele	10 A6	53 17N	3 35W
Abersychan	10 D7	51 44N	3 3W
Abertillery	10 D7	51 44N	3 9W
Aberystwyth	10 C5	52 25N	4 6W
Abingdon	8 C6	51 40N	1 17W
Aboyne	3 H12	57 4N	2 48W
Accrington	7 E4	53 46N	2 22W
Achill Hd.	12 D1	53 59N	10 15W
Achill I.	12 D1	53 58N	10 5W
A'Chralaig	2 H7	57 11N	5 10W
Adlington	7 E3	53 36N	2 36W
Adwick le Street . .	7 E6	53 35N	1 12W
Agnews Hill	13 B10	54 51N	5 55W
Ailsa Craig	4 D5	55 15N	5 7W
Ainsdale	7 E2	53 37N	3 2W
Aird Brenish	2 F3	58 8N	7 8W
Airdrie	5 C8	55 53N	3 57W
Aire ➜	7 E7	53 42N	0 55W
Alcester	8 B5	52 13N	1 52W
Aldbrough	7 E8	53 50N	0 7W
Aldeburgh	9 B12	52 9N	1 35 E
Alderley Edge . . .	7 F4	53 18N	2 15W
Alderney	11 H9	49 42N	2 12W
Aldershot	9 D7	51 15N	0 43W
Aldridge	7 G5	52 36N	1 55W
Alexandria	4 C6	55 59N	4 40W
Alford, *Aberds.* . .	3 H12	57 13N	2 42W
Alford, *Lincs.* . . .	7 F9	53 16N	0 10 E
Alfreton	7 F6	53 6N	1 22W
Allen, Bog of . . .	15 B9	53 15N	7 0W
Allen, L.	12 C5	54 12N	8 5W
Alloa	5 B8	56 7N	3 49W
Alness	3 G9	57 41N	4 15W
Alnmouth	6 B5	55 24N	1 37W
Alnwick	6 B5	55 25N	1 42W
Alsager	7 F4	53 7N	2 20W
Alsh, L.	2 H6	57 15N	5 39W
Alston	6 C4	54 48N	2 26W
Alton	9 D7	51 8N	0 59W
Altrincham	7 F4	53 25N	2 21W

Alva	5 B8	56 9N	3 49W
Alyth	5 A9	56 38N	3 15W
Amble	6 B5	55 20N	1 36W
Ambleside	6 D3	54 26N	2 58W
Amersham	9 C7	51 40N	0 38W
Amesbury	8 D5	51 10N	1 46W
Amlwch	10 A5	53 24N	4 21W
Ammanford	10 D5	51 48N	4 0W
Ampthill	9 B8	52 3N	0 30W
An Teallach	2 G7	57 49N	5 18W
An Uaimh	13 D8	53 39N	6 40W
Andover	8 D6	51 13N	1 29W
Anglesey □	10 A5	53 16N	4 18W
Angus □	5 A10	56 46N	2 56W
Angus, Braes of . .	3 J11	56 51N	3 10W
Annagh Hd.	12 C1	54 15N	10 5W
Annalee ➜	13 C7	54 3N	7 15W
Annan	5 E9	54 57N	3 17W
Annan ➜	5 E9	54 58N	3 18W
Annandale	5 D9	55 10N	3 25W
Anstey	7 G6	52 41N	1 14W
Anstruther	5 B10	56 14N	2 40W
Antrim	13 B9	54 43N	6 13W
Antrim □	13 B9	54 55N	6 20W
Antrim, Mts. of . .	13 B9	54 57N	6 8W
Appin	4 A5	56 37N	5 20W
Appleby-in-			
Westmorland . .	6 C4	54 35N	2 29W
Appledore	11 E5	51 3N	4 12W
Aran Fawddwy . .	10 B6	52 48N	3 40W
Aran I.	12 B4	55 0N	8 30W
Aran Is.	14 B3	53 5N	9 42W
Arbroath	5 A10	56 34N	2 35W
Arbury Hill	8 B6	52 13N	1 12W
Ardee	13 D8	53 51N	6 32W
Arderin	15 B7	53 3N	7 40W
Ardgour	4 A5	56 45N	5 25W
Ardivachar Pt. . .	2 H3	57 23N	7 25W
Ardmore Hd. . . .	15 E7	51 58N	7 43W
Ardmore Pt.	4 C3	55 40N	6 2W
Ardnamurchan . .	4 A4	56 43N	6 0W
Ardnamurchan, Pt.			
of	4 A3	56 44N	6 14W
Ardnave Pt.	4 C3	55 54N	6 20W
Ardrossan	4 C6	55 39N	4 50W
Ards Pen.	13 B10	54 30N	5 30W
Arenig Fawr	10 B6	52 56N	3 45W
Argyll	4 B5	56 14N	5 10W
Argyll & Bute □ . .	4 B5	56 13N	5 28W
Arisaig	2 J6	56 55N	5 50W
Arisaig, Sd. of . .	2 J6	56 50N	5 50W
Arkaig, L.	2 J7	56 58N	5 10W
Arklow	15 C10	52 48N	6 10W
Arklow Hd.	15 C10	52 46N	6 10W
Armadale	5 C8	55 54N	3 42W
Armagh	13 C8	54 22N	6 40W
Armagh □	13 C8	54 18N	6 37W
Armthorpe	7 E6	53 32N	1 3W
Arnold	7 F6	53 2N	1 8W
Arran	4 C5	55 34N	5 12W
Arrow, L.	12 C5	54 3N	8 20W

Arun ➜	9 E7	50 48N	0 33W
Arundel	9 E7	50 52N	0 32W
Ascot	9 D7	51 24N	0 41W
Ash	9 D7	51 14N	0 43W
Ashbourne	7 F5	53 2N	1 44W
Ashburton	11 F6	50 31N	3 45W
Ashby de la Zouch	7 G6	52 45N	1 29W
Ashdown Forest . .	9 D9	51 4N	0 2 E
Ashford	9 D10	51 8N	0 53 E
Ashington	6 B5	55 12N	1 35W
Ashton-in-			
Makerfield . . .	7 F3	53 29N	2 39W
Ashton under Lyne	7 F4	53 30N	2 8W
Aspatria	6 C2	54 45N	3 20W
Assynt	2 F7	58 20N	5 10W
Athboy	13 D8	53 37N	6 55W
Athenry	14 B5	53 18N	8 45W
Atherstone	7 G5	52 35N	1 32W
Atherton	7 E3	53 32N	2 30W
Athlone	14 B7	53 26N	7 57W
Atholl, Forest of . .	3 J10	56 51N	3 50W
Athy	15 C9	53 0N	7 0W
Attleborough	9 A11	52 32N	1 1 E
Auchterarder	5 B8	56 18N	3 43W
Auchtermuchty . .	5 B9	56 18N	3 15W
Aughnacloy	13 C8	54 25N	6 58W
Aviemore	3 H10	57 11N	3 50W
Avoca	15 C10	52 52N	6 13W
Avoca ➜	15 C10	52 48N	6 9W
Avon □	8 D3	51 30N	2 40W
Avon ➜, *Avon.* . .	8 D3	51 30N	2 43W
Avon ➜, *Hants.* . .	8 E5	50 44N	1 45W
Avon ➜, *Warks.* . .	8 C4	51 57N	2 9W
Avonmouth	8 C3	51 30N	2 42W
Awe, L.	4 B5	56 15N	5 15W
Axe Edge	7 F5	53 14N	1 59W
Axminster	11 F7	50 47N	3 1W
Aylesbury	9 C7	51 48N	0 49W
Aylsham	9 A11	52 48N	1 16 E
Ayr	4 D6	55 28N	4 37W
Ayr ➜	4 D6	55 29N	4 40W
Ayr, Heads of . . .	4 D6	55 25N	4 43W
Ayr, Pt. of	10 A7	53 21N	3 19W
Ayre, Pt. of	3 E12	58 55N	2 43W

B

Bacton	9 A11	52 50N	1 29 E
Bacup	7 E4	53 42N	2 12W
Badenoch	3 J9	56 59N	4 15W
Bagenalstown =			
Muine Bheag . .	15 C9	52 42N	6 57W
Baggy Pt.	11 E5	51 11N	4 12W
Bagh nam			
Faoileann . . .	2 H3	57 22N	7 13W
Baginbun Hd. . . .	15 D9	52 10N	6 50W
Bagshot	9 D7	51 22N	0 41W
Baildon	7 E5	53 52N	1 46W

Baile Atha Cliath =			
Dublin	15 B10	53 20N	6 18W
Bakewell	7 F5	53 13N	1 40W
Bala	10 B6	52 54N	3 36W
Bala, L.	10 B6	52 53N	3 38W
Balbriggan	13 D9	53 35N	6 10W
Baldock	9 C8	51 59N	0 11W
Ballachulish	4 A5	56 40N	5 10W
Ballaghaderreen . .	12 D4	53 55N	8 35W
Ballater	3 H11	57 2N	3 2W
Ballina, *Mayo* . . .	12 C3	54 7N	9 10W
Ballina, *Tipp.* . . .	14 C6	52 49N	8 27W
Ballinasloe	14 B6	53 20N	8 12W
Ballinderry ➜ . . .	13 B8	54 40N	6 32W
Ballinrobe	12 D3	53 36N	9 13W
Ballinskelligs B. . .	14 E2	51 46N	10 11W
Ballybunion	14 C3	52 30N	9 40W
Ballycastle	13 A9	55 12N	6 15W
Ballyclare	13 B10	54 46N	6 0W
Ballyconneely B. . .	14 B2	53 23N	10 8W
Ballydavid Hd. . .	14 D2	52 15N	10 20W
Ballydonegan B. . .	14 E2	51 38N	10 6W
Ballyhaunis	12 D4	53 47N	8 47W
Ballyhoura Mts. . .	14 D5	52 18N	8 33W
Ballymena	13 B9	54 53N	6 18W
Ballymoney	13 A8	55 5N	6 30W
Ballymote	12 C4	54 5N	8 31W
Ballynahinch	13 C10	54 24N	5 55W
Ballyquintin Pt. . .	13 C11	54 20N	5 30W
Ballyshannon . . .	12 B5	54 30N	8 10W
Balmoral Forest . .	3 J11	57 0N	3 15W
Baltimore	14 F4	51 29N	9 22W
Bamber Bridge . .	7 E3	53 44N	2 39W
Bamburgh	6 A5	55 36N	1 42W
Bamford	7 F5	53 21N	1 41W
Banbridge	13 C9	54 21N	6 17W
Banbury	8 B6	52 4N	1 21W
Banchory	3 H13	57 3N	2 30W
Bandon	14 E5	51 44N	8 45W
Bandon ➜	14 E5	51 40N	8 41W
Banff	3 G12	57 40N	2 32W
Bangor,			
Caerns. & Mers.	10 A5	53 13N	4 9W
Bangor, *Down* . .	13 B10	54 40N	5 40W
Bann ➜, *Down* . .	13 C8	54 30N	6 31W
Bann ➜, *L'derry* .	13 A8	55 10N	6 40W
Bannockburn . . .	5 B8	56 5N	3 55W
Bannow B.	15 D9	52 13N	6 48W
Banstead	9 D8	51 19N	0 10W
Bantry	14 E4	51 41N	9 27W
Bantry B.	14 E3	51 35N	9 50W
Bard Hd.	2 B15	60 6N	1 5W
Bardsey Sd.	10 B4	52 47N	4 46W
Bargoed	10 D7	51 42N	3 22W
Barking and			
Dagenham . . .	9 C9	51 31N	0 10 E
Barmouth	10 B5	52 44N	4 3W
Barnard Castle . .	6 C5	54 33N	1 55W
Barnet	9 C8	51 37N	0 15W
Barnoldswick . . .	7 E4	53 55N	2 11W
Barns Ness	5 C11	55 59N	2 27W

Barnsley	7 E6	53 33N	1 29W
Barnstaple	11 E5	51 5N	4 3W
Barnstaple B. . . .	11 E5	51 5N	4 20W
Barra	2 J3	57 0N	7 30W
Barra Hd.	2 J2	56 47N	7 40W
Barrhead	4 C7	55 48N	4 23W
Barrow ➜	15 D9	52 14N	6 58W
Barrow-in-Furness	6 D2	54 8N	3 15W
Barrow upon			
Humber	7 E8	53 41N	0 22W
Barrowford	7 E4	53 51N	2 14W
Barry	11 E7	51 23N	3 19W
Barry I.	11 E7	51 23N	3 17W
Barry's Pt.	14 E5	51 36N	8 40W
Barton upon			
Humber	7 E8	53 41N	0 27W
Basildon	9 C9	51 34N	0 29 E
Basingstoke	8 D6	51 15N	1 5W
Bass Rock	5 B10	56 5N	2 40W
Bath	8 D4	51 22N	2 22W
Bathgate	5 C8	55 54N	3 38W
Batley	7 E5	53 43N	1 38W
Battle	9 E9	50 55N	0 30 E
Beachy Hd.	9 E9	50 44N	0 16 E
Beaconsfield	9 C7	51 36N	0 39W
Beaminster	8 E3	50 48N	2 44W
Bearsden	4 C7	55 55N	4 21W
Beauly	3 H9	57 29N	4 27W
Beauly ➜	3 H9	57 26N	4 28W
Beauly Firth	3 H9	57 30N	4 20W
Beaumaris	10 A5	53 16N	4 7W
Bebington	7 F2	53 23N	3 1W
Beccles	9 B12	52 27N	1 33 E
Bedford	9 B8	52 8N	0 29W
Bedford Level . . .	9 A8	52 35N	0 15W
Bedfordshire □ . .	9 B8	52 4N	0 28W
Bedlington	6 B5	55 8N	1 35W
Bedwas	11 D7	51 36N	3 10W
Bedworth	8 B6	52 28N	1 29W
Bee, L.	2 H3	57 22N	7 21W
Beeston	7 G6	52 55N	1 11W
Beighton	7 F6	53 21N	1 21W
Beinn a' Ghlo . . .	3 J10	56 51N	3 42W
Beinn Mhor	2 G4	57 59N	6 39W
Beith	4 C6	55 45N	4 38W
Belfast	13 B10	54 35N	5 56W
Belfast L.	13 B10	54 40N	5 50W
Belmullet	12 C2	54 13N	9 58W
Belper	7 F6	53 2N	1 29W
Belturbet	12 C7	54 6N	7 28W
Bembridge	8 E6	50 41N	1 4W
Ben Alder	3 J9	56 50N	4 30W
Ben Avon	3 H11	57 6N	3 28W
Ben Bheigeir	4 C3	55 43N	6 6W
Ben Chonzie	5 B8	56 27N	4 0W
Ben Cruachan . . .	4 B5	56 26N	5 8W
Ben Dearg, *Highl.*	3 G8	57 47N	4 58W
Ben Dearg,			
Perths. & Kinr. .	3 J10	56 52N	3 53W
Ben Dhorain	3 F10	58 7N	3 50W
Ben Dorain	4 A6	56 32N	4 42W

Ben Eighie **2 G7** 57 37N 5 30W
Ben Hee **3 F8** 58 16N 4 43W
Ben Hiant **4 A3** 56 42N 6 1W
Ben Hope **3 F8** 58 24N 4 36W
Ben Ime **4 B6** 56 14N 4 49W
Ben Klibreck **3 F9** 58 14N 4 25W
Ben Lawers **4 A7** 56 33N 4 13W
Ben Lomond **4 B6** 56 12N 4 39W
Ben Loyal **3 F9** 58 25N 4 25W
Ben Lui **4 B6** 56 24N 4 50W
Ben Macdhui **3 H10** 57 4N 3 40W
Ben Mholach **2 F4** 58 14N 6 33W
Ben Mhor **2 H3** 57 16N 7 21W
Ben More, *Arg. & Bute* **4 B3** 56 26N 6 2W
Ben More, *Stirl.* **4 B6** 56 23N 4 31W
Ben More Assynt **3 F8** 58 7N 4 51W
Ben Nevis **3 J7** 56 48N 5 2W
Ben Rinnes **3 H11** 57 25N 3 15W
Ben Stack **3 F8** 58 20N 4 58W
Ben Tharsuinn **3 G9** 57 47N 4 20W
Ben Venue **4 B7** 56 13N 4 28W
Ben Vorlich **4 B7** 56 22N 4 15W
Ben Wyvis **3 G8** 57 40N 4 35W
Benbane Hd. **13 A9** 55 15N 6 30W
Benbaun **12 D2** 53 30N 9 50W
Benbecula **2 H3** 57 26N 7 21W
Benderloch **4 A5** 56 30N 5 22W
Beneraird **4 D6** 55 4N 4 57W
Bennane Hd. **4 D6** 55 8N 4 59W
Bentley **7 E6** 53 33N 1 9W
Benwee Hd. **12 C2** 54 20N 9 50W
Berkeley **8 C4** 51 41N 2 28W
Berkhamsted **9 C7** 51 45N 0 33W
Berkshire □ **8 D6** 51 30N 1 20W
Berkshire Downs **8 C5** 51 30N 1 30W
Berry Hd. **11 G7** 50 24N 3 29W
Berst Ness **3 D12** 59 16N 3 0W
Bertraghboy B. **14 B3** 53 22N 9 54W
Berwick-upon-Tweed **6 A5** 55 47N 2 0W
Berwyn Mts. **10 B7** 52 54N 3 26W
Betws-y-Coed **10 A6** 53 4N 3 49W
Beverley **7 E8** 53 52N 0 26W
Bewdley **8 B4** 52 23N 2 19W
Bexhill **9 E9** 50 51N 0 29 E
Bexley **9 D9** 51 26N 0 10 E
Bicester **8 C6** 51 53N 1 9W
Biddulph **7 F4** 53 8N 2 11W
Bidean nam Bian **4 A5** 56 39N 5 6W
Bideford **11 E5** 51 1N 4 13W
Bideford B. = Barnstaple B. **11 E5** 51 5N 4 20W
Bigbury B. **11 G6** 50 18N 3 58W
Biggar **5 C8** 55 38N 3 31W
Biggleswade **9 B8** 52 6N 0 16W
Billericay **9 C9** 51 38N 0 25 E
Billinge Hill **7 E3** 53 32N 2 42W
Billingham **6 C6** 54 36N 1 18W
Billingshurst **9 D8** 51 2N 0 28W
Bilston **7 G4** 52 34N 2 5W
Bingley **7 E5** 53 51N 1 50W
Birdlip **8 C4** 51 50N 2 7W
Birkenhead **7 F2** 53 24N 3 1W
Birmingham **8 B5** 52 30N 1 55W
Birr **14 B7** 53 7N 7 55W
Birtley **6 C5** 54 53N 1 34W
Bishop Auckland **6 C5** 54 40N 1 40W
Bishop's Stortford **9 C9** 51 52N 0 11 E
Bishop's Waltham **8 E6** 50 57N 1 13W
Bla Bheinn **2 H5** 57 14N 6 7W
Black Combe **6 D2** 54 16N 3 20W
Black Hd., *Ireland* **14 B4** 53 9N 9 18W
Black Hd., *Ant.* **13 B10** 54 56N 5 42W
Black Hd., *Corn.* **11 H3** 50 0N 5 6W
Black Isle **3 G9** 57 35N 4 15W
Black Mts. **10 D7** 51 52N 3 5W
Black Mt. = Mynydd Du **10 D6** 51 45N 3 45W
Blackburn **7 E4** 53 44N 2 30W
Blackdown Hill **8 D7** 51 4N 41 7W
Blackdown Hills **8 E2** 50 57N 3 15W
Blackhill **7 E5** 53 32N 1 53W
Blackhope Scar **5 C9** 55 44N 3 5W
Blackmoor Vale **8 E4** 50 54N 2 28W
Blackpool **7 E2** 53 48N 3 3W
Blacksod B. **12 C2** 54 6N 10 0W
Blacksod Pt. **12 C1** 54 7N 10 5W
Blackstairs Mt. **15 C9** 52 33N 6 50W
Blackwater →, *Munst.* **14 E7** 51 55N 7 50W
Blackwater →, *Essex* **9 C10** 51 44N 0 53 E
Blackwater →, *Tyrone* **13 B8** 54 31N 6 35W
Blackwood **10 D7** 51 40N 3 13W
Blaenau Ffestiniog **10 B6** 52 59N 3 57W
Blaenau Gwent □ **10 D2** 51 47N 3 12W
Blaenavon **10 D7** 51 46N 3 5W
Blaina **10 D7** 51 46N 3 10W
Blair Atholl **3 J10** 56 46N 3 50W
Blairgowrie **5 A9** 56 36N 3 20W
Blakeney **9 A11** 52 57N 1 0 E
Blandford Forum **8 E4** 50 52N 2 10W
Blarney **14 E5** 51 57N 8 35W
Blaydon **6 C5** 54 56N 1 47W
Bletchley **9 C7** 51 59N 0 44W
Bloody Foreland **12 A5** 55 10N 8 18W
Bluemull Sd. **2 A16** 60 45N 1 0W
Blyth **6 B5** 55 8N 1 32W
Blyth Bridge **7 G4** 52 58N 2 4W
Boderg, L. **12 D6** 53 55N 8 0W
Bodmin **11 G4** 50 28N 4 44W
Bodmin Moor **11 F4** 50 33N 4 36W
Boggeragh Mts. **14 D5** 52 2N 8 55W
Bognor Regis **9 E7** 50 47N 0 40W
Bogrie Hill **5 D8** 55 8N 3 54W
Boisdale, L. **2 H3** 57 9N 7 19W
Boldon **6 C6** 54 57N 1 26W
Bolsover **7 F6** 53 14N 1 18W
Bolt Hd. **11 G6** 50 13N 3 48W
Bolt Tail **11 G6** 50 13N 3 55W
Bolton **7 E4** 53 35N 2 26W
Bolus Hd. **14 E2** 51 48N 10 20W
Bo'ness **5 B8** 56 1N 3 38W
Bonnyrigg **5 C9** 55 52N 3 8W
Bootle, *Cumb.* **6 D2** 54 17N 3 24W
Bootle, *Mersey.* **7 F2** 53 28N 3 1W
Borders □ **5 C10** 55 35N 2 50W
Borehamwood **9 C8** 51 40N 0 15W
Boroughbridge **6 D6** 54 6N 1 23W
Borth **10 C5** 52 29N 4 3W
Boscastle **11 F4** 50 42N 4 42W
Boston **7 G8** 52 59N 0 2W
Bourne **7 G8** 52 46N 0 22W
Bournemouth **8 E5** 50 43N 1 53W
Bourton-on-the-Water **8 C5** 51 53N 1 45W
Bowland, Forest of **7 E3** 54 0N 2 30W
Bowmore **4 C3** 55 45N 6 18W
Bowness-on-Windermere **6 D3** 54 22N 2 56W
Box Hill **9 D8** 51 16N 0 16W
Boyle **12 D5** 53 58N 8 19W
Boyne → **13 D9** 53 43N 6 15W
Bracadale, L. **2 H4** 57 20N 6 30W
Brackley **8 B6** 52 3N 1 9W
Bracknell **9 D7** 51 24N 0 45W
Bradda Hd. **13 C12** 54 6N 4 46W
Bradford **7 E5** 53 47N 1 45W
Bradford on Avon **8 D4** 51 20N 2 15W
Bradwell-on-Sea **9 C10** 51 44N 0 55 E
Braemar **3 J11** 57 0N 3 25W
Braeriach **3 H10** 57 4N 3 44W
Braich-y-pwll **10 B4** 52 47N 4 46W
Braintree **9 C10** 51 53N 0 34 E
Brampton **6 C3** 54 56N 2 43W
Branderburgh **3 G11** 57 43N 3 17W
Brandon, *Kilk.* **15 C9** 52 31N 6 58W
Brandon, *Durham* **6 C5** 54 46N 1 37W
Brandon, *Suffolk* **9 B10** 52 27N 0 37 E
Brandon B. **14 D2** 52 17N 10 8W
Brandon Mt. **14 D2** 52 15N 10 15W
Brandon Pt. **14 D2** 52 18N 10 10W
Braunton **11 E5** 51 6N 4 9W
Bray **15 B10** 53 12N 6 6W
Bray Hd., *Kerry* **14 E2** 51 52N 10 26W
Bray Hd., *Wick.* **15 B10** 53 12N 6 2W
Breadalbane **4 A7** 56 30N 4 15W
Brechin **5 A10** 56 44N 2 40W
Breckland **9 B10** 52 30N 0 40 E
Brecon **10 D7** 51 57N 3 23W
Brecon Beacons **10 D7** 51 53N 3 27W
Bredon Hill **8 B4** 52 3N 2 2W
Brendon Hills **8 D2** 51 6N 3 25W
Brenig, L. **10 A6** 53 6N 3 30W
Brent **9 C8** 51 33N 0 18W
Brentwood **9 C9** 51 37N 0 19 E
Bressay Sd. **2 B15** 60 8N 1 10W
Brianne, L. **10 C6** 52 8N 3 45W
Bridge of Don **3 H13** 57 10N 2 8W
Bridgend **11 D6** 51 30N 3 35W
Bridgnorth **7 G4** 52 33N 2 25W
Bridgwater **8 D3** 51 7N 3 0W
Bridlington **6 D8** 54 6N 0 11W
Bridport **11 E3** 50 43N 2 45W
Brierfield **7 E4** 53 49N 2 15W
Brierley Hill **8 B4** 52 29N 2 7W
Brigg **7 E8** 53 33N 0 30W
Brighouse **7 E5** 53 42N 1 47W
Brightlingsea **9 C11** 51 49N 1 1 E
Brighton **9 E8** 50 50N 0 9W
Bristol **8 D3** 51 26N 2 35W
Bristol Channel **11 E4** 51 18N 4 30W
Brixham **11 G6** 50 24N 3 31W
Brize Norton **8 C5** 51 46N 1 35W
Broad Bay **2 F5** 58 14N 6 16W
Broad Haven **12 C2** 54 20N 9 55W
Broad Law **5 C9** 55 31N 3 22W
Broad Sd. **11 H1** 49 56N 6 19W
Broadstairs **9 D11** 51 21N 1 28 E
Broadway **8 B5** 52 2N 1 51W
Broadwindsor **8 E3** 50 49N 2 49W
Brockenhurst **8 E5** 50 49N 1 34W
Brodick **4 C5** 55 34N 5 9W
Bromfield **8 B3** 52 25N 2 45W
Bromley **9 D9** 51 20N 0 5 E
Bromsgrove **8 B4** 52 20N 2 3W
Bromyard **8 B4** 52 12N 2 30W
Broom, L. **2 G7** 57 55N 5 15W
Brora **3 F10** 58 3N 3 50W
Brosna → **14 B7** 53 8N 8 0W
Brotton **6 C7** 54 34N 0 55W
Brough **6 C4** 54 32N 2 19W
Brough Hd. **3 D11** 59 8N 3 20W
Broughty Ferry **5 B10** 56 29N 2 50W
Brown Clee Hill **8 B3** 52 28N 2 36W
Brown Willy **11 F4** 50 35N 4 34W
Brownhills **7 G5** 52 38N 1 57W
Broxburn **5 C9** 55 56N 3 23W
Bruernish Pt. **2 J3** 57 0N 7 22W
Bruton **8 D4** 51 6N 2 28W
Brynmawr **10 D7** 51 48N 3 11W
Buchan **3 G13** 57 32N 2 8W
Buchan Ness **3 H14** 57 29N 1 48W
Buckfastleigh **11 G6** 50 28N 3 47W
Buckhaven **5 B9** 56 10N 3 2W
Buckie **3 G12** 57 40N 2 58W
Buckingham **9 C7** 52 0N 0 59W
Buckinghamshire □ **9 C7** 51 50N 0 55W
Buckley **10 A7** 53 10N 3 5W
Buddon Ness **5 B10** 56 29N 2 42W
Bude **11 F4** 50 49N 4 33W
Budle B. **6 A5** 55 37N 1 45W
Budleigh Salterton **11 F7** 50 37N 3 19W
Buie, L. **4 B4** 56 20N 5 55W
Builth Wells **10 C7** 52 10N 3 26W
Bulkington **8 B6** 52 29N 1 25W
Bunclody **15 C9** 52 40N 6 40W
Buncrana **12 A7** 55 8N 7 28W
Bundoran **12 C5** 54 24N 8 17W
Bungay **9 B11** 52 27N 1 26 E
Burford **8 C5** 51 48N 1 38W
Burgess Hill **9 E8** 50 57N 0 7W
Burghead B. **3 G10** 57 40N 3 33W
Burnham **9 C7** 51 32N 0 40W
Burnham Market **9 A10** 52 57N 0 43 E
Burnham-on-Crouch **9 C10** 51 37N 0 50 E
Burnham-on-Sea **8 D3** 51 14N 3 0W
Burnley **7 E4** 53 47N 2 15W
Burntisland **5 B9** 56 4N 3 14W
Burntwood **7 G5** 52 41N 1 55W
Burrow Hd. **4 E7** 54 40N 4 23W
Burry Port **10 D5** 51 41N 4 17W
Burscough Bridge **7 E3** 53 36N 2 52W
Burton Latimer **9 B7** 52 23N 0 41W
Burton upon Trent **7 G5** 52 48N 1 39W
Bury **7 E4** 53 36N 2 19W
Bury St. Edmunds **9 B10** 52 15N 0 42 E
Bushey **9 C8** 51 38N 0 20W
Bushmills **13 A8** 55 14N 6 32W
Bute **4 C5** 55 48N 5 2W
Bute, Kyles of **4 C5** 55 55N 5 10W
Bute, Sd. of **4 C5** 55 43N 5 8W
Buttevant **14 D5** 52 14N 8 40W
Buxton **7 F5** 53 16N 1 54W
Byfleet **9 D7** 51 20N 0 32W

C

Cader Idris **10 B6** 52 43N 3 56W
Caernarfon **10 A5** 53 8N 4 17W
Caernarfon B. **10 A4** 53 4N 4 40W
Caernarfonshire & Merionethshire □ **10 B6** 52 52N 3 59W
Caernarvon = Caernarfon **10 A5** 53 8N 4 17W
Caerphilly **11 D7** 51 34N 3 13W
Caha Mts. **14 E3** 51 45N 9 40W
Caher **14 D7** 52 23N 7 56W
Cahirciveen **14 E2** 51 57N 10 13W
Cahore Pt. **15 C10** 52 34N 6 11W
Cairn Gorm **3 H10** 57 7N 3 40W
Cairn Table **5 C7** 55 30N 4 0W
Cairngorm Mts. **3 H10** 57 6N 3 42W
Cairnsmore of Fleet **4 E7** 54 59N 4 20W
Caister-on-Sea **9 A12** 52 38N 1 43 E
Caithness **3 F10** 58 25N 3 35W
Caithness, Ord of **3 F10** 58 9N 3 37W
Calder → **7 E6** 53 44N 1 21W
Caledonian Canal **2 J7** 56 50N 5 6W
Caliach Pt. **4 A3** 56 37N 6 20W
Callan **15 C8** 52 33N 7 25W
Callander **4 B7** 56 15N 4 14W
Calne **8 D5** 51 26N 2 0W
Cam → **9 B9** 52 21N 0 16 E
Camberley **9 D7** 51 20N 0 44W
Camborne **11 G3** 50 13N 5 18W
Cambrian Mts. **10 C6** 52 25N 3 52W
Cambridge **9 B9** 52 13N 0 8 E
Cambridgeshire □ **9 B9** 52 12N 0 7 E
Camden **9 C8** 51 33N 0 10W
Camelford **11 F4** 50 37N 4 41W
Campbeltown **4 D4** 55 25N 5 36W
Canbane East **13 D7** 53 45N 7 6W
Canna, Sd. of **2 H5** 57 1N 6 30W
Cannock **7 G4** 52 42N 2 2W
Cannock Chase **7 G5** 52 43N 2 0W
Canterbury **9 D11** 51 17N 1 5 E
Canvey **9 C10** 51 32N 0 35 E
Caolisport, L. **4 C4** 55 54N 5 40W
Cardiff **11 E7** 51 28N 3 11W
Cardigan **10 C4** 52 6N 4 41W
Cardigan B. **10 B4** 52 30N 4 30W
Cardiganshire □ **10 C6** 52 16N 3 58W
Carisbrooke **8 E6** 50 42N 1 19W
Carlingford L. **13 C9** 54 2N 6 5W
Carlisle **6 C3** 54 54N 2 55W
Carlow **15 C9** 52 50N 6 58W
Carlow □ **15 C9** 52 43N 6 50W
Carlton **7 G6** 52 58N 1 6W
Carluke **5 C8** 55 44N 3 50W
Carmarthen **10 D5** 51 52N 4 20W
Carmarthen B. **10 D4** 51 40N 4 30W
Carmarthenshire □ **10 D5** 51 55N 4 13W
Carmel Hd. **10 A4** 53 24N 4 34W
Carn Ban **3 H9** 57 6N 4 15W
Carn Eige **2 H7** 57 17N 5 9W
Carn Glas-choire **3 H10** 57 20N 3 50W
Carn Mor **3 H11** 57 14N 3 13W
Carn na Saobhaidhe **3 H9** 57 12N 4 20W
Carndonagh **13 A7** 55 15N 7 16W
Carnedd Llewelyn **10 A6** 53 9N 3 58W
Carnforth **6 D3** 54 8N 2 47W
Carnoustie **5 A10** 56 30N 2 41W
Carnsore Pt. **15 D10** 52 10N 6 20W
Carra, L. **12 D3** 53 41N 9 12W
Carrauntoohill **14 E3** 52 0N 9 49W
Carrick **4 D6** 55 12N 4 38W
Carrick-on-Shannon **12 D5** 53 57N 8 7W
Carrick-on-Suir **15 D8** 52 22N 7 30W
Carrickfergus **13 B10** 54 43N 5 50W
Carrickmacross **13 D8** 53 58N 6 43W
Carrigan Hd. **12 B4** 54 38N 8 40W
Carron → **2 H7** 57 30N 5 30W
Carron, L. **2 H6** 57 22N 5 35W
Carstairs **5 C8** 55 42N 3 41W
Cashel **14 C7** 52 31N 7 53W
Cashla B. **14 B3** 53 12N 9 37W
Castle Cary **8 D3** 51 5N 2 32W
Castle Donington **7 G6** 52 50N 1 20W
Castle Douglas **5 E8** 54 57N 3 57W
Castlebar **12 D3** 53 52N 9 17W
Castleblaney **13 C8** 54 7N 6 44W
Castlederg **12 B6** 54 43N 7 35W
Castleford **7 E6** 53 43N 1 21W
Castleisland **14 D4** 52 14N 9 28W
Castlemaine Harbour **14 D3** 52 8N 9 50W
Castlepollard **12 D7** 53 40N 7 20W
Castlerea **12 D5** 53 47N 8 30W
Castletown **13 C12** 54 4N 4 40W
Castletown Bearhaven **14 E3** 51 40N 9 54W
Caterham **9 D8** 51 16N 0 4W
Cavan **12 D7** 54 0N 7 22W
Cavan □ **13 D7** 53 58N 7 10W
Ceanannus Mor **13 D8** 53 42N 6 53W
Cefn-mawr **10 B7** 52 58N 3 3W
Cefnfford **10 D6** 51 42N 3 39W
Celbridge **15 B9** 53 20N 6 33W
Cellar Hd. **2 F5** 58 25N 6 10W
Celyn, L. **10 B6** 52 56N 3 42W
Cemaes Hd. **10 C4** 52 7N 4 44W
Chadwell St. Mary **9 D9** 51 28N 0 22 E
Chandler's Ford **8 E6** 50 59N 1 23W
Channel Is. **11 J9** 49 30N 2 40W
Chapel en le Frith **7 F5** 53 19N 1 54W
Chard **8 E3** 50 52N 2 59W
Charlbury **8 C6** 51 52N 1 29W
Charlestown of Aberlour **3 H11** 57 27N 3 13W
Charleville = Rath Luirc **14 D5** 52 21N 8 40W
Charlton Kings **8 C4** 51 52N 2 3W
Charnwood Forest **7 G6** 52 43N 1 18W
Chatham **9 D10** 51 22N 0 32 E
Chatteris **9 B9** 52 27N 0 3 E
Cheadle, *Gt. Man.* **7 F4** 53 23N 2 14W
Cheadle, *Staffs.* **7 G5** 52 59N 1 59W
Cheddar **8 D3** 51 16N 2 47W
Chelmsford **9 C9** 51 44N 0 29 E
Cheltenham **8 C4** 51 55N 2 5W
Chepstow **10 D8** 51 38N 2 40W
Chertsey **9 D7** 51 23N 0 30W
Cherwell → **8 C6** 51 46N 1 18W
Chesham **9 C7** 51 42N 0 36W
Cheshire □ **7 F3** 53 14N 2 30W
Cheshunt **9 C8** 51 42N 0 1W
Chesil Beach **11 F8** 50 37N 2 33W
Chester **7 F3** 53 12N 2 53W
Chester-le-Street **6 C5** 54 53N 1 34W
Chesterfield **7 F6** 53 14N 1 26W
Cheviot Hills **6 B3** 55 20N 2 30W
Chichester **9 E7** 50 50N 0 47W
Chicken Hd. **2 F5** 58 10N 6 15W
Chigwell **9 C9** 51 37N 0 4 E
Chiltern Hills **9 C7** 51 44N 0 42W
Chippenham **8 D4** 51 27N 2 7W
Chipping Norton **8 C5** 51 56N 1 32W
Chipping Ongar **9 C9** 51 42N 0 11 E
Chipping Sodbury **8 C4** 51 31N 2 23W
Chobham **9 D7** 51 20N 0 36W
Chorley **7 E3** 53 39N 2 39W
Chorleywood **9 C8** 51 39N 0 29W
Christchurch **8 E5** 50 44N 1 45W
Chulmleigh **11 F6** 50 55N 3 52W
Church Stretton **8 A3** 52 32N 2 49W
Churchdown **8 C4** 51 53N 2 9W
Chwarel y Fan **10 D7** 51 56N 3 5W
Cill Chainnigh = Kilkenny **15 C8** 52 40N 7 17W
Cinderford **8 C3** 51 49N 2 30W
Cirencester **8 C5** 51 43N 1 59W
Clach Leathad **4 A6** 56 36N 4 52W
Clackmannan □ **5 B8** 56 9N 3 49W
Clacton-on-Sea **9 C11** 51 47N 1 10 E
Clara **15 B7** 53 20N 7 38W
Clare □ **14 C4** 52 45N 9 0W
Clare → **14 B4** 53 22N 9 5W
Clare I. **12 D2** 53 48N 10 0W
Clay Cross **7 F6** 53 11N 1 26W
Clear, C. **14 F3** 51 26N 9 30W
Cleator Moor **6 C2** 54 31N 3 30W
Clee Hills **8 B3** 52 26N 2 35W
Cleethorpes **7 E8** 53 33N 0 2W
Cleeve Cloud **8 C5** 51 56N 1 57W
Clent Hills **8 B4** 52 25N 2 6W
Clevedon **8 D3** 51 26N 2 52W
Cleveland □ **6 C6** 54 35N 1 8W
Cleveland Hills **6 D6** 54 25N 1 11W
Cleveleys **7 E2** 53 53N 3 3W
Clew B. **12 D2** 53 54N 9 50W
Clifden **12 E1** 53 30N 10 2W
Clifden B. **12 E1** 53 29N 10 5W
Clift Sd. **2 B15** 60 4N 1 17W
Clisham **2 G4** 57 57N 6 50W
Clitheroe **7 E4** 53 52N 2 23W
Clogher Hd. **13 D9** 53 48N 6 15W
Clonakilty **14 E5** 51 37N 8 53W
Clondalkin **15 B10** 53 20N 6 25W
Clones **13 C7** 54 10N 7 13W
Clonmel **15 D7** 52 22N 7 42W
Clovelly **11 F5** 51 0N 4 25W
Clun Forest **8 B2** 52 27N 3 7W
Clwyd → **10 A6** 53 20N 3 30W
Clydach **10 D6** 51 42N 3 54W
Clyde → **4 C7** 55 56N 4 29W
Clyde, Firth of **4 D6** 55 20N 5 0W
Clydebank **4 C7** 55 54N 4 25W
Clydesdale **5 C8** 55 42N 3 50W
Clywedog, L. **10 C6** 52 29N 3 40W
Cnoc Moy **4 D4** 55 23N 5 44W
Coalisland **13 B8** 54 33N 6 42W
Coalville **7 G6** 52 43N 1 21W
Coatbridge **4 C7** 55 52N 4 2W
Cóbh **14 E6** 51 50N 8 18W
Cockenzie **5 C10** 55 58N 2 59W
Cockermouth **6 C2** 54 40N 3 22W
Cods Hd. **14 E2** 51 40N 10 7W
Coigach **2 G7** 57 55N 5 10W
Colchester **9 C10** 51 54N 0 55 E
Cold Fell **6 C3** 54 54N 2 40W
Coldstream **5 C11** 55 39N 2 14W
Coleraine **13 A8** 55 8N 6 40W
Coleshill **8 B5** 52 30N 1 42W
Colgrave Sd. **2 A16** 60 35N 1 0W
Colinton **5 C9** 55 54N 3 15W
Coll **4 A2** 56 40N 6 35W
Collier Law **6 C5** 54 47N 1 59W
Collooney **12 C5** 54 11N 8 28W
Colne **7 E4** 53 51N 2 11W
Colonsay **4 B3** 56 4N 6 12W
Colwyn Bay **10 A6** 53 17N 3 44W
Combe Martin **11 E5** 51 12N 4 2W
Comber **13 B10** 54 33N 5 45W
Comeragh Mts. **15 D7** 52 17N 7 35W
Congleton **7 F4** 53 10N 2 12W
Conisbrough **7 F6** 53 29N 1 12W
Coniston **6 D2** 54 22N 3 6W
Conn, L. **12 C3** 54 3N 9 15W
Connacht **14 D4** 53 45N 8 40W
Connah's Quay **10 A7** 53 13N 3 6W
Connel **4 B5** 56 27N 5 24W
Connemara **12 E2** 53 29N 9 45W
Cononbridge **3 G9** 57 32N 4 30W
Consett **6 C5** 54 52N 1 50W
Conway = Conwy **10 A6** 53 17N 3 50W
Conwy **10 A6** 53 17N 3 50W
Conwy B. **10 A6** 53 17N 3 57W
Cookstown **13 B8** 54 40N 6 43W
Cootehill **13 C7** 54 5N 7 5W
Coquet → **6 B5** 55 18N 1 45W
Corbridge **6 C5** 54 58N 2 0W
Corby **9 A7** 52 30N 0 41W
Corby Glen **7 G7** 52 49N 0 31W
Corcaigh = Cork **14 E6** 51 54N 8 30W
Corfe Castle **8 E4** 50 37N 2 3W
Cork **14 E6** 51 54N 8 30W
Cork □ **14 E5** 51 50N 8 50W
Cork Harbour **14 E6** 51 46N 8 16W
Corn Hill **12 D6** 53 48N 7 43W
Cornwall □ **11 G4** 50 26N 4 40W
Cornwall, C. **11 G2** 50 8N 5 42W
Corrib, L. **14 B4** 53 5N 9 10W
Corringham **9 C10** 51 30N 0 26 E
Corry Mt. **12 C5** 54 8N 8 8W
Corryvreckan, G. of **4 B4** 56 10N 5 44W
Corsewall Pt. **4 E5** 55 0N 5 10W
Corsham **8 D4** 51 25N 2 11W
Coseley **7 G4** 52 33N 2 6W
Cot Nab **7 D7** 54 1N 0 45W
Cotswold Hills **8 C4** 51 42N 2 10W
Cottingham **7 E8** 53 47N 0 23W
Coul Pt. **4 C2** 55 50N 6 30W
Coupar Angus **5 A9** 56 33N 3 17W
Courtmacsherry B. **14 E5** 51 37N 8 37W
Cove **4 B6** 56 2N 4 50W
Coventry **8 B6** 52 25N 1 28W
Cow Green Res. **6 C4** 54 40N 2 20W
Cowal **4 B5** 56 5N 5 8W
Cowdenbeath **5 B9** 56 7N 3 20W
Cowes **8 E6** 50 45N 1 18W
Craigavon **13 C9** 54 28N 6 20W
Craignish, L. **4 B4** 56 11N 5 32W
Crail **5 B10** 56 16N 2 38W
Cramlington **6 B5** 55 5N 1 36W
Cranborne Chase **8 E4** 50 56N 2 6W
Cranbrook **9 D10** 51 6N 0 33 E
Cranfield Pt. **13 C9** 54 1N 6 3W
Cranleigh **9 D8** 51 8N 0 29W
Crawley **9 D8** 51 7N 0 10W
Creag Meagaidh **3 J8** 56 57N 4 38W
Crediton **11 F6** 50 47N 3 39W
Cree → **4 E7** 54 51N 4 24W
Creran, L. **4 A5** 56 30N 5 20W
Crewe **7 F4** 53 6N 2 28W
Crewkerne **8 E3** 50 53N 2 48W
Criccieth **10 B5** 52 55N 4 15W
Cricklade **8 C5** 51 38N 1 50W
Crieff **5 B8** 56 22N 3 50W
Criffell **5 E8** 54 56N 3 38W
Crinan Canal **4 B5** 56 4N 5 30W
Croagh Patrick **12 D2** 53 46N 9 40W
Croghan Mt. **15 C10** 52 48N 6 20W
Crohy Hd. **12 B5** 54 55N 8 28W
Cromarty **3 G9** 57 40N 4 2W
Cromarty Firth **3 G9** 57 40N 4 15W
Cromdale, Hills of **3 H11** 57 20N 3 28W
Cromer **9 A11** 52 56N 1 18 E
Crook **6 C5** 54 43N 1 45W
Crosby **7 E2** 53 30N 3 2W
Cross Fell **6 C4** 54 44N 2 29W
Crossfarnoge Pt. **15 D9** 52 10N 6 37W
Crosshaven **14 E6** 51 48N 8 19W
Crossmaglen **13 C8** 54 5N 6 37W
Crow Hd. **14 E2** 51 34N 10 9W
Crow Sd. **11 H1** 49 56N 6 16W
Crowborough **9 D9** 51 3N 0 9 E
Crowthorne **9 D7** 51 22N 0 50W
Croydon **9 D8** 51 18N 0 5W
Cruden Bay **3 H14** 57 25N 1 50W
Cuckfield **9 D8** 51 1N 0 8W
Cuffley **9 C8** 51 43N 0 9W
Cuilcagh **12 C6** 54 12N 7 50W
Cuillin Hills **2 H5** 57 14N 6 15W
Cuillin Sd. **2 H5** 57 4N 6 20W
Cullen **3 G12** 57 45N 2 50W
Cullin, L. **12 D3** 53 58N 9 12W
Culloden **3 H9** 57 29N 4 7W
Cullompton **11 F7** 50 52N 3 23W
Culm → **11 F6** 50 46N 3 31W
Culter Fell **5 C8** 55 35N 3 30W
Cults **3 H13** 57 8N 2 10W
Culvain **2 J7** 56 55N 5 19W
Cumbernauld **5 C8** 55 57N 3 58W
Cumbrae Is. **4 C6** 55 46N 4 54W
Cumbria □ **6 C3** 54 35N 2 55W
Cumbrian Mts. **6 D2** 54 30N 3 0W
Cumnock **4 D7** 55 27N 4 18W
Cunninghame **4 C6** 55 38N 4 35W
Cupar **5 B9** 56 20N 3 3W
Cupidstown Hill **15 B9** 53 15N 6 31W
Currane, L. **14 E2** 51 50N 10 8W
Cwmbran **10 D7** 51 39N 3 3W

D

Daingean **15 B8** 53 18N 7 15W
Dalbeattie **5 E8** 54 55N 3 50W
Dalkeith **5 C9** 55 54N 3 5W
Dalmellington **4 D7** 55 20N 4 25W
Dalry **4 C6** 55 44N 4 42W
Dalton-in-Furness **6 D2** 54 3N 3 10W

35
Danbury Hoy Sd.

Danbury 9 C10 51 43N 0 34 E
Darlington 6 C5 54 33N 1 33W
Dart → 11 G6 50 24N 3 36W
Dartford 9 D9 51 26N 0 15 E
Dartmoor 11 F6 50 36N 4 0W
Dartmouth 11 G6 50 21N 3 35W
Darton 7 E5 53 36N 1 32W
Darvel 4 C7 55 37N 4 20W
Darwen 7 E4 53 42N 2 29W
Daventry 8 B6 52 16N 1 10W
Dawlish 11 F7 50 34N 3 28W
Dawros Hd. 12 B4 54 48N 8 32W
Deal 9 D11 51 13N 1 25 E
Dean, Forest of 8 C3 51 50N 2 35W
Dearne 7 E6 53 32N 1 17W
Dee →, *Aberds.* 3 H13 57 4N 2 7W
Dee →, *Flints.* 10 A7 53 15N 3 7W
Deer Sd. 3 E12 58 58N 2 50W
Denbigh 10 A7 53 12N 3 26W
Denbighshire □ 10 A7 53 8N 3 22W
Denby Dale 7 E5 53 35N 1 40W
Dennis Hd. 3 D13 59 23N 2 26W
Denny 5 B8 56 1N 3 55W
Denton 7 F4 53 26N 2 10W
Derby 7 G6 52 27N 1 28W
Derbyshire □ 7 F5 53 0N 1 30W
Derg, L. 14 C6 53 0N 8 20W
Derravaragh, L. 12 D7 53 38N 7 22W
Derry = Londonderry 12 B7 55 0N 7 23W
Derry → 15 C9 52 43N 6 35W
Derrynsaggart Mts. 14 E4 51 58N 9 15W
Derwent →, *Derby* 7 G6 52 53N 1 17W
Derwent →, *N. Yorks.* 7 E7 53 45N 0 57W
Desborough 9 B7 52 27N 0 50W
Deveron → 3 G12 57 40N 2 31W
Devilsbit 14 C7 52 50N 7 58W
Devizes 8 D5 51 21N 2 0W
Devon □ 8 F6 50 50N 3 40W
Devonport 11 G5 50 23N 4 11W
Dewsbury 7 E5 53 42N 1 38W
Didcot 8 C6 51 36N 1 14W
Dinas Hd. 10 C4 52 2N 4 56W
Dingle 14 D2 52 9N 10 17W
Dingle B. 14 D2 52 3N 10 20W
Dingwall 3 G9 57 36N 4 26W
Dinnington 7 F6 53 21N 1 12W
Diss 9 B11 52 23N 1 6 E
Ditchling Beacon 9 E8 50 49N 0 7W
Dizzard Pt. 11 F4 50 46N 4 38W
Dodman Pt. 11 G4 50 13N 4 49W
Dolgellau 10 B6 52 44N 3 53W
Dolgelley = Dolgellau 10 B6 52 44N 3 53W
Dollar 5 B8 56 9N 3 41W
Don →, *Aberds.* 3 H13 57 14N 2 5W
Don →, *S. Yorks.* 7 E7 53 41N 0 51W
Donaghadee 13 B10 54 38N 5 32W
Doncaster 7 E6 53 31N 1 9W
Donegal 12 B5 54 39N 8 8W
Donegal □ 12 B6 54 53N 8 0W
Donegal B. 12 B4 54 30N 8 35W
Donegal Harbour 12 B5 54 35N 8 15W
Donna Nook 7 F9 53 29N 0 9 E
Dooega Hd. 12 D1 53 54N 10 3W
Doon, L. 4 D7 55 15N 4 22W
Dorchester 11 E4 50 42N 2 28W
Dorking 9 D8 51 14N 0 20W
Dornoch 3 G9 57 52N 4 5W
Dornoch Firth 3 G10 57 52N 4 0W
Dorridge 8 B5 52 22N 1 45W
Dorset □ 8 E4 50 48N 2 25W
Douglas 13 C13 54 9N 4 29W
Doulus Hd. 14 E2 51 57N 10 19W
Doune 4 B7 56 12N 4 3W
Dounreay 3 E10 58 34N 3 44W
Dove → 7 G5 52 51N 1 36W
Dover 9 D11 51 7N 1 19 E
Dovey = Dyfi → 10 B6 52 32N 4 0W
Down □ 13 C10 54 20N 5 47W
Downham Market 9 A9 52 36N 0 22 E
Downpatrick 13 C10 54 20N 5 43W
Downpatrick Hd. 12 C3 54 20N 9 21W
Driffield 7 D8 54 1N 0 25W
Drogheda 13 D9 53 45N 6 20W
Droichead Atha = Drogheda 13 D9 53 45N 6 20W
Droichead Nua 15 B9 53 11N 6 50W
Droitwich 8 B4 52 16N 2 10W
Dromore 12 B7 54 31N 7 28W
Dronfield 7 F6 53 18N 1 29W
Druridge B. 6 B5 55 16N 1 32W
Drygarn Fawr 10 C6 52 13N 3 39W
Dublin 15 B10 53 20N 6 18W
Dublin □ 15 B10 53 24N 6 20W
Dudley 8 A4 52 30N 2 5W
Dufftown 3 H11 57 26N 3 9W
Dukinfield 7 F4 53 29N 2 5W
Dulas B. 10 A5 53 22N 4 16W
Dumbarton 4 C6 55 58N 4 35W
Dumbarton & Clydebank □ 4 C6 55 58N 4 35W
Dumfries 5 D8 55 4N 3 37W
Dumfries & Galloway □ 5 D8 55 5N 4 0W
Dún Dealgan = Dundalk 13 C9 54 1N 6 25W
Dun Laoghaire 15 B10 53 17N 6 9W
Dunaff Hd. 12 A6 55 18N 7 30W
Dunany Pt. 13 D9 53 51N 6 15W
Dunbar 5 C10 56 0N 2 32W
Dunblane 5 B8 56 10N 3 58W
Duncansby Hd. 3 E12 58 39N 3 0W
Dundalk 13 C9 54 1N 6 25W
Dundalk B. 13 D9 53 55N 6 15W
Dundee 5 B10 56 29N 3 0W
Dundrum 13 C10 54 17N 5 50W
Dunfermline 5 B9 56 5N 3 28W
Dungannon 13 B8 54 30N 6 47W
Dungarvan 15 D7 52 6N 7 40W
Dungarvan Harbour 15 D7 52 5N 7 35W
Dungeness 9 E10 50 54N 0 59 E
Dunipace 5 B8 56 4N 3 55W
Dunkeld 5 A8 56 34N 3 36W
Dunkery Beacon 8 D1 51 15N 3 37W
Dúnleary = Dun Laoghaire 15 B10 53 17N 6 9W
Dunmanway 14 E4 51 43N 9 8W
Dunnet B. 3 E11 58 37N 3 23W
Dunoon 4 C6 55 57N 4 56W
Duns 5 C11 55 47N 2 20W
Dunstable 9 C7 51 53N 0 31W
Dunster 8 D2 51 11N 3 28W
Dunvegan Hd. 2 G4 57 30N 6 42W
Durham 6 C5 54 47N 1 34W
Durham □ 6 C5 54 42N 1 45W
Durlston Hd. 8 E5 50 35N 1 58W
Durness 3 E8 58 34N 4 45W
Dursley 8 C4 51 41N 2 21W
Dury Voe 2 B15 60 20N 1 8W
Dyce 3 H13 57 12N 2 11W
Dyfi → 10 B6 52 32N 4 0W
Dymchurch 9 D11 51 2N 1 0 E

E

Ealing 9 C8 51 30N 0 19W
Earadale Pt. 4 D4 55 24N 5 50W
Earby 7 E4 53 55N 2 8W
Earl Shilton 7 G6 52 35N 1 20W
Earlsferry 5 B10 56 11N 2 50W
Earn → 5 B9 56 20N 3 19W
Earn, L. 4 B7 56 23N 4 14W
Easington 6 C6 54 50N 1 24W
Easington Colliery 6 C6 54 49N 1 19W
East Ayrshire □ 4 D7 55 26N 4 11W
East Cowes 8 E6 50 45N 1 17W
East Dereham 9 A10 52 40N 0 57 E
East Dunbartonshire □ 4 C7 55 57N 4 20W
East Grinstead 9 D9 51 8N 0 0 E
East Kilbride 4 C7 55 46N 4 10W
East Linton 5 C10 56 0N 2 40W
East Lothian □ 5 C10 55 57N 2 48W
East Renfrewshire □ 4 C7 55 48N 4 23W
East Retford = Retford 7 F7 53 19N 0 55W
East Sussex □ 9 E9 51 0N 0 20 E
East Wittering 9 E7 50 46N 0 53W
Eastbourne 9 E9 50 46N 0 18 E
Easter Ross 3 G8 57 50N 4 35W
Eastleigh 8 E6 50 58N 1 21W
Eastwood 7 F6 53 2N 1 17W
Eaval 2 G3 57 33N 7 12W
Ebbw Vale 10 D7 51 47N 3 12W
Eccleshall 7 G4 52 52N 2 14W
Eckington 7 F6 53 19N 1 21W
Eday Sd. 3 D12 59 12N 2 45W
Eddrachillis B. 2 F7 58 16N 5 10W
Eddystone 11 G5 50 11N 4 16W
Eden → 6 C2 54 57N 3 2W
Edenbridge 9 D9 51 12N 0 4 E
Edenderry 15 B8 53 21N 7 3W
Edge Hill 8 B6 52 7N 1 28W
Edinburgh 5 C9 55 57N 3 12W
Egham 9 D7 51 25N 0 33W
Egremont 6 D1 54 28N 3 33W
Eigg 2 J5 56 54N 6 10W
Eil, L. 2 J7 56 50N 5 15W
Eishort, L. 2 H6 57 9N 6 0W
Elan → 10 C6 52 17N 3 30W
Elan Valley Reservoirs 10 C6 52 12N 3 42W
Elgin 3 G11 57 39N 3 20W
Elie 5 B10 56 11N 2 50W
Elland 7 E5 53 41N 1 49W
Ellesmere Port 7 F3 53 17N 2 55W
Ellon 3 H13 57 21N 2 5W
Ely 9 B9 52 24N 0 16 E
Emsworth 9 E7 50 51N 0 56W
Enard B. 2 F7 58 5N 5 20W
Enfield 9 C8 51 39N 0 4W
Ennell, L. 12 E7 53 29N 7 25W
Ennis 14 C5 52 51N 8 59W
Enniscorthy 15 D9 52 30N 6 35W
Enniskillen 12 C6 54 20N 7 40W
Ennistimon 14 C4 52 56N 9 18W
Eport, L. 2 G3 57 33N 7 10W
Epping 9 C9 51 42N 0 8 E
Epsom 9 D8 51 19N 0 16W
Eriboll, L. 3 F8 58 28N 4 41W
Ericht, L. 3 J9 56 50N 4 25W
Eriskay, Sd. of 2 H3 57 5N 7 20W
Erisort L. 2 F4 58 5N 6 30W
Erne → 12 C5 54 30N 8 16W
Erne, Lower L. 12 C6 54 26N 7 46W
Erne, Upper L. 12 C7 54 14N 7 22W
Errigal 12 A5 55 2N 8 8W
Erris Hd. 12 C2 54 19N 10 0W
Erskine 4 C7 55 52N 4 27W
Esha Ness 2 A14 60 30N 1 36W
Esher 9 D8 51 21N 0 22W
Esk → 5 E9 54 58N 3 4W
Eskdale 5 D9 55 12N 3 4W
Essex □ 9 C9 51 55N 0 30 E
Eston 6 C6 54 33N 1 6W
Etive, L. 4 A5 56 30N 5 12W
Ettrick Water → 5 C10 55 31N 2 55W
Evesham 8 B5 52 6N 1 57W
Ewe, L. 2 G6 57 49N 5 38W
Ewell 9 D8 51 20N 0 15W
Exe → 11 F7 50 38N 3 27W
Exeter 11 F6 50 43N 3 31W
Exmoor 11 E6 51 10N 3 59W
Exmouth 11 F7 50 37N 3 26W
Eye, *Cambs.* 7 G8 52 36N 0 11W
Eye, *Suffolk* 9 B11 52 19N 1 9 E
Eye Pen. 2 F5 58 13N 6 10W
Eyemouth 5 C11 55 53N 2 5W
Eynhallow Sd. 3 D11 59 8N 3 7W
Eynort, L. 2 H3 57 13N 7 18W

F

Fair Hd. 13 A9 55 14N 6 10W
Fair Isle 2 C14 59 32N 1 36W
Fairford 8 C5 51 42N 1 48W
Fakenham 9 A10 52 50N 0 51 E
Faldingworth 7 F8 53 21N 0 22W
Falkirk 5 B8 56 1N 3 47W
Falkland 5 B9 56 15N 3 13W
Falmouth 11 G3 50 9N 5 5W
Fanad Hd. 12 A6 55 17N 7 40W
Faraid Hd. 3 E8 58 35N 4 48W
Fareham 8 E6 50 52N 1 11W
Faringdon 8 C5 51 39N 1 34W
Farnborough 9 D7 51 17N 0 46W
Farne Is. 6 A5 55 38N 1 37W
Farnham 9 D7 51 13N 0 49W
Farnworth 7 E4 53 33N 2 24W
Fauldhouse 5 C8 55 50N 3 44W
Faversham 9 D10 51 18N 0 54 E
Fawley 8 E6 50 49N 1 20W
Feale → 14 D3 52 26N 9 40W
Featherbed Moss 7 E5 53 31N 1 56W
Felixstowe 9 C11 51 58N 1 22 E
Felton 6 B5 55 18N 1 42W
Fergus → 14 C5 52 45N 9 0W
Fermanagh □ 12 C6 54 21N 7 40W
Fermoy 14 D6 52 4N 8 18W
Ferndown 8 E5 50 48N 1 53W
Ferryhill 6 C5 54 42N 1 32W
Fethaland, Pt. of 2 A15 60 39N 1 20W
Ffestiniog 10 B6 52 58N 3 56W
Fife □ 5 B9 56 13N 3 2W
Fife Ness 5 B10 56 17N 2 35W
Filey 6 D8 54 13N 0 18W
Filton 8 C3 51 30N 2 34W
Findhorn → 3 G10 57 38N 3 38W
Findochty 3 G12 57 42N 2 53W
Finn → 12 B6 54 50N 7 55W
Fionn L. 2 G7 57 46N 5 30W
Fishguard 10 D4 51 59N 4 59W
Fitful Hd. 2 C15 59 54N 1 20W
Five Sisters 2 H7 57 11N 5 21W
Flamborough Hd. 6 D8 54 8N 0 4W
Fleet 9 D7 51 16N 0 50W
Fleet, L. 3 G9 57 57N 4 2W
Fleetwood 7 E2 53 55N 3 1W
Flint 10 A7 53 15N 3 7W
Flintshire □ 10 A7 53 15N 3 10W
Flitwick 9 C8 51 59N 0 30W
Flodden 6 A4 55 37N 2 8W
Foinaven 3 F8 58 30N 4 53W
Folkestone 9 D11 51 5N 1 11 E
Fordingbridge 8 E5 50 56N 1 48W
Foreland Pt. 11 E6 51 14N 3 47W
Forfar 5 A10 56 40N 2 53W
Formartine 3 H13 57 20N 2 15W
Formby 7 E2 53 33N 3 3W
Forres 3 G10 57 37N 3 38W
Fort Augustus 3 H8 57 9N 4 40W
Fort William 2 J7 56 48N 5 8W
Forth 5 B8 56 8N 3 48W
Forth, Firth of 5 B10 56 5N 2 55W
Fortrose 3 G9 57 35N 4 10W
Fortuneswell 11 F9 50 33N 2 26W
Foulness I. 9 C10 51 36N 0 55 E
Fowey 11 G4 50 20N 4 39W
Fowey → 11 G4 50 20N 4 39W
Foyle → 13 B7 55 0N 7 13W
Foyle, L. 13 A7 55 6N 7 8W
Foynes 14 C4 52 37N 9 5W
Framlingham 9 B11 52 14N 1 20 E
Fraserburgh 3 G13 57 41N 2 3W
Frimley 9 D7 51 18N 0 43W
Frinton-on-Sea 9 C11 51 50N 1 16 E
Frodsham 7 F3 53 17N 2 45W
Frome 8 D4 51 16N 2 17W
Frome → 8 E4 50 44N 2 5W
Frower Pt. 14 E6 51 40N 8 30W
Fulwood 7 E3 53 47N 2 41W
Furness 6 D2 54 14N 3 8W
Fyne, L. 4 C5 56 0N 5 20W

G

Gaillimh = Galway 14 B4 53 16N 9 4W
Gainsborough 7 F7 53 23N 0 46W
Gairloch 2 G6 57 42N 5 40W
Gairloch, L. 2 G6 57 43N 5 45W
Galashiels 5 C10 55 37N 2 50W
Gallan Hd. 2 F3 58 14N 7 2W
Galley Hd. 14 E5 51 32N 8 56W
Galloway 4 D7 55 1N 4 25W
Galloway, Mull of 4 E6 54 38N 4 50W
Galston 4 C7 55 36N 4 22W
Galty Mts. 14 D6 52 22N 8 10W
Galtymore 14 D6 52 22N 8 12W
Galway 14 B4 53 16N 9 4W
Galway □ 14 B4 53 16N 9 3W
Galway B. 14 B4 53 10N 9 20W
Gamlingay 9 B8 52 9N 0 11W
Gara, L. 12 D5 53 57N 8 26W
Garforth 7 E6 53 48N 1 22W
Garioch 3 H12 57 18N 2 40W
Garron Pt. 13 A10 55 3N 6 0W
Garry, L. 3 H8 57 5N 4 52W
Garstang 7 E3 53 53N 2 47W
Gatehouse of Fleet 4 E7 54 53N 4 10W
Gateshead 6 C5 54 57N 1 37W
Gatley 7 F4 53 25N 2 15W
Gerrans B. 11 G4 50 12N 4 57W
Gerrards Cross 9 C7 51 35N 0 32W
Giants Causeway 13 A8 55 15N 6 30W
Gibraltar Pt. 7 F9 53 6N 0 20 E
Gill, L. 12 C5 54 15N 8 25W
Gillingham, *Dorset* 8 D4 51 2N 2 15W
Gillingham, *Kent* 9 D10 51 23N 0 34 E
Girdle Ness 3 H13 57 9N 2 2W
Girvan 4 D6 55 15N 4 50W
Gisborough Moor 6 D7 54 30N 1 2W
Glanaruddery Mts. 14 D4 52 20N 9 27W
Glandore Harbour 14 E4 51 33N 9 8W
Glas Maol 3 J11 56 52N 3 20W
Glasgow 4 C7 55 52N 4 14W
Glastonbury 8 D3 51 9N 2 42W
Glen Affric 3 H8 57 15N 5 0W
Glen B. 12 B4 54 43N 8 45W
Glen Garry, *Highl.* 2 H7 57 3N 5 7W
Glen Garry, *Perths. & Kinr.* 3 J9 56 47N 4 5W
Glen Mor 3 H8 57 12N 4 37W
Glen Shiel 2 H7 57 8N 5 20W
Glencoe 4 A5 56 40N 5 6W
Gleneagles 5 B8 56 16N 3 44W
Glengad Hd. 13 A7 55 19N 7 11W
Glengarriff 14 E3 51 45N 9 33W
Glennamaddy 12 D4 53 37N 8 33W
Glenrothes 5 B9 56 12N 3 11W
Glenties 12 B5 54 48N 8 18W
Glossop 7 F5 53 27N 1 56W
Gloucester 8 C4 51 52N 2 15W
Gloucestershire □ 8 C4 51 44N 2 10W
Goat Fell 4 C5 55 37N 5 11W
Godalming 9 D7 51 12N 0 37W
Goil, L. 4 B6 56 8N 4 52W
Golden Vale 14 C6 52 33N 8 17W
Golspie 3 G10 57 58N 3 58W
Goodwick 10 C3 52 1N 5 0W
Goole 7 E7 53 42N 0 52W
Gorebridge 5 C9 55 51N 3 2W
Gorey 15 C10 52 41N 6 18W
Goring-by-Sea 9 E8 50 49N 0 26W
Gorleston 9 A12 52 35N 1 44 E
Gorseinon 10 D5 51 40N 4 2W
Gort 14 B5 53 4N 8 50W
Gosport 8 E6 50 48N 1 8W
Gourock 4 C6 55 58N 4 49W
Gower 11 D5 51 35N 4 10W
Grafham Water 9 B8 52 18N 0 17W
Gragareth 6 D4 54 12N 2 29W
Grampian Highlands = Grampian Mts. 3 J10 56 50N 4 0W
Grampian Mts. 3 J10 56 50N 4 0W
Granard 12 D6 53 47N 7 30W
Grand Union Canal 9 B7 52 5N 0 52W
Grange-over-Sands 6 D3 54 12N 2 55W
Grangemouth 5 B8 56 1N 3 43W
Grantham 7 G7 52 55N 0 39W
Grantown-on-Spey 3 H10 57 19N 3 36W
Grassington 6 D5 54 5N 2 0W
Gravesend 9 D9 51 25N 0 22 E
Grays 9 D9 51 28N 0 23 E
Great Blasket I. 14 D1 52 5N 10 30W
Great Driffield = Driffield 7 D8 54 1N 0 25W
Great Dunmow 9 C9 51 52N 0 22 E
Great Harwood 7 E4 53 47N 2 25W
Great I. 14 E6 51 52N 8 15W
Great Malvern 8 B4 52 7N 2 19W
Great Ormes Hd. 10 A6 53 20N 3 52W
Great Ouse → 9 A9 52 47N 0 22 E
Great Shunner Fell 6 D4 54 22N 2 16W
Great Stour = Stour → 9 D11 51 15N 1 20 E
Great Sugar Loaf 15 B10 53 10N 6 10W
Great Torrington 11 F5 50 57N 4 9W
Great Whernside 6 D5 54 9N 1 59W
Great Yarmouth 9 A12 52 40N 1 45 E
Greater London □ 9 C8 51 30N 0 5W
Greater Manchester □ 7 E4 53 30N 2 15W
Green Lowther 5 D8 55 22N 3 44W
Greenholm 4 C7 55 40N 4 20W
Greenock 4 C6 55 57N 4 46W
Greenore 13 C9 54 2N 6 8W
Greenore Pt. 15 D10 52 15N 6 20W
Greenstone Pt. 2 G6 57 55N 5 38W
Greenwich 9 D9 51 28N 0 0 E
Greian Hd. 2 H2 57 1N 7 30W
Gretna 5 E9 54 59N 3 4W
Gretna Green 5 E9 55 0N 3 3W
Greystones 15 B10 53 9N 6 4W
Griminish Pt. 2 G3 57 40N 7 29W
Grimsby 7 E8 53 35N 0 5W
Gruinard B. 2 G6 57 56N 5 35W
Gruinart, L. 4 C3 55 50N 6 20W
Gruting Voe 2 B14 60 12N 1 32W
Guernsey 11 J8 49 30N 2 35W
Guildford 9 D7 51 14N 0 34W
Guisborough 6 C6 54 32N 1 2W
Guiseley 7 E5 53 52N 1 43W
Gullane 5 B10 56 2N 2 50W
Gurnard's Hd. 11 G2 50 12N 5 37W
Gweebarra B. 12 B5 54 52N 8 21W
Gweedore 12 A5 55 4N 8 15W

H

Hackley Hd. 3 H14 57 19N 1 58W
Hackney 9 C8 51 33N 0 2W
Haddington 5 C10 55 57N 2 48W
Hadleigh, *Essex* 9 C10 51 33N 0 37 E
Hadleigh, *Suffolk* 9 B10 52 3N 0 58 E
Hags Hd. 14 C4 52 57N 9 28W
Hailsham 9 E9 50 52N 0 17 E
Halberry Hd. 3 F11 58 20N 3 11W
Halesowen 8 B4 52 27N 2 2W
Halesworth 9 B12 52 21N 1 31 E
Halifax 7 E5 53 43N 1 51W
Halkirk 3 E11 58 30N 3 30W
Halstead 9 C10 51 59N 0 39 E
Haltwhistle 6 C4 54 58N 2 27W
Hambleton Hills 6 D6 54 17N 1 12W
Hamilton 4 C7 55 47N 4 2W
Hammersmith and Fulham 9 D8 51 30N 0 15W
Hampshire □ 8 D6 51 3N 1 20W
Hampshire Downs 8 D6 51 10N 1 10W
Handa I. 2 F7 58 23N 5 10W
Haringey 9 C8 51 35N 0 7W
Harlech 10 B5 52 52N 4 7W
Harleston 9 B11 52 25N 1 18 E
Harlow 9 C9 51 47N 0 9 E
Harpenden 9 C8 51 48N 0 20W
Harris 2 G4 57 50N 6 55W
Harris, Sd. of 2 G3 57 44N 7 6W
Harrogate 7 E5 53 59N 1 32W
Harrow 9 C8 51 35N 0 15W
Hartland Pt. 11 E4 51 2N 4 32W
Hartlepool 6 C6 54 42N 1 11W
Harwich 9 C11 51 56N 1 18 E
Haslemere 9 D7 51 5N 0 41W
Haslingden 7 E4 53 43N 2 20W
Hastings 9 E10 50 51N 0 36 E
Hatfield, *Herts.* 9 C8 51 46N 0 11W
Hatfield, *S. Yorks.* 7 E7 53 34N 0 59W
Havant 9 E7 50 51N 0 59W
Haverfordwest 10 D4 51 48N 4 59W
Haverhill 9 B9 52 6N 0 27 E
Havering 9 C9 51 33N 0 20 E
Haweswater 6 C3 54 32N 2 48W
Hawick 5 D10 55 25N 2 48W
Hawkhurst 9 D10 51 2N 0 31 E
Hay-on-Wye 10 C7 52 4N 3 9W
Hayle 11 G3 50 12N 5 25W
Haywards Heath 9 D8 51 1N 0 6W
Hazel Grove 7 F4 53 23N 2 7W
Healaval Bheag 2 H4 57 24N 6 41W
Heanor 7 F6 53 1N 1 20W
Heathfield 9 E9 50 58N 0 18 E
Heaval 2 J3 56 58N 7 30W
Hebburn 6 C5 54 59N 1 30W
Hebden Bridge 7 E5 53 45N 2 0W
Hecla 2 H3 57 18N 7 15W
Hednesford 7 G5 52 43N 2 0W
Hedon 7 E8 53 44N 0 11W
Helensburgh 4 B6 56 1N 4 44W
Helli Ness 2 B15 60 3N 1 10W
Helmsdale 3 F10 58 8N 3 43W
Helmsley 6 D6 54 15N 1 2W
Helston 11 G3 50 7N 5 17W
Helvellyn 6 C2 54 31N 3 1W
Helvick Hd. 15 D7 52 3N 7 33W
Hemel Hempstead 9 C8 51 45N 0 28W
Hemsworth 7 E6 53 37N 1 21W
Henfield 9 E8 50 56N 0 17W
Hengoed 10 D7 51 39N 3 14W
Henley-on-Thames 9 C7 51 32N 0 53W
Hereford 8 B3 52 4N 2 42W
Hereford and Worcester □ 8 B3 52 10N 2 30W
Herma Ness 2 A16 60 50N 0 54W
Herne Bay 9 D11 51 22N 1 8 E
Hertford 9 C8 51 47N 0 4W
Hertfordshire □ 9 C8 51 51N 0 5W
Hessle 7 E8 53 44N 0 28W
Heswall 7 F2 53 19N 3 6W
Hetton-le-Hole 6 C6 54 49N 1 26W
Hexham 6 C4 54 58N 2 7W
Heysham 6 D3 54 5N 2 53W
Heywood 7 E4 53 35N 2 13W
High Pike 6 C2 54 43N 3 4W
High Willhays 11 F6 50 41N 3 59W
High Wycombe 9 C7 51 37N 0 45W
Higham Ferrers 9 B7 52 18N 0 36W
Highbridge 8 D3 51 13N 2 59W
Highland □ 3 H7 57 30N 5 0W
Highworth 8 C5 51 38N 1 42W
Hillingdon 9 C8 51 33N 0 29W
Hilpsford Pt. 6 D2 54 4N 3 12W
Hinckley 7 G6 52 33N 1 21W
Hindley 7 E3 53 32N 2 35W
Hinkley Pt. 8 D2 51 13N 3 9W
Hitchin 9 C8 51 57N 0 16W
Hockley 9 C10 51 35N 0 39 E
Hoddesdon 9 C8 51 45N 0 1W
Hog's Back 9 D7 51 13N 0 40W
Hogs Hd. 14 E2 51 46N 10 13W
Holbeach 7 G9 52 48N 0 1 E
Holborn Hd. 3 E10 58 37N 3 30W
Holderness 7 E8 53 45N 0 5W
Holmfirth 7 E5 53 34N 1 48W
Holsworthy 11 F5 50 48N 4 21W
Holt 9 A11 52 55N 1 4 E
Holy I., *Angl.* 10 A4 53 17N 4 37W
Holy I., *Northumb.* 6 A5 55 42N 1 48W
Holyhead 10 A4 53 18N 4 38W
Holywell 10 A7 53 16N 3 14W
Honiton 11 F7 50 48N 3 11W
Hook 9 D7 51 17N 0 55W
Hook Hd. 15 D9 52 8N 6 57W
Horden 6 C6 54 45N 1 17W
Horley 9 D8 51 10N 0 10W
Horn Hd. 12 A6 55 13N 8 0W
Horncastle 7 F8 53 13N 0 8W
Horndean 9 E6 50 50N 1 0W
Hornsea 7 E8 53 55N 0 10W
Horsforth 7 E5 53 50N 1 39W
Horsham 9 D8 51 4N 0 20W
Horwich 7 E3 53 37N 2 33W
Houghton-le-Spring 6 C6 54 51N 1 28W
Houghton Regis 9 C7 51 54N 0 32W
Hounslow 9 D8 51 29N 0 20W
Hourn, L. 2 H6 57 7N 5 35W
Hove 9 E8 50 50N 0 10W
Howden 7 E7 53 45N 0 52W
Howth Hd. 15 B10 53 21N 6 3W
Hoy Sd. 3 E11 58 57N 3 20W

Hoylake   **Mynydd Prescelly**

Naas Sleaford 37

N

Naas **15 B9** 53 12N 6 40W
Nagles Mts. **14 D5** 52 8N 8 30W
Nailsea **8 D3** 51 25N 2 44W
Nailsworth **8 C4** 51 41N 2 12W
Nairn **3 G10** 57 35N 3 54W
Nairn → **3 G10** 57 32N 3 58W
Nantwich **7 F3** 53 5N 2 31W
Narberth **10 D4** 51 48N 4 45W
Narrows **2 H5** 57 20N 6 5W
Nash Pt. **8 E6** 51 24N 3 34W
Navan = An Uaimh **13 D8** 53 39N 6 40W
Naver → **3 E9** 58 34N 4 15W
Neagh, L. **13 B9** 54 35N 6 25W
Neath **10 D6** 51 39N 3 49W
Neath → **10 D6** 51 38N 3 35W
Neath & Port Talbot □ **11 D6** 51 35N 3 48W
Neist Pt. **2 H4** 57 24N 6 48W
Nelson **7 E4** 53 50N 2 14W
Nenagh **14 C6** 52 52N 8 11W
Nenagh → **14 C6** 52 56N 8 16W
Nene → **9 A9** 52 38N 0 13 E
Nephin **12 C3** 54 1N 9 21W
Nephin Beg Range **12 D2** 54 0N 9 40W
Ness **2 F5** 58 27N 6 20W
Ness, L. **3 H8** 57 15N 4 30W
Neston **7 F2** 53 17N 3 3W
Nevis, L. **2 J6** 57 0N 5 43W
New Alresford **8 D6** 51 6N 1 10W
New Bedford R. → **9 A9** 52 34N 0 20 E
New Forest **8 E5** 50 53N 1 40W
New Galloway **4 D7** 55 4N 4 10W
New Holland **7 E8** 53 42N 0 22W
New Mills **7 F5** 53 22N 2 0W
New Milton **8 E5** 50 45N 1 40W
New Quay **10 C5** 52 13N 4 21W
New Radnor **10 C7** 52 15N 3 10W
New Romney **9 E10** 50 59N 0 57 E
New Ross **15 D9** 52 24N 6 58W
New Rossington **7 F6** 53 30N 1 4W
New Scone **5 B9** 56 25N 3 26W
New Tredegar **10 D7** 51 43N 3 15W
Newark-on-Trent **7 F7** 53 6N 0 48W
Newbiggin-by-the-Sea **6 B5** 55 12N 1 31W
Newbridge = Droichead Nua **15 B9** 53 11N 6 50W
Newburgh **5 B9** 56 21N 3 15W
Newburn **6 C5** 54 57N 1 45W
Newbury **8 D6** 51 24N 1 19W
Newcastle **13 C10** 54 13N 5 54W
Newcastle Emlyn **10 C5** 52 2N 4 29W
Newcastle-under-Lyme **7 F4** 53 2N 2 15W
Newcastle-upon-Tyne **6 C5** 54 59N 1 37W
Newcastle West **14 D4** 52 27N 9 3W
Newham **9 C9** 51 31N 0 2 E
Newhaven **9 E9** 50 47N 0 4 E
Newlyn **11 G2** 50 6N 5 33W
Newmarket, *Ireland* **14 D5** 52 13N 9 0W
Newmarket, *Suffolk* **9 B9** 52 15N 0 23 E
Newmilns **4 C7** 55 36N 4 20W
Newport, *Mayo* **12 D2** 53 50N 9 31W
Newport, *I. of W.* **8 E6** 50 42N 1 18W
Newport, *Newp.* **11 D8** 51 35N 3 0W
Newport, *Shrops.* **7 G4** 52 47N 2 22W
Newport B. **12 D2** 53 52N 9 38W
Newport-on-Tay **5 B10** 56 27N 2 56W
Newport Pagnell **9 B7** 52 5N 0 42W
Newquay **11 G3** 50 24N 5 6W
Newry **13 C9** 54 10N 6 20W
Newton Abbot **11 F6** 50 32N 3 37W
Newton Aycliffe **6 C5** 54 36N 1 33W
Newton le Willows **7 F3** 53 28N 2 40W
Newton Stewart **4 E6** 54 57N 4 30W
Newtongrange **5 C9** 55 52N 3 4W
Newtonmore **3 H9** 57 4N 4 7W
Newtown **10 B7** 52 31N 3 19W
Newtownabbey **13 B10** 54 40N 5 55W
Newtownards **13 B10** 54 37N 5 40W
Newtownbarry = Bunclody **15 C9** 52 40N 6 40W
Newtownstewart **12 B7** 54 43N 7 22W
Neyland **10 D4** 51 43N 4 58W
Nidd → **7 E6** 53 58N 1 28W
Nidderdale **6 D5** 54 5N 1 46W
Nigg B. **3 G9** 57 41N 4 5W
Nith → **5 D8** 55 20N 3 5W
Nithsdale **5 D8** 55 14N 3 50W
Nore → **15 D9** 52 24N 6 58W
Norfolk □ **9 A11** 52 39N 1 0 E
Norfolk Broads Nat. Park **9 A11** 52 45N 1 30 E
Normanton **7 E6** 53 41N 1 26W
North Ayrshire □ **4 C6** 55 38N 4 47W
North Berwick **5 B10** 56 4N 2 44W
North Channel **4 D4** 55 0N 5 30W
North Dorset Downs **8 E3** 50 50N 2 30W
North Downs **9 D9** 51 17N 0 30 E
North Esk → **5 A11** 56 44N 2 25W
North Foreland **9 D11** 51 22N 1 28 E
North Harris **2 G4** 58 0N 6 55W
North Lanarkshire □ **4 C7** 55 52N 4 2W
North Minch **2 F6** 58 5N 5 55W
North Roe **2 A15** 60 40N 1 22W
North Sd. **14 B3** 53 10N 9 48W
North Tyne → **6 C4** 54 59N 2 7W
North Uist **2 G3** 57 40N 7 15W
North Walsham **9 A11** 52 49N 1 22 E
North West Highlands **2 G8** 57 35N 5 0W
North York Moors **6 D7** 54 25N 0 50W
North Yorkshire □ **6 D6** 54 15N 1 25W
Northallerton **6 D6** 54 20N 1 26W
Northampton **9 B7** 52 14N 0 54W
Northamptonshire □ **9 B7** 52 16N 0 55W
Northern Ireland □ **13 B8** 54 45N 7 0W
Northfleet **9 D9** 51 26N 0 20 E
Northumberland □ **6 B5** 55 12N 2 0W
Northwich **7 F3** 53 16N 2 31W
Norton **6 D7** 54 9N 0 48W
Norwich **9 A11** 52 38N 1 17 E
Noss Hd. **3 F11** 58 29N 3 4W
Nottingham **7 G6** 52 57N 1 10W
Nottinghamshire □ **7 F7** 53 10N 1 0W
Noup Hd. **3 D11** 59 20N 3 2W
Nowen Hill **14 E4** 51 42N 9 15W
Nuneaton **8 A6** 52 32N 1 29W

O

Oa, Mull of **4 C3** 55 35N 6 20W
Oadby **7 G6** 52 37N 1 7W
Oakengates **7 G4** 52 42N 2 29W
Oakham **7 G7** 52 40N 0 43W
Oban **4 B5** 56 25N 5 30W
Ochil Hills **5 B8** 56 14N 3 40W
Offaly □ **15 B7** 53 15N 7 30W
Okehampton **11 F5** 50 44N 4 1W
Old Bedford R. → **9 A9** 52 36N 0 20 E
Old Fletton **7 G8** 52 34N 0 13W
Old Man of Hoy **3 E11** 58 53N 3 25W
Oldbury **8 C3** 51 38N 2 30W
Oldcastle **13 D7** 53 46N 7 10W
Oldham **7 E4** 53 33N 2 8W
Oldmeldrum **3 H13** 57 20N 2 19W
Olney **9 B7** 52 9N 0 42W
Omagh **12 B7** 54 36N 7 20W
Orford Ness **9 B12** 52 6N 1 31 E
Orkney □ **3 D11** 59 0N 3 0W
Ormskirk **7 E3** 53 35N 2 53W
Oronsay, Passage of **4 C3** 56 0N 6 10W
Orwell → **9 B11** 52 2N 1 12 E
Ossett **7 E5** 53 40N 1 35W
Oswaldtwistle **7 E4** 53 44N 2 27W
Oswestry **7 G2** 52 52N 3 3W
Otley **7 E5** 53 54N 1 41W
Ottery St. Mary **11 F7** 50 45N 3 16W
Oughter, L. **12 C7** 54 2N 7 30W
Oughterard **14 B4** 53 26N 9 20W
Oundle **9 B8** 52 28N 0 28W
Ouse → **7 E7** 53 33N 0 44W
Outer Hebrides **2 J2** 57 30N 7 40W
Owel, L. **12 D7** 53 34N 7 24W
Oxford **8 C6** 51 45N 1 15W
Oxfordshire □ **8 C6** 51 45N 1 15W
Oxted **9 D9** 51 14N 0 0 E
Oxwich Pt. **11 D5** 51 33N 4 8W
Oykel → **3 G9** 57 55N 4 26W

P

Pabbay, Sd. of **2 G3** 57 45N 7 4W
Paddock Wood **9 D9** 51 13N 0 24 E
Padiham **7 E4** 53 48N 2 20W
Padstow **11 F4** 50 33N 4 57W
Paignton **11 G6** 50 26N 3 33W
Painshawfield **6 C5** 54 56N 1 54W
Paisley **4 C7** 55 51N 4 27W
Papa, Sd. of **2 B14** 60 19N 1 40W
Papa Sd. **3 D12** 59 20N 2 56W
Parrett → **8 D3** 51 7N 3 0W
Partry Mts. **12 D3** 53 40N 9 28W
Parys Mt. **10 A5** 53 23N 4 18W
Passage West **14 E6** 51 52N 8 20W
Patna **4 D6** 55 21N 4 30W
Peak District Nat. Park **7 F5** 58 21N 1 6W
Peebles **5 C9** 55 40N 3 12W
Peel **13 C12** 54 13N 4 41W
Peel Fell **6 B3** 55 17N 2 35W
Pegwell B. **9 D11** 51 18N 1 22 E
Pembroke **10 D4** 51 41N 4 57W
Pembrokeshire □ **10 D4** 51 51N 4 56W
Pen-y-Ghent **6 D4** 54 10N 2 15W
Penarth **11 E7** 51 26N 3 11W
Pendle Hill **7 E4** 53 53N 2 18W
Penicuik **5 C9** 55 50N 3 14W
Penistone **7 E5** 53 31N 1 38W
Penkridge **7 G4** 52 44N 2 8W
Penmaenmawr **10 A6** 53 16N 3 55W
Pennines **6 C4** 54 50N 2 20W
Penrith **6 C3** 54 40N 2 45W
Penryn **11 G3** 50 10N 5 7W
Pentire Pt. **11 F4** 50 35N 4 57W
Pentland Firth **3 E11** 58 43N 3 10W
Pentland Hills **5 C9** 55 48N 3 25W
Penzance **11 G2** 50 7N 5 32W
Perranporth **11 G3** 50 21N 5 9W
Pershore **8 B4** 52 7N 2 4W
Perth **5 B9** 56 24N 3 27W
Perthshire & Kinross □ **5 A8** 56 45N 3 55W
Peterborough **7 G8** 52 35N 0 14W
Peterculter **3 H13** 57 5N 2 18W
Peterhead **3 G14** 57 30N 1 49W
Peterlee **6 C6** 54 45N 1 18W
Petersfield **9 D7** 51 0N 0 56W
Petworth **9 E7** 50 59N 0 37W
Pewsey, Vale of **8 D5** 51 20N 1 46W
Pickering **6 D7** 54 15N 0 46W
Pickering, Vale of **6 D7** 54 14N 0 45W
Pilsdon Pen **8 E3** 50 49N 2 51W
Pitlochry **5 A8** 56 43N 3 43W
Pittenweem **5 B10** 56 13N 2 43W
Plymouth **11 G5** 50 23N 4 9W
Plympton **11 G5** 50 24N 4 2W
Plymstock **11 G5** 50 22N 4 6W
Plynlimon = Pumlumon Fawr **10 C6** 52 29N 3 47W
Pocklington **7 E7** 53 56N 0 48W
Polegate **9 E9** 50 49N 0 15 E
Polperro **11 G4** 50 19N 4 31W
Pontardawe **10 D6** 51 43N 3 51W
Pontardulais **10 D5** 51 42N 4 3W
Pontefract **7 E6** 53 42N 1 19W
Ponteland **6 B5** 55 7N 1 45W
Pontypool **10 D7** 51 42N 3 1W
Pontypridd **11 D7** 51 36N 3 21W
Poole **8 E5** 50 42N 1 58W
Poole Harbour **8 E5** 50 41N 2 0W
Port Bannatyne **4 C5** 55 51N 5 4W
Port Ellen **4 C3** 55 38N 6 10W
Port Erin **13 C12** 54 5N 4 45W
Port Eynon Pt. **11 D5** 51 32N 4 12W
Port Glasgow **4 C6** 55 57N 4 40W
Port Isaac B. **11 F4** 50 36N 4 50W
Port Laigre = Waterford **15 D8** 52 16N 7 8W
Port Laoise **15 B8** 53 2N 7 20W
Port Talbot **11 D6** 51 35N 3 48W
Portadown **13 C9** 54 27N 6 26W
Portaferry **13 C10** 54 23N 5 32W
Portarlington **15 B8** 53 10N 7 10W
Porth Neigwl **10 B4** 52 48N 4 33W
Porthcawl **11 E6** 51 28N 3 42W
Porthleven **11 G3** 50 5N 5 19W
Porthmadog **10 B5** 52 55N 4 13W
Portishead **8 D3** 51 29N 2 46W
Portknockie **3 G12** 57 40N 2 52W
Portland, I. of **11 F9** 50 32N 2 25W
Portland Bill **11 F9** 50 31N 2 27W
Portmadoc = Porthmadog **10 B5** 52 55N 4 13W
Portpatrick **4 E5** 54 50N 5 7W
Portree **2 H5** 57 25N 6 11W
Portrush **13 A8** 55 13N 6 40W
Portslade **9 E8** 50 50N 0 11W
Portsmouth **8 E6** 50 48N 1 6W
Portsoy **3 G12** 57 41N 2 41W
Portstewart **13 A8** 55 12N 6 43W
Portumna **14 B6** 53 5N 8 12W
Potters Bar **9 C8** 51 42N 0 11W
Poulaphouca Res. **15 B10** 53 8N 6 30W
Poulton le Fylde **7 E3** 53 51N 2 59W
Powys □ **8 C7** 52 20N 3 20W
Prawle Pt. **11 G6** 50 13N 3 41W
Prestatyn **10 A7** 53 20N 3 24W
Prestbury **8 C4** 51 54N 2 2W
Presteigne **10 C7** 52 17N 3 0W
Preston **7 E3** 53 46N 2 42W
Prestonpans **5 C10** 55 58N 2 58W
Prestwich **7 E4** 53 32N 2 18W
Prestwick **4 D6** 55 30N 4 38W
Princes Risborough **9 C7** 51 43N 0 50W
Prudhoe **6 C5** 54 57N 1 52W
Pudsey **7 E5** 53 47N 1 40W
Pulborough **9 E8** 50 58N 0 30W
Pumlumon Fawr **10 C6** 52 29N 3 47W
Purbeck, I. of **8 E4** 50 40N 2 5W
Purfleet **9 D9** 51 29N 0 15 E
Pwllheli **10 B5** 52 54N 4 26W

Q

Quantock Hills **8 D2** 51 8N 3 10W
Queenborough **9 D10** 51 24N 0 46 E
Queensbury **7 E5** 53 46N 1 50W
Quendale, B. of **2 C15** 59 53N 1 20W
Quinag **2 F7** 58 13N 5 5W
Quoich, L. **2 H7** 57 4N 5 20W

R

Raasay **2 H5** 57 25N 6 4W
Radcliffe **7 E4** 53 35N 2 19W
Radcliffe-on-Trent **7 G6** 52 57N 1 3W
Radlett **9 C8** 51 41N 0 19W
Radnor Forest **10 C7** 52 17N 3 10W
Radstock **8 D4** 51 17N 2 25W
Rainham **9 D10** 51 22N 0 36 E
Rame Hd. **11 G5** 50 19N 4 14W
Ramsbottom **7 E4** 53 36N 2 20W
Ramsey, *Cambs.* **9 B8** 52 27N 0 6W
Ramsey, *I. of M.* **13 C13** 54 20N 4 21W
Ramsgate **9 D11** 51 20N 1 25 E
Randalstown **13 B9** 54 45N 6 20W
Rannoch **4 A7** 56 40N 4 20W
Rannoch, L. **4 A7** 56 41N 4 20W
Rannoch Moor **4 A6** 56 38N 4 48W
Rath Luirc **14 D5** 52 21N 8 40W
Rathdrum **15 C10** 52 57N 6 13W
Rathkeale **14 C5** 52 32N 8 57W
Rathlin I. **13 A9** 55 18N 6 14W
Rathmelton **12 A6** 55 3N 7 35W
Rattray **5 A9** 56 36N 3 20W
Rattray Hd. **3 G14** 57 38N 1 50W
Raunds **9 B7** 52 20N 0 32W
Ravenshead **7 F6** 53 5N 1 10W
Rawmarsh **7 F6** 53 27N 1 20W
Rawtenstall **7 E4** 53 42N 2 18W
Rayleigh **9 C10** 51 36N 0 38 E
Reading **9 D7** 51 27N 0 57W
Red B. **13 A9** 55 4N 6 2W
Red Wharf B. **10 A5** 53 18N 4 10W
Redbridge **9 C9** 51 35N 0 7 E
Redcar **6 C6** 54 37N 1 4W
Redditch **8 B5** 52 18N 1 57W
Redhill **9 D8** 51 14N 0 10W
Redruth **11 G3** 50 14N 5 14W
Ree, L. **12 D6** 53 35N 8 0W
Reigate **9 D8** 51 14N 0 11W
Renfrew **4 C7** 55 52N 4 24W
Renfrewshire □ **4 C6** 55 50N 4 31W
Renish Pt. **2 G4** 57 44N 6 59W
Retford **7 F7** 53 19N 0 55W
Rhayader **10 C7** 52 19N 3 30W
Rhinns Pt. **4 C3** 55 42N 6 29W
Rhois-Bheinn **2 J6** 56 50N 5 40W
Rhondda **10 D6** 51 39N 3 30W
Rhondda Cynon Taff □ **10 D7** 51 45N 3 27W
Rhosllanerchrugog **10 A7** 53 3N 3 4W
Rhossili B. **11 D5** 51 33N 4 15W
Rhum **2 J5** 57 0N 6 20W
Rhum, Sd. of **2 J5** 56 54N 6 14W
Rhyl **10 A7** 53 19N 3 29W
Rhymney **10 D7** 51 45N 3 17W
Ribble → **6 E3** 53 46N 2 42W
Richmond **6 D5** 54 24N 1 43W
Richmond-upon-Thames **9 D8** 51 28N 0 18W
Rickmansworth **9 C8** 51 38N 0 28W
Ringwood **8 E5** 50 50N 1 48W
Ripley **7 F6** 53 3N 1 24W
Ripon **6 D5** 54 8N 1 31W
Risca **11 D7** 51 36N 3 6W
Rishton **7 E4** 53 46N 2 26W
Roag, L. **2 F4** 58 10N 6 55W
Roaringwater B. **14 F3** 51 30N 9 30W
Robin Hood's Bay **6 D7** 54 26N 0 31W
Rochdale **7 E4** 53 36N 2 10W
Rochester **9 D10** 51 22N 0 30 E
Rochford **9 C10** 51 36N 0 42 E
Rockingham Forest **9 B7** 52 28N 0 42W
Roe → **13 A8** 55 10N 6 59W
Rogans Seat **6 D4** 54 25N 2 10W
Romney Marsh **9 D10** 51 4N 0 58 E
Romsey **8 E6** 51 0N 1 29W
Ronas Hill **2 A15** 60 33N 1 25W
Rora Hd. **3 E11** 58 51N 3 21W
Roscommon **12 D5** 53 38N 8 11W
Roscommon □ **12 D5** 53 40N 8 15W
Roscrea **14 C7** 52 58N 7 50W
Rose Ness **3 E12** 58 52N 2 50W
Ross-on-Wye **8 C3** 51 55N 2 34W
Rossall Pt. **7 E2** 53 55N 3 2W
Rossan Pt. **12 B4** 54 42N 8 47W
Rosscarbery B. **14 E5** 51 32N 9 0W
Rosses B. **12 A5** 55 2N 8 30W
Rosslare **15 D10** 52 17N 6 23W
Rosyth **5 B9** 56 2N 3 26W
Rotherham **7 F6** 53 26N 1 21W
Rothes **3 G11** 57 31N 3 12W
Rothesay **4 C5** 55 50N 5 3W
Rothwell, *Northants.* **9 B7** 52 25N 0 48W
Rothwell, *W. Yorks.* **7 E6** 53 46N 1 29W
Rottingdean **9 E8** 50 48N 0 3W
Rough Pt. **14 D2** 52 19N 10 2W
Royal Leamington Spa **8 B5** 52 18N 1 32W
Royal Tunbridge Wells **9 D9** 51 7N 0 16 E
Royston, *Herts.* **9 B8** 52 3N 0 1W
Royston, *S. Yorks.* **7 E6** 53 36N 1 27W
Royton **7 E4** 53 34N 2 7W
Rubh a' Mhail **4 C3** 55 55N 6 10W
Rubha Ardvule **2 H3** 57 17N 7 29W
Rubha Coigeach **2 F7** 58 6N 5 27W
Rubha Hunish **2 G5** 57 42N 6 20W
Rubha Robhanais = Lewis, Butt of **2 E5** 58 30N 6 12W
Rubh'an Dunain **2 H5** 57 10N 6 20W
Rugby **8 B6** 52 23N 1 16W
Rugeley **7 G5** 52 47N 1 56W
Runabay Hd. **13 A9** 55 10N 6 2W
Runcorn **7 F3** 53 20N 2 44W
Rush **13 D9** 53 31N 6 7W
Rushden **9 B7** 52 17N 0 37W
Rutherglen **4 C7** 55 50N 4 11W
Ruthin **10 A7** 53 7N 3 20W
Rutland Water **7 G7** 52 38N 0 38W
Ryan, L. **4 E5** 55 0N 5 2W
Ryde **8 E6** 50 44N 1 9W
Rye **9 E10** 50 57N 0 46 E

S

Sacquoy Hd. **3 D11** 59 12N 3 5W
Saddle Hd. **12 C1** 54 1N 10 10W
Saffron Walden **9 B9** 52 2N 0 15 E
St. Abb's Hd. **5 C11** 55 55N 2 10W
St. Agnes Hd. **11 G3** 50 19N 5 14W
St. Albans **9 C8** 51 44N 0 19W
St. Alban's Hd. **8 E4** 50 34N 2 3W
St. Andrews **5 B10** 56 20N 2 48W
St. Ann's Hd. **10 D3** 51 41N 5 11W
St. Asaph **10 A7** 53 15N 3 27W
St. Austell **11 G4** 50 20N 4 48W
St. Bee's Hd. **6 C1** 54 30N 3 38W
St. Brides B. **10 D3** 51 48N 5 15W
St. Catherine's Hill **8 E6** 50 36N 1 18W
St. Catherine's Pt. **8 E6** 50 34N 1 18W
St. David's **10 D3** 51 54N 5 16W
St. David's Hd. **10 D3** 51 55N 5 16W
St. Finan's B. **14 E2** 51 50N 10 22W
St. George's Channel **15 D11** 52 0N 6 0W
St. Govan's Hd. **11 D4** 51 35N 4 56W
St. Helens **7 F3** 53 28N 2 44W
St. Helier **11 J9** 49 11N 2 6W
St. Ives, *Cambs.* **9 B8** 52 20N 0 5W
St. Ives, *Corn.* **11 G3** 50 13N 5 29W
St. Ives B. **11 G3** 50 15N 5 27W
St. John's Pt., *Ireland* **12 B5** 54 35N 8 26W
St. John's Pt., *Down* **13 C10** 54 14N 5 40W
St. Just **11 G2** 50 7N 5 41W
St. Leonards **9 E10** 50 51N 0 33 E
St. Magnus B. **2 B14** 60 25N 1 35W
St. Mary's Sd. **11 H1** 49 53N 6 19W
St. Mawes **11 G3** 50 10N 5 1W
St. Michael's Mount **11 G3** 50 7N 5 30W
St. Monance **5 B10** 56 13N 2 46W
St. Neots **9 B8** 52 14N 0 16W
St. Ouens B. **11 J9** 49 13N 2 14W
St. Peter Port **11 J8** 49 27N 2 31W
Saintfield **13 C10** 54 28N 5 50W
Salcombe **11 G6** 50 14N 3 47W
Sale **7 F4** 53 26N 2 19W
Salford **7 F4** 53 30N 2 17W
Salisbury **8 D5** 51 4N 1 48W
Salisbury Plain **8 D5** 51 13N 1 50W
Saltash **11 G5** 50 25N 4 13W
Saltburn by the Sea **6 C7** 54 35N 0 58W
Saltcoats **4 C6** 55 38N 4 47W
Sanday Sd. **3 D12** 59 11N 2 31W
Sandbach **7 F4** 53 9N 2 23W
Sandgate **9 D11** 51 5N 1 9 E
Sandness **2 B14** 60 18N 1 38W
Sandown **8 E6** 50 39N 1 9W
Sandringham **9 A10** 52 50N 0 30 E
Sandwich **9 D11** 51 16N 1 21 E
Sandy **9 B8** 52 8N 0 18W
Sanquhar **5 D8** 55 21N 3 56W
Sawbridgeworth **9 C9** 51 49N 0 10 E
Sawel **13 B7** 54 48N 7 5W
Saxmundham **9 B12** 52 13N 1 31 E
Scafell Pike **6 D2** 54 26N 3 14W
Scalby **6 D8** 54 18N 0 26W
Scalloway **2 B15** 60 9N 1 16W
Scalpay **2 H6** 57 18N 6 0W
Scapa Flow **3 E11** 58 52N 3 6W
Scarborough **6 D8** 54 17N 0 24W
Scavaig, L. **2 H5** 57 8N 6 10W
Schiehallion **4 A7** 56 40N 4 6W
Scilly, Isles of **11 H1** 49 55N 6 15W
Score Hd. **2 B15** 60 12N 1 5W
Scotch Corner **6 D5** 54 27N 1 40W
Scridain, L. **4 B3** 56 23N 6 7W
Scunthorpe **7 E7** 53 35N 0 38W
Seaford **9 E9** 50 46N 0 8 E
Seaforth, L. **2 G4** 57 52N 6 36W
Seaham **6 C6** 54 51N 1 20W
Seahouses **6 A5** 55 35N 1 39W
Seascale **6 D2** 54 24N 3 29W
Seaton **11 F7** 50 42N 3 3W
Sedbergh **6 D3** 54 20N 2 31W
Selby **7 E6** 53 47N 1 5W
Selkirk **5 C10** 55 33N 2 50W
Selsey **9 E7** 50 44N 0 47W
Selsey Bill **9 E7** 50 44N 0 47W
Settle **6 D4** 54 5N 2 18W
Seven Heads **14 E5** 51 35N 8 43W
Sevenoaks **9 D9** 51 16N 0 11 E
Severn → **8 C3** 51 35N 2 38W
Sgurr a' Choire Ghlais **3 H8** 57 30N 4 56W
Sgurr Mor **3 G7** 57 42N 5 0W
Sgurr na Ciche **2 H7** 57 0N 5 29W
Sgurr na Lapaich **2 H7** 57 23N 5 5W
Shaftesbury **8 E4** 51 0N 2 12W
Shanklin **8 E6** 50 39N 1 9W
Shannon → **14 C3** 52 35N 9 38W
Shannon Airport **14 C5** 52 42N 8 57W
Shapinsay Sd. **3 D12** 59 0N 2 51W
Sheelin, L. **12 D7** 53 48N 7 20W
Sheep Haven **12 A6** 55 12N 7 55W
Sheeps Hd. **14 E3** 51 32N 9 50W
Sheerness **9 D10** 51 26N 0 47 E
Sheffield **7 F6** 53 23N 1 28W
Shehy Mts. **14 E4** 51 47N 9 15W
Shell, L. **2 F5** 58 0N 6 28W
Shenfield **9 C9** 51 39N 0 21 E
Sheppey, I. of **9 D10** 51 23N 0 50 E
Shepshed **7 G6** 52 47N 1 18W
Shepton Mallet **8 D3** 51 11N 2 31W
Sherborne **8 E3** 50 56N 2 31W
Sheringham **9 A11** 52 56N 1 11 E
Sherwood Forest **7 F6** 53 5N 1 5W
Shetland □ **2 B15** 60 30N 1 30W
Shiant, Sd. of **2 G5** 57 54N 6 30W
Shiel, L. **2 J6** 56 48N 5 32W
Shildon **6 C5** 54 37N 1 39W
Shillelagh **15 C9** 52 46N 6 32W
Shin → **3 G9** 57 58N 4 26W
Shin, L. **3 F8** 58 7N 4 30W
Shining Tor **7 F4** 53 15N 2 0W
Shipley **7 E5** 53 50N 1 47W
Shipston-on-Stour **8 B5** 52 4N 1 38W
Shirebrook **7 F6** 53 13N 1 11W
Shoeburyness **9 C10** 51 31N 0 49 E
Shoreham by Sea **9 E8** 50 50N 0 17W
Shotts **5 C8** 55 49N 3 47W
Shrewsbury **7 G3** 52 42N 2 45W
Shropshire □ **7 G3** 52 36N 2 45W
Sidlaw Hills **5 A9** 56 32N 3 10W
Sidmouth **11 F7** 50 40N 3 13W
Sighty Crag **6 B3** 55 8N 2 37W
Silloth **5 E9** 54 53N 3 25W
Silsden **7 E5** 53 55N 1 55W
Silvermine Mts. **14 C6** 52 47N 8 15W
Simonside **6 B5** 55 17N 1 58W
Sinclair's B. **3 E11** 58 30N 3 0W
Sion Mills **12 B7** 54 47N 7 29W
Sittingbourne **9 D10** 51 20N 0 43 E
Sixmilebridge **14 C5** 52 45N 8 46W
Sizewell **9 B12** 52 13N 1 38 E
Skaw Taing **2 B16** 60 23N 0 57W
Skegness **7 F9** 53 9N 0 20 E
Skelmersdale **7 E3** 53 34N 2 49W
Skelmorlie **4 C6** 55 52N 4 53W
Skelton **6 C7** 54 33N 0 59W
Skibbereen **14 E4** 51 33N 9 16W
Skiddaw **6 C2** 54 39N 3 9W
Skipton **7 E4** 53 57N 2 1W
Skokholm I. **10 D3** 51 42N 5 16W
Skomer I. **10 D3** 51 44N 5 19W
Skull **14 E3** 51 32N 9 40W
Skye **2 H5** 57 15N 6 10W
Slaney → **15 D10** 52 20N 6 30W
Slea Hd. **14 D2** 52 7N 10 30W
Sleaford **7 F8** 53 1N 0 22W

Sleat, Pt. of 2 H5 57 1N 6 0W
Sleat, Sd. of 2 H6 57 5N 5 47W
Slieve Anierin 12 C6 54 5N 7 58W
Slieve Aughty 14 B5 53 4N 8 30W
Slieve Beagh 13 C7 54 20N 7 12W
Slieve Bernagh 14 C5 52 50N 8 30W
Slieve Donard 13 C10 54 10N 5 57W
Slieve Elva 14 B4 53 5N 9 16W
Slieve Foye 13 C9 54 2N 6 11W
Slieve Gullion 13 C9 54 8N 6 26W
Slieve League 12 B4 54 40N 8 42W
Slieve More 12 C1 54 1N 10 3W
Slieve Snaght 12 A7 55 18N 7 20W
Slieve Tooey 12 B4 54 46N 8 39W
Slievecallan 14 C4 52 51N 9 16W
Slievefelim 14 C6 52 40N 8 20W
Slievenamon 15 D7 52 25N 7 37W
Sligeach = Sligo 12 C5 54 17N 8 28W
Sligo 12 C5 54 17N 8 28W
Sligo □ 12 C4 54 10N 8 35W
Sligo B. 12 C4 54 20N 8 40W
Slioch 2 G7 57 40N 5 20W
Slough 9 C7 51 30N 0 35W
Slyne Hd. 14 B2 53 25N 10 10W
Smerwick Harbour 14 D2 52 12N 10 23W
Smethwick 8 A5 52 30N 1 58W
Snaefell 13 C13 54 18N 4 26W
Snizort, L. 2 G5 57 33N 6 28W
Snowdon 10 A5 53 4N 4 8W
Snowdonia Nat. Park 10 A6 53 10N 4 0W
Soay Sd. 2 H5 57 10N 6 15W
Soham 9 B9 52 20N 0 20 E
Solihull 8 B5 52 26N 1 47W
Solway Firth 5 E8 54 45N 3 38W
Somerset □ 8 D3 51 9N 3 0W
Somerton 8 D3 51 3N 2 45W
South Ayrshire □ 4 D6 55 18N 4 41W
South Barrule 13 C12 54 9N 4 36W
South Benfleet 9 C10 51 33N 0 34 E
South Dorset Downs 8 E4 50 40N 2 26W
South Downs 9 E8 50 53N 0 10W
South Esk → 5 A10 56 44N 3 3W
South Foreland 9 D11 51 7N 1 23 E
South Harris 2 G4 57 50N 7 0W
South Hayling 9 E7 50 47N 0 56W
South Kirkby 7 E6 53 35N 1 19W
South Lanarkshire □ 5 C8 55 40N 3 48W
South Molton 11 E6 51 1N 3 50W
South Nesting B. 2 B15 60 18N 1 5W
South Queensferry 5 C9 56 0N 3 25W
South Sd. 14 B4 53 4N 9 28W
South Shields 6 C6 54 59N 1 26W
South Uist 2 H3 57 20N 7 15W
South Woodham Ferrers 9 C10 51 40N 0 37 E
South Yorkshire □ 7 F5 53 30N 1 20W
Southampton 8 E6 50 54N 1 23W
Southborough 9 D9 51 10N 0 15 E
Southend-on-Sea 9 C10 51 32N 0 42 E
Southern Uplands 5 D8 55 30N 3 0W
Southminster 9 C10 51 40N 0 51 E
Southport 7 E2 53 38N 3 1W
Southwark 9 D8 51 29N 0 5W
Southwell 7 F7 53 4N 0 57W
Southwick 9 E8 50 50N 0 14W
Southwold 9 B12 52 19N 1 41 E
Spalding 7 G8 52 47N 0 9W
Spanish Pt. 14 C4 52 51N 9 27W
Spean → 3 J8 56 50N 4 40W
Speke 7 F3 53 21N 2 51W
Spennymoor 6 C5 54 43N 1 35W
Sperrin Mts. 13 B8 54 50N 7 0W
Spey → 3 G11 57 26N 3 25W
Spey B. 3 G11 57 41N 3 0W
Spilsby 7 F9 53 10N 0 6 E
Spithead 8 E6 50 43N 1 5W
Spurn Hd. 7 E9 53 34N 0 8 E
Stackpole Hd. 11 D4 51 36N 4 52W
Stacks Mts. 14 D3 52 20N 9 34W
Staffa 4 B3 56 26N 6 21W
Stafford 7 G4 52 49N 2 9W
Staffordshire □ 7 G4 52 53N 2 10W
Staines 9 D8 51 26N 0 30W
Stainforth 7 E7 53 37N 0 59W
Staithes 6 C7 54 33N 0 47W
Stalybridge 7 F4 53 29N 2 4W
Stamford 7 G8 52 39N 0 29W
Standish 7 E3 53 35N 2 39W
Stanford le Hope 9 C9 51 30N 0 25 E
Stanhope 6 C4 54 45N 2 0W
Stanley 6 C5 54 53N 1 42W
Stansted Mountfitchet 9 C9 51 54N 0 13 E
Staple Hill 8 E2 50 56N 3 5W
Stapleford 7 G6 52 56N 1 16W
Staplehurst 9 D10 51 9N 0 35 E
Start B. 11 G6 50 15N 3 35W
Start Pt., *Devon* 11 G6 50 13N 3 38W
Start Pt., *Orkney* 3 D13 59 17N 2 25W
Staveley 7 F6 53 16N 1 20W
Stenhousemuir 5 B8 56 2N 3 46W
Steornabhaigh = Stornoway 2 F5 58 12N 6 23W
Stevenage 9 C8 51 54N 0 11W
Stevenston 4 C6 55 38N 4 46W
Stewarton 4 C7 55 40N 4 30W
Steyning 9 E8 50 54N 0 19W
Stiperstones 7 G3 52 36N 2 57W
Stirling 5 B8 56 7N 3 57W
Stirling □ 4 B7 56 15N 4 14W
Stockbridge 8 D6 51 7N 1 28W
Stockport 7 F4 53 25N 2 11W
Stocksbridge 7 F5 53 30N 1 36W
Stockton-on-Tees 6 C6 54 34N 1 20W
Stoer, Pt. of 2 F7 58 15N 5 22W
Stoke on Trent 7 F4 53 1N 2 11W
Stone 7 G4 52 55N 2 10W
Stonehaven 3 J13 56 58N 2 11W
Stonehouse, *Gloucs.* 8 C4 51 45N 2 18W
Stonehouse, *S. Lanarks.* 5 C8 55 42N 4 0W
Stony Stratford 9 B7 52 4N 0 51W
Stornoway 2 F5 58 12N 6 23W
Stour →, *Dorset* 8 E5 50 48N 1 45W
Stour →, *Here. & Worcs.* 8 B4 52 25N 2 13W
Stour →, *Kent* 9 D11 51 15N 1 20 E
Stour →, *Suffolk* 9 C11 51 55N 1 5 E
Stourbridge 8 B4 52 28N 2 8W
Stourport-on-Severn 8 B4 52 21N 2 18W
Stow-on-the-Wold 8 C5 51 55N 1 42W
Stowmarket 9 B11 52 11N 1 0 E
Strabane 12 B7 54 50N 7 28W
Strangford L. 13 C10 54 30N 5 37W
Stranraer 4 E5 54 54N 5 1W
Stratford-upon-Avon 8 B5 52 12N 1 42W
Strath Earn 5 B8 56 20N 3 50W
Strath Spey 3 H10 57 15N 3 40W
Strath Tay 5 A8 56 38N 3 40W
Strathaven 4 C7 55 40N 4 4W
Strathbogie 3 H12 57 25N 2 45W
Strathmore 5 A10 56 40N 3 0W
Strathpeffer 3 G8 57 35N 4 32W
Strathy Pt. 3 E9 58 35N 4 3W
Stratton 11 F4 50 49N 4 31W
Stratton St. Margaret 8 C5 51 35N 1 45W
Street 8 D3 51 7N 2 43W
Stretford 7 F4 53 27N 2 19W
Striven, L. 4 C5 55 58N 5 9W
Stromeferry 2 H6 57 20N 5 33W
Stromness 3 E11 58 58N 3 18W
Stronsay Firth 3 D12 59 4N 2 50W
Stroud 8 C4 51 44N 2 12W
Strumble Hd. 10 C3 52 3N 5 6W
Studley 8 B5 52 16N 1 54W
Sturminster Newton 8 E4 50 56N 2 18W
Suck → 14 B6 53 17N 8 18W
Sudbury 9 B10 52 2N 0 44 E
Suffolk □ 9 B11 52 16N 1 0 E
Suir → 15 D8 52 15N 7 10W
Sullom Voe 2 B15 60 27N 1 20W
Sumburgh Hd. 2 C15 59 52N 1 17W
Sunart 4 A4 56 40N 5 40W
Sunart, L. 4 A4 56 42N 5 43W
Sunderland 6 C6 54 54N 1 22W
Sunninghill 9 D7 51 25N 0 40W
Surrey □ 9 D7 51 16N 0 30W
Sutherland 3 F8 58 15N 4 40W
Sutton 9 D8 51 22N 0 13W
Sutton Coldfield 7 G5 52 33N 1 50W
Sutton in Ashfield 7 F6 53 7N 1 20W
Swadlincote 7 G5 52 47N 1 34W
Swaffham 9 A10 52 38N 0 42 E
Swale →, *Kent* 9 D10 51 22N 0 48 E
Swale →, *N. Yorks.* 6 D6 54 5N 1 20W
Swaledale 6 D5 54 20N 2 0W
Swanage 8 E5 50 36N 1 59W
Swanley 9 D9 51 23N 0 10 E
Swansea 11 D6 51 37N 3 57W
Sween, L. 4 C4 55 54N 5 51W
Swilly, L. 12 A6 55 12N 7 35W
Swindon 8 C5 51 33N 1 47W
Swinford 12 D4 53 57N 8 57W
Swinton, *Gt. Man.* 7 E4 53 31N 2 21W
Swinton, *S. Yorks.* 7 F6 53 28N 1 20W
Swords 13 E9 53 27N 6 15W
Sybil Pt. 14 D2 52 12N 10 28W
Symonds Yat 8 C3 51 50N 2 38W

T

Tacumshin L. 15 D10 52 12N 6 28W
Tadcaster 7 E6 53 53N 1 16W
Taff → 8 E7 51 28N 3 9W
Tain 3 G9 57 49N 4 4W
Tairbeart = Tarbert 2 G4 57 54N 6 49W
Tal-y-llyn 10 B6 52 40N 3 44W
Tamar → 11 G5 50 28N 4 15W
Tame → 7 G5 52 43N 1 45W
Tamworth 7 G5 52 38N 1 41W
Tan Hill 8 D5 51 23N 1 53W
Tandragee 13 C9 54 22N 6 23W
Tar → 14 D7 52 17N 7 50W
Taransay, Sd. of 2 G3 57 52N 7 0W
Tarbat Ness 3 G10 57 52N 3 48W
Tarbert, *Arg. & Bute* 4 C5 55 55N 5 25W
Tarbert, *W. Isles* 2 G4 57 54N 6 49W
Tarbert, East L. 2 G4 57 50N 6 45W
Tarbert, L. 4 C3 55 57N 6 0W
Tarbert, West L. 2 G4 57 55N 6 56W
Taunton 8 D2 51 1N 3 7W
Tavistock 11 F5 50 33N 4 9W
Tavy → 11 G5 50 28N 4 10W
Taw → 11 E5 51 4N 4 11W
Tay → 5 A8 56 37N 3 38W
Tay, Firth of 5 B9 56 25N 3 8W
Tay, L. 4 A7 56 30N 4 10W
Tayport 5 B10 56 27N 2 52W
Teermoyle Mt. 14 E2 51 57N 10 2W
Tees → 6 C6 54 36N 1 25W
Tees B. 6 C6 54 38N 1 8W
Teesdale 6 C4 54 37N 2 10W
Tegid, L. = Bala, L. 10 B6 52 53N 3 38W
Teifi → 10 C4 52 4N 4 44W
Teign → 11 F6 50 41N 3 42W
Teignmouth 11 F6 50 33N 3 30W
Telford 7 G4 52 42N 2 29W
Teme → 8 B4 52 23N 2 15W
Templemore 14 C7 52 48N 7 50W
Tenby 10 D4 51 40N 4 42W
Tenterden 9 D10 51 4N 0 42 E
Test → 8 E5 50 54N 1 36W
Tetbury 8 C4 51 37N 2 9W
Teviot → 5 D10 55 21N 2 51W
Teviotdale 5 D10 55 25N 2 50W
Tewkesbury 8 C4 51 59N 2 8W
Thame 9 C7 51 44N 0 58W
Thames → 9 D10 51 30N 0 35 E
Thanet, I. of 9 D11 51 21N 1 20 E
Thatcham 8 D6 51 24N 1 17W
The Aird 3 H8 57 27N 4 39W
The Buck 3 H12 57 19N 3 0W
The Cheviot 6 B4 55 29N 2 8W
The Faither 2 A14 60 34N 1 30W
The Fens 7 G9 52 45N 0 2 E
The Glenkens 4 D7 55 10N 4 15W
The Long Mynd 7 G3 52 35N 2 50W
The Machars 4 E6 54 46N 4 31W
The Mumbles 11 D6 51 34N 4 0W
The Naze 9 C11 51 53N 1 19 E
The Needles 8 E5 50 39N 1 35W
The North Sd. 3 D12 59 18N 2 45W
The Paps 14 D4 52 2N 9 15W
The Peak = Kinder Scout 7 F5 53 24N 1 53W
The Potteries 7 F4 53 5N 2 10W
The Rhins 4 E5 54 52N 5 3W
The Saddle 2 H7 57 10N 5 27W
The Snap 2 A16 60 35N 0 50W
The Solent 8 E6 50 45N 1 25W
The Sound 11 G5 50 20N 4 10W
The Storr 2 G5 57 30N 6 12W
The Trossachs 4 B7 56 14N 4 24W
The Wash 9 A9 52 58N 0 20 E
The Weald 9 D9 51 7N 0 29 E
The Wrekin 7 G3 52 41N 2 35W
Thetford 9 B10 52 25N 0 44 E
Thirsk 6 D6 54 15N 1 20W
Thornaby on Tees 6 C6 54 36N 1 19W
Thornbury 8 C3 51 36N 2 31W
Thorne 7 E7 53 36N 0 56W
Thrapston 9 B7 52 24N 0 32W
Thurcroft 7 F6 53 24N 1 13W
Thurles 14 C7 52 40N 7 53W
Thurmaston 7 G6 52 40N 1 8W
Thurso 3 E10 58 34N 3 31W
Tilbury 9 D9 51 27N 0 24 E
Tillicoultry 5 B8 56 9N 3 44W
Tintagel 11 F4 50 40N 4 45W
Tintagel Hd. 11 F4 50 40N 4 46W
Tipperary 14 D6 52 28N 8 10W
Tipperary □ 14 C7 52 37N 7 55W
Tipton 8 A4 52 32N 2 4W
Tiptree 9 C10 51 48N 0 46 E
Tiree 4 A2 56 31N 6 55W
Tiree, Passage of 4 B2 56 30N 6 30W
Tiumpan Hd. 2 F5 58 15N 6 10W
Tiverton 11 F7 50 54N 3 30W
Tobermory 4 A3 56 37N 6 4W
Todhead Pt. 3 J13 56 53N 2 12W
Todmorden 7 E4 53 43N 2 7W
Toe Hd., *Ireland* 14 F4 51 29N 9 13W
Toe Hd., *W. Isles* 2 G3 57 50N 7 10W
Tolsta Hd. 2 F5 58 20N 6 10W
Tomnavoulin 3 H11 57 19N 3 18W
Tonbridge 9 D9 51 12N 0 18 E
Tongue 3 F9 58 29N 4 25W
Tongue, Kyle of 3 E9 58 30N 4 30W
Tonyrefail 11 D7 51 35N 3 26W
Tor B. 11 G6 50 26N 3 31W
Tor Ness 3 E11 58 47N 3 18W
Torbay 11 G6 50 26N 3 31W
Torfaen □ 10 D7 51 42N 3 1W
Torpoint 11 G5 50 23N 4 12W
Torquay 11 G6 50 27N 3 31W
Torridge → 11 F5 50 51N 4 10W
Torridon, L. 2 G6 57 35N 5 50W
Tory I. 12 A5 55 17N 8 12W
Totland 8 E5 50 41N 1 32W
Totnes 11 G6 50 26N 3 41W
Totton 8 E6 50 55N 1 29W
Towcester 9 B7 52 7N 0 56W
Tower Hamlets 9 C8 51 32N 0 2W
Trá Li = Tralee 14 D3 52 16N 9 42W
Tralee 14 D3 52 16N 9 42W
Tramore 15 D8 52 10N 7 10W
Tranent 5 C10 55 57N 2 58W
Trawbreaga B. 12 A7 55 20N 7 25W
Tredegar 10 D7 51 47N 3 16W
Tregaron 10 C6 52 14N 3 56W
Treharris 10 D7 51 40N 3 17W
Treig, L. 3 J8 56 48N 4 42W
Tremadog B. 10 B5 52 51N 4 18W
Trent → 7 E7 53 43N 0 44W
Treorchy 10 D7 51 39N 3 25W
Tresco 11 H1 49 57N 6 20W
Trevose Hd. 11 F3 50 33N 5 3W
Trim 13 D8 53 34N 6 48W
Tring 9 C7 51 47N 0 39W
Troon 4 C6 55 33N 4 40W
Trostan 13 A9 55 4N 6 10W
Trotternish 2 G5 57 32N 6 15W
Troup Hd. 3 G13 57 41N 2 18W
Trowbridge 8 D4 51 18N 2 12W
Truro 11 G3 50 17N 5 2W
Truskmore 12 C5 54 23N 8 20W
Trwyn Cilan 10 B4 52 47N 4 31W
Tuam 12 D4 53 30N 8 50W
Tuath, L. 4 A3 56 30N 6 15W
Tulla 14 C5 52 53N 8 45W
Tullamore 15 B7 53 17N 7 31W
Tullow 15 C9 52 48N 6 45W
Tummel → 4 A7 56 42N 4 5W
Tummel, L. 5 A8 56 43N 3 55W
Tunbridge Wells = Royal Tunbridge Wells 9 D9 51 7N 0 16 E
Turners Hill 8 A4 52 30N 2 3W
Turriff 3 G13 57 32N 2 28W
Tweed → 6 A5 55 42N 1 59W
Twyford 9 D7 51 29N 0 51W
Tyne → 6 C6 54 58N 1 28W
Tyne & Wear □ 6 C6 54 55N 1 25W
Tynemouth 6 B6 55 1N 1 27W
Tyrone □ 13 B7 54 40N 7 15W
Tywi → 10 D5 51 48N 4 20W
Tywyn 10 B5 52 36N 4 5W

U

Uckfield 9 E9 50 58N 0 6 E
Uddingston 4 C7 55 50N 4 3W
Ugie 3 G14 57 32N 1 50W
Ullapool 2 G7 57 54N 5 10W
Ullswater 6 C3 54 35N 2 52W
Ulster 13 B8 54 35N 6 30W
Ulverston 6 D2 54 13N 3 7W
Unshin → 12 C5 54 8N 8 26W
Unst 2 A16 60 50N 0 55W
Uppingham 7 G7 52 36N 0 43W
Upton 7 F3 53 14N 2 52W
Upton-upon-Severn 8 B4 52 4N 2 12W
Ure → 6 D6 54 20N 1 25W
Urie → 3 H13 57 19N 2 20W
Urmston 7 F4 53 28N 2 22W
Usk 10 D8 51 42N 2 53W
Usk → 11 D8 51 37N 2 56W
Uttoxeter 7 G5 52 53N 1 50W

V

Vale of Belvoir 7 G7 52 55N 0 58W
Vale of Glamorgan □ 11 E7 51 25N 3 20W
Valencia I. 14 E2 51 54N 10 22W
Vaternish Pt. 2 G4 57 36N 6 40W
Ventnor 8 E6 50 35N 1 12W
Verwood 8 E5 50 53N 1 53W
Veryan B. 11 G4 50 12N 4 51W
Virginia Water 9 D7 51 23N 0 33W
Vyrnwy → 10 B7 52 43N 3 15W
Vyrnwy, L. 10 B7 52 48N 3 30W

W

Wadebridge 11 F4 50 31N 4 51W
Wakefield 7 E6 53 41N 1 30W
Walbury Hill 8 D6 51 22N 1 28W
Wallasey 7 F2 53 26N 3 2W
Wallingford 8 C6 51 36N 1 8W
Wallsend 6 C5 54 59N 1 31W
Walney, I. of 6 D2 54 5N 3 15W
Walsall 7 G5 52 36N 1 59W
Waltham Abbey 9 C9 51 40N 0 1 E
Waltham Forest 9 C9 51 37N 0 2 E
Walton-on-Thames 9 D8 51 21N 0 22W
Walton-on-the-Naze 9 C11 51 52N 1 17 E
Wandsworth 9 D8 51 28N 0 15W
Wantage 8 C6 51 35N 1 25W
Ward Hill 3 E11 58 52N 3 20W
Ward's Stone 6 D3 54 2N 2 39W
Ware 9 C8 51 48N 0 2W
Wareham 8 E4 50 41N 2 8W
Warley 8 B5 52 30N 1 58W
Warminster 8 D4 51 12N 2 11W
Warrenpoint 13 C9 54 7N 6 15W
Warrington 7 F3 53 25N 2 38W
Warsop 7 F6 53 13N 1 9W
Warwick 8 B5 52 17N 1 36W
Warwickshire □ 8 B5 52 20N 1 30W
Washington 6 C6 54 55N 1 30W
Wast Water 6 D2 54 26N 3 18W
Watchet 8 D2 51 10N 3 20W
Waterford 15 D8 52 16N 7 8W
Waterford □ 15 D7 52 10N 7 40W
Waterford Harbour 15 D9 52 10N 6 58W
Watergate B. 11 G3 50 26N 5 4W
Waterlooville 8 E6 50 53N 1 2W
Watford 9 C8 51 38N 0 23W
Wath upon Dearne 7 E6 53 30N 1 21W
Wear → 6 C6 54 55N 1 22W
Weardale 6 C4 54 44N 2 5W
Weaver → 7 F3 53 17N 2 35W
Wednesbury 7 G4 52 33N 2 1W
Wednesfield 7 G4 52 36N 2 3W
Weisdale Voe 2 B15 60 14N 1 20W
Welland → 7 G8 52 43N 0 10W
Wellingborough 9 B7 52 18N 0 41W
Wellington, *Shrops.* 7 G3 52 42N 2 31W
Wellington, *Somst.* 8 E2 50 58N 3 13W
Wells 8 D3 51 12N 2 39W
Wells-next-the-Sea 9 A10 52 57N 0 51 E
Welshpool 10 B7 52 40N 3 9W
Welwyn Garden City 9 C8 51 49N 0 11W
Wem 7 G3 52 52N 2 45W
Wendover 9 C7 51 46N 0 45W
Wenlock Edge 8 A3 52 30N 2 43W
Wensleydale 6 D5 54 18N 2 0W
West Auckland 6 C5 54 38N 1 42W
West Bridgford 7 G6 52 56N 1 8W
West Bromwich 8 A5 52 32N 1 59W
West Kirby 7 F2 53 22N 3 11W
West Lomond 5 B9 56 15N 3 16W
West Lothian □ 5 C8 55 54N 3 38W
West Mersea 9 C10 51 46N 0 55 E
West Midlands □ 8 B5 52 30N 1 55W
West Sussex □ 9 E7 50 55N 0 30W
West Yorkshire □ 7 E5 53 45N 1 40W
Westbury 8 D4 51 16N 2 11W
Wester Ross 3 G8 57 37N 5 0W
Westerham 9 D9 51 16N 0 5 E
Western Isles □ 2 F4 57 30N 7 10W
Westhill 3 H13 57 8N 2 17W
Westhoughton 7 E3 53 34N 2 30W
Westmeath □ 12 D7 53 30N 7 30W
Westminster 9 C8 51 30N 0 8W
Weston 7 G4 52 50N 2 2W
Weston-super-Mare 8 D3 51 20N 2 59W
Westport 12 D2 53 44N 9 31W
Westray Firth 3 D12 59 15N 3 0W
Westward Ho! 11 E5 51 2N 4 16W
Wetheral 6 C3 54 52N 2 50W
Wetherby 7 E6 53 56N 1 23W
Wexford 15 D10 52 20N 6 28W
Wexford □ 15 D10 52 20N 6 25W
Wey → 9 D8 51 19N 0 29W
Weybridge 9 D8 51 22N 0 28W
Weymouth 8 E4 50 36N 2 28W
Whale Firth 2 A15 60 40N 1 10W
Whaley Bridge 7 F5 53 20N 2 0W
Wharfe → 7 E6 53 55N 1 30W
Wharfedale 6 D4 54 7N 2 4W
Wheathampstead 9 C8 51 49N 0 18W
Wheatley Hill 6 C6 54 45N 1 23W
Whernside 6 D4 54 14N 2 24W
Whickham 6 C5 54 56N 1 41W
Whipsnade 9 C7 51 51N 0 32W
Whitburn 5 C8 55 52N 3 41W
Whitby 6 D7 54 29N 0 37W
Whitchurch, *Hants.* 8 D6 51 14N 1 20W
Whitchurch, *Shrops.* 7 G3 52 58N 2 42W
White Coomb 5 D9 55 24N 3 19W
White Horse, Vale of 8 C5 51 37N 1 30W
White Horse Hill 8 C5 51 35N 1 35W
Whitehaven 6 C1 54 33N 3 35W
Whitehead 13 B10 54 45N 5 42W
Whiten Hd. 3 E8 58 34N 4 35W
Whitesand B. 11 G5 50 18N 4 20W
Whithorn 4 E7 54 44N 4 25W
Whitley Bay 6 B6 55 4N 1 28W
Whitstable 9 D11 51 21N 1 2 E
Whittlesey 7 G8 52 34N 0 8W
Whitworth 7 E4 53 40N 2 11W
Wick 3 F11 58 26N 3 5W
Wickford 9 C10 51 37N 0 33 E
Wickham 8 E6 50 54N 1 11W
Wickham Market 9 B11 52 9N 1 21 E
Wicklow 15 C10 53 0N 6 2W
Wicklow □ 15 C10 52 59N 6 25W
Wicklow Hd. 15 C10 52 59N 6 3W
Wicklow Mts. 15 C10 53 0N 6 30W
Wide Firth 3 D12 59 2N 3 0W
Widnes 7 F3 53 22N 2 44W
Wigan 7 E3 53 33N 2 38W
Wigston 7 G6 52 35N 1 6W
Wigton 6 C2 54 50N 3 9W
Wigtown 4 E7 54 52N 4 27W
Willaston 7 F3 53 17N 2 59W
Willenhall 7 G4 52 36N 2 3W
Willington 6 C5 54 43N 1 42W
Wilmslow 7 F4 53 19N 2 14W
Wilton 8 D5 51 5N 1 52W
Wiltshire □ 8 D5 51 20N 2 0W
Wimborne Minster 8 E5 50 48N 2 0W
Wincanton 8 D4 51 3N 2 24W
Winchelsea 9 E10 50 55N 0 43 E
Winchester 8 D6 51 4N 1 19W
Windermere 6 D3 54 24N 2 56W
Windsor 9 D7 51 28N 0 36W
Winsford 7 F3 53 12N 2 31W
Wirksworth 7 F5 53 5N 1 34W
Wirral 7 F3 53 25N 3 0W
Wisbech 7 G9 52 39N 0 10 E
Wishaw 5 C8 55 46N 3 55W
Witham 9 C10 51 48N 0 39 E
Witham → 7 F8 53 3N 0 8W
Withernsea 7 E9 53 43N 0 2 E
Witney 8 C6 51 47N 1 29W
Wivenhoe 9 C10 51 51N 0 59 E
Woking 9 D7 51 18N 0 33W
Wokingham 9 D7 51 25N 0 50W
Wolf Rock 11 H2 49 56N 5 50W
Wolverhampton 7 G4 52 35N 2 6W
Wolverton 9 B7 52 3N 0 48W
Wombwell 7 E6 53 31N 1 23W
Woodbridge 9 B11 52 6N 1 19 E
Woodhall Spa 7 F8 53 10N 0 12W
Woodley 9 D7 51 26N 0 54W
Woodstock 8 C6 51 51N 1 20W
Woolacombe 11 E5 51 10N 4 12W
Wooler 6 A5 55 33N 2 0W
Wootton Bassett 8 C5 51 32N 1 55W
Worcester 8 B4 52 12N 2 12W
Worcestershire Beacon 8 B4 52 6N 2 21W
Workington 6 C1 54 39N 3 34W
Worksop 7 F6 53 19N 1 9W
Worms Hd. 11 D5 51 33N 4 19W
Worsbrough 7 E6 53 31N 1 29W
Worthing 9 E8 50 49N 0 21W
Wotton under Edge 8 C4 51 37N 2 20W
Wragby 7 F8 53 17N 0 18W
Wrath, C. 3 E7 58 38N 5 0W
Wrexham 10 A8 53 5N 3 0W
Wroxham 9 A11 52 42N 1 23 E
Wye → 8 C3 51 36N 2 40W
Wylfa Hd. 10 A5 53 25N 4 28W
Wymondham, *Leics.* 7 G7 52 45N 0 42W
Wymondham, *Norfolk* 9 A11 52 34N 1 7 E

Y

Yare → 9 A12 52 36N 1 45 E
Yate 8 C4 51 32N 2 26W
Yatton 8 D3 51 23N 2 50W
Yell 2 A15 60 35N 1 5W
Yell Sd. 2 A15 60 33N 1 15W
Yeovil 8 E3 50 57N 2 38W
Yes Tor 11 F6 50 41N 3 59W
York 7 E6 53 58N 1 7W
York, Vale of 6 D6 54 15N 1 25W
Yorkshire Dales Nat. Park 6 D4 54 12N 2 10W
Yorkshire Wolds 7 E7 54 0N 0 30W
Youghal 14 E7 51 58N 7 51W

WORLD MAPS

EUROPE 4-15, ASIA 16-25, AFRICA 26-33, AUSTRALIA AND OCEANIA 34-37,
NORTH AMERICA 38-45, SOUTH AMERICA 46-47

SETTLEMENTS

◌ PARIS ▪ Berne ◉ Livorno ◉ Brugge ◎ Algeciras ⊙ Frejus ○ Oberammergau ○ Thira

Settlement symbols and type styles vary according to the scale of each map and indicate the importance
of towns on the map rather than specific population figures

∴ Ruins or Archæological Sites ˇ Wells in Desert

ADMINISTRATION

———— International Boundaries

– – – International Boundaries
(Undefined or Disputed)

·········· Internal Boundaries

◌ National Parks

Country Names

NICARAGUA

Administrative
Area Names

K E N T

CALABRIA

International boundaries show the *de facto* situation where there are rival claims to territory

COMMUNICATIONS

———— Principal Roads

‿‿ Other Roads

--‿- Trails and Seasonal Roads

≍ Passes

✿ Airfields

‿ Principal Railways

----- Railways
Under Construction

‿ Other Railways

⇥--⇤ Railway Tunnels

·········· Principal Canals

PHYSICAL FEATURES

‿ Perennial Streams

······· Intermittent Streams

◯ Perennial Lakes

⬭ Intermittent Lakes

Swamps and Marshes

Permanent Ice
and Glaciers

▴ 8848 Elevations in metres

▾ 8050 Sea Depths in metres

_1134_ Height of Lake Surface
Above Sea Level
in metres

ELEVATION AND DEPTH TINTS

Height of Land Above Sea Level									Land Below Sea Level					Depth of Sea	
in metres	6000	4000	3000	2000	1500	1000	400	200	0						
in feet	18 000	12 000	9000	6000	4500	3000	1200	600		6000	12 000	15 000	18 000	24 000	in feet
									0	200	2000	4000	5000	6000	8000	in metres

Some of the maps have different contours to highlight and clarify the principal relief features

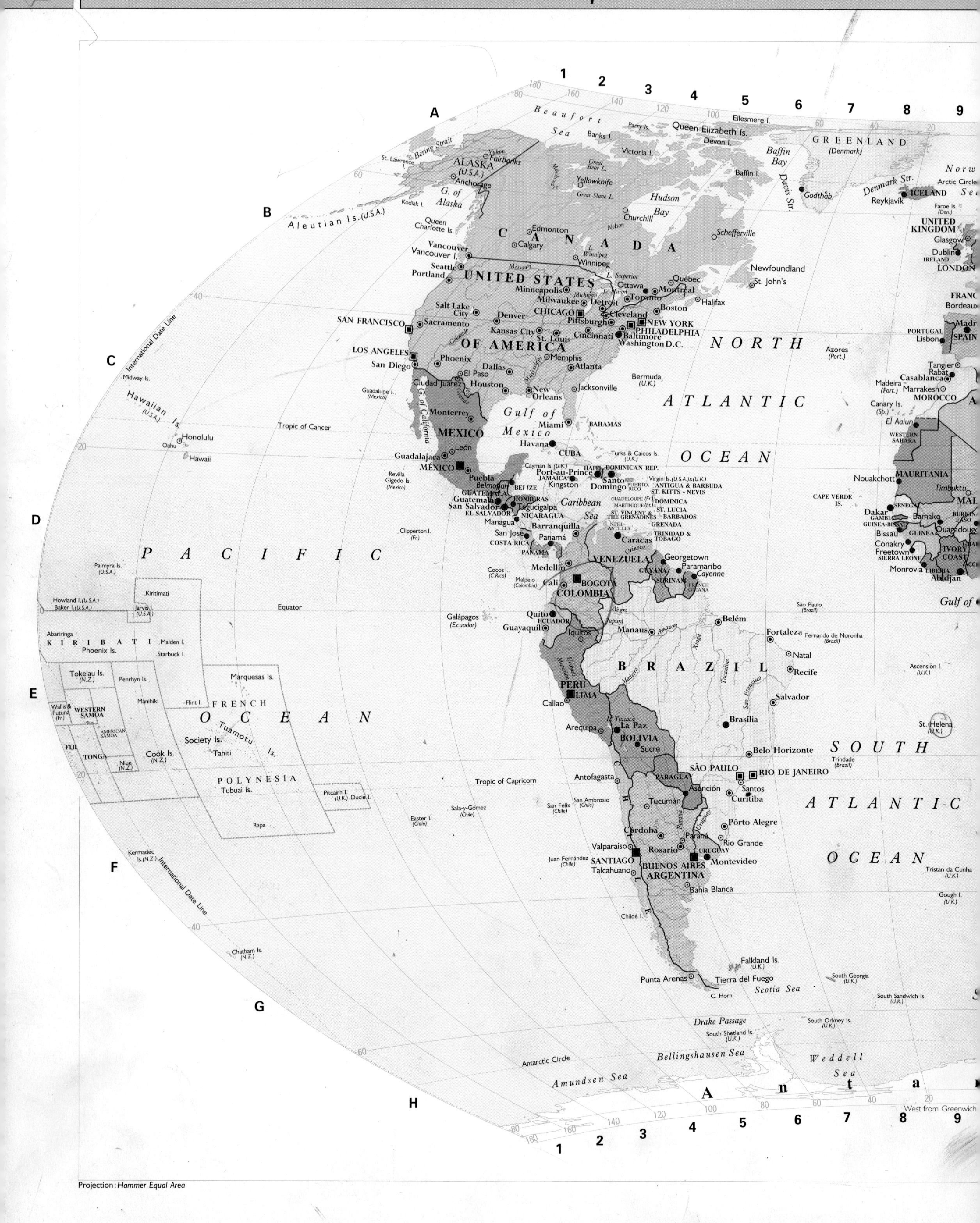

Beaufort Sea
Banks I.
Parry Is.
Queen Elizabeth Is.
Ellesmere I.
Devon I.
Victoria I.
GREENLAND
(Denmark)
Baffin Bay
Baffin I.
Davis Str.
Godthåb
Denmark Str.
ICELAND
Reykjavík
Arctic Circle
Faroe Is. (Den.)
UNITED KINGDOM
Glasgow
Dublin
IRELAND
LONDON
Bering Strait
St. Lawrence I.
ALASKA (U.S.A.)
Fairbanks
Yukon
Anchorage
G. of Alaska
Kodiak I.
Aleutian Is. (U.S.A.)
Great Bear L.
Yellowknife
Great Slave L.
Mackenzie
Hudson Bay
Churchill
Nelson
Queen Charlotte Is.
Edmonton
Calgary
CANADA
L. Winnipeg
Winnipeg
Schefferville
Vancouver
Vancouver I.
Seattle
Portland
Missouri
L. Superior
Newfoundland
St. John's
Québec
Ottawa
Montréal
L. Huron
Toronto
Halifax
UNITED STATES OF AMERICA
Minneapolis
Michigan
Milwaukee
Detroit
CHICAGO
Cleveland
Boston
Salt Lake City
Denver
Pittsburgh
NEW YORK
PHILADELPHIA
Baltimore
Washington D.C.
SAN FRANCISCO
Sacramento
Kansas City
St. Louis
Cincinnati
Colorado
LOS ANGELES
San Diego
Phoenix
Memphis
Dallas
Atlanta
El Paso
Ciudad Juárez
Houston
New Orleans
Jacksonville
Mississippi
Grande
NORTH ATLANTIC OCEAN
Azores (Port.)
Bermuda (U.K.)
FRANCE
Bordeaux
PORTUGAL
Lisbon
SPAIN
Madrid
Tangier
Rabat
Casablanca
Madeira (Port.)
Marrakesh
MOROCCO
Canary Is. (Sp.)
El Aaiun
WESTERN SAHARA
International Date Line
Midway Is.
Hawaiian Is. (U.S.A.)
Guadalupe I. (Mexico)
G. of California
Monterrey
Gulf of Mexico
Miami
BAHAMAS
Tropic of Cancer
Honolulu
Oahu
Hawaii
MEXICO
León
Guadalajara
MÉXICO
Havana
CUBA
Turks & Caicos Is. (U.K.)
Revilla Gigedo Is. (Mexico)
Puebla
Cayman Is. (U.K.)
Port-au-Prince
HAITI
DOMINICAN REP.
JAMAICA
Kingston
Santo Domingo
PUERTO RICO
Virgin Is. (U.S.A.)&(U.K.)
ANTIGUA & BARBUDA
ST. KITTS - NEVIS
Belmopan
BELIZE
GUATEMALA
Guatemala
HONDURAS
Tegucigalpa
San Salvador
EL SALVADOR
NICARAGUA
Managua
Caribbean Sea
GUADELOUPE (Fr.)
MARTINIQUE (Fr.)
DOMINICA
ST. LUCIA
ST. VINCENT & THE GRENADINES
BARBADOS
GRENADA
NETH. ANTILLES
TRINIDAD & TOBAGO
Barranquilla
San José
COSTA RICA
Panamá
PANAMA
Caracas
Orinoco
VENEZUELA
Georgetown
GUYANA
Paramaribo
SURINAM
Cayenne
FRENCH GUIANA
Clipperton I. (Fr.)
Cocos I. (C.Rica)
Malpelo (Colombia)
Medellín
Cali
BOGOTA
COLOMBIA
OCEAN
Nouakchott
MAURITANIA
Timbuktu
CAPE VERDE IS.
Dakar
SENEGAL
GAMBIA
GUINEA-BISSAU
Bissau
Bamako
Ouagadougou
GUINEA
Conakry
Freetown
SIERRA LEONE
Monrovia
LIBERIA
IVORY COAST
Abidjan
Gulf of
PACIFIC OCEAN
Palmyra Is. (U.S.A.)
Kiritimati
Howland I. (U.S.A.)
Baker I. (U.S.A.)
Jarvis I. (U.S.A.)
Equator
Galápagos (Ecuador)
Quito
ECUADOR
Guayaquil
Negro
Japurá
Amazon
Manaus
Iquitos
Belém
Fortaleza
Fernando de Noronha (Brazil)
São Paulo (Brazil)
Abariringa
KIRIBATI
Phoenix Is.
Malden I.
Starbuck I.
Natal
Recife
Xingu
Tocantins
Madeira
Ucayali
Marañón
BRAZIL
São Francisco
Ascension I. (U.K.)
Tokelau Is. (N.Z.)
Penrhyn Is.
Marquesas Is.
Manihiki
Flint I.
FRENCH POLYNESIA
Wallis & Futuna (Fr.)
WESTERN SAMOA
AMERICAN SAMOA
FIJI
TONGA
Niue (N.Z.)
Cook Is. (N.Z.)
Society Is.
Tahiti
Tuamotu Is.
Tubuai Is.
Pitcairn I. (U.K.)
Ducie I.
Rapa
PERU
LIMA
Callao
Salvador
Brasília
L. Titicaca
La Paz
Arequipa
BOLIVIA
Sucre
Belo Horizonte
SOUTH ATLANTIC OCEAN
St. Helena (U.K.)
Trindade (Brazil)
Antofagasta
SÃO PAULO
RIO DE JANEIRO
PARAGUAY
Asunción
Santos
Curitiba
Tropic of Capricorn
Easter I. (Chile)
Sala-y-Gomez (Chile)
San Felix (Chile)
San Ambrosio (Chile)
CHILE
Tucumán
Paraná
Uruguay
Pôrto Alegre
Córdoba
Rio Grande
Valparaíso
Rosario
URUGUAY
Montevideo
Juan Fernández (Chile)
SANTIAGO
Talcahuano
BUENOS AIRES
ARGENTINA
Bahía Blanca
Tristan da Cunha (U.K.)
Gough I. (U.K.)
Kermadec Is.(N.Z.)
Chiloé I.
Chatham Is. (N.Z.)
Falkland Is. (U.K.)
Punta Arenas
Tierra del Fuego
Scotia Sea
C. Horn
South Georgia (U.K.)
South Sandwich Is. (U.K.)
Drake Passage
South Orkney Is. (U.K.)
South Shetland Is. (U.K.)
Bellingshausen Sea
Weddell Sea
Antarctic Circle
Amundsen Sea
Antarctica
West from Greenwich

Projection: *Hammer Equal Area*

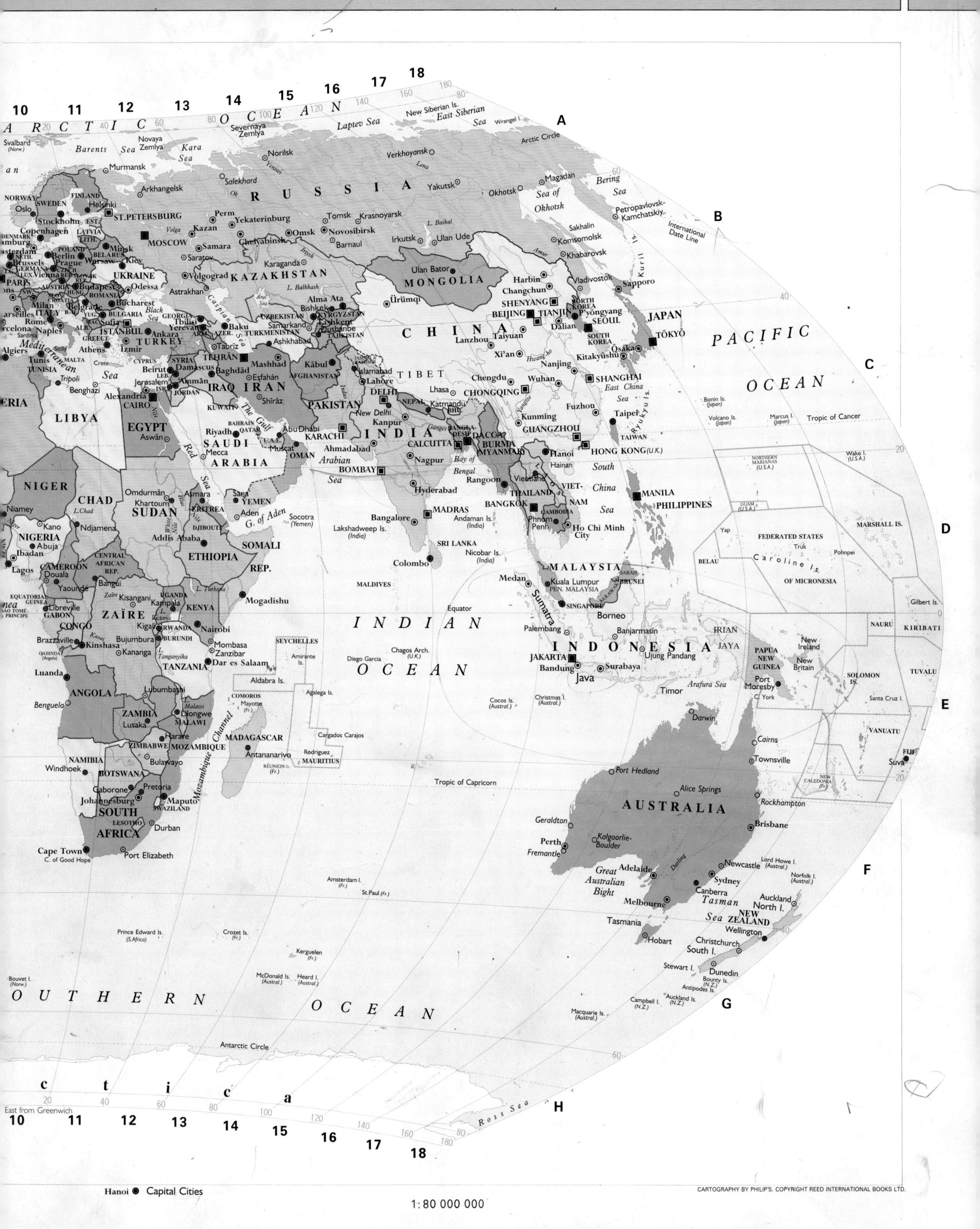

A R C T I C O C E A N
Svalbard (Norw.)
Barents Sea
Novaya Zemlya
Kara Sea
Severnaya Zemlya
Laptev Sea
New Siberian Is.
East Siberian Sea
Wrangel I.
Arctic Circle
Murmansk
Norilsk
Verkhoyansk
Salekhard
Arkhangelsk
R U S S I A
Yakutsk
Okhotsk
Magadan
Sea of Okhotsk
Bering Sea
Petropavlovsk-Kamchatskiy
International Date Line
Sakhalin
Komsomolsk
Khabarovsk
Kuril Is.
NORWAY
SWEDEN
FINLAND
Oslo
Helsinki
Stockholm
ST.PETERSBURG
Copenhagen
LATVIA
MOSCOW
Perm
Yekaterinburg
Kazan
Tomsk
Krasnoyarsk
Omsk
Novosibirsk
Barnaul
Irkutsk
Ulan Ude
L. Baikal
Chelyabinsk
Samara
Saratov
POLAND
Berlin
Minsk
BELARUS
Warsaw
Prague
Kiev
Brussels
UKRAINE
Vienna
Odessa
Budapest
ROMANIA
Bucharest
Belgrade
BULGARIA
Sofia
Milan
ITALY
Rome
Naples
Athens
GREECE
Volgograd
Astrakhan
K A Z A K H S T A N
Karaganda
L. Balkhash
Alma Ata
Bishkek
KYRGYZSTAN
UZBEKISTAN
Tashkent
Samarkand
Dushanbe
TAJIKISTAN
TURKMENISTAN
Ashkhabad
Caspian Sea
Aral Sea
Black Sea
GEORGIA
Tbilisi
Yerevan
Baku
ISTANBUL
Ankara
TURKEY
Izmir
Tabriz
Mediterranean Sea
Algiers
Tunis
TUNISIA
MALTA
Crete
CYPRUS
SYRIA
Beirut
Damascus
Jerusalem
Ammān
JORDAN
Baghdād
IRAQ
IRAN
TEHRĀN
Mashhad
Esfahān
Shīrāz
Tripoli
Benghazi
LIBYA
Alexandria
CAIRO
EGYPT
Aswân
KUWAIT
The Gulf
BAHRAIN
QATAR
Riyadh
U.A.E.
Abu Dhabi
Muscat
OMAN
SAUDI ARABIA
Mecca
Red Sea
Kābul
AFGHANISTAN
Islamabad
Lahore
PAKISTAN
KARACHI
DELHI
New Delhi
Kanpur
NEPAL
Katmandu
BHUTAN
I N D I A
Ahmadabad
CALCUTTA
DACCA
BANGLADESH
Nagpur
Arabian Sea
BOMBAY
Bay of Bengal
Hyderabad
Bangalore
MADRAS
Andaman Is. (India)
Lakshadweep Is. (India)
SRI LANKA
Colombo
Nicobar Is. (India)
MALDIVES
MONGOLIA
Ulan Bator
Ürümqi
C H I N A
TIBET
Lhasa
Lanzhou
Taiyuan
Xi'an
Chengdu
CHONGQING
Wuhan
Nanjing
SHANGHAI
Kunming
GUANGZHOU
Fuzhou
Taipei
TAIWAN
HONG KONG (U.K.)
Hainan
Harbin
Changchun
SHENYANG
BEIJING
TIANJIN
Dalian
NORTH KOREA
P'yongyang
SEOUL
SOUTH KOREA
Vladivostok
Sapporo
JAPAN
TŌKYŌ
Ōsaka
Kitakyūshū
East China Sea
Ryukyu Is.
PACIFIC OCEAN
Bonin Is. (Japan)
Volcano Is. (Japan)
Marcus I. (Japan)
Tropic of Cancer
Wake I. (U.S.A.)
NORTHERN MARIANAS (U.S.A.)
GUAM (U.S.A.)
MARSHALL IS.
FEDERATED STATES OF MICRONESIA
Caroline Is.
Yap
Truk
Pohnpei
BELAU
BURMA (MYANMAR)
Rangoon
Hanoi
Vientiane
THAILAND
BANGKOK
VIETNAM
CAMBODIA
Phnom Penh
Ho Chi Minh City
South China Sea
MANILA
PHILIPPINES
MALAYSIA
Medan
Kuala Lumpur
PEN. MALAYSIA
SINGAPORE
BRUNEI
SABAH
SARAWAK
Sumatra
Borneo
Palembang
Banjarmasin
I N D O N E S I A
JAKARTA
Bandung
Surabaya
Java
Ujung Pandang
IRIAN JAYA
Timor
Arafura Sea
PAPUA NEW GUINEA
Port Moresby
C. York
New Ireland
New Britain
SOLOMON IS.
NAURU
KIRIBATI
Gilbert Is.
TUVALU
Santa Cruz I.
VANUATU
FIJI
Suva
NEW CALEDONIA (Fr.)
Equator
I N D I A N O C E A N
SEYCHELLES
Amirante Is.
Chagos Arch. (U.K.)
Diego Garcia
Aldabra Is.
COMOROS
Mayotte (Fr.)
Agalega Is.
Cargados Carajos
MADAGASCAR
Antananarivo
Rodriguez
MAURITIUS
RÉUNION (Fr.)
Cocos Is. (Austral.)
Christmas I. (Austral.)
Tropic of Capricorn
NIGER
Niamey
CHAD
L. Chad
Ndjamena
Kano
NIGERIA
Abuja
Ibadan
Lagos
CAMEROON
Douala
Yaoundé
CENTRAL AFRICAN REP.
Bangui
Omdurmân
Khartoum
SUDAN
Asmara
ERITREA
DJIBOUTI
Sana
YEMEN
Aden
G. of Aden
Socotra (Yemen)
Addis Ababa
ETHIOPIA
SOMALI REP.
Mogadishu
L. Turkana
EQUATORIAL GUINEA
SÃO TOMÉ & PRÍNCIPE
Libreville
GABON
CONGO
ZAÏRE
Kisangani
UGANDA
Kampala
KENYA
Nairobi
Kigali
RWANDA
BURUNDI
Bujumbura
Brazzaville
Kinshasa
Kananga
L. Tanganyika
Mombasa
Zanzibar
Dar es Salaam
TANZANIA
Luanda
ANGOLA
Benguela
Lubumbashi
ZAMBIA
Lusaka
MALAWI
Lilongwe
Harare
ZIMBABWE
MOZAMBIQUE
Mozambique Channel
NAMIBIA
Windhoek
BOTSWANA
Gaborone
Pretoria
Johannesburg
Maputo
SWAZILAND
SOUTH AFRICA
LESOTHO
Durban
Cape Town
C. of Good Hope
Port Elizabeth
Bulawayo
Darwin
Cairns
Townsville
Port Hedland
Alice Springs
AUSTRALIA
Rockhampton
Geraldton
Brisbane
Kalgoorlie-Boulder
Perth
Fremantle
Darling
Great Australian Bight
Adelaide
Newcastle
Sydney
Canberra
Melbourne
Tasmania
Hobart
Lord Howe I. (Austral.)
Norfolk I. (Austral.)
Tasman Sea
Auckland
North I.
NEW ZEALAND
Wellington
Christchurch
South I.
Stewart I.
Dunedin
Bounty Is. (N.Z.)
Antipodes Is.
Auckland Is. (N.Z.)
Campbell I. (N.Z.)
Macquarie Is. (Austral.)
Amsterdam I. (Fr.)
St.Paul (Fr.)
Prince Edward Is. (S.Africa)
Crozet Is. (Fr.)
Kerguelen (Fr.)
McDonald Is. (Austral.)
Heard I. (Austral.)
Bouvet I. (Norw.)
S O U T H E R N O C E A N
Antarctic Circle
Ross Sea
A n t a r c t i c a
East from Greenwich
10 11 12 13 14 15 16 17 18
A B C D E F G H
Hanoi ● Capital Cities
1:80 000 000
CARTOGRAPHY BY PHILIP'S. COPYRIGHT REED INTERNATIONAL BOOKS LTD.

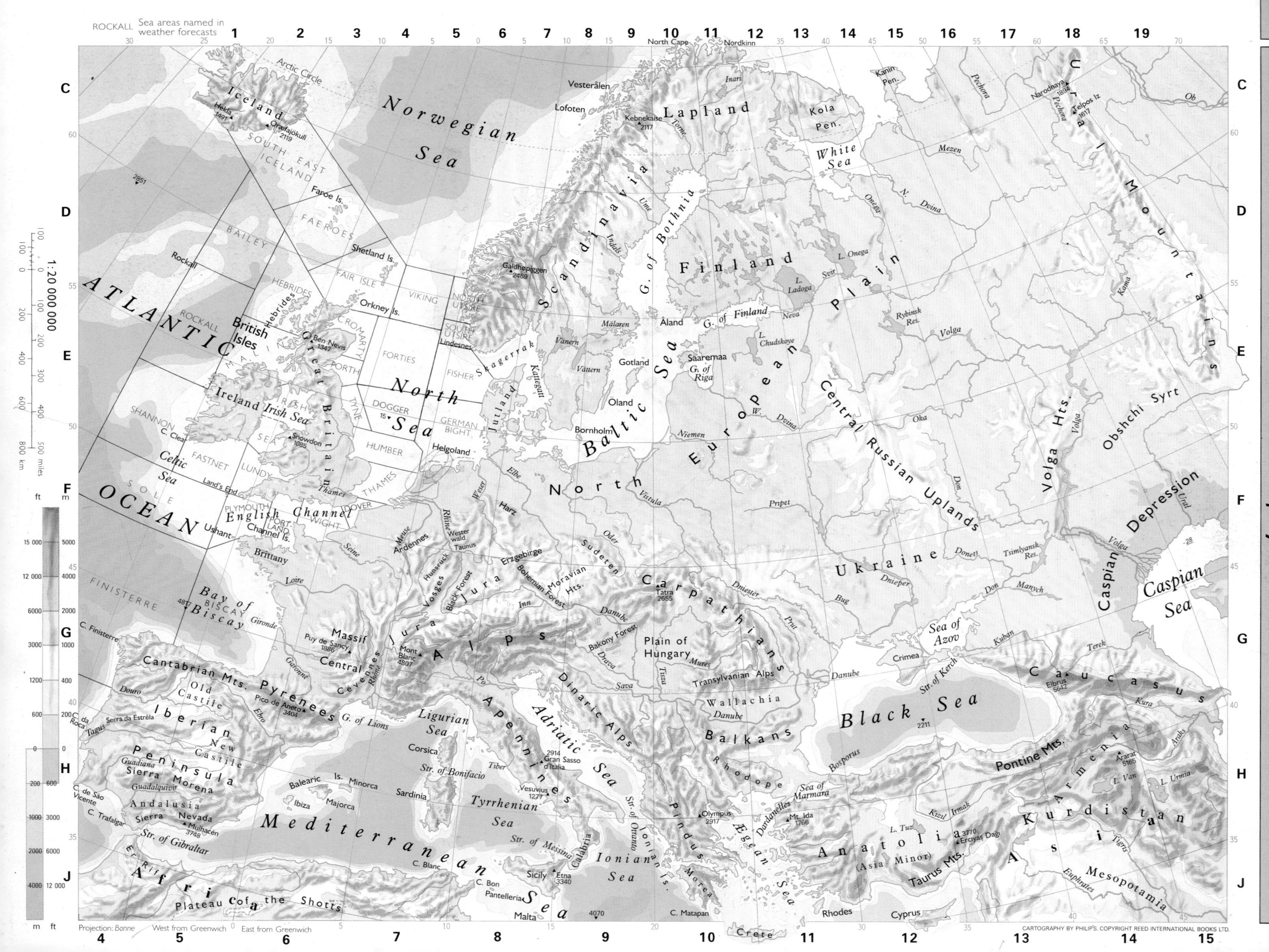

ROCKALL Sea areas named in weather forecasts

1:20 000 000

CARTOGRAPHY BY PHILIP'S. COPYRIGHT REED INTERNATIONAL BOOKS LTD.

Projection: Bonne

West from Greenwich   East from Greenwich

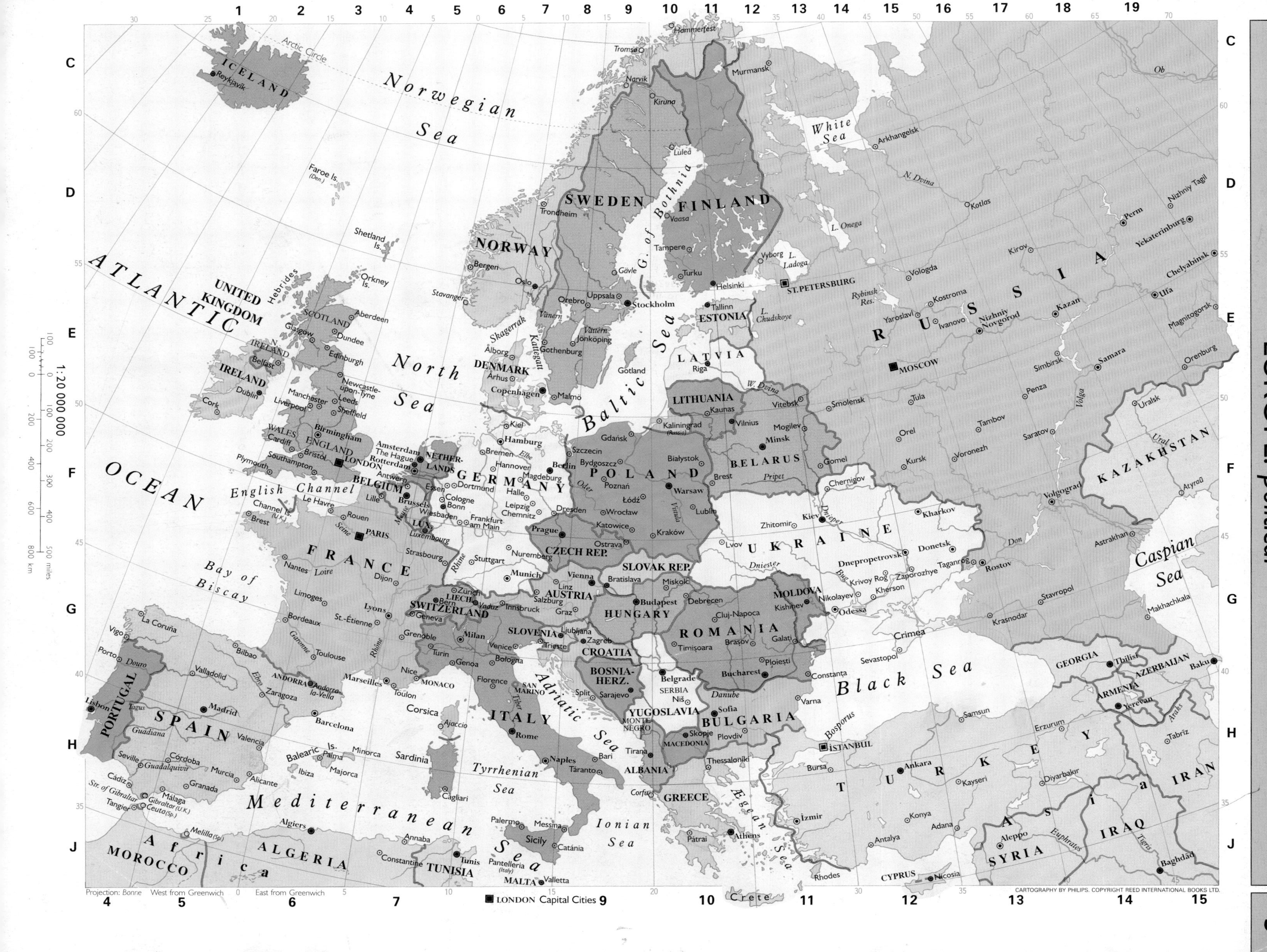

Scale 1 : 20 000 000

100 0 100 200 300 400 500 miles

100 0 200 400 600 800 km

Projection: Bonne

West from Greenwich   0   East from Greenwich

■ LONDON Capital Cities

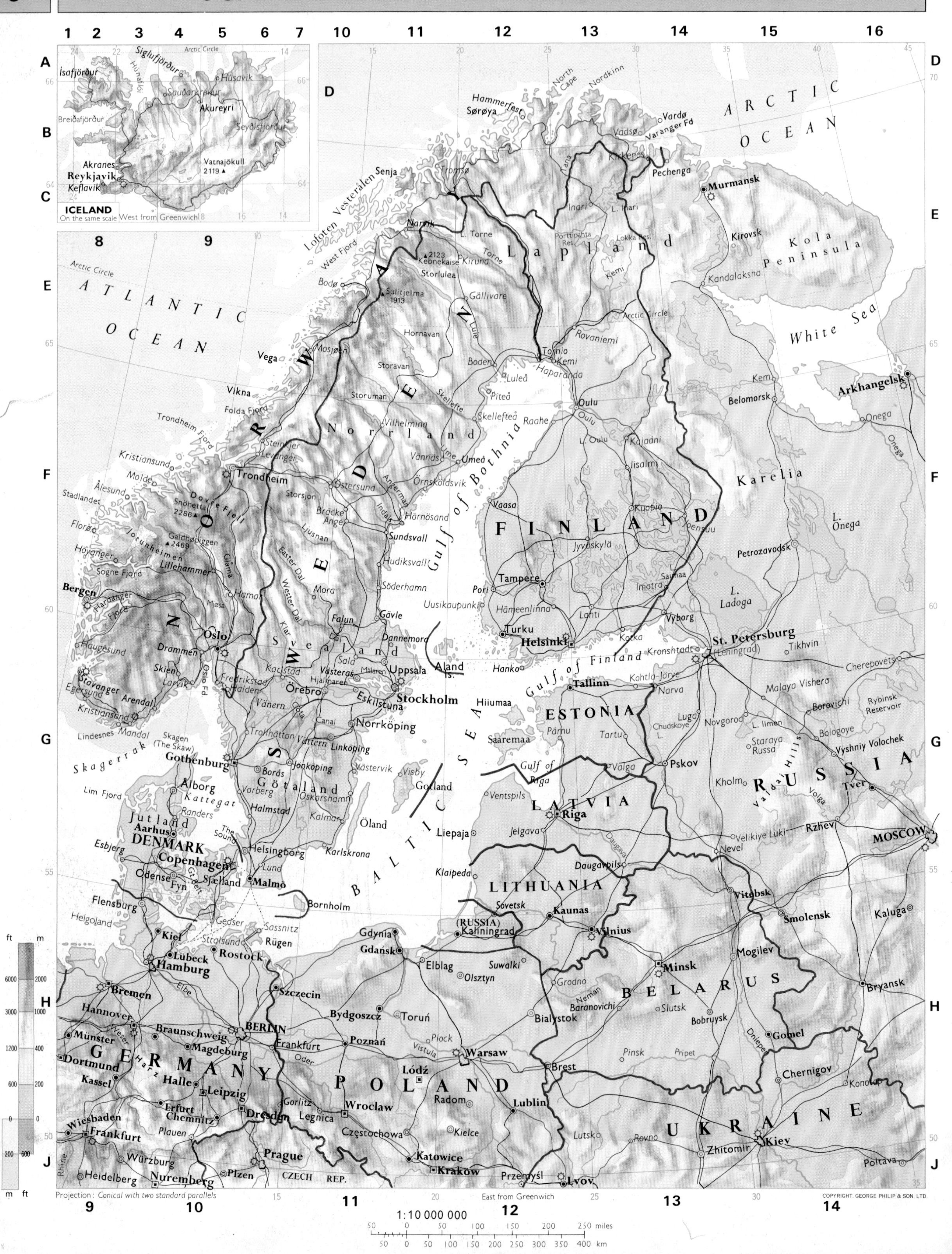

ICELAND
On the same scale   West from Greenwich

Projection: Conical with two standard parallels

1:10 000 000

East from Greenwich

COPYRIGHT GEORGE PHILIP & SON, LTD.

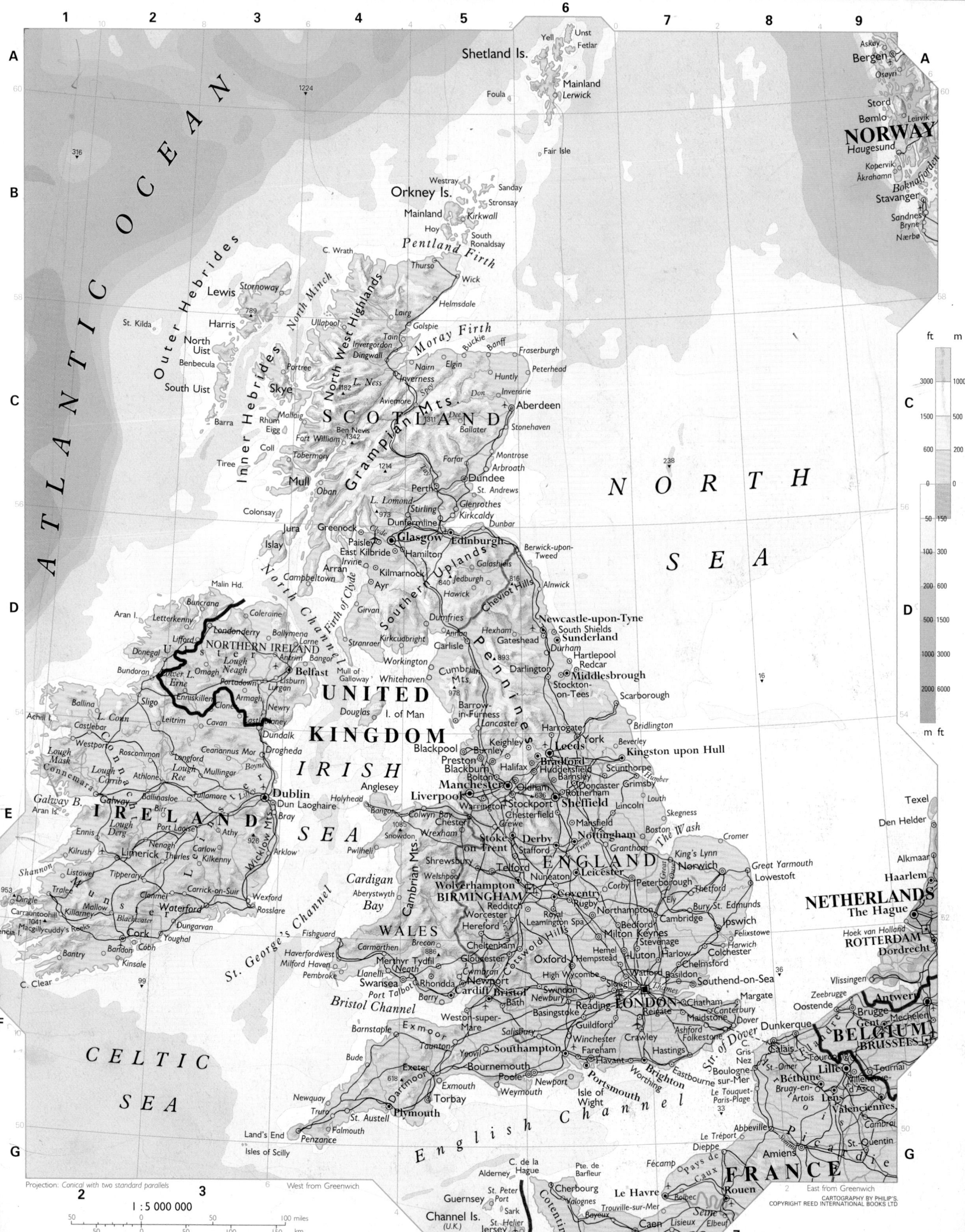
ATLANTIC OCEAN
NORTH SEA
IRISH SEA
CELTIC SEA
English Channel
UNITED KINGDOM
SCOTLAND
ENGLAND
WALES
IRELAND
NORTHERN IRELAND
NORWAY
NETHERLANDS
BELGIUM
FRANCE
Shetland Is.
Yell
Unst
Fetlar
Mainland
Lerwick
Foula
Fair Isle
Orkney Is.
Westray
Sanday
Stronsay
Kirkwall
Hoy
South Ronaldsay
Pentland Firth
C. Wrath
Thurso
Wick
Helmsdale
Outer Hebrides
Lewis
Stornoway
Harris
St. Kilda
North Uist
Benbecula
South Uist
Barra
North Minch
North West Highlands
Ullapool
Lairg
Golspie
Tain
Invergordon
Dingwall
Moray Firth
Buckie
Banff
Fraserburgh
Peterhead
Nairn
Elgin
Inverness
Huntly
Inverurie
Aberdeen
Stonehaven
Portree
Skye
L. Ness
Aviemore
Inner Hebrides
Mallaig
Rhum
Eigg
Coll
Tiree
Ben Nevis
Fort William
Tobermory
Mull
Oban
Grampian Mts.
Ballater
Forfar
Montrose
Arbroath
Dundee
St. Andrews
Perth
Glenrothes
Kirkcaldy
L. Lomond
Stirling
Dunfermline
Dunbar
Colonsay
Jura
Islay
Greenock
Paisley
Glasgow
Edinburgh
East Kilbride
Hamilton
Irvine
Arran
Kilmarnock
Ayr
Campbeltown
Southern Uplands
Galashiels
Jedburgh
Hawick
Berwick-upon-Tweed
Cheviot Hills
Alnwick
North Channel
Firth of Clyde
Girvan
Stranraer
Kirkcudbright
Dumfries
Mull of Galloway
Malin Hd.
Buncrana
Aran I.
Letterkenny
Londonderry
Coleraine
Ballymena
Larne
Lifford
Donegal
Ulster
Lough Neagh
Antrim
Bangor
Belfast
Lisburn
Omagh
Lower L. Erne
Bundoran
Portadown
Lurgan
Enniskillen
Armagh
Newry
Sligo
Ballina
Achill I.
L. Conn
Castlebar
Westport
Lough Mask
Connemara
Roscommon
Leitrim
Cavan
Dundalk
Drogheda
Longford
Ceanannus Mor
Boyne
Mullingar
Lough Ree
Athlone
Lough Corrib
Galway
Galway B.
Aran Is.
Ballinasloe
Tullamore
Dublin
Dun Laoghaire
Bray
Birr
Port Laoise
Athy
Wicklow Mts.
Ennis
Lough Derg
Nenagh
Carlow
Kilkenny
Arklow
Kilrush
Limerick
Thurles
Shannon
Listowel
Tipperary
Munster
Tralee
Mallow
Clonmel
Carrick-on-Suir
Wexford
Rosslare
Dingle
Carrauntoohill
Killarney
Blackwater
Waterford
Dungarvan
Macgillycuddy's Reeks
Cork
Cobh
Youghal
Bandon
Bantry
Kinsale
C. Clear
Carlisle
Workington
Whitehaven
Cumbrian Mts.
I. of Man
Douglas
Barrow-in-Furness
Lancaster
Pennines
Hexham
Newcastle-upon-Tyne
South Shields
Gateshead
Sunderland
Durham
Hartlepool
Redcar
Darlington
Middlesbrough
Stockton-on-Tees
Scarborough
Harrogate
York
Bridlington
Beverley
Kingston upon Hull
Keighley
Leeds
Blackpool
Burnley
Preston
Blackburn
Bradford
Halifax
Huddersfield
Bolton
Barnsley
Scunthorpe
Humber
Grimsby
Manchester
Oldham
Doncaster
Rotherham
Liverpool
Warrington
Stockport
Sheffield
Lincoln
Louth
Skegness
Anglesey
Holyhead
Bangor
Colwyn Bay
Chester
Crewe
Chesterfield
Mansfield
Boston
The Wash
Snowdon
Wrexham
Stoke on Trent
Derby
Nottingham
Grantham
Cromer
Pwllheli
Stafford
King's Lynn
Norwich
Great Yarmouth
Lowestoft
Shrewsbury
Telford
Leicester
Cardigan Bay
Aberystwyth
Welshpool
Wolverhampton
BIRMINGHAM
Nuneaton
Coventry
Corby
Peterborough
Thetford
Cambrian Mts.
Redditch
Rugby
Ely
Bury St. Edmunds
Worcester
Royal Leamington Spa
Northampton
Cambridge
Ipswich
Hereford
Bedford
Felixstowe
St. George's Channel
Fishguard
Brecon
Cheltenham
Milton Keynes
Stevenage
Harwich
Carmarthen
Cotswold Hills
Haverfordwest
Milford Haven
Pembroke
Merthyr Tydfil
Neath
Gloucester
Oxford
Hemel Hempstead
Luton
Harlow
Colchester
Chelmsford
Llanelli
Swansea
Port Talbot
Rhondda
Cwmbran
Newport
Cardiff
Barry
High Wycombe
Watford
Basildon
Southend-on-Sea
Bristol
Swindon
Slough
Thames
LONDON
Margate
Bristol Channel
Bath
Newbury
Reading
Chatham
Canterbury
Basingstoke
Reigate
Maidstone
Dover
Barnstaple
Exmoor
Weston-super-Mare
Guildford
Ashford
Folkestone
Salisbury
Winchester
Crawley
Taunton
Southampton
Hastings
Str. of Dover
Yeovil
Fareham
Havant
Bude
Bournemouth
Portsmouth
Brighton
Worthing
Eastbourne
Exeter
Poole
Newport
Dartmoor
Exmouth
Weymouth
Isle of Wight
Torbay
Newquay
Plymouth
Truro
St. Austell
Falmouth
Penzance
Land's End
Isles of Scilly
Alderney
C. de la Hague
Pte. de Barfleur
Guernsey
St. Peter Port
Sark
Channel Is. (U.K.)
Jersey
St. Helier
Cherbourg
Cotentin
Valognes
Bayeux
Le Havre
Trouville-sur-Mer
Caen
Lisieux
Fécamp
Pays de Caux
Bolbec
Seine
Rouen
Elbeuf
Dieppe
Le Tréport
Abbeville
Amiens
Picardie
St.-Quentin
Cambrai
Valenciennes
Lens
Arras
Bruay-en-Artois
Béthune
Lille
Villeneuve-d'Ascq
Tournai
Le Touquet-Paris-Plage
Boulogne-sur-Mer
C. Gris-Nez
Calais
St.-Omer
Dunkerque
Tourcoing
Oostende
Brugge
Gent
Zeebrugge
Antwerp
Mechelen
BRUSSELS
Vlissingen
Dordrecht
ROTTERDAM
Hoek van Holland
The Hague
Haarlem
Alkmaar
Den Helder
Texel
Askøy
Bergen
Os
Stord
Bømlo
Leirvik
Haugesund
Kopervik
Åkrahamn
Boknafjorden
Stavanger
Sandnes
Bryne
Nærbø
ft
m
Projection: Conical with two standard parallels
West from Greenwich
East from Greenwich
1 : 5 000 000
miles
km
CARTOGRAPHY BY PHILIP'S.
COPYRIGHT REED INTERNATIONAL BOOKS LTD

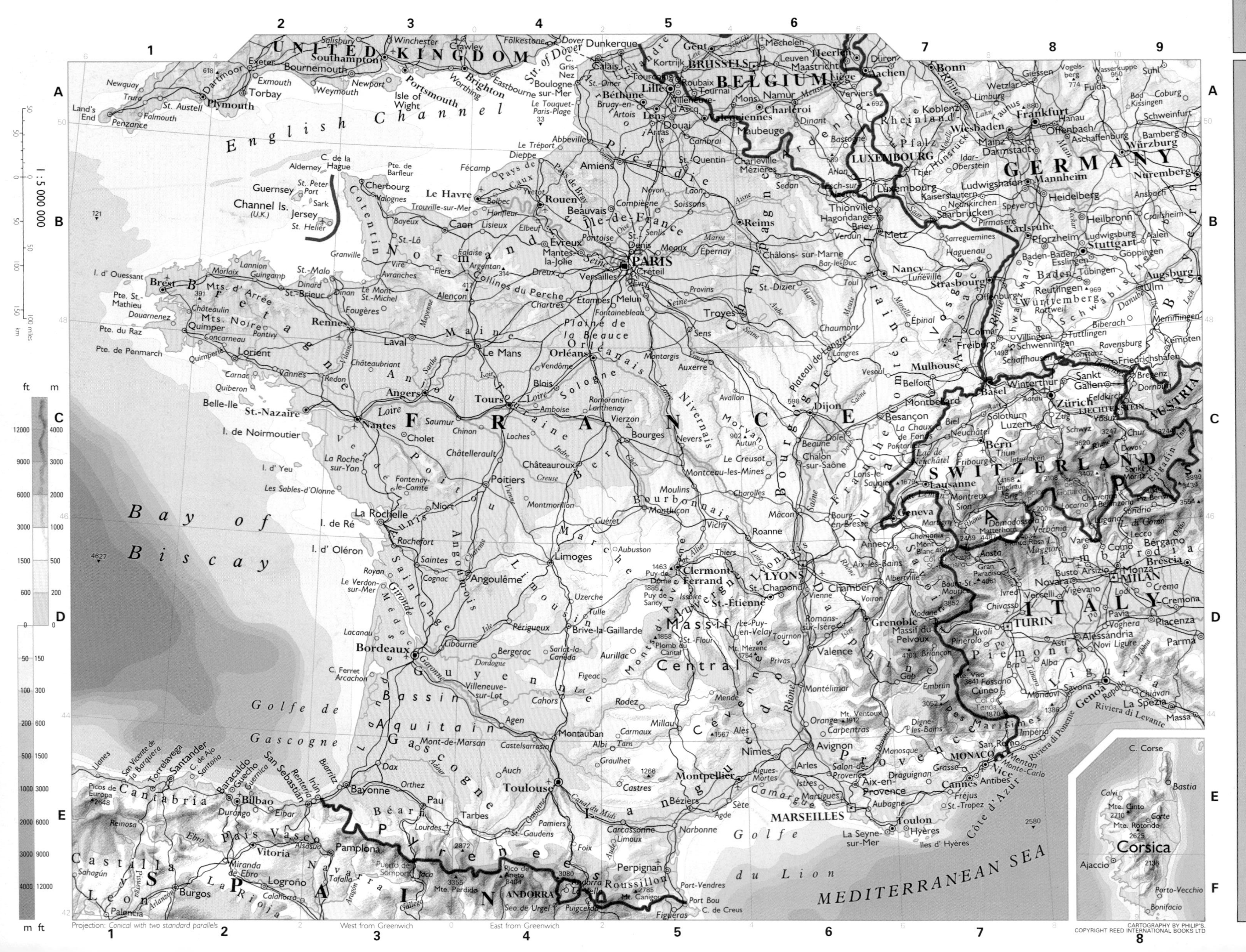

1 : 5 000 000

CARTOGRAPHY BY PHILIP'S.
COPYRIGHT REED INTERNATIONAL BOOKS LTD

Projection: Conical with two standard parallels

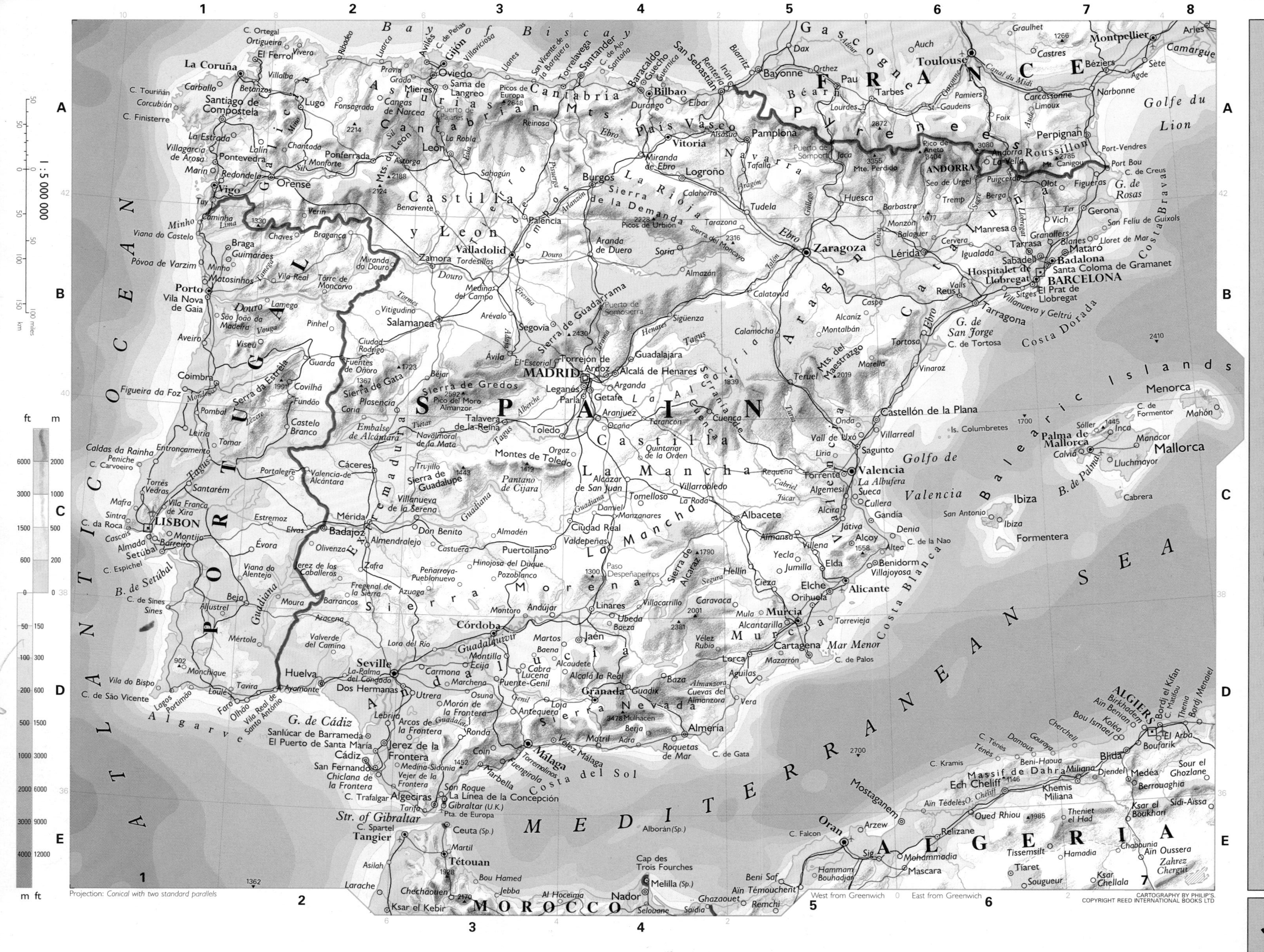
SPAIN
PORTUGAL
FRANCE
ANDORRA
ALGERIA
MOROCCO
MEDITERRANEAN SEA
ATLANTIC OCEAN
Bay of Biscay
Golfe du Lion
Balearic Islands
Mallorca
Menorca
Ibiza
Formentera
Golfo de Valencia
G. de Cádiz
Str. of Gibraltar
Pyrenees
MADRID
LISBON
BARCELONA
ALGIERS
Porto
Valencia
Zaragoza
Seville
Málaga
Bilbao
Granada
Córdoba
Gibraltar (U.K.)
Ceuta (Sp.)
Melilla (Sp.)
Tangier
Oran
1 : 5 000 000
50 0 50 100 miles
50 0 50 100 150 km
ft m
Projection: Conical with two standard parallels
West from Greenwich 0 East from Greenwich
CARTOGRAPHY BY PHILIP'S. COPYRIGHT REED INTERNATIONAL BOOKS LTD

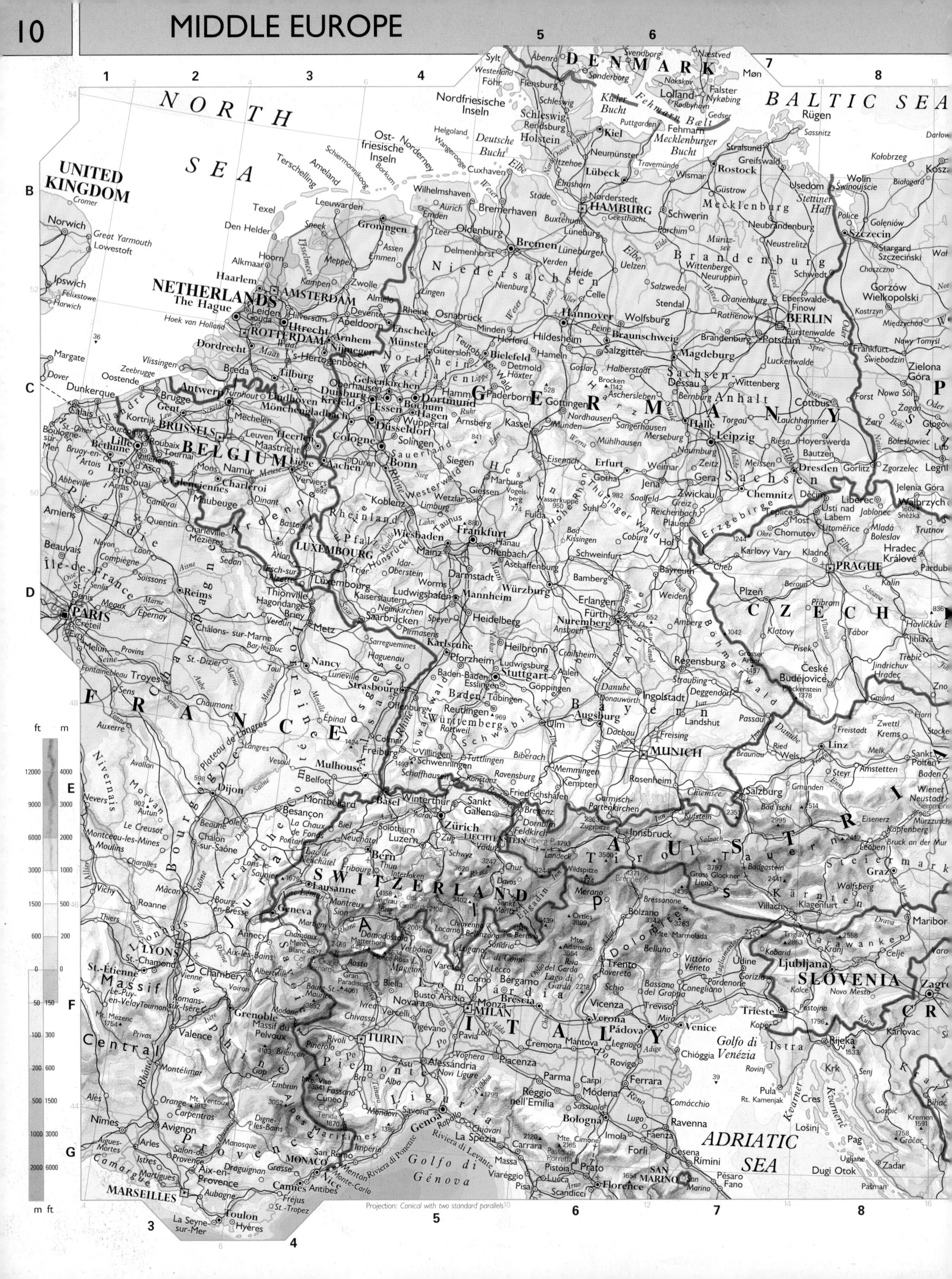
NORTH SEA
BALTIC SEA
UNITED KINGDOM
NETHERLANDS
BELGIUM
LUXEMBOURG
FRANCE
GERMANY
DENMARK
CZECH
AUSTRIA
SWITZERLAND
LIECHTENSTEIN
ITALY
SLOVENIA
MONACO
SAN MARINO
ADRIATIC SEA
Golfo di Venézia
Golfo di Génova
Deutsche Bucht
Kieler Bucht
Fehmarn Bælt
Mecklenburger Bucht
Nordfriesische Inseln
Ost-friesische Inseln
Stettiner Haff
Norwich
Great Yarmouth
Lowestoft
Ipswich
Felixstowe
Harwich
Margate
Dover
Cromer
AMSTERDAM
The Hague
ROTTERDAM
Utrecht
Haarlem
Leiden
Groningen
Arnhem
Nijmegen
Eindhoven
Tilburg
Breda
Dordrecht
Den Helder
Leeuwarden
Zwolle
Enschede
Maastricht
Heerlen
BRUSSELS
Antwerp
Gent
Brugge
Oostende
Zeebrugge
Liège
Namur
Charleroi
Mons
Mechelen
Leuven
Kortrijk
Tournai
PARIS
Lille
Calais
Dunkerque
Amiens
Reims
Metz
Nancy
Strasbourg
Mulhouse
Dijon
Besançon
LYONS
Grenoble
MARSEILLES
Toulon
Nice
Avignon
Nîmes
Valence
St.-Étienne
Troyes
Épinal
Colmar
Belfort
Chambéry
Annecy
Massif Central
Jura
Vosges
Île-de-France
Picardie
Champagne
Lorraine
Alsace
Bourgogne
Franche-Comté
Provence
Dauphiné
Camargue
HAMBURG
BERLIN
MUNICH
Frankfurt
Cologne
Düsseldorf
Dortmund
Essen
Duisburg
Bochum
Bonn
Aachen
Bremen
Bremerhaven
Hannover
Braunschweig
Magdeburg
Leipzig
Dresden
Chemnitz
Halle
Erfurt
Kassel
Göttingen
Münster
Osnabrück
Bielefeld
Kiel
Lübeck
Rostock
Schwerin
Stralsund
Rügen
Potsdam
Wiesbaden
Mainz
Koblenz
Mannheim
Heidelberg
Karlsruhe
Stuttgart
Nuremberg
Würzburg
Regensburg
Augsburg
Ulm
Freiburg
Saarbrücken
Trier
Kaiserslautern
Wolfsburg
Flensburg
Niedersachsen
Nordrhein-Westfalen
Rheinland-Pfalz
Hessen
Thüringer Wald
Sachsen
Sachsen-Anhalt
Brandenburg
Mecklenburg
Harz
Bayern
Schwarzwald
Schwäbische Alb
Erzgebirge
Böhmerwald
Baden-Württemberg
Rhine
Elbe
Danube
Oder
PRAGUE
Plzeň
Karlovy Vary
České Budějovice
Liberec
Ústí nad Labem
Linz
Salzburg
Innsbruck
Graz
Klagenfurt
Villach
Wiener Neustadt
Zürich
Basel
Bern
Geneva
Lausanne
Luzern
Lugano
St. Moritz
MILAN
TURIN
Genoa
Venice
Verona
Pádova
Bologna
Florence
Trieste
Trento
Bolzano
Brescia
Bergamo
Parma
Modena
Ferrara
Ravenna
Rimini
Pisa
Livorno
La Spezia
Alessándria
Piemonte
Lombardia
Liguria
Dolomites
Alpes Maritimes
Ljubljana
Maribor
Rijeka
Zagreb
Szczecin
Wrocław
Zielona Góra
Kołobrzeg
Gorzów Wielkopolski
Frankfurt-Świebodzin
Projection: Conical with two standard parallels
ft m
12000 4000
9000 3000
6000 2000
3000 1000
1500 500
600 200
0 0
50 150
100 300
200 600
500 1500
1000 3000
2000 6000
m ft

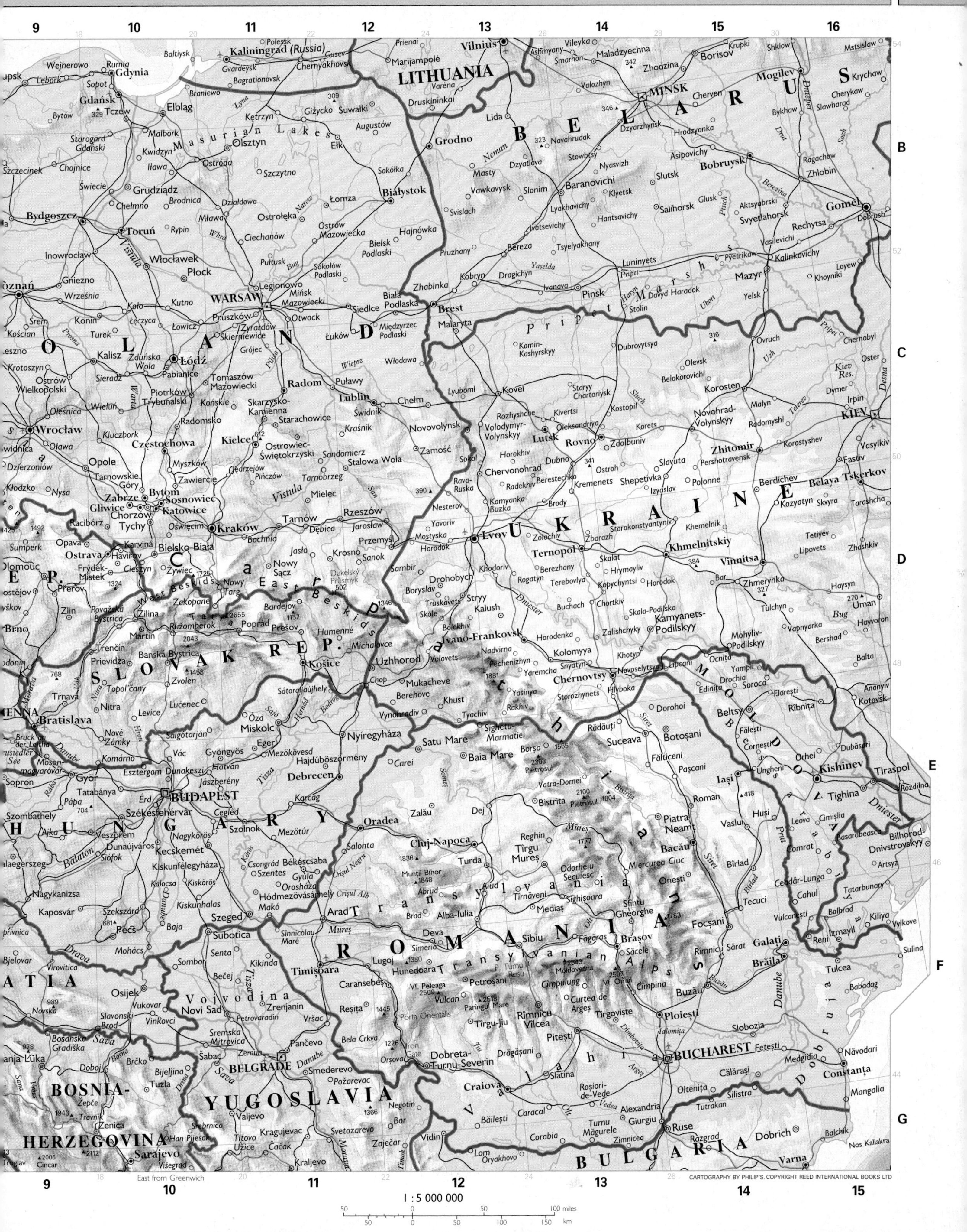
9
10
11
12
13
14
15
16
LITHUANIA
B E L A R U S
P O L A N D
U K R A I N E
SLOVAK REP.
H U N G A R Y
R O M A N I A
M O L D O V A
YUGOSLAVIA
BOSNIA-
HERZEGOVINA
B U L G A R I A
C R O A T I A
Kaliningrad (Russia)
Vilnius
Minsk
Grodno
Gdańsk
Gdynia
Elbląg
Olsztyn
Masurian Lakes
Białystok
Bydgoszcz
Toruń
Włocławek
Płock
WARSAW
Brest
Pinsk
Pripet Marshes
Gomel
Mogilev
Bobruysk
Baranovichi
Poznań
Łódź
Radom
Lublin
Kielce
Częstochowa
Wrocław
Opole
Katowice
Kraków
Tarnów
Rzeszów
Przemyśl
Lvov
Lutsk
Rovno
Zhitomir
KIEV
Vinnitsa
Ternopol
Khmelnitskiy
Ivano-Frankovsk
Chernovtsy
Ostrava
Bielsko-Biała
Nowy Sącz
West Beskids
East Beskids
Tatra
Carpathians
Košice
Uzhhorod
Bratislava
Miskolc
Debrecen
BUDAPEST
Győr
Székesfehérvár
Balaton
Szeged
Pécs
Danube
Tisza
Vistula
Dniester
Kishinev
Tiraspol
Iaşi
Suceava
Botoşani
Bacău
Galaţi
Brăila
Constanţa
Cluj-Napoca
Oradea
Arad
Timişoara
Transylvania
Transylvanian Alps
Braşov
Ploieşti
BUCHAREST
Craiova
Walachia
Dobruja
Bessarabia
Novi Sad
BELGRADE
Vojvodina
Osijek
Sarajevo
Ruse
Varna
Dobrich
B
C
D
E
F
G
East from Greenwich
1 : 5 000 000
50 0 50 100 miles
50 0 50 100 150 km
CARTOGRAPHY BY PHILIP'S. COPYRIGHT REED INTERNATIONAL BOOKS LTD

Countries / Regions: FRANCE, SWITZERLAND, AUSTRIA, SLOVENIA, CROATIA, ITALY, ALGERIA, TUNISIA, MALTA, HERZ

Seas: LIGURIAN SEA, TYRRHENIAN SEA, ADRIATIC SEA, MEDITERR

Islands / Regions: Corsica, Sardinia, SICILIA, Elba, Capraia, Pianosa, Montecristo, Giglio, Asinara, Maddalena

Grid numbers: 1 2 3 4 5 6 7 (top and bottom); B C D E F G (sides)

Elevation scale:
ft / m
12000 / 4000
9000 / 3000
6000 / 2000
3000 / 1000
1500 / 500
600 / 200
0 / 0
50 / 150
100 / 300
200 / 600
500 / 1500
1000 / 3000
2000 / 6000
4000 / 12000
m / ft

Cities and places (selection):
Lyons, Annecy, Aix-les-Bains, Chambéry, Albertville, Chamonix, Grenoble, Valence, Montélimar, Avignon, Orange, Carpentras, Digne-les-Bains, Manosque, Aix-en-Provence, MARSEILLES, Toulon, Hyères, Cannes, Antibes, Nice, MONACO, Monte-Carlo, Menton, San Remo, Imperia, Savona, Genoa, La Spézia, Carrara, Massa, Viaréggio, Pisa, Livorno, TURIN, Pinerolo, Cuneo, Mondovi, Alba, Asti, Alessandria, Novara, Vercelli, Biella, Ivrea, MILAN, Monza, Bergamo, Brescia, Como, Lecco, Varese, Pavia, Lodi, Crema, Cremona, Mantova, Piacenza, Parma, Modena, Reggio nell'Emilia, Carpi, Ferrara, Bologna, Imola, Faenza, Forli, Cesena, Rimini, Ravenna, Comácchio, Verona, Vicenza, Pádova, Venice, Trieste, Treviso, Belluno, Trento, Rovereto, Bolzano, Bressanone, Merano, Udine, Gorizia, Pordenone, Conegliano, Bassano del Grappa, Schio, Rovigo, Legnago, Adria, Chióggia, Koper, Rijeka, Pula, Krk, Cres, Lošinj, Zadar, Ljubljana, Zagreb, Karlovac, Sisak, Novo Mesto, Celje, Maribor, Varaždin, Koprivnica, Bjelovar, Virovitica, Banja Luka, Bihač, Graz, Wolfsberg, Klagenfurt, Villach, Villa
Florence, Prato, Pistóia, Lucca, Scandicci, Arezzo, Siena, Volterra, Grosseto, Orbetello, Perugia, Assisi, Foligno, Spoleto, Terni, Viterbo, Orvieto, Civitavécchia, ROME, VATICAN CITY, Tivoli, Frosinone, Latina, Ánzio, Aprilia, Terracina, Fondi, Cassino, Fórmia, Gaeta, Pomézia, Velletri, L'Aquila, Rieti, Avezzano, Pescara, Chieti, Lanciano, Vasto, Térmoli, Campobasso, Isérnia, Benevento, Avellino, NAPLES, Caserta, Pozzuoli, Ischia, Capri, Salerno, Battipáglia, Nocera Inferiore, Torre del Greco, Castellammare di Stábia, Potenza, Matera, Bari, Barletta, Trani, Molfetta, Andria, Corato, Monópoli, Fasano, Martina Franca, Putignano, Altamura, Cerignola, Fóggia, Manfredónia, San Severo, Táranto, Ancona, Macerata, Fermo, Ascoli Piceno, Téramo, Senigállia, Pésaro, Fano, Urbino, SAN MARINO, Iesi, Fabriano, Città di Castello, Montesilvano Marina

Reggio di Calábria, Messina, Catánia, Siracusa, Ragusa, Módica, Gela, Caltagirone, Vittória, Licata, Agrigento, Enna, Caltanissetta, Marsala, Trápani, Mazara del Vallo, Castelvetrano, Sciacca, PALERMO, Cefalù, Milazzo, Taormina, Acireale, Giarre, Paternò, Adrano, Lentini, Augusta, Avola, Partinico, Alcamo, Bagheria, Términi Imerese, Barcellona-Pozzo di Gotto, Monti Nébrodi, Etna, Strómboli, Lípari, Vulcano, Salina, Ísole Eólie, Ustica, Pantelleria, Lampedusa, Ísole Pelagie, Linosa, Gozo, Valletta, MALTA, Rabat

Tunis, Bizerte, Béja, Nabeul, Hammamet, Sousse, Monastir, Mahdia, Kairouan, Kasserine, Sbeïtla, Gafsa (?), El Kef, Menzel-Bourguiba, Mateur, Manouba, Bardo, Ben Arous, Korba, Kelibia, Soliman, Menzel-Temime, Tábarka, Jendouba, Bou Salem, Le Kef, El Fahs, Zaghouan, Moknine, Msaken, Kalaa-Kebira, Akouda, Hamman Sousse
Annaba, Constantine, Skikda, Collo, El Milia, Guelma, Souk-Ahras, El Khroub, Sedrata, Ain Beida, Oum-el-Bouaghi, Khenchela, Tébessa, Cheria, Babor, Mila, El Kala, Azzaba

ALPS, PYRENEES (?), Massif du Pelvoux, Côte d'Azur, Riviera di Ponente, Riviera di Levante, Golfo di Génova, Golfo di Venézia, Golfo di Táranto, Lago di Garda, L. Trasimeno, L. di Bolsena, L. di Bracciano, Mte. Cinto, Mte. Rotondo, Gran Sasso d'Italia, Gennargentu, C. Spartivento, C. Carbonara, Str. di Messina

Projection: Conical with two standard parallels

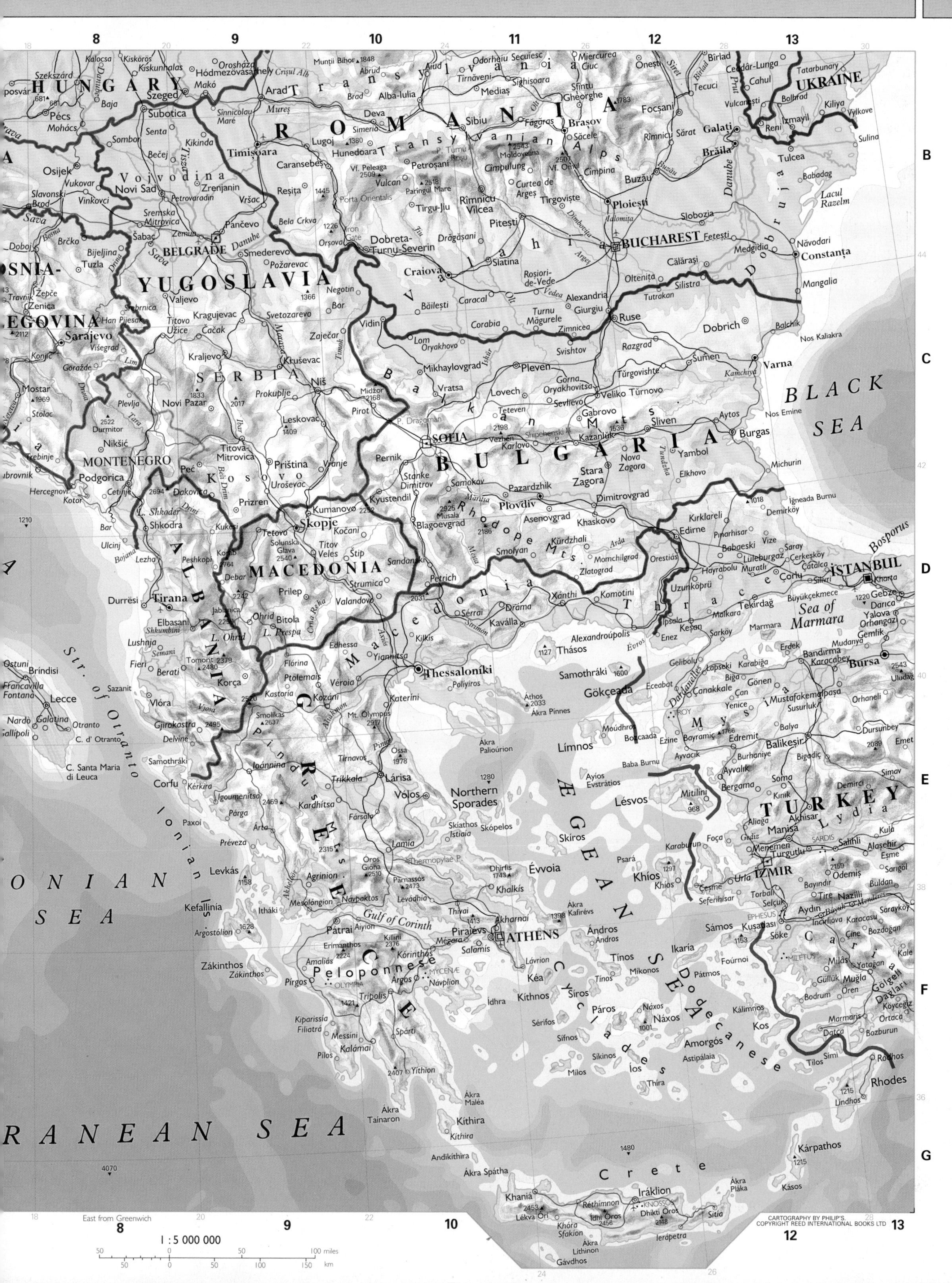

HUNGARY
ROMANIA
UKRAINE
YUGOSLAVIA
SERBIA
MONTENEGRO
MACEDONIA
ALBANIA
BULGARIA
GREECE
TURKEY
BLACK SEA
IONIAN SEA
MEDITERRANEAN SEA
AEGEAN SEA
Sea of Marmara
Str. of Otranto
Transylvania
Transylvanian Alps
Walachia
Dobruja
Vojvodina
Kosovo
Balkan Mts
Rhodope Mts
Macedonia
Thrace
Pindus Mts
Peloponnese
Cyclades
Dodecanese
Crete
Rhodes
Gulf of Corinth
Northern Sporades
Mysia
Lydia
Caria
BUCHAREST
BELGRADE
SOFIA
Skopje
Tirana
Sarajevo
ATHENS
Thessaloníki
İSTANBUL
İZMIR
Bursa
Constanța
Varna
Burgas
Plovdiv
Timișoara
Brașov
Ploiești
Craiova
Novi Sad
Niš
Podgorica
Iráklion
East from Greenwich
1 : 5 000 000
miles
km
CARTOGRAPHY BY PHILIP'S.
COPYRIGHT REED INTERNATIONAL BOOKS LTD

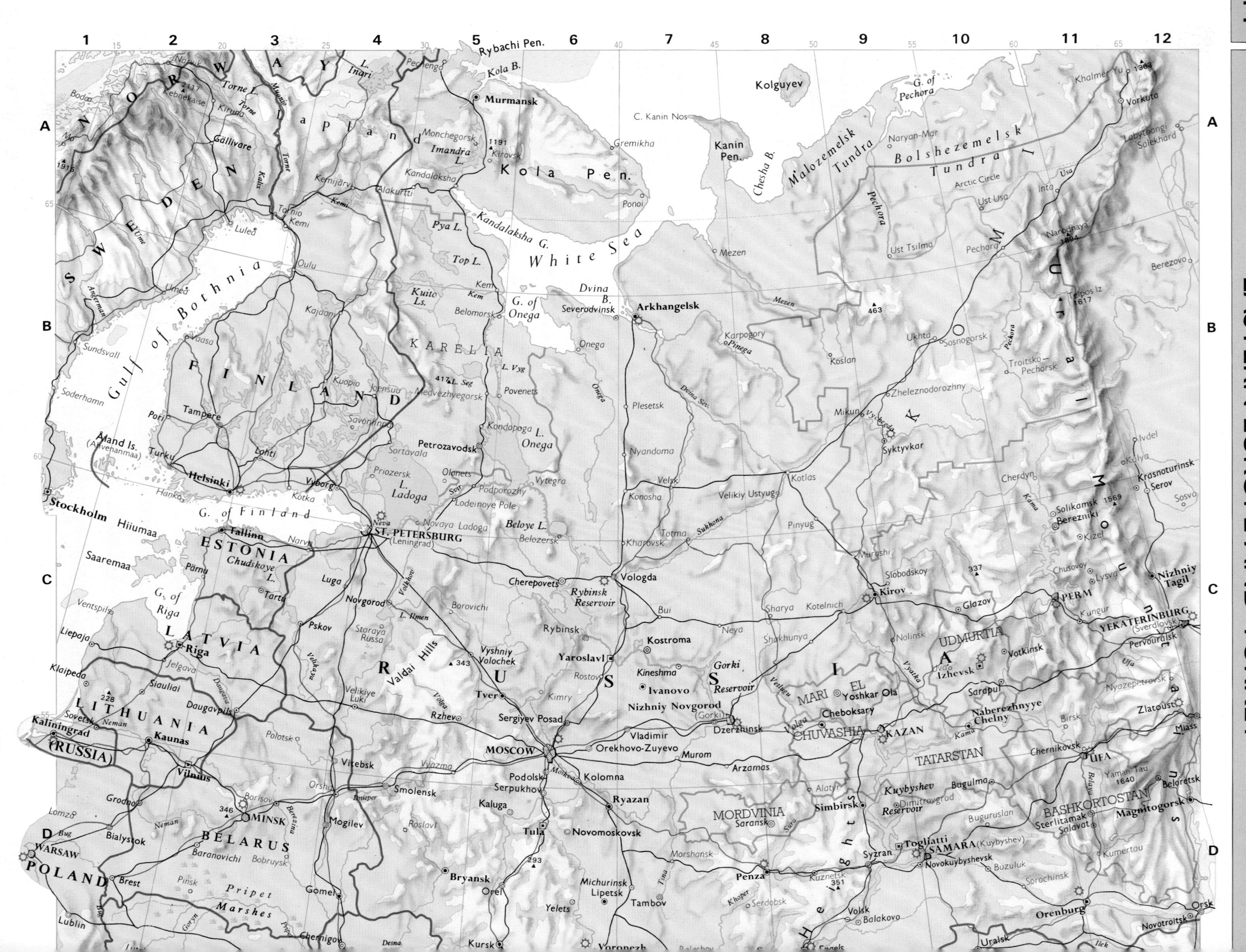
Murmansk
Kola Pen.
Kola B.
Rybachi Pen.
White Sea
Kandalaksha G.
G. of Onega
Dvina B.
Arkhangelsk
Severodvinsk
Kanin Pen.
C. Kanin Nos
Chesha B.
Kolguyev
G. of Pechora
Naryan-Mar
Bolshezemelsk Tundra
Malozemelsk Tundra
Pechora
Arctic Circle
Vorkuta
Ukhta
Syktyvkar
Kotlas
Kirov
PERM
YEKATERINBURG
(Sverdlovsk)
Nizhniy Tagil
UFA
BASHKORTOSTAN
Orenburg
UDMURTIA
Izhevsk
TATARSTAN
KAZAN
Naberezhnyye Chelny
MARI EL
Yoshkar Ola
CHUVASHIA
Cheboksary
SAMARA
(Kuybyshev)
Togliatti
Syzran
Simbirsk
MORDVINIA
Saransk
Penza
Kostroma
Ivanovo
Nizhniy Novgorod
(Gorki)
Dzerzhinsk
Vladimir
Yaroslavl
Rybinsk Reservoir
Vologda
Cherepovets
Onega L.
Ladoga L.
ST. PETERSBURG
(Leningrad)
Petrozavodsk
KARELIA
Novgorod
Pskov
Valdai Hills
Tver
MOSCOW
Ryazan
Tula
Kaluga
Smolensk
Bryansk
Orel
Kursk
Lipetsk
Tambov
Vitebsk
Mogilev
Gomel
MINSK
BELARUS
Pripet Marshes
Vilnius
Kaunas
LITHUANIA
Kaliningrad
(RUSSIA)
LATVIA
Riga
G. of Riga
ESTONIA
Tallinn
G. of Finland
Helsinki
FINLAND
Tampere
Turku
Gulf of Bothnia
Oulu
Åland Is.
Stockholm
SWEDEN
NORWAY
Luleå
POLAND
WARSAW
Brest
Lublin

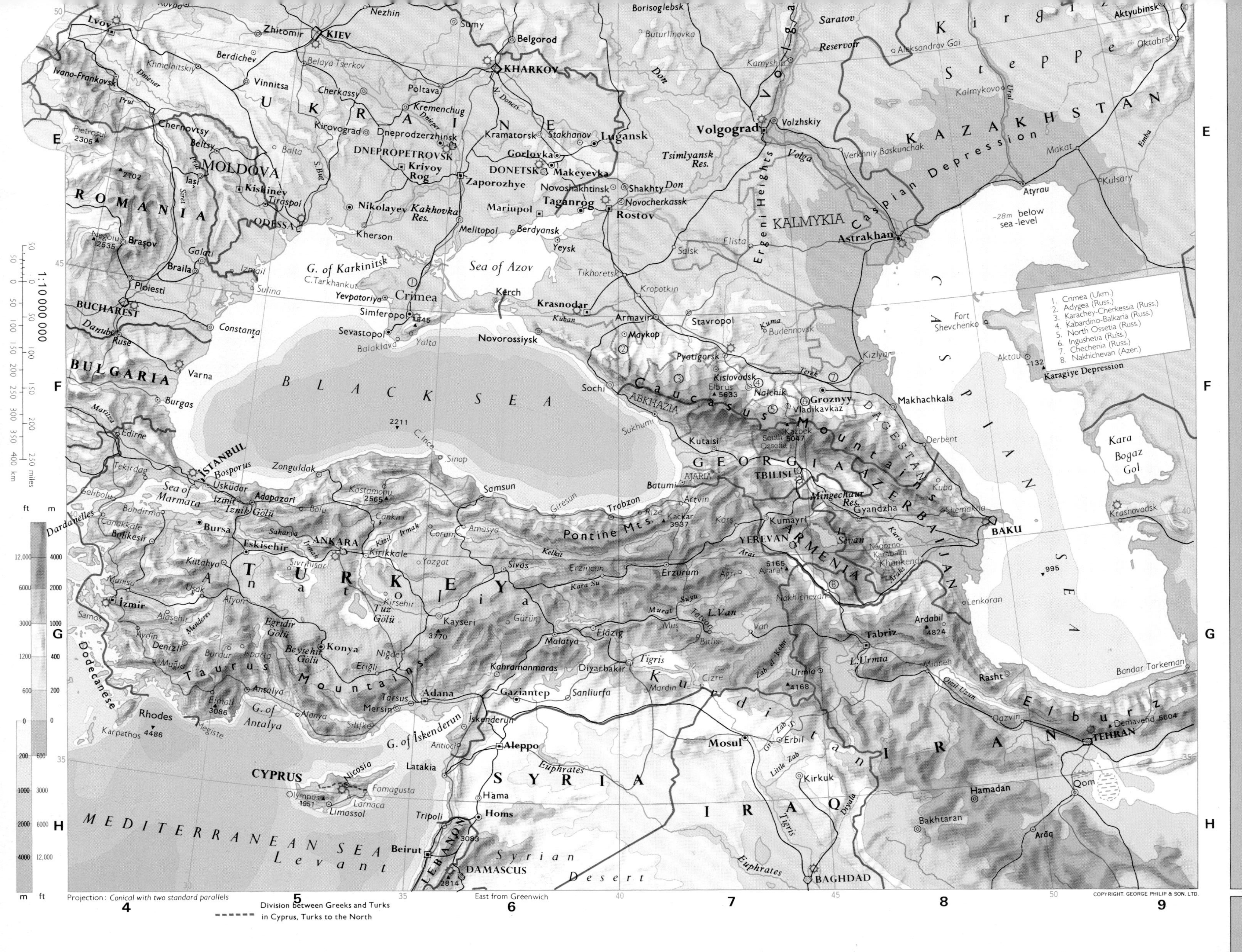

1. Crimea (Ukr.)
2. Adygea (Russ.)
3. Karachay-Cherkessia (Russ.)
4. Kabardino-Balkaria (Russ.)
5. North Ossetia (Russ.)
6. Ingushetia (Russ.)
7. Chechenia (Russ.)
8. Nakhichevan (Azer.)
9. Karabye Depression

1:10 000 000

Projection: Conical with two standard parallels

Division Between Greeks and Turks
in Cyprus, Turks to the North

East from Greenwich

COPYRIGHT. GEORGE PHILIP & SON, LTD.

ASIA: physical

ARCTIC OCEAN
PACIFIC OCEAN
INDIAN OCEAN
ATLANTIC OCEAN
Greenland
Norwegian Sea
Svalbard
Severnaya Zemlya
C. Chelyuskin
Taimyr Peninsula
Laptev Sea
New Siberian Is.
Wrangel I.
Chukot Ra.
C. Dezhneva
Bering Strait
Alaska
Bering Sea
Aleutian Is.
Aleutian Trench 7822
Iceland
Arctic Circle
British Isles
North Sea
Barents Sea
Novaya Zemlya
Kara Sea
North Cape
Scandinavia
Finland
Kola Pen.
White Sea
Baltic Sea
Europe
North European Plain
Central Russian Uplands
Alps
Carpathians
Danube
Adriatic Sea
Rhine
Ural Mts.
Narodnaya 1894
West Siberian Plain
Siberia
Central Siberian Plateau
Verkhoyansk Ra.
Cherski Ra.
Kolyma Ra.
Koryak Ra.
Kamchatka Pen.
Sredinny Ra.
Klyuchevskaya 4750
Sea of Okhotsk
Sakhalin
Kuril Is.
Kuril Trench 10 542
Hokkaido
Stanovoy Ra.
Yablonovyy Ra.
L. Baikal
Sayan Mts.
Altai
Belukha 4506
Steppe
Black Sea
Bosporus
Caucasus
Elbrus 5642
Caspian Sea
Aral Sea
Anatolia
Taurus Mts.
Pontine Mts.
Ararat 5165
Cyprus
Mediterranean Sea
Middle East
Mesopotamia
Tigris
Euphrates
Dead Sea
Syrian Desert
Sinai
Nile
Libyan Desert
Red Sea
Arabia
Nafud Desert
Rub' al Khali (Empty Quarter)
The Gulf
G. of Oman
Elburz Mts.
Damavend 5604
Zagros
Plateau of Iran
Kyzyl Kum
Kara Kum
Hindu Kush
Pamirs
Communism Pk. 7495
Tian Shan
Turfan Basin
Tarim Basin
Takla Makan
Kunlun Shan
Plateau of Tibet
Karakoram Ra.
K2 8611
Himalaya
Mt. Everest 8848
Nan Shan
Gobi
Plateau of Mongolia
Great Khingan Mts.
Manchurian Plain
Great Plain of China
China
Korea
Sea of Japan
Japan
Honshu
Fuji-San 3776
Japan Trench 10 554
Bonin Is.
Yellow Sea
East China Sea
Ryukyu Is.
Taiwan
Tropic of Cancer
Guam
Mariana Trench 11 022
Thar Desert
India
Ganges
Deccan
Western Ghats
Eastern Ghats
Arabian Sea
Bay of Bengal
Andaman Is.
Nicobar Is.
Ceylon
Lakshadweep Is.
Maldives
Chagos Arch.
Indo-China
G. of Thailand
Malay Pen.
South China Sea
Hainan
Philippines
Luzon
Mindanao
Mindanao Trench 10 497
Borneo
Sumatra
Java
East Indies
Celebes
New Guinea
Australia
Arafura Sea
Timor Sea
Africa
Ethiopian Highlands
Somali Pen.
G. of Aden
Socotra
Equator
Amirante Is.
Seychelles
L. Victoria
L. Tanganyika
L. Malawi
Projection: Bonne
East of Greenwich
CARTOGRAPHY BY PHILIP'S.COPYRIGHT REED INTERNATIONAL BOOKS LTD.
1: 50 000 000
200 0 200 400 600 800 1000 miles
200 0 400 800 1200 1600 km

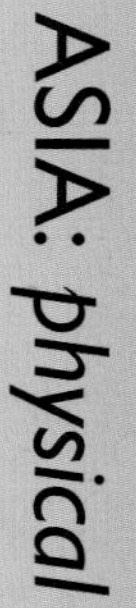

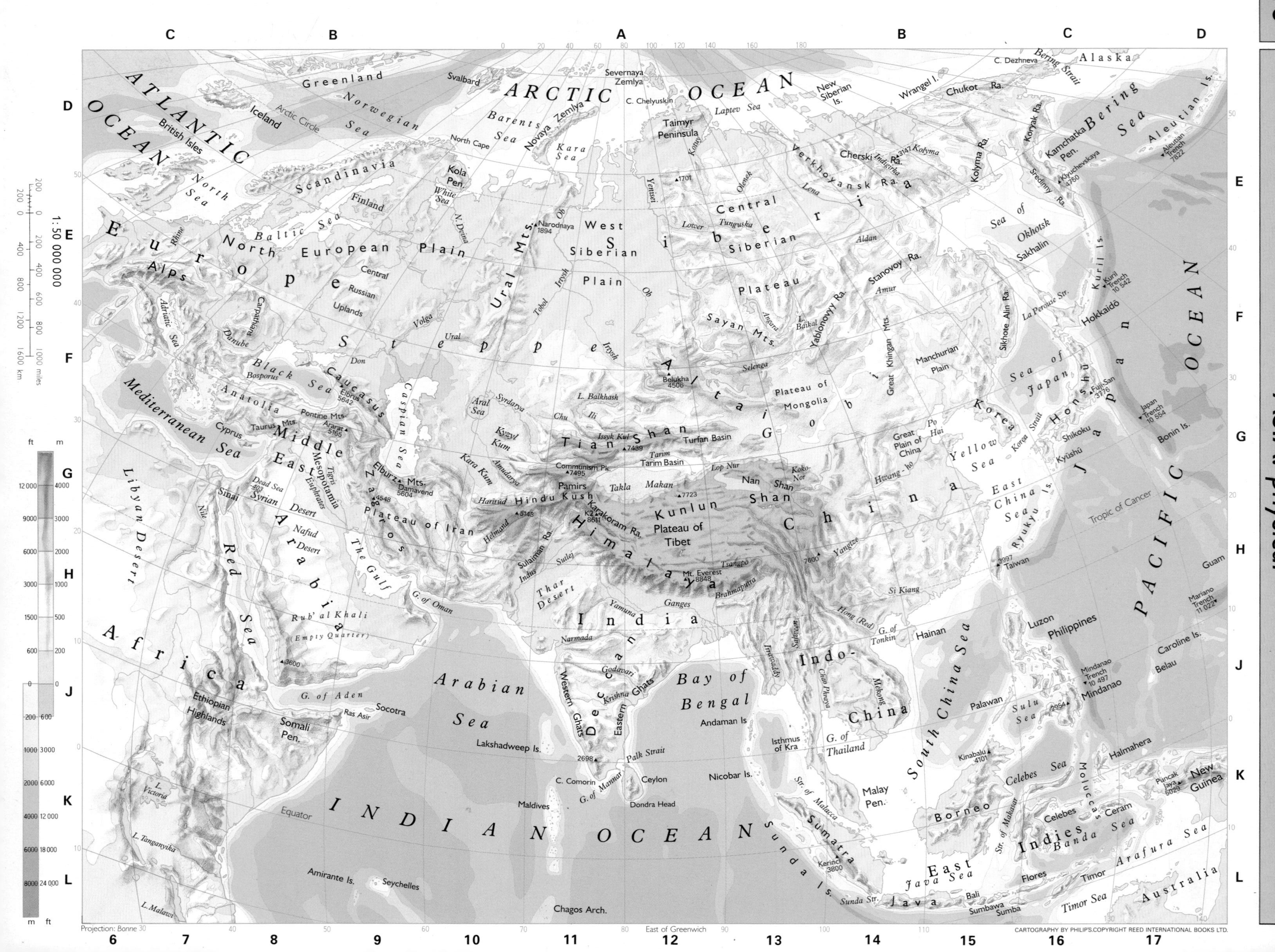

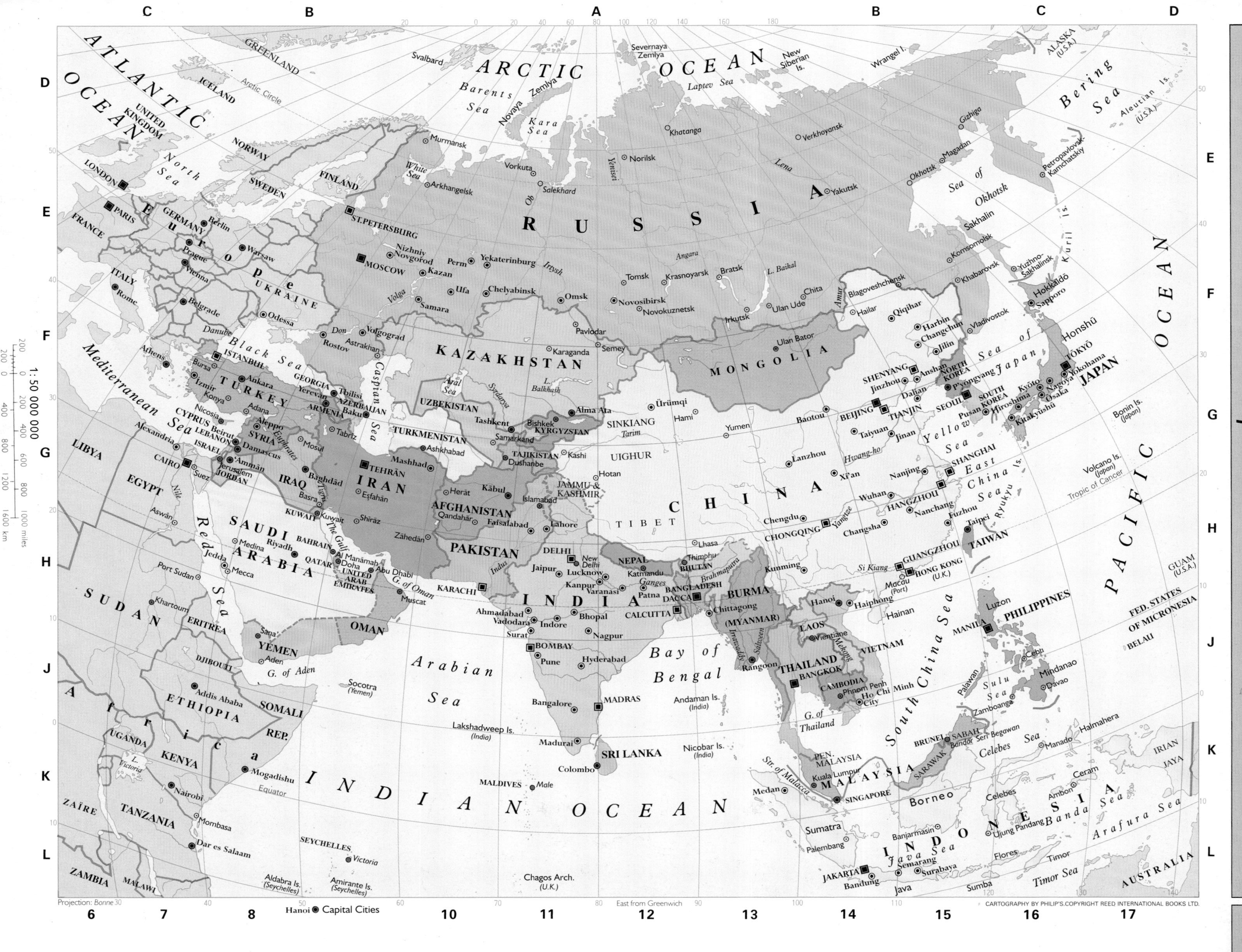

1:50 000 000

200 0 200 400 600 800 1000 miles

200 0 400 800 1200 1600 km

Hanoi ● Capital Cities

Projection: Bonne

CARTOGRAPHY BY PHILIP'S. COPYRIGHT REED INTERNATIONAL BOOKS LTD.

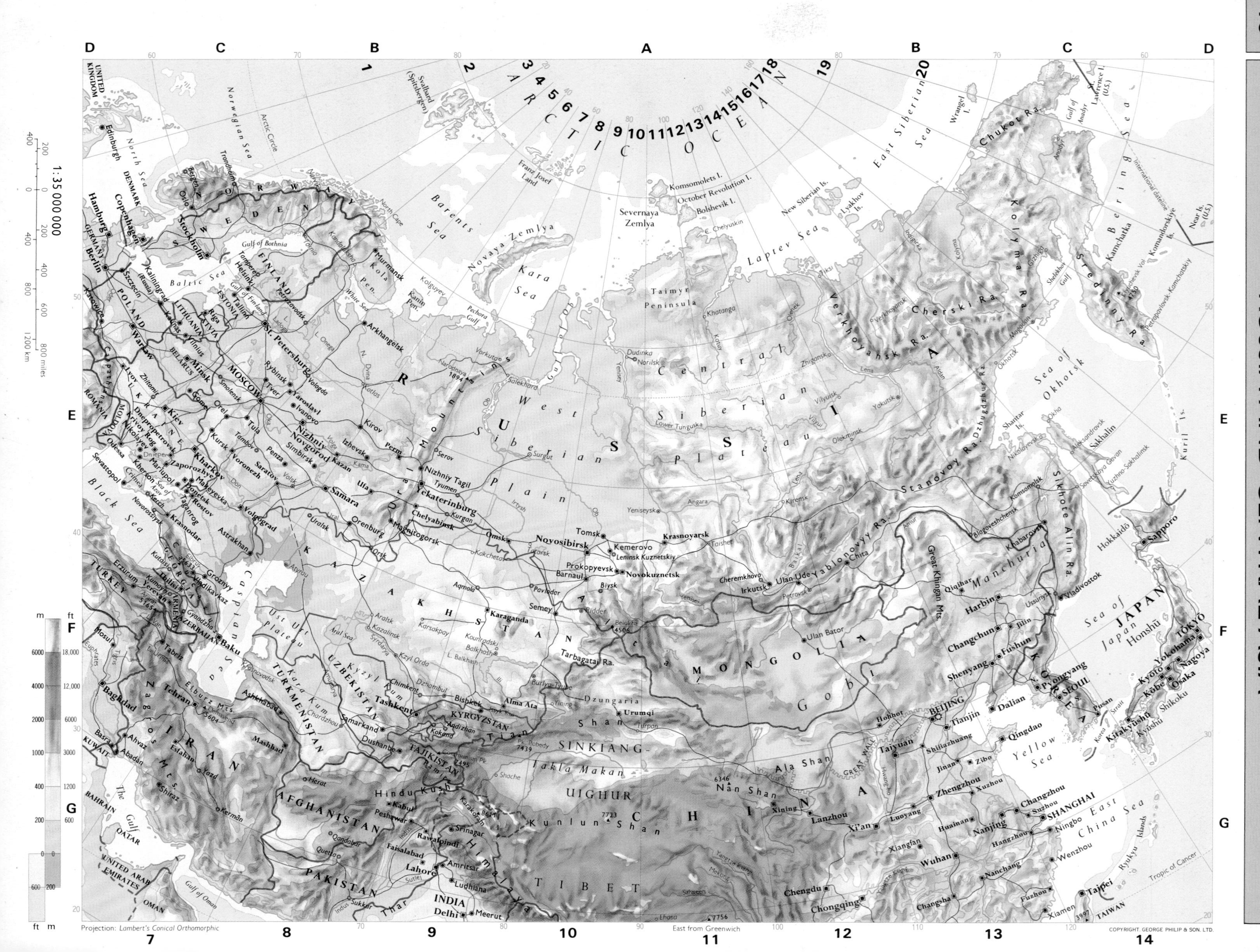

1:35 000 000

Projection: Lambert's Conical Orthomorphic

COPYRIGHT GEORGE PHILIP & SON LTD

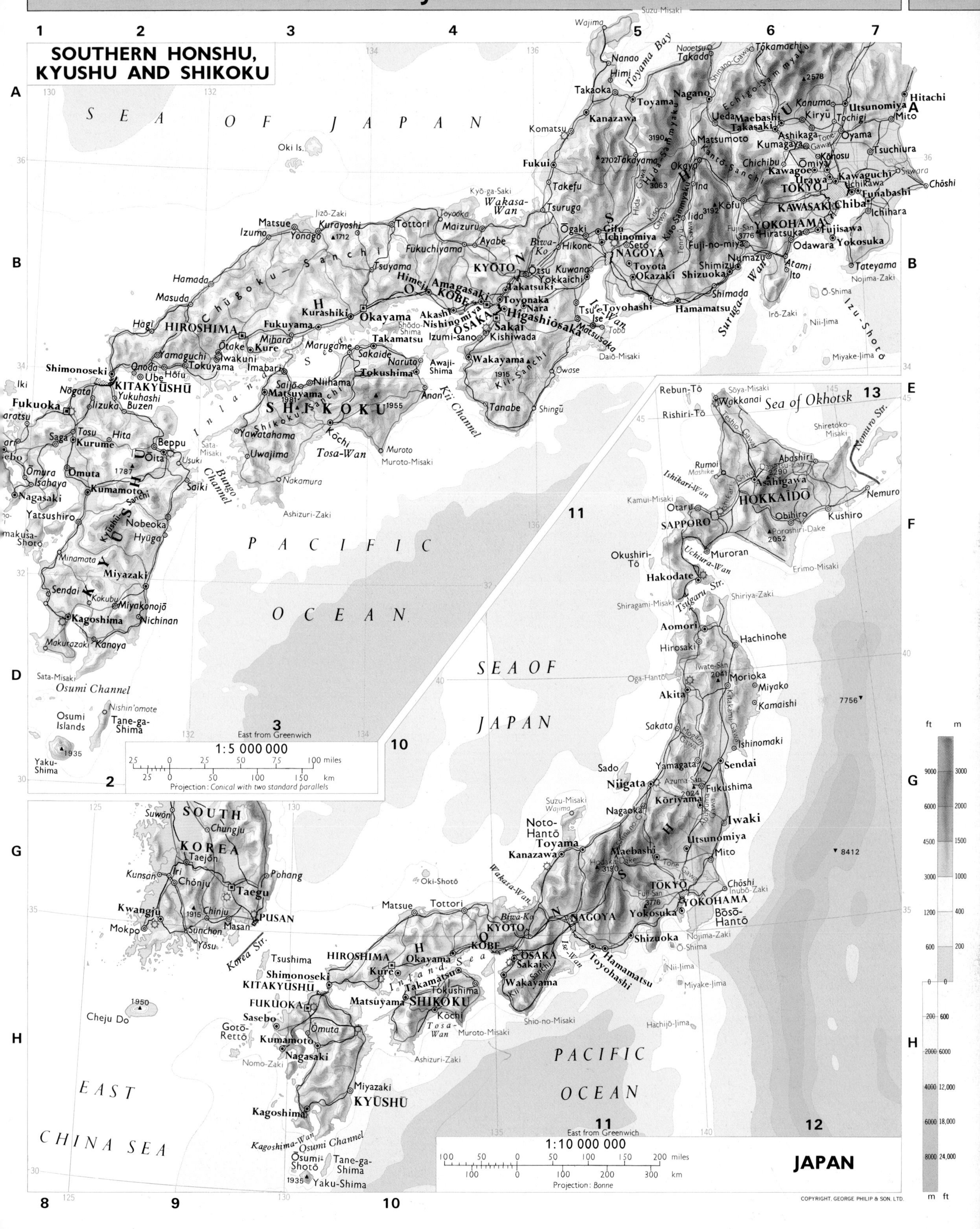
SOUTHERN HONSHU, KYUSHU AND SHIKOKU
SEA OF JAPAN
PACIFIC OCEAN
Inland Sea
Kii Channel
Bungo Channel
Osumi Channel
Tosa-Wan
SHIKOKU
KYUSHU
HONSHU
TOKYO
YOKOHAMA
KAWASAKI
NAGOYA
KYOTO
OSAKA
KOBE
HIROSHIMA
KITAKYUSHU
Fukuoka
Nagasaki
Kagoshima
1:5 000 000
Projection: Conical with two standard parallels
East from Greenwich
SEA OF JAPAN
PACIFIC OCEAN
EAST CHINA SEA
Sea of Okhotsk
HOKKAIDO
SAPPORO
SOUTH KOREA
PUSAN
Korea Str.
Tsugaru Str.
1:10 000 000
Projection: Bonne
JAPAN

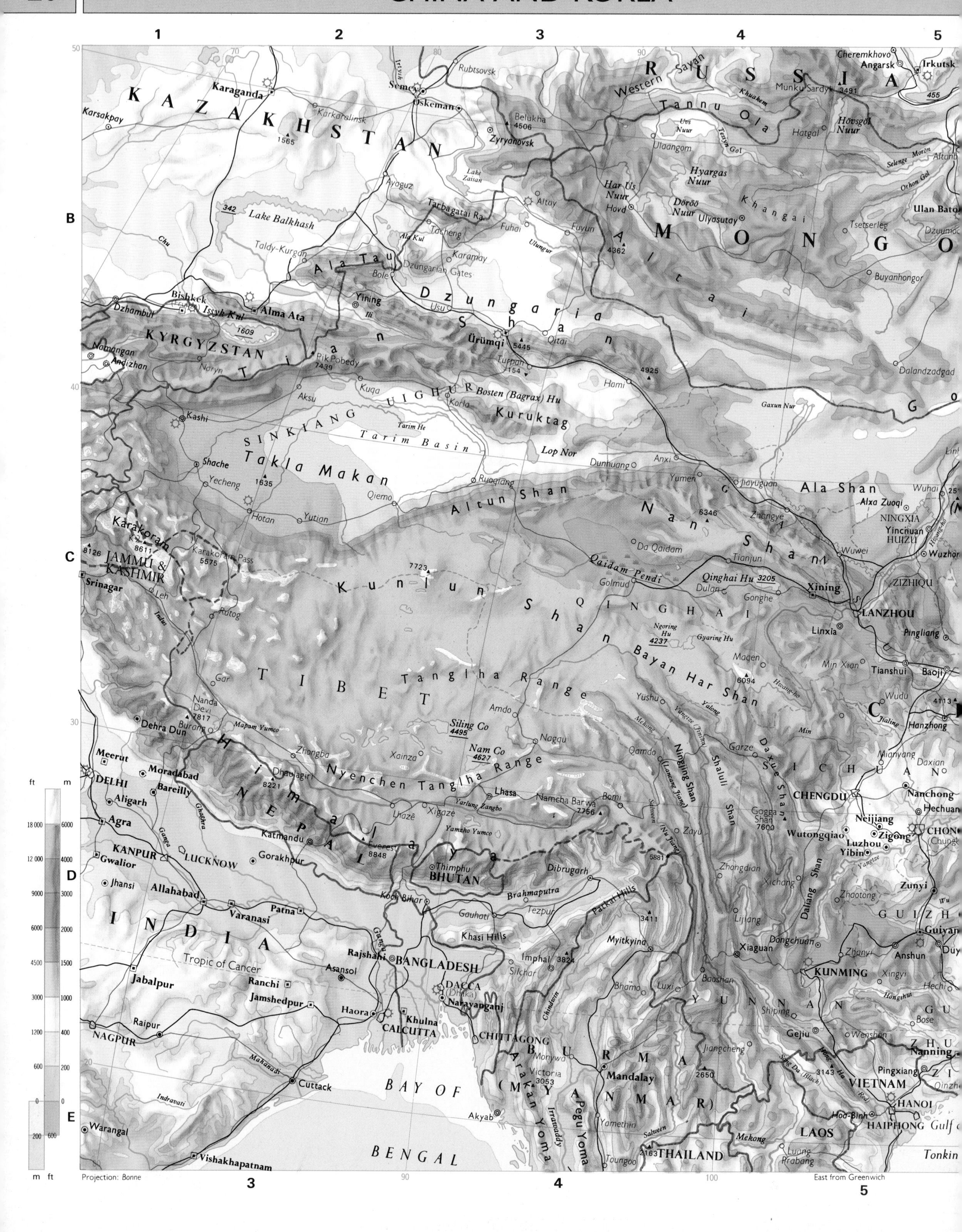
KAZAKHSTAN
Karaganda
Karsakpay
Karkaralinsk
Semey
Oskeman
Rubtsovsk
Zyryanovsk
Belukha 4506
Lake Zaisan
Ayaguz
Lake Balkhash
Chu
Taldy-Kurgan
Tarbagatai Ra.
Tacheng
Ala Kul
Karamay
Ala Tau
Dzungarian Gates
Bole
Bishkek
Dzhambul
Issyk Kul
Alma Ata
KYRGYZSTAN
Namangan
Andizhan
Naryn
Yining
Ili
Usu
Dzungaria
Ürümqi
Qitai
Tian Shan
Pik Pobedy 7439
Turpan
Hami
Aksu
Kuqa
Korla
Bosten (Bagrax) Hu
UIGHUR
SINKIANG
Kashi
Kuruktag
Tarim He
Tarim Basin
Lop Nor
Shache
Takla Makan
Yecheng
Hotan
Yutian
Qiemo
Ruoqiang
Altun Shan
Dunhuang
Anxi
Yumen
Jiayuguan
Ala Shan
Nan Shan
Zhangye
Da Qaidam
Qaidam Pendi
Golmud
Tianjun
Qinghai Hu 3205
Dulan
Xining
Gonghe
Karakoram
Karakoram Pass
JAMMU & KASHMIR
Srinagar
Leh
Rutog
Indus
Kunlun Shan
QINGHAI
Ngoring Hu 4237
Gyaring Hu
Bayan Har Shan
Maqen
TIBET
Tanglha Range
Gar
Amdo
Yushu
Nanda Devi 7817
Mapam Yumco
Siling Co 4495
Nagqu
Nam Co 4627
Zhongba
Xainza
Nyenchen Tanglha Range
Dhaulagiri 8221
Lhasa
Namcha Barwa 7766
Bomi
Qamdo
Lhazê
Xigaze
Yarlung Zangbo
Yamzho Yumco
Katmandu
Everest 8848
NEPAL
Himalaya
Thimphu
BHUTAN
Dibrugarh
Brahmaputra
Tezpur
Gauhati
Khasi Hills
Koch Bihar
Dehra Dun
Meerut
DELHI
Moradabad
Bareilly
Aligarh
Agra
KANPUR
LUCKNOW
Gorakhpur
Gwalior
Jhansi
Allahabad
Varanasi
Patna
INDIA
Tropic of Cancer
Jabalpur
Ranchi
Jamshedpur
Asansol
Rajshahi
BANGLADESH
DACCA (Dhaka)
Narayanganj
Haora
Khulna
CALCUTTA
CHITTAGONG
Raipur
NAGPUR
Mahanadi
Cuttack
Indravati
Warangal
Vishakhapatnam
BAY OF BENGAL
Akyab
Imphal
Silchar
Myitkyina
Bhamo
Chindwin
Monywa
Mandalay
BURMA (MYANMAR)
Arakan Yoma
Pegu Yoma
Irrawaddy
Yamethin
Toungoo
Salween
THAILAND
LAOS
Mekong
Luang Prabang
VIETNAM
HANOI
HAIPHONG
Gulf of Tonkin
Hoa Binh
RUSSIA
Western Sayan
Tannu Ola
Uvs Nuur
Ulaangom
Munku Sardyk 3491
Irkutsk
Angarsk
Cheremkhovo
Hövsgöl Nuur
Hatgal
Selenge Mörön
Orhon Gol
Ulan Bator
Hyargas Nuur
Har Us Nuur
Hovd
Döröö Nuur
Uliastay
Khangai
MONGOLIA
Altai
Tsetserleg
Buyanhongor
Dalandzadgad
Gaxun Nur
Gobi
Altay
Fuhai
Fuyun
Ulungur
Wuhai
Alxa Zuoqi
NINGXIA HUIZU ZIZHIQU
Yinchuan
Wuwei
Wuzhong
LANZHOU
Linxia
Pingliang
Tianshui
Baoji
Min Xian
Wudu
Hanzhong
Jialing
Mianyang
Daxian
Nanchong
SICHUAN
CHENGDU
Neijiang
Zigong
Luzhou
Yibin
Wutongqiao
Gongga Shan 7600
Daxue Shan
Garze
Shaluli Shan
Ningjing Shan
Zayü
Zhongdian
Xichang
Lijiang
Daliang Shan
Zhaotong
Zunyi
GUIZHOU
Guiyang
Anshun
Dongchuan
Zhanyi
KUNMING
Xiaguan
Baoshan
Luxi
YUNNAN
Shiping
Gejiu
Jiangcheng
Wenshan
Nanning
Pingxiang
Hechi
Hongshui
Xingyi
Projection: Bonne
East from Greenwich

7

6

8

9

120

130

140

50

Lake Baykal

Ilan Ude

Yablonovyy Range

Chita

Nerchinsk

Borzya

Manzhouli

Hulun Nur

Hailar

Chita

Svobodny

Chegdomyn

Aleksandrovsk

L. Bolon

Komsomolsk

C. Terpeniya

Poronoysk

Sakhalin

Yuzhno-Sakhalinsk

Blagoveshchensk

Anhui

Orogen Zizhiqi

Khabarovsk

Bikin

Amur

Buir Nur

Chaybalsan

Kerulen

Nenjiang

Bei'an

Yichun

Hegang

Jiamusi

Shuangyashan

Mishan

Lake Khanka

B

La Perouse Str.

Wakkanai

Amur

Little Khingan Mts

Saynshand

Abagnar Qi

Manchuria

Qiqihar

Anda

Suihua

Songhua

HARBIN

Mudanjiang

Jixi

Ussuriysk

Asahigawa

2290

Hokkaido

Otaru

SAPPORO

Kushiro

Dzamin Uud

Erenhot

Horqin Youyi Qianqi

Tao'an

Jilin

Butha Qi

Sikhote Alin Ra.

C. Erimo

Hakodate

Aomori

Hachinohe

Morioka

INNER MONGOLIA

1949

CHANGCHUN

Shuangliao

Tongliao

Siping

Liaoyuan

Songhua Lake

Yanji

2744

Chongjin

Vladivostok

Nakhodka

Tsugaru Strait

Akita

40

Sado

Sendai

Hohhot

Jining

Zhangjiakou

Xuanhua

Chifeng

Fuxin

FUSHUN

SHENYANG

Benxi

Tonghua

NORTH

SEA OF

JAPAN

Niigata

Koriyama

Utsunomiya

Baotou

Datong

3058

HEBEI

Liaoyang

Chaoyang

Chengde

Jinzhou

ANSHAN

Yingkou

Dandong

Yalu

KOREA

Hungnam

Wonsan

Kanazawa

Toyama

TOKYO

KAWASAKI

YOKOHAMA

C

GREAT WALL

TAIYUAN

SHANXI

BEIJING (Peking)

Baoding

Tangshan

Qinghuangdao

G. of Liaodong

Liaodong Pen.

Korea Bay

PYONGYANG

Haeju

Kaesong

SEOUL

Fuji 3776

NAGOYA

KYOTO

OSAKA

Sakai

Shizuoka

Yokosuka

Hamamatsu

Fenyang

Yuci

Shijiazhuang

TIANJIN (Tientsin)

Cangzhou

DALIAN

INCHON

SOUTH

Okayama

KOBE

Wakayama

Yangquan

Dezhou

G. of Chihli (Bo Hai)

Yantai

Weihai

Taejon

TAEGU

Hiroshima

HONSHU

JAPAN

Handan

Xinxiang

JINAN

Weifang

Ye Xian

YELLOW

Masan

PUSAN

Shimonoseki

Shikoku

Kochi

Matsuyama

Changzhi

Anyang

Zibo

Tai'an

SHANDONG

Jining

QINGDAO

SEA

Kwangju

1915

KITAKYUSHU

FUKUOKA

Sasebo

Nagasaki

Kumamoto

Kyushu

Tongchuan

Sanmenxia

Luoyang

Kaifeng

Shangqiu

Xuzhou

Lianyungang

Qingjiang

Cheju Do

1950

Ko

Kagoshima

XI'AN (Sian)

ZHENGZHOU

HENAN

Pingdingshan

Nanyang

Shangshui

Bengbu

Hongze Hu

JIANGSU

Zhumadian

Huainan

NANJING (Nanking)

Zhenjiang

Changzhou

Wuxi

Suzhou

Nantong

Tanega

Ankang

Han Shui

Xiangfan

Dabie Shan

Hefei

ANHUI

Wuhu

Tongling

SHANGHAI

HUBEI

WUHAN

Anqing

Hangzhou

Hangzhou Wan

Yichang

Shashi

Huangshi

Yangtze

Tunxi

Shaoxing

Ningbo

EAST CHINA

Amami-o-Shima

D

Changde

Dongting L.

Yiyang

Nanchang

Jingdezhen

ZHEJIANG

Jinhua

SEA

Da Shan

Poyang L.

Shangrao

Wenzhou

Ryukyu Islands

HUNAN

Changsha

Xiangtan

JIANGXI

Wuyi Shan

2120

PACIFIC

Shaoyang

Zhuzhou

Jian

Nanping

Naha

Okinawa

Hengyang

Min

Sanming

Fuzhou

Nan Ling

Ganzhou

FUJIAN

Sakishima Gunto

Tropic of Cancer

Guilin

Shaoguan

Zhangzhou

Quanzhou

Chilung

OCEAN

GUANGXI

Wuzhou

GUANGDONG

Mei Xian

Xiamen (Amoy)

Chiai

Chao'an

Yu Shan

3997

TAIPEI

Taichung

TAIWAN

Formosa Strait

Jiangmen

Foshan

GUANGZHOU (Canton)

Shantou

Tainan

KAOHSIUNG

Maoming

HONG KONG (U.K.)

Macau (Port.)

Batan Is.

E

Zhanjiang

SOUTH CHINA

Haikou

HAINAN

1879

SEA

Babuyan Is.

110

120

130

6

7

8

COPYRIGHT GEORGE PHILIP & SON LTD

1:15 000 000

100   0   100   200   300   400 miles

100   0   100   200   300   400   500   600 km

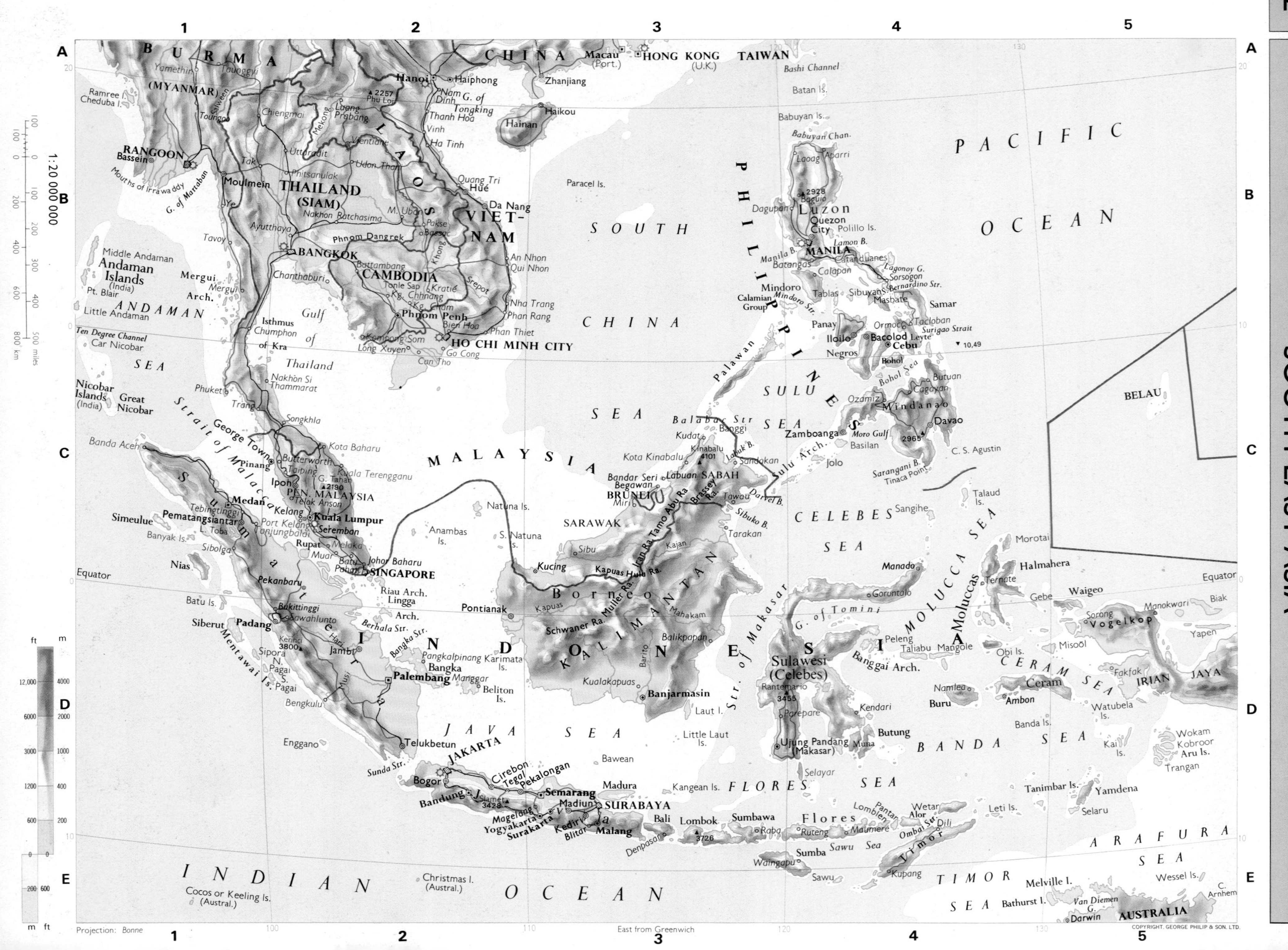
PACIFIC OCEAN
SOUTH CHINA SEA
PHILIPPINES
SULU SEA
CELEBES SEA
MOLUCCA SEA
CERAM SEA
BANDA SEA
FLORES SEA
JAVA SEA
ARAFURA SEA
TIMOR SEA
INDIAN OCEAN
ANDAMAN SEA
Gulf of Thailand
Strait of Malacca
BURMA (MYANMAR)
THAILAND (SIAM)
LAOS
VIET-NAM
CAMBODIA
MALAYSIA
INDONESIA
Borneo
KALIMANTAN
Sumatera
Jawa
Sulawesi (Celebes)
IRIAN JAYA
CHINA
HONG KONG (U.K.)
Macau (Port.)
TAIWAN
BELAU
AUSTRALIA
RANGOON
BANGKOK
Hanoi
HO CHI MINH CITY
Phnom Penh
Kuala Lumpur
SINGAPORE
JAKARTA
SURABAYA
MANILA
Cebu
Davao
Zamboanga
BRUNEI
SARAWAK
SABAH
Banjarmasin
Ujung Pandang (Makasar)
Palembang
Medan
Padang
Ambon
Darwin
Christmas I. (Austral.)
Cocos or Keeling Is. (Austral.)
Andaman Islands (India)
Nicobar Islands (India)
Equator
1:20 000 000
miles
km
East from Greenwich
Projection: Bonne
COPYRIGHT GEORGE PHILIP & SON, LTD.

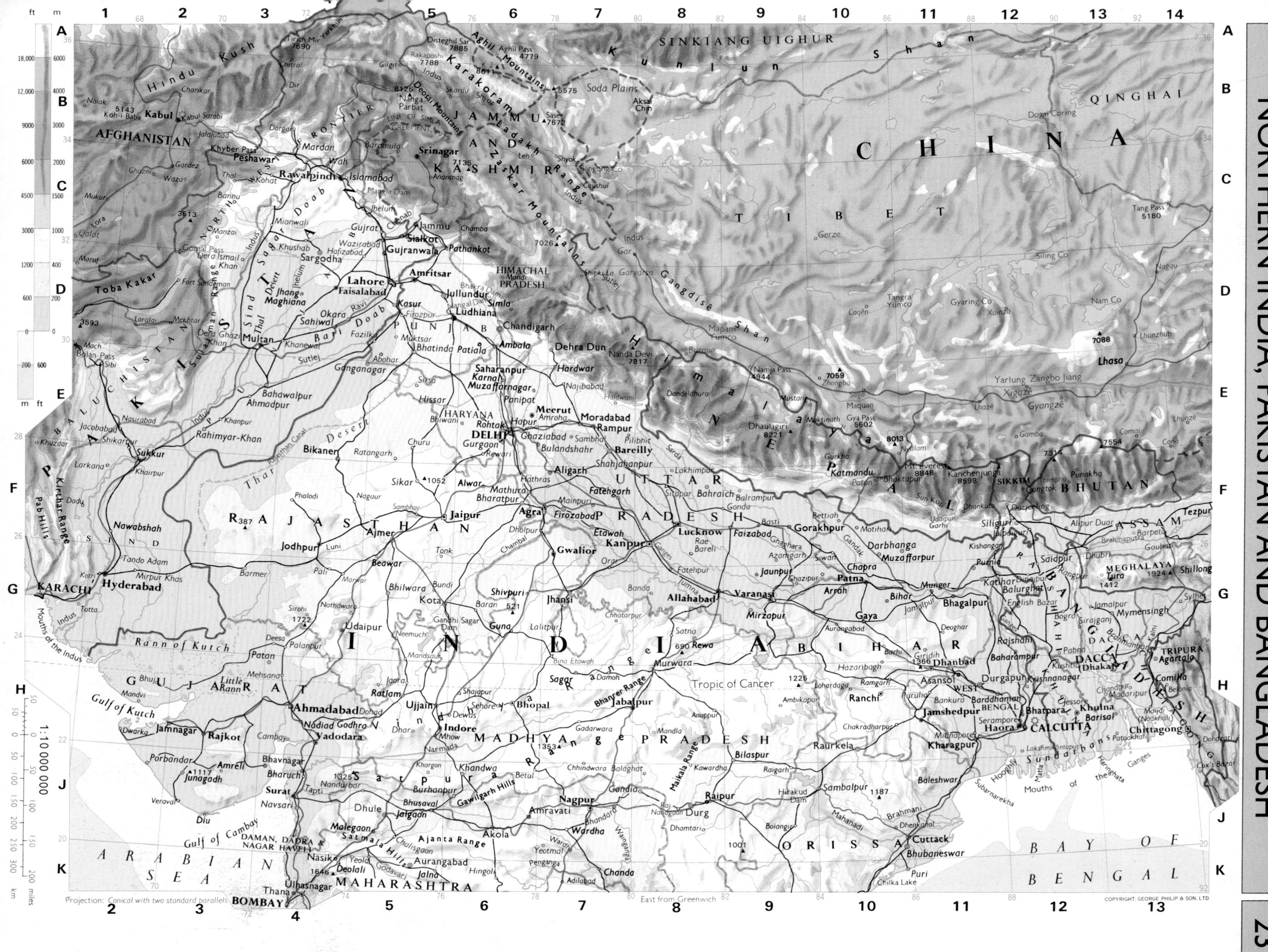

Projection: Conical with two standard parallels

1:10 000 000

COPYRIGHT GEORGE PHILIP & SON, LTD.

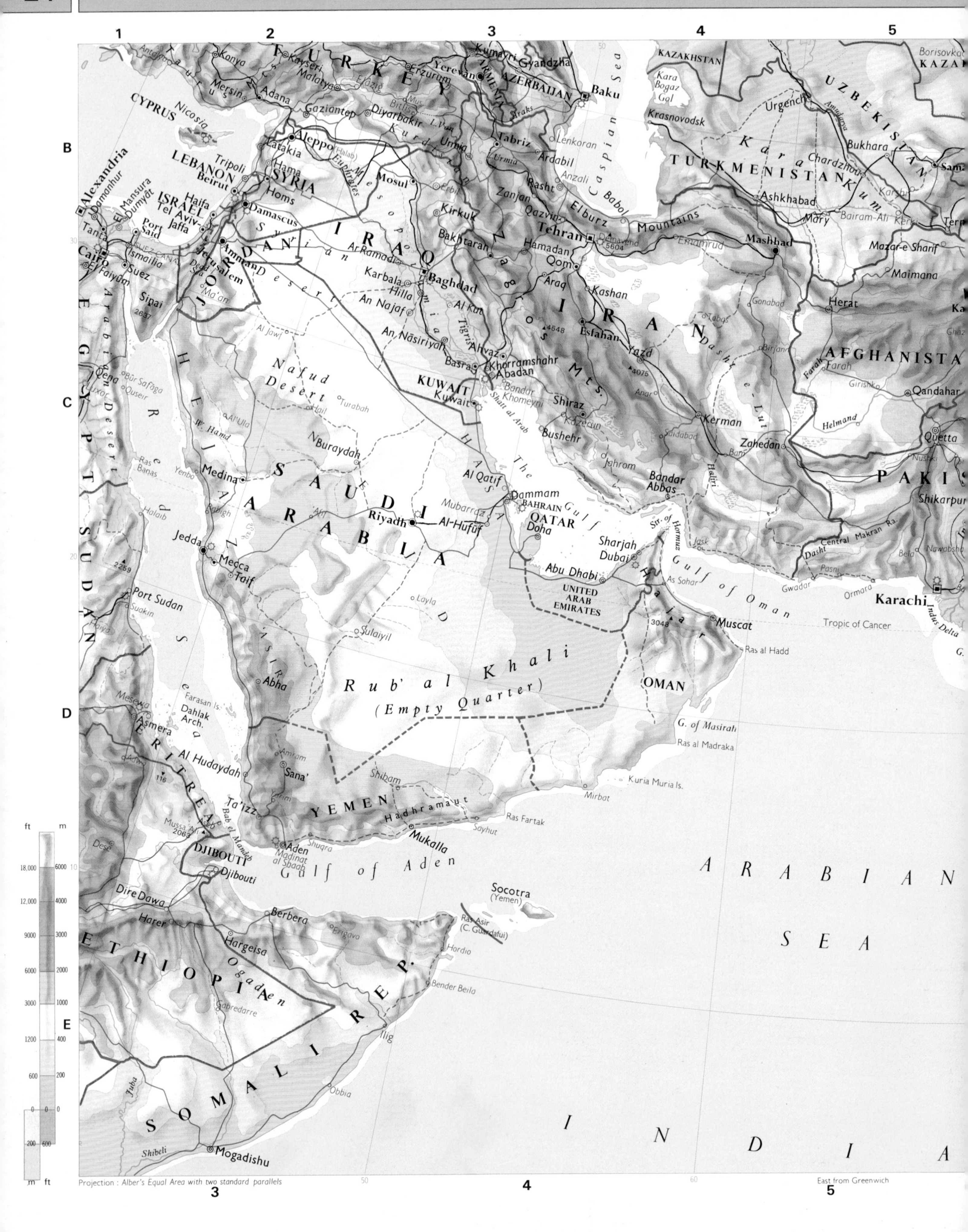

ft | m
18,000 | 6000 10
12,000 | 4000
9000 | 3000
6000 | 2000
3000 | 1000
1200 | 400 E
600 | 200
0 | 0
200 | 600
m | ft

Projection : Alber's Equal Area with two standard parallels

East from Greenwich

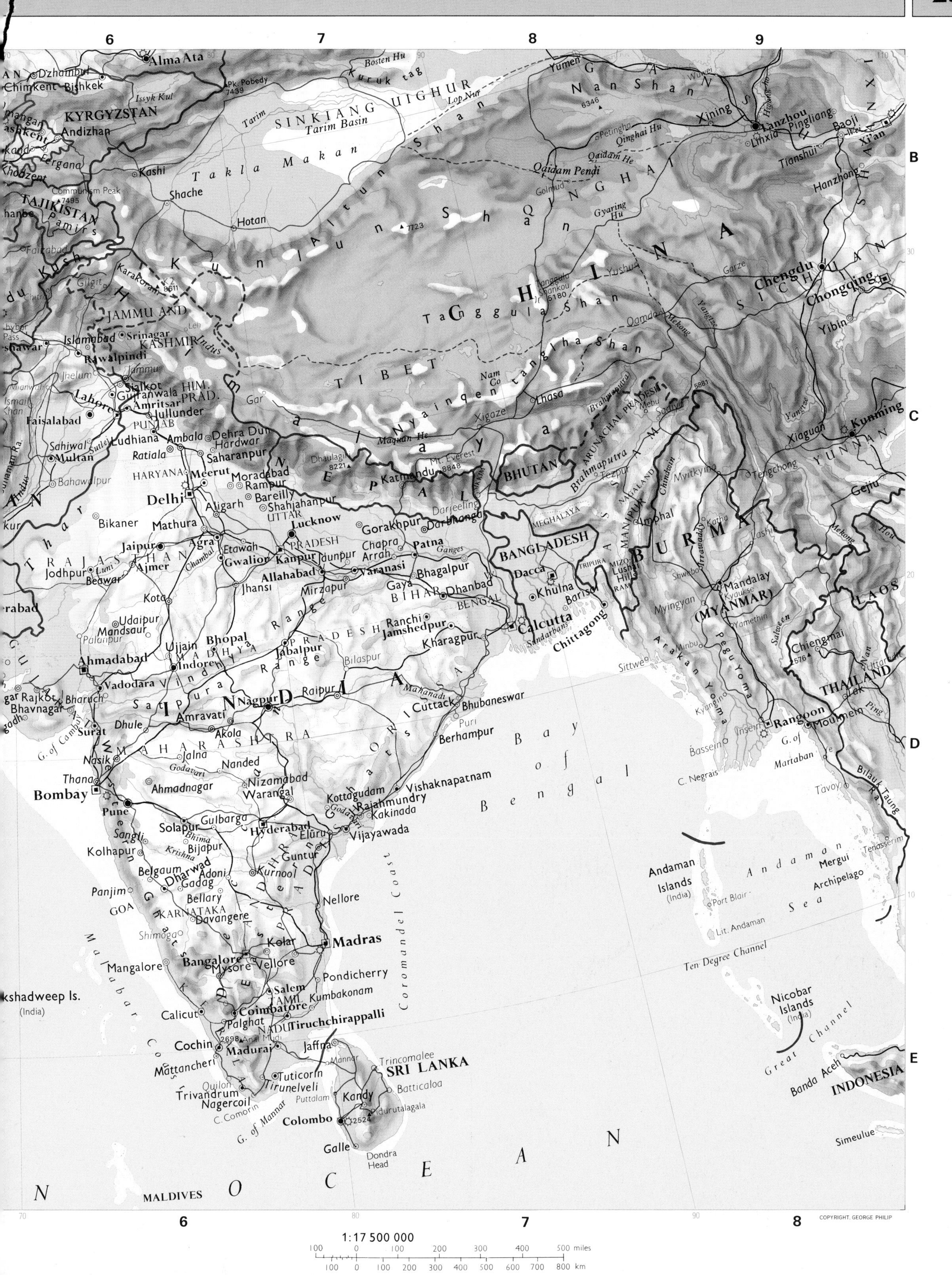

1:17 500 000

100   0   100   200   300   400   500 miles

100   0   100   200   300   400   500   600   700   800 km

EUROPE

British Isles

Carpathians

B. of Biscay
Mont Blanc 4807
Alps
Pyrénées
Apennines
Dinaric Alps
Adriatic Sea
Elbrus 5633
Caucasus
Caspian Sea
Aral Sea

NORTH ATLANTIC OCEAN

Azores

Iberian Peninsula
Corsica
Sardinia
Sicily
Black Sea
Anatolia
Asia

Madeira
6578
Str. of Gibraltar
C. Bon
Malta
5121
Crete
Cyprus
Levant
Mesopotamia
Tigris
Euphrates
Syrian Desert
The Gulf

Canary Is.
Tenerife
Middle Atlas 4165
High Atlas
Toubkal
High Plateaux
Saharan Atlas
Mediterranean Sea
G. of Gabès
Chott Djerid
G. of Sidra
Tripolitania
Cyrenaica
Siwa Oasis
Mt. Sinai 4642
Arabian Desert
Arabia
Hejaz
Red Sea

Anti Atlas
Ras Nouâdhibou

S a h a r a
Tasili Plateau
Hoggar
Tropic of Cancer
El Djouf
Adrar
Aïr
Bilma
Tibesti
Al Kufrah
El Khârga
Libyan Desert
Egypt
Nile
Nubia
Nubian Desert

Cape Verde Is.
C. Vert
Senegal
Senegambia
Gambia
Fouta Djalon
Niger
Volta
S a h e l
G u i n e a
Niger
Benue
L. Chad
Bahr el Ghazal
Wadai
Chari
Darfûr
Kordofân
Athara
White Nile
Blue Nile
Ras Dashen 4620
116
L. Tana
Barïm
Bab el Mandeb
G. of Aden
Ras Asir
Soco

Grain Coast
Ivory Coast
C. Palmas
Gold Coast
Slave Coast
Bight of Benin
Mt. Cameroon 4070
Bioko
Bight of Bonny
I. de Principe
São Tomé
Adamawa Highlands
Dar Banda
Ubangi
Uele
Congo
Zaïre
Bahr el Ghazâl
Bahr el Jebel
Ethiopian Highlands
L. Turkana
Shaballe
Juba
Somali Peninsula

Equator
Gulf of Guinea
C. Lopez
Annobón
Ogooué
Basin
Zaïre
Kasai
Sankuru
Lualaba
Chutes Boyoma
L. Albert
Ruwenzori 5109
Mt. Elgon 4321
L. Edward
L. Kivu
L. Victoria
Mt. Kenya 5199
Kilimanjaro 5895
Tana
Pemba I.
INDIAN OCEAN
Seychelle

Ascension I.
SOUTH ATLANTIC OCEAN
St. Helena
Cuanza
Cuango
Kasai
L. Tanganyika
Luena
L. Mweru
Rungwe 2961
Shaba
Bängweulu Swamp
L. Nyasa (L. Malawi)
Aldabra Is.
C. Delgado
Comoros

Bié Plateau
Luapula
Cuando
Cubango
Cunene
C. Fria
Zambezi
Zumbezi
Shire
Victoria Falls
Mozambique Channel
Madagascar
2643
Maurit
Réunion

Tropic of Capricorn
Walvis Bay
Namib Desert
Okavango Swamps
Kalahari
Limpopo
Delagoa B.

Orange
Vaal
High Veld
Compass Mt. 2505
3482
Drakensberg
Nieveldberge
Great Karoo
Swartberge
Algoa B.
C. of Good Hope
C. Agulhas

Tristan da Cunha

ft m
12000 4000
9000 3000
6000 2000
3000 1000
1500 500
600 200
0 0
200 600
1000 3000
2000 6000
4000 12000
m ft

1 : 42 000 000

200 0 200 400 600 800 1000 1200 miles
200 0 200 400 600 800 1000 1200 1400 1600 1800 km

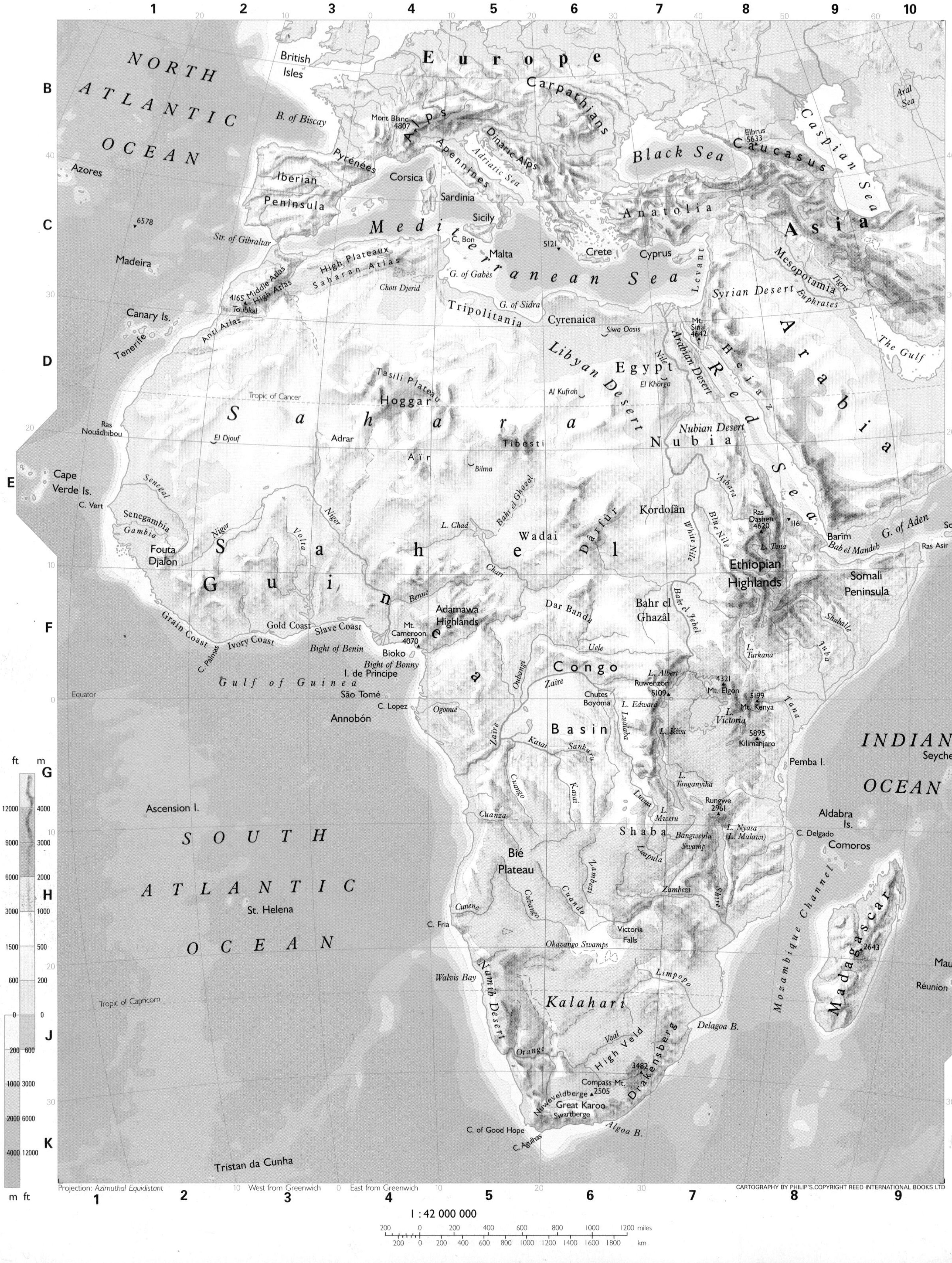

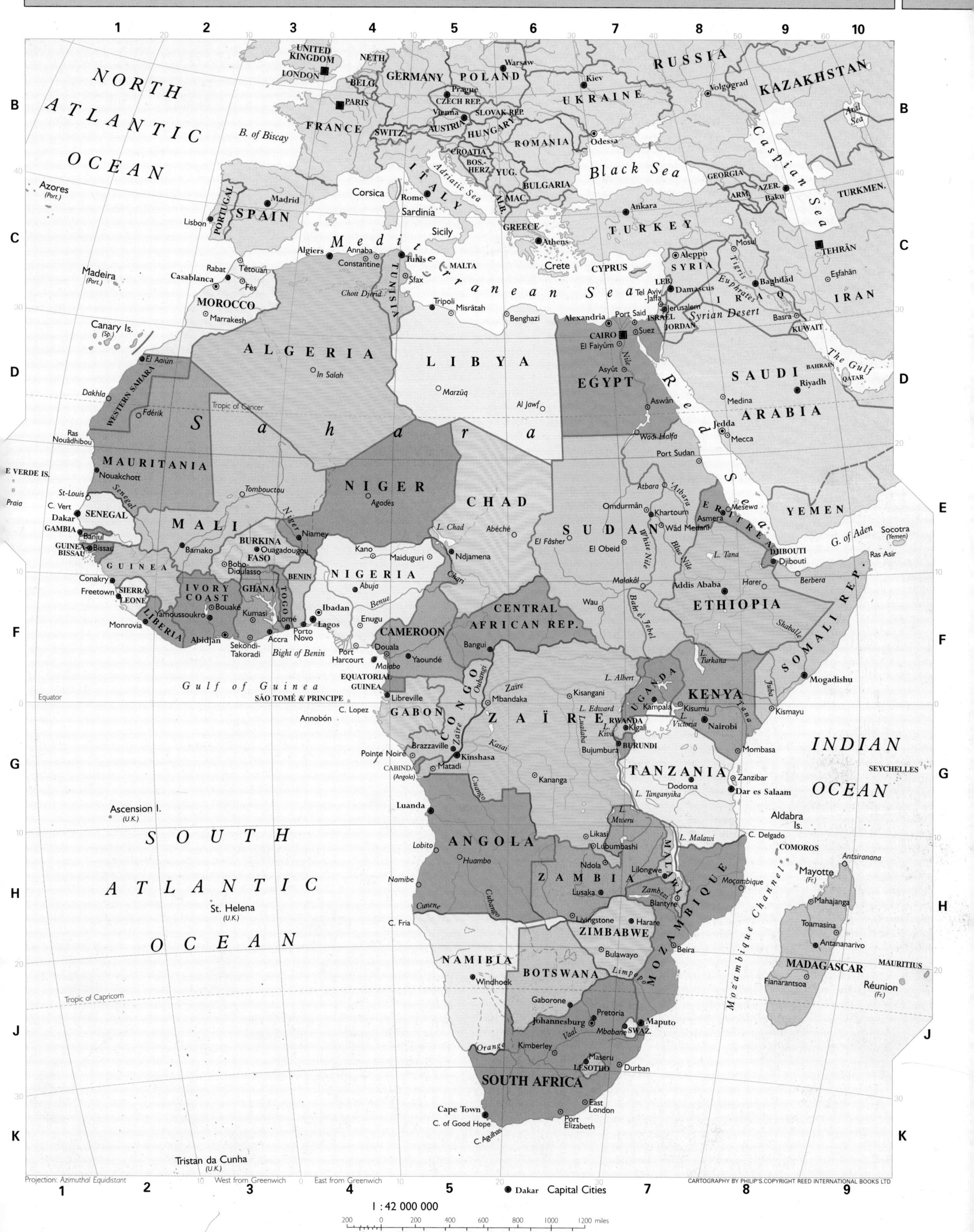

AFRICA : *political*

Capital Cities ● Dakar

1 : 42 000 000

200   0   200   400   600   800   1000   1200 miles

200   0   200   400   600   800   1000   1200   1400   1600   1800 km

Projection: Azimuthal Equidistant

West from Greenwich   East from Greenwich

CARTOGRAPHY BY PHILIP'S. COPYRIGHT REED INTERNATIONAL BOOKS LTD

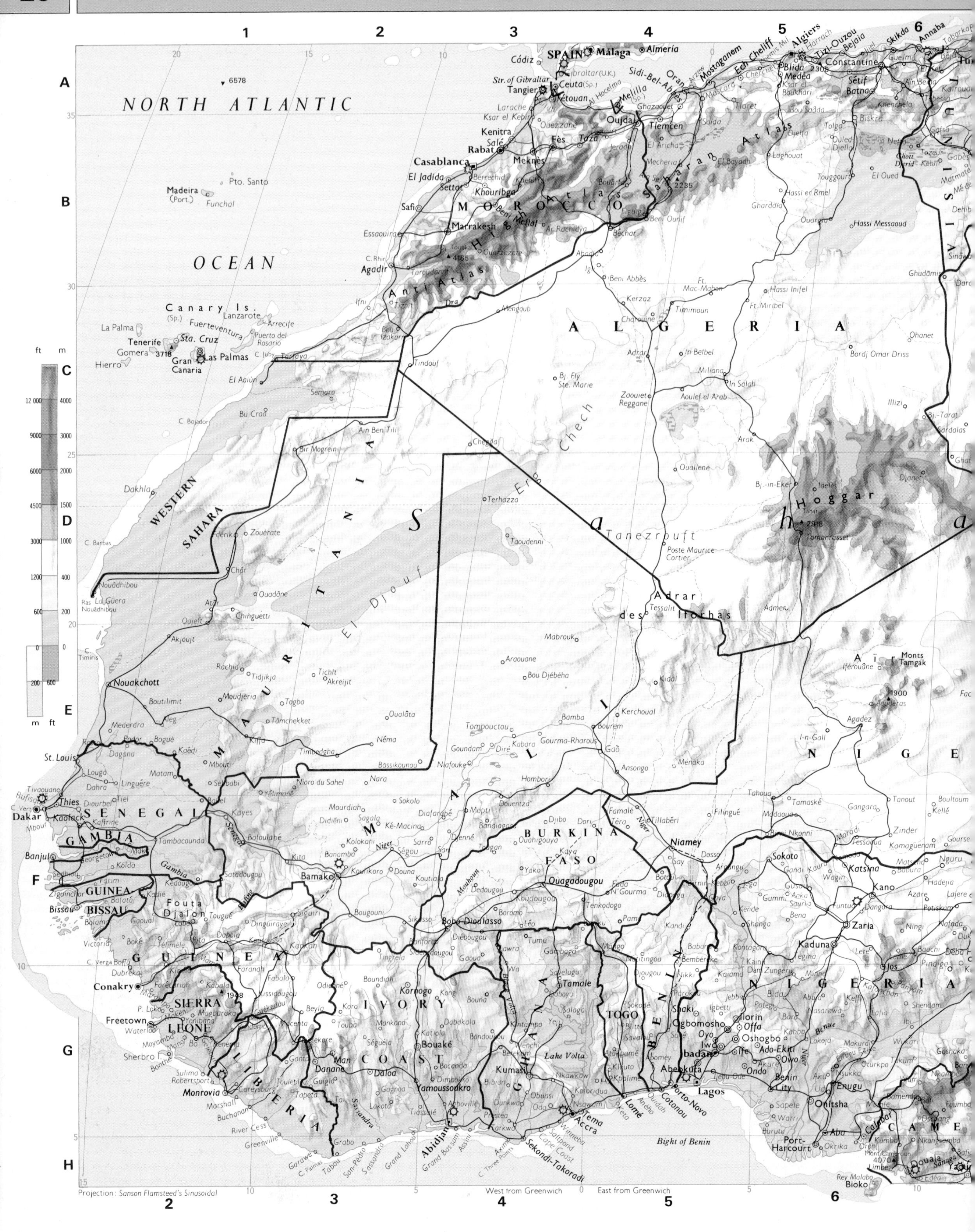

Projection: Sanson Flamsteed's Sinusoidal

West from Greenwich   East from Greenwich

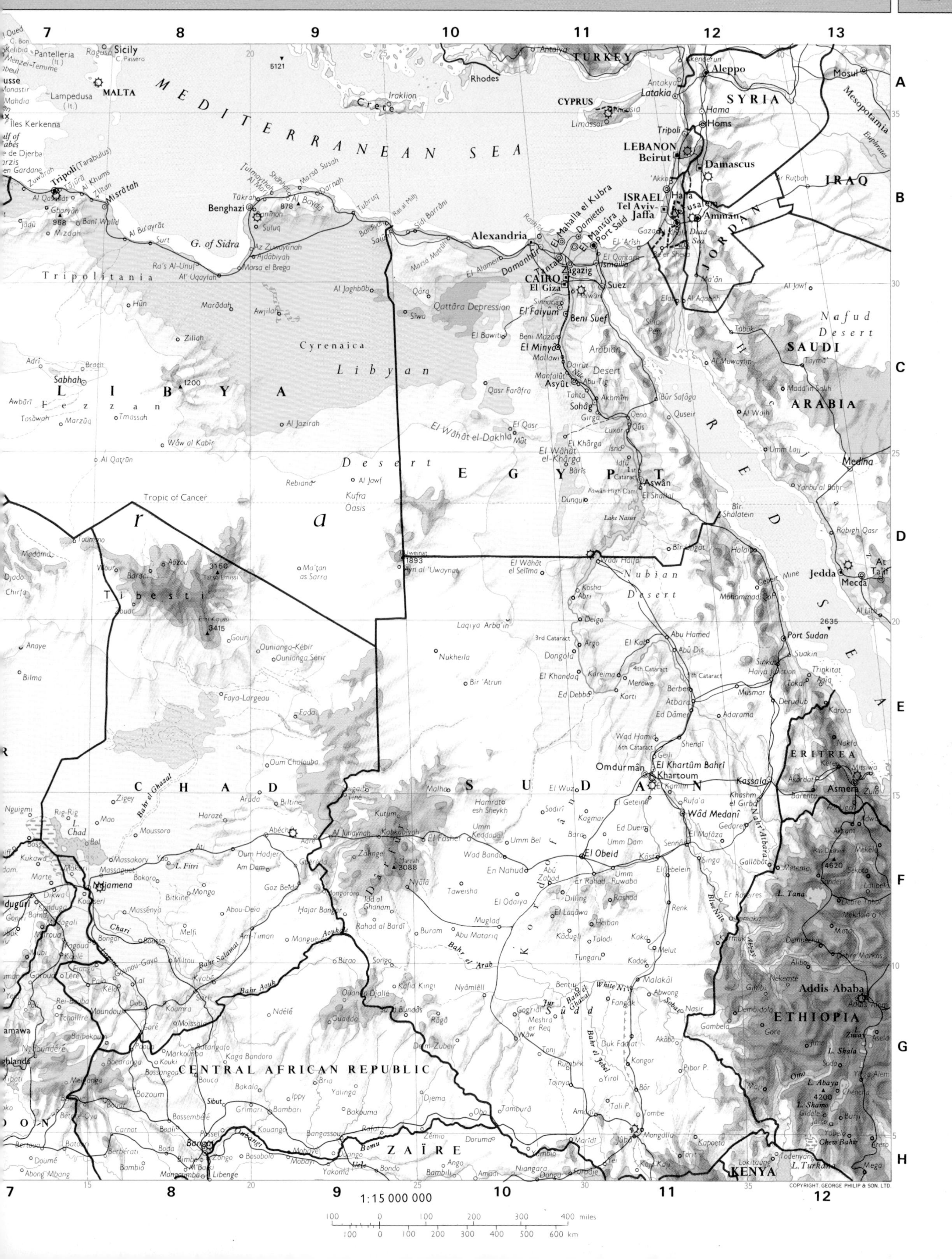
MEDITERRANEAN SEA
TURKEY
SYRIA
LEBANON
ISRAEL
JORDAN
IRAQ
CYPRUS
MALTA
Sicily
Pantelleria
Lampedusa
Crete
Rhodes
Iraklion
Aleppo
Latakia
Hama
Homs
Tripoli
Beirut
Damascus
Tel Aviv-Jaffa
Ammān
Dead Sea
Mosul
Mesopotamia
Euphrates
LIBYA
Tripolitania
Cyrenaica
Fezzan
Tripoli (Tarabulus)
Misrātah
Benghazi
G. of Sidra
Sabhah
Tibesti
Emi Koussi
3415
3150
EGYPT
Alexandria
Port Said
CAIRO
El Giza
Suez
Zagazig
Tanta
El Faiyûm
Beni Suef
El Minya
Asyût
Sohâg
Luxor
Aswân
Lake Nasser
Qattâra Depression
Siwa
Libyan Desert
Arabian Desert
Sinai Pen.
Kufra Oasis
Tropic of Cancer
Nubian Desert
Wadi Halfa
SAUDI ARABIA
Nafud Desert
Medina
Jedda
Mecca
Tabūk
RED SEA
SUDAN
Khartoum
Omdurmân
El Khartûm Bahrî
Port Sudan
Kassala
Wad Medanî
El Obeid
El Fasher
Atbara
Berber
Dongola
Kordofan
Darfur
Sudd
White Nile
Blue Nile
Bahr el Ghazal
Bahr el Jebel
Juba
Malakâl
ERITREA
Asmera
ETHIOPIA
Addis Ababa
L. Tana
L. Abaya
L. Shamo
L. Turkana
KENYA
CHAD
L. Chad
Ndjamena
Abéché
Faya-Largeau
CENTRAL AFRICAN REPUBLIC
Bangui
ZAÏRE
1:15 000 000
100 0 100 200 300 400 miles
100 0 100 200 300 400 500 600 km
COPYRIGHT, GEORGE PHILIP & SON, LTD.

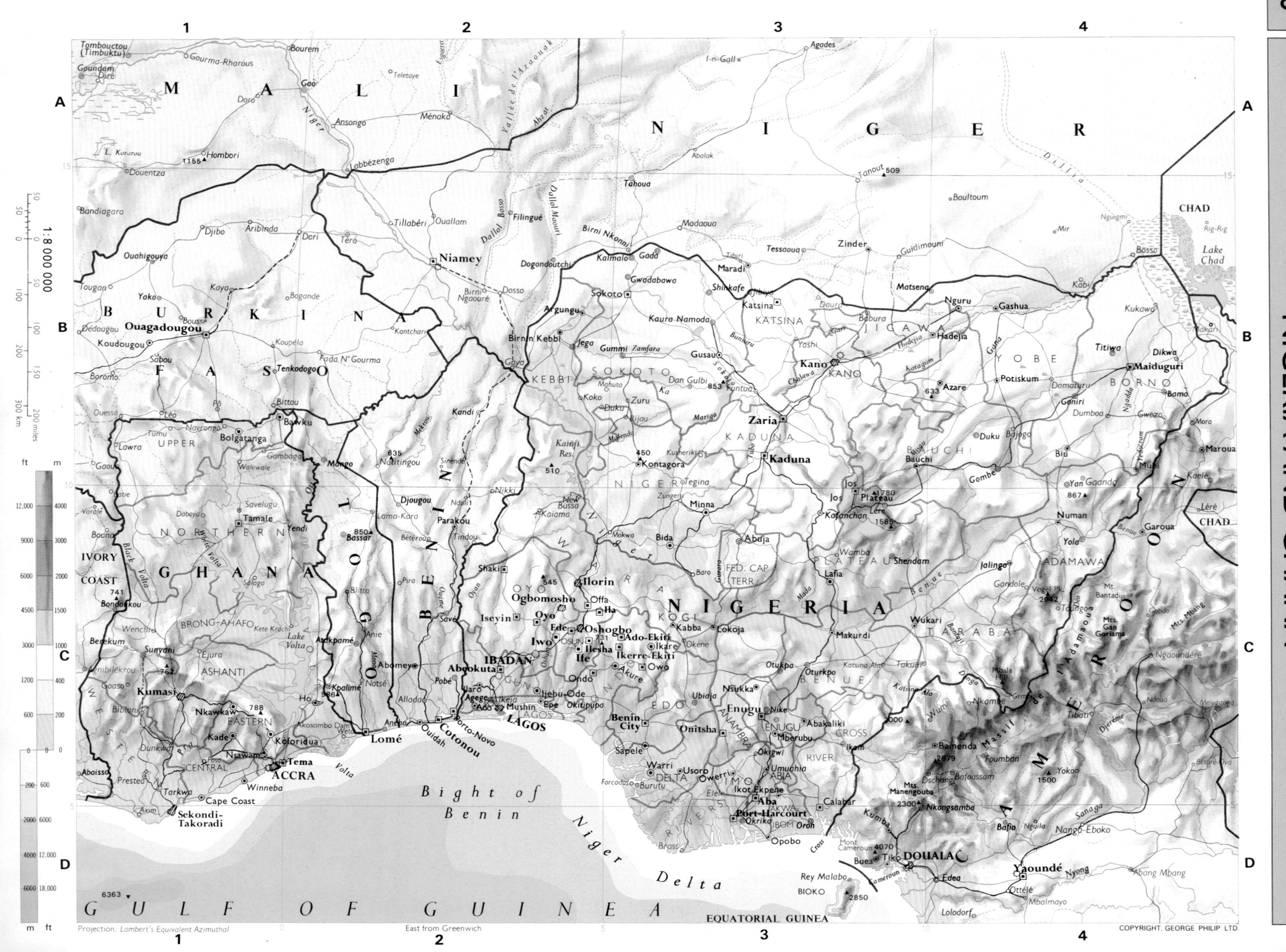

1 : 8 000 000

Projection: Lambert's Equivalent Azimuthal

East from Greenwich

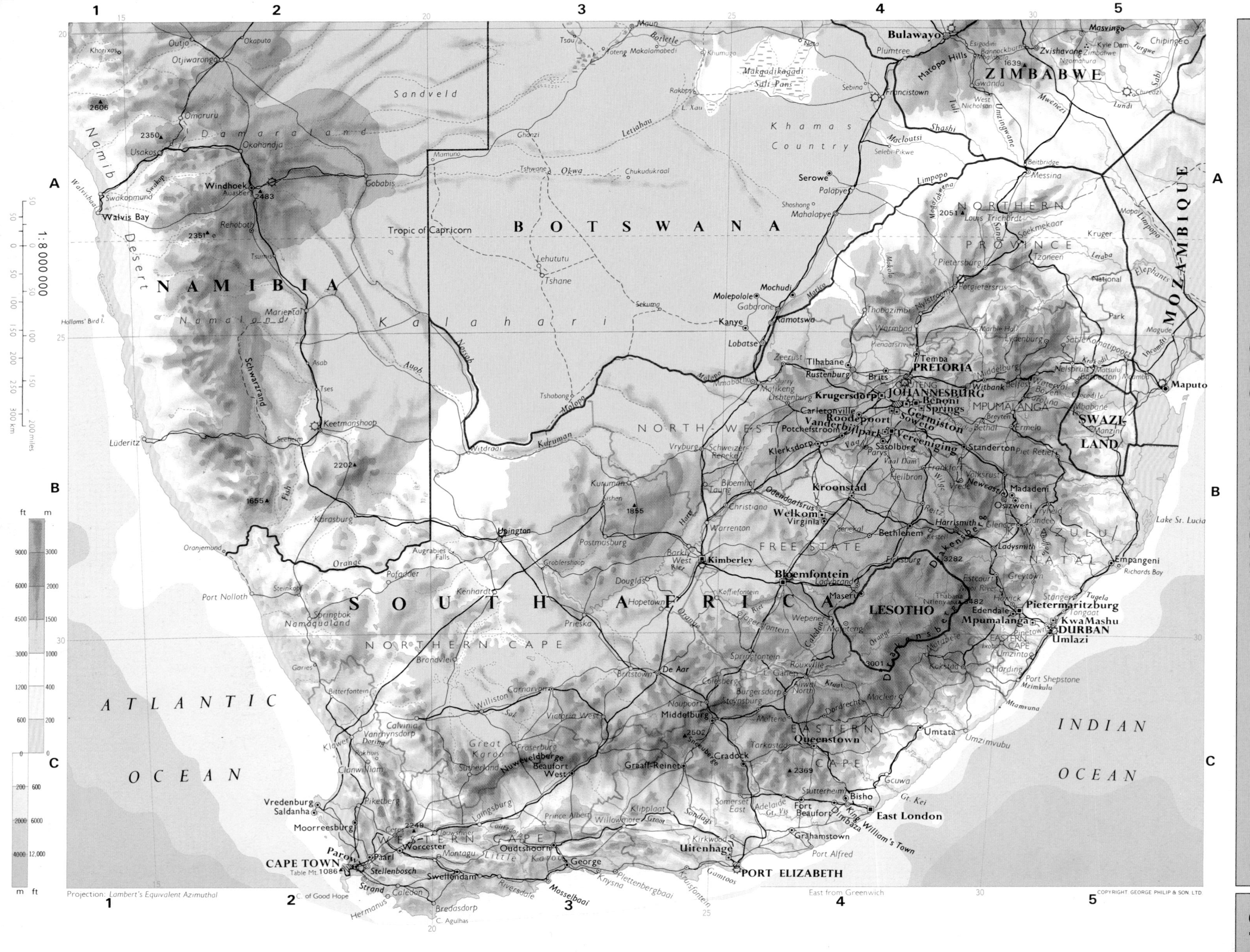
SOUTH AFRICA
NAMIBIA
BOTSWANA
ZIMBABWE
MOZAMBIQUE
LESOTHO
SWAZILAND
ATLANTIC OCEAN
INDIAN OCEAN
Kalahari
Namib Desert
Tropic of Capricorn
NORTHERN CAPE
WESTERN CAPE
EASTERN CAPE
FREE STATE
NORTH WEST
NORTHERN PROVINCE
MPUMALANGA
KWAZULU/NATAL
PRETORIA
JOHANNESBURG
CAPE TOWN
DURBAN
PORT ELIZABETH
East London
Bloemfontein
Kimberley
Pietermaritzburg
Windhoek
Walvis Bay
Maputo
Bulawayo
1:8 000 000
Projection: Lambert's Equivalent Azimuthal
COPYRIGHT GEORGE PHILIP & SON LTD
East from Greenwich

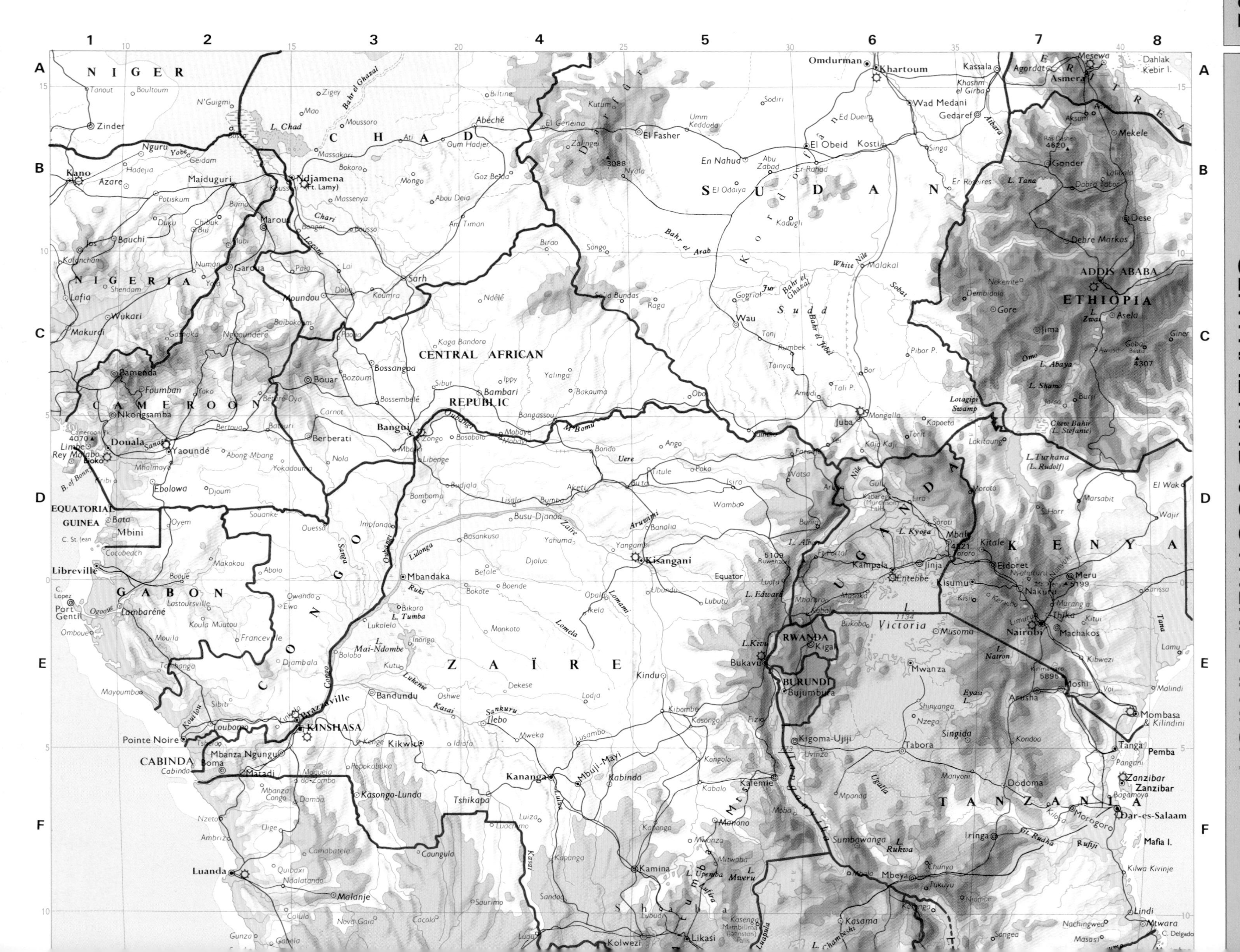
NIGER
Zinder
CHAD
Ndjamena
L. Chad
Abéché
SUDAN
Omdurman
Khartoum
Wad Medani
Kassala
El Obeid
El Fasher
Wau
Juba
ETHIOPIA
ADDIS ABABA
Asmera
NIGERIA
Kano
Maiduguri
CAMEROON
Yaoundé
Douala
CENTRAL AFRICAN
REPUBLIC
Bangui
EQUATORIAL
GUINEA
GABON
Libreville
Port Gentil
CONGO
Brazzaville
Pointe Noire
CABINDA
ZAÏRE
KINSHASA
Kisangani
Mbandaka
Kananga
UGANDA
Kampala
KENYA
Nairobi
Mombasa
RWANDA
BURUNDI
Bujumbura
L. Victoria
TANZANIA
Dar-es-Salaam
Zanzibar
Dodoma
Tabora
Luanda

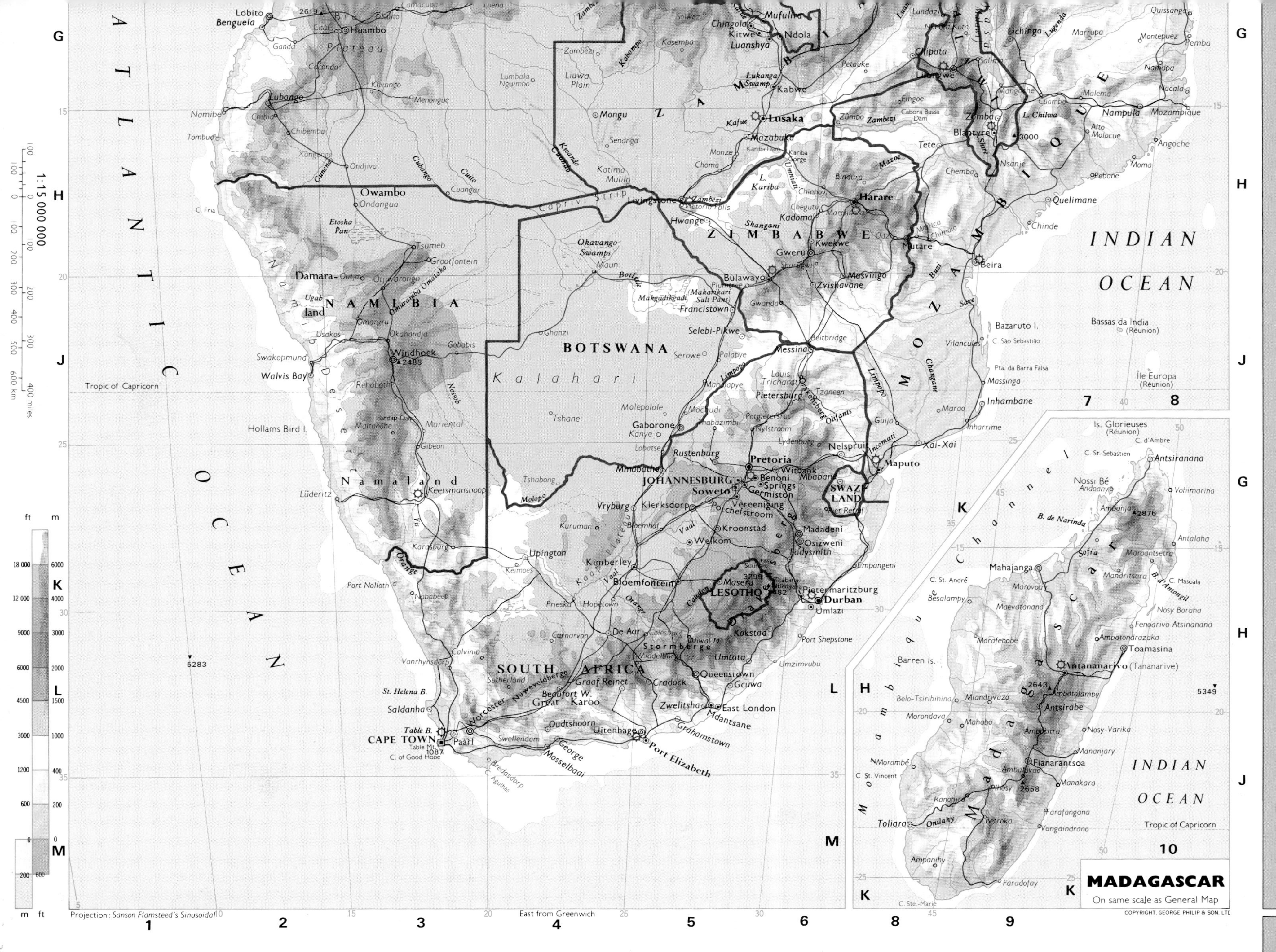

MADAGASCAR
On same scale as General Map

COPYRIGHT GEORGE PHILIP & SON LTD

INDIAN

OCEAN

ATLANTIC OCEAN

1:15 000 000

Projection Sanson Flamsteed's Sinusoidal

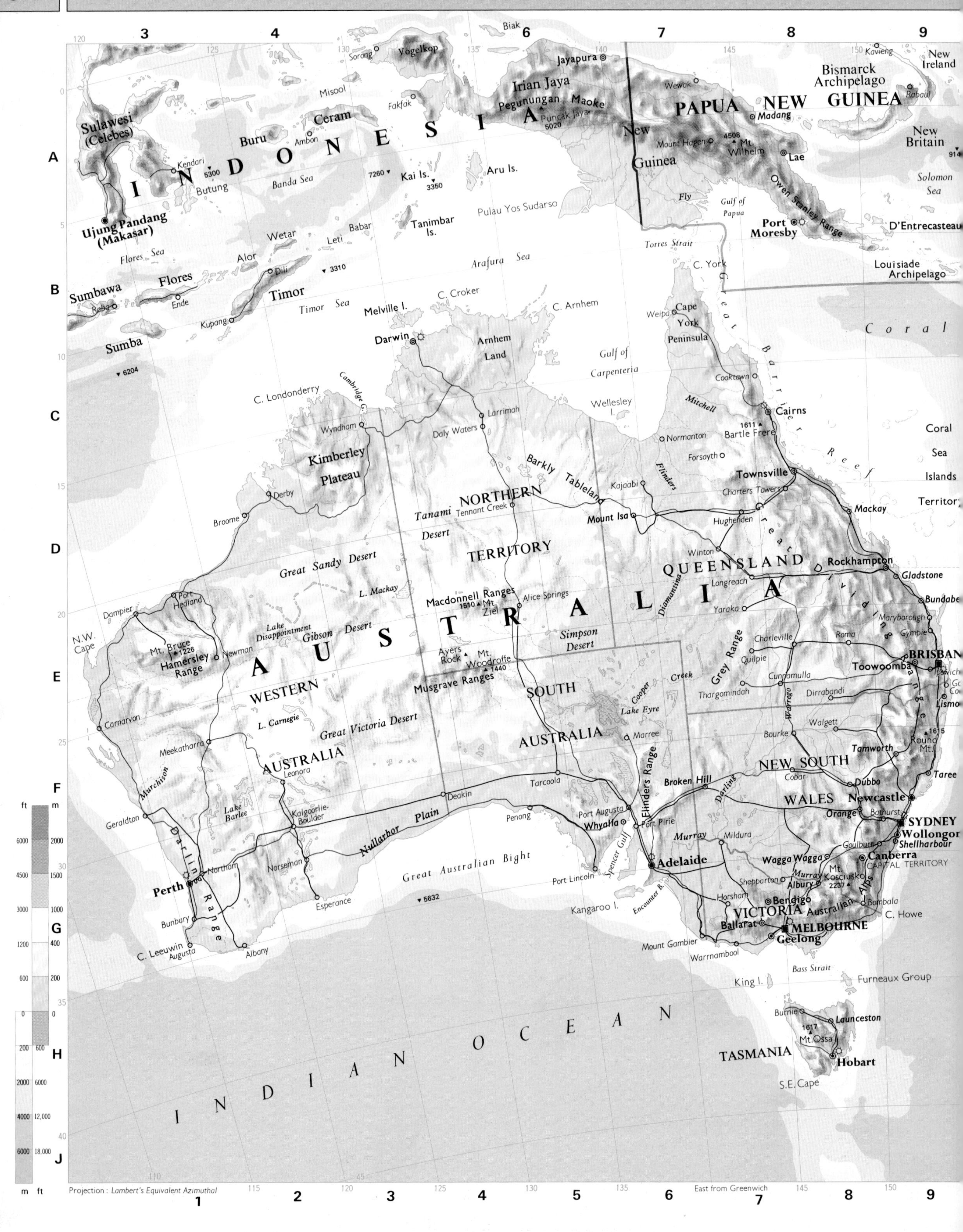

INDONESIA
Sulawesi (Celebes)
Ujung Pandang (Makasar)
Kendari
Butung
Banda Sea
Buru
Ambon
Ceram
Misool
Sorong
Vogelkop
Biak
Fakfak
Kai Is.
Aru Is.
Tanimbar Is.
Pulau Yos Sudarso
Irian Jaya
Jayapura
Pegunungan Maoke
Puncak Jaya 5020
PAPUA NEW GUINEA
New Guinea
Wewak
Madang
Mount Hagen
Mt. Wilhelm 4508
Lae
Fly
Gulf of Papua
Port Moresby
Owen Stanley Range
Bismarck Archipelago
Kavieng
New Ireland
Rabaul
New Britain
Solomon Sea
D'Entrecasteaux
Louisiade Archipelago
Torres Strait
Flores Sea
Wetar
Babar
Leti
Alor
Dili
Flores
Sumbawa
Raba
Ende
Timor
Kupang
Timor Sea
Sumba
Arafura Sea
Melville I.
C. Croker
C. Arnhem
Darwin
Arnhem Land
Gulf of Carpentaria
C. York
Weipa
Cape York Peninsula
Coral Sea
Great Barrier Reef
Cooktown
Cairns
Bartle Frere 1611
Coral Sea Islands Territory
C. Londonderry
Cambridge G.
Wyndham
Larrimah
Daly Waters
Wellesley I.
Mitchell
Normanton
Forsayth
Flinders
Kimberley Plateau
Derby
Broome
Barkly Tableland
Kajaabi
Townsville
Charters Towers
Mackay
Tanami Desert
Tennant Creek
NORTHERN TERRITORY
Mount Isa
Hughenden
Winton
Great Dividing Range
QUEENSLAND
Rockhampton
Gladstone
Longreach
Bundaberg
Great Sandy Desert
L. Mackay
Macdonnell Ranges
Mt. Ziel 1510
Alice Springs
Diamantina
AUSTRALIA
Port Hedland
Dampier
N.W. Cape
Mt. Bruce 1226
Hamersley Range
Newman
Lake Disappointment
Gibson Desert
Ayers Rock
Mt. Woodroffe 1440
Musgrave Ranges
Simpson Desert
Yaraka
Maryborough
Gympie
Charleville
Roma
Quilpie
Grey Range
BRISBANE
Toowoomba
Ipswich
Cunnamulla
Thargomindah
Cooper Creek
Warrego
Dirranbandi
Lismore
WESTERN AUSTRALIA
SOUTH AUSTRALIA
Lake Eyre
Marree
Carnarvon
L. Carnegie
Great Victoria Desert
Walgett
Bourke
Round Mt. 1615
Tamworth
Meekatharra
Murchison
Leonora
NEW SOUTH WALES
Cobar
Taree
Dubbo
Newcastle
Tarcoola
Flinders Range
Broken Hill
Darling
Deakin
Lake Barlee
Kalgoorlie-Boulder
Geraldton
Nullarbor Plain
Penong
Port Augusta
Whyalla
Port Pirie
Orange
Bathurst
SYDNEY
Wollongong
Shellharbour
Murray
Mildura
Goulburn
Canberra
AUSTRALIAN CAPITAL TERRITORY
Darling Range
Northam
Norseman
Great Australian Bight
Spencer Gulf
Adelaide
Wagga Wagga
Perth
Port Lincoln
Shepparton
Albury
Mt. Kosciusko 2237
Australian Alps
Esperance
5632
Kangaroo I.
Encounter B.
Horsham
Bendigo
VICTORIA
Bombala
C. Howe
Bunbury
Ballarat
MELBOURNE
Geelong
C. Leeuwin
Augusta
Albany
Mount Gambier
Warrnambool
Bass Strait
King I.
Furneaux Group
Burnie
Launceston
Mt. Ossa 1617
TASMANIA
Hobart
S.E. Cape
INDIAN OCEAN
Projection: Lambert's Equivalent Azimuthal
East from Greenwich

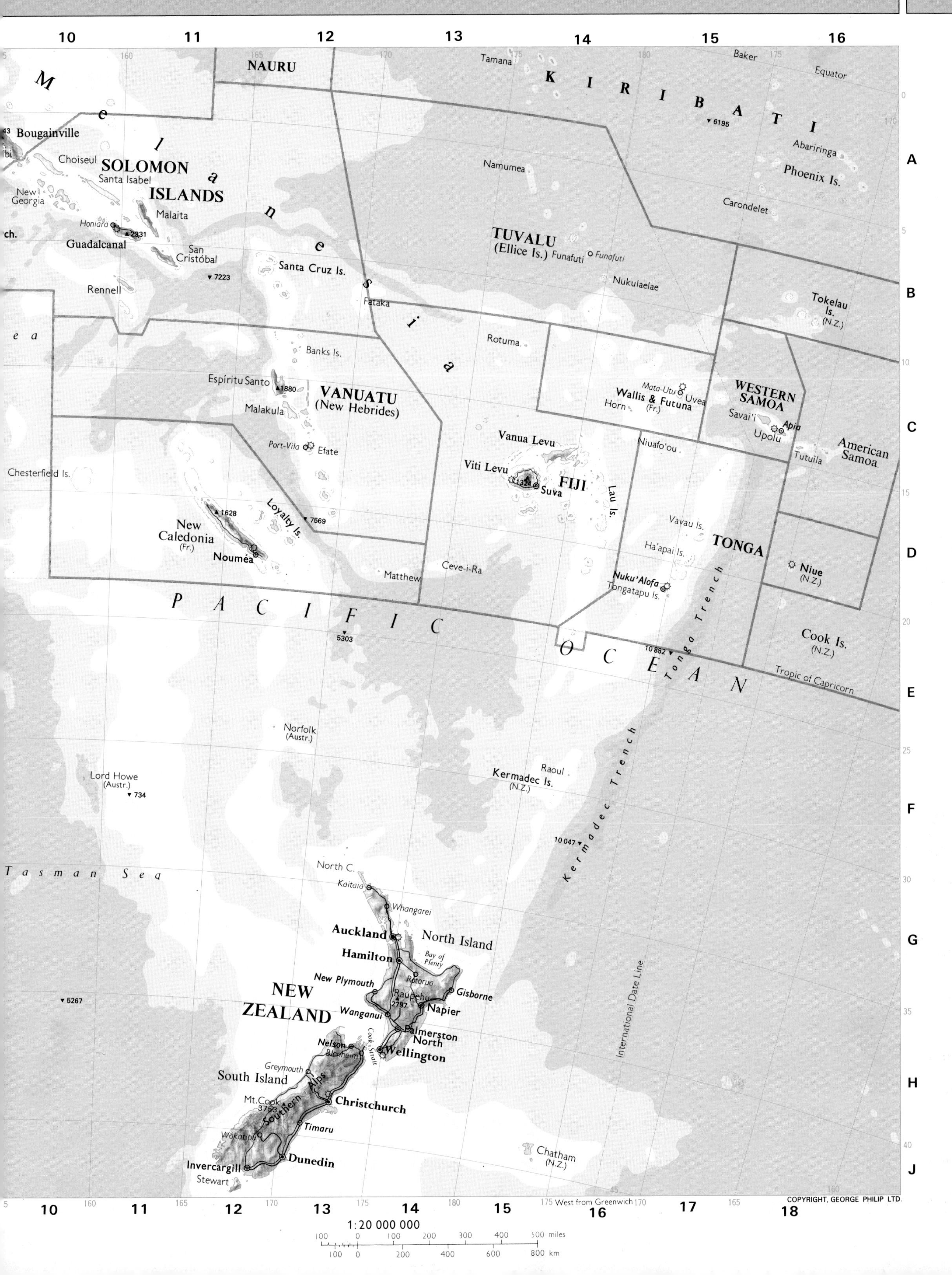

M e l a n e s i a

NAURU

K I R I B A T I

Tamana

Baker
Equator

▲43 Bougainville

Choiseul

SOLOMON
ISLANDS

Santa Isabel

New
Georgia

Malaita

Honiara

Guadalcanal

▲2331

San
Cristóbal

Rennell

Namumea

Abariringa

Phoenix Is.

Carondelet

▼6195

TUVALU
(Ellice Is.)

Funafuti ○ Funafuti

Nukulaelae

Tokelau
Is.
(N.Z.)

Santa Cruz Is.

▼7223

Fataka

Banks Is.

Rotuma.

Espíritu Santo

▲1880

VANUATU
(New Hebrides)

Malakula

Port-Vila ○ Efate

Loyalty Is.

▲1628

New
Caledonia
(Fr.)

Nouméa

Matthew

Chesterfield Is.

▼7569

Vanua Levu

Viti Levu

▲1324

Suva

FIJI

Wallis & Futuna
(Fr.)

Mata-Utu ○ Uvea

Horn

Niuafo'ou

Lau Is.

Vavau Is.

Ha'apai Is.

TONGA

Nuku'Alofa
Tongatapu Is.

Ceve-i-Ra

WESTERN
SAMOA

Savai'i

Upolu

Apia

American
Samoa

Tutuila

Niue
(N.Z.)

Cook Is.
(N.Z.)

P A C I F I C

O C E A N

▼5303

▼10 882

Tonga Trench

Tropic of Capricorn

Norfolk
(Austr.)

Raoul

Kermadec Is.
(N.Z.)

Kermadec Trench

International Date Line

Lord Howe
(Austr.)

▼734

▼10 047

T a s m a n   S e a

North C.

Kaitaia

Whangarei

▼5267

Auckland

Hamilton

New Plymouth

Wanganui

NEW
ZEALAND

North Island

Bay of
Plenty

Rotorua

Ruapehu
2797

Gisborne

Napier

Palmerston
North

Nelson

Blenheim

Cook Strait

Wellington

Greymouth

South Island

Mt.Cook
3753

Southern

Alps

Christchurch

Wakatipu

Timaru

Invercargill

Stewart

Dunedin

Chatham
(N.Z.)

West from Greenwich

COPYRIGHT. GEORGE PHILIP LTD.

1:20 000 000

100   0   100   200   300   400   500 miles

100   0   200   400   600   800 km

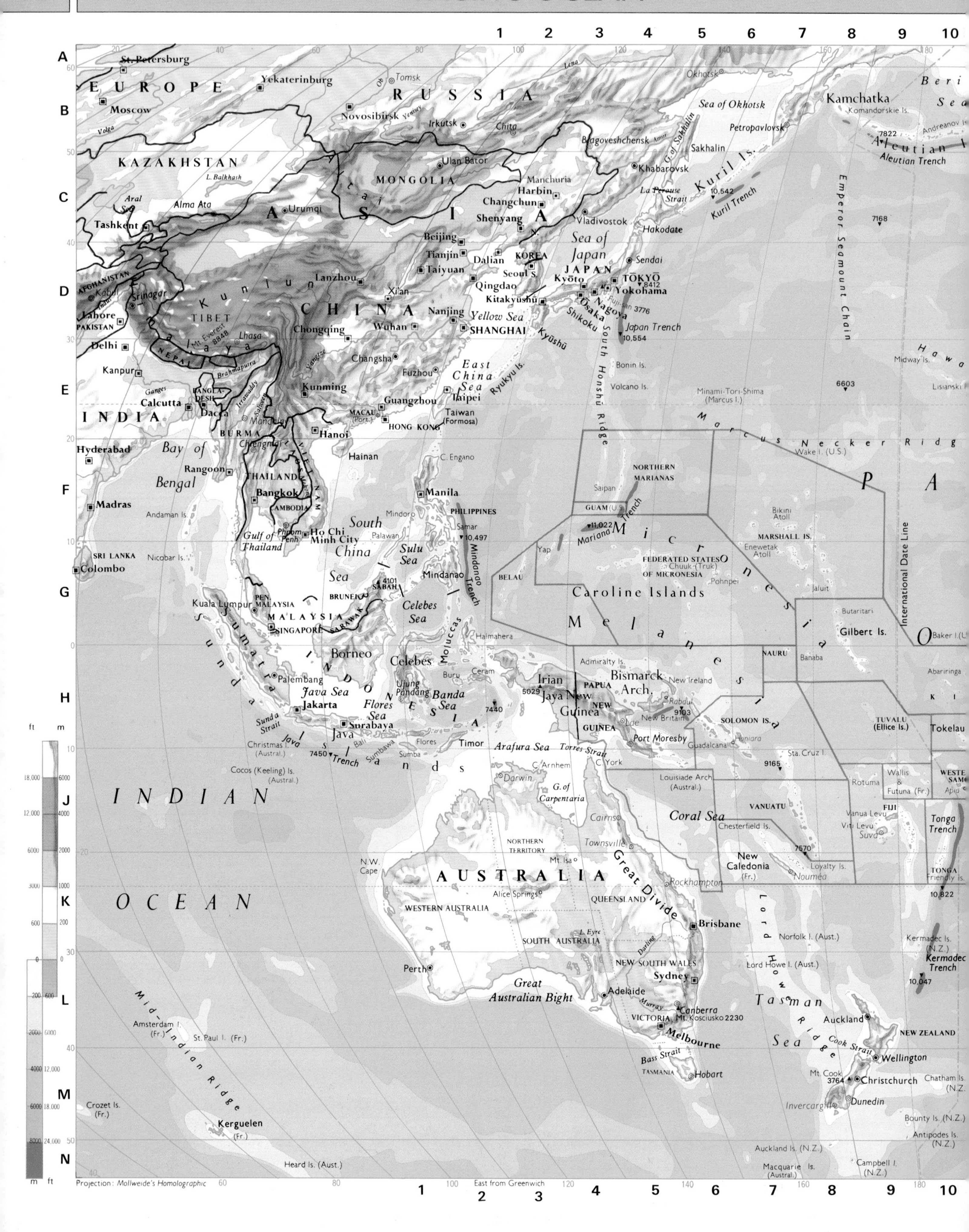

PACIFIC OCEAN

1 2 3 4 5 6 7 8 9 10

EUROPE St. Petersburg Yekaterinburg Tomsk **RUSSIA** Lena Okhotsk Beri
Moscow Novosibirsk Yenisey Irkutsk Chita Blagoveshchensk Sea of Okhotsk **Kamchatka** Komandorskie Is.
Volga Ob Amur Gse of Sakhalin Petropavlovsk 7822 Andreanov I.
KAZAKHSTAN Ulan Bator Manchuria Khabarovsk Sakhalin Kuril Is. Aleutian I.
L. Balkhash **MONGOLIA** Harbin Vladivostok La Perouse Strait 10,542 Kuril Trench Aleutian Trench
Aral Sea Alma Ata Urumqi **A S I A** Changchun Hakodate 7168
Tashkent Altai Shenyang KOREA Sea of Japan Emperor Seamount Chain
Beijing Sendai **JAPAN**
AFGHANISTAN Kabul Tianjin Dalian Seoul S. Kyōto TŌKYŌ 8412 Yokohama
Srinagar Taiyuan Qingdao Osaka Nagoya Fujisan 3776 Midway Is. Hawa
Lahore Lanzhou Xi'an Kitakyūshū Shikoku South Honshu Ridge Japan Trench
PAKISTAN TIBET **CHINA** Nanjing Yellow Sea Kyūshū 10,554
Delhi Mt. Everest 8848 Lhasa Chongqing Wuhan **SHANGHAI** Bonin Is. 6603
Kanpur Himalaya Brahmaputra Changsha Ryukyu Is. Volcano Is. Minami-Tori-Shima Lisianski I.
Ganges Nepal Fuzhou East China Sea (Marcus I.)
INDIA Calcutta BANGLA-DESH Kunming Guangzhou Taipei Marcus Necker Ridg
Dacca Mandalay MACAU Taiwan Wake I. (US) **P** **A**
Hyderabad **BURMA** Chengmai HONG KONG (Formosa) **NORTHERN MARIANAS**
Rangoon Hainan C. Engano Saipan **GUAM (U.S.)** Bikini Atoll
Madras Bay of **THAILAND** Manila **PHILIPPINES** 11,022 Mariana **MARSHALL IS.**
Andaman Is. Bengal Bangkok Mindoro Samar Mariana Mi Enewetak Atoll
CAMBODIA 10,497 Yap FEDERATED STATES Jaluit
SRI LANKA Nicobar Is. Gulf of Phnom Penh Palawan Mindanao **OF MICRONESIA** Chuuk (Truk) Pohnpei
Colombo Thailand Ho Chi Minh City South Sulu Sea BELAU Caroline Islands n e
PEN. MALAYSIA China 4101 SABAH Celebes Melan Butaritari
Kuala Lumpur BRUNEI Sea Celebes Sea Halmahera Gilbert Is. Baker I. (U
MALAYSIA SARAWAK Moluccas Admiralty Is. New Ireland **NAURU** Banaba Abariringa
SINGAPORE Borneo Celebes Buru Ceram Irian Bismarck New Britain 9103 **SOLOMON IS.** **TUVALU** Tokelau
Sumatra Ujung Pandang Banda Sea 5029 Jaya New Guinea Rabaul (Ellice Is.) **WESTE**
Palembang Java Sea 7440 **NEW GUINEA** New Britain Guadalcanal Honiara **SAMA**
JAKARTA Flores Sea **PAPUA** Port Moresby 9165 **FIJI** Apia
Christmas I. (Austral.) Surabaya Bali Flores Timor Arafura Sea Torres Strait Sta. Cruz I. Rotuma Wallis & Futuna (Fr.)
7450 Java Trench Sumbawa Sumba C. York C. Arnhem 9165 Vanua Levu Viti Levu Suva Tonga
Cocos (Keeling) Is. (Austral.) Java Darwin G. of Carpentaria **VANUATU** Trench
INDIAN N.W. Cape Cairns Coral Sea Chesterfield Is. Vanua Lava TONGA
NORTHERN TERRITORY Townsville 7670 Friendly Is.
OCEAN **AUSTRALIA** Great Divide Rockhampton New Caledonia (Fr.) Loyalty Is. Nouméa 10,822
Mt. Isa **QUEENSLAND** Brisbane Norfolk I. (Aust.) Kermadec Is. (N.Z.)
Alice Springs **WESTERN AUSTRALIA** L. Eyre **SOUTH AUSTRALIA** **NEW SOUTH WALES** Lord Howe I. (Aust.) Kermadec Trench
Perth Darling Sydney 10,047
Murray Adelaide Canberra Mt. Kosciusko 2230 **Tasman** Auckland
Amsterdam I. (Fr.) Great **VICTORIA** Melbourne Sea Ridge **NEW ZEALAND**
St. Paul I. (Fr.) Australian Bight Bass Strait Cook Strait Wellington
Mid-Indian Ridge **TASMANIA** Hobart Mt. Cook Chatham Is. (N.Z.)
Crozet Is. (Fr.) 3764 Christchurch
Invercargill Dunedin
Kerguelen (Fr.) Bounty Is. (N.Z.)
Antipodes Is. (N.Z.)
Heard Is. (Aust.) Auckland Is. (N.Z.) Campbell I. (Austral.)
Macquarie Is. (Austral.)

ft m
18,000 6000
12,000 4000
6000 2000
3000 1000
600 200
0 0
200 600
2000 6000
4000 12,000
6000 18,000
8000 24,000
m ft

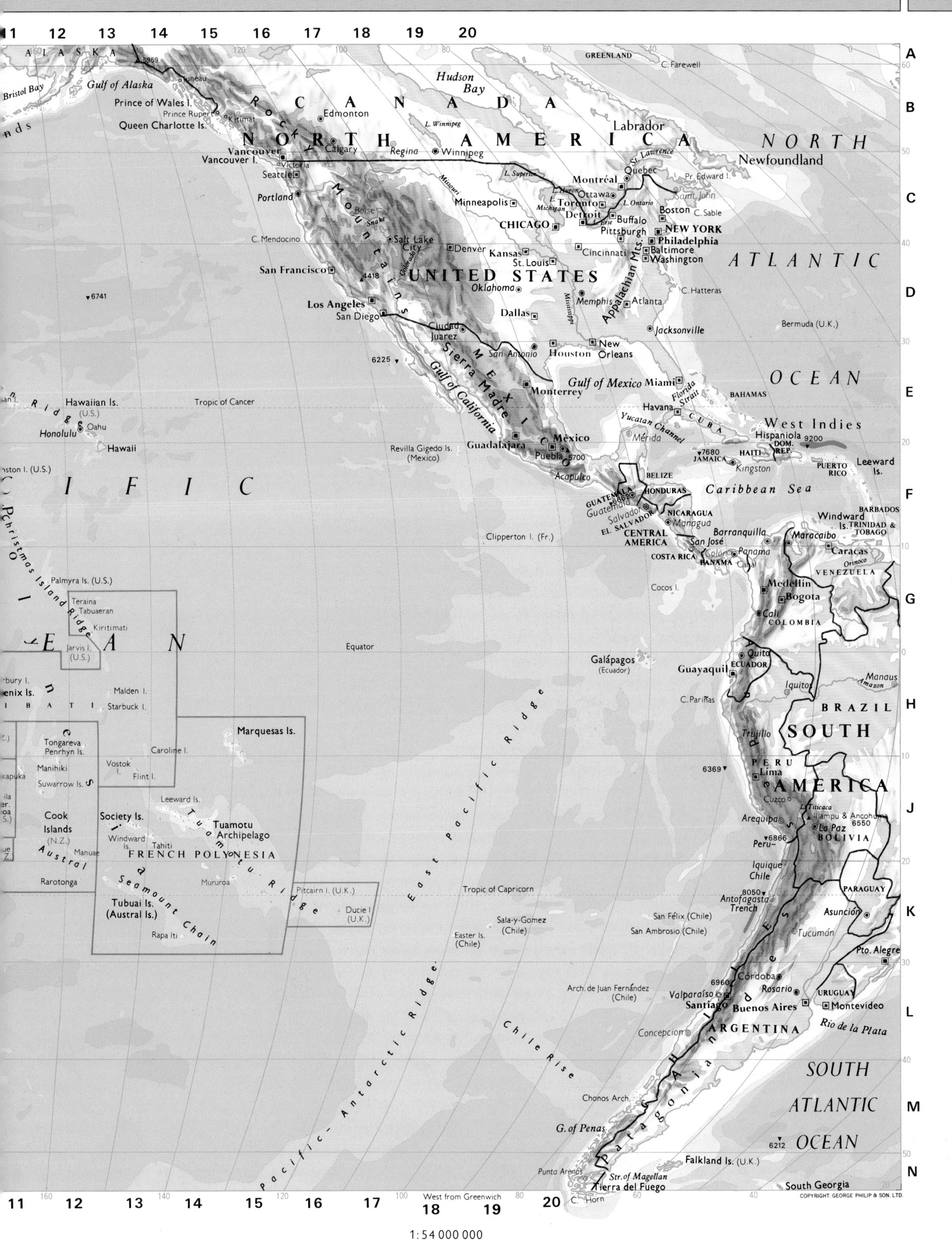

CANADA
NORTH AMERICA
UNITED STATES
MEXICO
Hudson Bay
Gulf of Alaska
Rocky Mountains
Appalachian Mts.
Labrador
Newfoundland
NORTH ATLANTIC OCEAN
Gulf of Mexico
Caribbean Sea
West Indies
CENTRAL AMERICA
SOUTH AMERICA
BRAZIL
COLOMBIA
VENEZUELA
ECUADOR
PERU
BOLIVIA
PARAGUAY
URUGUAY
ARGENTINA
SOUTH ATLANTIC OCEAN
East Pacific Ridge
Pacific–Antarctic Ridge
Chile Rise
FRENCH POLYNESIA
Hawaiian Is. (U.S.)
Tropic of Cancer
Tropic of Capricorn
Equator
Galápagos (Ecuador)
Falkland Is. (U.K.)
South Georgia
Tierra del Fuego
C. Horn
West from Greenwich
COPYRIGHT. GEORGE PHILIP & SON. LTD.

1:54 000 000

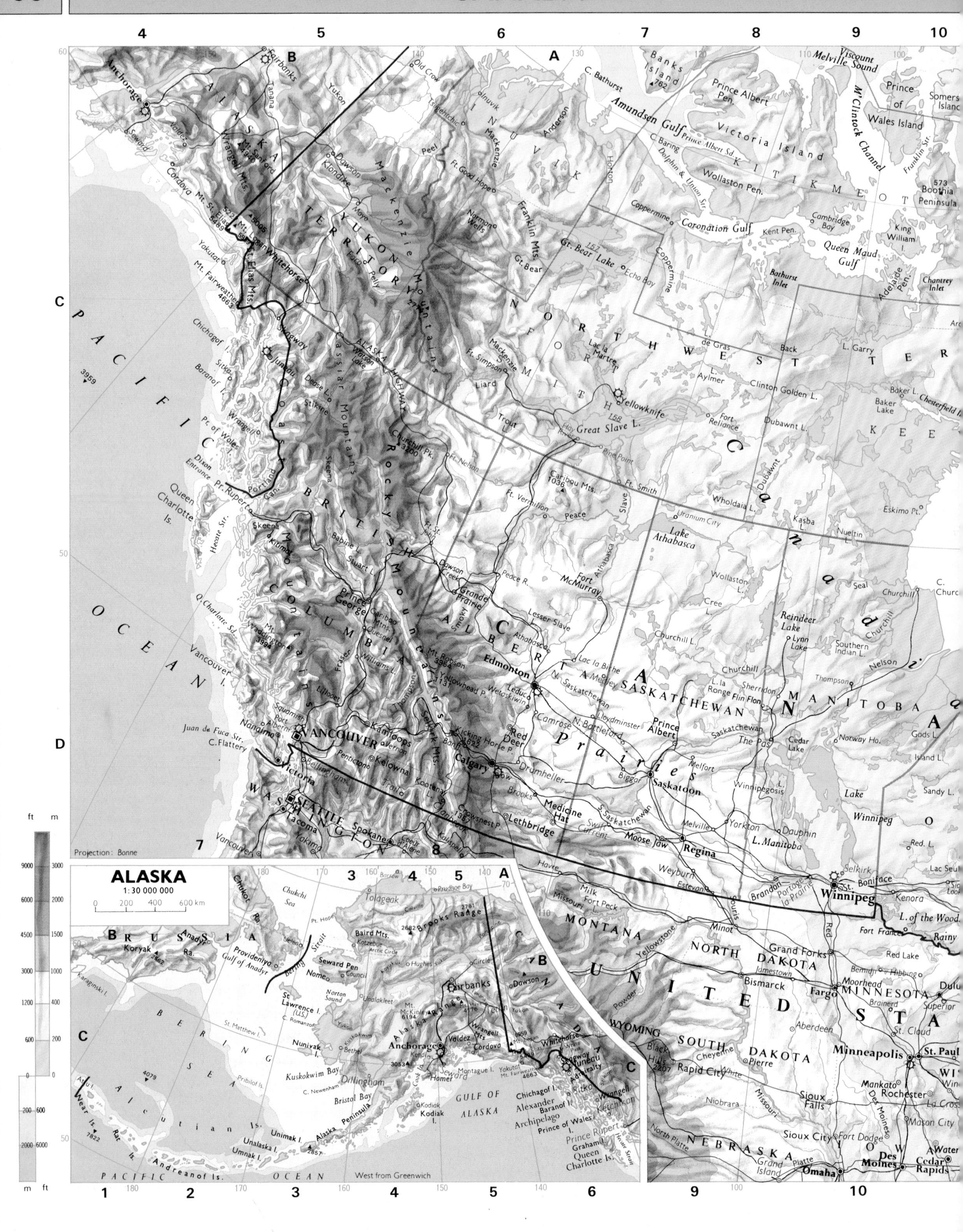

ALASKA

1:30 000 000

0   200   400   600 km

Projection: Bonne

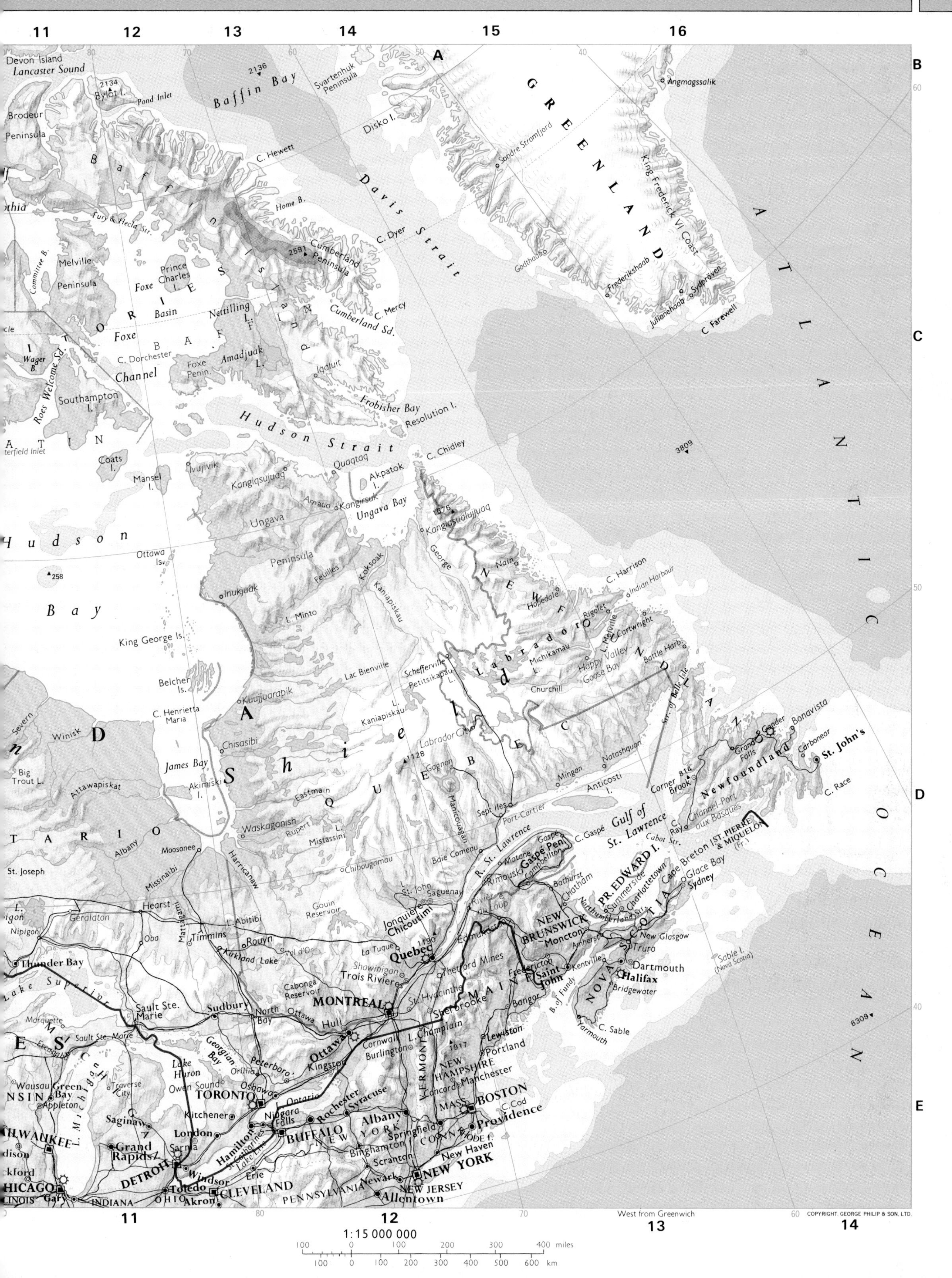

11 **12** **13** **14** **15** **16**

Devon Island
Lancaster Sound

Baffin Bay

2136

Svartenhuk
Peninsula

B

G R E E N L A N D

Angmagssalik

2134 I.
Bylot I.
Pond Inlet

Brodeur
Peninsula

Disko I.

King Frederick VI Coast

C. Hewett

Home B.

Davis Strait

Sondre Stromfjord

Melville
Peninsula

Prince
Charles

Foxe

Basin

C. Dyer

259

Cumberland
Peninsula

Godthaab

Frederikshaab
Sydproven

A T L A N T I C

C

Commerce B.

Foxe
Penin.

Nettilling
L.

C. Mercy
Cumberland Sd.

Julianehaab

C. Farewell

rcle

Foxe
Basin

C. Dorchester

Amadjuak
L.

Igaluit

Channel

Wager
B.

Southampton
I.

Frobisher Bay

Roes Welcome Sd.

Coats
I.

Resolution I.

N
T
I
N

terfield Inlet

Mansel
I.

Hudson Strait

C. Chidley

Quaqtaq

Akpatok
I.

3809

Hudson

Ivujivik

Kangiqsujuaq

Kangirsuk

Ungava Bay

N E W

Ottawa
Is.

Kangiqsualujjuaq

Nain

C. Harrison

Bay

258

Ungava
Peninsula

Feuilles

Amaud

George

1676

F
O
U
N
D

Inukjuak

Koksoak

Indian Harbour
Hopedale

Rigolet
L. Melville
Cartwright
Happy Valley

50

King George Is.

L. Minto

Kaniapiskau

Michikamau

Goose Bay

Battle Harb.

L
A

Belcher
Is.

Schefferville
Petitsikapau L.

Churchill

Str. of Belle Isle

Lac Bienville

C. Henrietta
Maria

Severn

Winisk

S h i e l d

Labrador City

Natashquan

Newfoundland
Grand
Falls
Bonavista
Carbonear

Z

D

Big
Trout L.

A

James Bay

Chisasibi

128

Gagnon

Q U E B E C

Corner B.d
Brook

St. John's

C. Race

Attawapiskat

Akimiski
I.

Eastmain

Mistassini

Mingan

Anticosti
I.

Channel-Port
aux Basques

D

O
N
T
A
R
I
O

Albany

Waskaganish

Rupert

L.

Sept Iles

ST. PIERRE
& MIQUELON
(Fr.)

St. Joseph

Moosonee

Missinaibi

Hurricanaw

Chibougamau

Port-Cartier

C. Gaspé

Gulf of
St. Lawrence

Cabot Str.

Cape Breton

Glace Bay

O
C
E
A
N

igon

Geraldton

Hearst

L. Abitibi

Gouin
Reservoir

Baie Comeau

R. St. Lawrence
Matane
Rimouski
Campbellton

Gaspé
Gaspé Pen.

PR. EDWARD I.
Charlottetown

Sydney

Nipigon

Oba

Mattagami

Rouyn

St. John

Saguenay

Bathurst
Chatham

Summerside

New Glasgow

Thunder Bay

Timmins

Kirkland Lake

Val d'Or

Jonquiere
Chicoutimi

La Tuque

Rivière
du Loup

Edmundston

NEW
BRUNSWICK
Moncton

Northumberland Str.

Amherst

Truro
Dartmouth

Lake Superior

Sault Ste.
Marie

Cabonga
Reservoir

190

Quebec

Thetford Mines

Fredericton

Kentville

N
O
V
A

Halifax

Sable I.
(Nova Scotia)

6309

E S C

Marquette

Sudbury

North
Bay

Shawinigan
Trois Rivieres

MAIN

Saint
John

Bridgewater

Sault Ste. Marie

Georgian
Bay

Ottawa

MONTREAL

St. Hyacinthe

Sherbrooke

Bangor

B. of Fundy

ES
NSIN

Escanaba

Lake
Huron

Peterboro

Hull

Kingston

Cornwall

L. Champlain

917

Lewiston

Portland

C. Sable

Wausau
Green
Bay

Traverse
City

Orillia
Owen Sound

Oshawa

Ontario

Burlington

VERMONT
NEW
HAMPSHIRE

Yarmouth

E

Appleton

Saginaw

TORONTO

Niagara
Falls

L.
Rochester

Syracuse

Albany

Concord
Manchester

BOSTON

adison

Kitchener

London

Hamilton

NEW

Springfield

MASS.

C. Cod

Providence

ckford

Grand
Rapids

Sarnia

Erie

BUFFALO

YORK

CONN.
New Haven

RODE I.

HWAUKEE

Lake Michigan

DETROIT

Windsor

Lake Erie

Binghamton

Scranton

CHICAGO

Gary

INDIANA

Toledo

Akron

CLEVELAND

PENNSYLVANIA

Newark

NEW YORK

NEW JERSEY

LINOIS

OHIO

Allentown

1:15 000 000

100   0   100   200   300   400 miles

100   0   100   200   300   400   500   600 km

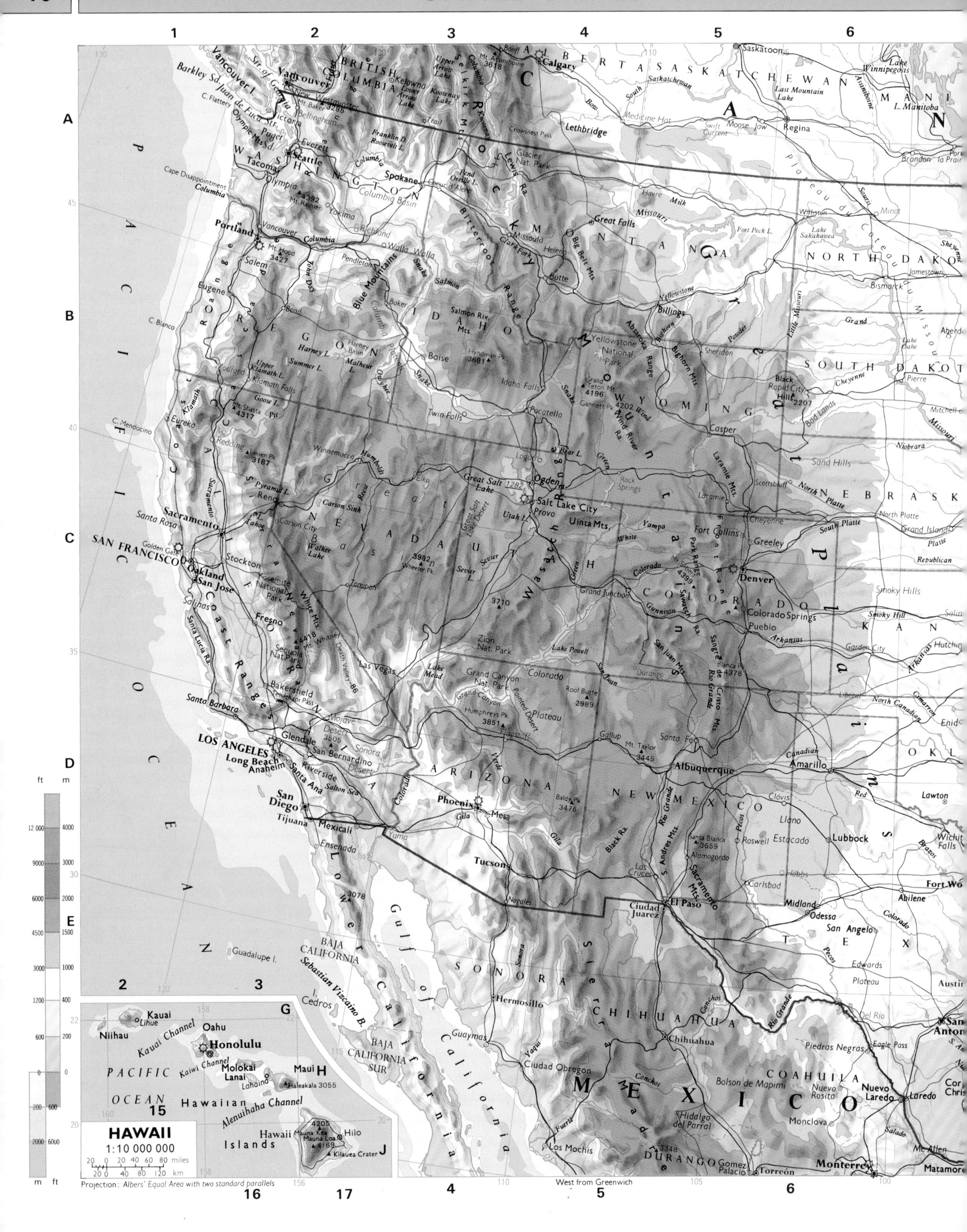

HAWAII
1:10 000 000

0 20 40 60 80 miles
20 0 40 80 120 km

Projection: Albers' Equal Area with two standard parallels

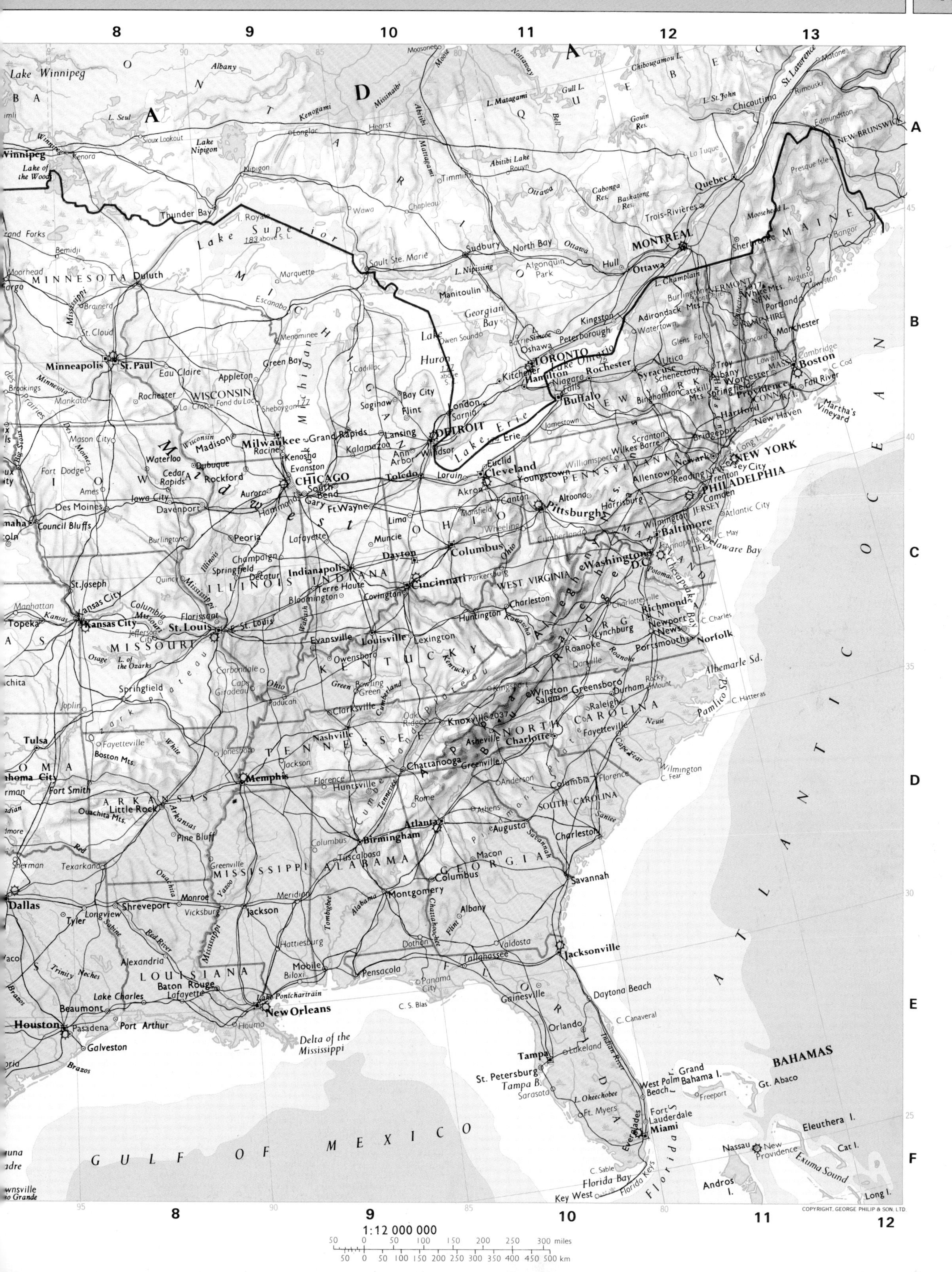

GULF OF MEXICO

ATLANTIC OCEAN

BAHAMAS

1:12 000 000

50 0   50 100 150 200 250   300 miles
50 0 50 100 150 200 250 300 350 400 450 500 km

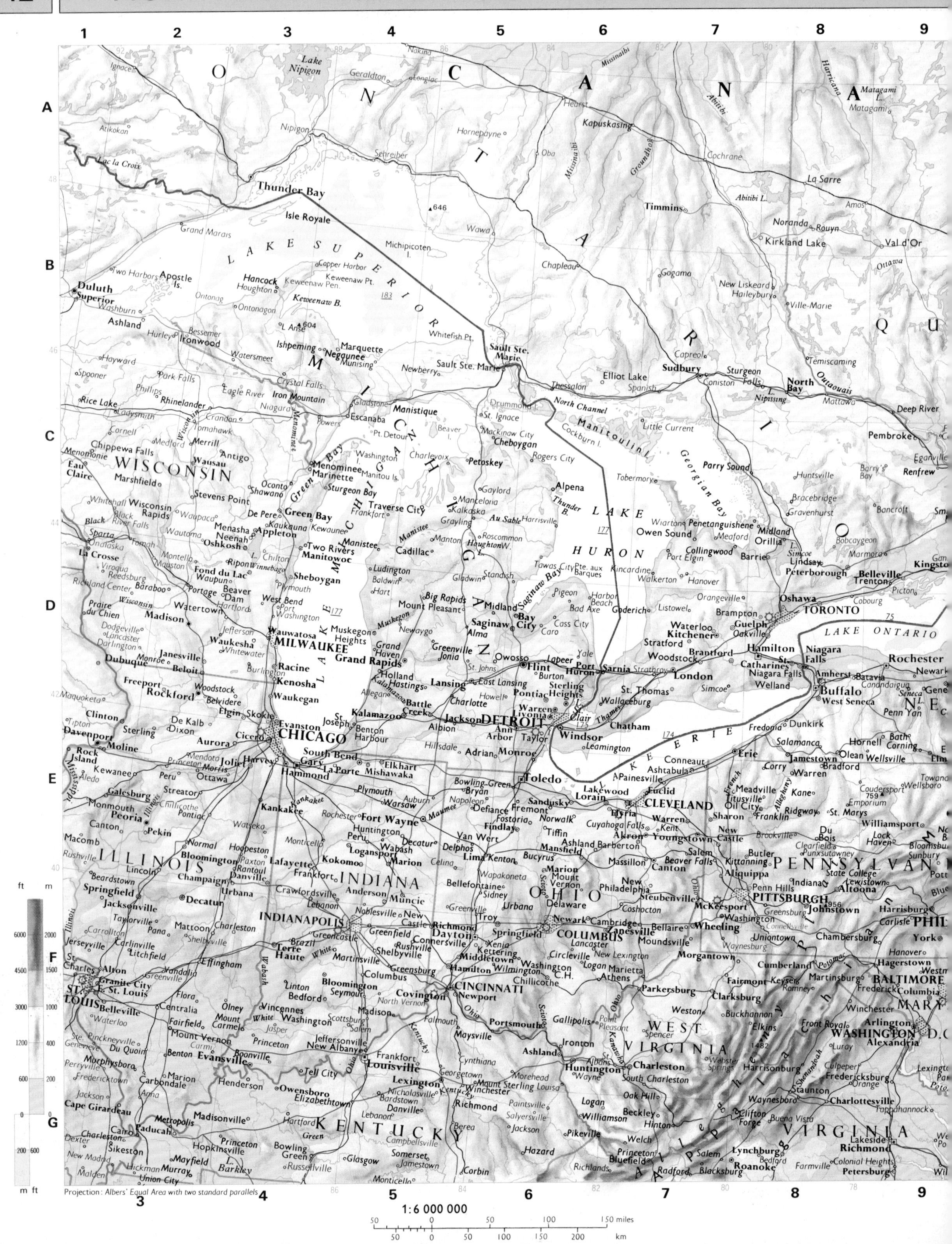
ONTARIO
QUEBEC
LAKE SUPERIOR
LAKE MICHIGAN
LAKE HURON
LAKE ERIE
LAKE ONTARIO
WISCONSIN
MICHIGAN
ILLINOIS
INDIANA
OHIO
KENTUCKY
WEST VIRGINIA
VIRGINIA
PENNSYLVANIA
Lake Nipigon
Thunder Bay
Isle Royale
Duluth
Superior
Sault Ste. Marie
Manitoulin I.
Georgian Bay
Saginaw Bay
Green Bay
Sudbury
Timmins
Kapuskasing
North Bay
Toronto
Hamilton
Niagara Falls
Buffalo
Rochester
London
Windsor
DETROIT
CHICAGO
MILWAUKEE
Madison
Grand Rapids
Lansing
Flint
Toledo
CLEVELAND
Akron
Youngstown
Erie
PITTSBURGH
COLUMBUS
Dayton
CINCINNATI
INDIANAPOLIS
Fort Wayne
South Bend
Louisville
Lexington
Frankfort
Evansville
St. Louis
Peoria
Springfield
Charleston
Huntington
Harrisburg
BALTIMORE
WASHINGTON D.C.
Richmond
Lynchburg
Roanoke
Appalachian Mountains
Projection: Albers' Equal Area with two standard parallels
1:6 000 000
miles
km

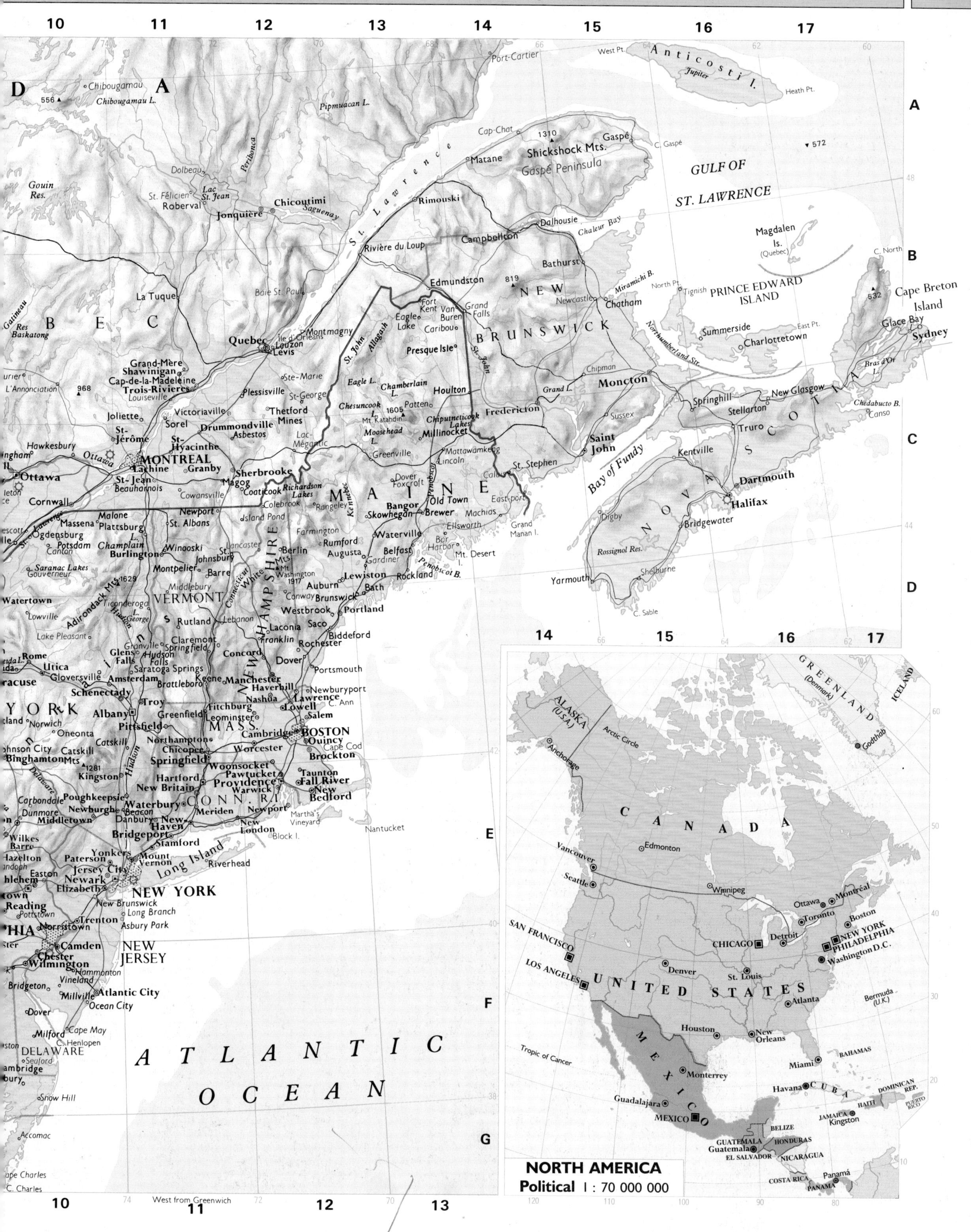
NORTH AMERICA
Political 1 : 70 000 000
GULF OF ST. LAWRENCE
ATLANTIC OCEAN
NEW BRUNSWICK
NOVA SCOTIA
PRINCE EDWARD ISLAND
MAINE
VERMONT
NEW HAMPSHIRE
MASS.
CONN.
R.I.
NEW JERSEY
DELAWARE
CANADA
UNITED STATES
MEXICO

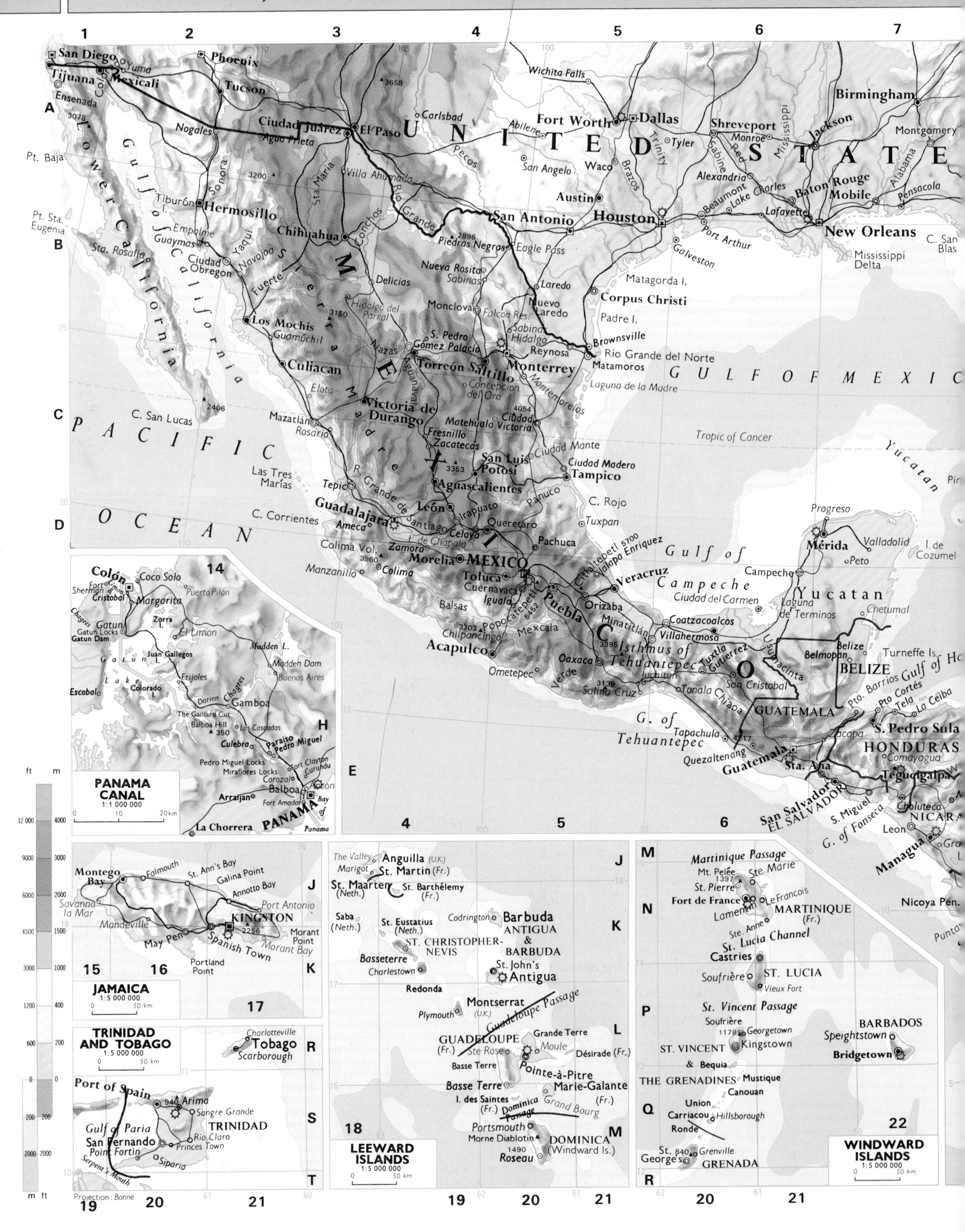

1   2   3   4   5   6   7

San Diego, Yuma
Tijuana, Mexicali   Phoenix
Ensenada   Tucson
3078
Pt. Baja   Nogales   Ciudad Juárez   El Paso   U N I T E D   Wichita Falls   Birmingham
A   Agua Prieta   Carlsbad   Fort Worth   Dallas   Shreveport   Jackson   Montgomery
Pt. Sta.   Abilene   Monroe   S T A T E
Eugenia   Tiburón   Hermosillo   3200   Pecos   San Angelo   Tyler   Alabama   Pensacola
3658   Waco   Alexandria   Baton Rouge   Mobile
Empalme   Villa Ahumada   Austin   Beaumont   Lafayette
B   Guaymas   Chihuahua   2896   San Antonio   Houston   Port Arthur   New Orleans   C. San
Sta. Rosalía   Ciudad   Piedras Negras   Eagle Pass   Galveston   Blas
Obregón   Delicias   Nueva Rosita   Laredo   Matagorda I.   Mississippi
Navojoa   Hidalgo del   Sabinas   Nuevo   Corpus Christi   Delta
Parral   3150   Monclova   Laredo
Los Mochis   Falcon Res.   Padre I.
Guamúchil   S. Pedro   Sabinas   Reynosa   G U L F   O F   M E X I C O
C   Culiacán   Gómez Palacio   Hidalgo   Brownsville
2406   Torreón   Saltillo   Monterrey   Matamoros
C. San Lucas   Mazatlán   Concepción   Rio Grande del Norte
Rosario   del Oro   Montemorelos   Laguna de la Madre
Victoria de   4054   Tropic of Cancer   Yucatan
Durango   Matehuala   Ciudad
Las Tres   Fresnillo   Victoria
Marías   Tepic   3353   Zacatecas   Ciudad Mante
León   San Luis   Ciudad Madero   Progreso
D   Guadalajara   Aguascalientes   Potosí   Tampico   Mérida   Valladolid   I. de
Ameca   Irapuato   Panuco   Peto   Cozumel
C. Corrientes   Santiago   Querétaro   C. Rojo
Zamora   de Chapala   Celaya   Pachuca   Tuxpan   Gulf of   Campeche   Chetumal
Colima Vol.   3960   Jalapa Enriquez   Campeche   Yucatan
Colón   14   Manzanillo   Morelia   MEXICO   5700   Veracruz   Ciudad del Carmen
Coco Solo   Colima   Toluca   Puebla   Orizaba   Laguna de
Cuernavaca   5452   Coatzacoalcos   Terminos

PANAMA CANAL
1:1 000 000
0   10   20 km

JAMAICA
1:5 000 000

TRINIDAD AND TOBAGO
1:5 000 000

LEEWARD ISLANDS
1:5 000 000

WINDWARD ISLANDS
1:5 000 000

Projection : Bonne

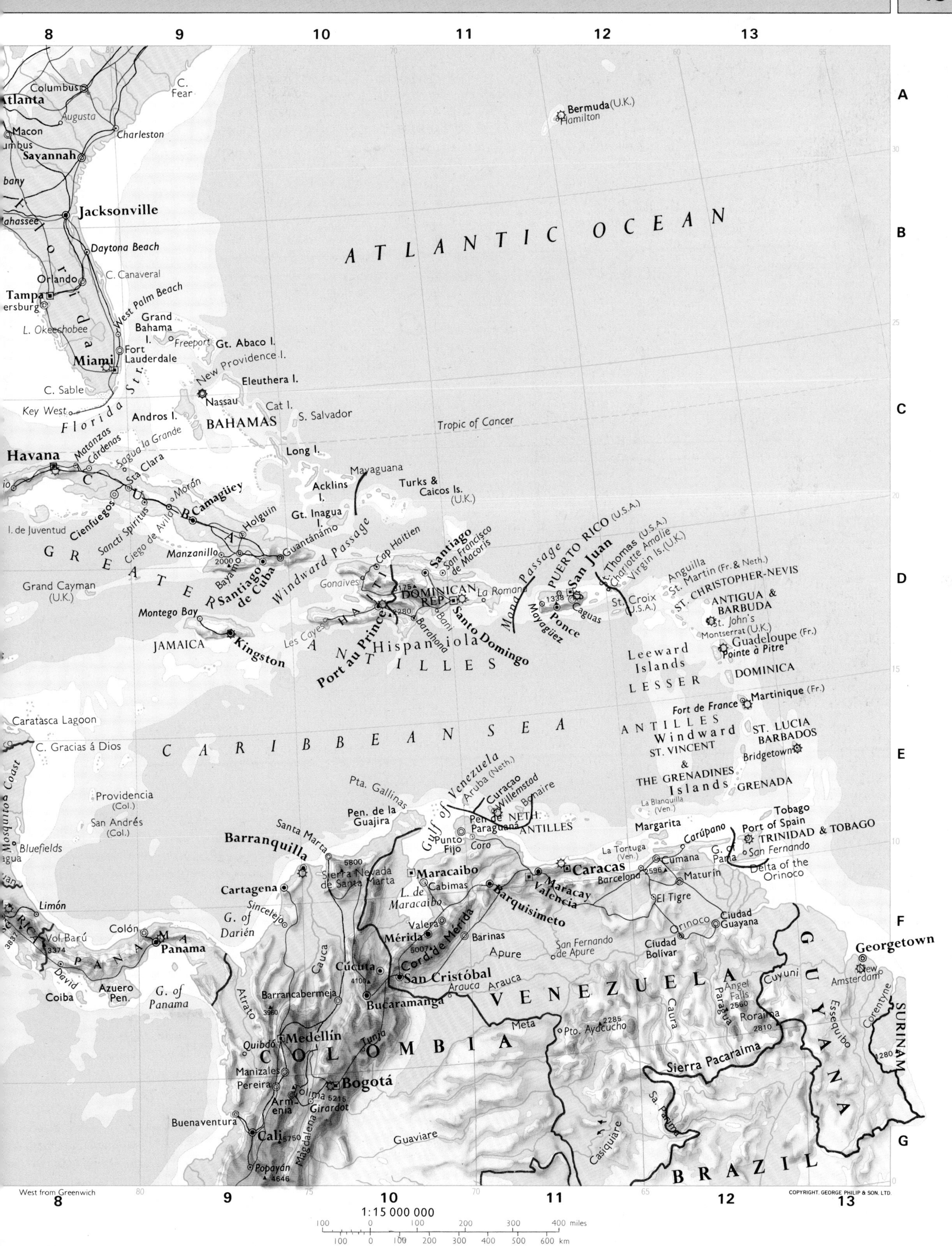

8   9   10   11   12   13

A

B

C

Columbus
C. Fear
Atlanta
Macon
Augusta
Charleston
umbus
Savannah
bany
Tallahassee
Jacksonville
Daytona Beach
Orlando
C. Canaveral
Tampa
ersburg
West Palm Beach
L. Okeechobee
Grand Bahama I.
Miami
Freeport
Gt. Abaco I.
Fort Lauderdale
C. Sable
New Providence I.
Eleuthera I.
Key West
Nassau
Cat I.
Andros I.
BAHAMAS
S. Salvador
Havana
Matanzas
Cárdenas
Long I.
Tropic of Cancer
Sagua la Grande
Sta. Clara
Morón
Mayaguana
Cienfuegos
Sancti Spíritus
Acklins I.
Turks & Caicos Is. (U.K.)
I. de Juventud
Ciego de Ávila
C U B A
Camagüey
Gt. Inagua
Holguín
G R E A T E R
Manzanillo
2000
Bayamo
Guantánamo
Cap Haitien
Santiago
San Francisco de Macorís
PUERTO RICO (U.S.A.)
St. Thomas (U.S.A.)
Anguilla
Grand Cayman (U.K.)
Santiago de Cuba
Gonaïves
1750
DOMINICAN REP.
La Romana
San Juan
Charlotte Amalie
Virgin Is.(U.K.)
St. Martin (Fr. & Neth.)
ST. CHRISTOPHER-NEVIS
Montego Bay
2280
Baní
Santo Domingo
H A I T I
Barahona
Mayagüez
Caguas
St. Croix (U.S.A.)
ANTIGUA & BARBUDA
St. John's
JAMAICA
Kingston
Les Cayes
A N T I L L E S
Port au Prince
Hispaniola
Ponce
1338
Montserrat (U.K.)
Guadeloupe (Fr.)
Pointe à Pitre
Leeward Islands
DOMINICA
LESSER
Martinique (Fr.)
Fort de France
Caratasca Lagoon
C. Gracias á Dios
ANTILLES
Windward
ST. LUCIA
BARBADOS
ST. VINCENT
Bridgetown
C A R I B B E A N   S E A
&
THE GRENADINES
Islands
GRENADA
Providencia (Col.)
Gulf of Venezuela
Pta. Gallinas
Aruba (Neth.)
Curaçao
Willemstad
La Blanquilla (Ven.)
San Andrés (Col.)
Bonaire
Tobago
Bluefields
Pen. de la Guajira
PEN. DE NETH.
Margarita
Port of Spain
TRINIDAD & TOBAGO
gua
Santa Marta
Paraguaná
ANTILLES
Carúpano
San Fernando
Mosquito Coast
Barranquilla
Punto Fijo
Coro
La Tortuga (Ven.)
G. of Paria
Cumaná
Limón
5800
Sierra Nevada de Santa Marta
Maracaibo
Caracas
Barcelona
2596
Maturín
Delta of the Orinoco
Cartagena
Sincelejo
L. de Maracaibo
Cabimas
Maracay
Valencia
El Tigre
Vol. Barú
3374
Colón
G. of Darién
Barquisimeto
Ciudad Guayana
3837
PANAMA
Valera
Mérida
Barinas
Orinoco
David
Panama
Cúcuta
Cord. de Mérida
5007
Apure
San Fernando de Apure
Ciudad Bolívar
Georgetown
Coiba
Azuero Pen.
G. of Panama
Atrato
4100
San Cristóbal
Arauca
Meta
Pto. Ayacucho
2285
New Amsterdam
Barrancabermeja
Bucaramanga
Arauca
V E N E Z U E L A
Caura
Roraima
2810
SURINAM
3960
Cauca
Tunja
Caroní
Paragua
2560
Quibdó
Medellín
C O L O M B I A
Meta
Sierra Pacaraima
G U Y A N A
280
Manizales
Pereira
Tolima 5215
Bogotá
Sa. Parú
Essequibo
Corentyne
Armenia
Girardot
Buenaventura
Cali
5750
Guaviare
Casiquiare
Magdalena
Popayán
4646
B R A Z I L

A T L A N T I C   O C E A N

Bermuda (U.K.)
Hamilton

Florida Str.

Cayuni
Angel Falls

1 : 15 000 000

100   0   100   200   300   400 miles
100   0   100   200   300   400   500   600 km

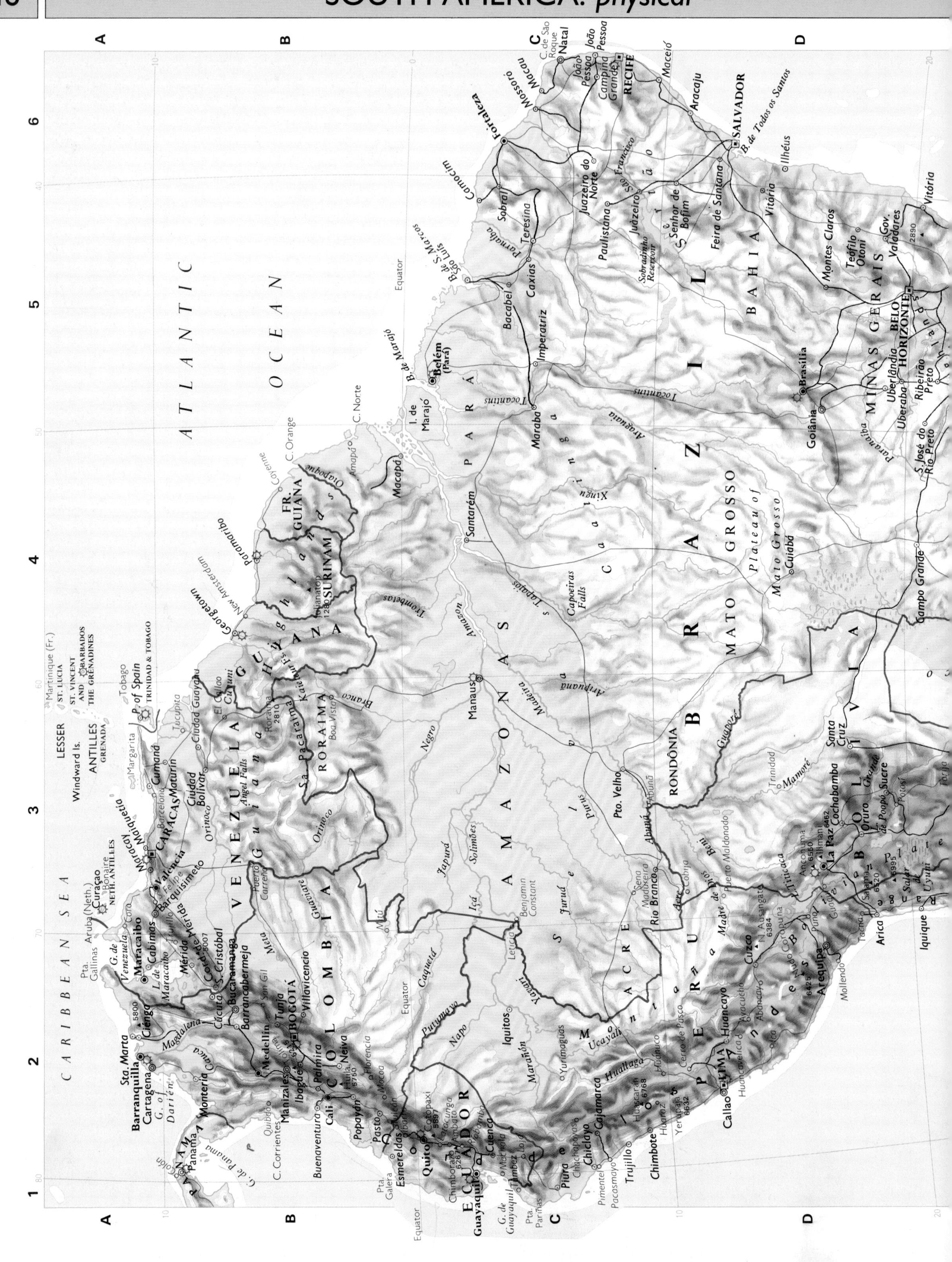
CARIBBEAN SEA
ATLANTIC OCEAN
LESSER ANTILLES
Windward Is.
NETH. ANTILLES
TRINIDAD & TOBAGO
VENEZUELA
COLOMBIA
ECUADOR
PERU
BOLIVIA
BRAZIL
GUYANA
SURINAM
FR. GUIANA
Guiana Highlands
AMAZONAS
ACRE
RONDÔNIA
RORAIMA
PARÁ
BAHIA
MINAS GERAIS
MATO GROSSO
Plateau of Mato Grosso
Amazon
Equator
Caracas
Bogotá
Quito
Lima
La Paz
Manaus
Belém (Pará)
Brasília
Belo Horizonte
Salvador
Recife
Fortaleza
Georgetown
Paramaribo
Cayenne
Santarém
Maracaibo
Medellín
Cali
Guayaquil
Iquitos
Cuzco
Arequipa
Arica
Iquique
Cochabamba
Sucre
Oruro
Santa Cruz
Cuiabá
Campo Grande
Goiânia
Teresina
São Luís
Natal
João Pessoa
Maceió
Aracaju
Vitória
Chimborazo 6267
Cotopaxi 5897
Huascarán 6768
Roraima 2810
Angel Falls

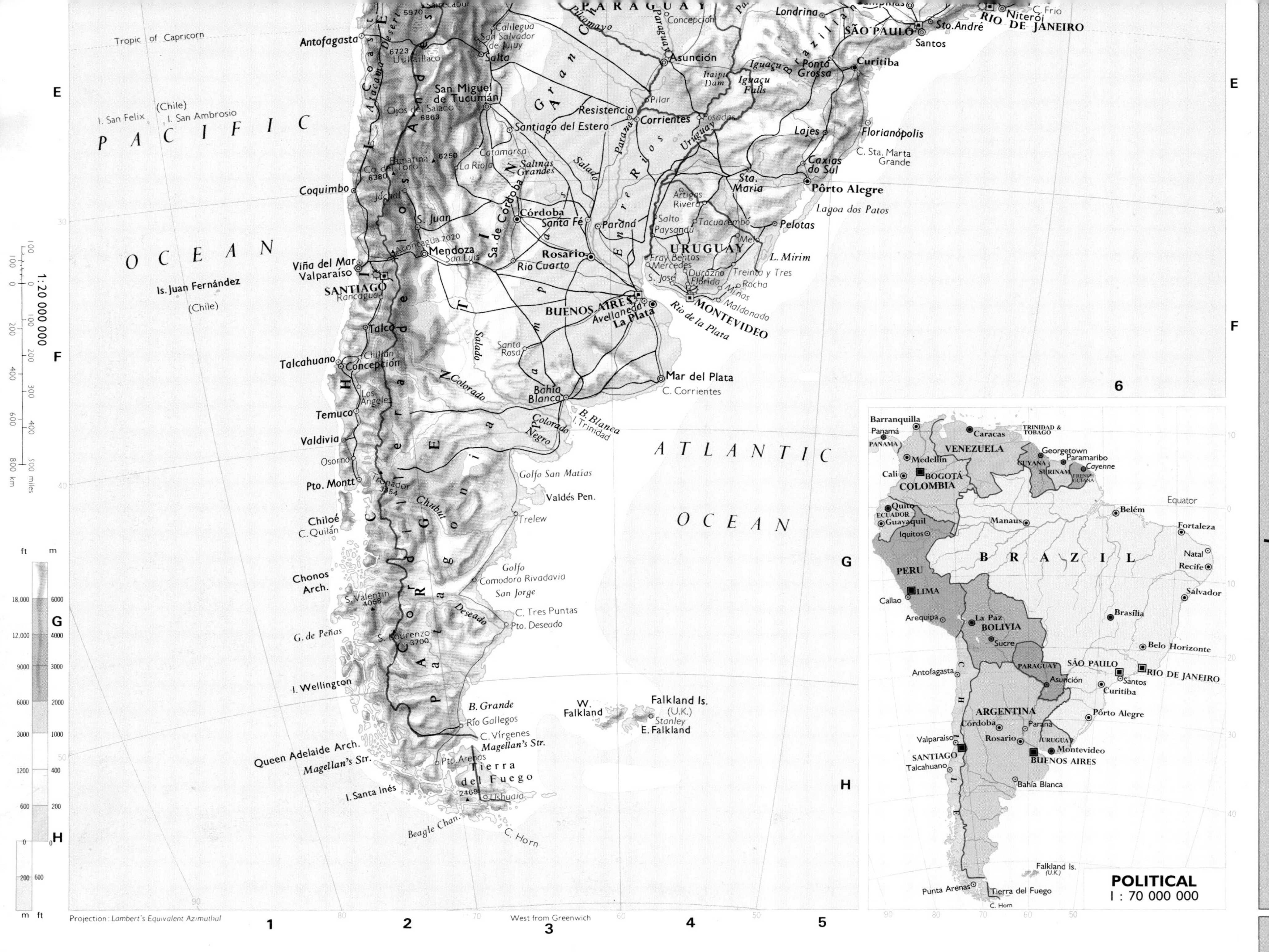

POLITICAL
1 : 70 000 000

1:20 000 000

1:20 000 000

Projection Lambert's Equivalent Azimuthal

100   0   100   200   300   400   500 miles
100   0   200   400   600   800 km

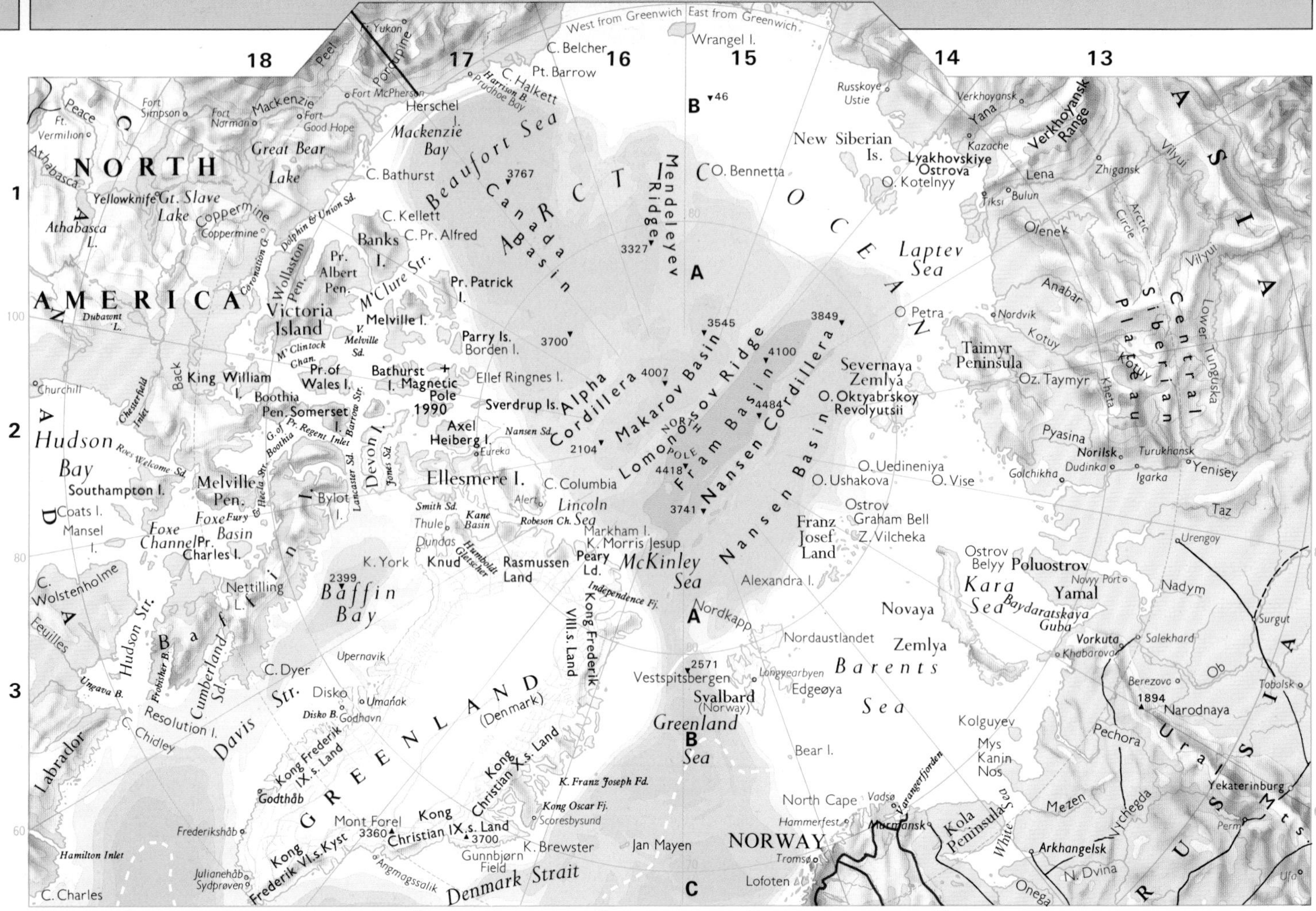

West from Greenwich / East from Greenwich

The Arctic

NORTH AMERICA

Yukon · Porcupine · Peace · Ft. Vermilion · Athabasca · Athabasca L. · Yellowknife · Gt. Slave Lake · Fort Simpson · Fort Norman · Mackenzie · Fort Good Hope · Fort McPherson · Herschel I. · Mackenzie Bay · Great Bear Lake · Coppermine · Coppermine G. · Dubawnt L. · Dubawnt L. · Churchill · Back · Chesterfield Inlet

Beaufort Sea · C. Bathurst · C. Kellett · C. Pr. Alfred · Banks I. · Pr. Patrick I. · Borden I. · Ellef Ringnes I. · Melville I. · M'Clure Str. · Pr. Albert Pen. · Wollaston Pen. · Victoria Island · Dolphin & Union Sd. · Coronation G. · King William I. · Boothia Pen. · Pr. of Wales I. · Somerset I. · Bathurst I. · Magnetic Pole 1990 · Sverdrup I. · Axel Heiberg I. · Devon I. · Ellesmere I. · Eureka · Alert · Parry Is. · M'Clintock Chan. · Melville Sd. · Gulf of Boothia · Pr. Regent Inlet · Lancaster Sd. · Barrow Str. · Jones Sd. · Bylot I. · Baffin Bay

Hudson Bay · Southampton I. · Coats I. · Mansel I. · Melville Pen. · Foxe Pen. · Fury · Foxe Basin · Foxe Channel · Pr. Charles I. · Wolstenholme · Ungava B. · Labrador · C. Chidley · Hamilton Inlet · C. Charles · Hudson Str. · Frobisher B. · Resolution I. · Cumberland Sd. · Davis Str. · C. Dyer · Baffin I. · Nettilling · 2399 · Feuilles

CANADA · ARCTIC OCEAN · Canada Basin · Alpha Cordillera · Makarov Basin · Lomonosov Ridge · Fram Basin · Nansen Cordillera · Nansen Basin · Mendeleyev Ridge · 3767 · 3327 · 3700 · 3545 · 3849 · 4007 · 4100 · 4484 · 2104 · 4418 · 3741 · NORTH POLE

GREENLAND (Denmark) · Smith Sd. · Kane Basin · Thule · Dundas · Humboldt Glacier · K. York · Knud Rasmussen Land · Peary Ld. · Lincoln Sea · Robeson Ch. · Markham I. · K. Morris Jesup · C. Columbia · McKinley Sea · Independence Fj. · Kong Frederik VIII.s Land · Nordkapp · Alexandra I. · Franz Josef Land · Graham Bell · Z. Vilcheka · Ostrov Ushakova · O. Uedineniya · O. Vise · Kong Christian X.s Land · K. Franz Joseph Fd. · Kong Oscar Fj. · Scoresbysund · K. Brewster · Gunnbjørn Field · 3700 · Denmark Strait · Disko · Umanak · Disko B. · Godhavn · Upernavik · C. Dyer · Godthåb · Mont Forel · 3360 · Kong Frederik VI.s Kyst · Frederikshåb · Julianehåb · Sydprøven · Angmagssalik · Kong Christian IX.s Land

Svalbard (Norway) · Vestspitsbergen · Longyearbyen · Edgeøya · Nordaustlandet · 2571 · Greenland Sea · Barents Sea · Bear I. · Jan Mayen · North Cape · Hammerfest · Vadsø · Varangerfjorden · NORWAY · Tromsø · Lofoten

ASIA · Verkhoyansk Range · Verkhoyansk · Yana · Lena · Kazache · Zhigansk · Central Siberian Plateau · Vilyuy · Vilyui · Olenek · Anabar · Kotuy · Khatanga · Nordvik · O. Petra · Taimyr Peninsula · Oz. Taymyr · Severnaya Zemlya · O. Oktyabrskoy Revolyutsii · Laptev Sea · New Siberian Is. · Lyakhovskiye Ostrova · O. Kotelnyy · O. Bennetta · Russkoye Ustie · Wrangel I. · Pt. Barrow · C. Halkett · Harrison B. · Prudhoe Bay · C. Belcher · Tiksi · Bulun · Olenek · Pyasina · Norilsk · Dudinka · Igarka · Turukhansk · Yenisey · Golchikha · Taz · Urengoy · Nadym · Surgut · Ob · Tobolsk · Salekhard · Vorkuta · Khabarovo · Kara Sea · Baydaratskaya Guba · Yamal · Novaya Zemlya · Kolguyev · Mys Kanin Nos · Pechora · Mezen · N. Dvina · Arkhangelsk · Onega · Kola Peninsula · Murmansk · White Sea · URSS / RUSSIA · Ural Mts. · Narodnaya 1894 · Yekaterinburg · Perm · Poluostrov Belyy · Ostrov Graham Bell · Berezovo · Novyy Port · Nichegda · Ufa

Antarctica

Projection: Zenithal Equidistant
1 : 35 000 000

PACIFIC OCEAN · ATLANTIC (Drake Passage) · Tierra del Fuego · C. de Hornos · Falkland Is. (U.K.) · Stanley (U.K.) · South Georgia · Elephant I. · Clarence I. · South Shetland Is. · Kg. George I. · Capitan Arturo Prat (Chile) · Deception I. · Orcadas (Arg.) · Signy I. (U.K.) · Coronation I. · South Orkney Is. (U.K.) · Gen. Bernardo O'Higgins (Chile) · Joinville I. · Esperanza (Arg.) · Marambio (Arg.) · James Ross I. · Robertson I. · Graham Land · Palmer (U.S.A.) · Anvers I. · Faraday (U.K.) · Biscoe Is. · Adelaide I. · Rothera (U.K.) · Alexander I. · Charcot I. · C. Byrd · Antarctic Peninsula · Palmer Land · Larsen Ice Shelf · San Martín (Arg.) · Dyer Plateau · George VI Sound · 4191 · 3658 · 2987 · 2896 · 1036

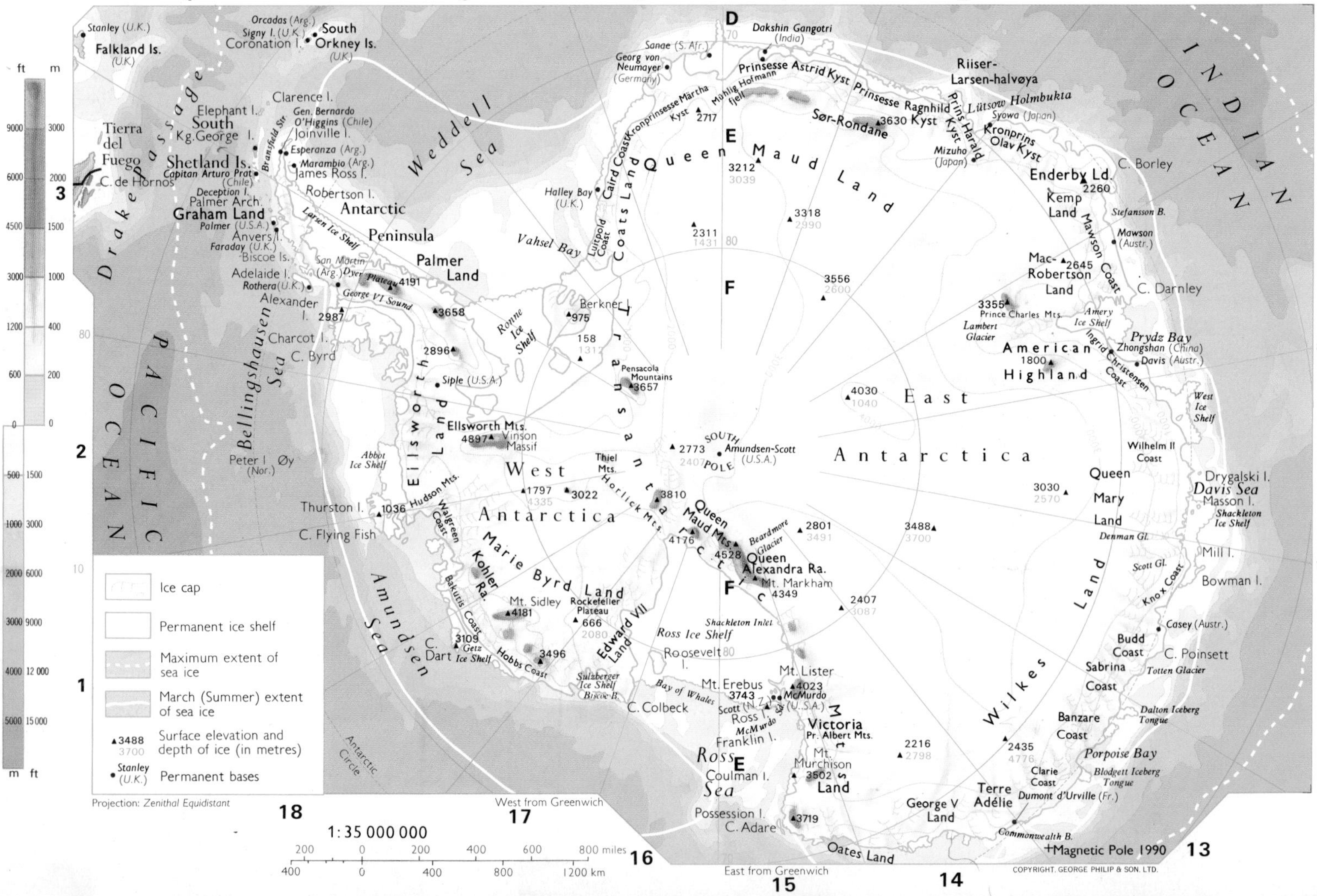

Weddell Sea · Coats Land · Caird Coast · Luitpold Coast · Vahsel Bay · Filchner Ice Shelf · Ronne Ice Shelf · Berkner I. · Pensacola Mountains · 3657 · 158 · Halley Bay (U.K.) · Ellsworth Land · Ellsworth Mts. · Vinson Massif 4897 · Siple (U.S.A.) · West Antarctica · Marie Byrd Land · Thurston I. · Abbot Ice Shelf · Peter I. Øy (Nor.) · Bellingshausen Sea · Amundsen Sea · Kohler Ra. · Mt. Sidley 4181 · Executive Committee Ra. · 3109 · Getz Ice Shelf · C. Dart · Hobbs Coast · Bakutis Coast · Walgreen Coast · Hudson Mts. · 1797 · 3022 · 2773 · Thiel Mts. · Horlick Mts. · 3810 · 4176 · 4528 · Queen Maud Mts. · Beardmore Glacier · Rockefeller Plateau · 666 · Edward VII Land · Sulzberger Ice Shelf · C. Colbeck · Roosevelt I. · Ross Ice Shelf · Bay of Whales · 3496

SOUTH POLE · Amundsen-Scott (U.S.A.) 2407 · 2801 3491 · 3488 3700 · EAST Antarctica

INDIAN OCEAN · Dakshin Gangotri (India) · Sanae (S. Afr.) · Georg von Neumayer (Germany) · Prinsesse Astrid Kyst · Prinsesse Ragnhild Kyst · Prins Harald Kyst · Lützow Holmbukta · Syowa (Japan) · Mizuho (Japan) · Riiser-Larsen-halvøya · Mühlig Hofmann fjell · Sør-Rondane · Kronprins Olav Kyst · Kronprinsesse Martha Kyst · 2717 · 3630 · Queen Maud Land · 3212 3039 · 3318 2990 · 2311 1431 · 3556 2600 · Enderby Ld. · 2260 · Kemp Land · Stefansson B. · Mawson (Austr.) · Mac-Robertson Land · 2645 · C. Darnley · Prince Charles Mts. · 3355 · Lambert Glacier · Amery Ice Shelf · Prydz Bay · Zhongshan (China) · Davis (Austr.) · American Highland 1800 · Ingrid Christensen Coast · 4030 1040

Wilhelm II Coast · Queen Mary Land · 3030 2570 · Drygalski I. · Davis Sea · Masson I. · Shackleton Ice Shelf · Denman Gl. · Mill I. · Scott Gl. · Knox Coast · Budd Coast · Casey (Austr.) · C. Poinsett · Sabrina Coast · Totten Glacier · Banzare Coast · Dalton Iceberg Tongue · Clarie Coast · Porpoise Bay · 2216 2798 · 2435 4776 · Dumont d'Urville (Fr.) · Terre Adélie · George V Land · Commonwealth B. · Magnetic Pole 1990 · Oates Land · C. Adare 3719 · Possession I. · Ross Sea · Coulman I. · Victoria Land · Mt. Murchison 3502 · Pr. Albert Mts. · Mt. Lister · Mt. Erebus 4023 · McMurdo (U.S.A.) · Scott (N.Z.) · Ross I. · 3743 · Franklin I. · Transantarctic Mts. · Mt. Markham 4349 · Shackleton Inlet · Queen Alexandra Ra. · West Ice Shelf

Legend

Ice cap
Permanent ice shelf
Maximum extent of sea ice
March (Summer) extent of sea ice
▲3488 / 3700 — Surface elevation and depth of ice (in metres)
● Stanley (U.K.) — Permanent bases

ft | m
9000 | 3000
6000 | 2000
4500 | 1500
3000 | 1000
1200 | 400
600 | 200
0 | 0
500 | 1500
1000 | 3000
2000 | 6000
3000 | 9000
4000 | 12 000
5000 | 15 000
m | ft

Scale 1 : 35 000 000
200 · 0 · 200 · 400 · 600 · 800 miles
400 · 0 · 400 · 800 · 1200 km

WORLD THEMATIC MAPS

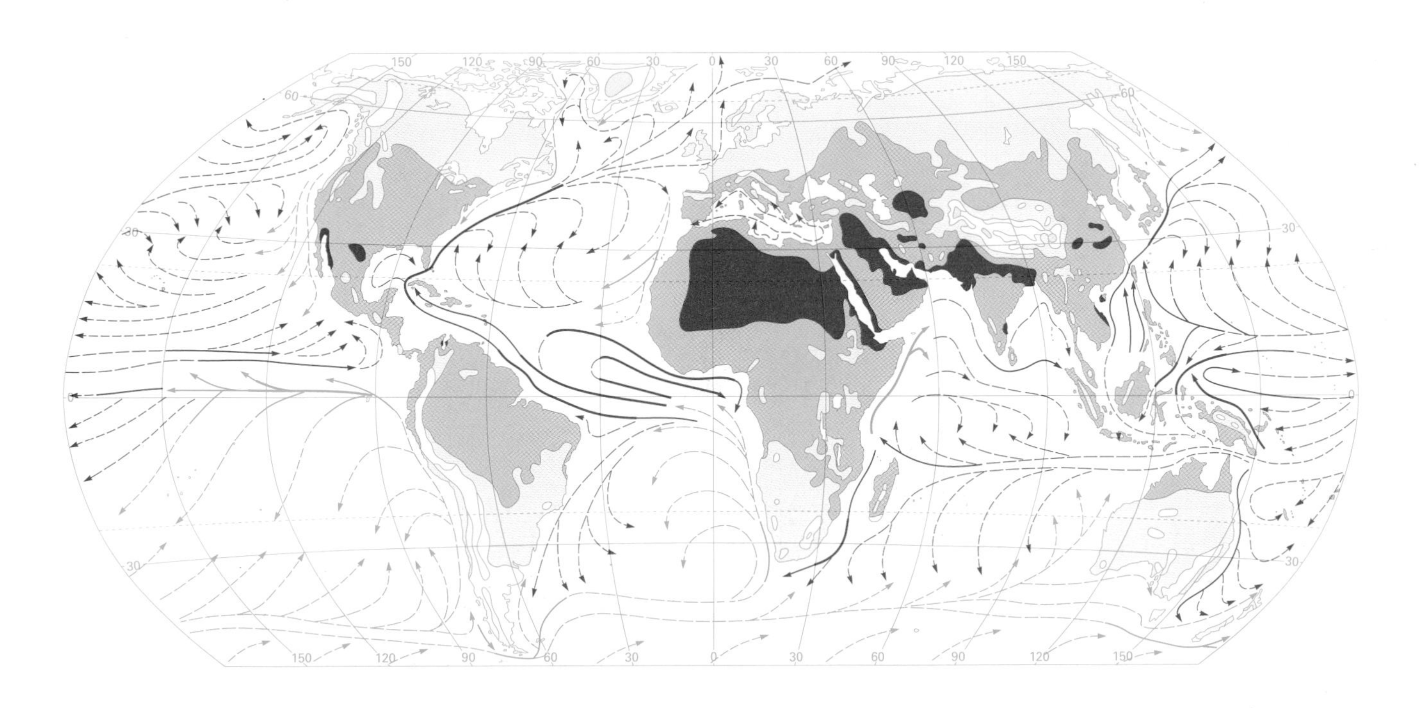

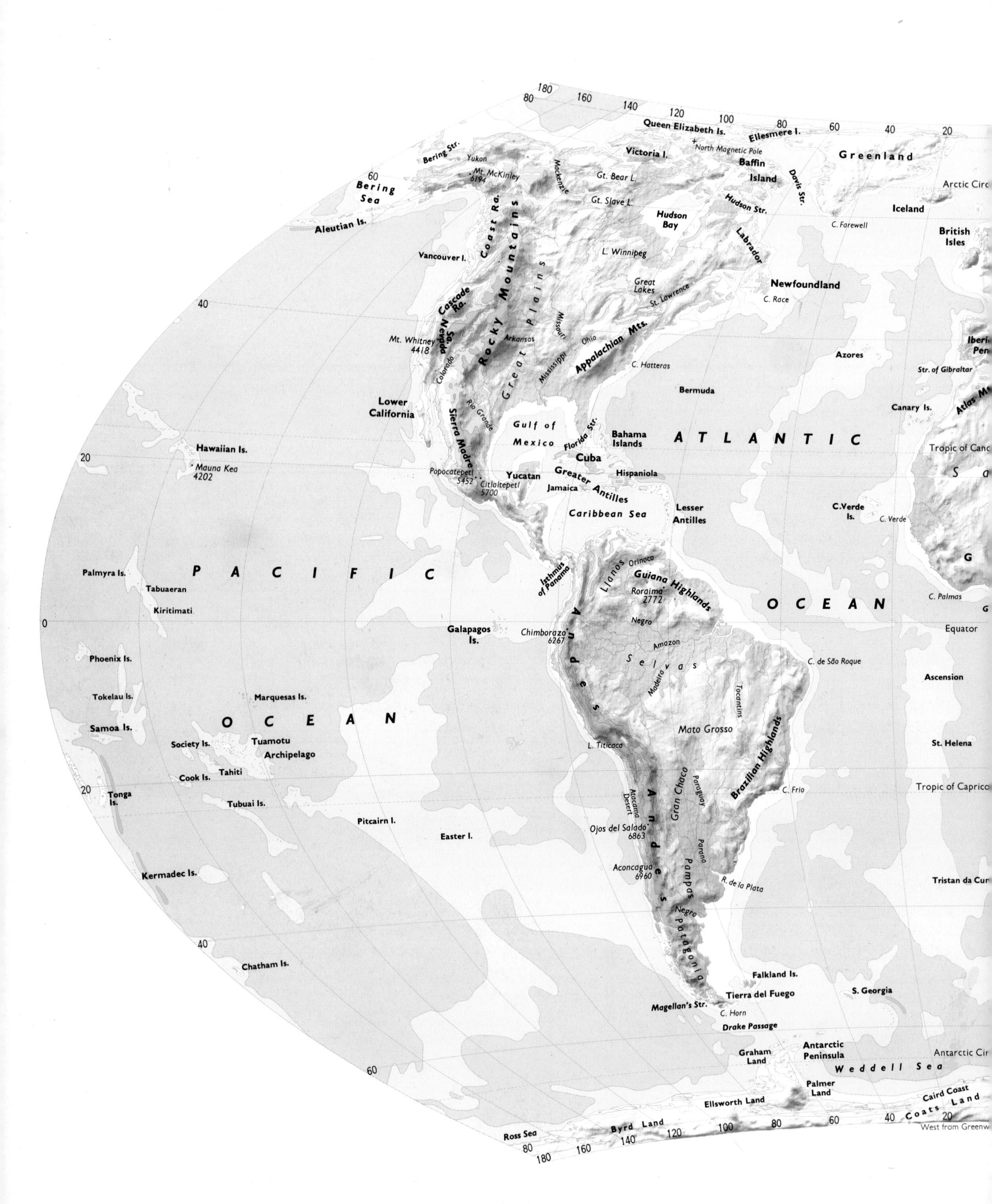

180 80 160 140 120 100 80 60 40 20

Queen Elizabeth Is. Ellesmere I. Greenland

Bering Str. Yukon Victoria I. North Magnetic Pole Baffin Arctic Circle

60 Mt. McKinley Mackenzie Gt. Bear L. Island Iceland

Bering 6194 Gt. Slave L. Davis Str.

Sea Hudson Str. British

Coast Ra. Hudson Labrador Isles

Aleutian Is. Bay

Vancouver I. L. Winnipeg Newfoundland

40 Great St. Lawrence C. Race

Cascade Ra. Rocky Mountains Lakes

Great Plains Iberian

Mt. Whitney Sierra Nevada Arkansas Missouri Ohio Appalachian Mts. Azores Pen.

4418 Colorado Mississippi C. Hatteras Str. of Gibraltar

Lower Rio Grande Bermuda Canary Is. Atlas Mts

California ATLANTIC Tropic of Cancer

Gulf of Bahama S

20 Hawaiian Is. Sierra Madre Mexico Florida Str. Islands

Mauna Kea Popocatepetl Cuba

4202 5452 Yucatan Citlaltepetl Greater Antilles Hispaniola C. Verde

5700 Jamaica Is. C. Verde

Caribbean Sea Lesser G

Palmyra Is. Antilles OCEAN

Tabuaeran P A C I F I C Isthmus Orinoco Guiana Highlands C. Palmas

Kiritimati of Panama Llanos Roraima

0 2772 Equator

Galapagos Chimborazo Negro Ascension

Phoenix Is. Is. 6267 Amazon C. de São Roque

Selvas

Tokelau Is. Madeira St. Helena

Marquesas Is. Andes

Samoa Is. O C E A N Mato Grosso

Society Is. Tuamotu Brazilian Highlands

Cook Is. Tahiti Archipelago L. Titicaca Paraguay C. Frio

20 Tonga Tubuai Is. Gran Chaco Tropic of Capricorn

Is. Atacama Paraná

Pitcairn I. Desert Andes R. de la Plata Tristan da Cunha

Easter I. Ojos del Salado Pampas

6863

Kermadec Is. Aconcagua Negro

6960 Patagonia

40 Chatham Is. Falkland Is. S. Georgia

Tierra del Fuego

Magellan's Str. C. Horn

Drake Passage Antarctic

Graham Antarctic Circle

60 Land Peninsula Weddell Sea

Palmer

Land Caird Coast

Ellsworth Land Coats Land

Ross Sea Byrd Land 100 80 60 40 20

180 140 120 West from Greenwich

160

Projection: Hammer Equal Area

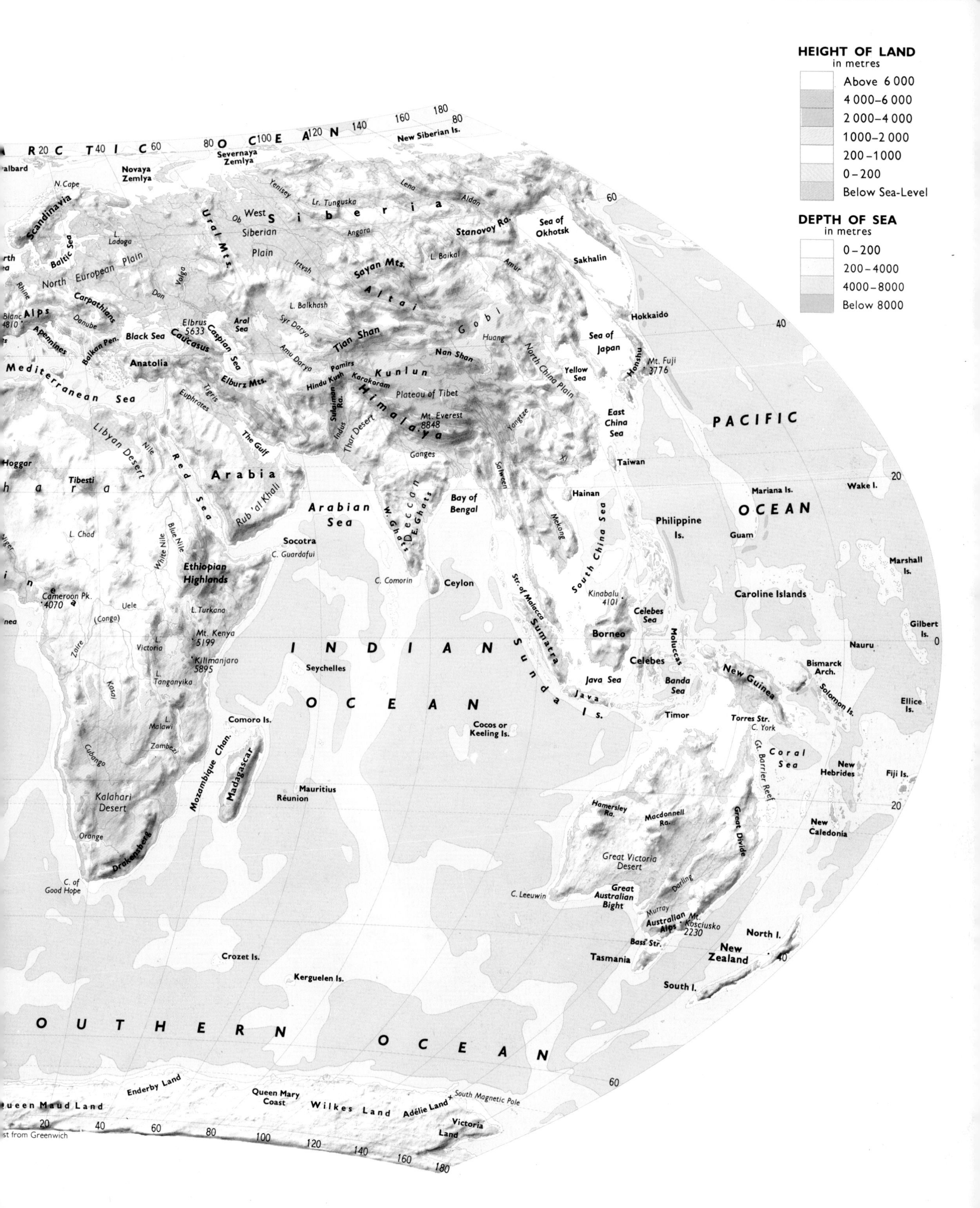

HEIGHT OF LAND
in metres

Above 6 000
4 000–6 000
2 000–4 000
1000–2 000
200–1000
0–200
Below Sea-Level

DEPTH OF SEA
in metres

0–200
200–4000
4000–8000
Below 8000

ARCTIC OCEAN

Svalbard
N. Cape
Novaya Zemlya
Severnaya Zemlya
New Siberian Is.
Scandinavia
N. Cape
Baltic Sea
North Sea
Rhine
North European Plain
Ural Mts.
Ob
West Siberian Plain
S i b e r i a
Yenisey
Lr. Tunguska
Lena
Aldan
Angara
Stanovoy Ra.
Sea of Okhotsk
Irtysh
Sayan Mts.
Altai
L. Baikal
Amur
Sakhalin
Hokkaido
Alps
Blanc 4810
Apennines
Carpathians
Danube
Volga
Don
L. Ladoga
L. Balkhash
Gobi
Sea of Japan
Honshu
Mt. Fuji 3776
Black Sea
Balkan Pen.
Caucasus
Elbrus 5633
Caspian Sea
Aral Sea
Syr Darya
Amu Darya
Tian Shan
Pamirs
Nan Shan
Huang
North China Plain
Yellow Sea
East China Sea
Anatolia
Elburz Mts.
Euphrates
Tigris
Hindu Kush
Karakoram
Kunlun
Plateau of Tibet
Mediterranean Sea
Libyan Desert
Nile
Red Sea
The Gulf
Suleiman Ra.
Indus
Thar Desert
H i m a l a y a
Mt. Everest 8848
Ganges
Yangtze
Salween
Xi
Taiwan
PACIFIC
Hoggar
Tibesti
Sahara
Arabia
Rub' al Khali
Arabian Sea
W. Ghats
Deccan
E. Ghats
Bay of Bengal
Mekong
Hainan
South China Sea
Philippine Is.
Guam
Mariana Is.
Wake I.
OCEAN
Niger
L. Chad
Socotra
C. Guardafui
C. Comorin
Ceylon
Str. of Malacca
Kinabalu 4101
Caroline Islands
Marshall Is.
Cameroon Pk. 4070
Guinea
Uele
(Congo)
Ethiopian Highlands
L. Turkana
Mt. Kenya 5199
Sumatra
Borneo
Celebes Sea
Celebes
Moluccas
Nauru
Gilbert Is.
Zaire
L. Victoria
Kilimanjaro 5895
INDIAN
Seychelles
Java Sea
Java
Banda Sea
New Guinea
Bismarck Arch.
Solomon Is.
Ellice Is.
Kasai
L. Tanganyika
Comoro Is.
OCEAN
Timor
Torres Str.
C. York
L. Malawi
Zambezi
Madagascar
Mozambique Chan.
Mauritius
Réunion
Cocos or Keeling Is.
Coral Sea
New Hebrides
Fiji Is.
Cubango
Kalahari Desert
Drakensberg
Hamersley Ra.
Macdonnell Ra.
Great Barrier Reef
New Caledonia
Orange
C. of Good Hope
Great Victoria Desert
Great Divide
Darling
C. Leeuwin
Great Australian Bight
Murray
Australian Alps
Mt. Kosciusko 2230
North I.
New Zealand
Bass Str.
Tasmania
South I.
Crozet Is.
Kerguelen Is.
S O U T H E R N   O C E A N
Queen Maud Land
Enderby Land
Queen Mary Coast
Wilkes Land
Adélie Land
South Magnetic Pole
Victoria Land
East from Greenwich

1 : 80 000 000

Copyright, George Philip & Son, Ltd.

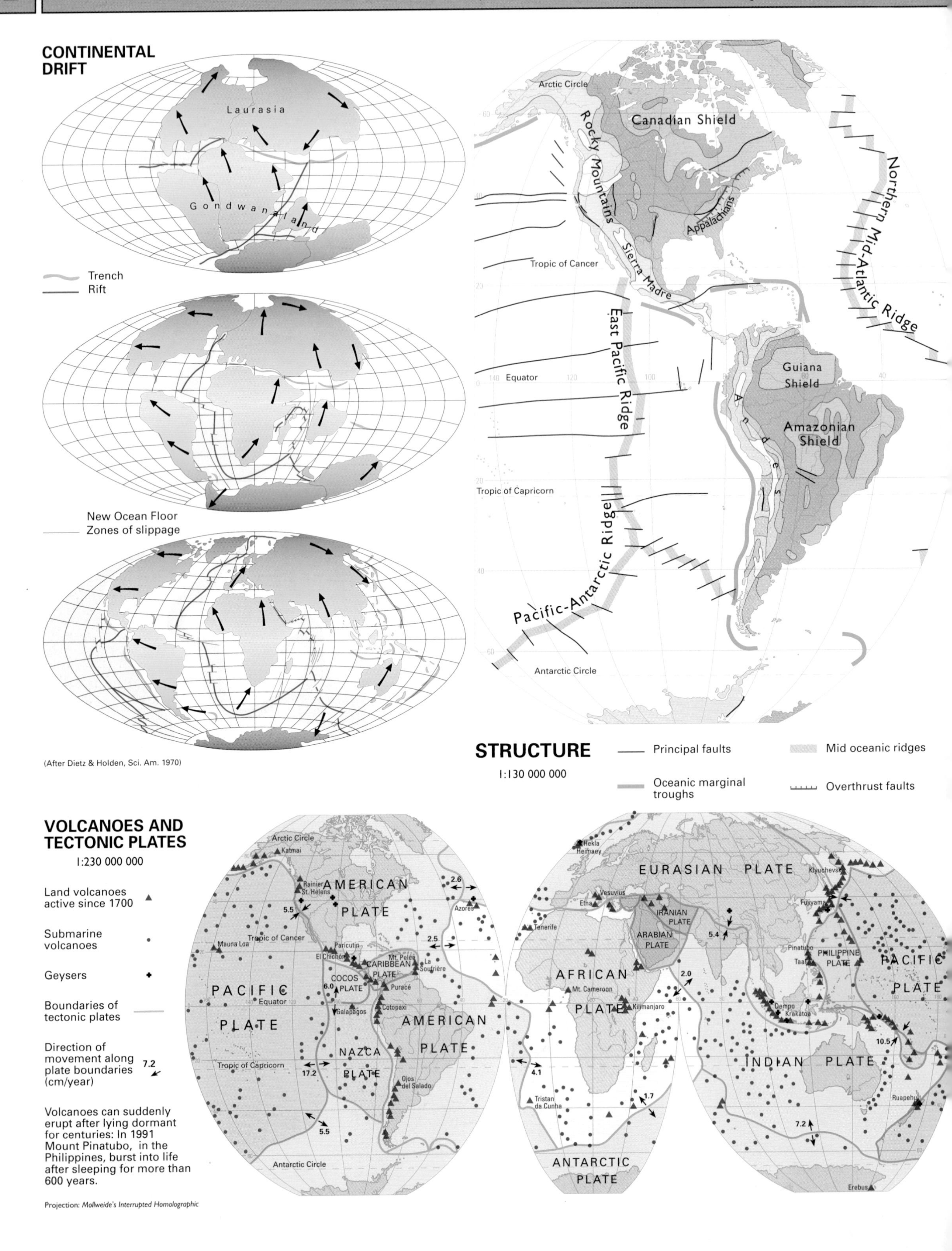

CONTINENTAL DRIFT

Laurasia

Gondwanaland

~ Trench
— Rift

New Ocean Floor
Zones of slippage

(After Dietz & Holden, Sci. Am. 1970)

Arctic Circle

Canadian Shield

Rocky Mountains

Appalachians

Tropic of Cancer

Sierra Madre

East Pacific Ridge

Northern Mid-Atlantic Ridge

Equator

Guiana Shield

Andes

Amazonian Shield

Tropic of Capricorn

Pacific-Antarctic Ridge

Antarctic Circle

STRUCTURE

1:130 000 000

— Principal faults

Oceanic marginal troughs

Mid oceanic ridges

ᴜᴜᴜ Overthrust faults

VOLCANOES AND TECTONIC PLATES

1:230 000 000

Land volcanoes
active since 1700 ▲

Submarine
volcanoes ·

Geysers +

Boundaries of
tectonic plates

Direction of
movement along
plate boundaries
(cm/year) 7.2 ↙

Volcanoes can suddenly
erupt after lying dormant
for centuries: In 1991
Mount Pinatubo, in the
Philippines, burst into life
after sleeping for more than
600 years.

Projection: Mollweide's Interrupted Homolographic

Arctic Circle
Katmai
Rainier
St. Helens
AMERICAN
PLATE
Azores
2.6

5.5

Mauna Loa
Tropic of Cancer
Paricutin
El Chichón
CARIBBEAN
PLATE
Mt. Pelée
La Soufrière
2.5

PACIFIC
PLATE
COCOS
PLATE
6.0
Puracé
Equator

PLATE

Galapagos
Cotopaxi
AMERICAN
PLATE

NAZCA
PLATE

Tropic of Capricorn
17.2
Ojos
del Salado
7.2

5.5

Antarctic Circle

Hekla
Heimaey
EURASIAN PLATE
Klyuchevsk

Vesuvius
Etna
IRANIAN PLATE
Fujiyama
5.4

Tenerife
ARABIAN PLATE
Pinatubo
Taal
PHILIPPINE
PLATE
PACIFIC
PLATE

AFRICAN
PLATE
Mt. Cameroon
2.0
Kilimanjaro
Dempo
Krakatoa

4.1
INDIAN PLATE
10.5

Tristan
da Cunha
1.7

ANTARCTIC
PLATE
7.2
Ruapehu

Erebus

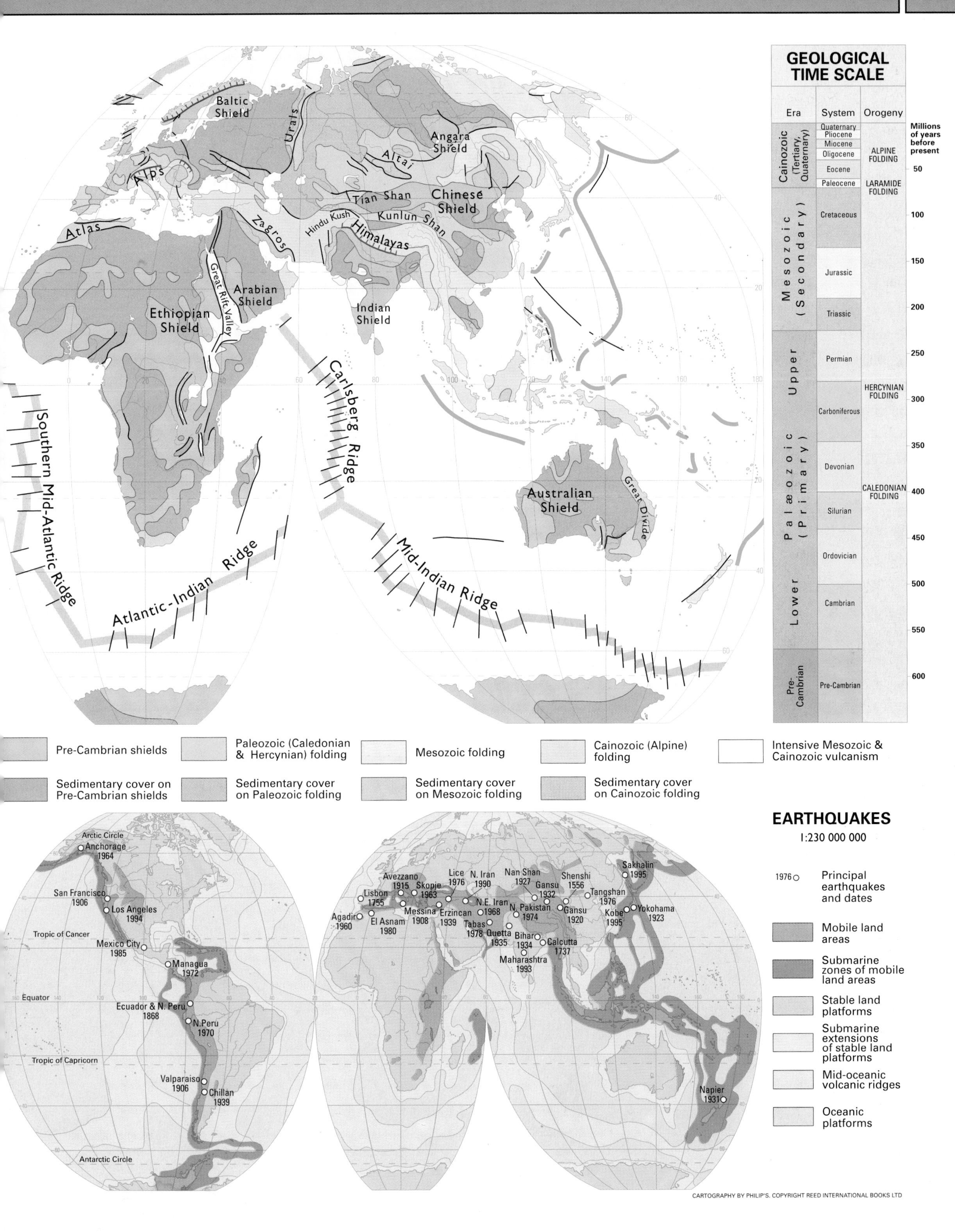

GEOLOGICAL TIME SCALE

Era	System	Orogeny	Millions of years before present
Cainozoic (Tertiary, Quaternary)	Quaternary		
	Pliocene	ALPINE FOLDING	
	Miocene		50
	Oligocene		
	Eocene	LARAMIDE FOLDING	
	Paleocene		
Mesozoic (Secondary)	Cretaceous		100
	Jurassic		150
	Triassic		200
Upper Palæozoic (Primary)	Permian		250
	Carboniferous	HERCYNIAN FOLDING	300
	Devonian		350
	Silurian	CALEDONIAN FOLDING	400
Lower Palæozoic (Primary)	Ordovician		450
	Cambrian		500
			550
Pre-Cambrian	Pre-Cambrian		600

Pre-Cambrian shields

Sedimentary cover on Pre-Cambrian shields

Paleozoic (Caledonian & Hercynian) folding

Sedimentary cover on Paleozoic folding

Mesozoic folding

Sedimentary cover on Mesozoic folding

Cainozoic (Alpine) folding

Sedimentary cover on Cainozoic folding

Intensive Mesozoic & Cainozoic vulcanism

Map labels: Baltic Shield, Urals, Angara Shield, Altai, Alps, Tian Shan, Chinese Shield, Atlas, Zagros, Hindu Kush, Kunlun Shan, Himalayas, Great Rift Valley, Arabian Shield, Ethiopian Shield, Indian Shield, Carlsberg Ridge, Australian Shield, Great Divide, Southern Mid-Atlantic Ridge, Atlantic-Indian Ridge, Mid-Indian Ridge

EARTHQUAKES

1:230 000 000

1976 ○ Principal earthquakes and dates

Mobile land areas

Submarine zones of mobile land areas

Stable land platforms

Submarine extensions of stable land platforms

Mid-oceanic volcanic ridges

Oceanic platforms

Earthquake labels: Arctic Circle, Anchorage 1964, San Francisco 1906, Los Angeles 1994, Tropic of Cancer, Mexico City 1985, Managua 1972, Equator, Ecuador & N. Peru 1868, N. Peru 1970, Tropic of Capricorn, Valparaiso 1906, Chillan 1939, Antarctic Circle, Avezzano 1915, Lisbon 1755, Skopje 1963, Lice 1976, N. Iran 1990, Nan Shan 1927, Shenshi 1556, Sakhalin 1995, Agadir 1960, Messina 1908, Erzincan 1939, N.E. Iran 1968, N. Pakistan 1974, Gansu 1932, Gansu 1920, Tangshan 1976, Kobe 1995, Yokohama 1923, El Asnam 1980, Tabas 1978, Quetta 1935, Bihar 1934, Calcutta 1737, Maharashtra 1993, Napier 1931

CARTOGRAPHY BY PHILIP'S. COPYRIGHT REED INTERNATIONAL BOOKS LTD

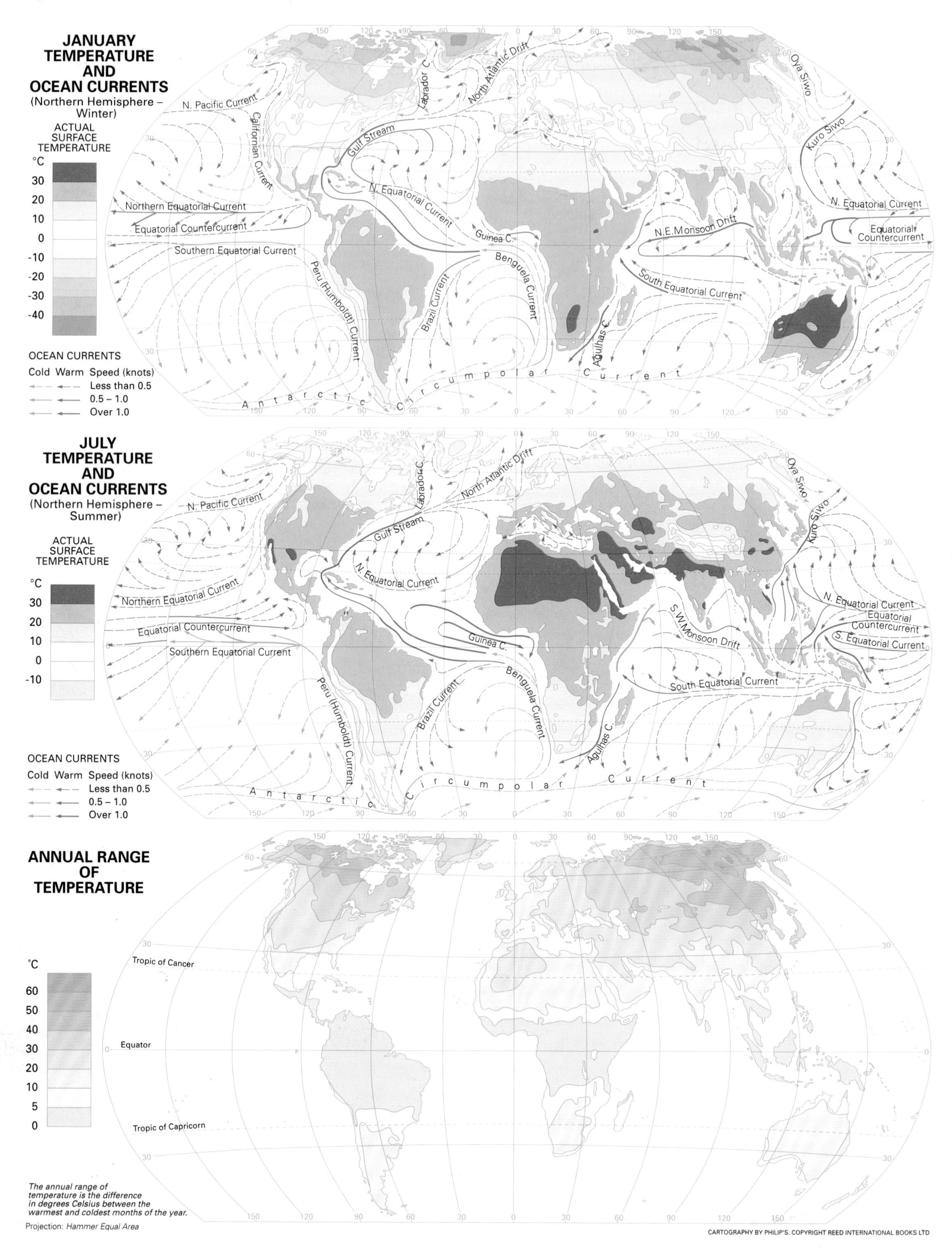

JANUARY TEMPERATURE AND OCEAN CURRENTS
(Northern Hemisphere – Winter)

ACTUAL SURFACE TEMPERATURE

°C
30
20
10
0
-10
-20
-30
-40

OCEAN CURRENTS

Cold Warm Speed (knots)
Less than 0.5
0.5 – 1.0
Over 1.0

JULY TEMPERATURE AND OCEAN CURRENTS
(Northern Hemisphere – Summer)

ACTUAL SURFACE TEMPERATURE

°C
30
20
10
0
-10

OCEAN CURRENTS

Cold Warm Speed (knots)
Less than 0.5
0.5 – 1.0
Over 1.0

ANNUAL RANGE OF TEMPERATURE

°C
60
50
40
30
20
10
5
0

Tropic of Cancer

Equator

Tropic of Capricorn

The annual range of temperature is the difference in degrees Celsius between the warmest and coldest months of the year.

Projection: *Hammer Equal Area*

CARTOGRAPHY BY PHILIP'S. COPYRIGHT REED INTERNATIONAL BOOKS LTD

1:190 000 000

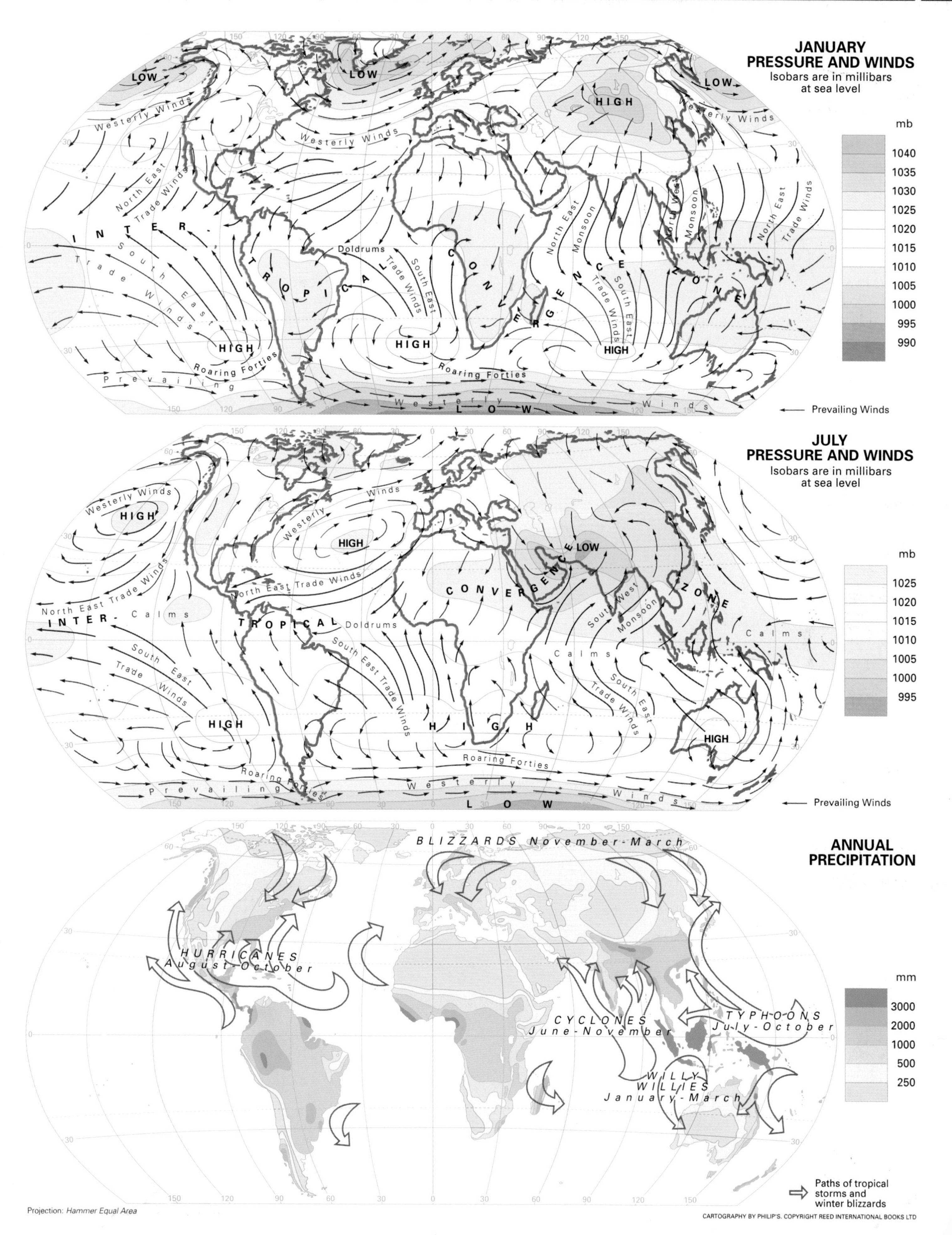

**JANUARY
PRESSURE AND WINDS**
Isobars are in millibars
at sea level

mb

1040
1035
1030
1025
1020
1015
1010
1005
1000
995
990

LOW
LOW
HIGH
LOW
Westerly Winds
Westerly Winds
Westerly Winds
North East Trade Winds
North East Trade Winds
North East Monsoon
North West Monsoon
I N T E R -
T R O P I C A L
Doldrums
South East Trade Winds
C O N V E R G E N C E   Z O N E
South East Trade Winds
HIGH
HIGH
HIGH
Roaring Forties
Roaring Forties
Prevailing
W e s t e r l y   W i n d s
L O W

⟶ Prevailing Winds

**JULY
PRESSURE AND WINDS**
Isobars are in millibars
at sea level

mb

1025
1020
1015
1010
1005
1000
995

Westerly Winds
HIGH
HIGH
Westerly Winds
LOW
North East Trade Winds
North East Trade Winds
I N T E R -
C a l m s
C O N V E R G E N C E   Z O N E
T R O P I C A L
Doldrums
South East Trade Winds
South West Monsoon
C a l m s
South East Trade Winds
HIGH
H I G H
Calms
Calms
HIGH
Roaring Forties
P r e v a i l i n g
Roaring Forties
W e s t e r l y   W i n d s
L O W

⟶ Prevailing Winds

**ANNUAL
PRECIPITATION**

BLIZZARDS November–March
HURRICANES August–October
CYCLONES June–November
TYPHOONS July–October
WILLY WILLIES January–March

mm

3000
2000
1000
500
250

⟹ Paths of tropical
storms and
winter blizzards

Projection: *Hammer Equal Area*

CARTOGRAPHY BY PHILIP'S. COPYRIGHT REED INTERNATIONAL BOOKS LTD

1:190 000 000

CLIMATIC REGIONS after Köppen

Köppen's classification recognises five major climatic regions corresponding broadly to the five principal vegetation types and these are designated by the letters A, B, C, D and E. Each one of these are subdivided on the basis of temperature and rainfall.

TROPICAL RAINY CLIMATES A

Af	Rain Forest Climate	All mean monthly temperatures above 18°C and an annual variation in temperature of less than 6°C
Am	Monsoon Climate	
Aw	Savanna Climate	All monthly temperatures above 18°C but with an annual variation in temperature of less than 12°C

DRY CLIMATES B

BS	Steppe Climate	The principal difference between this grouping and groups A, C, D and E is the combination of a wide range of temperatures with low rainfall
BW	Desert Climate	

WARM TEMPERATE RAINY CLIMATES C

The climatic group is separated from group A by having the mean temperature of the coolest month below 18°C but above -3°C. The mean temperature of the warmest month is over 10°C.

Cw	Dry Winter Climate	The wettest month of summer has at least ten times as much rain as the driest winter month
Cs	Dry Summer Climate (Mediterranean)	The wettest month of winter has at least three times as much rain as the driest month of summer. The driest summer month itself has less than 30mm rainfall.
Cf	Climate with no Dry Season	Even rainfall throughout the year.

COLD TEMPERATE RAINY CLIMATES D

Dw	Dry Winter Climate	The mean temperature of the coldest month is below -3°C but the mean temperature of the warmest month is still over 10°C.
Df	Climate with no Dry Season	

POLAR CLIMATES E

ET	Tundra Climate	The mean temperature of the warmest month is below 10°C giving permanently frozen subsoil.
EF	Polar Climate	The mean temperature of the warmest month is below 0°C giving permanent ice and snow.

The classification is in some cases subdivided by the addition of the following letters after the major types :-

Used with groups C and D	**a**	Hot summer – mean temperature of the hottest month above 22°C and with more than four months of over 10°C.
	b	Warm summer – mean temperature of the hottest month below 22°C but still with more than four months of over 10°C.
	c	Cool short summer – mean temperature of the hottest month below 22°C but with less than four months of over 10°C.
Used with group D	**d**	Cool short summer and cold winter – mean temperature of the hottest month below 22°C and of the coolest month below -38°C.
Used with group B	**h**	Hot dry climate – mean annual temperature above 18°C.
	k	Cool dry climate – mean annual temperature below 18°C.
Used with group E	**H**	Polar climate due to elevation being over 1500m.

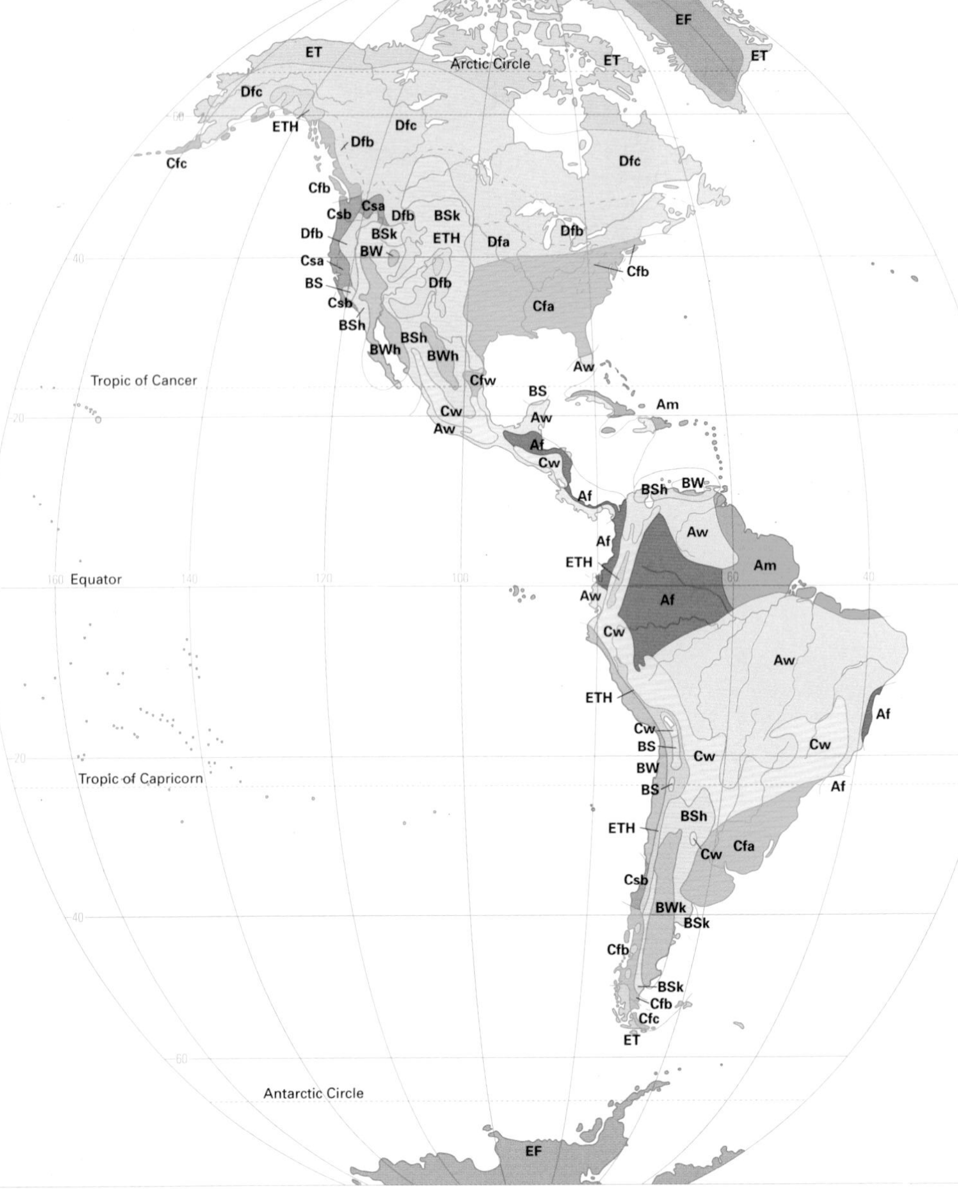

SOIL REGIONS

1:220 000 000

after Glinka, Stremme, Marbut, and others

- Tundra soil
- Podzols
- Brown forest soil
- Lightly leached dry forest soil
- Red and yellow sub-tropical forest soil
- Reddish savanna soil and tropical red earths
- Laterites
- Chernozem
- Degraded chernozem
- Black savanna soil
- Chestnut steppe soil
- Grey and brown desert steppe soils
- Alluvium
- Mountain and high plateau soils
- Oases soil
- Tropical and mangrove swamp

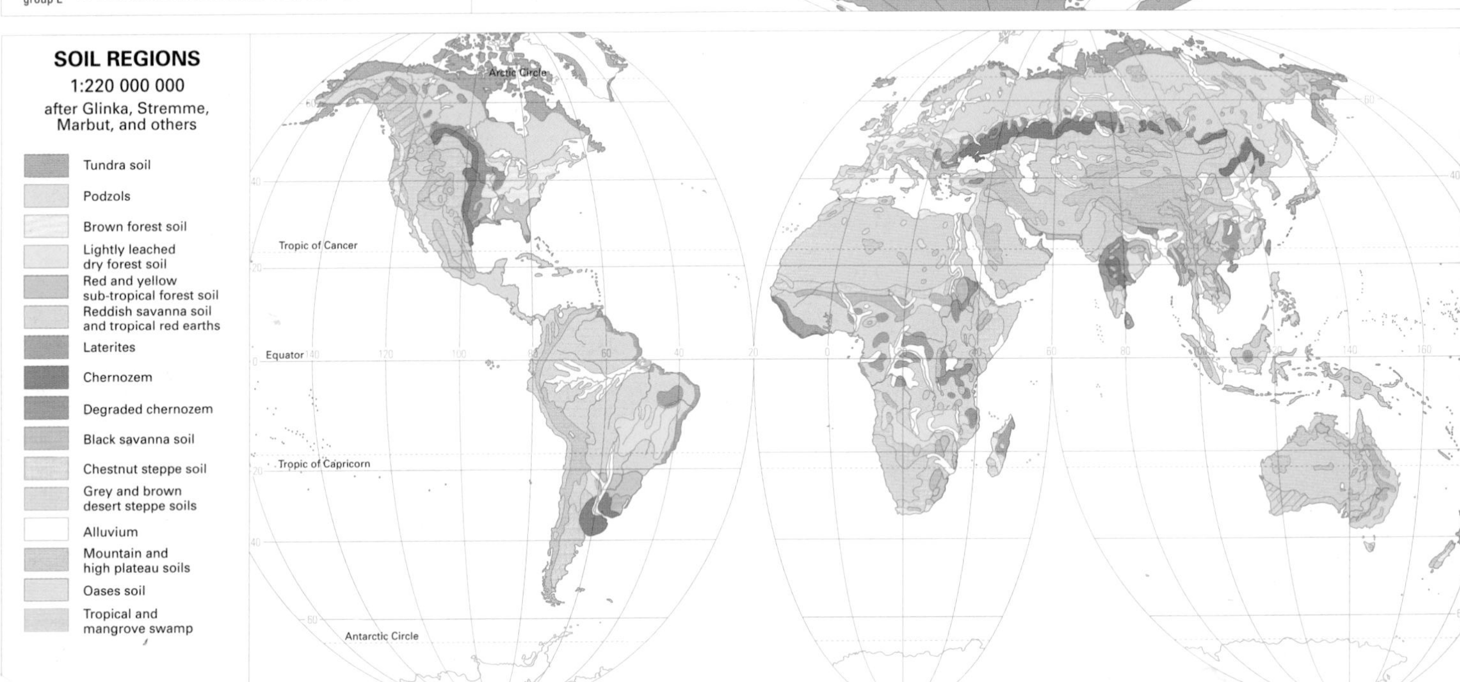

Projection: Interrupted Mollweide's Homolographic

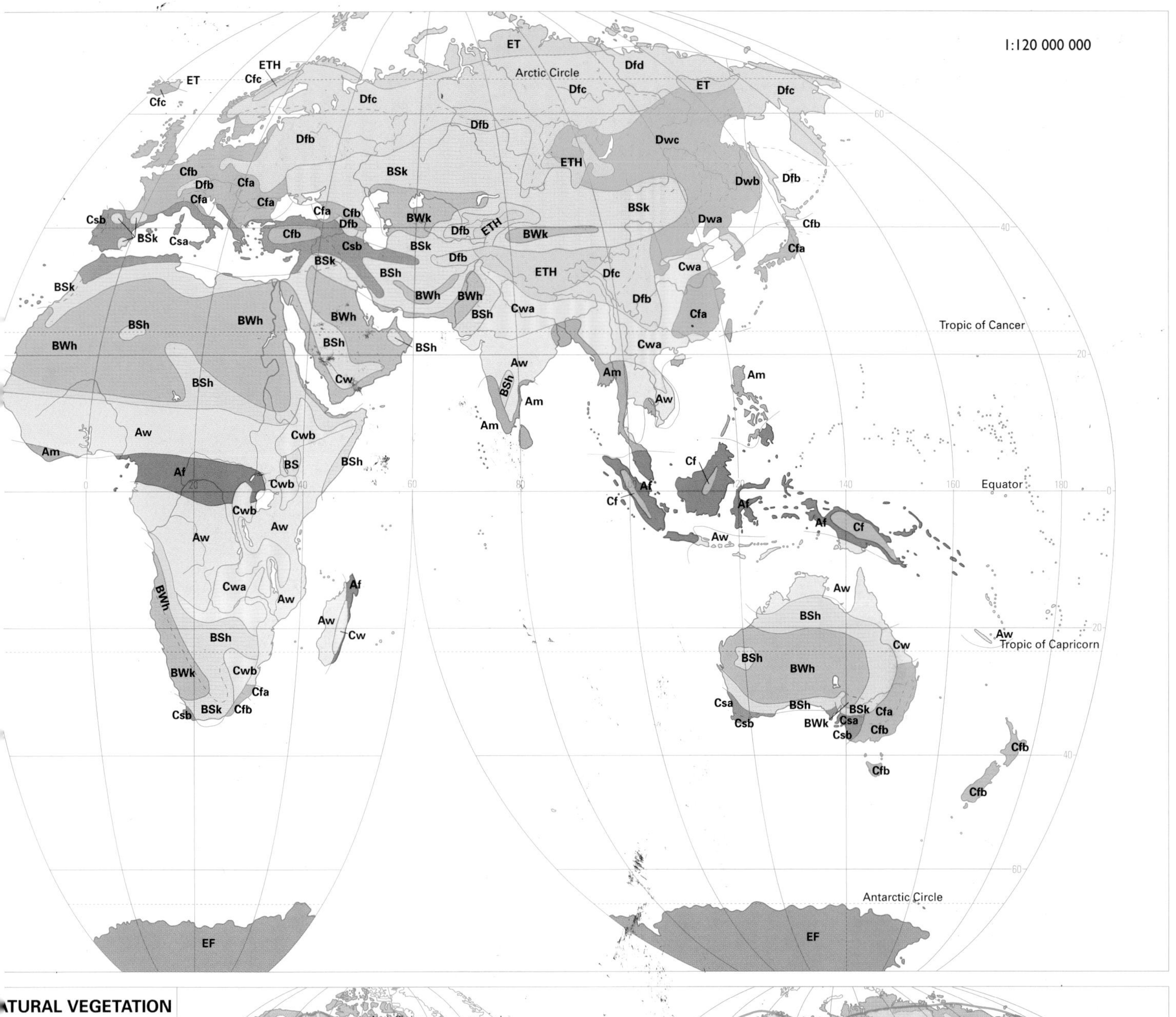

1:120 000 000

ETH
Cfc
ET
Cfc
Cfc
ET
Arctic Circle
Dfd
Dfc
ET
Dfc
Dfb
Dfc
Dfb
Dfb
Dwc
Cfb
BSk
Cfb
Cfa
ETH
Csb
Dfb
Cfa
Cfa
Dwb
Dfb
Csb
Cfb
Cfa
Cfb
BWk
Dwa
Cfb
BSk
Csa
Csb
Dfb
ETH
Cwa
Cfa
BSk
BSk
BSh
BWk
ETH
Dwa
Tropic of Cancer
BSh
BWh
BWh
BSh
Dfc
Cwa
BWh
BWh
Cfa
BWh
BSh
BSh
Cwa
BSh
BSh
Cw
Aw
Am
BSh
Cwb
Am
Aw
Am
Af
Cwb
Am
BSh
Cf
Equator
Cwb
Aw
Af
Cf
Cwa
Aw
Cf
Af
Af
BWh
Aw
Af
Cf
Aw
Aw
Aw
Cw
Aw
Cwa
Aw
BSh
Aw
Tropic of Capricorn
BWk
Cwb
BSh
Cfa
BWh
Cw
Csb
BSk
Cfb
BSh
Csa
BSk
Cfa
Csb
BWk
Cfb
Csb
Cfb
Cfb
Cfb

Arctic Circle

Antarctic Circle

EF
EF

CARTOGRAPHY BY PHILIP'S. COPYRIGHT REED INTERNATIONAL BOOKS LTD

ATURAL VEGETATION

1:220 000 000
after Austin Miller

- Tropical rainforest
- Subtropical and temperate rainforest
- Monsoon woodland and open jungle
- Subtropical and temperate woodland, scrub and bush
- Tropical savanna, with low trees and bush
- Tropical savanna and grasslands
- Dry semi-desert, with shrub and grass
- Desert shrub
- Desert
- Dry steppe and shrub
- Temperate grasslands, prairie and steppe
- Mediterranean hardwood forest and scrub
- Temperate deciduous forest and meadow
- Temperate deciduous and coniferous forest
- Northern coniferous forest (taiga)
- Mountainous forest, mainly coniferous
- High plateau steppe and tundra
- Arctic tundra
- Polar and mountainous ice desert

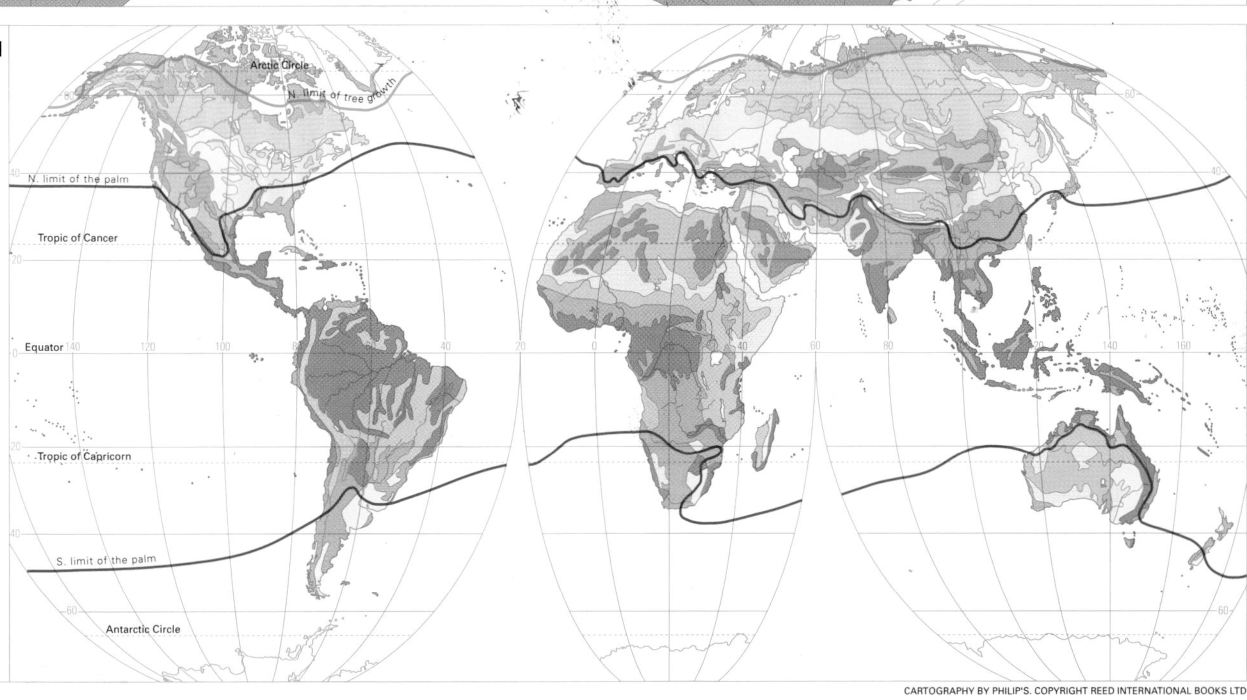

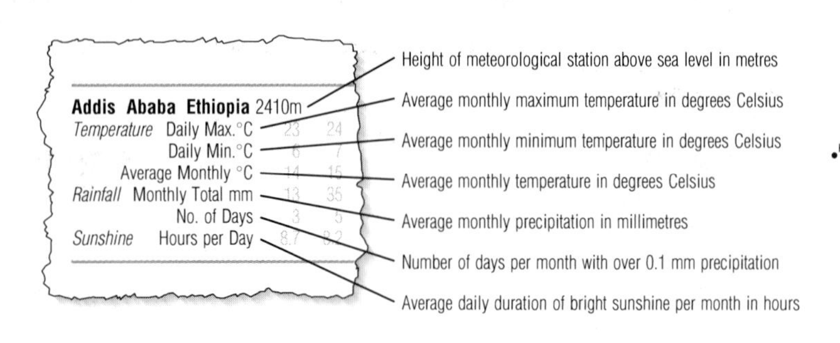

Addis Ababa Ethiopia 2410m — Height of meteorological station above sea level in metres

Temperature Daily Max.°C 23 24 — Average monthly maximum temperature in degrees Celsius

Daily Min.°C 6 7 — Average monthly minimum temperature in degrees Celsius

Average Monthly °C 14 15 — Average monthly temperature in degrees Celsius

Rainfall Monthly Total mm 13 35 — Average monthly precipitation in millimetres

No. of Days 3 5 — Number of days per month with over 0.1 mm precipitation

Sunshine Hours per Day 8.7 8.2 — Average daily duration of bright sunshine per month in hours

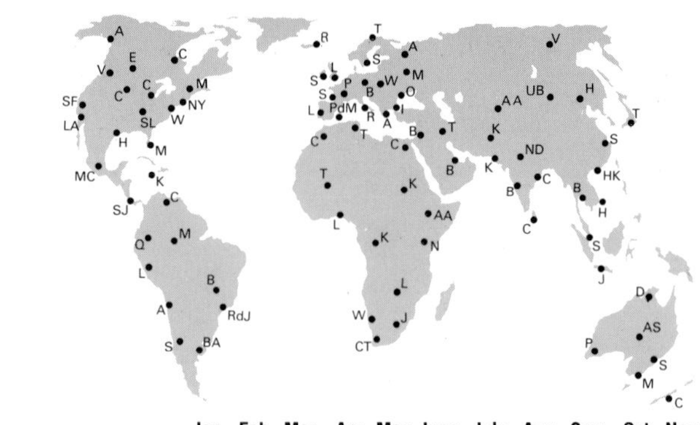

	Jan	Feb	Mar	Apr	May	June	July	Aug	Sep	Oct	Nov	Dec	Year
Addis Ababa Ethiopia 2410m													
Temperature Daily Max.°C	23	24	25	24	25	23	20	20	21	22	23	22	23
Daily Min.°C	6	7	9	10	9	10	11	11	10	7	5	5	8
Average Monthly °C	14	15	17	17	17	16	16	15	15	15	14	14	15
Rainfall Monthly Total mm	13	35	67	91	81	117	247	255	167	29	8	5	1115
No. of Days	3	5	10	12	10	20	27	28	21	7	2	1	146
Sunshine Hours per Day	8.7	8.2	7.6	8.1	6.5	4.8	2.8	3.2	5.2	7.6	6.7	7	6.4
Alice Springs Australia 580m													
Temperature Daily Max.°C	35	35	32	27	23	19	19	23	27	31	33	35	28
Daily Min.°C	21	20	17	12	8	5	4	6	10	15	18	20	13
Average Monthly °C	28	27	25	20	15	12	12	14	18	23	25	27	21
Rainfall Monthly Total mm	44	33	27	10	15	13	7	8	7	18	29	38	249
No. of Days	4	3	3	2	2	2	1	2	3	3	4	4	31
Sunshine Hours per Day	10.3	10.4	9.3	9.2	8	8	8.9	9.8	10	9.7	10.1	10	9.5
Alma Ata Kazakhstan 848m													
Temperature Daily Max.°C	-3	-2	6	17	22	27	29	28	19	14	5	-1	13
Daily Min.°C	-14	-13	-6	3	9	13	16	14	5	1	-7	-12	1
Average Monthly °C	-9	-7	0	10	15	20	22	21	12	8	-1	-6	7
Rainfall Monthly Total mm	26	32	64	89	99	59	35	23	25	46	48	35	581
No. of Days	8	8	11	12	11	10	9	6	5	7	9	9	105
Sunshine Hours per Day	3.7	3.8	4.5	6.3	7.8	9.1	10.2	9.6	8	6.4	4.2	3.6	6.6
Anchorage USA 183m													
Temperature Daily Max.°C	-7	-3	0	7	13	18	19	17	13	6	-2	-6	-6
Daily Min.°C	-15	-12	-9	-2	4	8	10	9	5	-2	-9	-14	-2
Average Monthly °C	-11	-7	-4	3	9	13	15	13	9	2	-5	-10	-4
Rainfall Monthly Total mm	20	18	13	11	13	25	47	64	64	47	28	24	374
No. of Days	5	10	7	7	7	9	13	13	13	11	10	11	116
Sunshine Hours per Day	2.4	4.1	6.6	8.3	8.3	9.2	8.5	6	4.4	3.1	2.6	1.6	5.4
Antofagasta Chile 95m													
Temperature Daily Max.°C	25	25	24	21	20	19	17	17	18	19	21	22	21
Daily Min.°C	17	17	16	15	13	11	11	11	12	13	15	16	14
Average Monthly °C	21	21	20	18	16	15	14	14	15	16	18	19	17
Rainfall Monthly Total mm	0	0	0	1	1	3	5	3	1	3	1	0	18
No. of Days	0	0	0	0.1	0.1	0.2	0.5	0.4	0.5	0.2	0.3	0	2.3
Sunshine Hours per Day	10.5	10.3	8	7.3	6.3	6.1	6	5.5	6	5.5	6.5	8.9	7.2
Archangel Russia 4m													
Temperature Daily Max.°C	-9	-8	-2	5	11	18	22	17	13	6	-2	-7	6
Daily Min.°C	-17	-17	-14	-7	0	6	9	10	3	-3	-8	-14	-4
Average Monthly °C	-13	-12	-8	-1	6	12	16	13	8	1	-5	-10	1
Rainfall Monthly Total mm	33	28	28	28	39	59	63	57	66	55	44	39	539
No. of Days	22	19	19	15	14	14	12	14	19	21	21	23	213
Sunshine Hours per Day	0.2	1.3	3.9	6	7.2	9.2	9.8	7.4	3.3	1.9	0.6	0.1	4.3
Athens Greece 107m													
Temperature Daily Max.°C	13	14	16	20	25	30	33	33	29	24	19	15	23
Daily Min.°C	6	7	8	11	16	20	23	23	19	15	12	8	14
Average Monthly °C	10	10	12	16	20	25	28	28	24	20	15	11	18
Rainfall Monthly Total mm	62	37	37	23	23	14	6	7	15	51	56	71	402
No. of Days	6	11	11	9	8	4	2	3	4	8	12	15	103
Sunshine Hours per Day	3.9	5.2	5.8	7.7	8.9	10.7	11.9	11.5	9.4	6.8	4.8	3.8	7.3
Bahrain City Bahrain 2m													
Temperature Daily Max.°C	20	21	25	29	33	36	37	38	36	32	27	22	30
Daily Min.°C	14	15	18	22	25	29	31	32	29	25	22	16	23
Average Monthly °C	17	18	21	25	29	32	34	35	32	29	25	19	26
Rainfall Monthly Total mm	18	12	10	9	2	0	0	0	0	0.4	3	16	70
No. of Days	3	3	3	2	1	0	0	0	0	0	0.1	3	15
Sunshine Hours per Day	5.9	6.9	7.9	8.8	10.6	13.2	12.1	12	12	10.3	7.7	6.4	9.5
Bangkok Thailand 10m													
Temperature Daily Max.°C	32	33	34	35	34	33	32	32	32	31	31	31	33
Daily Min.°C	20	23	24	26	25	25	25	24	24	24	23	20	24
Average Monthly °C	26	28	29	30	30	29	28	28	28	27	27	26	28
Rainfall Monthly Total mm	9	30	36	82	165	153	168	183	310	239	55	8	1438
No. of Days	2	2	4	5	14	16	19	21	23	17	7	1	131
Sunshine Hours per Day	8.2	8	8	10	7.5	6.1	4.7	5.2	5.2	6.1	7.3	7.8	7
Beirut Lebanon 35m													
Temperature Daily Max.°C	16	17	19	22	26	29	31	32	30	27	23	19	24
Daily Min.°C	11	11	12	15	18	21	23	24	23	20	16	13	17
Average Monthly °C	13	14	16	19	22	25	27	28	26	24	20	16	21
Rainfall Monthly Total mm	195	156	94	51	17	3	0.5	0.5	7	48	130	185	887
No. of Days	16	14	11	6	3	1	0.1	0.2	1	4	9	14	79
Sunshine Hours per Day	4.8	5.4	6.3	7.5	9.9	12.1	11.9	11.3	9.2	8.2	6.6	4.7	8.2
Berlin Germany 55m													
Temperature Daily Max.°C	2	3	8	14	19	22	24	23	20	13	7	3	13
Daily Min.°C	-4	-3	0	4	8	11	13	13	9	5	2	-1	5
Average Monthly °C	-1	0	4	9	14	17	19	18	14	9	4	1	9
Rainfall Monthly Total mm	43	40	31	41	46	62	70	68	46	47	46	41	581
No. of Days	11	9	8	9	9	9	11	9	8	9	10	9	111
Sunshine Hours per Day	1.6	2.5	4.3	5.3	6.9	7.8	7.1	6.6	5.7	3.4	1.6	1.1	4.5
Bombay India 10m													
Temperature Daily Max.°C	28	28	30	32	33	31	30	29	30	32	32	30	31
Daily Min.°C	19	20	22	24	27	26	25	24	24	24	23	21	23
Average Monthly °C	24	24	26	28	30	29	27	27	27	28	27	25	27
Rainfall Monthly Total mm	2	1	0	3	16	520	709	419	297	88	21	2	2078
No. of Days	0	0	0	0	1	16	26	20	14	3	1	0	81
Sunshine Hours per Day	9	9.3	9	9.1	9.3	5	3.1	2.5	5.4	7.7	9.7	9.6	7.4
Brasilia Brazil 910m													
Temperature Daily Max.°C	28	28	28	28	27	27	27	29	30	29	28	27	28
Daily Min.°C	18	18	18	17	15	13	13	14	16	18	18	18	16
Average Monthly °C	23	23	23	22	21	20	20	21	23	24	23	22	22
Rainfall Monthly Total mm	252	204	227	93	17	3	6	3	30	127	255	343	1560
No. of Days	21	16	18	13	5	2	1	3	7	12	19	23	140
Sunshine Av. Monthly Dur.	5.8	5.7	6	7.4	8.7	9.3	9.6	9.8	7.9	6.5	4.8	4.4	7.2
Buenos Aires Argentina 25m													
Temperature Daily Max.°C	30	29	26	22	18	14	14	16	18	21	25	28	22
Daily Min.°C	17	17	16	12	9	5	6	6	8	10	14	16	11
Average Monthly °C	23	23	21	17	13	10	10	11	13	15	19	22	16
Rainfall Monthly Total mm	79	71	109	89	76	61	56	61	79	86	84	99	950
No. of Days	7	6	7	8	7	7	8	9	8	9	9	8	93
Sunshine Hours per Day	9.2	8.5	7.5	6.8	4.9	3.5	3.8	5.2	6	6.8	8.1	8.5	6.6
Cairo Egypt 75m													
Temperature Daily Max.°C	19	21	24	28	32	35	35	35	33	30	26	21	28
Daily Min.°C	9	9	12	14	18	20	22	22	20	18	14	10	16
Average Monthly °C	14	15	18	21	25	28	29	28	26	24	20	16	22
Rainfall Monthly Total mm	4	4	3	1	2	1	0	0	1	1	3	7	25
No. of Days	3	2	1	1	1	0	0	0	1	1	1	2	12
Sunshine Hours per Day	6.9	8.4	8.7	9.7	10.5	11.9	11.7	11.3	10.4	9.4	8.3	6.4	9.5
Calcutta India 5m													
Temperature Daily Max.°C	27	29	34	36	35	34	32	32	32	32	29	26	31
Daily Min.°C	13	15	21	24	25	26	26	26	26	23	18	13	21
Average Monthly °C	20	22	27	30	30	30	29	29	29	28	23	20	26
Rainfall Monthly Total mm	10	30	34	44	140	297	325	332	253	114	20	5	1604
No. of Days	3	4	3	5	9	17	23	23	18	9	1	1	116
Sunshine Hours per Day	8.6	8.7	8.9	9	8.7	5.4	4.1	4.1	5.1	6.5	8.3	8.4	7.1
Cape Town South Africa 44m													
Temperature Daily Max.°C	26	26	25	23	20	18	17	18	19	21	24	25	22
Daily Min.°C	15	15	14	11	9	7	7	7	8	10	13	15	11
Average Monthly °C	21	20	20	17	14	13	12	12	14	16	18	20	16
Rainfall Monthly Total mm	12	19	17	42	67	98	68	76	36	45	12	13	505
No. of Days	5	5	5	9	12	13	12	13	10	9	5	5	103
Sunshine Hours per Day	11.4	10.2	9.4	7.7	6.1	5.7	6.4	6.6	7.6	8.6	10.2	10.9	8.4
Caracas Venezuela 1040m													
Temperature Daily Max.°C	24	25	26	27	27	26	26	26	27	26	25	26	26
Daily Min.°C	14	14	15	16	17	17	16	16	16	16	16	15	16
Average Monthly °C	19	19	20	21	22	21	21	21	21	21	20	20	21
Rainfall Monthly Total mm	23	10	15	33	79	102	109	109	107	109	94	46	836
No. of Days	6	3	4	9	14	15	15	13	12	13	10	11	116
Sunshine Hours per Day	7.6	7.8	7.5	6.4	6.4	6.4	7.3	7.4	7.2	6.8	6.9	6.7	7

Casablanca Morocco 59m

	Jan	Feb	Mar	Apr	May	June	July	Aug	Sep	Oct	Nov	Dec	Year
Temperature Daily Max.°C	17	18	20	21	22	24	26	26	26	24	21	18	22
Daily Min.°C	8	9	11	12	15	18	19	20	18	15	12	10	14
Average Monthly °C	13	13	15	16	18	21	23	23	22	20	17	14	18
Rainfall Monthly Total mm	78	61	54	37	20	3	0	1	6	28	58	94	440
No. of Days	11	8	9	5	4	2	0	1	2	6	9	10	67
Sunshine Hours per Day	5.2	6.3	7.3	9	9.4	9.7	10.2	9.7	9.1	7.4	5.9	5.3	7.9

Cheyenne USA 1869m

	Jan	Feb	Mar	Apr	May	June	July	Aug	Sep	Oct	Nov	Dec	Year
Temperature Daily Max.°C	3	4	6	12	18	24	29	28	23	16	8	5	15
Daily Min.°C	-9	-9	-7	-2	4	9	12	12	7	1	-5	-7	1
Average Monthly °C	-3	-2	0	5	11	16	21	20	15	9	2	-1	8
Rainfall Monthly Total mm	13	14	31	48	64	55	46	37	28	21	16	11	384
No. of Days	6	7	10	10	13	11	11	10	7	5	6	5	101
Sunshine Hours per Day	6	6.9	7.8	8	8.4	10.3	10.1	9.2	9.1	8	6	5.5	7.9

Chicago USA 186m

	Jan	Feb	Mar	Apr	May	June	July	Aug	Sep	Oct	Nov	Dec	Year
Temperature Daily Max.°C	0.6	1.5	6.4	14.1	20.6	26.4	28.9	28	23.8	17.4	8.4	2.1	14.9
Daily Min.°C	-7	-6	-2	5	11	16	20	19	14	8	0	-5	-6
Average Monthly °C	-3	-2	2	9	16	21	24	23	19	13	4	-2	4
Rainfall Monthly Total mm	47	41	70	77	96	103	86	80	69	71	56	48	843
No. of Days	10	10	12	12	13	11	9	9	8	8	10	10	122
Sunshine Hours per Day	4	5	6.6	6.9	8.9	10.2	10	9.2	8.2	6.9	4.5	3.7	7

Christchurch New Zealand 5m

	Jan	Feb	Mar	Apr	May	June	July	Aug	Sep	Oct	Nov	Dec	Year
Temperature Daily Max.°C	21	21	19	17	13	11	10	11	14	17	19	21	16
Daily Min.°C	12	12	10	7	4	2	1	3	5	7	8	11	7
Average Monthly °C	16	16	15	12	9	6	6	7	9	12	13	16	11
Rainfall Monthly Total mm	56	46	43	46	76	69	61	58	51	51	51	61	669
No. of Days	10	8	9	10	12	13	14	11	10	11	10	11	129
Sunshine Hours per Day	7	6.5	5.6	4.7	4.3	3.9	4.1	4.7	5.6	6.1	6.9	6.3	5.5

Churchill Canada 35m

	Jan	Feb	Mar	Apr	May	June	July	Aug	Sep	Oct	Nov	Dec	Year
Temperature Daily Max.°C	-24	-22	-15	-7	1	10	17	16	9	2	-7	-18	-3
Daily Min.°C	-32	-31	-24	-15	-5	2	7	8	3	-4	-15	-26	-11
Average Monthly °C	-28	-27	-19	-11	-2	6	12	12	6	-1	-11	-22	-7
Rainfall Monthly Total mm	14	16	18	30	34	44	30	62	53	42	42	25	410
No. of Days	9	9	10	13	11	10	12	13	15	16	17	14	149
Sunshine Hours per Day	2.6	6.6	6.1	6.2	5.6	7.1	9.2	7.5	3.4	2.2	1.6	1.9	4.8

Colombo Sri Lanka 10m

	Jan	Feb	Mar	Apr	May	June	July	Aug	Sep	Oct	Nov	Dec	Year
Temperature Daily Max.°C	30	31	31	31	30	30	29	29	30	29	29	30	30
Daily Min.°C	22	22	23	24	25	25	25	25	25	24	23	22	24
Average Monthly °C	26	26	27	28	28	27	27	27	27	27	26	26	27
Rainfall Monthly Total mm	101	66	118	230	394	220	140	102	174	348	333	142	2368
No. of Days	10	6	11	17	23	22	16	14	17	22	20	12	190
Sunshine Hours per Day	7.9	9	8.1	7.2	6.4	5.4	6.1	6.3	6.2	6.5	6.4	7.8	6.9

Darwin Australia 30m

	Jan	Feb	Mar	Apr	May	June	July	Aug	Sep	Oct	Nov	Dec	Year
Temperature Daily Max.°C	32	32	33	33	33	31	31	32	33	34	34	33	33
Daily Min.°C	25	25	25	24	23	21	19	21	23	25	26	26	24
Average Monthly °C	29	29	29	29	28	26	25	26	28	29	30	29	28
Rainfall Monthly Total mm	405	309	279	77	8	2	0	1	15	48	108	214	1466
No. of Days	20	18	17	6	1	1	0.1	0.1	2	5	10	15	95
Sunshine Hours per Day	5.8	5.8	6.6	9.8	9.3	10	9.9	10.4	10.1	9.4	9.6	6.8	8.6

Edmonton Canada 676m

	Jan	Feb	Mar	Apr	May	June	July	Aug	Sep	Oct	Nov	Dec	Year
Temperature Daily Max.°C	-9	-7	0	10	17	20	24	22	17	11	0	-5	8
Daily Min.°C	-19	-17	-10	-2	4	8	11	9	5	-1	-9	-14	-3
Average Monthly °C	-14	-12	-5	4	11	14	17	15	11	5	-4	-10	3
Rainfall Monthly Total mm	24	22	20	26	42	77	82	70	34	21	20	22	460
No. of Days	11	11	10	8	9	13	13	12	9	7	8	11	122
Sunshine Hours per Day	2.9	4.1	5.3	7.3	8.5	8.4	9.8	8.5	6.3	5.1	3.5	2.6	6

Harbin China 175m

	Jan	Feb	Mar	Apr	May	June	July	Aug	Sep	Oct	Nov	Dec	Year
Temperature Daily Max.°C	-14	-9	0	12	21	26	29	27	20	12	-1	-11	9
Daily Min.°C	-26	-23	-12	-1	7	14	18	16	8	0	-12	-22	-3
Average Monthly °C	-20	-16	-6	6	14	20	23	22	14	6	-7	-17	3
Rainfall Monthly Total mm	4	6	17	23	44	92	167	119	52	36	12	5	577
No. of Days	5	5	6	7	11	15	16	13	12	7	6	6	109
Sunshine Hours per Day	6.4	7.8	8	7.8	8.3	8.6	8.6	8.2	7.2	6.9	6.1	5.7	7.5

Ho Chi Minh Vietnam 10m

	Jan	Feb	Mar	Apr	May	June	July	Aug	Sep	Oct	Nov	Dec	Year
Temperature Daily Max.°C	32	33	34	35	33	32	31	31	31	31	31	31	32
Daily Min.°C	21	22	23	24	24	24	24	24	23	23	23	22	23
Average Monthly °C	26	27	29	30	29	28	28	28	27	27	27	26	28
Rainfall Monthly Total mm	16	3	13	42	220	331	314	269	336	269	115	56	1984
No. of Days	2	1	2	5	17	22	23	21	22	20	11	7	153
Sunshine Hours per Day	6.3	7.1	6.8	6.7	5.1	5	3.9	5	4	4.5	5.2	5.7	5.4

Hong Kong Hong Kong 35m

	Jan	Feb	Mar	Apr	May	June	July	Aug	Sep	Oct	Nov	Dec	Year
Temperature Daily Max.°C	18	18	20	24	28	30	31	31	30	27	24	20	25
Daily Min.°C	13	13	16	19	23	26	26	26	25	23	19	15	20
Average Monthly °C	16	15	18	22	25	28	28	28	27	25	21	17	23
Rainfall Monthly Total mm	30	60	70	133	332	479	286	415	364	33	46	17	2265
No. of Days	6	8	11	11	16	21	19	17	15	8	5	5	142
Sunshine Hours per Day	4.7	3.5	3.1	3.8	5	5.4	6.8	6.5	6.6	7	6.2	5.5	5.3

Honolulu Hawaii 5m

	Jan	Feb	Mar	Apr	May	June	July	Aug	Sep	Oct	Nov	Dec	Year
Temperature Daily Max.°C	26	26	26	27	28	29	29	29	30	29	28	26	28
Daily Min.°C	19	19	19	20	21	22	23	23	23	22	21	20	21
Average Monthly °C	23	22	23	23	24	26	26	26	26	26	24	23	24
Rainfall Monthly Total mm	96	84	73	33	25	8	11	23	25	47	55	76	556
No. of Days	10	10	9	9	6	6	8	7	7	10	10	11	103
Sunshine Hours per Day	7.3	7.7	8.3	8.6	8.8	9.1	9.4	9.3	9.2	8.3	7.5	6.2	8.3

Houston USA 12m

	Jan	Feb	Mar	Apr	May	June	July	Aug	Sep	Oct	Nov	Dec	Year
Temperature Daily Max.°C	17	18	22	25	29	32	34	34	31	28	21	18	26
Daily Min.°C	8	9	12	16	20	23	24	24	22	17	12	9	16
Average Monthly °C	12	14	17	21	25	28	29	29	27	22	16	14	21
Rainfall Monthly Total mm	94	82	61	87	113	97	131	90	97	91	103	104	1150
No. of Days	11	10	9	8	7	8	10	9	9	6	8	10	105
Sunshine Hours per Day	5.1	5.6	6.6	7.3	9.3	10.9	10.4	9.7	8.7	8.3	6.6	5.5	7.8

Istanbul Turkey 40m

	Jan	Feb	Mar	Apr	May	June	July	Aug	Sep	Oct	Nov	Dec	Year
Temperature Daily Max.°C	9	9	11	16	21	26	29	29	25	21	15	11	18
Daily Min.°C	3	2	3	7	12	16	18	20	15	12	8	5	10
Average Monthly °C	6	6	7	12	16	21	23	24	20	16	12	8	14
Rainfall Monthly Total mm	88	80	61	37	32	27	27	22	49	61	87	96	667
No. of Days	18	15	14	9	8	5	4	3	6	10	13	17	122
Sunshine Hours per Day	2.6	3.8	4.5	6.3	8.6	10.6	11.6	10.9	8.2	5.3	3.7	2.8	6.6

Jakarta Indonesia 10m

	Jan	Feb	Mar	Apr	May	June	July	Aug	Sep	Oct	Nov	Dec	Year
Temperature Daily Max.°C	29	29	30	31	31	31	31	31	31	31	30	29	30
Daily Min.°C	23	23	23	24	24	23	23	23	23	23	23	23	23
Average Monthly °C	26	26	27	27	27	27	27	27	27	27	27	26	27
Rainfall Monthly Total mm	300	300	211	147	114	97	64	43	66	112	142	203	1799
No. of Days	18	17	15	11	9	7	5	4	5	8	12	14	125
Sunshine Av. Monthly Dur.	6.1	6.5	7.7	8.5	8.4	8.5	9.1	9.5	9.6	9	7.7	7.1	8.1

Johannesburg South Africa 1692m

	Jan	Feb	Mar	Apr	May	June	July	Aug	Sep	Oct	Nov	Dec	Year
Temperature Daily Max.°C	25	25	24	21	19	16	17	19	23	24	24	25	22
Daily Min.°C	14	14	13	10	7	4	4	6	9	11	13	14	10
Average Monthly °C	20	20	18	16	13	10	10	13	16	18	18	19	16
Rainfall Monthly Total mm	112	97	75	61	22	9	8	5	25	69	116	111	710
No. of Days	15	11	10	10	5	2	1	2	3	10	15	15	99
Sunshine Av. Monthly Dur.	8.4	8.3	7.9	9.1	8.8	8.8	9.2	9.7	9.5	8.9	8.3	8.4	

Kabul Afghanistan 1791 m

	Jan	Feb	Mar	Apr	May	June	July	Aug	Sep	Oct	Nov	Dec	Year
Temperature Daily Max.°C	2	4	12	19	26	31	33	33	30	22	17	8	20
Daily Min.°C	-8	-6	1	6	11	13	16	15	11	6	1	-3	5
Average Monthly °C	-3	-1	6	13	18	22	25	24	20	14	9	3	12
Rainfall Monthly Total mm	28	61	72	117	33	1	7	1		1	37	14	372
No. of Days	6	7	9	11	8	3	2	1	1	3	2	5	58
Sunshine Av. Monthly Dur.	5.9	6	5.7	6.8	10.1	11.5	11.4	11.2	9.8	9.4	7.8	6.1	8.5

Karachi Pakistan 5m

	Jan	Feb	Mar	Apr	May	June	July	Aug	Sep	Oct	Nov	Dec	Year
Temperature Daily Max.°C	24	25	28	30	31	32	31	30	30	31	30	26	29
Daily Min.°C	14	16	20	23	26	28	27	26	25	23	19	16	22
Average Monthly °C	19	21	24	27	29	30	29	28	27	27	25	21	26
Rainfall Monthly Total mm	13	10	8	3	3	18	81	41	13	0.5	3	5	198
No. of Days	2	3	1	1	0.1	1	6	3	1	0.2	0.4	1.3	20
Sunshine Av. Monthly Dur.	8.8	9.3	9	9.9	10.1	7.8	4.4	4.8	7.1	9.3	9.3	8.7	8.2

Khartoum Sudan 380m

	Jan	Feb	Mar	Apr	May	June	July	Aug	Sep	Oct	Nov	Dec	Year
Temperature Daily Max.°C	32	33	37	40	42	41	38	36	38	39	35	32	37
Daily Min.°C	16	17	20	23	26	27	26	25	25	25	21	17	22
Average Monthly °C	24	25	28	32	34	34	32	30	32	32	28	25	30
Rainfall Monthly Total mm	0	0	0	1	7	5	56	80	28	2	0	0	179
No. of Days	0	0	0	0	1	1	6	8	3	1	0	0	20
Sunshine Av. Monthly Dur.	10.6	11.2	10.4	10.8	10.4	10.1	8.6	8.6	9.6	10.3	10.8	10.6	10.2

Kingston Jamaica 35m

	Jan	Feb	Mar	Apr	May	June	July	Aug	Sep	Oct	Nov	Dec	Year
Temperature Daily Max.°C	30	30	30	31	31	32	32	32	32	31	31	31	31
Daily Min.°C	20	20	20	21	22	24	23	23	23	23	22	21	22
Average Monthly °C	25	25	25	26	26	28	28	28	27	27	26	26	26
Rainfall Monthly Total mm	23	15	23	31	102	89	38	91	99	180	74	36	801
No. of Days	3	3	2	3	4	5	4	7	6	9	5	4	55
Sunshine Av. Monthly Dur.	8.3	8.8	8.7	8.7	8.3	7.8	8.5	8.5	7.6	7.3	8.3	7.7	8.2

Kinshasa Zaire 311m

	Jan	Feb	Mar	Apr	May	June	July	Aug	Sep	Oct	Nov	Dec	Year
Temperature Daily Max.°C	31	31	32	32	31	28	27	29	30	31	31	30	30
Daily Min.°C	22	22	22	22	22	19	17	18	20	21	21	22	21
Average Monthly °C	26	26	27	27	26	24	22	23	25	26	26	26	25
Rainfall Monthly Total mm	128	142	173	222	129	4	3	3	46	145	246	161	1402
No. of Days	9	10	13	15	10	1	0	1	5	10	16	13	103
Sunshine Av. Monthly Dur.	4.3	4.8	4.8	5.5	4.5	4.6	4	4.7	4.3	4.7	4.4	4.6	4.6

Lagos Nigeria 40m

	Jan	Feb	Mar	Apr	May	June	July	Aug	Sep	Oct	Nov	Dec	Year
Temperature Daily Max.°C	32	33	33	32	31	29	28	28	29	30	31	32	31
Daily Min.°C	22	23	23	23	23	22	22	21	22	22	23	22	22
Average Monthly °C	27	28	28	28	27	26	25	24	25	26	27	27	26
Rainfall Monthly Total mm	28	41	99	99	203	300	180	56	180	190	63	25	1464
No. of Days	1	4	7	8	14	18	14	9	16	16	7	2	116
Sunshine Av. Monthly Dur.	5.9	6.8	6.3	6.1	5.6	3.8	2.8	3.3	3	5.1	6.6	6.5	5.2

Lima Peru 120m

	Jan	Feb	Mar	Apr	May	June	July	Aug	Sep	Oct	Nov	Dec	Year
Temperature Daily Max.°C	28	29	29	27	24	20	20	19	20	22	24	26	24
Daily Min.°C	19	20	19	17	16	15	14	14	14	15	16	17	16
Average Monthly °C	24	24	24	22	20	17	17	16	17	18	20	21	20
Rainfall Monthly Total mm	1	1	1	1	5	5	8	8	8	3	3	1	45
No. of Days	1	0	0	0	1	1	1	2	1	0	0	0	7
Sunshine Av. Monthly Dur.	6.3	6.8	6.9	6.7	4	1.4	1.1	1	1.1	2.5	4.1	5	3.9

Lisbon Portugal 77m

	Jan	Feb	Mar	Apr	May	June	July	Aug	Sep	Oct	Nov	Dec	Year
Temperature Daily Max.°C	14	15	17	20	21	25	27	28	26	22	17	15	21
Daily Min.°C	8	8	10	12	13	15	17	17	17	14	11	9	13
Average Monthly °C	11	12	14	16	17	20	22	23	21	18	14	12	17
Rainfall Monthly Total mm	111	76	109	54	44	16	3	4	33	62	93	103	708
No. of Days	15	12	14	10	10	5	2	2	6	9	13	15	113
Sunshine Av. Monthly Dur.	4.7	5.9	6	8.3	9.1	10.6	11.4	10.7	8.4	6.7	5.2	4.6	7.7

London (Kew) United Kingdom 5m

	Jan	Feb	Mar	Apr	May	June	July	Aug	Sep	Oct	Nov	Dec	Year
Temperature Daily Max.°C	6	7	10	13	17	20	22	21	19	14	10	7	14
Daily Min.°C	2	2	3	6	8	12	14	13	11	8	5	4	7
Average Monthly °C	4	5	7	9	12	16	18	17	15	11	8	5	11
Rainfall Monthly Total mm	54	40	37	37	46	45	57	59	49	57	64	48	593
No. of Days	15	13	11	12	12	11	12	11	13	13	15	15	153
Sunshine Av. Monthly Dur.	1.7	2.3	3.5	5.7	6.7	7	6.6	6	5	3.3	1.9	1.4	4.3

Los Angeles USA 30m

	Jan	Feb	Mar	Apr	May	June	July	Aug	Sep	Oct	Nov	Dec	Year
Temperature Daily Max.°C	18	18	18	19	20	22	24	24	24	23	22	19	21
Daily Min.°C	7	8	9	11	13	15	17	17	16	14	11	9	12
Average Monthly °C	12	13	14	15	17	18	21	21	20	18	16	14	17
Rainfall Monthly Total mm	69	74	46	28	3	3	0	0	5	10	28	61	327
No. of Days	7	6	5	4	1	1	0	1	1	2	3	6	37
Sunshine Av. Monthly Dur.	6.9	8.2	8.9	8.8	9.5	10.3	11.7	11	10.1	8.6	8.2	7.6	9.2

Lusaka Zambia 1154m

	Jan	Feb	Mar	Apr	May	June	July	Aug	Sep	Oct	Nov	Dec	Year
Temperature Daily Max.°C	26	26	26	27	25	23	23	26	29	31	29	27	27
Daily Min.°C	17	17	16	15	12	10	9	11	15	18	18	17	15
Average Monthly °C	22	22	21	21	18	17	16	19	22	25	23	22	21
Rainfall Monthly Total mm	224	173	90	19	3	1	0	1	1	17	85	196	810
No. of Days	19	18	12	3	1	0	0	0	0	3	10	18	84
Sunshine Av. Monthly Dur.	5.1	5.4	6.9	8.9	9	9	9.1	9.6	9.5	9	7	5.5	7.8

Manaus Brazil 45m

	Jan	Feb	Mar	Apr	May	June	July	Aug	Sep	Oct	Nov	Dec	Year
Temperature Daily Max.°C	31	31	31	31	31	31	32	33	34	34	33	32	32
Daily Min.°C	24	24	24	24	24	24	24	24	24	25	25	24	24
Average Monthly °C	28	28	28	27	28	28	28	29	29	29	29	28	28
Rainfall Monthly Total mm	278	278	300	287	193	99	61	41	62	112	165	220	2096
No. of Days	20	19	20	19	18	11	8	6	7	11	12	16	167
Sunshine Av. Monthly Dur.	3.9	4	3.6	3.9	5.4	6.9	7.9	8.2	7.5	6.6	5.9	4.9	5.7

Melbourne Australia 35m

	Jan	Feb	Mar	Apr	May	June	July	Aug	Sep	Oct	Nov	Dec	Year
Temperature Daily Max.°C	26	26	24	20	17	14	13	15	17	19	22	24	20
Daily Min.°C	14	14	13	11	8	7	6	6	8	9	11	12	10
Average Monthly °C	20	20	18	15	13	10	9	11	13	14	16	18	15
Rainfall Monthly Total mm	47	50	56	57	48	52	48	51	55	66	58	60	648
No. of Days	9	8	9	13	14	16	17	17	15	14	13	11	156
Sunshine Av. Monthly Dur.	8.3	8.4	6.7	5.3	4.4	3.6	4.1	4.9	5.7	6.4	7.6	7.9	6.1

Mexico City Mexico 2309m

	Jan	Feb	Mar	Apr	May	June	July	Aug	Sep	Oct	Nov	Dec	Year
Temperature Daily Max.°C	21	23	26	27	26	25	23	24	23	22	21	21	24
Daily Min.°C	5	6	7	9	10	11	11	11	11	9	6	5	8
Average Monthly °C	13	15	16	18	18	18	17	17	17	16	14	13	16
Rainfall Monthly Total mm	8	4	9	23	57	111	160	149	119	46	16	7	709
No. of Days	2	3	4	6	14	17	22	22	20	11	3	3	127
Sunshine Av. Monthly Dur.	7.3	8.1	8.5	8.1	7.8	7	6.2	6.4	5.6	6.3	7	7.3	7.1

Miami USA 2m

	Jan	Feb	Mar	Apr	May	June	July	Aug	Sep	Oct	Nov	Dec	Year
Temperature Daily Max.°C	24	25	27	28	30	31	32	32	31	29	27	25	28
Daily Min.°C	14	15	16	19	21	23	24	24	24	22	18	15	20
Average Monthly °C	19	20	21	23	25	27	28	28	27	25	22	20	24
Rainfall Monthly Total mm	51	48	58	99	163	188	170	178	241	208	71	43	1518
No. of Days	6	6	6	8	10	13	17	16	19	15	9	7	132
Sunshine Av. Monthly Dur.	7.7	8.3	8.7	9.4	8.9	8.5	8.7	8.4	7.1	6.5	7.5	7.1	8.1

Montreal Canada 57m

	Jan	Feb	Mar	Apr	May	June	July	Aug	Sep	Oct	Nov	Dec	Year
Temperature Daily Max.°C	-6	-4	2	11	18	23	26	25	20	14	5	-3	11
Daily Min.°C	-13	-11	-5	2	9	14	17	16	11	6	0	-9	3
Average Monthly °C	-9	-8	-2	6	13	19	22	20	16	10	3	-6	7
Rainfall Monthly Total mm	87	76	86	83	81	91	98	87	96	84	89	89	1047
No. of Days	17	15	15	14	13	12	13	10	13	12	15	17	166
Sunshine Av. Monthly Dur.	2.8	3.4	4.5	5.2	6.7	7.7	8.2	7.7	5.6	4.3	2.4	2.2	5.1

Moscow Russia 156m

	Jan	Feb	Mar	Apr	May	June	July	Aug	Sep	Oct	Nov	Dec	Year
Temperature Daily Max.°C	-6	-4	1	9	18	22	24	22	17	10	1	-5	9
Daily Min.°C	-14	-16	-11	-1	5	9	12	9	4	-2	-6	-12	-2
Average Monthly °C	-10	-10	-5	4	12	15	18	16	10	4	-2	-8	4
Rainfall Monthly Total mm	31	28	33	35	52	67	74	74	58	51	36	36	575
No. of Days	17	15	14	13	12	15	16	16	17	16	17	19	187
Sunshine Av. Monthly Dur.	1	1.9	3.7	5.2	7.8	8.3	8.4	7.1	4.4	2.4	1	0.6	4.4

Nairobi Kenya 1616m

	Jan	Feb	Mar	Apr	May	June	July	Aug	Sep	Oct	Nov	Dec	Year
Temperature Daily Max.°C	27	28	28	26	25	24	23	23	26	27	25	25	25
Daily Min.°C	13	13	14	15	14	12	11	12	12	13	14	14	13
Average Monthly °C	20	21	21	20	19	18	17	17	19	20	19	19	19
Rainfall Monthly Total mm	49	36	85	153	126	32	13	18	21	48	132	75	788
No. of Days	5	4	8	16	14	5	4	5	4	7	16	11	99
Sunshine Av. Monthly Dur.	8.8	9.4	8.7	7.3	5.9	5.9	4.3	4.2	5.8	7.1	7	8.1	6.9

New Delhi India 220m

	Jan	Feb	Mar	Apr	May	June	July	Aug	Sep	Oct	Nov	Dec	Year
Temperature Daily Max.°C	21	24	29	36	41	39	35	34	34	34	28	23	32
Daily Min.°C	6	10	14	20	26	28	27	26	24	17	11	7	18
Average Monthly °C	14	17	22	28	33	34	31	30	29	26	20	15	25
Rainfall Monthly Total mm	25	21	13	8	13	77	178	184	123	10	2	11	665
No. of Days	3	4	2	2	2	6	14	11	7	0.4	0.3	2	54
Sunshine Av. Monthly Dur.	7.7	8.2	8.2	8.7	9.2	7.9	6	6.3	6.9	9.4	8.7	8.3	8

New York USA 3m

	Jan	Feb	Mar	Apr	May	June	July	Aug	Sep	Oct	Nov	Dec	Year
Temperature Daily Max.°C	4	4	9	15	21	26	28	27	24	18	12	6	16
Daily Min.°C	-3	-2	1	6	12	17	20	19	16	10	4	-1	8
Average Monthly °C	1	1	5	11	16	21	24	23	20	14	8	2	12
Rainfall Monthly Total mm	89	74	104	89	91	86	102	119	89	84	89	84	1100
No. of Days	11	10	12	11	12	10	10	10	8	8	9	10	121
Sunshine Av. Monthly Dur.	4.9	5.9	6.7	7.1	8.1	10	9.9	8.9	7.9	7	5.7	5.1	7.3

Odessa Ukraine 64m

	Jan	Feb	Mar	Apr	May	June	July	Aug	Sep	Oct	Nov	Dec	Year
Temperature Daily Max.°C	1	2	6	12	19	24	27	26	21	15	8	4	14
Daily Min.°C	-6	-7	-2	4	11	15	18	17	12	8	1	-4	6
Average Monthly °C	-3	-2	2	8	15	19	22	21	17	11	5	0	10
Rainfall Monthly Total mm	28	26	20	27	34	45	34	37	29	35	43	31	389
No. of Days	11	10	10	9	9	9	7	6	6	8	10	11	106
Sunshine Av. Monthly Dur.	2.3	2.6	4.6	6.7	9	9.9	11.3	10.4	8.2	5.7	2.2	1.9	6.3

Palma Spain 93m

	Jan	Feb	Mar	Apr	May	June	July	Aug	Sep	Oct	Nov	Dec	Year
Temperature Daily Max.°C	13	14	16	18	21	25	28	28	25	21	16	13	20
Daily Min.°C	6	7	9	11	14	18	21	21	19	15	11	8	13
Average Monthly °C	10	10	12	15	18	22	24	24	22	18	13	10	17
Rainfall Monthly Total mm	31	39	48	43	54	37	27	49	76	86	52	45	587
No. of Days	5	5	8	9	8	6	4	6	7	9	6	6	79
Sunshine Av. Monthly Dur.	4.8	5.9	5.7	7.1	8.1	9.3	10.1	8.8	6.7	5.7	5	4.3	6.8

Paris France 75m

	Jan	Feb	Mar	Apr	May	June	July	Aug	Sep	Oct	Nov	Dec	Year
Temperature Daily Max.°C	6	7	12	16	20	23	25	24	21	16	10	7	16
Daily Min.°C	1	1	4	6	10	13	15	14	12	8	5	2	8
Average Monthly °C	3	4	8	11	15	18	20	19	17	12	7	4	12
Rainfall Monthly Total mm	56	46	35	42	57	54	59	64	55	50	51	50	619
No. of Days	17	14	12	13	12	12	12	13	13	13	15	16	162
Sunshine Av. Monthly Dur.	2	2.9	4.9	6.6	7.3	7.2	7.3	6.6	6	4	2.1	1.5	4.9

Perth Australia 60m

	Jan	Feb	Mar	Apr	May	June	July	Aug	Sep	Oct	Nov	Dec	Year
Temperature Daily Max.°C	29	30	27	25	21	18	17	18	19	21	25	27	23
Daily Min.°C	17	18	16	14	12	10	9	9	10	11	14	16	13
Average Monthly °C	23	24	22	19	16	14	13	13	15	16	19	22	18
Rainfall Monthly Total mm	8	13	22	44	128	189	177	145	84	58	19	13	900
No. of Days	3	3	5	8	15	17	19	19	15	12	7	5	128
Sunshine Av. Monthly Dur.	10.4	9.8	8.8	7.5	5.7	4.8	5.4	6	7.2	8.1	9.6	10.4	7.8

Quito Ecuador 2875m

	Jan	Feb	Mar	Apr	May	June	July	Aug	Sep	Oct	Nov	Dec	Year
Temperature Daily Max.°C	22	22	22	21	21	22	22	23	23	22	22	22	22
Daily Min.°C	8	9	9	9	9	7	7	7	7	8	7	8	8
Average Monthly °C	15	15	15	15	15	14	14	15	15	15	15	15	15
Rainfall Monthly Total mm	119	131	154	185	130	54	20	25	81	134	96	104	1233
No. of Days	16	17	20	22	21	12	7	9	14	18	14	16	186
Sunshine Av. Monthly Dur.	5.4	5	4.2	4.5	5.2	6.3	7.2	7.1	6.1	5.4	5.6	5.6	5.6

Reykjavik Iceland 18m

	Jan	Feb	Mar	Apr	May	June	July	Aug	Sep	Oct	Nov	Dec	Year
Temperature Daily Max.°C	2	3	5	6	10	13	15	14	12	8	5	4	8
Daily Min.°C	-3	-3	-1	1	4	7	9	8	6	3	0	-2	3
Average Monthly °C	0	0	2	4	7	10	12	11	9	5	3	1	5
Rainfall Monthly Total mm	89	64	62	56	42	42	50	56	67	94	78	79	779
No. of Days	20	17	18	18	16	15	15	16	19	21	18	20	213
Sunshine Av. Monthly Dur.	0.8	2	3.6	4.5	5.9	6.1	5.8	5.4	3.5	2.3	1.1	0.3	3.7

Rio de Janeiro Brazil 60m

	Jan	Feb	Mar	Apr	May	June	July	Aug	Sep	Oct	Nov	Dec	Year
Temperature Daily Max.°C	29	30	29	27	25	25	24	25	24	25	26	28	26
Daily Min.°C	23	23	22	21	19	18	17	18	19	19	20	22	20
Average Monthly °C	26	26	25	24	22	21	21	21	21	22	23	25	23
Rainfall Monthly Total mm	125	122	130	107	79	53	41	43	66	79	104	137	1086
No. of Days	13	11	12	10	10	7	7	7	11	13	13	14	128
Sunshine Av. Monthly Dur.	6.9	6.9	6.8	6.3	6.2	6.3	6.5	6.6	5.1	5.1	5.7	5.6	6.2

Rome Italy 46m

	Jan	Feb	Mar	Apr	May	June	July	Aug	Sep	Oct	Nov	Dec	Year
Temperature Daily Max.°C	11	12	15	19	23	27	30	30	26	21	16	12	20
Daily Min.°C	4	4	7	9	13	17	19	19	16	13	8	6	11
Average Monthly °C	7	8	11	14	18	22	25	25	21	17	12	9	16
Rainfall Monthly Total mm	76	89	77	73	63	48	14	22	70	128	117	107	882
No. of Days	7	6	8	9	6	4	2	2	5	6	8	8	68
Sunshine Av. Monthly Dur.	4.3	4.7	6.6	7	8.6	9.4	10.8	9.9	8.1	6.4	4.1	3.3	6.9

St Denis Réunion 10m

	Jan	Feb	Mar	Apr	May	June	July	Aug	Sep	Oct	Nov	Dec	Year
Temperature Av. Daily Max.	30	30	29	28	27	26	25	25	25	26	27	29	27
Av. Daily Min.	23	23	23	21	20	18	17	17	17	19	20	22	20
Av. Monthly	26	26	26	25	23	22	21	21	21	22	24	25	24
Rainfall Monthly Total mm	263	216	290	160	81	75	70	49	47	44	95	151	1541
No. of Days	19	17	18	13	14	14	17	16	14	12	13	16	183
Sunshine Av. Monthly Dur.	7.7	7.7	6.7	7.4	7.6	7.3	7.2	7.1	7.2	7.1	7.1	7	7.3

St Louis USA 172m

	Jan	Feb	Mar	Apr	May	June	July	Aug	Sep	Oct	Nov	Dec	Year
Temperature Daily Max.°C	5	7	12	19	24	30	32	31	27	21	12	6	19
Daily Min.°C	-5	-4	0	7	12	17	19	19	14	8	1	-3	7
Average Monthly °C	0	2	6	13	18	23	26	25	21	15	7	2	13
Rainfall Monthly Total mm	50	52	78	94	95	109	84	77	70	73	65	50	897
No. of Days	7	8	10	11	10	9	9	7	9	8	8	9	105
Sunshine Av. Monthly Dur.	4.4	5.3	6.8	7.7	9.2	9.9	10.6	9.4	8.8	7.9	5.7	4.3	7.6

San Francisco USA 5m

	Jan	Feb	Mar	Apr	May	June	July	Aug	Sep	Oct	Nov	Dec	Year
Temperature Daily Max.°C	13	15	16	17	17	18	18	18	21	20	18	14	17
Daily Min.°C	8	9	9	10	11	12	12	12	13	12	11	9	11
Average Monthly °C	10	12	13	13	14	15	15	15	17	16	14	0	14
Rainfall Monthly Total mm	116	93	74	37	16	4	0.3	1	6	23	51	108	528
No. of Days	11	10	10	6	3	1	1	1	1	4	8	11	67
Sunshine Av. Monthly Dur.	4.9	6.9	7.9	9.1	9.6	11	9.3	8.3	8.8	7.5	6.3	4.6	7.9

San Jose Costa Rica 1145m

	Jan	Feb	Mar	Apr	May	June	July	Aug	Sep	Oct	Nov	Dec	Year
Temperature Daily Max.°C	24	25	26	26	27	26	25	26	26	25	25	24	25
Daily Min.°C	15	15	15	17	17	17	17	16	16	16	16	15	16
Average Monthly °C	19	20	21	21	22	21	21	21	21	20	20	19	20
Rainfall Monthly Total mm	8	5	10	37	244	284	230	233	342	333	172	46	1944
No. of Days	3	1	2	7	19	22	23	24	24	25	14	6	170
Sunshine Av. Monthly Dur.	7	7.8	8	7	5.2	4	4	4.4	5	4.4	4.5	5.9	5.6

Santander Spain 66m

	Jan	Feb	Mar	Apr	May	June	July	Aug	Sep	Oct	Nov	Dec	Year
Temperature Daily Max.°C	12	12	14	15	17	20	22	22	21	18	15	13	17
Daily Min.°C	7	7	8	10	11	14	16	16	15	12	10	8	11
Average Monthly °C	9	9	11	12	14	17	19	19	18	15	12	10	14
Rainfall Monthly Total mm	119	88	78	83	89	63	54	84	114	133	125	159	1189
No. of Days	16	14	13	13	14	13	11	14	14	14	15	18	169
Sunshine Av. Monthly Dur.	2.7	3.5	4.5	5.5	6	6.7	6.8	6.4	5.2	4.3	3.2	2.4	4.8

Santiago Chile 520m

	Jan	Feb	Mar	Apr	May	June	July	Aug	Sep	Oct	Nov	Dec	Year
Temperature Daily Max.°C	30	29	27	24	19	15	15	17	19	22	26	29	23
Daily Min.°C	12	11	10	7	5	3	3	4	6	7	9	11	7
Average Monthly °C	21	20	18	15	12	9	9	10	12	15	17	20	15
Rainfall Monthly Total mm	3	3	5	13	64	84	76	56	31	15	8	5	363
No. of Days	0	0	1	1	5	6	6	5	3	3	1	0	31
Sunshine Av. Monthly Dur.	10.8	8.9	8.5	5.5	3.6	3.3	3.3	3.6	4.8	6.1	8.7	10.1	6.4

Shanghai China 5m

	Jan	Feb	Mar	Apr	May	June	July	Aug	Sep	Oct	Nov	Dec	Year
Temperature Daily Max.°C	8	8	13	19	24	28	32	32	27	23	17	10	20
Daily Min.°C	-1	0	4	9	14	19	23	23	19	13	7	2	11
Average Monthly °C	3	4	8	14	19	23	27	27	23	18	12	6	15
Rainfall Monthly Total mm	48	59	84	94	94	180	147	142	130	71	51	36	1136
No. of Days	10	10	12	13	12	14	11	11	12	9	8	8	130
Sunshine Av. Monthly Dur.	4	3.7	4.4	4.8	5.4	4.7	6.9	7.5	5.3	5.6	4.7	4.5	5.1

Shannon Ireland 2m

	Jan	Feb	Mar	Apr	May	June	July	Aug	Sep	Oct	Nov	Dec	Year
Temperature Daily Max.°C	8	9	11	13	16	19	19	20	17	14	11	9	14
Daily Min.°C	2	2	4	5	7	10	12	12	10	7	5	3	7
Average Monthly °C	5	5	7	9	12	14	16	16	14	11	8	6	10
Rainfall Monthly Total mm	94	67	56	53	61	57	77	79	86	86	96	117	929
No. of Days	15	11	11	11	11	11	14	14	14	14	15	18	159
Sunshine Av. Monthly Dur.	1.8	2.6	3.4	5.1	6.8	5.8	4.9	5.1	3.7	2.8	2.1	1.4	3.8

Singapore Singapore 10m

	Jan	Feb	Mar	Apr	May	June	July	Aug	Sep	Oct	Nov	Dec	Year
Temperature Daily Max.°C	31	31	31	31	31	31	31	31	30	31	30	30	31
Daily Min.°C	23	23	24	24	24	25	25	24	24	24	24	23	24
Average Monthly °C	27	27	27	27	28	28	28	27	27	27	27	27	27
Rainfall Monthly Total mm	252	175	200	196	173	171	165	191	178	206	251	265	2423
No. of Days	17	12	14	15	15	13	13	15	14	16	19	19	182
Sunshine Av. Monthly Dur.	5.1	5.7	6	5.8	5.7	5.7	5.9	5.7	5.6	5	4.6	4.3	5.4

Stockholm Sweden 44m

	Jan	Feb	Mar	Apr	May	June	July	Aug	Sep	Oct	Nov	Dec	Year
Temperature Daily Max.°C	-1	-1	2	8	15	19	22	20	15	9	5	2	10
Daily Min.°C	-5	-6	-4	1	6	10	14	13	9	5	1	-2	4
Average Monthly °C	-3	-3	-1	5	10	15	18	17	12	7	3	0	7
Rainfall Monthly Total mm	46	32	27	33	36	45	61	77	59	50	56	50	572
No. of Days	10	7	6	7	7	8	9	10	9	9	10	11	103
Sunshine Av. Monthly Dur.	1.3	2.4	5	6.8	8.7	9.6	9.1	7.3	5.6	2.8	1.3	0.7	5.1

Sydney Australia 40m

	Jan	Feb	Mar	Apr	May	June	July	Aug	Sep	Oct	Nov	Dec	Year
Temperature Daily Max.°C	26	26	25	22	19	17	17	18	20	22	24	25	22
Daily Min.°C	18	19	17	14	11	9	8	9	11	13	16	17	14
Average Monthly °C	22	22	21	18	15	13	12	13	16	18	20	21	18
Rainfall Monthly Total mm	89	101	127	135	127	117	117	76	74	71	74	74	1182
No. of Days	13	13	14	13	13	12	12	11	12	12	12	13	150
Sunshine Av. Monthly Dur.	7.5	7	6.4	6.1	5.7	5.3	6.1	7	7.3	7.5	7.5	7.5	6.8

Tehran Iran 1191m

	Jan	Feb	Mar	Apr	May	June	July	Aug	Sep	Oct	Nov	Dec	Year
Temperature Daily Max.°C	9	11	16	21	29	30	37	36	29	24	16	11	22
Daily Min.°C	-1	1	4	10	16	20	23	23	18	12	6	1	11
Average Monthly °C	4	6	10	15	22	25	30	29	23	18	11	6	17
Rainfall Monthly Total mm	37	23	36	31	14	2	1	1	1	5	29	27	207
No. of Days	4	4	3	6	3	0.6	0.2	0.3	0.4	2	4	5	32
Sunshine Av. Monthly Dur.	5.9	6.7	7.5	7.4	8.6	11.6	11.2	11	10.1	7.6	6.9	6.3	8.4

Timbuktu Mali 269m

	Jan	Feb	Mar	Apr	May	June	July	Aug	Sep	Oct	Nov	Dec	Year
Temperature Daily Max.°C	31	35	38	41	43	42	38	35	38	40	37	31	37
Daily Min.°C	13	16	18	22	26	27	25	24	24	23	18	14	21
Average Monthly °C	22	25	28	31	34	34	32	30	31	31	28	23	29
Rainfall Monthly Total mm	0	0	0	1	4	20	54	93	31	3	0	0	206
No. of Days	0	0	0	0	1	4	8	10	5	1	0	0	29
Sunshine Av. Monthly Dur.	9.1	9.6	9.6	9.7	9.8	9.4	9.6	9	9.3	9.5	9.5	8.9	9.4

Tokyo Japan 5m

	Jan	Feb	Mar	Apr	May	June	July	Aug	Sep	Oct	Nov	Dec	Year
Temperature Daily Max.°C	9	9	12	18	22	25	29	30	27	20	16	11	19
Daily Min.°C	-1	-1	3	4	13	17	22	23	19	13	7	1	10
Average Monthly °C	4	4	8	11	18	21	25	26	23	17	11	6	14
Rainfall Monthly Total mm	48	73	101	135	131	182	146	147	217	220	101	61	1562
No. of Days	6	7	10	11	12	12	11	10	13	12	8	5	117
Sunshine Av. Monthly Dur.	6	5.9	5.7	6	6.2	5	5.8	6.6	4.5	4.4	4.8	5.4	5.5

Tromsø Norway 100m

	Jan	Feb	Mar	Apr	May	June	July	Aug	Sep	Oct	Nov	Dec	Year
Temperature Daily Max.°C	-2	-2	0	3	7	12	16	14	10	5	2	0	5
Daily Min.°C	-6	-6	-5	-2	1	6	9	8	5	1	-2	-4	0
Average Monthly °C	-4	-4	-3	0	4	9	13	11	7	3	0	-2	3
Rainfall Monthly Total mm	96	79	91	65	61	59	56	80	109	115	88	95	994
No. of Days	14	12	15	12	11	11	10	14	15	16	13	13	156
Sunshine Av. Monthly Dur.	0.1	1.6	2.9	6.1	5.7	6.9	7.9	4.8	3.5	1.7	0.3	0	3.5

Tunis Tunisia 65m

	Jan	Feb	Mar	Apr	May	June	July	Aug	Sep	Oct	Nov	Dec	Year
Temperature Daily Max.°C	15	16	18	21	25	29	32	33	30	25	20	16	23
Daily Min.°C	7	7	9	11	14	18	20	21	19	15	11	7	13
Average Monthly °C	11	12	13	16	19	23	26	27	25	20	15	12	18
Rainfall Monthly Total mm	65	49	43	40	22	10	2	7	34	56	54	62	444
No. of Days	13	12	11	9	6	5	2	3	7	9	11	14	102
Sunshine Av. Monthly Dur.	5.6	6.7	7.2	7.8	9.9	10.6	12.1	11.3	8.6	7	6.1	5.3	8.2

Ulan Bator Mongolia 1305m

	Jan	Feb	Mar	Apr	May	June	July	Aug	Sep	Oct	Nov	Dec	Year
Temperature Daily Max.°C	-19	-13	-4	7	13	21	22	21	14	6	-6	-16	104
Daily Min.°C	-32	-29	-22	-8	-2	7	11	8	2	-8	-20	-28	-10
Average Monthly °C	-26	-21	-13	-1	6	14	16	14	8	-1	-13	-22	47
Rainfall Monthly Total mm	1	1	2	5	10	28	76	51	23	5	5	2	209
No. of Days	1	1	2	2	4	5	10	8	3	2	2	1	41
Sunshine Av. Monthly Dur.	6.4	7.8	8	7.8	8.3	8.6	8.6	8.2	7.2	6.9	6.1	5.7	7.5

Vancouver Canada 5m

	Jan	Feb	Mar	Apr	May	June	July	Aug	Sep	Oct	Nov	Dec	Year
Temperature Daily Max.°C	6	7	10	14	17	20	23	22	19	14	9	7	14
Daily Min.°C	0	1	3	5	8	11	13	12	10	7	3	2	6
Average Monthly °C	3	4	6	9	13	16	18	17	14	10	6	4	10
Rainfall Monthly Total mm	214	161	151	90	69	65	39	44	83	172	198	243	1529
No. of Days	20	16	17	13	10	10	7	7	10	15	18	21	164
Sunshine Av. Monthly Dur.	1.6	3	3.8	5.9	7.5	7.4	9.5	8.2	6	3.7	2	1.4	5

Verkhoyansk Russia 137m

	Jan	Feb	Mar	Apr	May	June	July	Aug	Sep	Oct	Nov	Dec	Year
Temperature Daily Max.°C	-47	-40	-20	-1	11	21	24	21	12	-8	-33	-42	-8
Daily Min.°C	-51	-48	-40	-25	-7	4	6	1	-6	-20	-39	-50	-23
Average Monthly °C	-49	-44	-30	-13	2	12	15	11	3	-14	-36	-46	-16
Rainfall Monthly Total mm	7	5	5	4	5	25	33	30	13	11	10	7	155
No. of Days	9	8	7	5	6	10	9	9	8	10	12	11	104
Sunshine Av. Monthly Dur.	0	2.6	6.9	9.6	9.7	10	9.7	7.5	4.1	2.4	0.6	0	5.4

Warsaw Poland 110m

	Jan	Feb	Mar	Apr	May	June	July	Aug	Sep	Oct	Nov	Dec	Year
Temperature Daily Max.°C	0	0	6	12	20	23	24	23	19	13	6	2	12
Daily Min.°C	-6	-6	-2	3	9	12	15	14	10	5	1	-3	4
Average Monthly °C	-3	-3	2	7	14	17	19	18	14	9	3	0	8
Rainfall Monthly Total mm	27	32	27	37	46	69	96	65	43	38	31	44	555
No. of Days	15	14	11	13	11	13	16	13	12	12	12	16	158
Sunshine Av. Monthly Dur.	1.7	2	3.7	5.3	8.1	8.1	7.1	6.9	5.3	3.8	1.6	1.3	4.6

Washington USA 22m

	Jan	Feb	Mar	Apr	May	June	July	Aug	Sep	Oct	Nov	Dec	Year
Temperature Daily Max.°C	7	8	12	19	25	29	31	30	26	20	14	8	19
Daily Min.°C	-1	-1	2	8	13	18	21	20	16	10	4	-1	9
Average Monthly °C	3	3	7	13	19	24	26	25	21	15	9	4	14
Rainfall Monthly Total mm	84	68	96	85	103	88	108	120	100	78	75	75	1080
No. of Days	11	9	12	10	12	10	11	10	9	8	9	10	121
Sunshine Av. Monthly Dur.	4.4	5.7	6.7	7.4	8.2	8.8	8.6	8.2	7.5	6.5	5.3	4.5	6.8

Windhoek Namibia 1728m

	Jan	Feb	Mar	Apr	May	June	July	Aug	Sep	Oct	Nov	Dec	Year
Temperature Daily Max.°C	30	29	27	26	23	20	21	24	27	29	30	30	26
Daily Min.°C	17	17	15	13	9	7	7	9	12	15	16	17	13
Average Monthly °C	24	23	21	19	16	13	14	16	20	22	23	24	20
Rainfall Monthly Total mm	71	76	77	41	5	2	1	1	3	13	35	39	364
No. of Days	12	11	10	5	2	0	0	0	1	3	7	7	58
Sunshine Av. Monthly Dur.	8.9	8.6	8.3	9.5	10	10	10	10.5	10.4	10.2	9.7	9.8	9.7

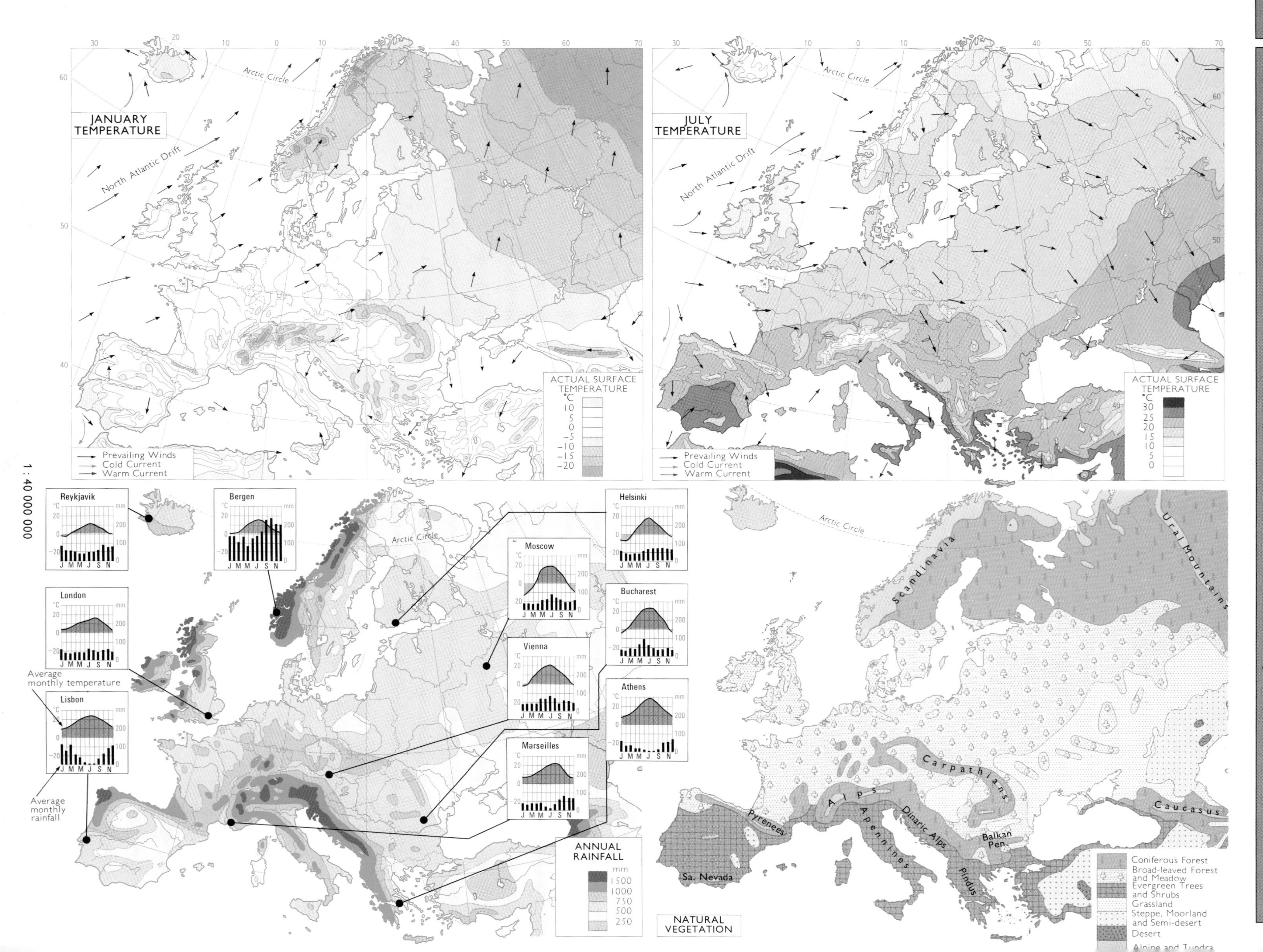

JULY TEMPERATURE

ACTUAL SURFACE TEMPERATURE
°C 30 25 20 15 10 5 0

North Atlantic Drift

Prevailing Winds
Cold Current
Warm Current

JANUARY TEMPERATURE

ACTUAL SURFACE TEMPERATURE
°C 10 5 -5 -10 -15 -20

North Atlantic Drift

Prevailing Winds
Cold Current
Warm Current

NATURAL VEGETATION

Coniferous Forest
Broad-leaved Forest and Meadow
Evergreen Trees and Shrubs
Grassland
Steppe, Moorland and Semi-desert
Desert
Alpine and Tundra

Ural Mountains
Scandinavia
Carpathians
Caucasus
Balkan Pen.
Pindus
Dinaric Alps
Alps
Apennines
Pyrenees
Sa. Nevada

ANNUAL RAINFALL
mm 1500 1000 750 500 250

Helsinki
Bucharest
Athens
Moscow
Vienna
Marseilles
Bergen
Reykjavik
London
Lisbon

Average monthly temperature
Average monthly rainfall

1 : 40 000 000

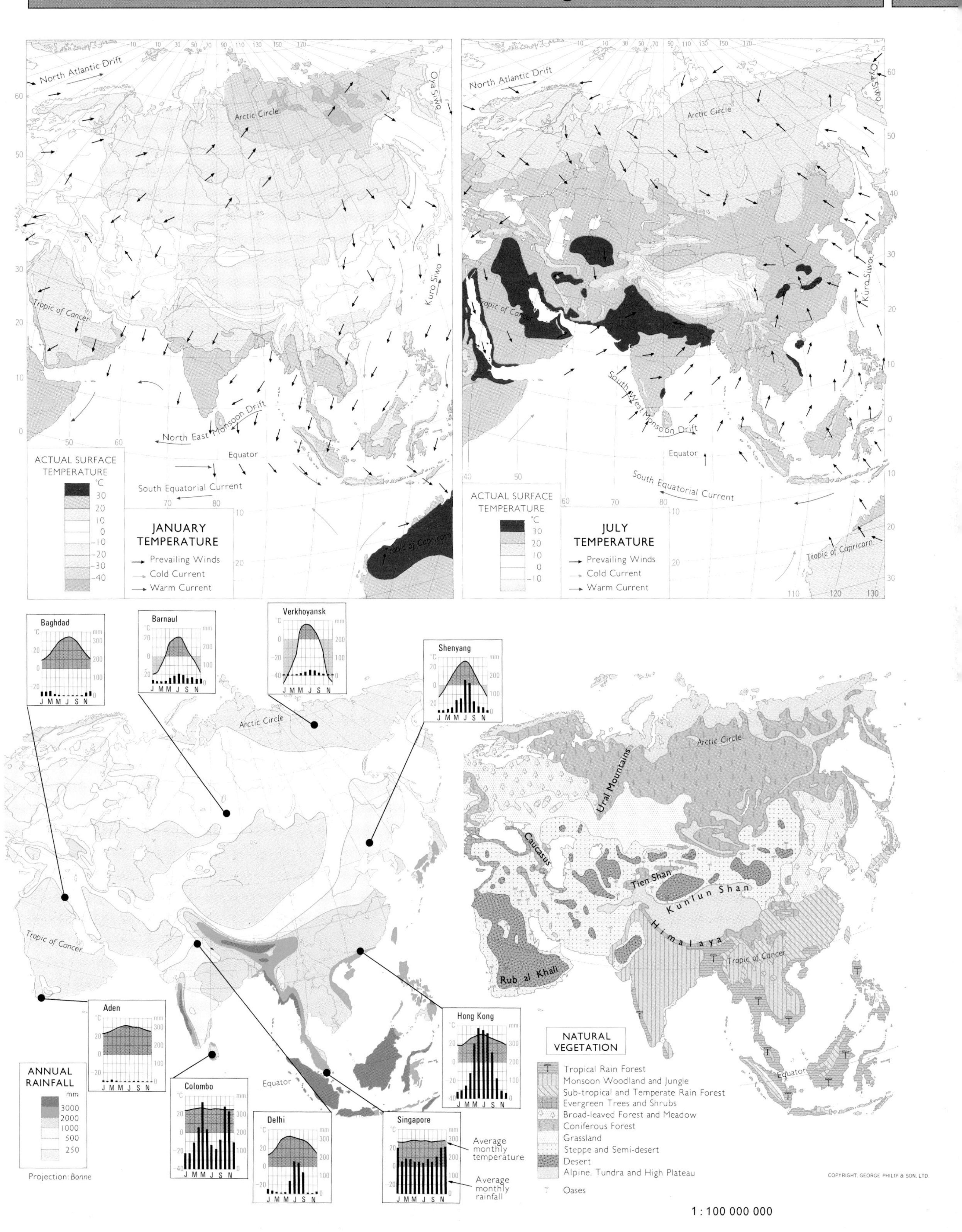

ACTUAL SURFACE TEMPERATURE

°C
30
20
10
0
-10
-20
-30
-40

JANUARY TEMPERATURE

→ Prevailing Winds
→ Cold Current
→ Warm Current

ACTUAL SURFACE TEMPERATURE

°C
30
20
10
0
-10

JULY TEMPERATURE

→ Prevailing Winds
→ Cold Current
→ Warm Current

North Atlantic Drift
Arctic Circle
Tropic of Cancer
Kuro Siwo
Oya Siwo
North East Monsoon Drift
Equator
South Equatorial Current
Tropic of Capricorn

South West Monsoon Drift
Equator
South Equatorial Current
Tropic of Capricorn
Kura Siwo

Baghdad
Barnaul
Verkhoyansk
Shenyang
Aden
Colombo
Delhi
Singapore
Hong Kong

Arctic Circle
Tropic of Cancer
Equator

ANNUAL RAINFALL

mm
3000
2000
1000
500
250

Projection: Bonne

NATURAL VEGETATION

T Tropical Rain Forest
Monsoon Woodland and Jungle
Sub-tropical and Temperate Rain Forest
Evergreen Trees and Shrubs
Broad-leaved Forest and Meadow
Coniferous Forest
Grassland
Steppe and Semi-desert
Desert
Alpine, Tundra and High Plateau

Oases

Ural Mountains
Arctic Circle
Caucasus
Tien Shan
Kunlun Shan
Himalaya
Rub al Khali
Tropic of Cancer
Equator

Average monthly temperature
Average monthly rainfall

COPYRIGHT GEORGE PHILIP & SON LTD

1 : 100 000 000

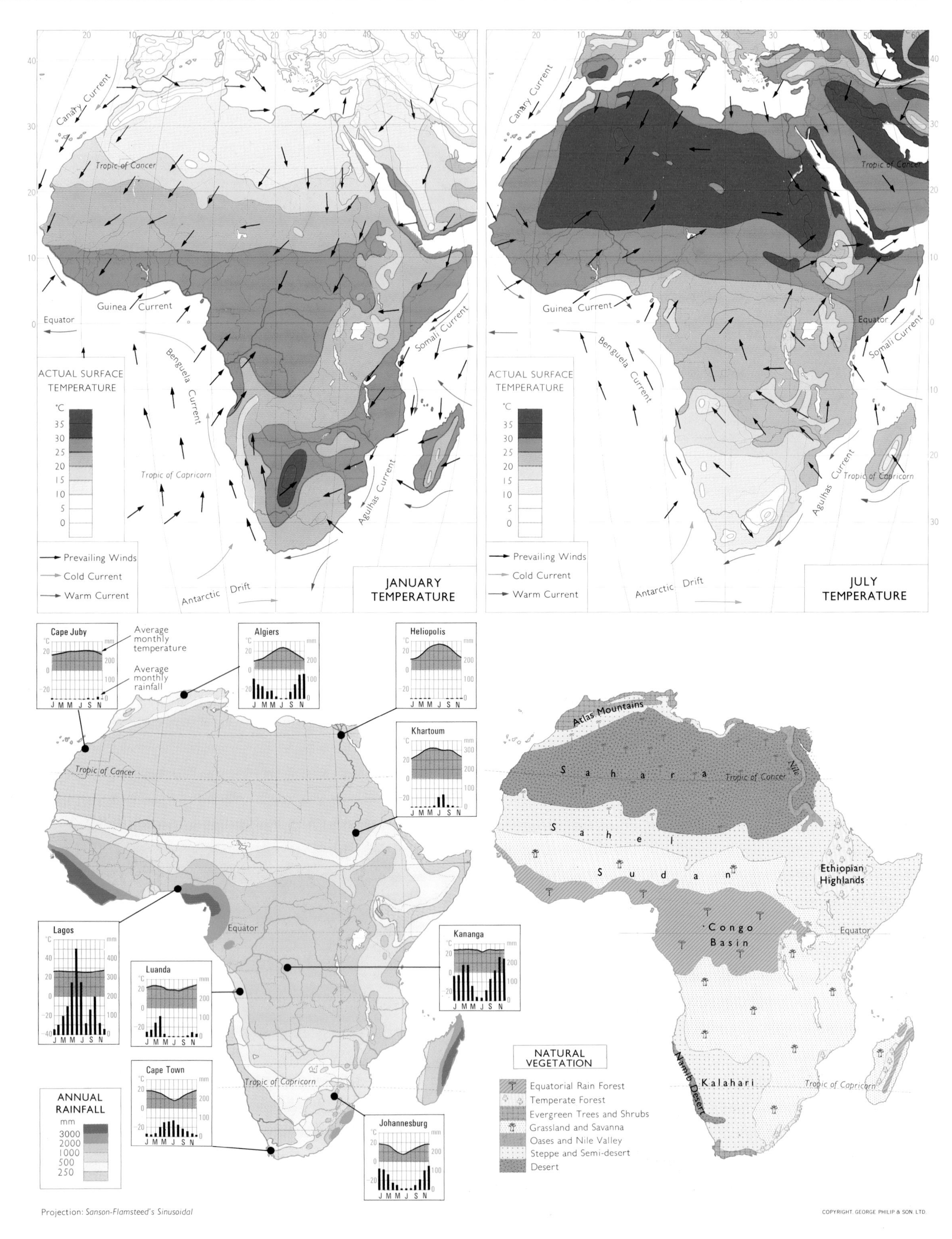

ACTUAL SURFACE TEMPERATURE

°C
35
30
25
20
15
10
5
0

→ Prevailing Winds
→ Cold Current
→ Warm Current

JANUARY TEMPERATURE

ACTUAL SURFACE TEMPERATURE

°C
35
30
25
20
15
10
5
0

→ Prevailing Winds
→ Cold Current
→ Warm Current

JULY TEMPERATURE

Cape Juby
Average monthly temperature
Average monthly rainfall

Algiers

Heliopolis

Khartoum

Lagos

Luanda

Kananga

Cape Town

Johannesburg

ANNUAL RAINFALL

mm
3000
2000
1000
500
250

NATURAL VEGETATION

⊤ Equatorial Rain Forest
Temperate Forest
Evergreen Trees and Shrubs
🌴 Grassland and Savanna
Oases and Nile Valley
Steppe and Semi-desert
Desert

Atlas Mountains

Sahara

Sahel

Sudan

Congo Basin

Ethiopian Highlands

Kalahari

Namib Desert

Nile

Tropic of Cancer

Equator

Tropic of Capricorn

Projection: Sanson-Flamsteed's Sinusoidal

1 : 80 000 000

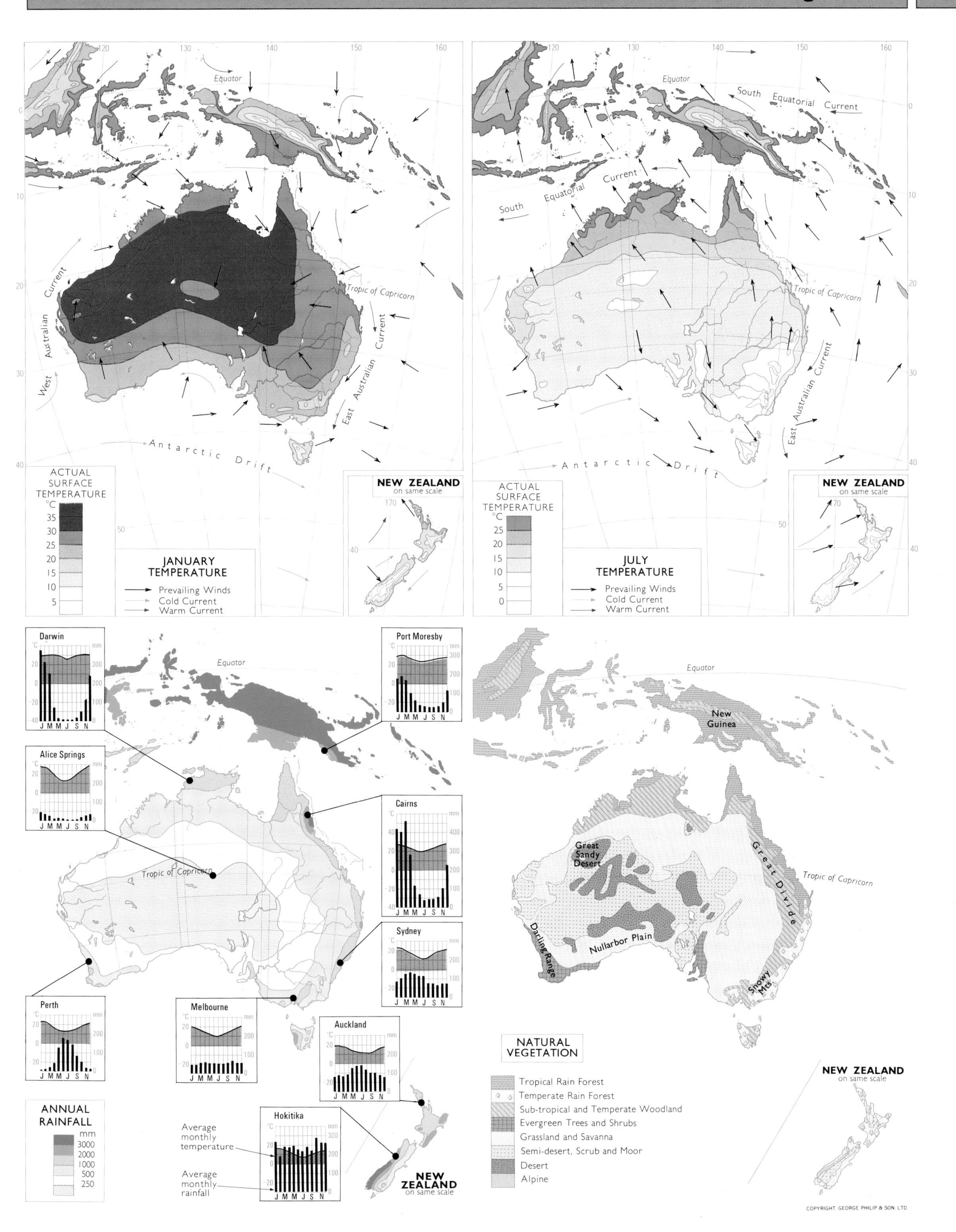

ACTUAL SURFACE TEMPERATURE
°C
35
30
25
20
15
10
5

JANUARY TEMPERATURE
→ Prevailing Winds
→ Cold Current
→ Warm Current

NEW ZEALAND
on same scale

ACTUAL SURFACE TEMPERATURE
°C
25
20
15
10
5
0

JULY TEMPERATURE
→ Prevailing Winds
→ Cold Current
→ Warm Current

NEW ZEALAND
on same scale

Darwin
Port Moresby
Alice Springs
Cairns
Sydney
Perth
Melbourne
Auckland
Hokitika

Average monthly temperature
Average monthly rainfall

ANNUAL RAINFALL
mm
3000
2000
1000
500
250

NEW ZEALAND
on same scale

Equator
Tropic of Capricorn

New Guinea

Great Sandy Desert

Darling Range

Nullarbor Plain

Great Divide

Snowy Mts.

Tropic of Capricorn

NATURAL VEGETATION
- Tropical Rain Forest
- Temperate Rain Forest
- Sub-tropical and Temperate Woodland
- Evergreen Trees and Shrubs
- Grassland and Savanna
- Semi-desert, Scrub and Moor
- Desert
- Alpine

NEW ZEALAND
on same scale

1:60 000 000

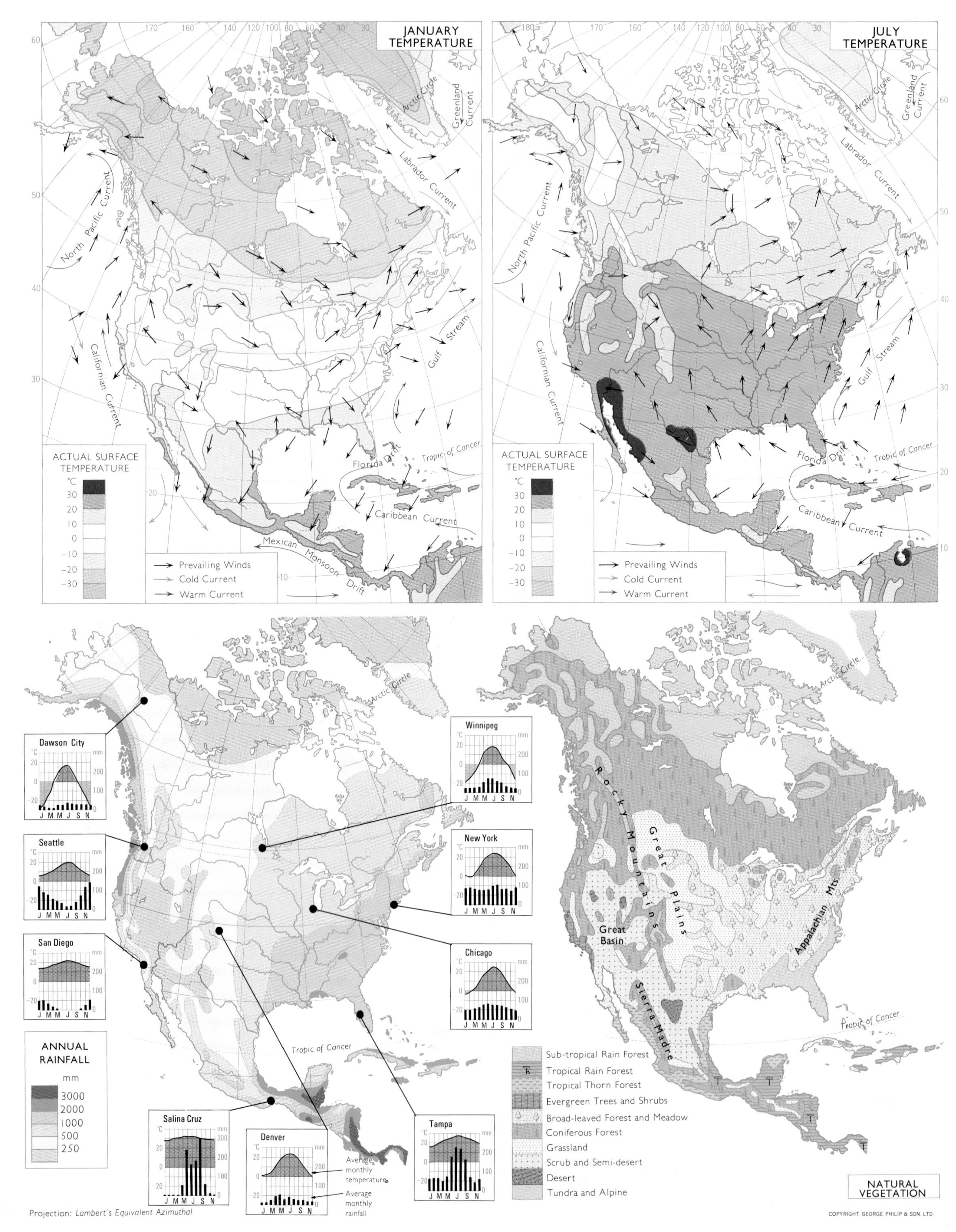

JANUARY TEMPERATURE

JULY TEMPERATURE

ACTUAL SURFACE TEMPERATURE
°C
30
20
10
0
-10
-20
-30

→ Prevailing Winds
→ Cold Current
→ Warm Current

ACTUAL SURFACE TEMPERATURE
°C
30
20
10
0
-10
-20
-30

→ Prevailing Winds
→ Cold Current
→ Warm Current

Dawson City
Seattle
San Diego
Winnipeg
New York
Chicago
Salina Cruz
Denver
Tampa

ANNUAL RAINFALL
mm
3000
2000
1000
500
250

Average monthly temperature

Average monthly rainfall

Sub-tropical Rain Forest
Tropical Rain Forest
Tropical Thorn Forest
Evergreen Trees and Shrubs
Broad-leaved Forest and Meadow
Coniferous Forest
Grassland
Scrub and Semi-desert
Desert
Tundra and Alpine

Rocky Mountains
Great Plains
Great Basin
Sierra Madre
Appalachian Mts

NATURAL VEGETATION

Projection: Lambert's Equivalent Azimuthal

1 : 70 000 000

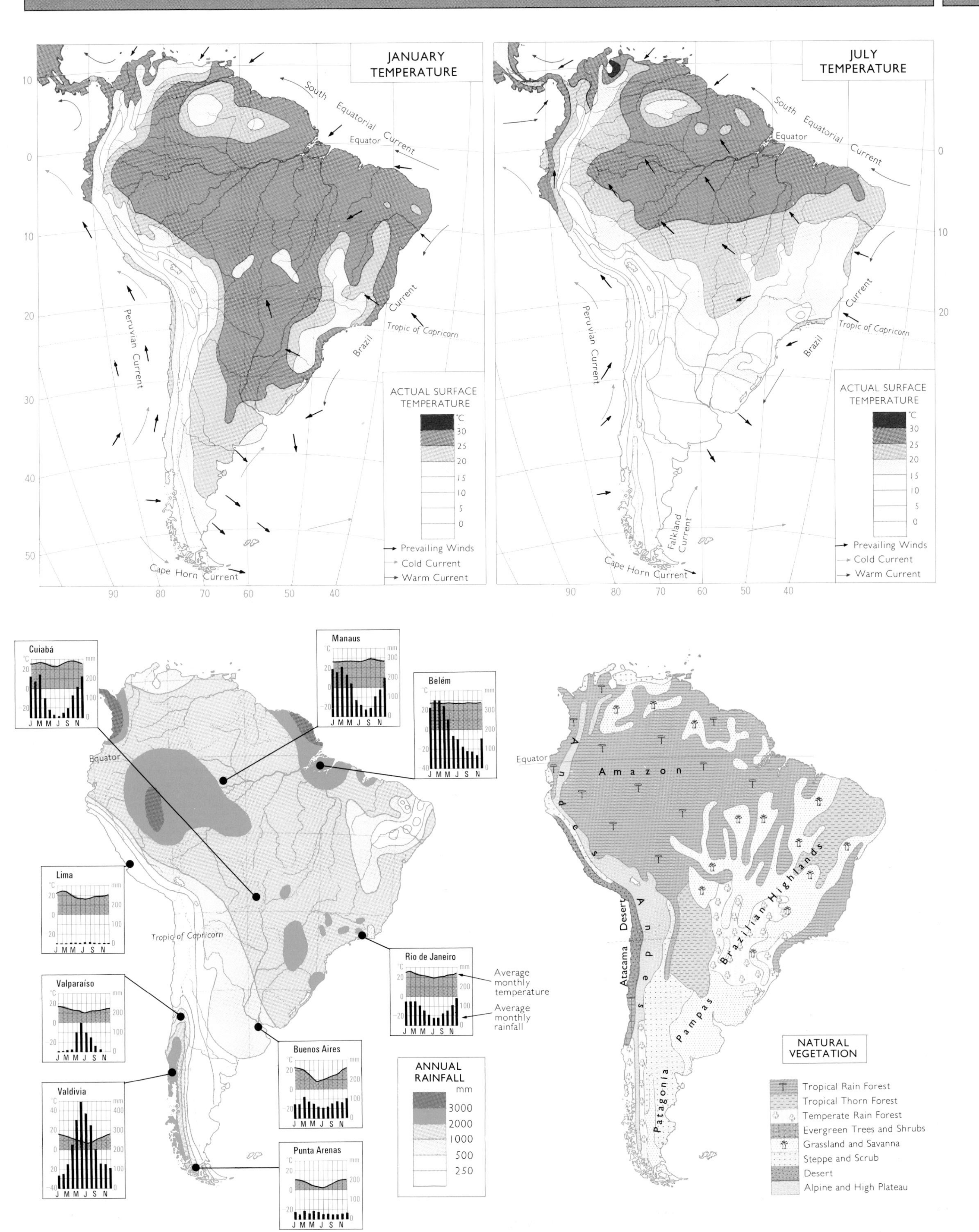

JANUARY TEMPERATURE

JULY TEMPERATURE

South Equatorial Current

Equator

Peruvian Current

Brazil Current

Tropic of Capricorn

Falkland Current

Cape Horn Current

ACTUAL SURFACE TEMPERATURE
°C
30
25
20
15
10
5
0

→ Prevailing Winds
→ Cold Current
→ Warm Current

Cuiabá

Manaus

Belém

Equator

Lima

Tropic of Capricorn

Valparaíso

Rio de Janeiro

Average monthly temperature

Average monthly rainfall

Buenos Aires

Valdivia

ANNUAL RAINFALL

mm
3000
2000
1000
500
250

Punta Arenas

Amazon

Andes

Atacama Desert

Brazilian Highlands

Pampas

Patagonia

NATURAL VEGETATION

- Tropical Rain Forest
- Tropical Thorn Forest
- Temperate Rain Forest
- Evergreen Trees and Shrubs
- Grassland and Savanna
- Steppe and Scrub
- Desert
- Alpine and High Plateau

Projection: *Lambert's Equivalent Azimuthal*

COPYRIGHT GEORGE PHILIP & SON LTD

1 : 70 000 000

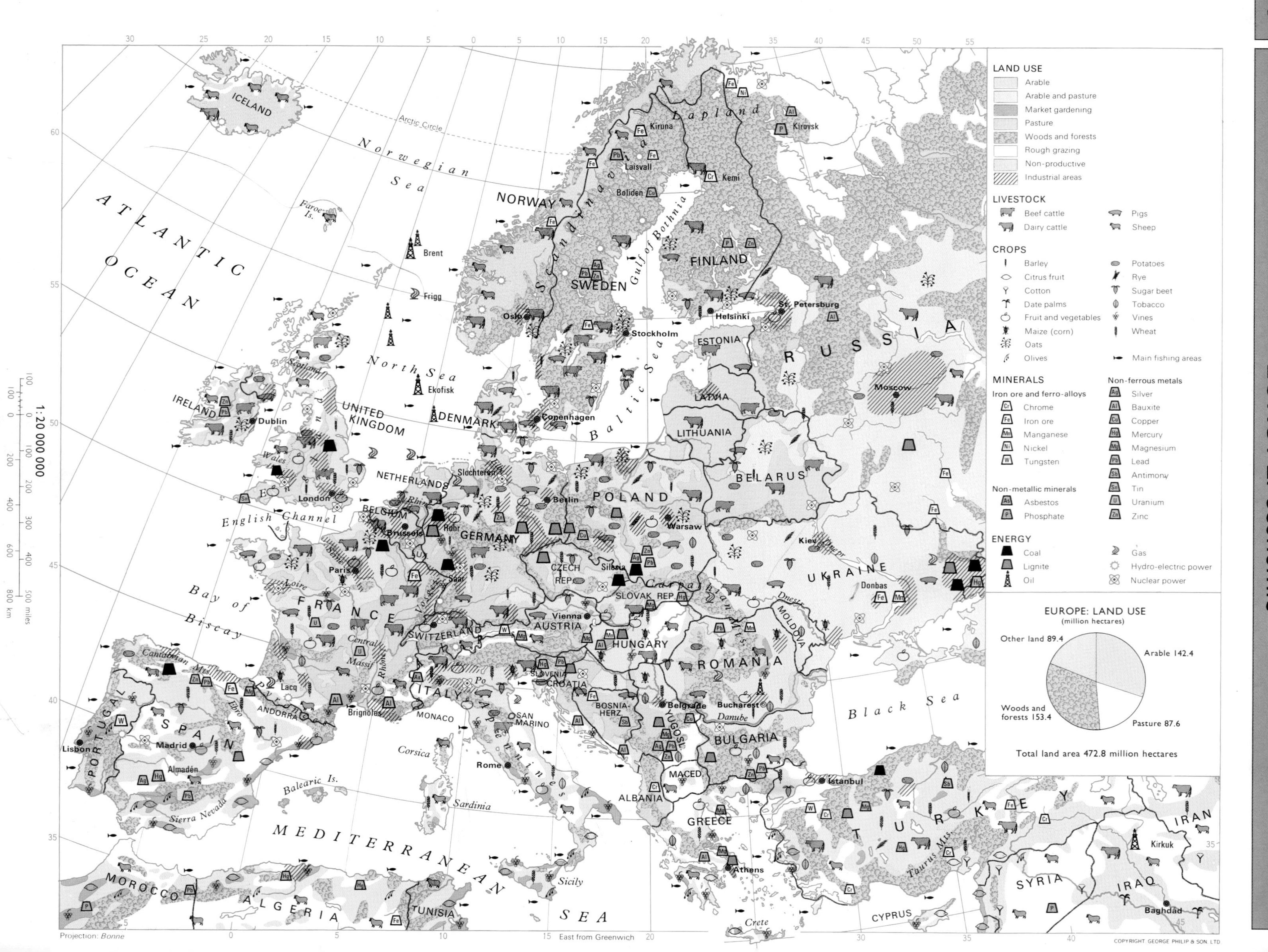

LAND USE
Arable
Arable and pasture
Market gardening
Pasture
Woods and forests
Rough grazing
Non-productive
Industrial areas

LIVESTOCK
Beef cattle
Dairy cattle
Pigs
Sheep

CROPS
Barley
Citrus fruit
Cotton
Date palms
Fruit and vegetables
Maize (corn)
Oats
Olives
Potatoes
Rye
Sugar beet
Tobacco
Vines
Wheat
Main fishing areas

MINERALS
Iron ore and ferro-alloys
Chrome
Iron ore
Manganese
Nickel
Tungsten

Non-ferrous metals
Silver
Bauxite
Copper
Mercury
Magnesium
Lead
Antimony
Tin
Uranium
Zinc

Non-metallic minerals
Asbestos
Phosphate

ENERGY
Coal
Lignite
Oil
Gas
Hydro-electric power
Nuclear power

EUROPE: LAND USE
(million hectares)

Other land 89.4
Arable 142.4
Pasture 87.6
Woods and forests 153.4

Total land area 472.8 million hectares

1:20 000 000

Projection: *Bonne*

COPYRIGHT GEORGE PHILIP & SON, LTD

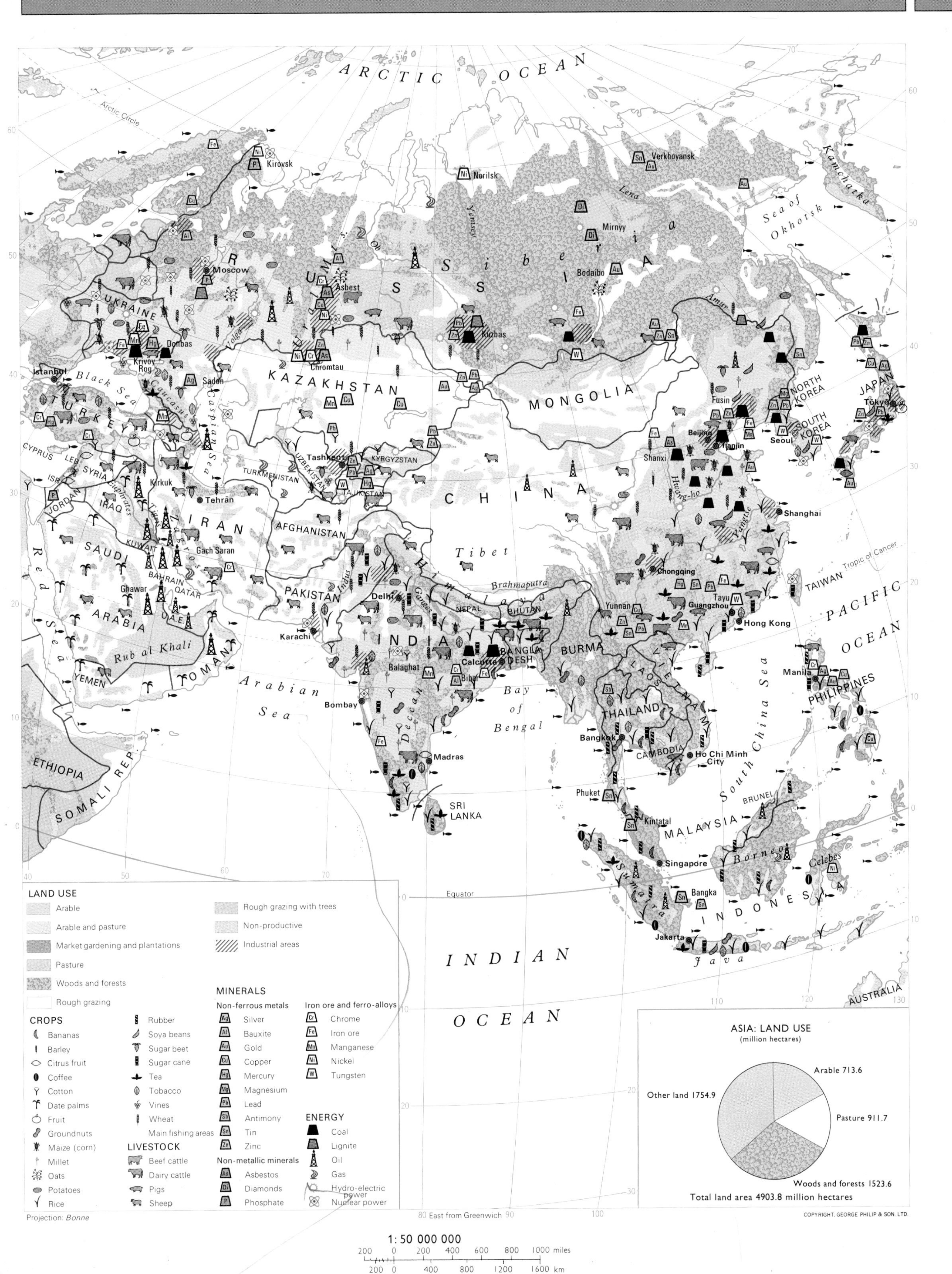
ARCTIC OCEAN
Arctic Circle
Kirovsk
Norilsk
Verkhoyansk
Sea of Okhotsk
Kamchatka
Lena
Yenisey
Ob
Mirnyy
Bodaibo
Siberia
RUSSIA
Moscow
Asbest
Kuzbas
Amur
Urals
UKRAINE
Donbas
Krivoy Rog
Volga
Chromtau
KAZAKHSTAN
MONGOLIA
NORTH KOREA
SOUTH KOREA
JAPAN
Tokyo
Seoul
Fusin
Beijing
Tianjin
Shanxi
Hwang-ho
Yangtze
Shanghai
Istanbul
Black Sea
Caucasus
Sadon
Caspian Sea
TURKEY
CYPRUS
LEB.
SYRIA
ISR.
JORDAN
IRAQ
Euphrates
Tigris
Kirkuk
Tehran
IRAN
Zagros
TURKMENISTAN
UZBEKISTAN
Tashkent
KYRGYZSTAN
TAJIKISTAN
AFGHANISTAN
CHINA
Tibet
Brahmaputra
Himalaya
KUWAIT
BAHRAIN
QATAR
U.A.E.
Gach Saran
SAUDI ARABIA
Ghawar
Red Sea
Rub al Khali
YEMEN
OMAN
PAKISTAN
Indus
Karachi
Delhi
Ganges
NEPAL
BHUTAN
BANGLADESH
Calcutta
INDIA
Balaghat
Bihar
Deccan
Bombay
Madras
Arabian Sea
Bay of Bengal
SRI LANKA
ETHIOPIA
SOMALI REP.
Chongqing
Yunnan
Guangzhou
Tayu
Hong Kong
TAIWAN
Tropic of Cancer
PACIFIC OCEAN
BURMA
LAOS
VIETNAM
THAILAND
Bangkok
CAMBODIA
Ho Chi Minh City
South China Sea
Manila
PHILIPPINES
Phuket
Kintatal
BRUNEI
MALAYSIA
Singapore
Borneo
Celebes
Sumatra
Bangka
INDONESIA
Jakarta
Java
Equator
INDIAN OCEAN
AUSTRALIA
LAND USE
Arable
Arable and pasture
Market gardening and plantations
Pasture
Woods and forests
Rough grazing
Rough grazing with trees
Non-productive
Industrial areas
CROPS
Bananas
Barley
Citrus fruit
Coffee
Cotton
Date palms
Fruit
Groundnuts
Maize (corn)
Millet
Oats
Potatoes
Rice
Rubber
Soya beans
Sugar beet
Sugar cane
Tea
Tobacco
Vines
Wheat
Main fishing areas
LIVESTOCK
Beef cattle
Dairy cattle
Pigs
Sheep
MINERALS
Non-ferrous metals
Ag Silver
Al Bauxite
Au Gold
Cu Copper
Hg Mercury
Mg Magnesium
Pb Lead
Sb Antimony
Sn Tin
Zn Zinc
Non-metallic minerals
As Asbestos
Di Diamonds
P Phosphate
Iron ore and ferro-alloys
Cr Chrome
Fe Iron ore
Mn Manganese
Ni Nickel
W Tungsten
ENERGY
Coal
Lignite
Oil
Gas
Hydro-electric power
Nuclear power
ASIA: LAND USE
(million hectares)
Arable 713.6
Pasture 911.7
Woods and forests 1523.6
Other land 1754.9
Total land area 4903.8 million hectares
Projection: Bonne
80 East from Greenwich 90
COPYRIGHT GEORGE PHILIP & SON LTD.
1: 50 000 000
200 0 200 400 600 800 1000 miles
200 0 400 800 1200 1600 km

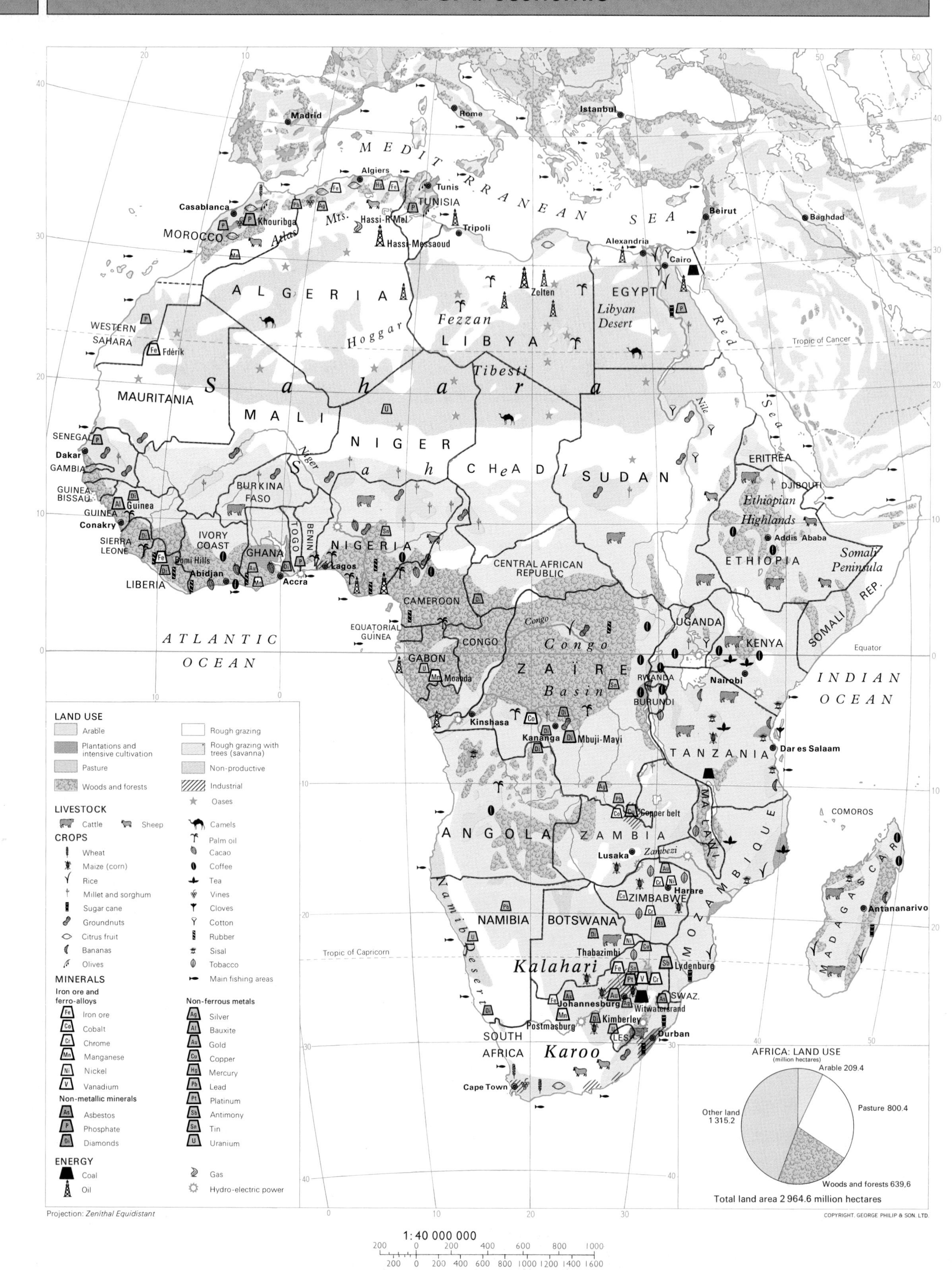
MEDITERRANEAN SEA
Madrid
Rome
Istanbul
Algiers
Tunis
TUNISIA
Casablanca
Khouribga
MOROCCO
Atlas Mts.
Hassi-R'Mel
Hassi-Messaoud
Tripoli
Beirut
Baghdad
Alexandria
Cairo
ALGERIA
Zelten
EGYPT
Libyan Desert
Fezzan
LIBYA
Hoggar
WESTERN SAHARA
Fdérik
Red Sea
Tropic of Cancer
Tibesti
Sahara
MAURITANIA
MALI
NIGER
Nile
SENEGAL
Dakar
GAMBIA
Niger
Sahel
CHAD
SUDAN
ERITREA
DJIBOUTI
GUINEA-BISSAU
GUINEA
Guinea
BURKINA FASO
Ethiopian Highlands
Conakry
SIERRA LEONE
IVORY COAST
GHANA
TOGO
BENIN
NIGERIA
Addis Ababa
ETHIOPIA
Somali Peninsula
Bomi Hills
Abidjan
Accra
Lagos
CENTRAL AFRICAN REPUBLIC
LIBERIA
CAMEROON
SOMALI REP.
EQUATORIAL GUINEA
Congo
UGANDA
ATLANTIC OCEAN
CONGO
Congo Basin
KENYA
Equator
GABON
Moanda
ZAÏRE
RWANDA
BURUNDI
Nairobi
INDIAN OCEAN
Kinshasa
Kananga
Mbuji-Mayi
TANZANIA
Dar es Salaam
MALAWI
Copper belt
COMOROS
ANGOLA
ZAMBIA
Lusaka
Zambezi
MOZAMBIQUE
MADAGASCAR
Harare
ZIMBABWE
Antananarivo
Namib Desert
NAMIBIA
BOTSWANA
Tropic of Capricorn
Thabazimbi
Kalahari
Lydenburg
SWAZ.
Johannesburg
Witwatersrand
Postmasburg
Kimberley
LES.
Durban
SOUTH AFRICA
Karoo
Cape Town
LAND USE
Arable
Plantations and intensive cultivation
Pasture
Woods and forests
Rough grazing
Rough grazing with trees (savanna)
Non-productive
Industrial
Oases
LIVESTOCK
Cattle
Sheep
Camels
CROPS
Wheat
Maize (corn)
Rice
Millet and sorghum
Sugar cane
Groundnuts
Citrus fruit
Bananas
Olives
Palm oil
Cacao
Coffee
Tea
Vines
Cloves
Cotton
Rubber
Sisal
Tobacco
Main fishing areas
MINERALS
Iron ore and ferro-alloys
Iron ore
Cobalt
Chrome
Manganese
Nickel
Vanadium
Non-metallic minerals
Asbestos
Phosphate
Diamonds
Non-ferrous metals
Silver
Bauxite
Gold
Copper
Mercury
Lead
Platinum
Antimony
Tin
Uranium
ENERGY
Coal
Oil
Gas
Hydro-electric power
AFRICA: LAND USE
(million hectares)
Arable 209.4
Pasture 800.4
Woods and forests 639,6
Other land 1 315.2
Total land area 2 964.6 million hectares
Projection: Zenithal Equidistant
1:40 000 000

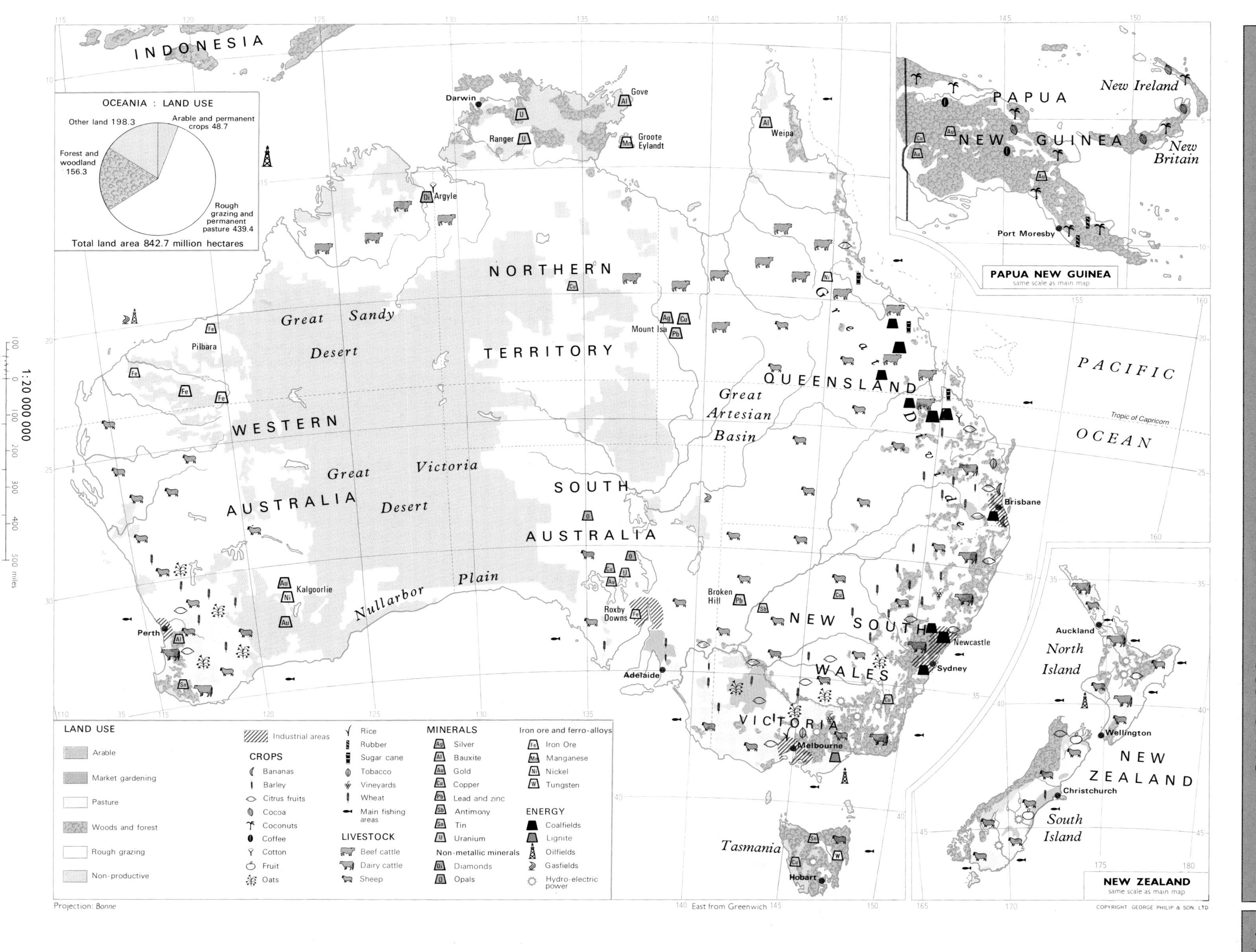

PACIFIC OCEAN

Tropic of Capricorn

PAPUA NEW GUINEA
same scale as main map

New Ireland

New Britain

PAPUA NEW GUINEA

Port Moresby

NEW ZEALAND
same scale as main map

COPYRIGHT GEORGE PHILIP & SON LTD

NEW ZEALAND

North Island

Auckland

Wellington

Christchurch

South Island

Brisbane

Newcastle

Sydney

QUEENSLAND

Great Dividing Range

Great Artesian Basin

NEW SOUTH WALES

VICTORIA

Melbourne

Broken Hill

Adelaide

Tasmania

Hobart

East from Greenwich 145

Weipa

SOUTH AUSTRALIA

Roxby Downs

Mount Isa

Gove

Groote Eylandt

NORTHERN TERRITORY

Ranger

Darwin

Argyle

Kalgoorlie

Great Sandy Desert

Great Victoria Desert

Nullarbor Plain

WESTERN AUSTRALIA

INDONESIA

Pilbara

Perth

OCEANIA : LAND USE

Other land 198.3

Arable and permanent crops 48.7

Rough grazing and permanent pasture 439.4

Forest and woodland 156.3

Total land area 842.7 million hectares

Projection: Bonne

LAND USE

- Arable
- Market gardening
- Pasture
- Woods and forest
- Rough grazing
- Non-productive

Industrial areas

CROPS
- Bananas
- Barley
- Citrus fruits
- Cocoa
- Coconuts
- Coffee
- Cotton
- Fruit
- Oats
- Rice
- Rubber
- Sugar cane
- Tobacco
- Vineyards
- Wheat
- Main fishing areas

LIVESTOCK
- Beef cattle
- Dairy cattle
- Sheep

MINERALS
- Silver
- Bauxite
- Gold
- Copper
- Lead and zinc
- Antimony
- Tin
- Uranium
- Non-metallic minerals
- Diamonds
- Opals

Iron ore and ferro-alloys
- Fe Iron Ore
- Manganese
- Nickel
- W Tungsten

ENERGY
- Coalfields
- Lignite
- Oilfields
- Gasfields
- Hydro-electric power

1:20 000 000

100 0 100 200 300 400 500 miles

100 0 200 400 600 800 km

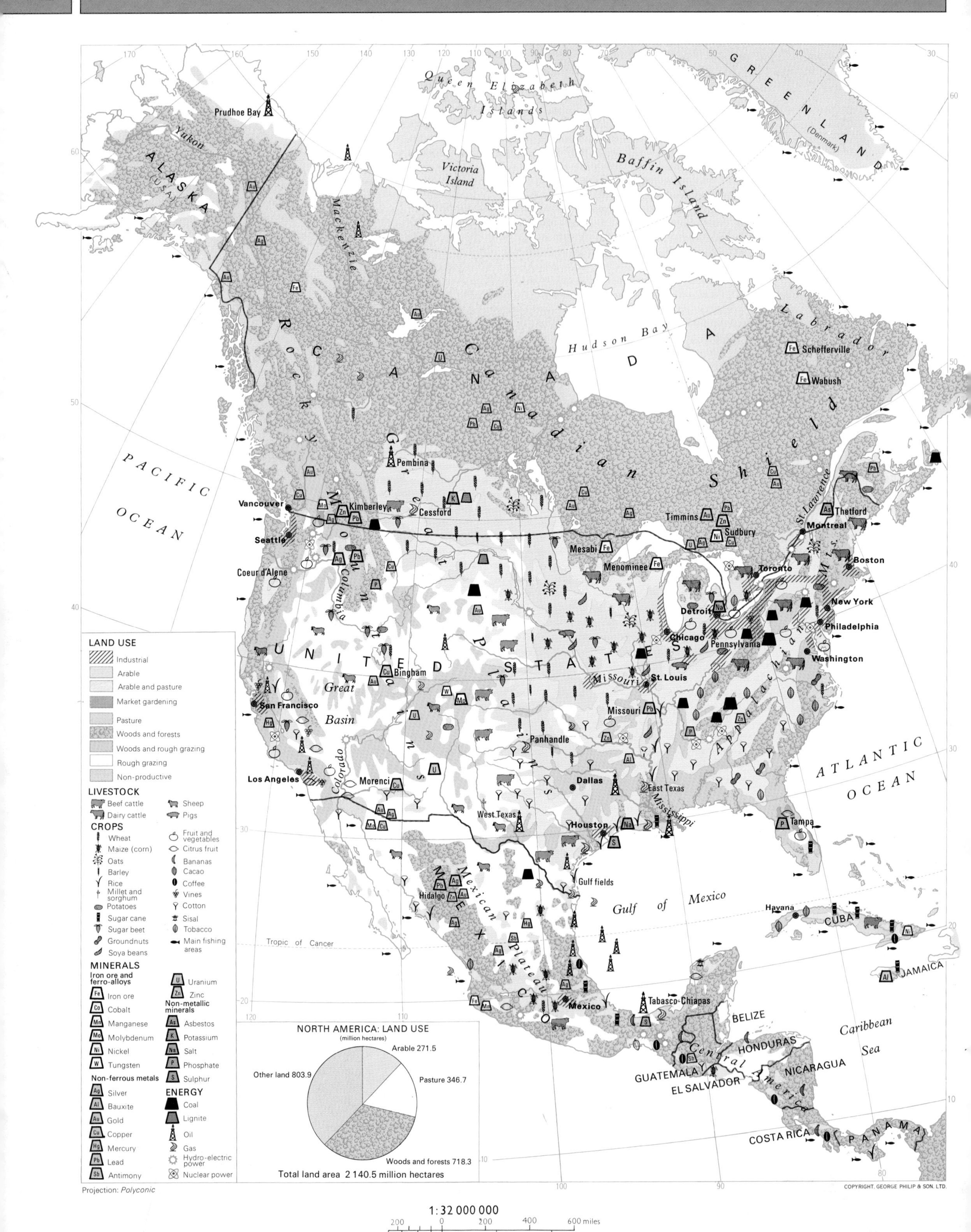

LAND USE
- Industrial
- Arable
- Arable and pasture
- Market gardening
- Pasture
- Woods and forests
- Woods and rough grazing
- Rough grazing
- Non-productive

LIVESTOCK
- Beef cattle
- Sheep
- Dairy cattle
- Pigs

CROPS
- Wheat
- Fruit and vegetables
- Maize (corn)
- Citrus fruit
- Oats
- Bananas
- Barley
- Cacao
- Rice
- Coffee
- Millet and sorghum
- Vines
- Potatoes
- Cotton
- Sugar cane
- Sisal
- Sugar beet
- Tobacco
- Groundnuts
- Main fishing areas
- Soya beans

MINERALS
Iron ore and ferro-alloys
- Fe Iron ore
- U Uranium
- Co Cobalt
- Zn Zinc
- Mn Manganese
- Mo Molybdenum

Non-metallic minerals
- As Asbestos
- Ni Nickel
- K Potassium
- W Tungsten
- Na Salt
- P Phosphate
Non-ferrous metals
- S Sulphur
- Ag Silver
- **ENERGY**
- Al Bauxite
- Coal
- Au Gold
- Lignite
- Cu Copper
- Oil
- Hg Mercury
- Gas
- Pb Lead
- Hydro-electric power
- Sb Antimony
- Nuclear power

NORTH AMERICA: LAND USE
(million hectares)

- Other land 803.9
- Arable 271.5
- Pasture 346.7
- Woods and forests 718.3

Total land area 2 140.5 million hectares

Projection: Polyconic

COPYRIGHT. GEORGE PHILIP & SON. LTD.

1: 32 000 000

200   0   200   400   600 miles
400   0   200   400   600   800 km

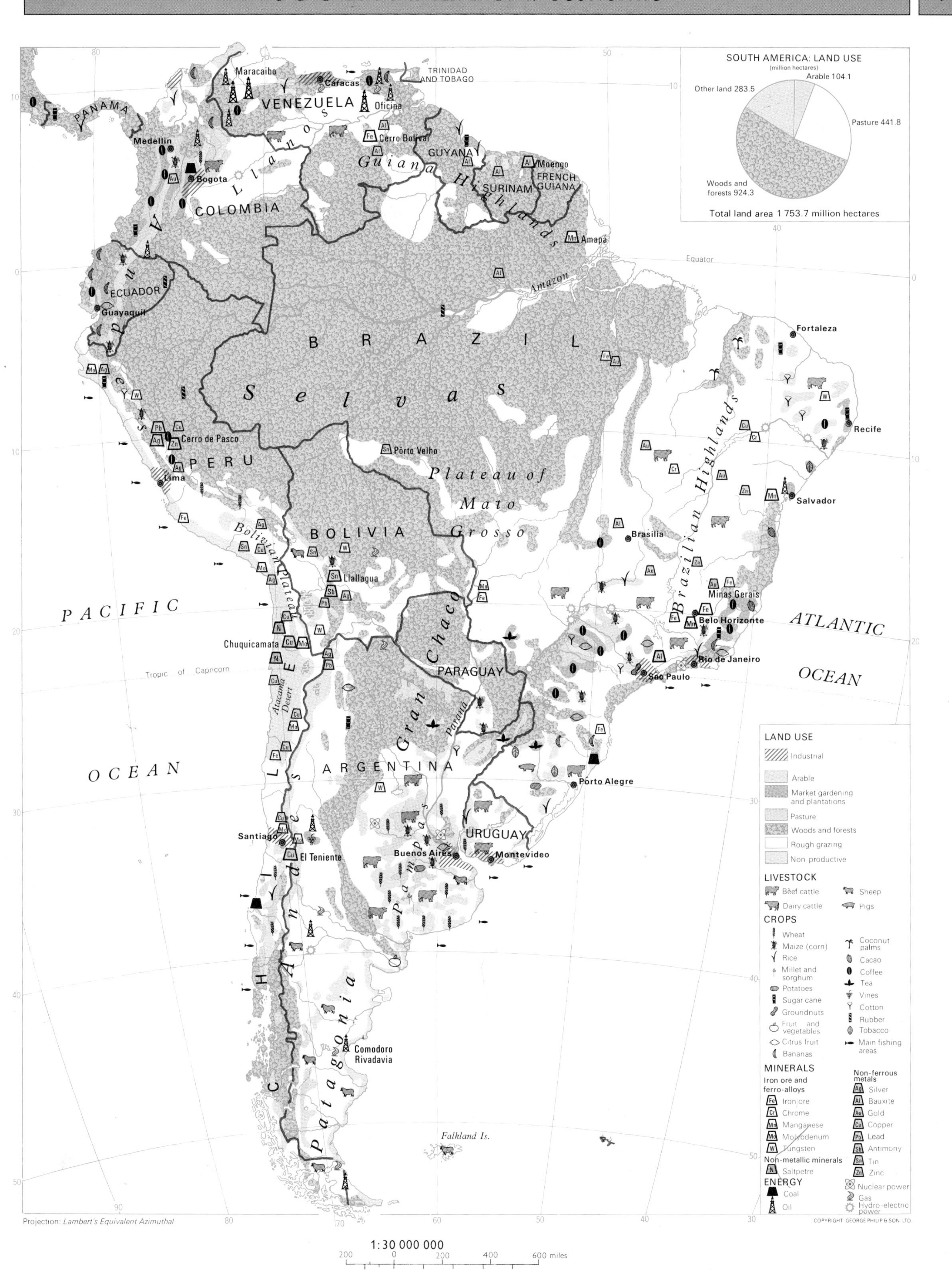

SOUTH AMERICA: LAND USE
(million hectares)

Arable 104.1
Other land 283.5
Pasture 441.8
Woods and forests 924.3

Total land area 1 753.7 million hectares

PANAMA

VENEZUELA
Maracaibo
Caracas
Oficina
TRINIDAD AND TOBAGO

Medellin
Bogota
COLOMBIA
Cerro Bolivar
GUYANA
SURINAM
FRENCH GUIANA
Moengo

ECUADOR
Guayaquil

Amapá

Equator

Amazon

B R A Z I L

S e l v a s

Fortaleza

Cerro de Pasco

PERU
Lima

Plateau of
Mato
Grosso

Pôrto Velho

Recife

BOLIVIA

Llallagua

Salvador

Brasília

Minas Gerais
Belo Horizonte

PACIFIC

Chuquicamata

Gran Chaco

PARAGUAY

Rio de Janeiro
São Paulo

ATLANTIC

OCEAN

Tropic of Capricorn

Atacama Desert

Paraná

OCEAN

ARGENTINA

Porto Alegre

Santiago

El Teniente

Buenos Aires

URUGUAY

Montevideo

Comodoro Rivadavia

Patagonia

Falkland Is.

LAND USE
- Industrial
- Arable
- Market gardening and plantations
- Pasture
- Woods and forests
- Rough grazing
- Non-productive

LIVESTOCK
- Beef cattle
- Dairy cattle
- Sheep
- Pigs

CROPS
- Wheat
- Maize (corn)
- Rice
- Millet and sorghum
- Potatoes
- Sugar cane
- Groundnuts
- Fruit and vegetables
- Citrus fruit
- Bananas
- Coconut palms
- Cacao
- Coffee
- Tea
- Vines
- Cotton
- Rubber
- Tobacco
- Main fishing areas

MINERALS
Iron ore and ferro-alloys
- Fe Iron ore
- Cr Chrome
- Mn Manganese
- Mo Molybdenum
- W Tungsten

Non-metallic minerals
- N Saltpetre

Non-ferrous metals
- Ag Silver
- Al Bauxite
- Au Gold
- Cu Copper
- Pb Lead
- Sb Antimony
- Sn Tin
- Zn Zinc

ENERGY
- Coal
- Oil
- Nuclear power
- Gas
- Hydro-electric power

Projection: *Lambert's Equivalent Azimuthal*

COPYRIGHT GEORGE PHILIP & SON LTD

1:30 000 000

200   0   200   400   600 miles

200   0   200   400   600   800 km

AGRICULTURAL PRODUCTION

Staple Crops

Wheat

China 18.6% | U.S.A. 11.6% | India 10.1% | Russia 7.5% | France 5.2% | Canada 4.9%

World total (1993): 564,457,000 tonnes

Rice

China 35.4% | India 21.0% | Indonesia 9.1% | Bangladesh 5.3% | Vietnam 4.2% | Thailand 3.6%

World total (1993): 527,413,000 tonnes

Millet

India 37.8% | China 15.0% | Nigeria 14.4% | Niger 5.4% | Russia 4.2%

World total (1993): 26,442,000 tonnes

Rye

Russia 34.9% | Poland 19.0% | Germany 11.2% | Belarus 10.7% | Ukraine 4.3%

World total (1993): 26,200,000 tonnes

Maize

U.S.A. 35.8% | China 22.9% | Brazil 6.7% | Mexico 4.1% | France 3.3%

World total (1993): 450,570,000 tonnes

Potatoes

Russia 13.2% | Poland 12.6% | China 12.2% | Ukraine 7.3% | U.S.A. 6.6% | India 5.5%

World total (1993): 288,183,000 tonnes

Soya

U.S.A. 44.3% | Brazil 20.5% | China 11.7% | Argentina 9.6% | India 4.1%

World total (1993): 111,011,000 tonnes

Cassava

Brazil 14.1% | Nigeria 13.7% | Zaïre 13.6% | Thailand 12.8% | Indonesia 10.6% | Tanzania 4.4%

World total (1993): 153,628,000 tonnes

Animal Products

Milk

U.S.A. 15.1% | Russia 9.4% | India 6.7% | Germany 6.2% | France 5.5% | Ukraine 4.0%

World total (1993): 453,733,000 tonnes

Butter

India 16.0% | Russia 10.1% | U.S.A. 9.0% | Germany 7.0% | France 6.4% | Pakistan 4.8% | Ukraine 4.5%

World total (1993): 6,956,000 tonnes

Lamb and Mutton

China 10.1% | Australia 9.3% | N. Zealand 7.2% | U.K. 4.9% | Turkey 4.4% | Pakistan 4.2%

World total (1993): 6,914,000 tonnes

Beef and Veal

U.S.A. 21.1% | Russia 6.8% | Brazil 6.1% | Argentina 5.4% | France 3.8% | China 3.8%

World total (1993): 50,239,000 tonnes

Pork

China 38.7% | U.S.A. 10.5% | Germany 4.9% | France 4.9% | Russia 3.4%

World total (1993): 73,891,000 tonnes

Sugars

Sugarcane

Brazil 24.2% | India 22.2% | China 6.6% | Cuba 4.2% | Mexico 4.0% | Pakistan 3.7%

World total (1993): 1,040,600,000 tonnes

Sugar beet

Ukraine 12.0% | France 11.3% | Germany 10.2% | Russia 9.1% | U.S.A. 8.5% | Poland 5.5% | Turkey 5.5%

World total (1993): 281,682,000 tonnes

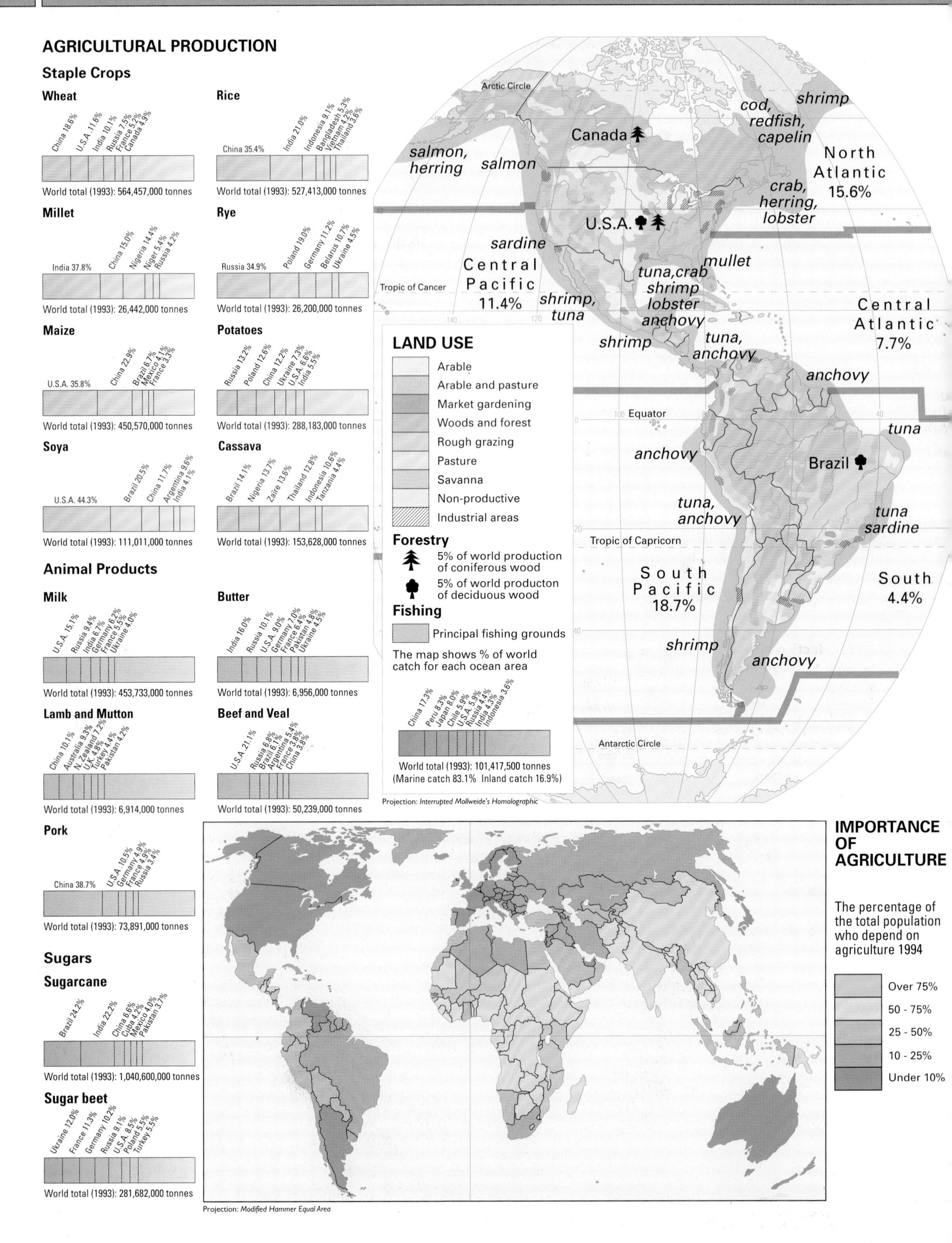

LAND USE

- Arable
- Arable and pasture
- Market gardening
- Woods and forest
- Rough grazing
- Pasture
- Savanna
- Non-productive
- Industrial areas

Forestry

- 5% of world production of coniferous wood
- 5% of world producton of deciduous wood

Fishing

Principal fishing grounds

The map shows % of world catch for each ocean area

China 17.3% | Peru 8.3% | Japan 8.0% | Chile 5.9% | U.S.A. 5.5% | Russia 4.4% | India 4.3% | Indonesia 3.6%

World total (1993): 101,417,500 tonnes
(Marine catch 83.1% Inland catch 16.9%)

Projection: *Interrupted Mollweide's Homolographic*

Arctic Circle
cod, redfish, capelin
shrimp
Canada
salmon, herring
salmon
North Atlantic 15.6%
crab, herring, lobster
U.S.A.
sardine
Central Pacific 11.4%
Tropic of Cancer
mullet
tuna, crab shrimp lobster anchovy
shrimp, tuna
shrimp
Central Atlantic 7.7%
tuna, anchovy
anchovy
Equator
tuna
anchovy
Brazil
tuna, anchovy
tuna sardine
Tropic of Capricorn
South Pacific 18.7%
South 4.4%
shrimp
anchovy
Antarctic Circle

IMPORTANCE OF AGRICULTURE

The percentage of the total population who depend on agriculture 1994

- Over 75%
- 50 – 75%
- 25 – 50%
- 10 – 25%
- Under 10%

Projection: *Modified Hammer Equal Area*

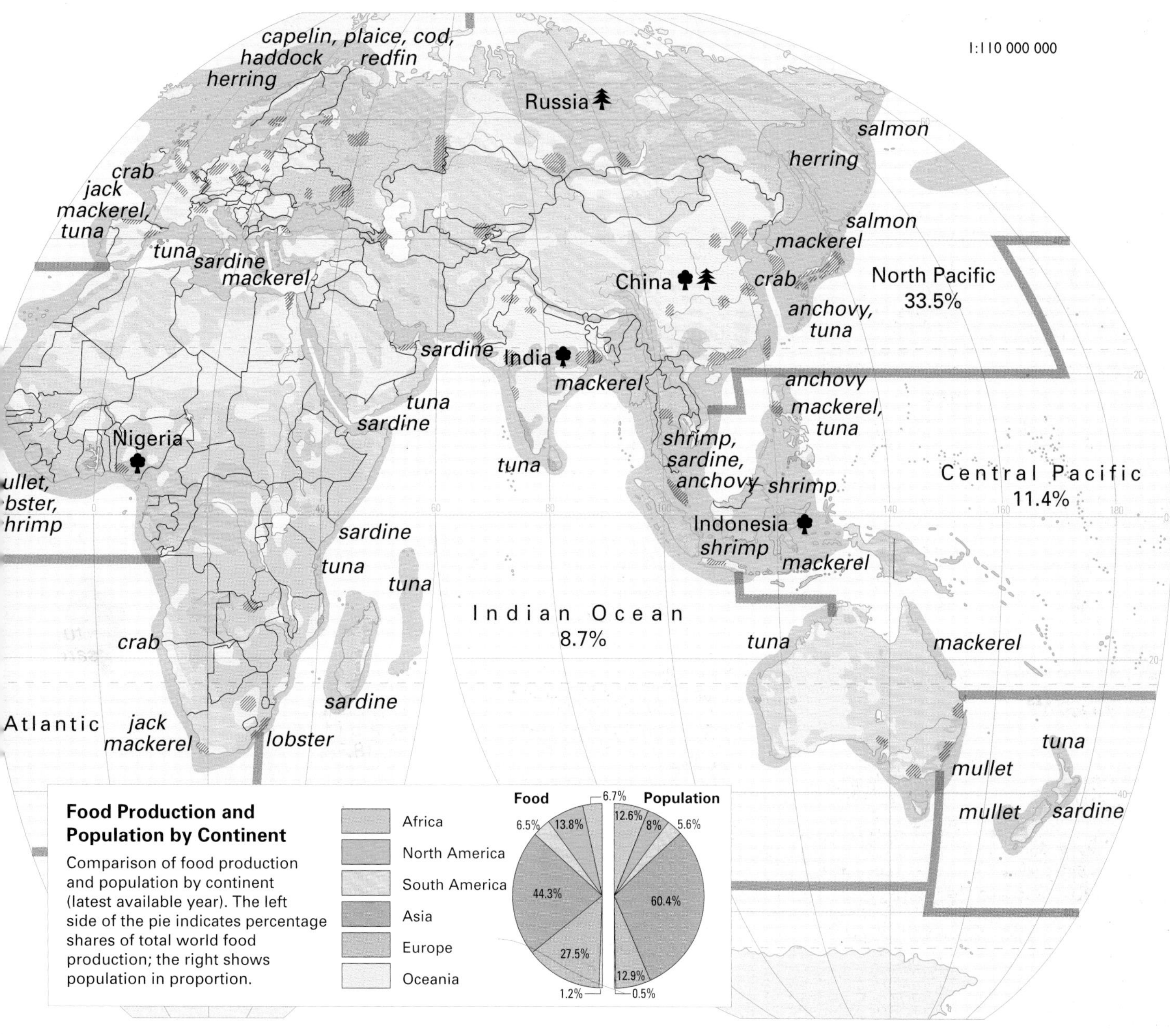

capelin, plaice, cod, haddock, redfin
herring

crab
jack mackerel, tuna

tuna sardine mackerel

Russia

salmon

herring

salmon

China

mackerel

crab

North Pacific
33.5%

sardine India

mackerel

anchovy, tuna

tuna
sardine

anchovy
mackerel, tuna

Nigeria

shrimp, sardine, anchovy

shrimp

Central Pacific
11.4%

mullet, lobster, shrimp

tuna

Indonesia
shrimp

sardine

mackerel

tuna

tuna
sardine

tuna

mackerel

crab

Indian Ocean
8.7%

tuna

sardine

Atlantic jack mackerel

lobster

mullet

mullet sardine

1:110 000 000

Food Production and Population by Continent

Comparison of food production and population by continent (latest available year). The left side of the pie indicates percentage shares of total world food production; the right shows population in proportion.

Africa
North America
South America
Asia
Europe
Oceania

Food | Population
6.7%
6.5% | 13.8% | 12.6% | 8% | 5.6%
44.3% | 60.4%
27.5%
1.2% | 12.9%
0.5%

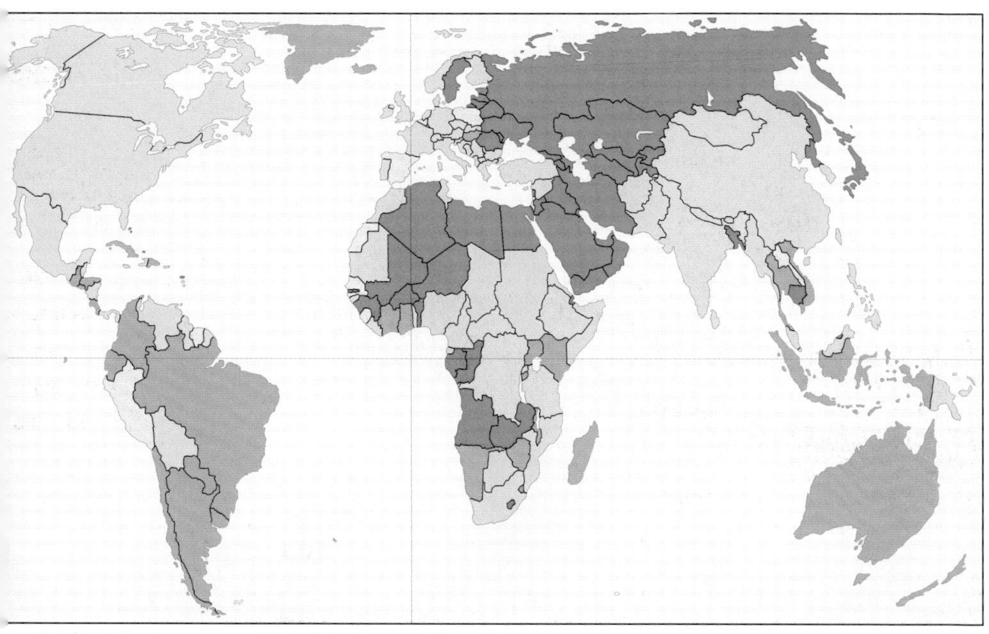

SELF-SUFFICIENCY IN FOOD

Balance of Trade in food products as a % of total trade in food products (S.I.T.C. Class 0,1 and 4).*

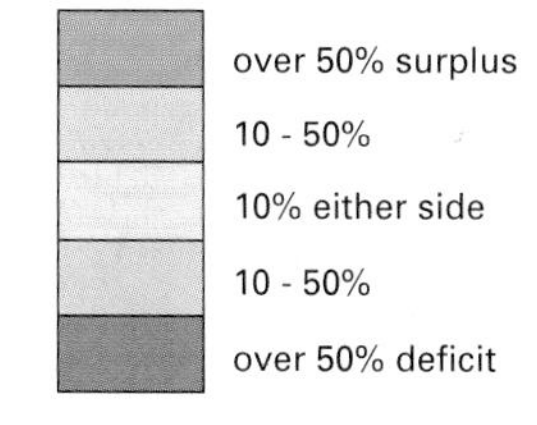

over 50% surplus
10 - 50%
10% either side
10 - 50%
over 50% deficit

*Statistics for the new republics of the former U.S.S.R., Czechoslovakia and Yugoslavia are not yet available. The map shows the statistics for the entire U.S.S.R., Czechoslovakia and Yugoslavia.

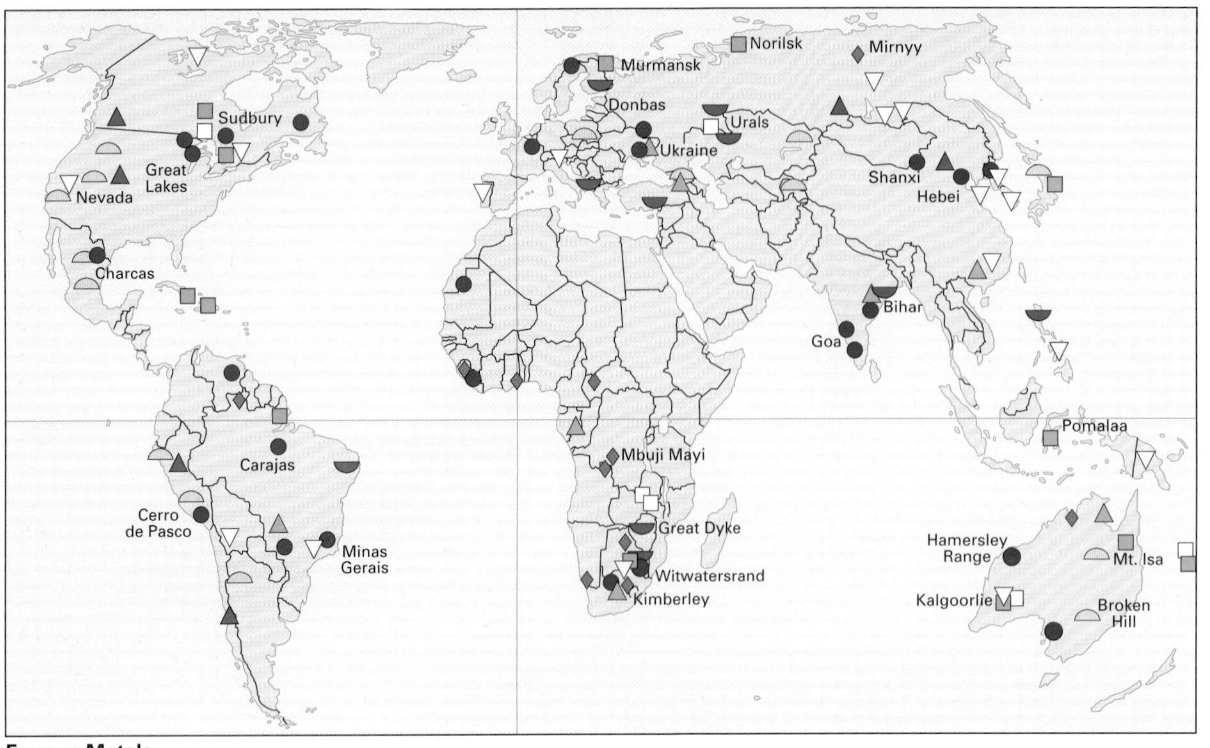

Precious Metals

▽ Gold
World total (1993)
1 900 tonnes

South Africa	32.6%
U.S.A.	17.7%
Australia	13.0%
Canada	7.9%
Russia	6.8%

◠ Silver
World total (1993)
13 000 tonnes

Mexico	16.1%
U.S.A.	11.5%
Peru	10.9%
Australia	8.1%
Russia	7.3%

◆ Diamonds
World total (1993)
100 850 000 carats

Australia	40.6%
Zaire	16.3%
Botswana	14.6%
Russia	11.4%
South Africa	9.7%

Ferrous Metals

● Iron Ore
World total (1993)
940 000 000 tonnes

China	25.0%
Brazil	16.4%
Australia	12.3%
Ukraine	7.4%
India	5.9%

■ Nickel
World total (1993)
790 000 tonnes

Russia	19.0%
Canada	14.9%
Japan	12.8%
Norway	7.2%
Australia	6.5%

◗ Chrome
World total (1993)
9 930 000 tonnes

Kazakhstan	35.2%
South Africa	28.5%
India	9.1%
Turkey	7.0%
Zimbabwe	5.2%

▲ Manganese
World total (1993)
22 000 000 tonnes

Ukraine	31.8%
China	19.1%
South Africa	15.9%
Brazil	9.1%
Gabon	8.2%

☐ Cobalt
World total (1992)
28 000 tonnes

Zaire	23.2%
Zambia	16.1%
Canada	16.1%
New Caledonia	8.9%
Australia	7.9%

▲ Molybdenum
World total (1991)
101 093 tonnes

U.S.A.	53.0%
China	15.8%
Chile	14.3%
Canada	10.9%
Peru	3.0%

▽ Tungsten
World total (1993)
34 240 tonnes

China	58.4%
Russia	10.2%
North Korea	8.8%
Bolivia	2.0%
Portugal	2.0%

Fertilizers

■ Nitrates
World total (1991)
82 270 000 tonnes

China	18.1%
U.S.A.	16.5%
Former U.S.S.R.	15.9%
India	8.5%
Canada	3.3%

△ Phosphates
World total (1993)
34 817 000 tonnes

U.S.A.	30.7%
China	13.5%
Russia	8.2%
India	6.8%
Ukraine	4.0%

▽ Potash
World total (1992)
23 382 000 tonnes

Canada	31.2%
Germany	15.1%
Russia	14.8%
Belarus	14.2%
Israel	5.5%

Non-Ferrous Metals

■ Copper
World total (1993)
9 500 000 tonnes

U.S.A.	18.9%
Chile	13.4%
Japan	12.5%
Germany	6.7%
Russia	6.1%

▲ Lead
World total (1993)
5 400 000 tonnes

U.S.A.	22.7%
Russia	9.3%
U.K.	6.7%
Germany	6.2%
Japan	5.7%

● Bauxite
World total (1993)
114 049 000 tonnes

Australia	36.2%
Guinea	14.9%
Brazil	8.2%
Former U.S.S.R.	6.4%
China	5.7%

▽ Tin
World total (1993)
220 000 tonnes

China	22.7%
Malaysia	20.7%
Indonesia	13.6%
Brazil	10.6%
Bolivia	7.6%

◆ Zinc
World total (1993)
7 127 000 tonnes

China	11.8%
Japan	10.3%
Canada	9.3%
Germany	7.7%
Belgium	5.6%

◠ Mercury
World total (1993)
4 200 tonnes

China	25.0%
Mexico	20.7%
Russia	14.3%
Algeria	8.9%
Kyrgyzstan	6.0%

Projection: *Modified Hammer Equal Area*

ENERGY PRODUCTION

Primary energy production
expressed in kilograms
of coal equivalent per
person 1992

	Over 10 000 kg per person
	1 000 - 10 000 kg per person
	100 - 1 000 kg per person
	10 - 100 kg per person
	Under 10 kg per person

● Oil

▽ Natural gas

▲ Coal and lignite

◇ Uranium *(the fuel used to generate nuclear power)*

In developing countries traditional fuels are still very important. Sometimes called biomass fuels, they include wood, charcoal and dried dung. The pie graph for Nigeria at the foot of the page shows their importance.

Map labels: Prudhoe Bay, Colorado, Texas, Appalachians, Gulf of Mexico, North Sea, Ruhr, Silesia, Donbas, Yamburg, Western Siberia, Kuzbas, Shanxi, The Gulf, Bihar, Brunei, Rum Jungle, Bowen Basin

Oil World total (1994) 3 183 500 000 tonnes		Natural Gas World total (1993) 2 658 000 000 tonnes of coal equivalent		Coal (bituminous) World total (1993) 3 160 000 000 tonnes		Coal (lignite) World total (1993) 1 265 000 000 tonnes		Uranium World total (1993) 32 532 tonnes (metal content)		Nuclear Power World total (1994) 820 000 000 tonnes of coal equivalent		Hydro-Electric Power World total (1994) 922 000 000 tonnes of coal equivalent	
...di Arabia	13.2%	Canada	28.2%	China	36.0%	U.S.A.	23.7%	Canada	28.2%	U.S.A.	31.0%	Canada	12.8%
...A.	12.6%	Nigeria	9.0%	U.S.A.	17.6%	Germany	17.5%	Niger	9.0%	France	16.3%	U.S.A.	12.2%
...sia	9.9%	Kazakhstan	8.3%	India	7.9%	Russia	9.1%	Kazakhstan	8.3%	Japan	11.8%	Former U.S.S.R.	10.4%
	5.7%	Uzbekistan	8.0%	Russia	6.3%	China	7.4%	Uzbekistan	8.0%	Former U.S.S.R.	7.9%	Brazil	10.3%
...xico	4.9%	Russia	7.4%	Australia South Africa }	5.8%	Poland	5.4%	Russia	7.4%	Germany	6.9%	China	6.9%

ENERGY CONSUMPTION

Primary energy consumption
expressed in kilograms
of coal equivalent per
person 1992

	Over 10 000 kg per person
	5 000 - 10 000 kg per person
	1 000 - 5 000 kg per person
	100 - 1 000 kg per person
	Under 100 kg per person

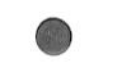

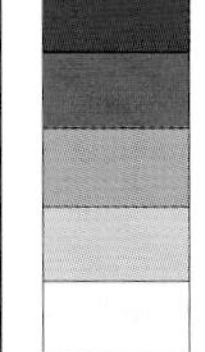

Energy consumption by Continent 1991

		Change 1990-91
Europe*	38.3%	*(-0.2%)*
North America	30.0%	*(+2.4%)*
Asia	25.0%	*(+1.9%)*
South America	3.0%	*(-2.9%)*
Africa	2.4%	*(-0.4%)*
Australasia	1.3%	*(no change)*

*includes former U.S.S.R.

Projection: Modified Hammer Equal Area

TYPE OF ENERGY CONSUMED BY SELECTED COUNTRIES 1993

Legend:
- Coal & Lignite
- Oil
- Natural gas
- Hydro-electricity
- Nuclear electricity
- Traditional Fuels

NIGERIA

CHINA

JAPAN

FRANCE

USA

NORWAY

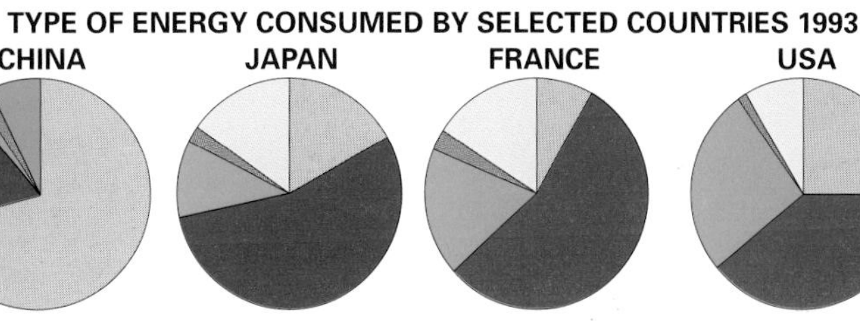

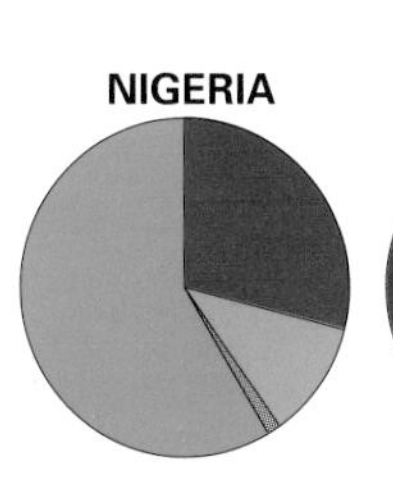

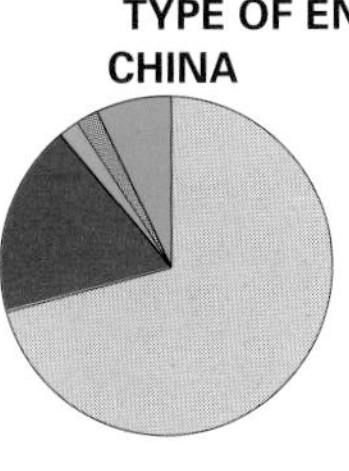

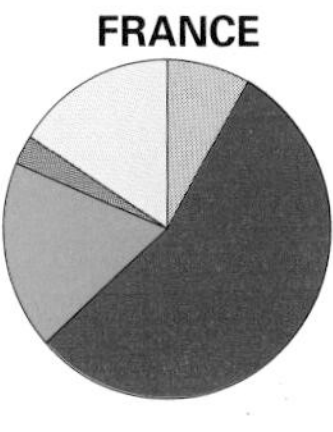

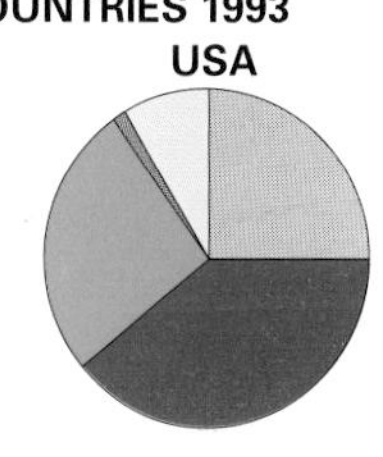

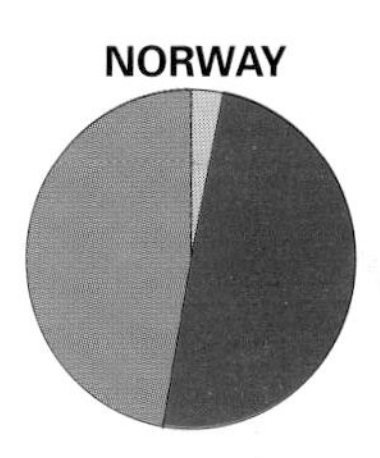

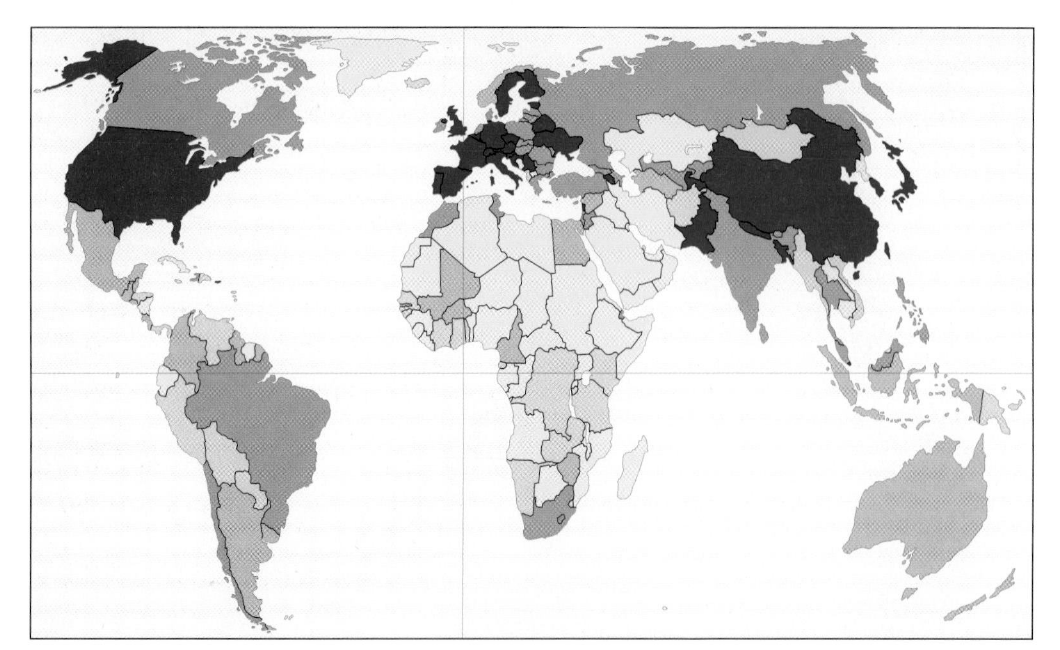

INDUSTRY AND TRADE

Manufactured goods (inc. machinery & transport) as a percentage of total exports (latest available year)

- Over 75%
- 50 - 75%
- 25 - 50%
- 10 - 25%
- Under 10%

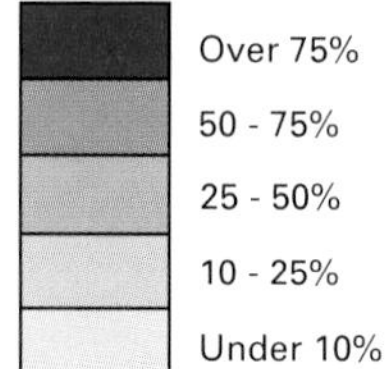

The Far East and South-East Asia (Japan 98.3%, Macau 97.8%, Taiwan 92.7%, Hong Kong 93.0%, South Korea 93.4%) are most dominant, but many countries in Europe (e.g. Slovenia 92.4%) are also heavily dependent on manufactured goods.

INDUSTRIAL PRODUCTION

Industrial output (mining, manufacturing, construction, energy and water production), top 40 nations, US $ billion (1991)

1. U.S.A.	1,627	21. Saudi Arabia	56
2. Japan	1,412	22. Indonesia	48
3. Germany	614	23. Spain	47
4. Italy	380	24. Argentina	46
5. France	348	25. Poland	39
6. U.K.	324	26. Norway	38
7. Former U.S.S.R.	250	27. Finland	37
8. Brazil	161	28. Thailand	36
9. China	155	29. Turkey	33
10. South Korea	127	30. Denmark	31
11. Canada	117	31. Israel	23
12. Australia	93	32. Iran	20
Netherlands	93	33. Ex- Czechoslovakia	19
14. Taiwan	86	34. Hong Kong	17
15. Mexico	85	Portugal (1989)	17
16. Sweden	70	36. Algeria	16
17. Switzerland (1989)	61	Greece	16
18. India	60	38. Iraq	15
19. Austria	59	Philippines	15
Belgium	59	Singapore	15

Graphs show the top ten producing countries for selected industrial goods.

RUBBER Natural and synthetic rubber in thousands of tonnes 1993 World production 13 081 thousand tonnes
Synthetic rubber

STEEL Production in thousand tonnes 1993

SHIPS Merchant vessels launched in thousand gross registered tonnes 1994 World production 16 340 thousand tonnes

TELEVISION SETS Production in thousands 1992

CLOTH Includes woven cotton and wool, silk, linen, jute, and man-made fabrics in thousands of tonnes 1991
Synthetic fabrics

PAPER Paper and paperboard in thousands of tonnes 1993 World production 253 586 thousand tonnes

CARS Passenger cars in thousands 1993

RADIO RECEIVERS Production in thousands 1991

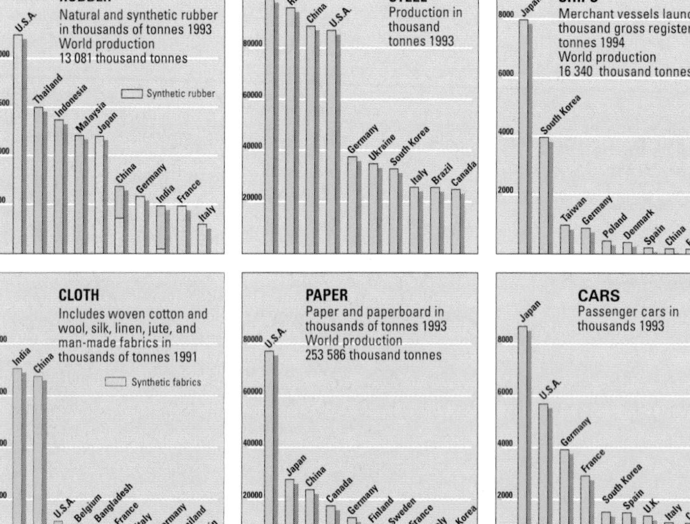

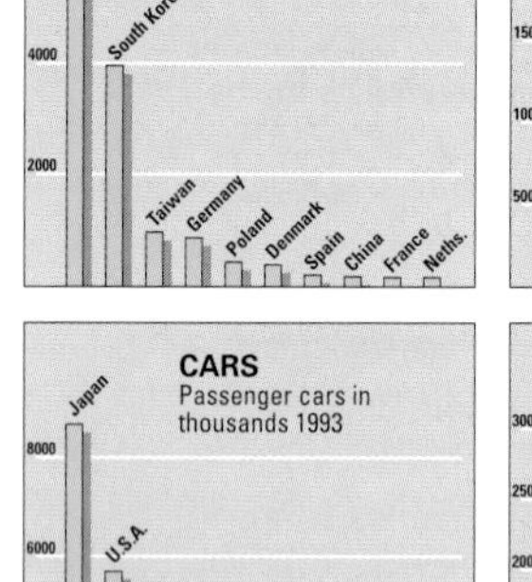

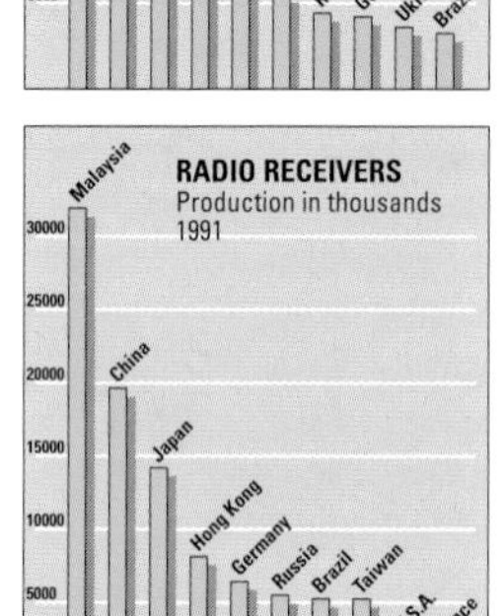

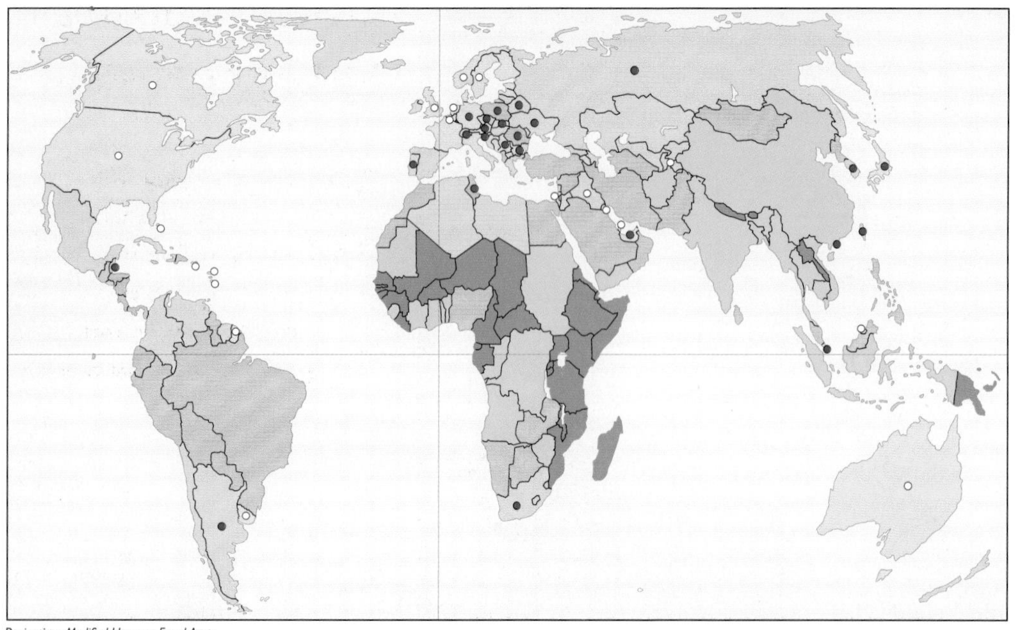

TYPE OF WORK

Percentage of total workforce employed in agriculture 1990-1992 †

- Over 75% in agriculture
- 50 - 75% in agriculture
- 25 - 50% in agriculture
- 10 - 25% in agriculture
- Under 10% in agriculture

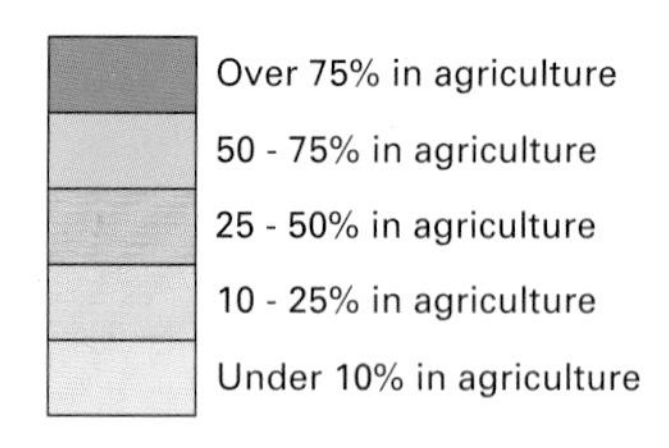

● Over a third of total workforce employed in manufacturing

○ Over two-thirds of total workforce employed in service industries (work in offices, shops, tourism, transport, construction and government)

† Includes forestry and fishing

Projection: *Modified Hammer Equal Area*

CARTOGRAPHY BY PHILIP'S. COPYRIGHT REED INTERNATIONAL BOOKS LTD

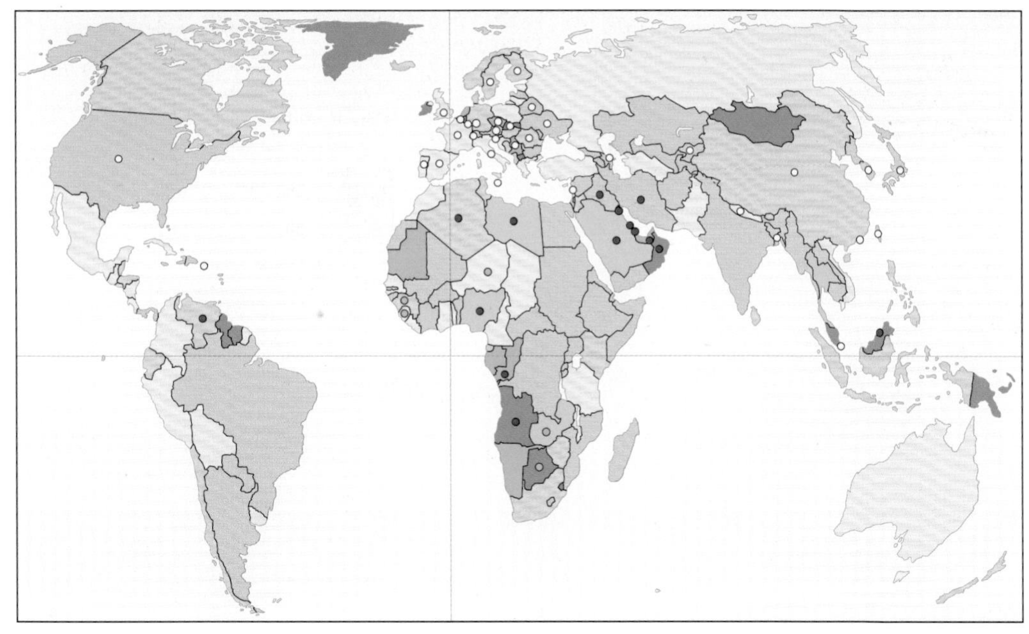

DEPENDENCE ON TRADE

Value of exports as a percentage
of G.N.P. (Gross National Product)
1993

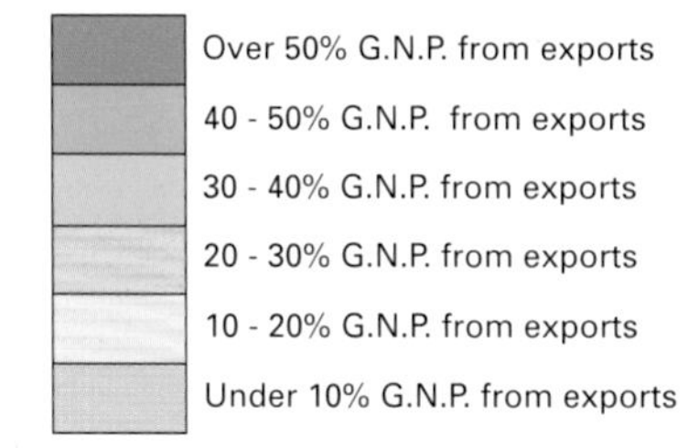

Over 50% G.N.P. from exports

40 - 50% G.N.P. from exports

30 - 40% G.N.P. from exports

20 - 30% G.N.P. from exports

10 - 20% G.N.P. from exports

Under 10% G.N.P. from exports

○ Most dependent on industrial
exports (over 75% of total exports)

● Most dependent on fuel exports
(over 75% of total exports)

◉ Most dependent on metal and
mineral exports (over 75% of total
exports)

BALANCE OF TRADE

Value of exports in proportion to
the value of imports 1993

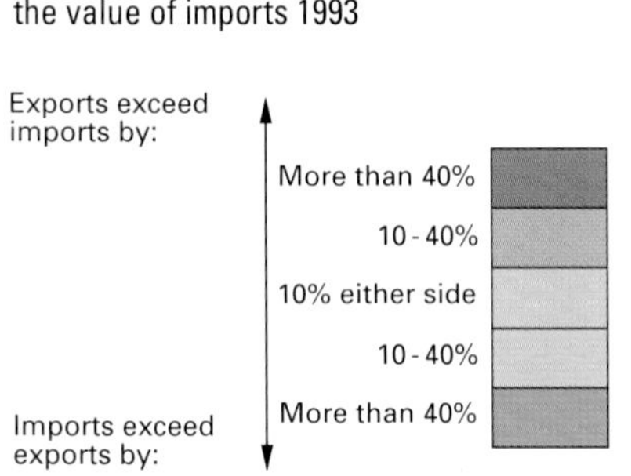

Exports exceed
imports by:

More than 40%

10 - 40%

10% either side

10 - 40%

Imports exceed
exports by:

More than 40%

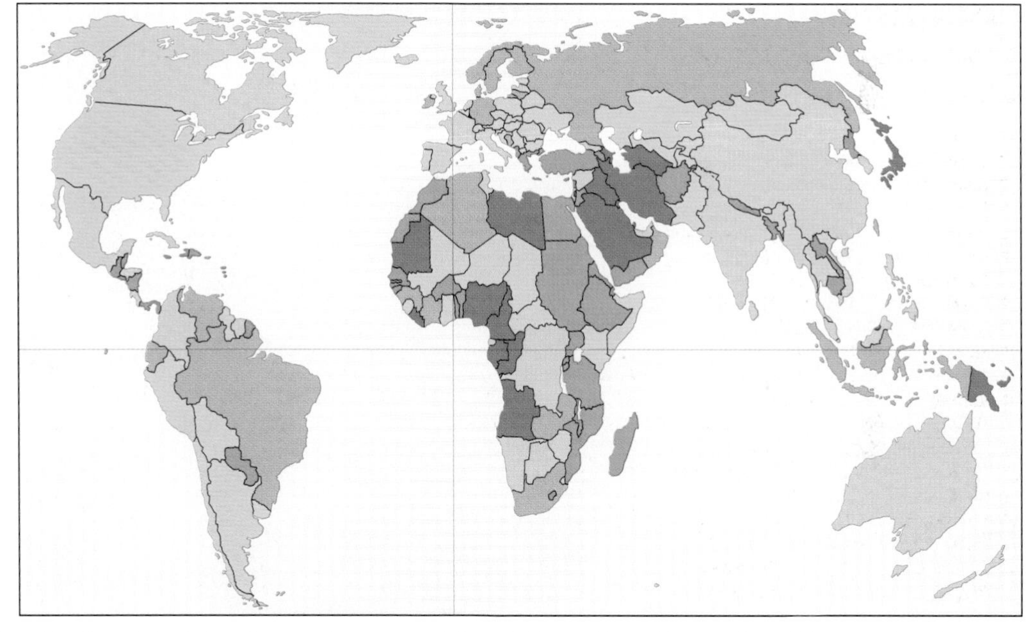

SHARE OF WORLD TRADE

Percentage share of total world
exports by value 1993

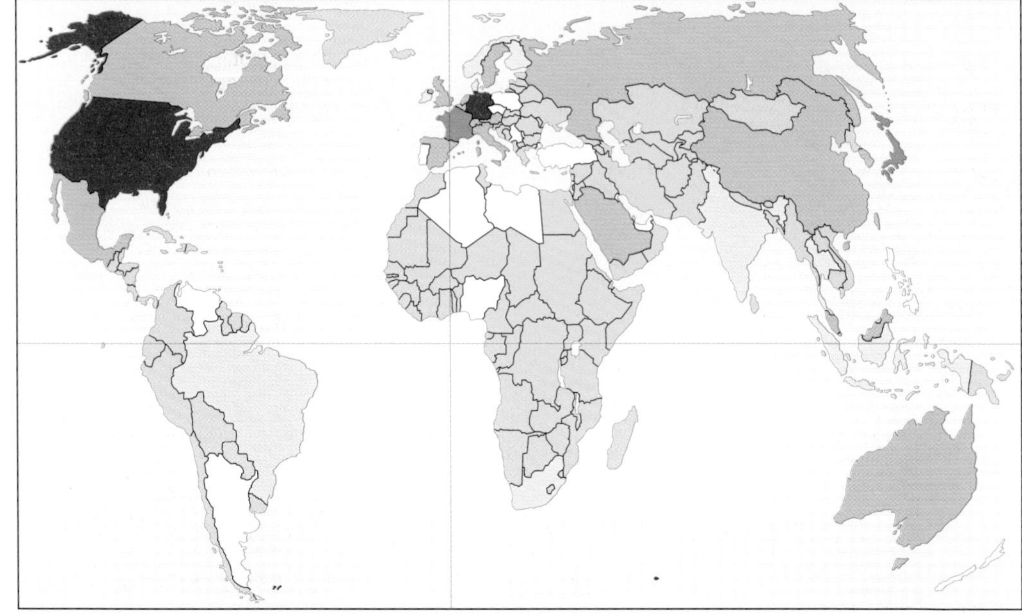

Over 10% of world trade

5 - 10% of world trade

1 - 5% of world trade

0.5 - 1% of world trade

0.25 - 0.5% of world trade

Under 0.25% of world trade

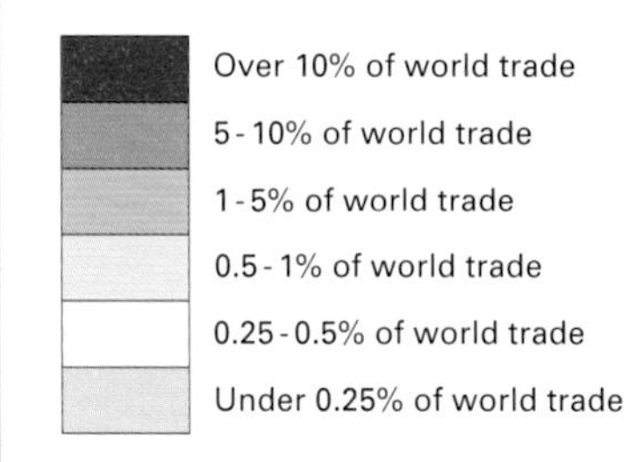

Projection: *Modified Hammer Equal Area*

CARTOGRAPHY BY PHILIP'S. COPYRIGHT REED INTERNATIONAL BOOKS LTD

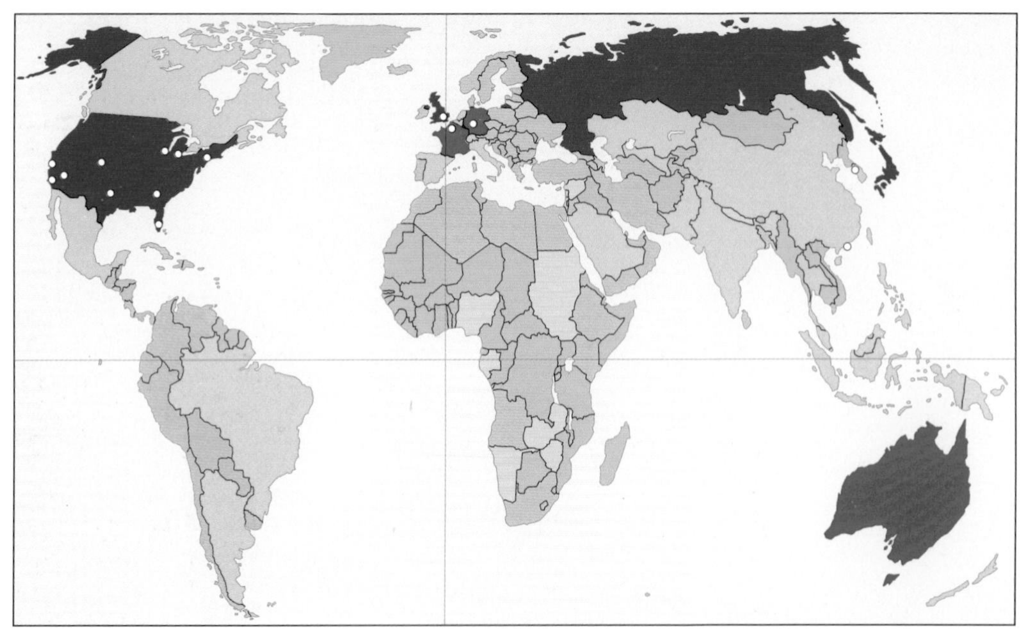

AIR TRAVEL

Passenger kilometres flown 1992

Passenger kilometres are the number of passengers (international and domestic) multiplied by the distance flown by each passenger from airport of origin.

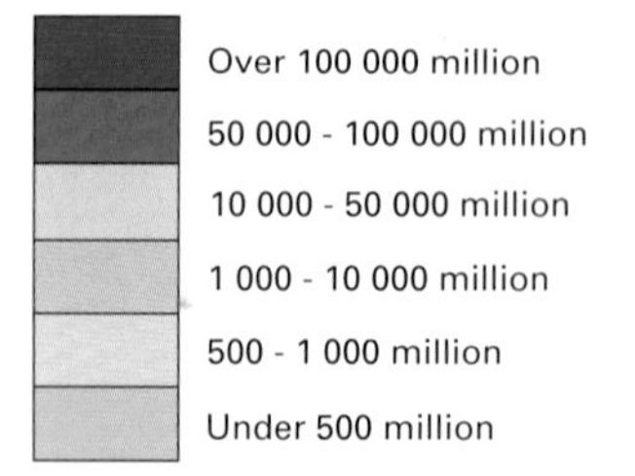

- Over 100 000 million
- 50 000 - 100 000 million
- 10 000 - 50 000 million
- 1 000 - 10 000 million
- 500 - 1 000 million
- Under 500 million

○ Major airports (handling over 25 million passengers in 1994)

World's busiest airports (total passengers)		World's busiest airports (international passengers)	
1. Chicago	(O'Hare)	1. London	(Heathrow)
2. Atlanta	(Hatsfield)	2. London	(Gatwick)
3. Dallas	(Dallas/Ft Worth)	3. Frankfurt	(International)
4. London	(Heathrow)	4. New York	(Kennedy)
5. Los Angeles	(Intern'l)	5. Paris	(De Gaulle)

TOURISM

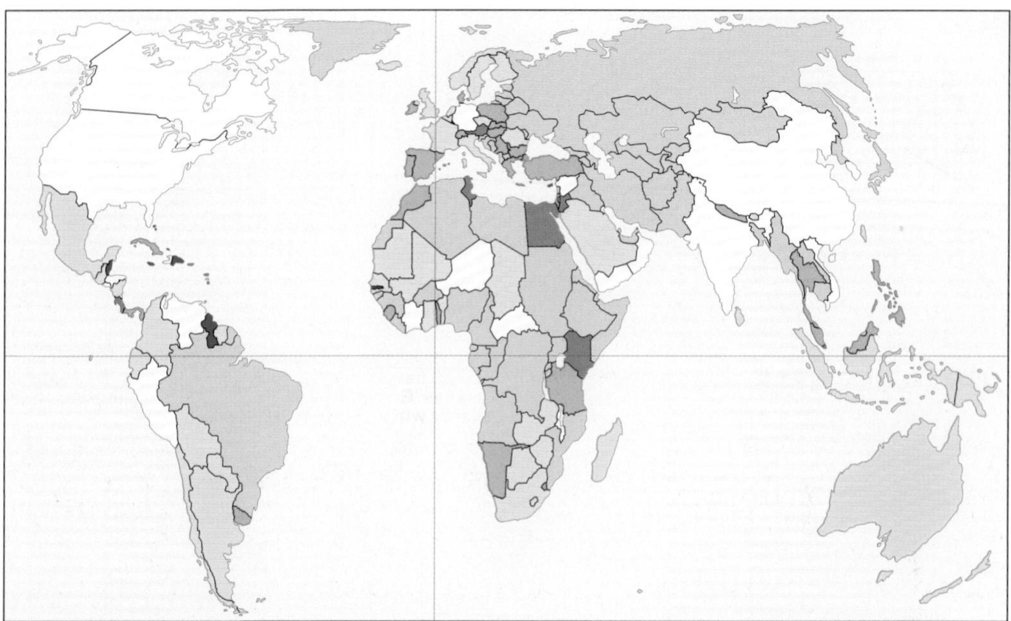

Tourism receipts as a percentage of G.N.P. (Gross National Product) 1992

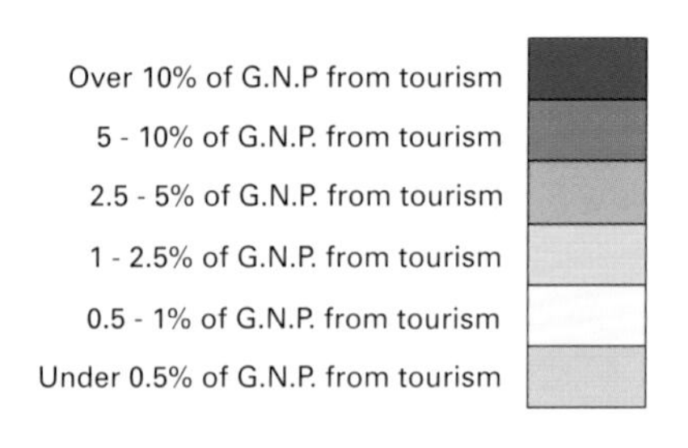

- Over 10% of G.N.P from tourism
- 5 - 10% of G.N.P. from tourism
- 2.5 - 5% of G.N.P. from tourism
- 1 - 2.5% of G.N.P. from tourism
- 0.5 - 1% of G.N.P. from tourism
- Under 0.5% of G.N.P. from tourism

Largest percentage share of total world spending on tourism 1993		Largest percentage share of total world receipts from tourism 1993	
U.S.A.	15%	U.S.A.	19%
Germany	14%	France	8%
Japan	10%	Italy	7%
U.K.	6%	Spain	6%
Italy	5%	Austria	4%

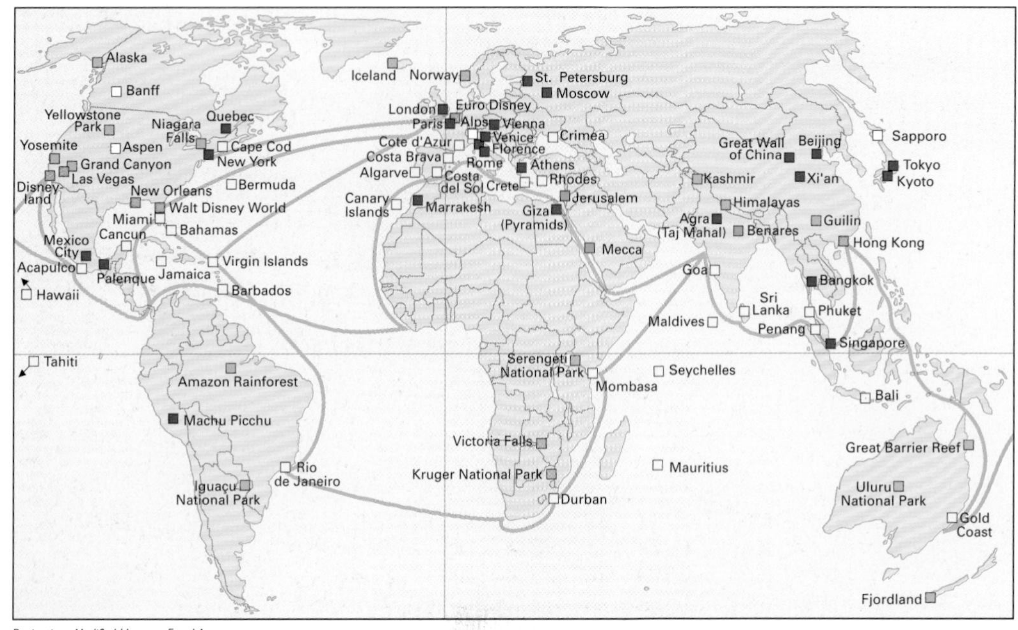

TOURIST DESTINATIONS

- ■ Cultural & historical centres
- ☐ Coastal resorts
- ☐ Ski resorts
- ▨ Centres of entertainment
- ▨ Places of pilgrimage
- ▨ Places of great natural beauty
- ～ Popular holiday cruise routes

UNESCO World Heritage Sites	Number of designated sites (1994)	
	Natural Heritage	Cultural Heritage
Europe	19	124
Middle East and Turkey	3	27
Former U.S.S.R.	0	7
South and East Asia	16	44
Canada and U.S.A.	15	10
Mexico and Central America	5	18
South America	12	18
Africa	30	40
Oceania	14	4

TIME ZONES

Note: Certain of the time zones are affected by the incidence of "Summer Time" in countries where it is adopted.

Zones using Greenwich Mean Time	Half hour zones
Zones slow of Greenwich Mean Time	Zones fast of Greenwich Mean Time

- - - - - International boundaries
Time zone boundaries
International date line
Selected air routes

10PM — Actual Solar Time when noon at Greenwich is shown along the top of the map.

10 — Hours slow or fast of Greenwich Mean Time

Equatorial scale: 1:220 000 000

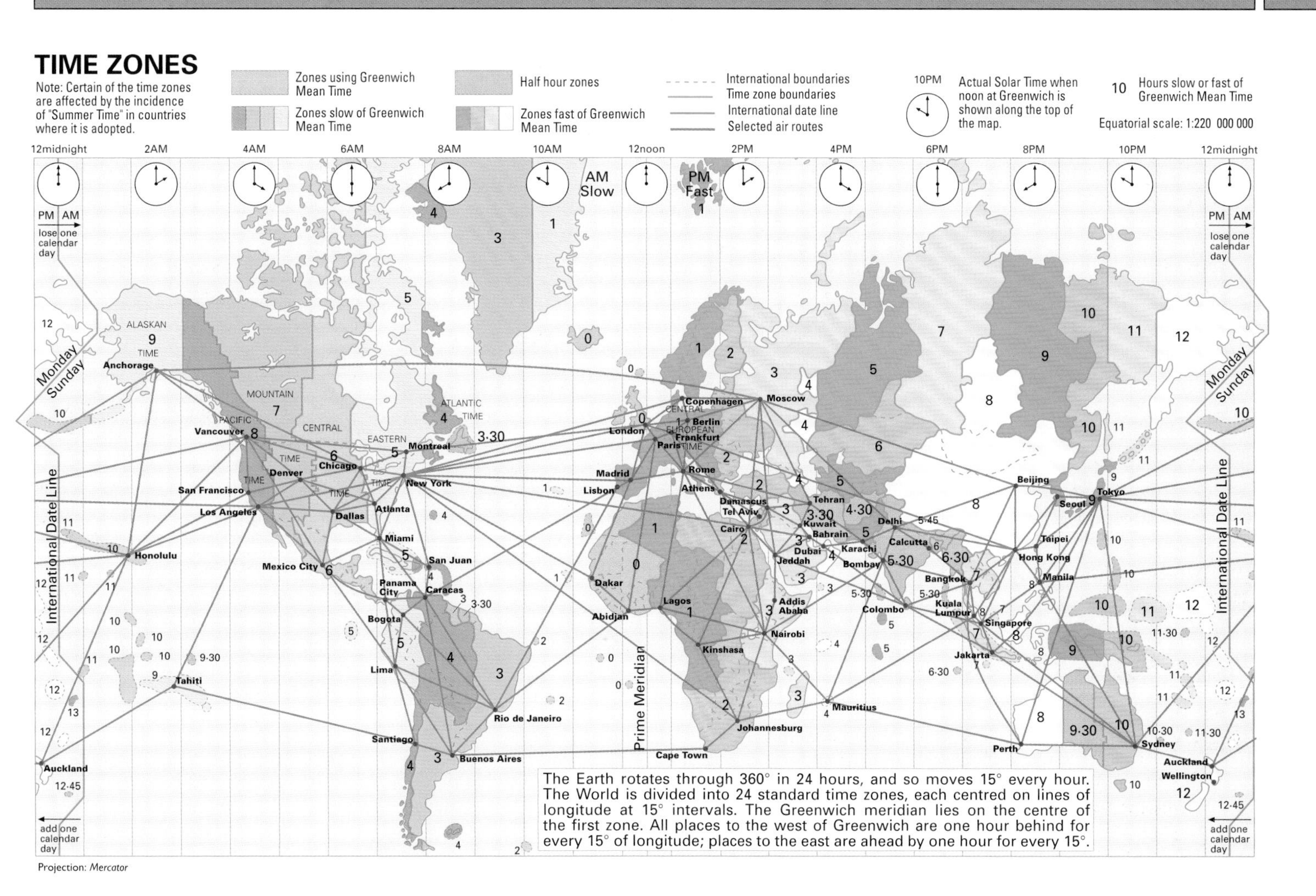

The Earth rotates through 360° in 24 hours, and so moves 15° every hour. The World is divided into 24 standard time zones, each centred on lines of longitude at 15° intervals. The Greenwich meridian lies on the centre of the first zone. All places to the west of Greenwich are one hour behind for every 15° of longitude; places to the east are ahead by one hour for every 15°.

Projection: Mercator

DISTANCE TABLE

The table shows air distances in miles and kilometres between twenty-four major cities. Known as 'Great Circle' distances, these measure the shortest routes between cities, which aircraft use where possible.

Kms (upper triangle)

from \ to	Bombay	Buenos Aires	Cairo	Calcutta	Caracas	Chicago	Hong Kong	Honolulu	Johannesburg	Lagos	London	Los Angeles	Mexico City	Moscow	Nairobi	New York	Paris	Rio de Janeiro	Rome	Singapore	Sydney	Tokyo	Wellington
Beijing	2956	11972	4688	2031	8947	6588	1220	5070	7276	7119	5057	6251	7742	3600	5727	6828	5106	10773	5049	2783	5561	1304	6700
Bombay		9275	2706	1034	9024	8048	2683	8024	4334	4730	4467	8700	9728	3126	2816	7793	4356	8332	3837	2432	6313	4189	7686
Buenos Aires			7341	10268	3167	5599	11481	7558	5025	4919	6917	6122	4591	8374	6463	5298	6867	1214	6929	9867	7332	11410	6202
Cairo				3541	6340	6127	5064	8838	3894	2432	2180	7580	7687	1803	2197	5605	1994	6149	1325	5137	8959	5947	10268
Calcutta					9609	7978	1653	7048	5256	5727	4946	8152	9494	3438	3839	7921	4883	9366	4486	1800	5678	3195	7055
Caracas						2502	10166	6009	6847	4810	4664	3612	2228	6175	7173	2131	4738	2825	5196	11407	9534	8801	8154
Chicago							7783	4247	8689	5973	3949	1742	1694	4971	8005	711	4132	5311	4809	9369	9243	6299	8358
Hong Kong								5543	6669	7360	5980	7232	8775	4439	5453	8047	5984	11001	5769	1615	4582	1786	5857
Honolulu									11934	10133	7228	2558	3781	7036	10739	4958	7437	8290	8026	6721	5075	3854	4669
Johannesburg										2799	5637	10362	9063	5692	1818	7979	5426	4420	4811	5381	6860	8418	7308
Lagos											3118	7713	6879	3886	2366	5268	2929	3750	2510	6925	9643	8376	9973
London												5442	5552	1552	4237	3463	212	5778	889	6743	10558	5942	11691
Los Angeles													1549	6070	9659	2446	5645	6310	6331	8776	7502	5475	6719
Mexico City														6664	9207	2090	5717	4780	6365	10321	8058	7024	6897
Moscow															3942	4666	1545	7184	1477	5237	9008	4651	10283
Nairobi																7358	4029	5548	3350	4635	7552	6996	8490
New York																	3626	4832	4280	9531	9935	6741	8951
Paris																		5708	687	6671	10539	6038	11798
Rio de Janeiro																			5725	9763	8389	11551	7367
Rome																				6229	10143	6127	11523
Singapore																					3915	3306	5298
Sydney																						4861	1383
Tokyo																							5762

Miles (lower triangle)

from \ to	Beijing	Bombay	Buenos Aires	Cairo	Calcutta	Caracas	Chicago	Hong Kong	Honolulu	Johannesburg	Lagos	London	Los Angeles	Mexico City	Moscow	Nairobi	New York	Paris	Rio de Janeiro	Rome	Singapore	Sydney	Tokyo
Bombay	4757																						
Buenos Aires	19268	14925																					
Cairo	7544	4355	11814																				
Calcutta	3269	1664	16524	5699																			
Caracas	14399	14522	5096	10203	15464																		
Chicago	10603	12953	9011	3206	12839	4027																	
Hong Kong	1963	4317	18478	8150	2659	16360	12526																
Honolulu	8160	12914	12164	14223	11343	9670	6836	8921															
Johannesburg	11710	6974	8088	6267	8459	11019	13984	10732	19206														
Lagos	11457	7612	7916	3915	9216	7741	9612	11845	16308	4505													
London	8138	7190	11131	3508	7961	7507	6356	9623	11632	9071	5017												
Los Angeles	10060	14000	9852	12200	13120	5812	2804	11639	4117	16676	12414	8758											
Mexico City	12460	15656	7389	12372	15280	3586	2726	14122	6085	14585	11071	8936	2493										
Moscow	5794	5031	13477	2902	5534	9938	8000	7144	11323	9161	6254	2498	9769	10724									
Nairobi	9216	4532	10402	3536	6179	11544	12883	8776	17282	2927	3807	6819	15544	14818	6344								
New York	10988	12541	8526	9020	12747	3430	1145	12950	7980	12841	8477	5572	3936	3264	7510	11842							
Paris	8217	7010	11051	3210	7858	7625	6650	9630	11968	8732	4714	342	9085	9200	2486	6485	5836						
Rio de Janeiro	17338	13409	1953	9896	15073	4546	8547	17704	13342	7113	6035	9299	10155	7693	11562	8928	7777	9187					
Rome	8126	6175	11151	2133	7219	8363	7739	9284	12916	7743	4039	1431	10188	10243	2376	5391	6888	1105	9214				
Singapore	4478	3914	15879	8267	2897	18359	15078	2599	10816	8660	11145	10852	14123	16610	8428	7460	15339	10737	15712	10025			
Sydney	8949	10160	11800	14418	9138	15343	14875	7374	8168	11040	15519	16992	12073	12969	14497	12153	15989	16962	13501	16324	6300		
Tokyo	2099	6742	18362	9571	5141	14164	10137	2874	6202	13547	13480	9562	8811	11304	7485	11260	10849	9718	18589	9861	5321	7823	
Wellington	10782	12370	9981	16524	11354	13122	13451	9427	7513	11761	16050	18814	10814	11100	16549	13664	14405	18987	11855	18545	8526	2226	9273

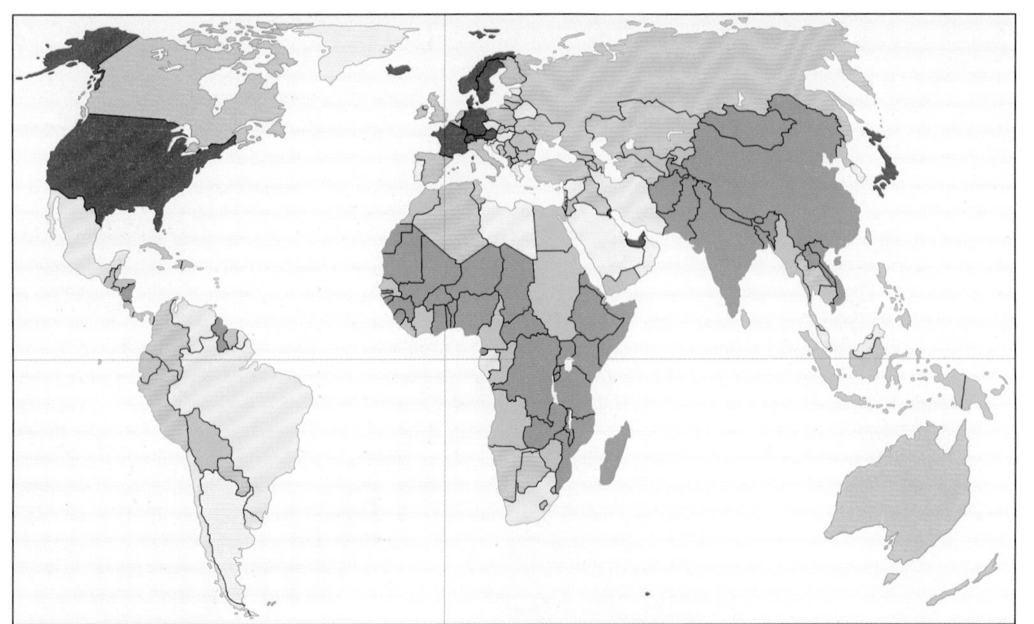

WEALTH

The value of total production in 1993 divided by the population.
(The Gross National Product per capita)

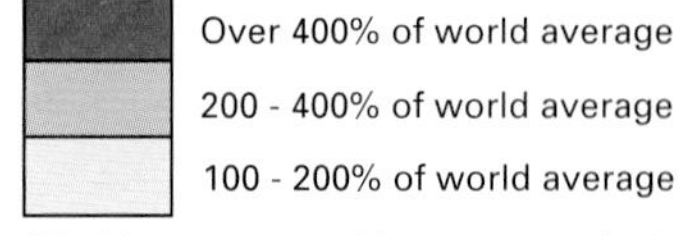

	Over 400% of world average
	200 - 400% of world average
	100 - 200% of world average

World average wealth per person $5 359

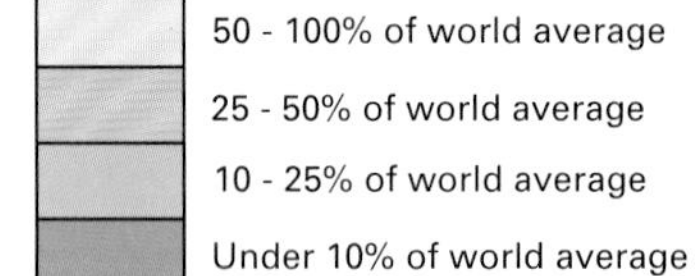

	50 - 100% of world average
	25 - 50% of world average
	10 - 25% of world average
	Under 10% of world average

Top 5 countries		Bottom 5 countries	
Switzerland	$36 410	Mozambique	$80
Luxembourg	$35 850	Ethiopia	$100
Liechtenstein	$33 510	Tanzania	$100
Japan	$31 450	Sierra Leone	$140
Bermuda	$27 000	Nepal	$160

U.K. $17 970

CAR OWNERSHIP

Number of people per car
(latest available year)

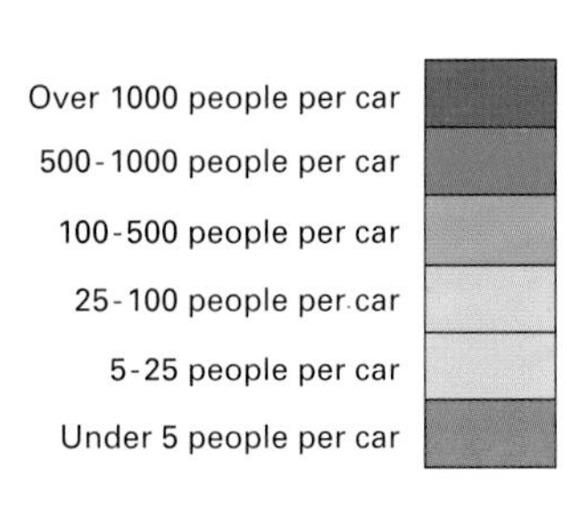

Over 1000 people per car	
500 - 1000 people per car	
100 - 500 people per car	
25 - 100 people per car	
5 - 25 people per car	
Under 5 people per car	

Most people per car		Most cars (millions)	
Nepal	4247	U.S.A.	143.8
Bangladesh	2618	Germany	39.1
Cambodia	2328	Japan	39.0
Somalia	1790	Italy	29.6
Ethiopia	1423	France	24.0

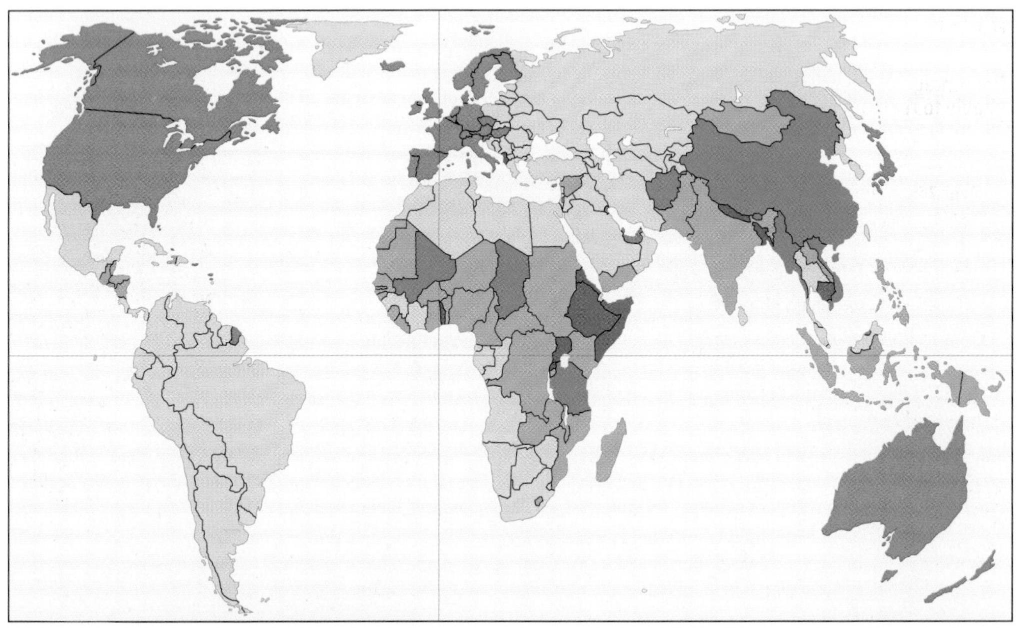

HUMAN DEVELOPMENT INDEX

The Human Development Index (H.D.I.) 1992 includes social and economic indicators and is calculated by the U.N. Development Programme as a measure of national human progress. Wealthy developed countries measure highest on the index.

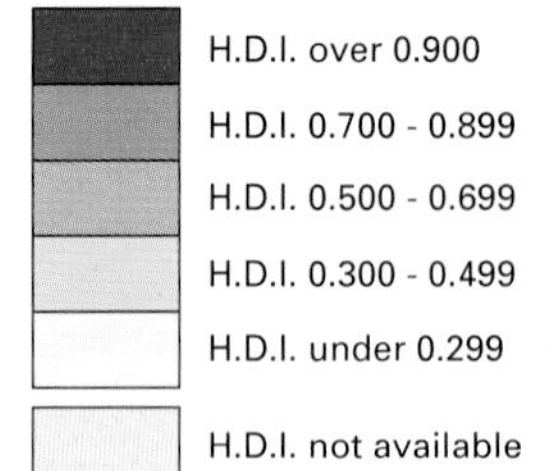

	H.D.I. over 0.900
	H.D.I. 0.700 - 0.899
	H.D.I. 0.500 - 0.699
	H.D.I. 0.300 - 0.499
	H.D.I. under 0.299
	H.D.I. not available

Top 5 countries		Bottom 5 countries	
Canada	0.950	Afghanistan	0.228
U.S.A.	0.937	Ethiopia	0.227
Japan	0.937	Mali	0.222
Netherlands	0.936	Sierra Leone	0.221
Finland	0.934	Niger	0.207

U.K.   0.916

Projection: *Modified Hammer Equal Area*

HEALTH CARE

Number of people per doctor 1988-1991

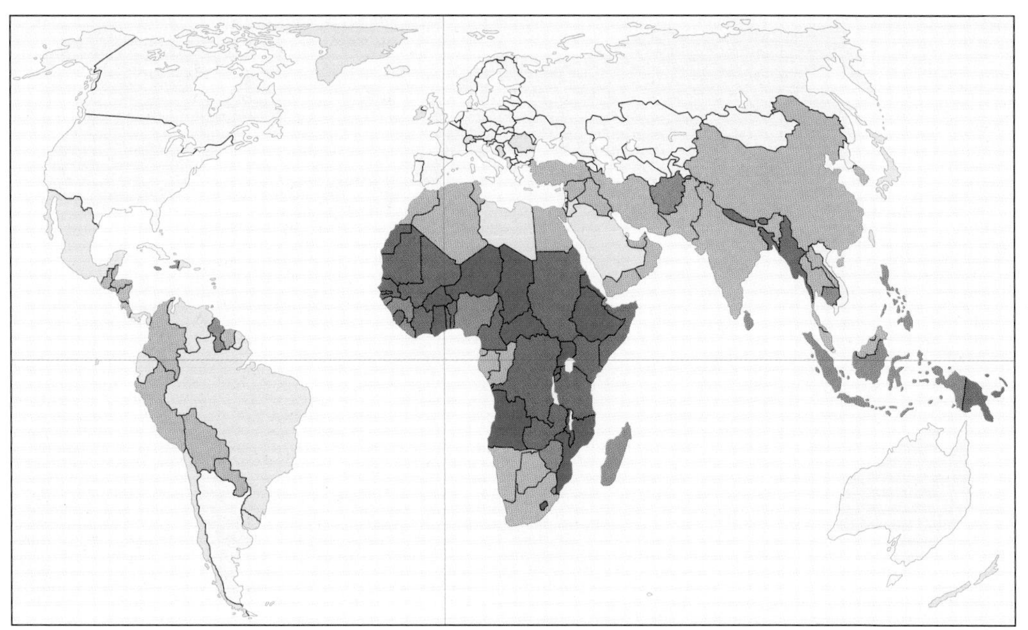

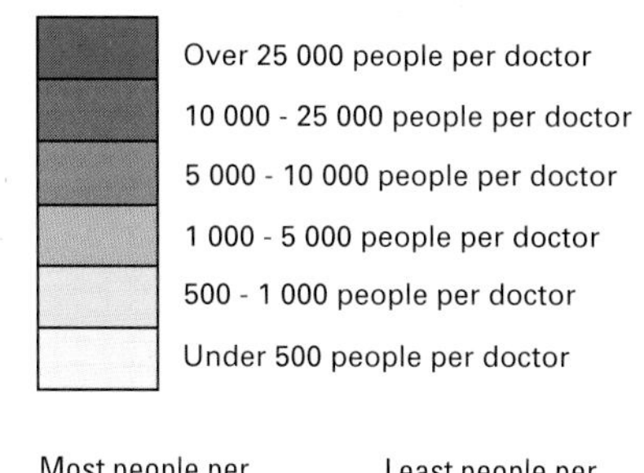

Over 25 000 people per doctor

10 000 - 25 000 people per doctor

5 000 - 10 000 people per doctor

1 000 - 5 000 people per doctor

500 - 1 000 people per doctor

Under 500 people per doctor

Most people per doctor 1990		Least people per doctor 1990	
Burkina Faso	57 310	Georgia	170
Malawi	45 740	Latvia	200
Rwanda	40 610	Italy	210
Niger	34 850	Russia	210
Ethiopia	32 500	Estonia	210
		U.K.	300

ILLITERACY

Percentage of the total population
unable to read or write 1992

Over 75% of population illiterate

50 - 75% of population illiterate

25 - 50% of population illiterate

10 - 25% of population illiterate

Under 10% of population illiterate

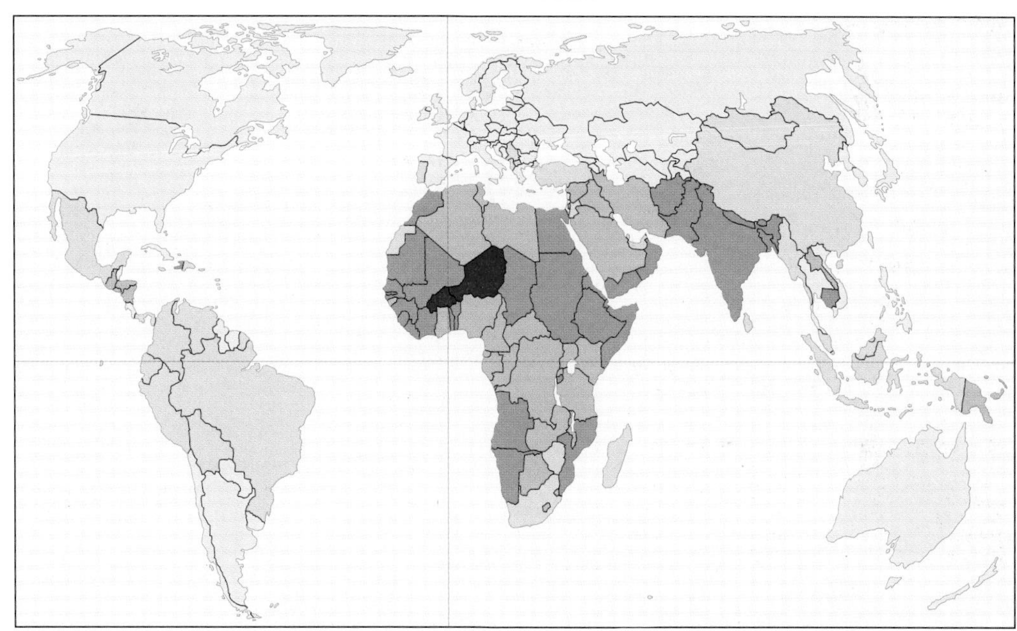

Educational expenditure per person
(latest available year)

Top 5 countries		Bottom 5 countries	
Sweden	$997	Chad	$2
Qatar	$989	Bangladesh	$3
Canada	$983	Ethiopia	$3
Norway	$971	Nepal	$4
Switzerland	$796	Somalia	$4
		U.K.	$447

FERTILITY & EDUCATION   Fertility rates compared with female education, selected countries (1990-1992)

Fertility rate: average number of
children borne per woman

Percentage of females aged 12 - 17
in secondary education

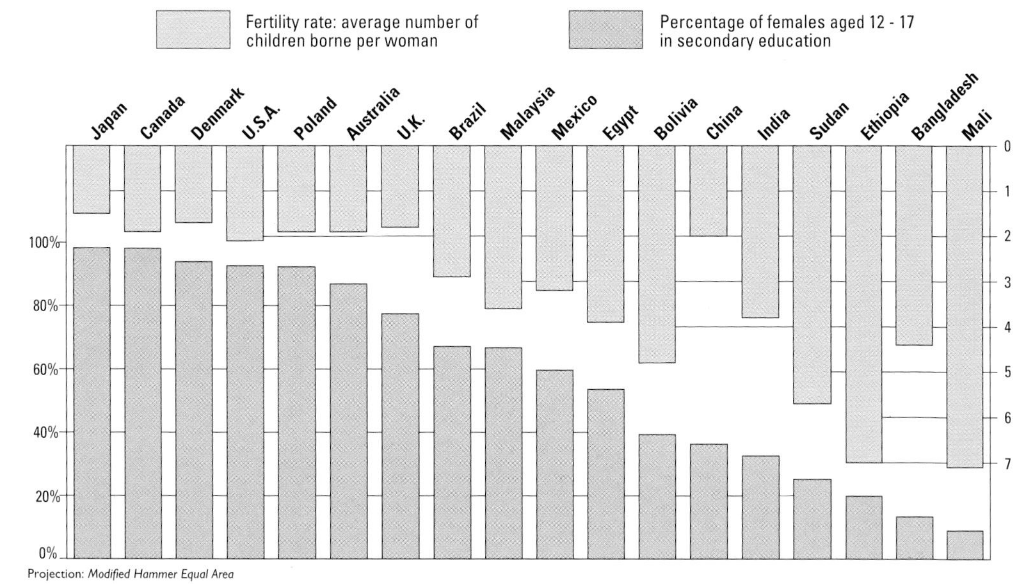

Projection: *Modified Hammer Equal Area*

CAUSES OF DEATH

Causes of death for selected countries by percentage
(1988-1992)

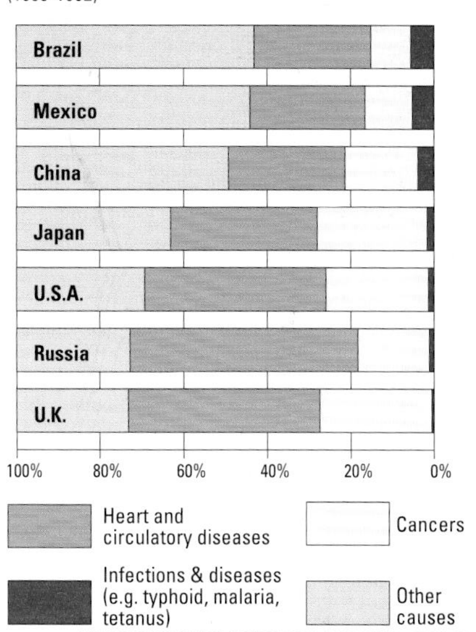

Heart and
circulatory diseases

Cancers

Infections & diseases
(e.g. typhoid, malaria,
tetanus)

Other
causes

AGE DISTRIBUTION PYRAMIDS

The bars represent the percentage of the total population (males plus females) in the age group shown.

Developed countries such as the U.K. have populations evenly spread across age groups and usually a growing percentage of elderly people. Developing countries such as Kenya have the great majority of their people in the younger age groups, about to enter their most fertile years.

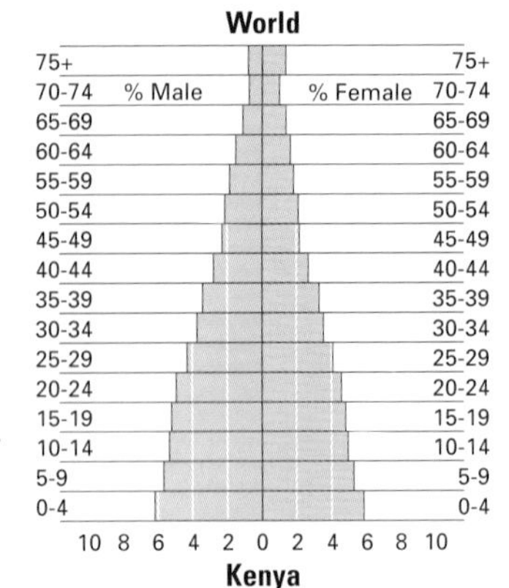

World

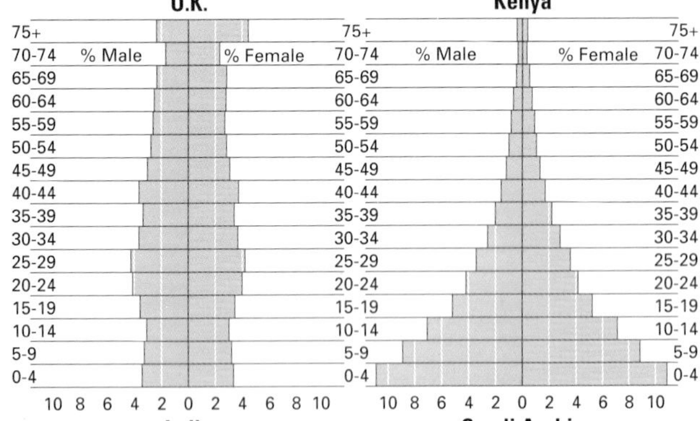

U.K.

Kenya

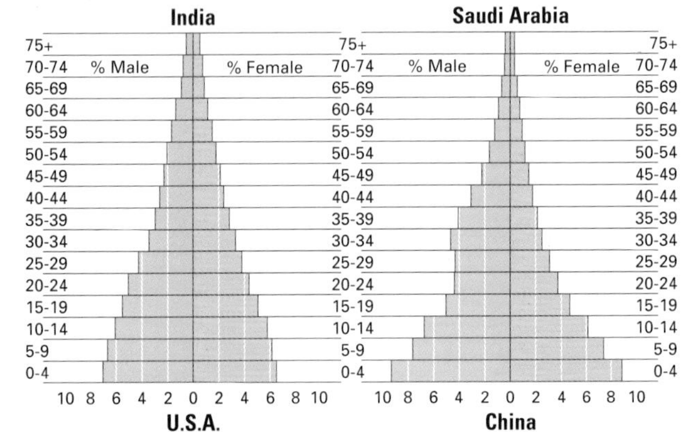

India

Saudi Arabia

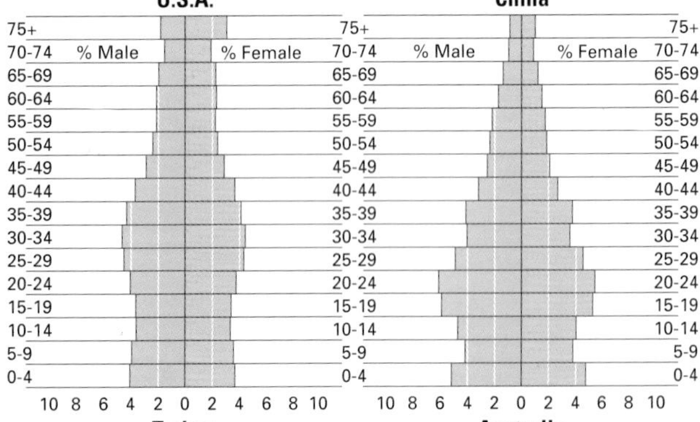

U.S.A.

China

Turkey

Australia

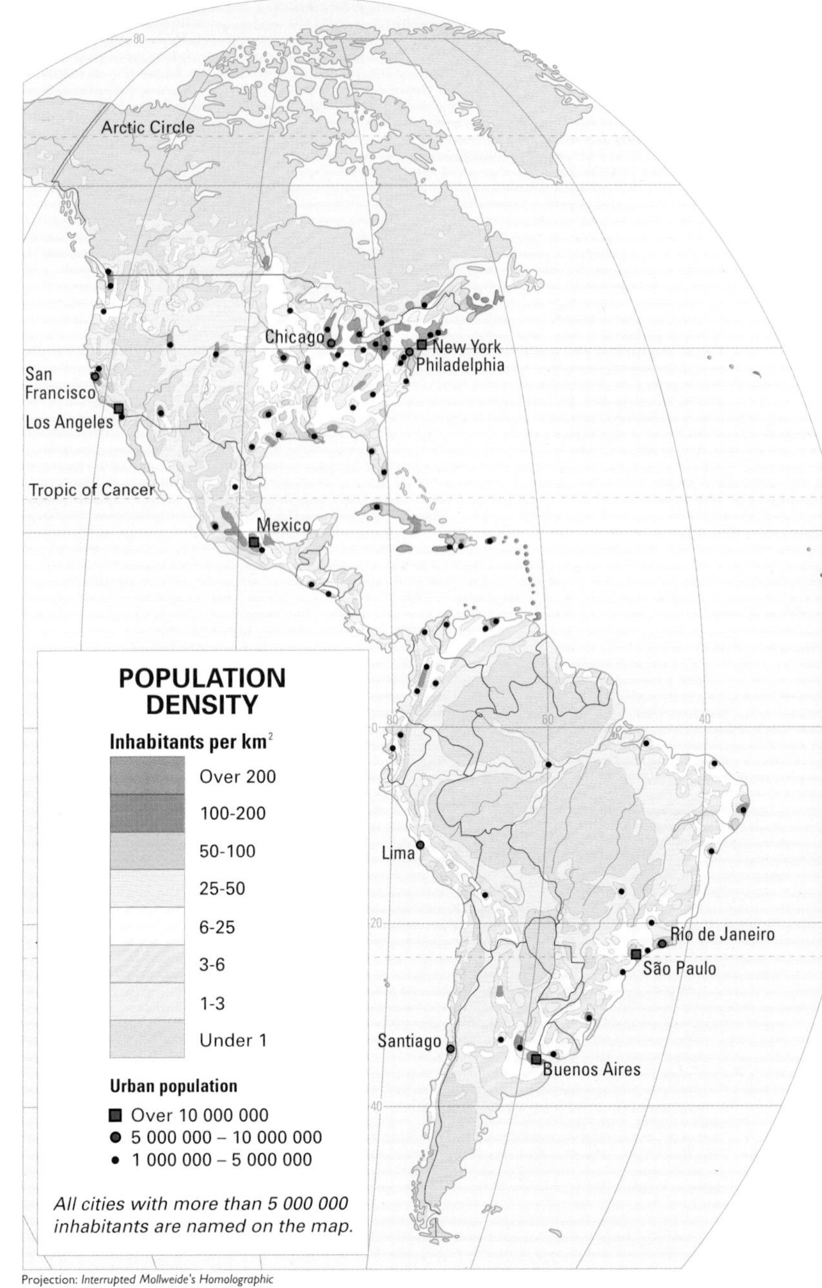

POPULATION DENSITY

Inhabitants per km²

- Over 200
- 100-200
- 50-100
- 25-50
- 6-25
- 3-6
- 1-3
- Under 1

Urban population

- ■ Over 10 000 000
- ● 5 000 000 – 10 000 000
- • 1 000 000 – 5 000 000

All cities with more than 5 000 000 inhabitants are named on the map.

Projection: Interrupted Mollweide's Homolographic

POPULATION CHANGE 1930-2020 Population totals are in millions

Figures in italics represent the percentage average annual increase for the period shown

	1930	1930-1960	1960	1960-1990	1990	1990-2020	2020
World	2013	*1.4%*	3019	*1.9%*	5292	*1.4%*	8062
Africa	155	*2.0%*	281	*2.85*	648	*2.7%*	1441
North America	135	*1.3%*	199	*1.1%*	276	*0.6%*	327
Latin America*	129	*1.8%*	218	*2.4%*	448	*1.6%*	719
Asia	1073	*1.5%*	1669	*2.1%*	3108	*1.4%*	4680
Europe	355	*0.6%*	425	*0.55*	498	*0.1%*	514
Oceania	10	*1.4%*	16	*1.75*	27	*1.1%*	37
C.I.S.†	176	*0.7%*	214	*1.0%*	288	*0.6%*	343

* South America plus Central America, Mexico, and the West Indies
† Commonwealth of Independent States, formerly the U.S.S.R.

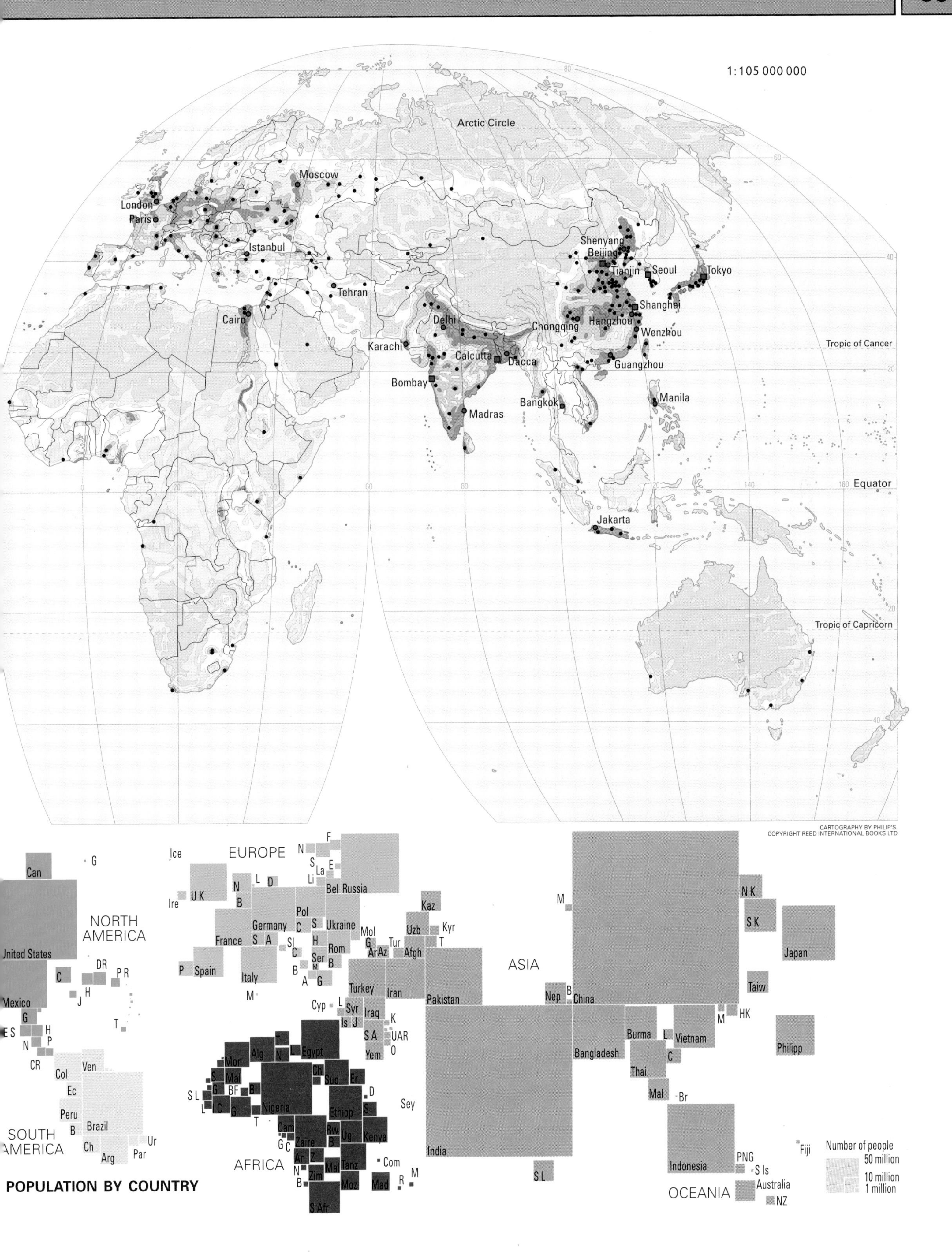

1:105 000 000

Arctic Circle

Moscow

London
Paris

Istanbul

Tehran

Cairo

Shenyang
Beijing
Tianjin · Seoul · Tokyo
Shanghai
Delhi · Hangzhou
Chongqing · Wenzhou
Karachi
Calcutta · Dacca · Guangzhou
Bombay
Madras · Bangkok · Manila

Tropic of Cancer

Equator

Jakarta

Tropic of Capricorn

CARTOGRAPHY BY PHILIP'S.
COPYRIGHT REED INTERNATIONAL BOOKS LTD

POPULATION BY COUNTRY

EUROPE

Ice · G

Can

NORTH
AMERICA

United States

Mexico

SOUTH
AMERICA

AFRICA

ASIA

Russia

China

Japan

India

Indonesia

Australia

OCEANIA

Number of people
50 million
10 million
1 million

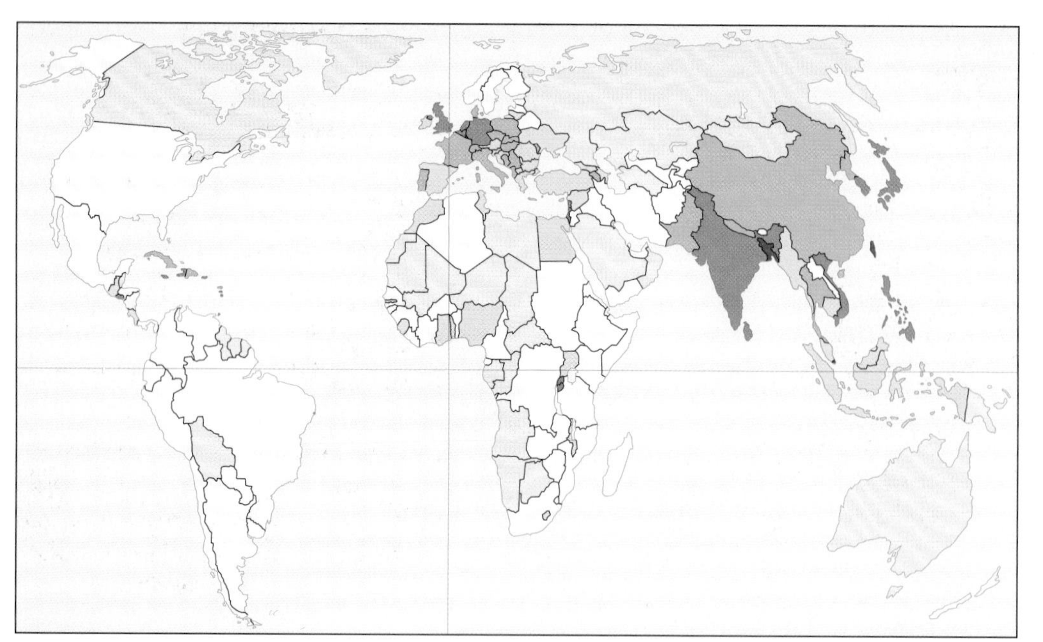

POPULATION DENSITY BY COUNTRY

Density of people per square kilometre 1993

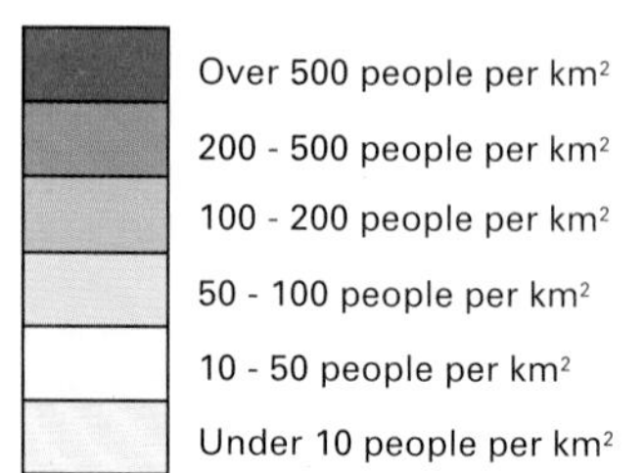

	Over 500 people per km²
	200 - 500 people per km²
	100 - 200 people per km²
	50 - 100 people per km²
	10 - 50 people per km²
	Under 10 people per km²

Top 5 countries		Bottom 5 countries	
Macau	21 000 per km²	Namibia	1.9 per km²
Monaco	15 641 per km²	French Guiana	1.5 per km²
Hong Kong	5 519 per km²	Mongolia	1.4 per km²
Gibraltar	5 017 per km²	W. Sahara	0.8 per km²
Singapore	4 501 per km²	Greenland	0.2 per km²

U.K. 238 per km²

POPULATION CHANGE 1990-2000

The predicted population change for the years 1990-2000

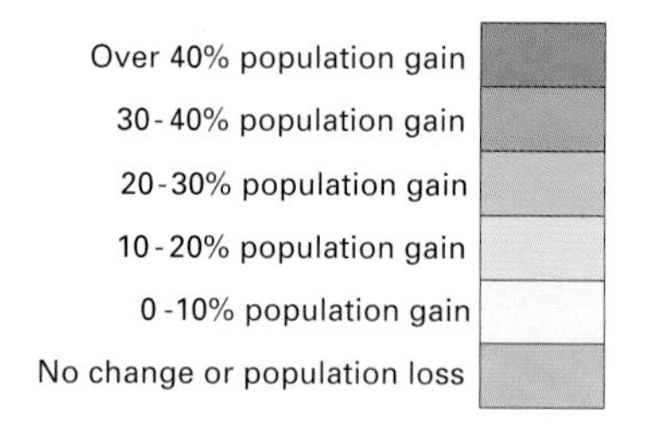

	Over 40% population gain
	30 - 40% population gain
	20 - 30% population gain
	10 - 20% population gain
	0 - 10% population gain
	No change or population loss

Top 5 countries		Bottom 5 countries	
Kuwait	+75.9%	Belgium	-0.1%
Namibia	+62.5%	Hungary	-0.2%
Afghanistan	+60.1%	Grenada	-2.4%
Mali	+55.5%	Germany	-3.2%
Tanzania	+54.6%	Tonga	-3.2%

U.K. +2.0%

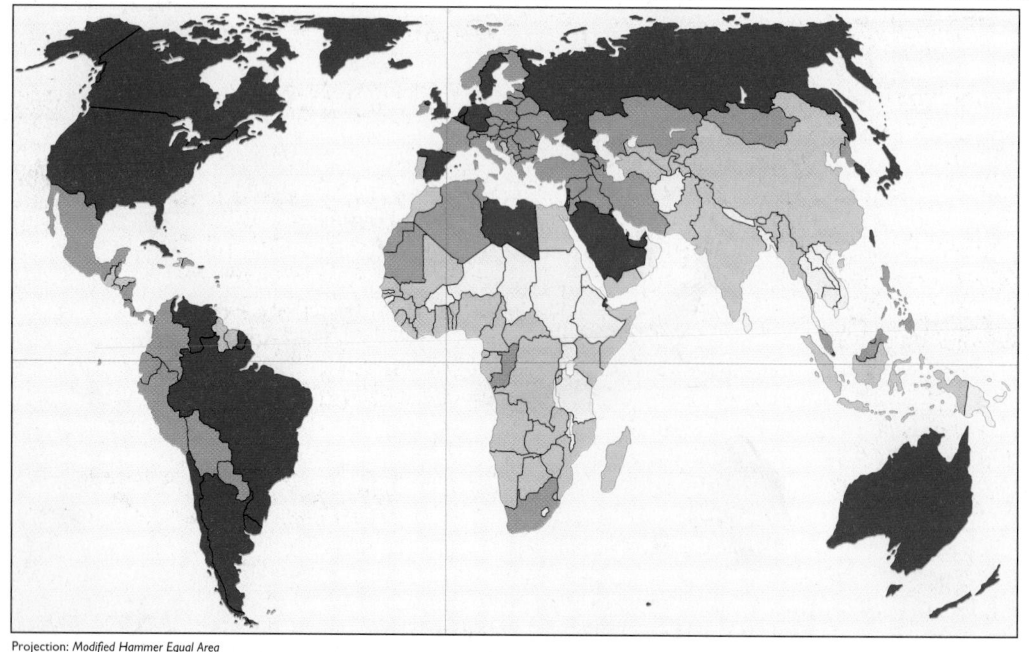

URBAN POPULATION

Percentage of total population living in towns and cities 1992

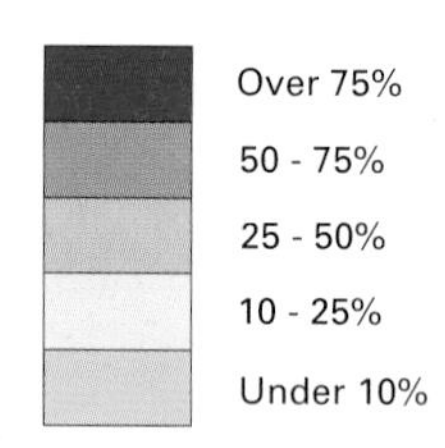

	Over 75%
	50 - 75%
	25 - 50%
	10 - 25%
	Under 10%

Most urbanized		Least urbanized	
Singapore	100%	Bhutan	6%
Belgium	97%	Rwanda	6%
Kuwait	95%	Burundi	7%
Hong Kong	94%	Malawi	12%
Venezuela	91%	Nepal	12%

U.K. 89%

Projection: *Modified Hammer Equal Area*

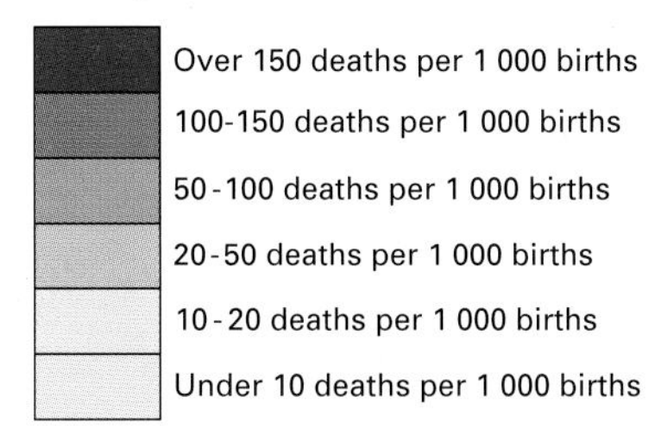

CHILD MORTALITY

The number of babies who will die under the age of one, per 1 000 births (average 1990-95)

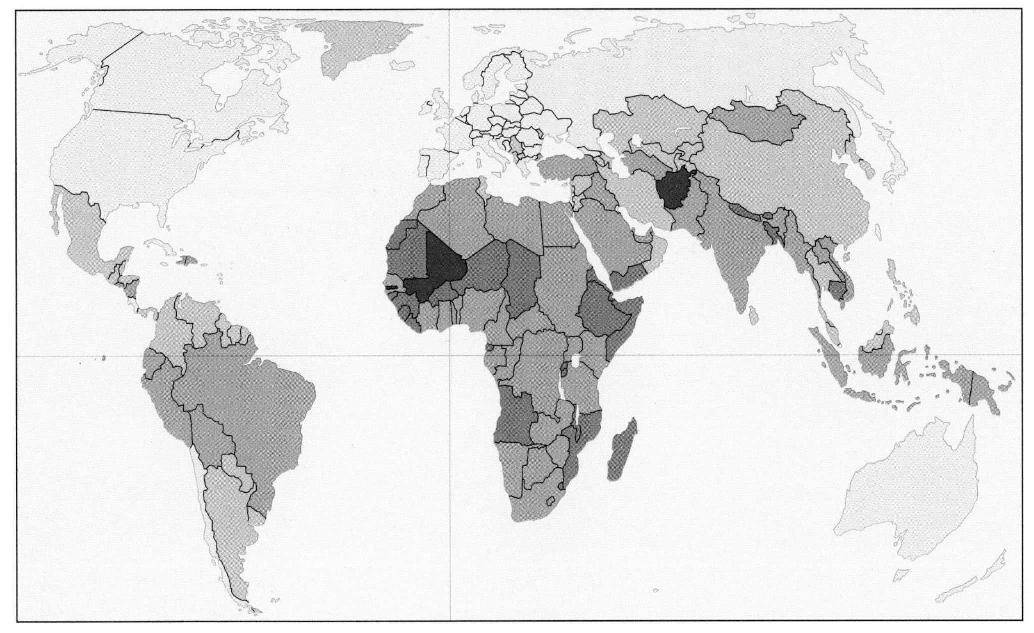

- Over 150 deaths per 1 000 births
- 100-150 deaths per 1 000 births
- 50-100 deaths per 1 000 births
- 20-50 deaths per 1 000 births
- 10-20 deaths per 1 000 births
- Under 10 deaths per 1 000 births

Highest child mortality		Lowest child mortality	
Afghanistan	162 deaths	Hong Kong	6 deaths
Mali	159 deaths	Denmark	6 deaths
Sierra Leone	143 deaths	Japan	5 deaths
Guinea-Bissau	140 deaths	Iceland	5 deaths
Malawi	138 deaths	Finland	5 deaths
		U.K.	8 deaths

LIFE EXPECTANCY

Average expected lifespan in years of babies born in the period 1990-95

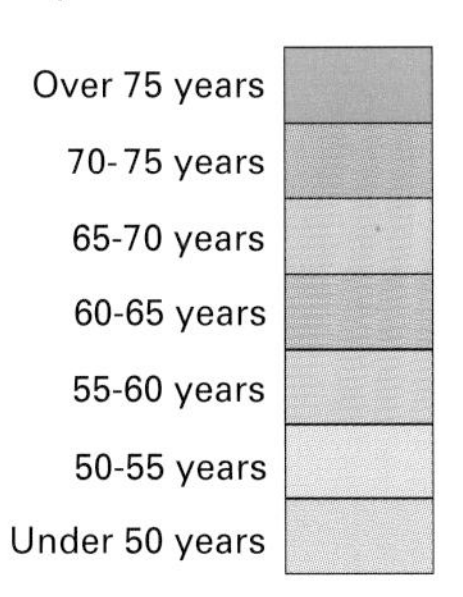

- Over 75 years
- 70-75 years
- 65-70 years
- 60-65 years
- 55-60 years
- 50-55 years
- Under 50 years

Highest life expectancy		Lowest life expectancy	
Japan	79 years	Gambia	45 years
Iceland	78 years	Guinea	45 years
Sweden	78 years	Afghanistan	44 years
Hong Kong	78 years	Guinea-Bissau	44 years
Switzerland	78 years	Sierra Leone	43 years
		U.K.	76 years

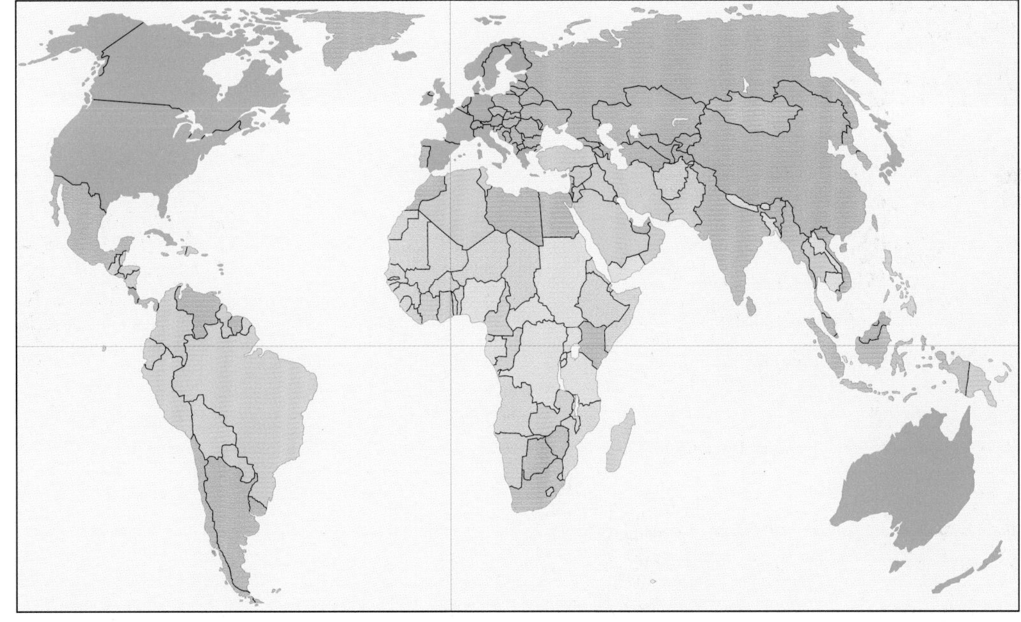

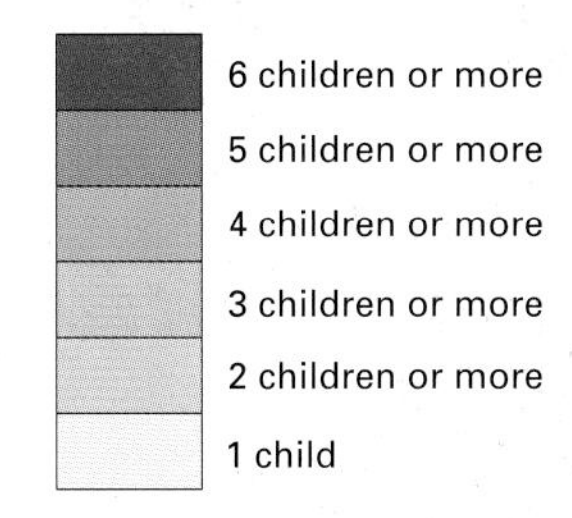

FAMILY SIZE

The average number of children a woman can expect to bear during her lifetime 1992

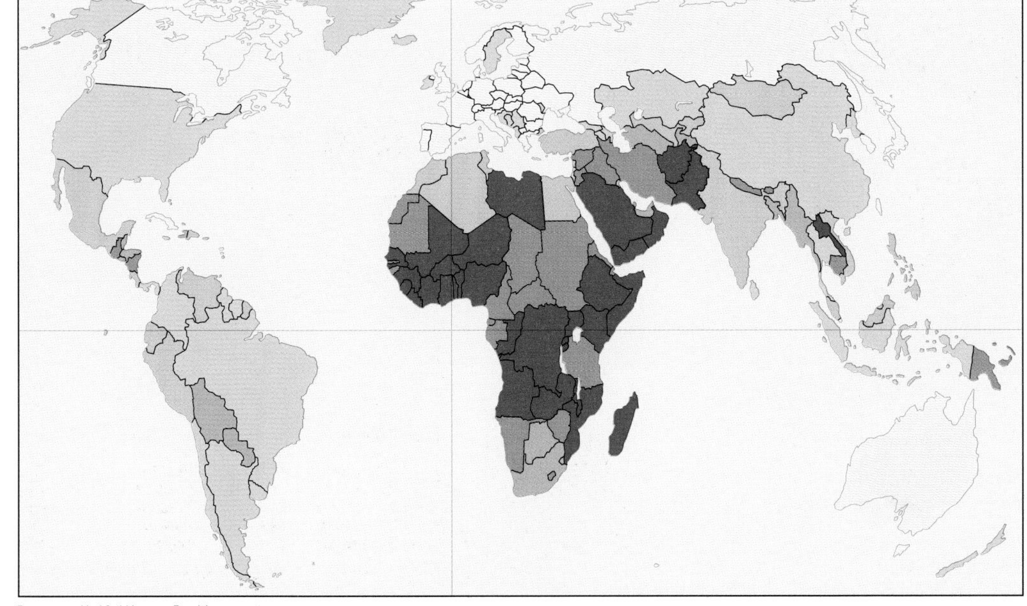

- 6 children or more
- 5 children or more
- 4 children or more
- 3 children or more
- 2 children or more
- 1 child

In the U.K. the average family size is 1.8 children per family, whilst in Kenya the average size is 6.3 children.

Projection: *Modified Hammer Equal Area*

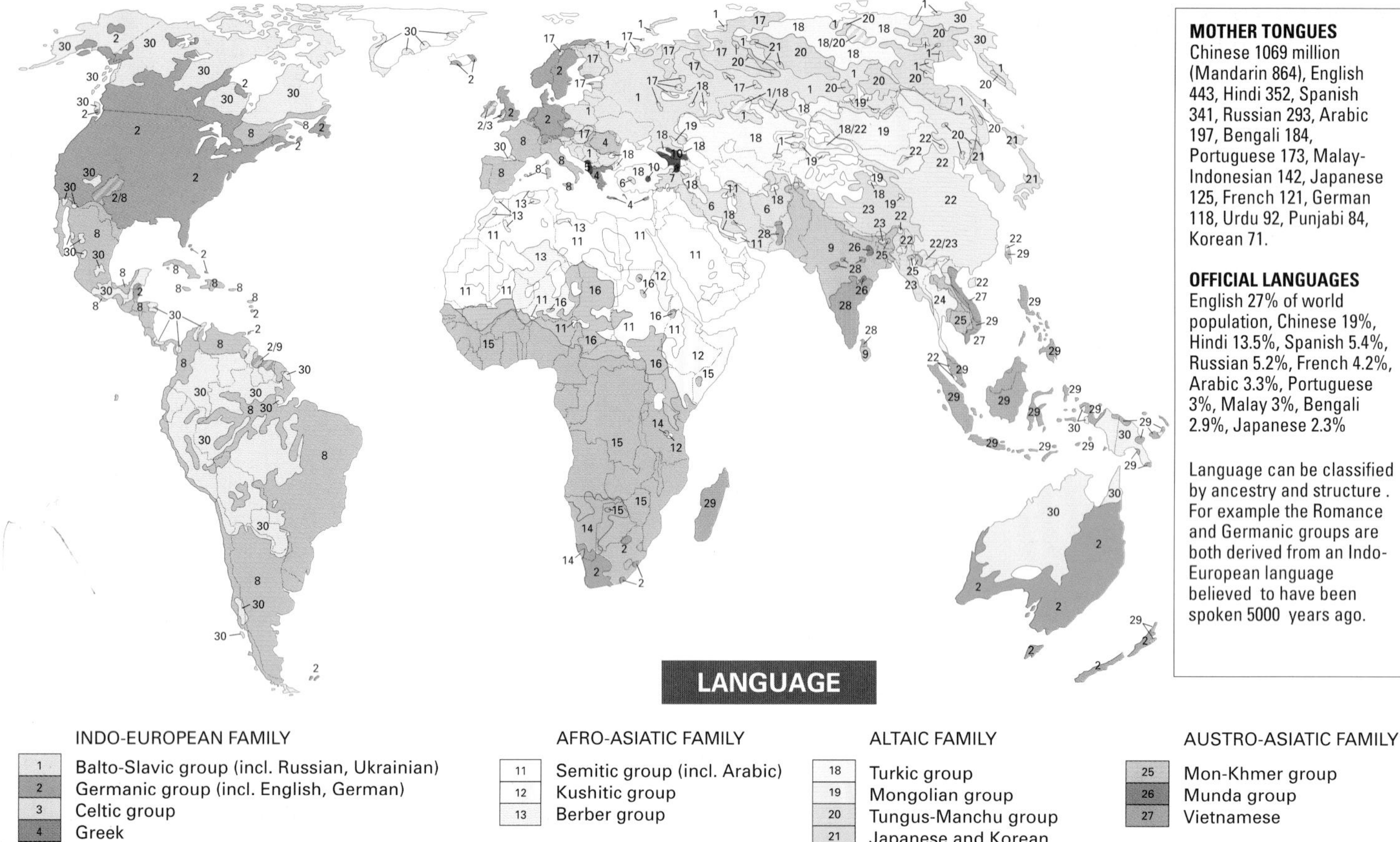

CARTOGRAPHY BY PHILIP'S. COPYRIGHT REED INTERNATIONAL BOOKS LTD

MOTHER TONGUES
Chinese 1069 million (Mandarin 864), English 443, Hindi 352, Spanish 341, Russian 293, Arabic 197, Bengali 184, Portuguese 173, Malay-Indonesian 142, Japanese 125, French 121, German 118, Urdu 92, Punjabi 84, Korean 71.

OFFICIAL LANGUAGES
English 27% of world population, Chinese 19%, Hindi 13.5%, Spanish 5.4%, Russian 5.2%, French 4.2%, Arabic 3.3%, Portuguese 3%, Malay 3%, Bengali 2.9%, Japanese 2.3%

Language can be classified by ancestry and structure. For example the Romance and Germanic groups are both derived from an Indo-European language believed to have been spoken 5000 years ago.

LANGUAGE

INDO-EUROPEAN FAMILY
1. Balto-Slavic group (incl. Russian, Ukrainian)
2. Germanic group (incl. English, German)
3. Celtic group
4. Greek
5. Albanian
6. Iranian group
7. Armenian
8. Romance group (incl. Spanish, Portuguese, French, Italian)
9. Indo-Aryan group (incl. Hindi, Bengali, Urdu, Punjabi, Marathi)
10. **CAUCASIAN FAMILY**

AFRO-ASIATIC FAMILY
11. Semitic group (incl. Arabic)
12. Kushitic group
13. Berber group
14. **KHOISAN FAMILY**
15. **NIGER-CONGO FAMILY**
16. **NILO-SAHARAN FAMILY**
17. **URALIC FAMILY**

ALTAIC FAMILY
18. Turkic group
19. Mongolian group
20. Tungus-Manchu group
21. Japanese and Korean

SINO-TIBETAN FAMILY
22. Sinitic (Chinese) languages
23. Tibetic-Burmic languages
24. **TAI FAMILY**

AUSTRO-ASIATIC FAMILY
25. Mon-Khmer group
26. Munda group
27. Vietnamese
28. **DRAVIDIAN FAMILY** (incl. Telugu, Tamil)
29. **AUSTRONESIAN FAMILY** (incl. Malay-Indonesian)
30. **OTHER LANGUAGES**

Roman Catholicism
Orthodox and other Eastern Churches
Protestantism
Sunni Islam
Shia Islam
Buddhism
Hinduism
Confucianism
Judaism
Shintoism
Primitive Religions

RELIGIOUS ADHERENTS

Christian	1667m	Hindu	663m
Roman Catholic	952m	Buddhist	312m
Protestant	337m	Chinese Folk	172m
Orthodox	162m	Tribal	92m
Anglican	70m	Jewish	18m
Other Christian	148m	Sikhs	17m
Muslim	881m		
Sunni	841m		
Shia	40m		

RELIGION

UNITED NATIONS

Created in 1945 to promote peace and co-operation and based in New York, the United Nations is the world's largest international organization, with 184 members and an annual budget of US $2.6 billion (1994–95). Each member of the General Assembly has one vote, while the permanent members of the 15-nation Security Council – USA, Russia, China, UK and France – hold a veto. The 54 members of the Economic and Social Council are responsible for economic, social, cultural, educational, health and related matters. The Secretariat is the UN's principal administrative arm; the only territory now administered by the Trusteeship Council is Belau (by the USA). The UN has 16 specialized agencies – based in Canada, France, Switzerland and Italy as well as the USA – which help members in fields such as education (UNESCO), agriculture (FAO), medicine (WHO) and finance (IFC).

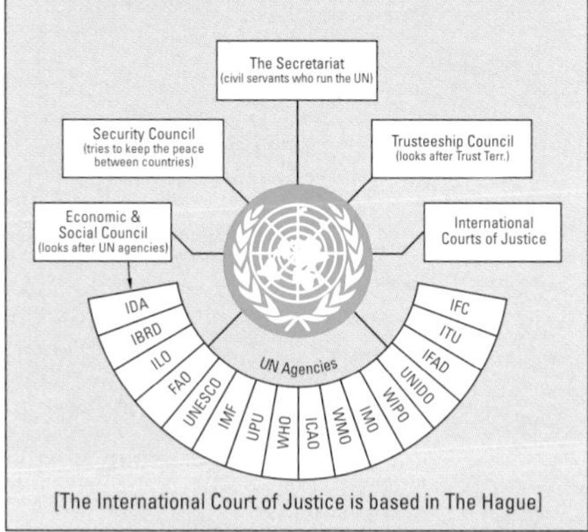

[The International Court of Justice is based in The Hague]

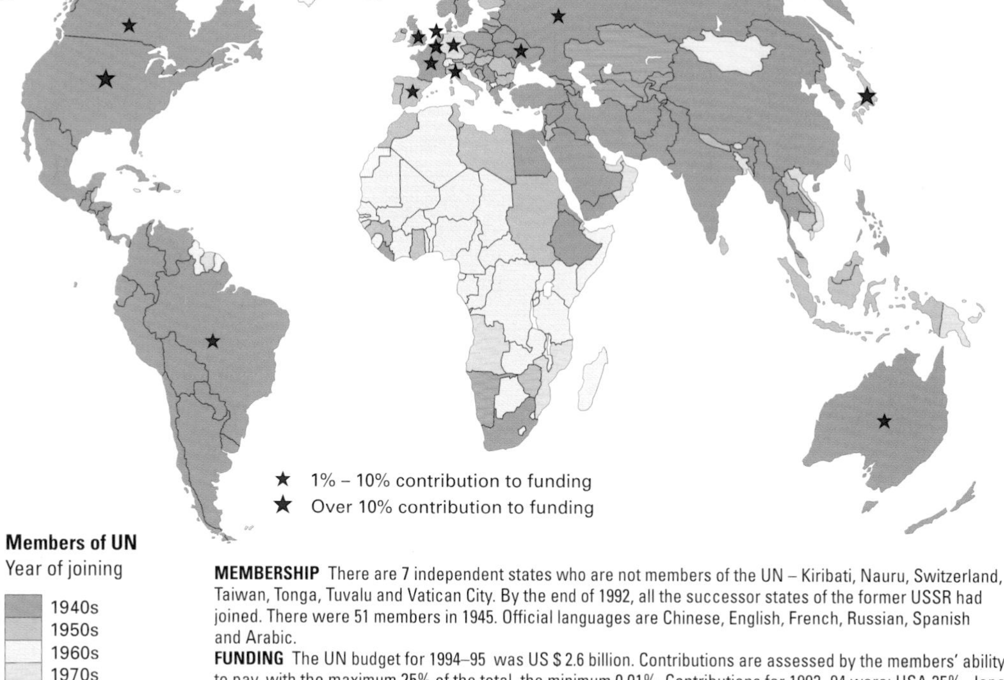

★ 1% – 10% contribution to funding
★ Over 10% contribution to funding

Members of UN
Year of joining

- 1940s
- 1950s
- 1960s
- 1970s
- 1980s
- 1990s
- Non members

MEMBERSHIP There are 7 independent states who are not members of the UN – Kiribati, Nauru, Switzerland, Taiwan, Tonga, Tuvalu and Vatican City. By the end of 1992, all the successor states of the former USSR had joined. There were 51 members in 1945. Official languages are Chinese, English, French, Russian, Spanish and Arabic.
FUNDING The UN budget for 1994–95 was US $ 2.6 billion. Contributions are assessed by the members' ability to pay, with the maximum 25% of the total, the minimum 0.01%. Contributions for 1992–94 were: USA 25%, Japan 12.45%, Germany 8.93%, Russia 6.71%, France 6%, UK 5.02%, Italy 4.29%, Canada 3.11% (others 28.49%).
PEACEKEEPING The UN has been involved in 33 peacekeeping operations worldwide since 1948 and there are currently 17 areas of UN patrol. In July 1993 there were 80,146 'blue berets' from 74 countries.

EU As from December 1993 the European Union (EU) refers to matters of foreign policy, security and justice. The European Community (EC) refers to all other matters. The 15 members – Austria, Belgium, Denmark, Finland, France, Germany, Greece, Ireland, Italy, Luxembourg, Netherlands, Portugal, Spain, Sweden and the UK – aim to integrate economies, co-ordinate social developments and bring about political union. These members of what is now the world's biggest market share agricultural and industrial policies and tariffs on trade.
EFTA European Free Trade Association (formed in 1960). Portugal left the 'Seven' in 1989 and Austria, Finland and Sweden left in 1995 to join the EU.
ACP African-Caribbean-Pacific (1963).
NATO North Atlantic Treaty Organization (formed in 1949). It continues after 1991 despite the winding up of the Warsaw Pact.
OAS Organization of American States (1949). It aims to promote social and economic co-operation between developed countries of North America and developing nations of Latin America.
ASEAN Association of South-east Asian Nations (1967).
OAU Organization of African Unity (1963). Its 53 members represent over 90% of Africa's population.
LAIA Latin American Integration Association (1980).
OECD Organization for Economic Co-operation and Development (1961). The 25 major Western free-market economies. 'G7' is its 'inner group' of USA, Canada, Japan, UK, Germany, Italy and France.
COMMONWEALTH The Commonwealth of Nations evolved from the British Empire; it comprises 16 nations recognizing the British monarch as head of state and 31 republics and 5 indigenous monarchies.

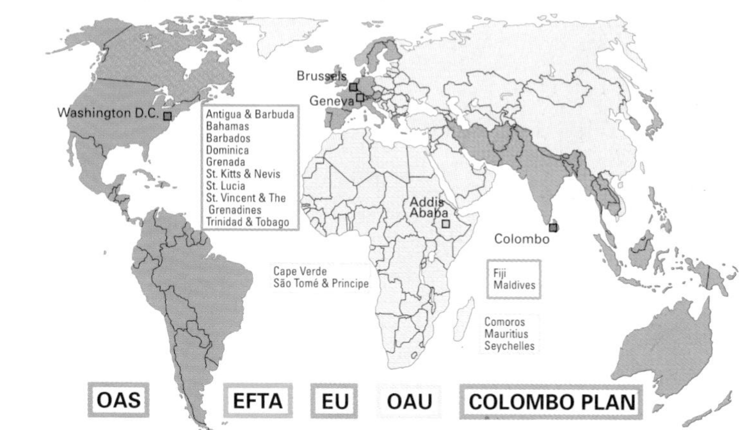

OAS   EFTA   EU   OAU   COLOMBO PLAN

OPEC Organization of Petroleum Exporting Countries (1960). It controls about three-quarters of the world's oil supply.
ARAB LEAGUE (1945) The League's aim is to promote economic, social, political and military co-operation.
COLOMBO PLAN (1951) Its 26 members aim to promote economic and social development in Asia and the Pacific.

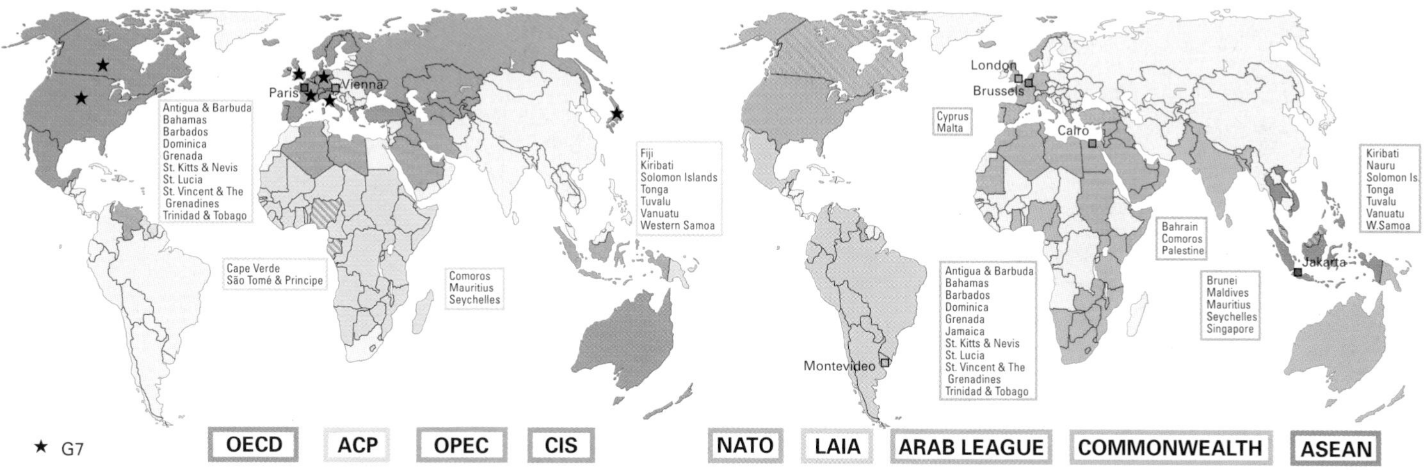

★ G7   OECD   ACP   OPEC   CIS   NATO   LAIA   ARAB LEAGUE   COMMONWEALTH   ASEAN

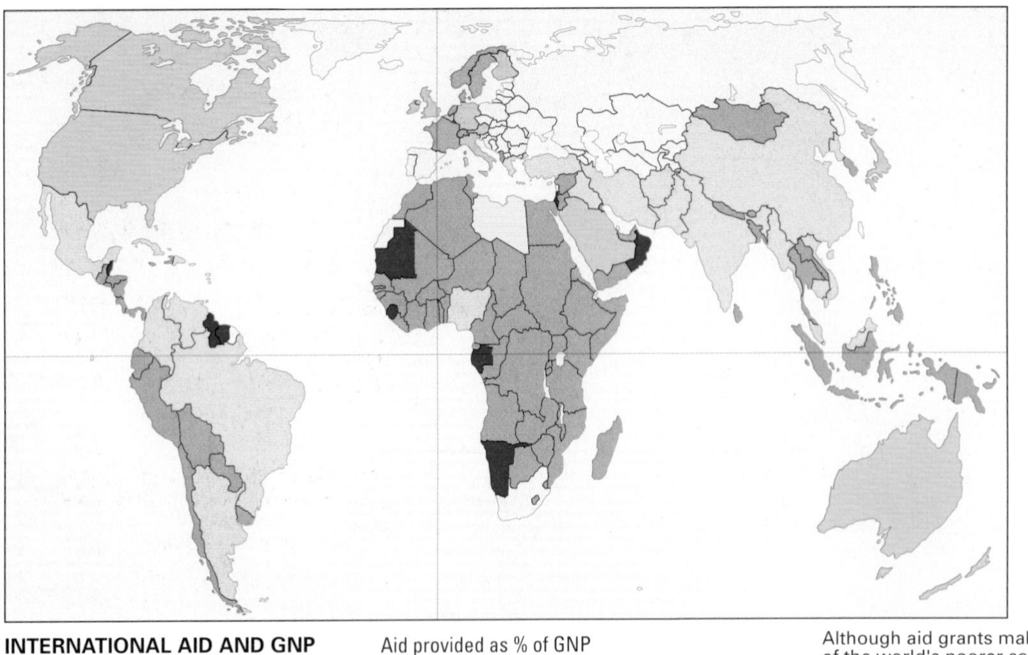

INTERNATIONAL AID

Aid provided or received,
divided by the total population 1993

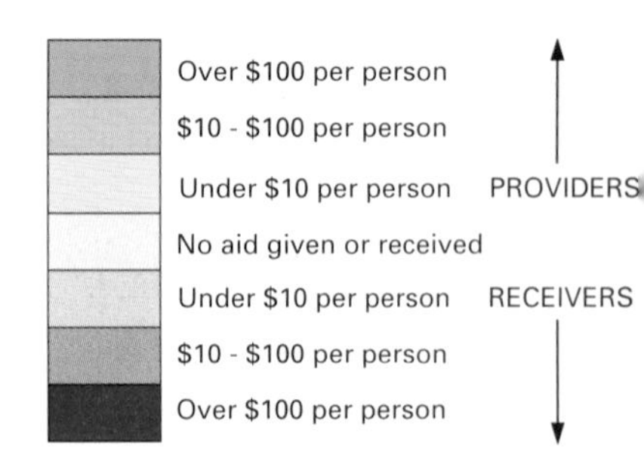

Over $100 per person
$10 - $100 per person
Under $10 per person — PROVIDERS
No aid given or received
Under $10 per person — RECEIVERS
$10 - $100 per person
Over $100 per person

INTERNATIONAL AID AND DEBT

Debt, US$ per capita 1992

Aid, US$ per capita 1992

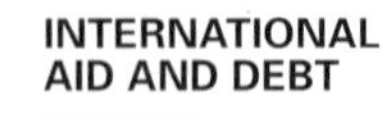

Although aid grants make a vital contribution to many
of the world's poorer countries, they are usually
dwarfed by the burden of debt that developing
economies are expected to repay.

Niger, Lesotho, Central Africa, Mali, Mozambique, Somalia, Botswana, Togo, El Salvador, Senegal, Bolivia, Honduras, Zambia, Papua N. Guinea, Mauritania, Mauritius, Costa Rica, Jamaica, Jordan $247, Gabon, Israel $352.5

$3628 $150 $100 $50

INTERNATIONAL AID AND GNP

Aid provided as % of GNP

(Total aid 1993)
- Denmark ($1.4 bn)
- Norway ($1.1 bn)
- Sweden ($2.3 bn)
- Netherlands ($42.6 bn)
- France ($8.2 bn)
- U.K. ($.3.2 bn)
- Japan ($9.3 bn)
- U.S.A. ($9.1 bn)

OECD target 0.7%

0.25% 0.5% 0.75% 1%

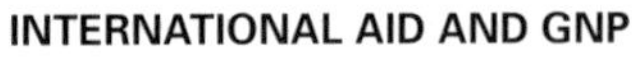

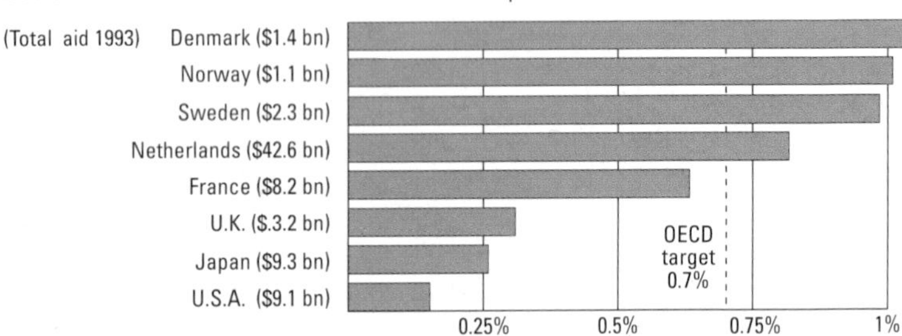

INTERNATIONAL MIGRATION

Foreign born as a %
of total population
(latest year)

more than 7.5%
3 - 7.5%
1.5 - 3%
less than 1.5%
no available data

Major migrations since 1945
1. 18m E. Europeans to Germany 1945 –
2. 4m Europeans to N. America 1945 –
3. 2.4m Jews to Israel 1945 –
4. 2m Irish & Commonwealth to U.K. 1945 –
5. 2m Europeans to Australia 1945
6. 2m N. Africans & S. Europeans to France 1946 –
7. 5m Chinese to Japan & Korea 1947 –
8. 2.9m Palestinian refugees 1947
9. 25m Indian & Pakistani refugees 1947–
10. 9m Mexicans to N. America 1950 –
11. 5m Korean refugees 1950 – 54

12. 4.7m C. Americans & W. Indians to N. America 1960–
13. 1.5m workers to S. Africa 1960 –
14. 2.4m S. Asian workers to the Gulf 1970 –
15. 3m workers to Nigeria & Ivory Coast 1970 –
16. 2m Bangladeshi & Pakistani refugees 1972 –
17. 1.5m Vietnamese & Cambodian refugees 1975 –
18. 6.1m Afghan refugees 1979 –
19. 2.9m Egyptian workers to Libya & the Gulf 1980 –
20. 2m workers to Argentina 1980 –
21. 1.7m Mozambique refugees 1985 –
22. 1.7m Yugoslav refugees 1992 –
23. 2.6m Rwanda - Burundi refugees 1994–

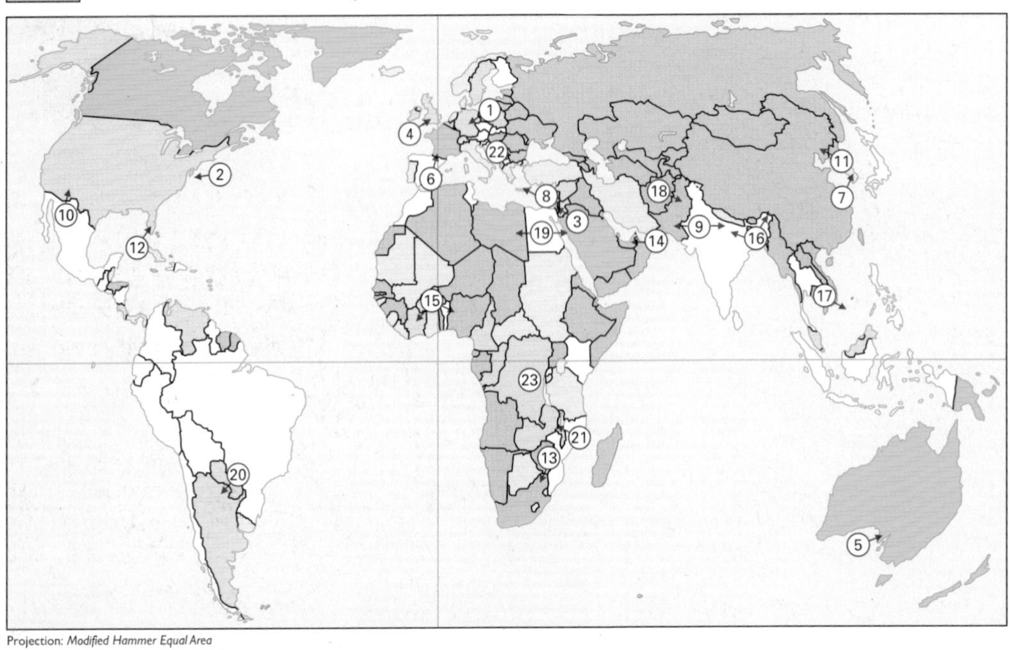

INTERNATIONAL REFUGEES

Origins of Refugees   World Total 1993 16.7 mill

North & South America 0.6%
Afghanistan 20.3%
Other Europe 4.3%
Former Yugoslavia 7.9%
Palestine 1
Other Africa 11.9%
Iraq 4.3%
Other Asia 7.7%
Mozambique 8%
Eritrea 2.5%
Rwanda 2.6%
Burundi 4.7%
Somalia 3.6%
Liberia 4.2%

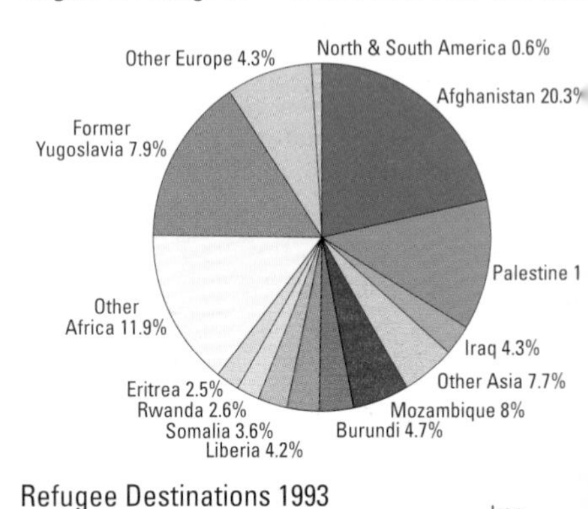

Refugee Destinations 1993

Refugees in host country

Refugees as a
proportion of host
country's population

Iran
Pakistan
Jordan
Malawi
Sudan
Guinea
Germany

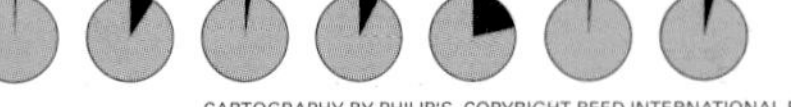

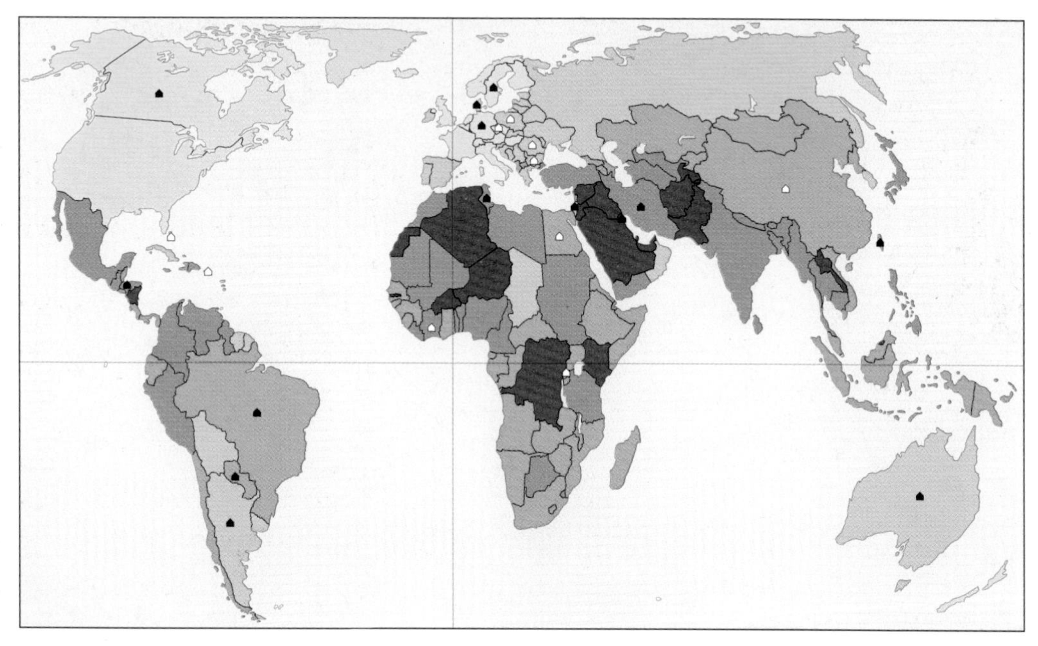

HOUSING

Number of people per household
(latest available year)

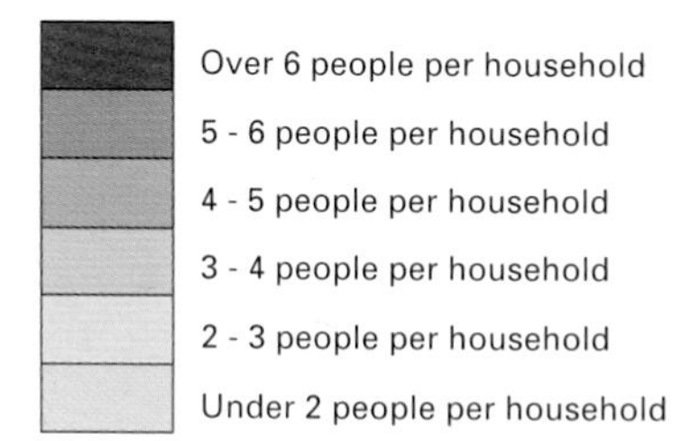

- Over 6 people per household
- 5 - 6 people per household
- 4 - 5 people per household
- 3 - 4 people per household
- 2 - 3 people per household
- Under 2 people per household

Expenditure on housing and energy as a
percentage of total consumer spending

- ▲ Over 20% spent
- △ Under 5% spent

WATER SUPPLY

Percentage of total population with
access to safe drinking water 1992

- Over 90% with safe water
- 75 - 90% with safe water
- 60 - 75% with safe water
- 45 - 60% with safe water
- 30 - 45% with safe water
- Under 30% with safe water

Least well provided countries

Central Africa	12%	Madagascar	23%
Uganda	15%	Guinea-Bissau	25%
Ethiopia	18%	Laos	28%
Mozambique	22%	Swaziland	30%
Afghanistan	23%	Tajikistan	30%

Average daily domestic water
consumption per person

△ Under 80 litres ▲ Over 320 litres

*80 litres of water a day is considered
necessary for a reasonable quality of life*

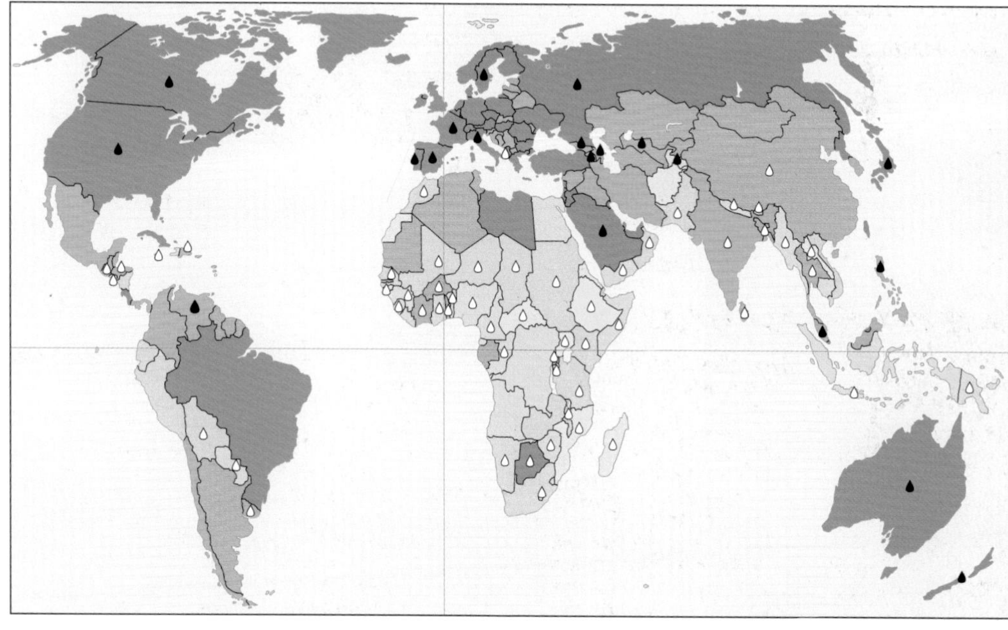

DAILY FOOD CONSUMPTION

Average daily food intake
in calories per person 1992

- Over 3 500 cals. per person
- 3 000 - 3 500 cals. per person
- 2 500 - 3 000 cals. per person
- 2 000 - 2 500 cals. per person
- Under 2 000 cals. per person
- No available data

Top 5 countries		Bottom 5 countries	
Ireland	3 847	Mozambique	1 680
Greece	3 815	Liberia	1 640
Cyprus	3 779	Ethiopia	1 610
U.S.A.	3 732	Afghanistan	1 523
Spain	3 708	Somalia	1 499
		U.K.	3 317

Projection: *Modified Hammer Equal Area*

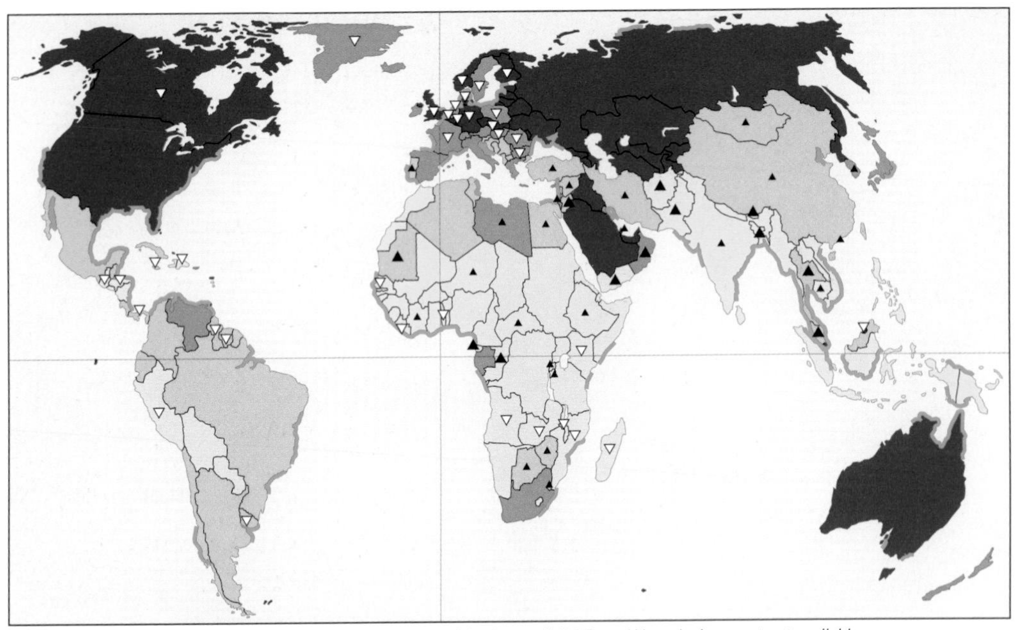

Statistics for each of the new republics of the former U.S.S.R. and Yugoslavia are not yet available.

GLOBAL WARMING

Carbon dioxide emissions in tonnes per person per year (1991)*

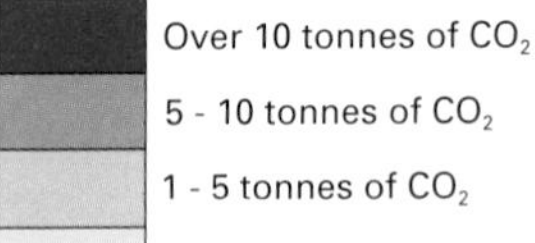

- Over 10 tonnes of CO_2
- 5 - 10 tonnes of CO_2
- 1 - 5 tonnes of CO_2
- Under 1 tonne of CO_2

Changes in CO_2 emissions 1980 - 1990

- ▲ Over 100% increase in emissions
- ▲ 50 - 100% increase in emissions
- ▽ Reduction in emissions
- ▬ Coasts in danger of flooding from rising sea levels caused by global warming

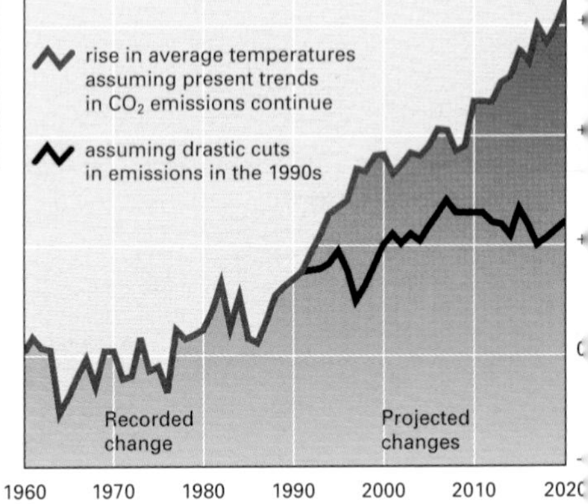

- ∿ rise in average temperatures assuming present trends in CO_2 emissions continue
- ∿ assuming drastic cuts in emissions in the 1990s

Recorded change

Projected changes

1960 1970 1980 1990 2000 2010 202O

Largest percentage share of total world greenhouse gas emissions 1991

5% 10% 15% 20%
U.S.A.
Former U.S.S.R.
China
Japan
Brazil
Germany
India
U.K.

Contribution to the greenhouse effect by the major heat-absorbing gases in the atmosphere

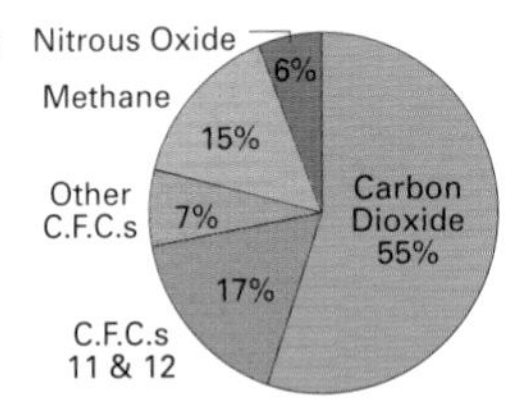

Nitrous Oxide 6%
Methane 15%
Other C.F.C.s 7%
Carbon Dioxide 55%
C.F.C.s 11 & 12 17%

THE GREENHOUSE EFFECT

Carbon dioxide is increased by burning fossil fuels and cutting forests

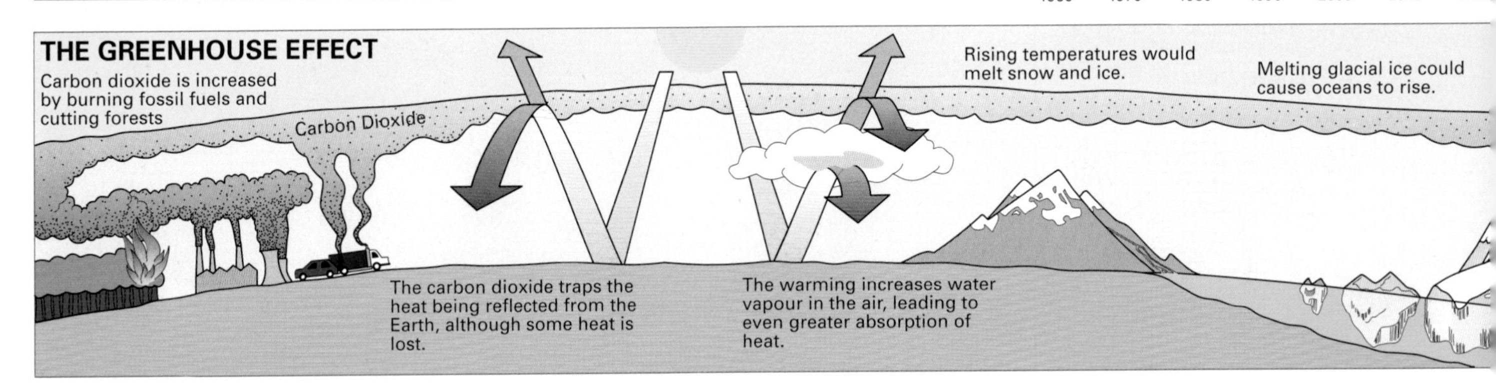

Carbon Dioxide

Rising temperatures would melt snow and ice.

Melting glacial ice could cause oceans to rise.

The carbon dioxide traps the heat being reflected from the Earth, although some heat is lost.

The warming increases water vapour in the air, leading to even greater absorption of heat.

ACID RAIN

Acid rain is caused by high levels of sulphur an nitrogen in the atmosphere. They combine with water vapour and oxygen to form acids (H_2SO_4 and HNO_3) which fall as precipitation.

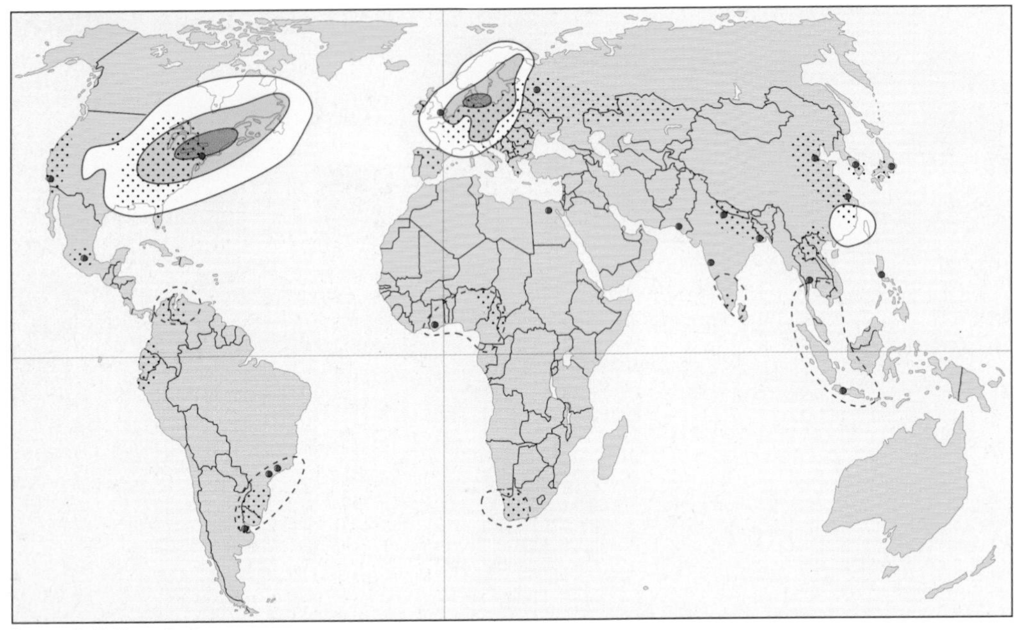

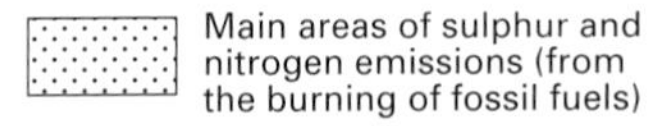

Main areas of sulphur and nitrogen emissions (from the burning of fossil fuels)

- Major cities with levels of air pollution exceding World Health Organisation guidelines

Areas of acid deposition

(pH numbers measure acidity: normal rain is pH 5

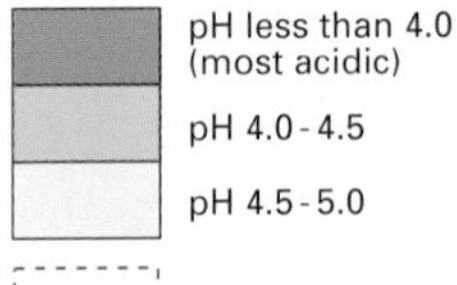

- pH less than 4.0 (most acidic)
- pH 4.0 - 4.5
- pH 4.5 - 5.0
- Potential problem areas

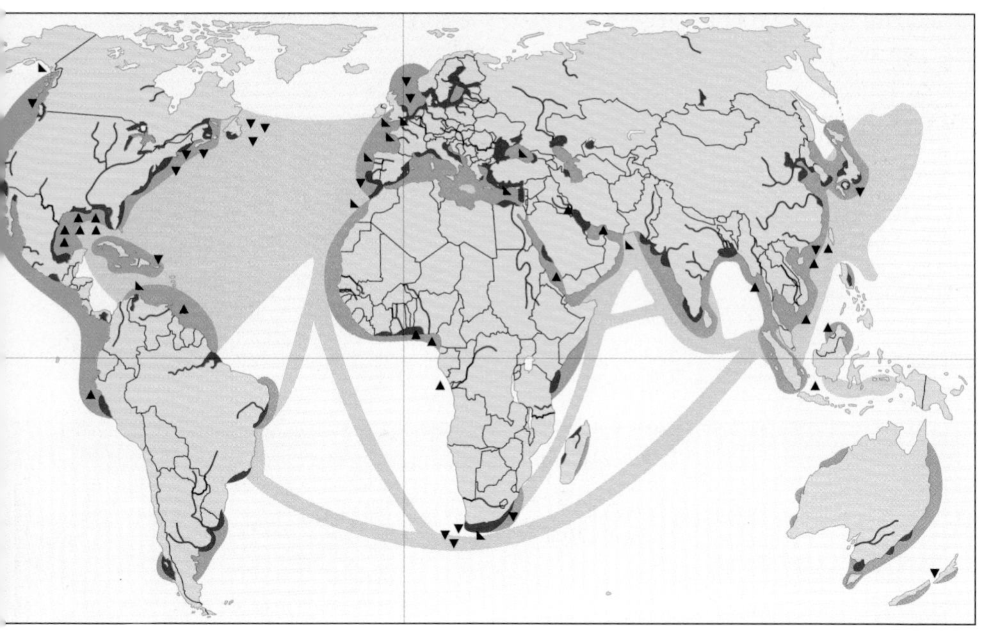

WATER POLLUTION

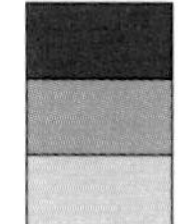

- Severely polluted sea areas and lakes
- Less polluted sea areas and lakes
- Areas of frequent oil pollution by shipping
- ◣ Major oil tanker spills
- ▲ Major oil rig blow-outs
- ▼ Offshore dumpsites for industrial and municipal waste
- ——— Severely polluted rivers and estuaries

Sources of marine oil pollution		Sources of river pollution	
Tanker operations	22%	Agriculture	64%
Municipal waste	22%	Mining	9%
Tanker accidents	13%	Land disposal	9%
River runoff	12%	Forestry	6%
Others	31%	Others	11%

DESERTIFICATION

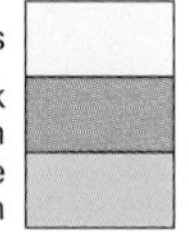

- Existing deserts
- Areas with a high risk of desertification
- Areas with a moderate risk of desertification

DEFORESTATION IN THE TROPICS

- Former areas of rainforest
- Existing rainforest

Deforestation 1981-1990

	Extent of forest cleared annually (thousand ha)	Annual deforestation rate (%)
Brazil	3 671	0.6
Indonesia	1 212	1.0
Zaire	732	0.6
Mexico	678	1.2
Bolivia	625	1.1
Venezuela	599	1.2
Thailand	515	2.9

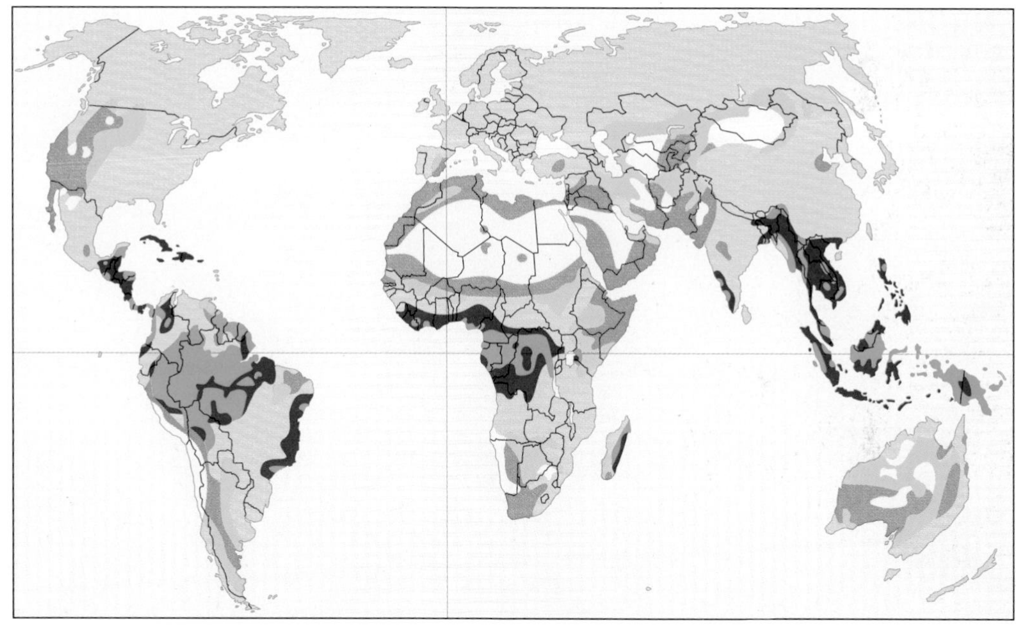

NATURAL DISASTERS

- ☐ Earthquake zones
- ● Major earthquakes since 1900 (with dates)
- ▲ Major volcanoes (notable eruptions since 1900 with dates)
- Areas liable to flood
- ⇨ Paths of tropical storms
- ⇨ Paths of winter blizzards
- ⠂ Areas liable to invasion by locusts
- ■ Major famines since 1900 (with dates)
- ⑨ Major storms and floods

1 Texas 1900
2 Central America 1966,1974
3 West Indies 1928, 1963, 1979, 1988
4 Bangladesh 1960, 1963, 1965, 1970, 1985, 1988, 1989, 1991
5 Huang He 1887, 1931
6 Yangtze 1911, 1989, 1995
7 Hunan 1991
8 Haiphong 1881
9 Philippines 1970, 1991
10 Mississippi 1993

Projection: Modified Hammer Equal Area

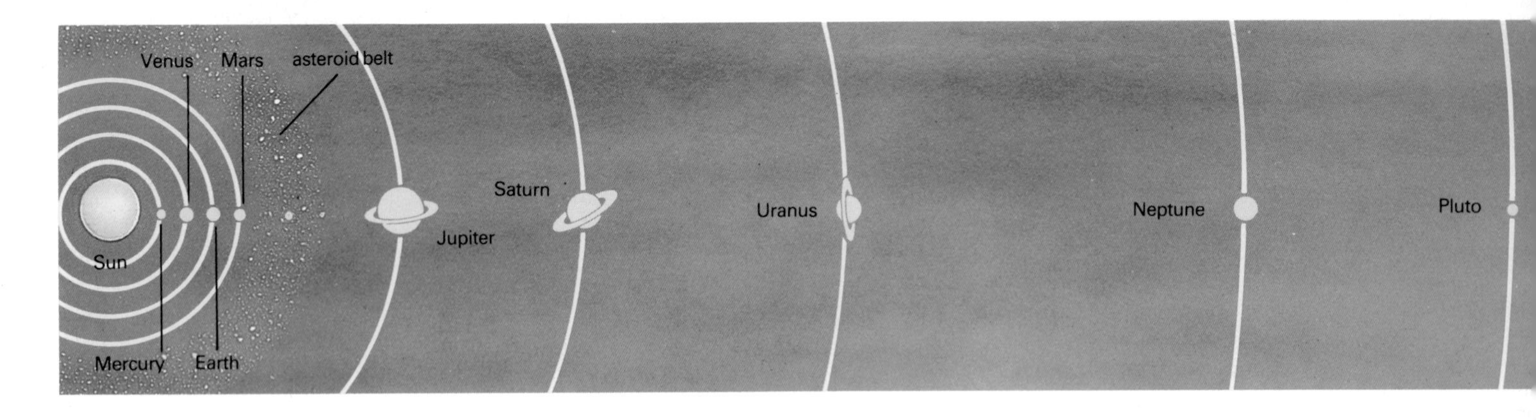

THE SOLAR SYSTEM

A minute part of one of the billions of galaxies (collections of stars) that comprise the Universe, the Solar System lies some 27,000 light-years from the centre of our own galaxy, the 'Milky Way'. Thought to be over 4,700 million years old, it consists of a central sun with nine planets and their moons revolving around it, attracted by its gravitational pull. The planets orbit the Sun in the same direction – anti-clockwise when viewed from the Northern Heavens – and almost in the same plane. Their orbital paths, however, vary enormously.

The Sun's diameter is 109 times that of Earth, and the temperature at its core – caused by continuous thermonuclear fusions of hydrogen into helium – is estimated to be 15 million degrees Celsius. It is the Solar System's only source of light and heat.

PROFILE OF THE PLANETS

	Mean distance from Sun (million km)	Mass (Earth = 1)	Period of orbit	Period of rotation (in days)	Diameter (km)	Number of known satellites
Mercury	58.3	0.06	88 days	58.67	4,878	0
Venus	107.7	0.8	224.7 days	243.00	12,104	0
Earth	149.6	1.0	365.24 days	0.99	12,756	1
Mars	227.3	0.1	1.88 years	1.02	6,794	2
Jupiter	777.9	317.8	11.86 years	0.41	142,800	16
Saturn	1,427.1	95.2	29.63 years	0.42	120,000	17
Uranus	2,872.3	14.5	83.97 years	0.45	52,000	15
Neptune	4,502.7	17.2	164.80 years	0.67	48,400	8
Pluto	5,894.2	0.002	248.63 years	6.38	3,000	1

All planetary orbits are elliptical in form, but only Pluto and Mercury follow paths that deviate noticeably from a circular one. Near Perihelion – its closest approach to the Sun – Pluto actually passes inside the orbit of Neptune, an event that last occurred in 1983. Pluto will not regain its station as outermost planet until February 1999.

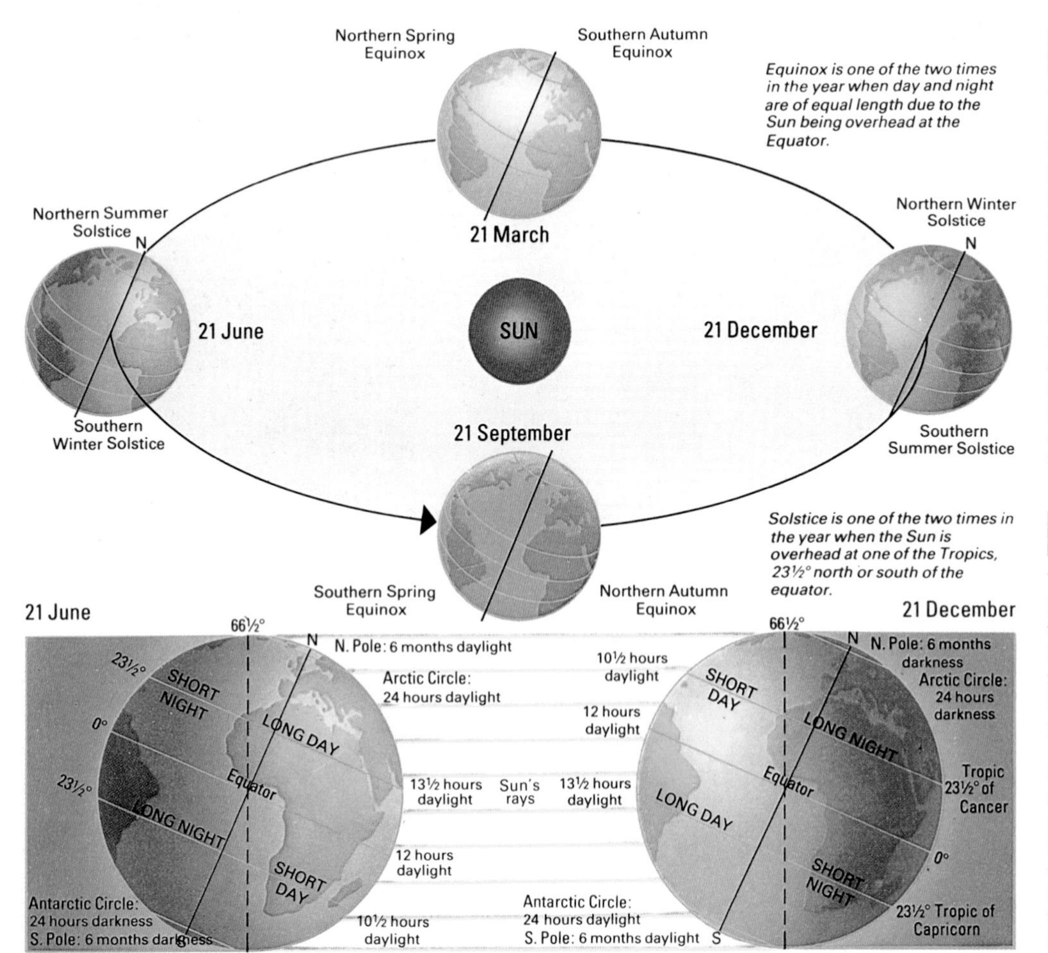

Equinox is one of the two times in the year when day and night are of equal length due to the Sun being overhead at the Equator.

Solstice is one of the two times in the year when the Sun is overhead at one of the Tropics, 23½° north or south of the equator.

THE SEASONS

The Earth revolves around the Sun once a year in an 'anti-clockwise' direction, tilted at a constant angle 66½°. In June, the northern hemisphere is tilted towards the Sun: as a result it receives more hours of sunshine in a day and therefore has its warmest season, summer. In December, the Earth has rotated halfway round the Sun so that the southern hemisphere is tilted towards the Sun and has its summer; the hemisphere that is tilted away from the Sun has winter. On 21 June the Sun is directly overhead at the Tropic of Cancer (23½° N), and this is midsummer in the northern hemisphere. Midsummer in the southern hemisphere occurs on 21 December, when the Sun is overhead at the Tropic of Capricorn (23½° S).

DAY AND NIGHT

The Sun appears to rise in the east, reach its highest point at noon, and then set in the west, to be followed by night. In reality it is not the Sun that is moving but the Earth revolving from west to east. Due to the tilting of the Earth the length of day and night varies from place to place and month to month.

At the summer solstice in the northern hemisphere (21 June), the Arctic has total daylight and the Antarctic total darkness. The opposite occurs at the winter solstice (21 December). At the Equator, the length of day and night are almost equal all year, at latitude 30° the length of day varies from about 14 hours to 10 hours, and at latitude 50° from about 16 hours to about 8 hours.

TIME

r: The time taken by the Earth to revolve und the Sun, or 365.24 days.

nth: The approximate time taken by the Moon evolve around the Earth. The 12 months of the r in fact vary from 28 (29 in a Leap Year) to 31 s.

ek: An artificial period of 7 days, not based on ronomical time.

·: The time taken by the Earth to complete one ation on its axis.

r: 24 hours make one day. Usually the day is ded into hours AM (ante meridiem or before n) and PM (post meridiem or after noon), ough most timetables now use the 24-hour tem, from midnight to midnight.

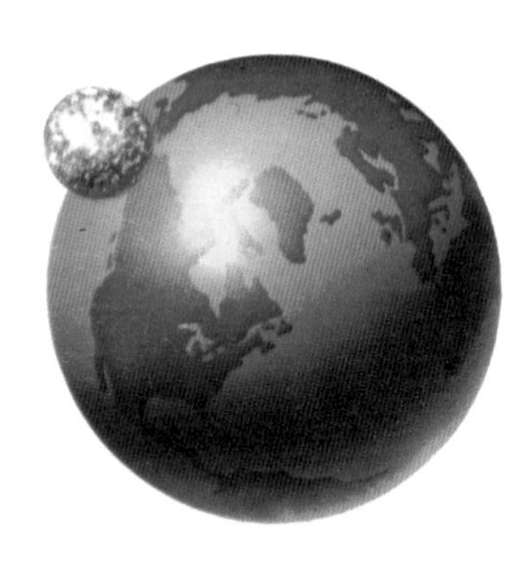

SUNRISE

Months of the year

SUNSET

Months of the year

THE MOON

Distance from Earth: 356,410 km – 406,685 km; Mean diameter: 3,475.1 km; Mass: approx. 1/81 that of Earth;
Surface gravity: one-sixth of Earth's; Daily range of temperature at lunar equator: 200°C; Average orbital speed: 3,683 km/h

PHASES OF THE MOON

New Moon | Crescent | First quarter | Gibbous | Full Moon | Gibbous | Last quarter | Crescent | New Moon

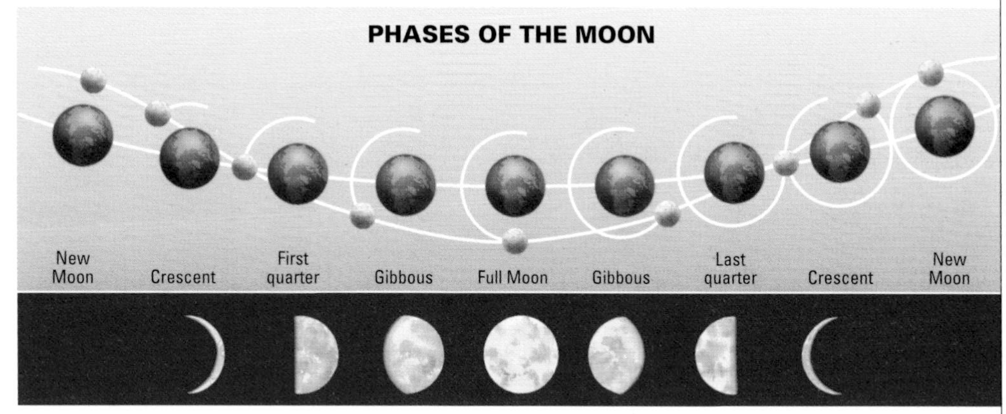

he Moon rotates more slowly than the Earth, making ne complete turn on its axis in just over 27 days. ince this corresponds to its period of revolution round the Earth, the Moon always presents the same hemisphere or face to us, and we never see 'the dark side'. The interval between one full Moon and the next (and between new Moons) is about 29½ days – a lunar month. The apparent changes in the shape of the Moon are caused by its changing position in relation to the Earth; like the planets, it produces no light of its own and shines only by reflecting the rays of the Sun.

Partial eclipse (1)

P   P   P

Total eclipse (2)

Lunar eclipse

ECLIPSES

When the Moon passes between the Sun and the Earth it causes a partial eclipse of the Sun (1) if the Earth passes through the Moon's outer shadow (P), or a total eclipse (2) if the inner cone shadow crosses the Earth's surface. In a lunar eclipse, the Earth's shadow crosses the Moon and, again, provides either a partial or total eclipse. Eclipses of the Sun and the Moon do not occur every month because of the 5° difference between the plane of the Moon's orbit and the plane in which the Earth moves. In the 1990s only 14 lunar eclipses are possible, for example, seven partial and seven total; each is visible only from certain, and variable, parts of the world. The same period witnesses 13 solar eclipses – six partial (or annular) and seven total.

TIDES

he daily rise and fall of the ocean's tides are the esult of the gravitational pull of the Moon and at of the Sun, though the effect of the latter is nly 46.6% as strong as that of the Moon. This ffect is greatest on the hemisphere facing the loon and causes a tidal 'bulge'. When lunar and olar forces pull together, with Sun, Earth and loon in line (near New and Full Moons), higher spring tides' (and lower low tides) occur; when unar and solar forces are least coincidental with e Sun and Moon at an angle (near the Moon's rst and third quarters), 'neap tides' occur, which ave a small tidal range.

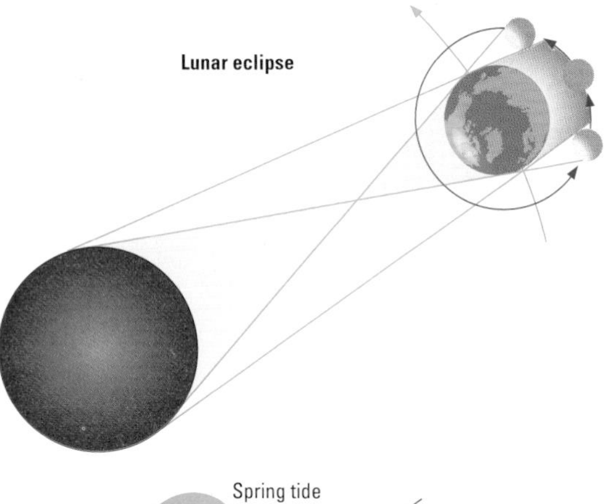

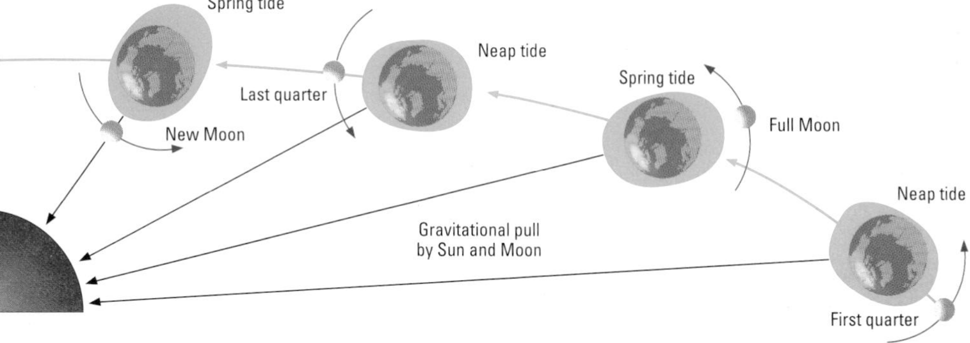

Spring tide
Neap tide
Last quarter
New Moon
Spring tide
Full Moon
Neap tide
Gravitational pull by Sun and Moon
First quarter

MAP PROJECTIONS

A map projection is the systematic depiction on a plane surface of the imaginary lines of latitude or longitude from a globe of the earth. This network of lines is called the graticule and forms the framework upon which an accurate depiction of the earth is made. The map graticule, which is the basis of any map, is constructed sometimes by graphical means, but often by using mathematical formulae to give the intersections of the graticule plotted as x and y co-ordinates. The choice between projections is based upon which properties the cartographer wishes the map to possess, the map scale and also the extent of the area to be mapped. Since the globe is three dimensional, it is not possible to depict its surface on a two dimensional plane without distortion. Preservation of one of the basic properties listed below can only be secured at the expense of the others and the choice of projection is often a compromise solution.

Correct Area

In these projections the areas from the globe are to scale on the map. For example, if you look at the diagram at the top right, areas of 10° x 10° are shown from the equator to the poles. The proportion of this area at the extremities are approximately 11:1. An equal area projection will retain that proportion in its portrayal of those areas. This is particularly useful in the mapping of densities and distributions. Projections with this property are termed **Equal Area, Equivalent or Homolographic.**

Correct Distance

In these projections the scale is correct along the meridians, or in the case of the Azimuthal Equidistant scale is true along any line drawn from the centre of the projection. They are called **Equidistant.**

Correct Shape

This property can only be true within small areas as it is achieved only by having a uniform scale distortion along both x and y axes of the projection. The projections are called **Conformal** or **Orthomorphic.**

In order to minimise the distortions at the edges of some projections, central portions of them are often selected for atlas maps. Below are listed some of the major types of projection.

Latitude and Longitude

prime meridian
plane of the prime meridian
centre of the earth
plane of the equator
North Pole
line of latitude of x° North (parallel)
line of longitude of y° East (meridian)

The area between 10 degrees of latitude and 10 degrees of longitude

108 583 km²	80°
322 195 km²	70°
525 317 km²	60°
711 527 km²	50°
875 171 km²	40°
1 011 536 km²	30°
1 116 918 km²	20°
1 188 622 km²	10°
1 224 902 km²	Equator 0°

The length of 10 degrees of longitude measured along line of latitude

80°	193 km
70°	381 km
60°	558 km
50°	717 km
40°	854 km
30°	965 km
20°	1047 km
10°	1096 km
	1107 km
0°	1113 km

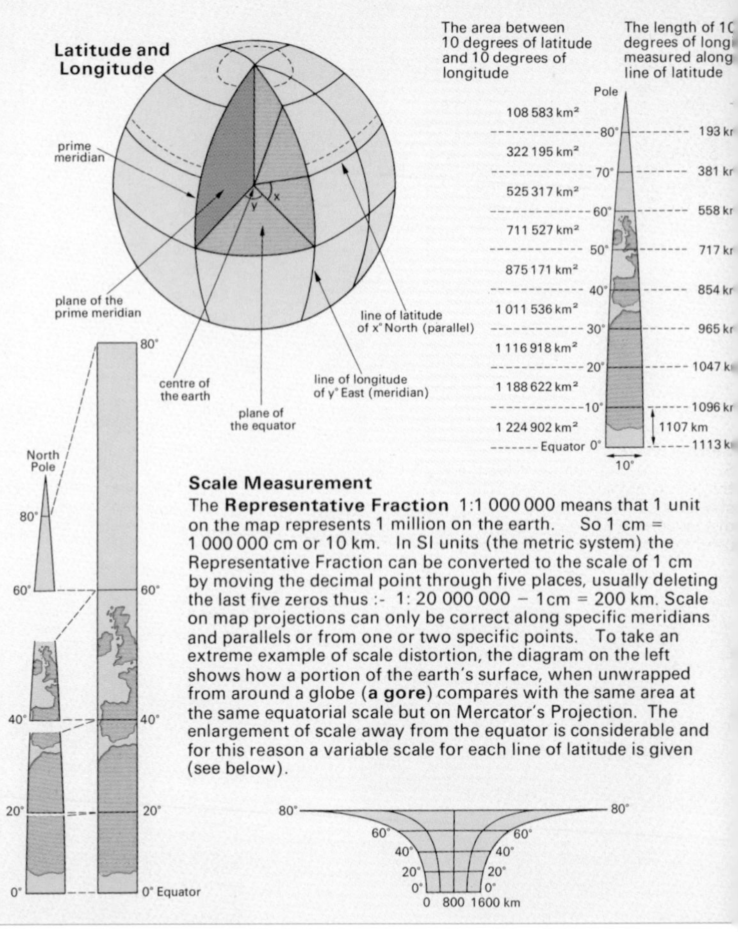

Scale Measurement

The **Representative Fraction** 1:1 000 000 means that 1 unit on the map represents 1 million on the earth. So 1 cm = 1 000 000 cm or 10 km. In SI units (the metric system) the Representative Fraction can be converted to the scale of 1 cm by moving the decimal point through five places, usually deleting the last five zeros thus :- 1: 20 000 000 − 1cm = 200 km. Scale on map projections can only be correct along specific meridians and parallels or from one or two specific points. To take an extreme example of scale distortion, the diagram on the left shows how a portion of the earth's surface, when unwrapped from around a globe (**a gore**) compares with the same area at the same equatorial scale but on Mercator's Projection. The enlargement of scale away from the equator is considerable and for this reason a variable scale for each line of latitude is given (see below).

0 800 1600 km

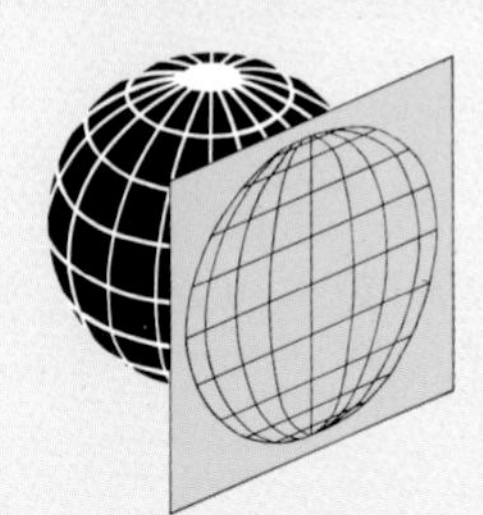

AZIMUTHAL OR ZENITHAL PROJECTIONS

These are constructed by the projection of part of the graticule from the globe onto a plane tangential to any single point on it. This plane may be tangential to the equator (**equatorial case**), the poles (**polar case**) or any other point (**oblique case**). Any straight line drawn from the point at which the plane touches the globe is the shortest distance from that point and is known as a **great circle**. In its **Gnomonic** construction *any* straight line on the map is a great circle, but there is great exaggeration towards the edges and this reduces its general uses. There are five different ways of transferring the graticule onto the plane and these are shown on the right. The central diagram below shows how the graticules vary, using the polar case as the example.

Equidistant | Equal-Area | Orthographic | Gnomonic | Stereographic (conformal)

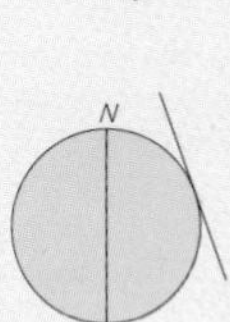

Oblique Case

The plane touches the globe at any point between the equator and poles. The oblique orthographic uses the distortion in azimuthal projections away from the centre to give a graphic depiction of the earth as seen from any desired point in space. It can also be used in both Polar and Equatorial cases. It is used not only for the earth but also for the moon and planets.

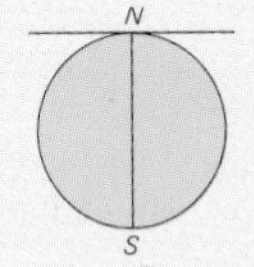

Polar Case

The polar case is the simplest to construct and the diagram below shows the differing effects of all five methods of construction comparing their coverage, distortion etc., using North America as the example.

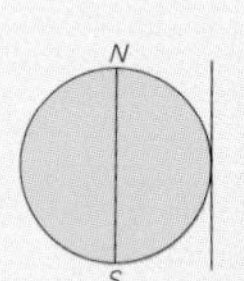

Equatorial Case

The example shown here is Lambert's Equivalent Azimuthal. It is the only projection which is both equal area and where bearing is true from the centre.

Equidistant | Equal-Area | Stereographic | Orthographic | Gnomonic

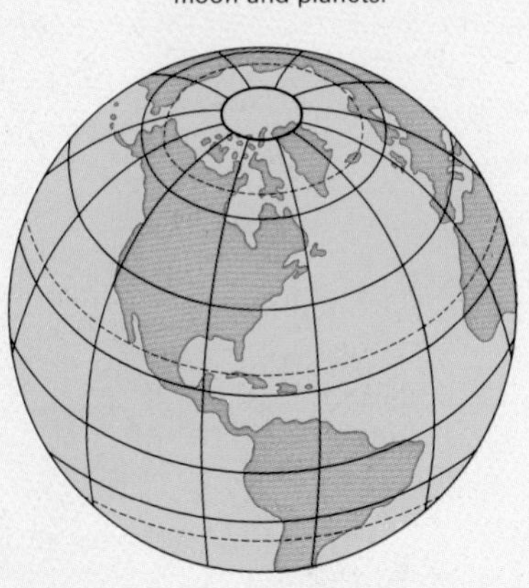

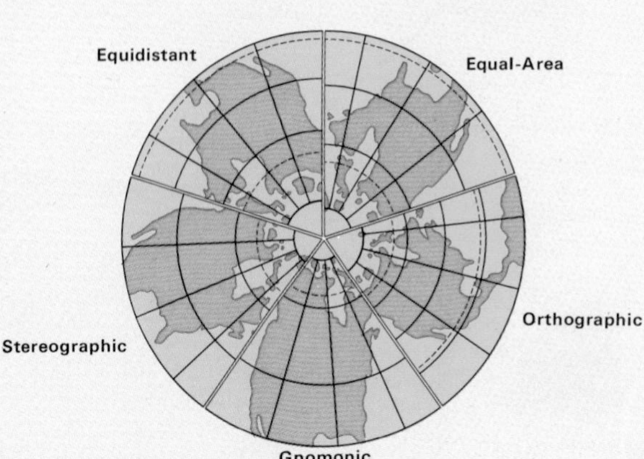

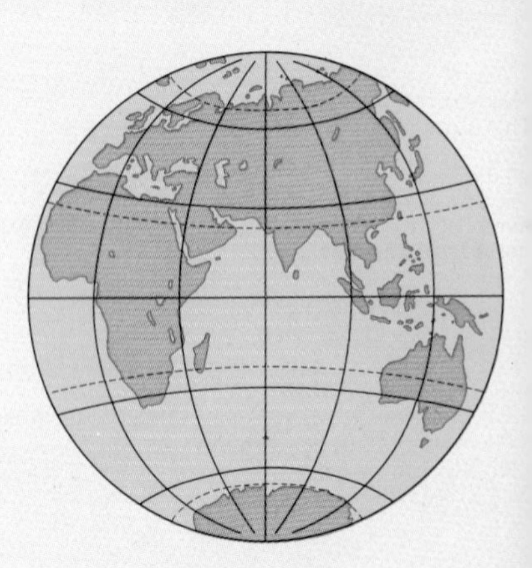

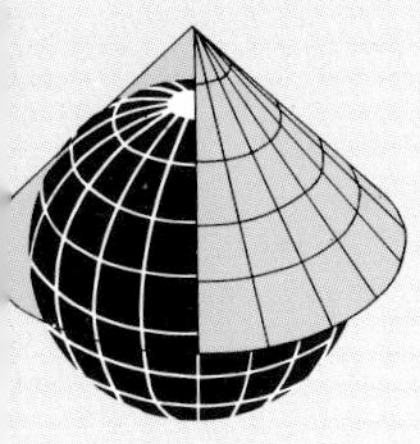

CONICAL PROJECTIONS

These use the projection of the graticule from the globe onto a cone which is tangential to a line of latitude (termed the **standard parallel**). This line is always an arc and scale is always true along it. Because of its method of construction it is used mainly for depicting the temperate latitudes around the standard parallel i.e. where there is least distortion. To reduce the distortion and include a larger range of latitudes, the projection may be constructed with the cone bisecting the surface of the globe so that there are two standard parallels each of which is true to scale. The distortion is thus spread more evenly between the two chosen parallels.

Simple Conical with one standard parallel

Conical with two standard parallels

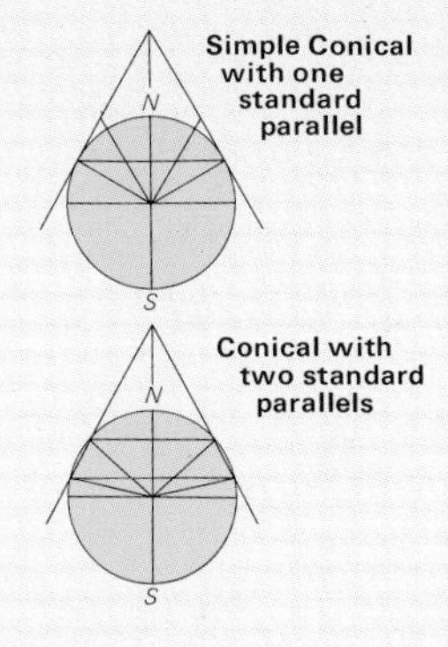

Bonne

This is a modification of the simple conic whereby the true scale along the meridians is sacrificed to enable the accurate representation of areas. However scale is true along each parallel but shapes are distorted at the edges.

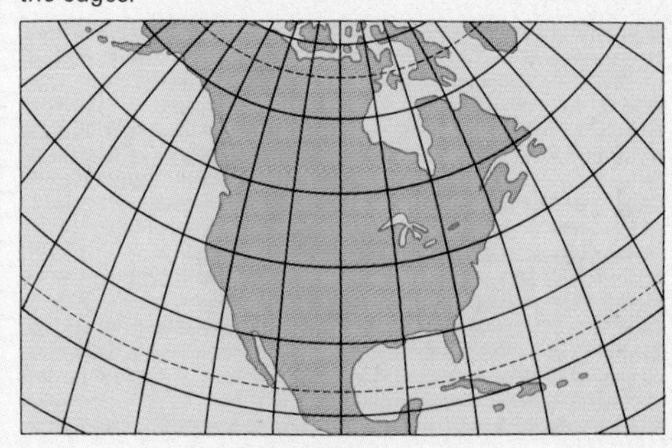

Simple Conic

Scale is correct not only along the standard parallel but also along all meridians. The selection of the standard parallel used is crucial because of the distortion away from it. The projection is usually used to portray regions or continents at small scales.

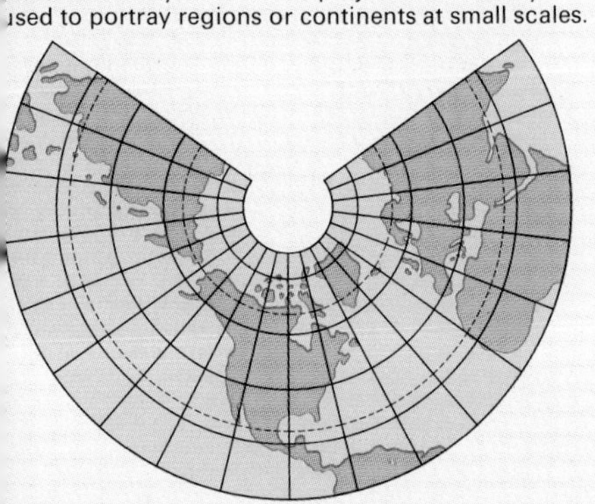

Lambert's Conformal Conic

This projection uses two standard parallels but instead of being equal area as Albers, it is Conformal. Because it has comparatively small distortion, direction and distances can be readily measured and it is therefore used for some navigational charts.

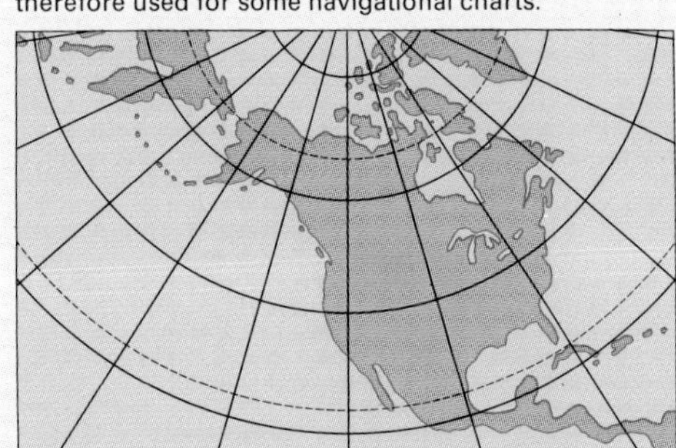

Albers Conical Equal Area

This projection uses two standard parallels and once again the selection of the two specific ones relative to the land area to be mapped is very important. It is equal area and is especially useful for large land masses oriented East-West, for example the U.S.A.

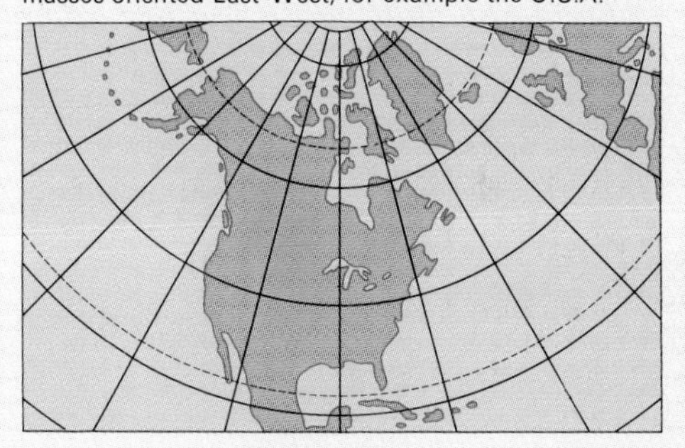

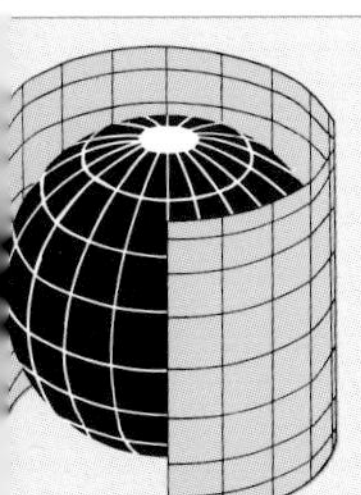

CYLINDRICAL AND OTHER WORLD PROJECTIONS

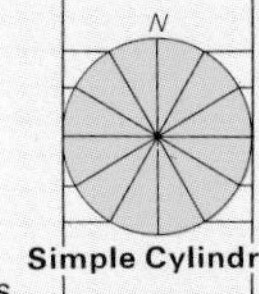

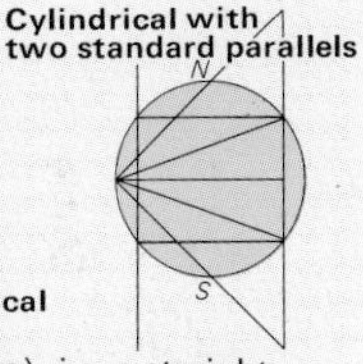

This group of projections are those which permit the whole of the Earth's surface to be depicted on one map. They are a very large group of projections and the following are only a few of them. Cylindrical projections are constructed by the projection of the graticule from the globe onto a cylinder tangential to the globe. In the examples shown here the cylinder touches the equator, but it can be moved through 90° so it touches the poles - this is called the **Transverse Aspect**. If the cylinder is twisted so that it touches anywhere between the equator and poles it is called the **Oblique Aspect**. Although cylindrical projections can depict all the main land masses, there is considerable distortion of shape and area towards the poles. One cylindrical projection, **Mercator** overcomes this shortcoming by possessing the unique navigational property that any straight drawn on it is a line of constant bearing (**loxodrome**), i.e. a straight line route on the globe crosses the parallels and meridians on the map at the same angles as on the globe. It is used for maps and charts between 15° either side of the equator. Beyond this enlargement of area is a serious drawback, although it is used for navigational charts at all latitudes.

Simple Cylindrical

Cylindrical with two standard parallels

Mercator

Mollweide

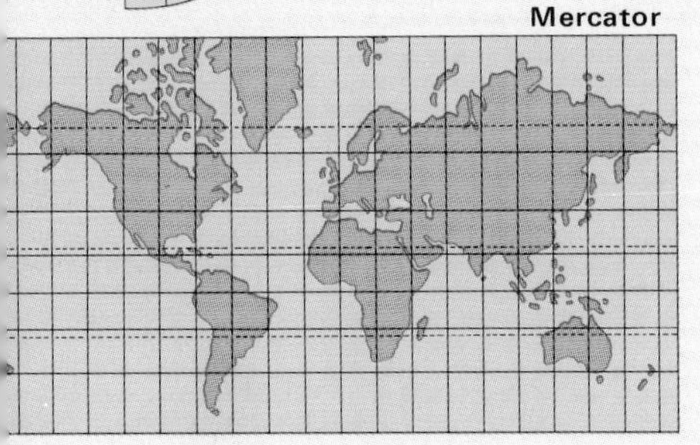

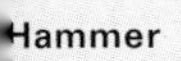

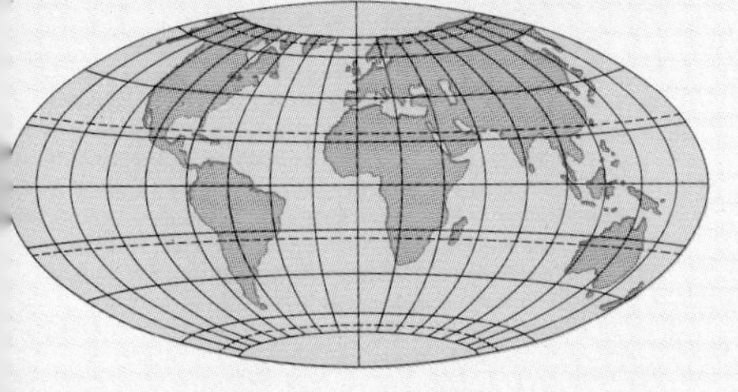

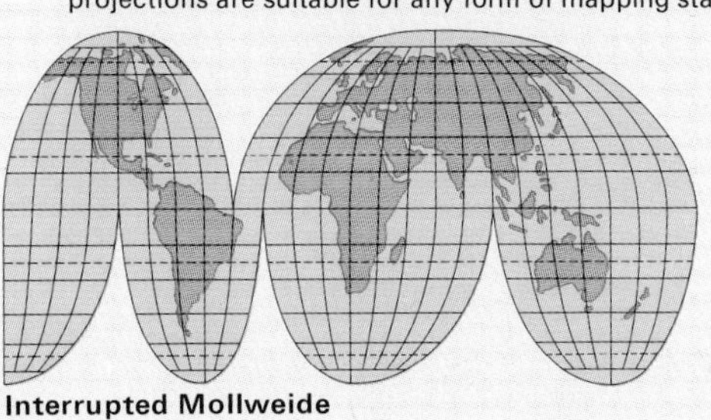

Interrupted Mollweide

Sanson-Flamsteed

Interrupted Sanson-Flamsteed

Hammer

This is not a cylindrical projection, but is developed from the Lambert Azimuthal Equal Area by doubling all the East-West distances along the parallels from the central meridian. Like both Sanson-Flamsteed and Mollweide it is distorted towards its edges but has curved parallels to lessen the distortion.

Mollweide and Sanson-Flamsteed

Both of these projections are termed **pseudo-cylindrical**. They are basically cylindrical projections where parallels have been progressively shortened and drawn to scale towards the poles. This allows them to overcome the gross distortions exhibited by the ordinary cylindrical projections and they are in fact Equal Area, Mollweide's giving a slightly better shape. To improve the shape of the continents still further they, like some other projections can be **Interrupted** as can be seen below, but this is at the expense of contiguous sea areas. These projections can have any central meridian and so can be 'centred' on the Atlantic, Pacific, Asia, America etc. In this form both projections are suitable for any form of mapping statistical distributions.

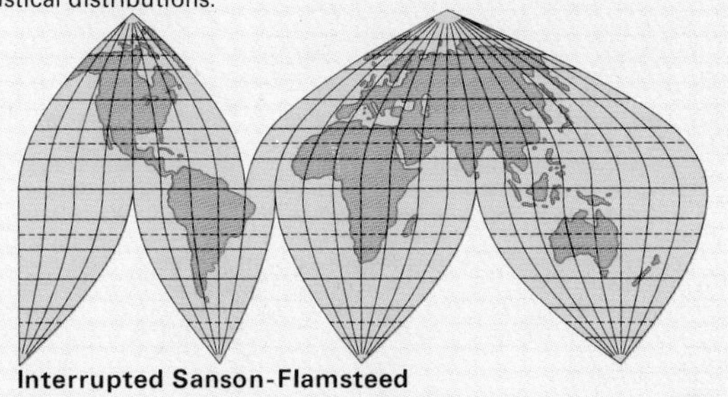

	Population									Land and Agriculture					Energy	Trade	
	Population Total 1995	Population Density 1995	Average annual change 1970-80	Average annual change 1990-95	Birth Rate average 1990-95	Death Rate average 1990-95	Fertility Rate 1992	Life Expectancy average 1990-95	Urban Population 1992	Land area	Arable and Permanent Crops	Permanent grassland	Forest	Agricultural Population 1993	Consumption per capita 1992	Imports per capita	Exports per capita
	millions	persons per km²	%	%	births per thousand population	deaths per thousand population	children	years	%	thousand km²	% of land area	% of land area	% of land area	% of active pop.	tonnes of coal	US $	US $
Afghanistan	19.5	30	1.7	3.3	52	22	6.9	44	22	652	12	46	3	53	0.04	37	11
Albania	3.5	126	2.3	1.3	22	5	2.9	73	36	27.4	25	15	38	46	0.57	128	76
Algeria	27.9	12	3.1	2.2	35	7	3.9	66	53	2,382	3	13	2	23	1.59	331	426
Angola	10.8	8.7	3.3	1.6	47	19	7.2	47	30	1,247	3	23	42	69	0.09	117	358
Argentina	34.7	13	1.7	1.4	20	9	2.8	71	87	2,737	10	52	22	10	1.99	495	382
Armenia	3.6	121	2	1.6	20	6	2.6	76	68	28.4	22	54	14	6	0.75	22	8
Australia	18.1	2.4	1.6	1.4	14	8	1.9	77	85	7,644	7	54	14	5	7.38	2,575	2,418
Austria	8	97	0.1	1.1	12	12	1.5	75	55	82.7	18	24	39	5	4.17	6,085	5,031
Azerbaijan	7.6	87	1.8	1.2	25	6	2.5	71	55	86.1	38	52	...	32	2.2	33	48
Bahamas	0.3	28	2.1	1.8	19	5	2	70	85	10	1	0.2	32	6	3.26	6,927	5,835
Bangladesh	118.3	909	2.8	0.5	41	14	4.4	53	17	130	69	5	15	67	0.08	35	20
Barbados	0.3	611	0.4	0.6	16	9	1.8	75	46	0.43	37	5	0	6	1.81	2,208	688
Belarus	10.5	51	0.7	0.5	15	10	1.7	70	68	208	46	15	33	19	5.1	72	69
Belgium	10.1	309	0.2	0.6	12	12	1.6	76	97	30.5	24	21	21	2	6.87	12,453	12,295
Benin	5.4	49	2.5	2.6	49	18	7.1	48	30	111	17	4	31	59	0.05	42	20
Bolivia	7.9	7.3	2.6	1.6	41	12	4.8	56	58	1,084	2	24	51	40	0.37	171	103
Bosnia-Herzegovina	3.8	75	1	-2.7	14	6	1.6	71	40	51.2	16	31	48	4	1.44	491	541
Botswana	1.5	2.6	3.8	2.6	44	10	4.9	61	25	567	2	58	19	61	...	1,298	1,235
Brazil	161.4	19	2.4	1.4	26	8	2.9	66	76	8,457	7	22	58	23	0.81	183	255
Bulgaria	8.8	79	0.4	-0.5	12	12	1.5	73	69	111	39	16	35	11	3.14	509	423
Burkina Faso	10.3	38	2.3	2.8	47	17	6.5	49	22	274	13	37	24	84	0.03	58	11
Burma	46.6	71	2.4	2.3	30	9	4.2	63	25	658	15	1	49	45	0.05	18	13
Burundi	6.4	250	1.6	3.3	47	16	6.8	50	7	25.7	53	36	3	91	0.02	34	12
Cambodia	10.5	59	-0.8	4.9	37	15	5.3	51	19	177	14	11	66	69	0.03	20	2
Cameroon	13.2	28	2.7	2.8	47	13	5.7	55	42	465	15	18	52	58	0.1	130	201
Canada	30	3.3	1.2	2.5	13	8	1.9	77	77	9,221	5	3	39	3	10.97	4,805	5,017
Central African Rep.	3.3	5.3	2.3	1.8	45	16	5.7	51	38	623	3	5	57	60	0.04	53	36
Chad	6.3	5	2.1	2.1	43	18	5.9	48	21	1,259	3	36	10	72	0.02	51	33
Chile	14.3	19	1.6	1.6	23	6	2.5	72	84	749	6	18	12	12	1.31	806	666
China	1,226.9	132	1.8	1.5	21	7	2	71	28	9,326	10	43	14	65	0.83	87	77
Colombia	34.9	34	2.3	1.2	26	6	2.7	69	71	1,039	5	39	47	25	0.85	195	207
Congo	2.6	7.6	2.8	3.1	46	13	6.3	55	56	342	0	29	62	59	0.34	277	437
Costa Rica	3.4	67	2.8	2.6	26	4	3.1	75	50	51.1	10	46	32	22	0.65	966	693
Croatia	4.9	88	0.4	0.5	12	11	1.7	71	52	56.4	24	36	37	17	1.82	1,162	947
Cuba	11	101	1.3	0.8	17	7	1.8	76	75	110	30	27	21	18	1.15	202	189
Cyprus	0.7	80	0.2	1.2	17	8	2.5	77	53	9.24	17	1	13	19	2.89	3,471	1,210
Czech Rep.	10.5	133	0.5	0.4	12	12	1.8	73	65	77.3	43	11	34	12	5.61	1,437	1,386
Denmark	5.2	123	0.4	0.3	11	11	1.7	76	86	42.4	60	5	10	4	4.66	5,687	6,920
Dominican Rep.	7.8	162	2.6	1.7	28	6	3.1	68	62	48.4	30	43	13	33	0.61	321	73
Ecuador	11.4	41	3	1.5	31	7	3.5	67	56	277	11	18	37	28	0.77	233	264
Egypt	64.1	64	2.1	4	31	9	3.9	62	44	995	3	0	0	39	0.7	145	40
El Salvador	5.7	277	2.3	1.8	36	7	4	66	44	20.7	35	29	5	35	0.4	348	133
Estonia	1.5	34	0.8	-0.7	15	12	1.6	70	72	43.2	33	21	43	12	5.36	1,114	872
Ethiopia	55.5	50	2.4	3.9	48	18	7	47	13	1,158	13	41	24	73	0.03	13	3
Finland	5.1	17	0.4	0.6	12	10	1.9	76	62	305	8	0.4	76	7	6.57	3,564	4,635
France	58.3	106	0.6	0.8	13	10	1.7	77	73	550	35	20	27	5	5.43	3,482	3,577
Gabon	1.3	5.1	4.8	2.6	43	16	5.3	54	48	258	2	18	77	65	0.86	749	1,926
Gambia, The	1.1	114	3.3	5.9	45	20	5.6	45	24	10	18	9	15	80	0.1	193	32
Georgia	5.4	78	0.8	0	16	9	2.1	73	57	69.7	70	29	0.4	15	1.29	61	38
Germany	82	235	0.1	0.6	11	12	1.3	75	86	349	34	15	30	4	5.89	4,496	5,318
Ghana	17.5	77	2.2	3.1	44	12	6	56	35	228	12	22	35	48	0.14	88	70
Greece	10.5	82	0.9	0.9	12	10	1.4	77	64	129	30	41	20	23	3.24	2,253	922
Guatemala	10.6	98	2.8	2.9	39	8	5.4	65	40	108	17	13	33	49	0.27	267	133
Guinea	6.7	27	1.4	3.1	51	20	7	45	28	246	3	22	59	72	0.08	103	118
Guinea-Bissau	1.1	38	4.2	2.2	43	21	5.8	44	21	28.1	12	38	38	77	0.1	78	18
Guyana	0.8	4.2	0.7	0.9	24	7	2.6	65	35	197	2	6	83	21	0.49	472	362
Haiti	7.2	261	1.7	2	35	12	4.8	57	30	27.6	33	18	1	62	0.05	56	16
Honduras	5.9	53	3.4	2.9	37	7	4.9	66	42	112	17	23	28	53	0.27	202	146
Hong Kong	6	6,061	2.5	0.5	12	6	1.2	78	94	0.99	7	1	22	1	2.29	23,422	22,339
Hungary	10.5	114	0.4	-0.1	12	13	1.7	72	63	92.3	54	13	19	10	3.34	1,217	836
Iceland	0.3	2.7	1.1	1.3	15	7	2.2	78	91	100	0	23	1	6	6.22	5,162	5,385
India	943	317	2.2	2.7	31	10	3.8	60	26	2,973	57	4	23	66	0.35	26	24

Wealth GNP 1993 million US $	GNP per capita 1993 US $	Annual rate of change GNP per capita 1985-93 %	GDP share agriculture %	GDP share industry %	GDP share services %	Real GDP per capita 1992 US $	Social Indicators Human Development Index 1992	Food Intake calories per day	Population per doctor 1988-91 persons	% of GNP spent on health 1991 %	% of GNP spent on education 1991 %	% of GNP spent on military 1992 %	Adult Illiteracy 1992 %	Aid given (*) and received per capita 1993 US $	
3,100	220	-6	52	33	15	819	0.228	1,523	7,692	...	2	7.7	71	12.7	Afghanistan
1,167	340	-7	37	18	46	3,500	0.739	2,605	730	4	...	2.3	15	...	Albania
44,347	1,650	-2.2	13	43	43	4,870	0.732	2,897	1,064	5.4	9.1	2.7	43	12.4	Algeria
5,700	600	-0.9	12	43	45	751	0.291	1,839	25,000	7.5	7.3	35.5	57	29.2	Angola
244,013	7,290	1.4	6	31	63	8,860	0.882	2,880	329	2.5	3.1	1.7	4	8.3	Argentina
2,471	660	-11.7	48	30	22	2,420	0.715	...	260	4.2	3.9	2.5	1	...	Armenia
309,967	17,510	1.1	3	29	68	18,220	0.927	3,179	400	8.6	5.5	2.4	1	54.0*	Australia
183,530	23,120	2.1	2	35	62	18,710	0.925	3,497	230	8.5	5.4	0.9	1	68.1*	Austria
5,424	730	-9.4	22	52	26	2,550	0.696	...	250	4.3	3.9	1.9	4	...	Azerbaijan
3,059	11,500	-0.2	2	14	83	17,360	0.894	2,624	750	14.5	4.4	2.3	2	7.5	Bahamas
25,882	220	1.8	30	17	52	1,230	0.364	2,019	12,500	1.4	2	1.3	64	11.8	Bangladesh
1,620	6,240	-0.4	7	21	73	9,667	0.9	3,207	1,000	12	8	0	3	3.8	Barbados
29,290	2,840	-0.2	17	54	29	6,440	0.866	...	282	3.2	3.9	4.5	2	...	Belarus
213,435	21,210	2.4	2	30	68	18,630	0.926	3,681	298	8.1	5.4	1.8	1	80.7*	Belgium
2,189	420	-1.1	36	13	51	1,630	0.332	2,532	14,286	2.8	5.1	1.3	67	50.7	Benin
5,472	770	1.4	33	32	35	2,410	0.588	2,094	2,564	2.4	3	1.9	19	80.7	Bolivia
10,000	2,500	1.8	11	61	28	...	...	...	624	...	...	...	1	...	Bosnia-Herzegovina
3,630	2,590	5.7	6	47	47	5,120	0.763	2,266	4,762	4.7	8.4	3.1	33	79.9	Botswana
471,978	3,020	-0.6	10	37	53	5,240	0.804	2,824	847	2.8	4.6	0.7	18	1.5	Brazil
9,773	1,160	-2.8	13	38	49	4,250	0.796	2,831	315	5.4	5.4	5.7	7	...	Bulgaria
2,928	300	0	44	20	37	810	0.228	2,387	57,310	7	2.3	4.3	83	43.6	Burkina Faso
41,000	950	5	63	9	28	751	0.457	2,598	12,500	6.8	1.9	3.1	18	2.3	Burma
1,102	180	0.6	52	21	27	720	0.286	1,941	16,667	1.7	3.5	5	67	45.8	Burundi
6,000	600	7.5	40	30	30	1,250	0.337	2,021	9,500	...	...	4.8	62	32.3	Cambodia
9,663	770	-7.3	29	25	47	2,390	0.503	1,981	12,500	1	3.4	1.6	40	51.3	Cameroon
574,884	20,670	0.4	3	32	65	20,520	0.95	3,094	446	9.9	7.4	2	1	82.0*	Canada
1,263	390	-3	50	14	36	1,130	0.361	1,690	25,000	2.6	2.8	2	46	57	Central African Rep.
1,248	200	0.5	44	22	35	760	0.296	1,989	30,030	4.7	2.3	2.6	55	38.3	Chad
42,454	3,070	6.1	8	41	50	8,410	0.88	2,582	943	3.4	3.7	2.7	5	12.8	Chile
581,109	490	6.5	19	48	33	1,950	0.594	2,727	1,000	2.1	2.3	5	21	2.7	China
50,119	1,400	2.3	16	35	50	5,480	0.836	2,677	1,064	1.8	2.9	2.4	10	3	Colombia
2,318	920	-1.9	11	35	53	2,870	0.538	2,296	3,571	...	5.6	3.8	29	54.4	Congo
7,041	2,160	2.6	15	26	59	5,480	0.883	2,883	1,136	30	4.6	0.9	6	30	Costa Rica
22,000	4,500	-20	12	50	38	...	...	...	500	...	...	...	1	...	Croatia
13,500	1,250	-10	16	52	32	3,412	0.769	2,833	332	...	6.6	5	5	2.9	Cuba
7,539	10,380	5.2	6	25	69	15,050	0.906	3,779	585	6.5	3.6	7.1	6	48.2	Cyprus
28,192	2,730	-2	9	74	17	7,690	0.872	...	250	5.9	5	2.6	1	...	Czech Rep.
137,610	26,510	1.1	4	27	69	19,080	0.92	3,664	360	7	6.1	2	1	258.2*	Denmark
8,039	1,080	0.3	15	23	62	3,280	0.705	2,286	935	2.1	1.5	1.4	19	...	Dominican Rep.
13,217	1,170	0.8	12	38	50	4,350	0.784	2,583	671	11	2.8	2.2	12	21.6	Ecuador
36,679	660	0.7	18	22	60	3,540	0.613	3,335	1,300	1	6.7	6	51	37.4	Egypt
7,233	1,320	1.2	9	25	66	2,250	0.579	2,663	1,563	2.6	1.8	1.7	30	69.2	El Salvador
4,703	3,040	-5.2	8	29	63	6,690	0.862	...	210	3.9	...	0.6	1	...	Estonia
5,200	100	-1.8	60	10	29	330	0.227	1,610	32,500	2.3	4.8	20.1	67	23.3	Ethiopia
96,220	18,970	-0.3	5	31	64	16,270	0.934	3,018	405	8.9	6.6	1.9	1	70.0*	Finland
1,289,235	22,360	1.8	3	29	69	19,510	0.93	3,633	333	9.1	6	3.4	1	137.3*	France
5,004	4,050	-1.7	8	45	47	3,913	0.579	2,500	2,500	...	5.7	3.7	41	81.7	Gabon
372	360	1	28	15	58	1,260	0.299	2,360	10,000	6.5	3.8	0.7	64	92.1	Gambia, The
3,071	560	-16.4	58	22	20	2,300	0.709	...	170	4.5	...	3.2	1	...	Georgia
1,902,995	23,560	1.9	1	38	61	21,120	0.921	3,344	370	9.1	5.4	2.4	1	85.7*	Germany
7,036	430	1.3	48	16	36	2,110	0.482	2,199	25,000	1.7	3.3	0.8	39	37.9	Ghana
76,698	7,390	1.3	18	32	50	8,310	0.907	3,815	313	4.8	3	5.6	6	...	Greece
11,092	1,110	0.8	25	19	55	3,330	0.591	2,255	4,000	2.1	1.4	1.1	46	20.1	Guatemala
3,170	510	1.3	24	31	45	592	0.237	2,389	7,692	2.3	2.2	1.3	67	66.6	Guinea
233	220	1.6	45	19	36	820	0.293	2,556	6,000	1.4	2.8	2.4	48	95.3	Guinea-Bissau
285	350	0.6	30	38	32	1,800	0.622	2,384	6,000	...	4.7	1	2	104.2	Guyana
5,200	800	-3.4	39	16	46	1,046	0.362	1,706	7,143	3.2	1.8	2.1	57	18.6	Haiti
3,220	580	0	20	30	50	2,000	0.578	2,305	1,266	2.9	4.6	1.5	29	58.9	Honduras
104,731	17,860	5.3	0	21	79	20,340	0.905	3,129	1,100	1.1	3	...	9	5.7	Hong Kong
34,254	3,330	0	6	28	66	6,580	0.856	3,503	312	6	6.7	3.5	1	...	Hungary
6,236	23,620	0.1	12	28	60	17,660	0.933	3,058	425	8.3	6	0	1	...	Iceland
262,810	290	3	31	27	41	1,230	0.439	2,395	2,439	1.3	3.5	2.5	50	1.7	India

	Population									Land and Agriculture					Energy	Trade	
	Population Total 1995	Population Density 1995	Average annual change 1970-80	Average annual change 1990-95	Birth Rate average 1990-95	Death Rate average 1990-95	Fertility Rate 1992	Life Expectancy average 1990-95	Urban Population 1992	Land area	Arable and Permanent Crops	Permanent grassland	Forest	Agricultural Population 1993	Consumption per capita 1992	Imports per capita	Exports per capita
	millions	persons per km²	%	%	births per thousand population	deaths per thousand population	children	years	%	thousand km²	% of land area	% of land area	% of land area	% of active pop.	tonnes of coal	US $	US $
Indonesia	198.6	110	2.3	2.1	27	9	2.9	63	33	1,812	12	7	60	46	0.38	148	178
Iran	68.9	42	3.2	4.8	33	7	5	67	57	1,636	11	27	11	25	1.66	186	209
Iraq	20.2	46	3.6	1.3	41	7	5.7	66	73	437	12	9	4	18	1.25	257	...
Ireland	3.6	52	1.4	0.5	18	8	2.1	75	57	68.9	13	68	5	12	4	6,008	8,121
Israel	5.7	276	2.7	4.4	21	7	2.9	76	92	20.6	21	7	6	4	3.27	4,301	2,810
Italy	57.2	194	0.5	0	11	11	1.3	76	67	294	41	17	23	6	4.02	3,316	3,133
Ivory Coast	14.3	45	4	3.6	50	13	7.4	55	42	318	12	41	22	53	0.21	189	254
Jamaica	2.7	249	1.3	1.9	22	6	2.4	74	52	10.8	20	24	17	26	1.51	879	439
Japan	125.2	332	1.1	0.3	12	8	1.5	79	77	377	12	2	67	6	4.74	1,940	2,909
Jordan	5.5	62	2.4	6.7	39	5	5.6	68	70	88.9	5	9	1	5	1.13	716	252
Kazakhstan	17.1	63	1.3	0.4	22	8	2.5	69	58	2,670	13	69	6	18	6.35	30	64
Kenya	28.2	50	3.8	3.3	47	10	6.3	61	25	570	4	67	4	76	0.11	61	49
Korea, North	23.9	199	2.2	1.9	25	5	2.4	71	60	120	17	0.4	74	31	4.26	95	52
Korea, South	45.1	457	1.8	1.1	15	6	1.7	71	77	98.7	21	1	65	22	3.19	1,902	1,865
Kyrgyzstan	4.7	24	2	1.5	29	7	3.7	69	39	191	14	85	0	33	1.77	25	25
Laos	4.9	21	1.7	3.5	44	15	6.7	51	20	231	3	3	54	70	0.04	41	21
Latvia	2.6	41	0.7	-1	14	12	1.6	70	72	64.1	68	32	...	17	3.24	487	388
Lebanon	3	290	0.8	1.9	30	8	3.1	67	86	10.2	30	1	8	7	1.78	1,401	186
Lesotho	2.1	68	2.3	3.4	40	11	5.2	59	21	30.4	11	66	0	77	...	332	28
Liberia	3.1	32	3.1	5.1	47	14	6.8	56	44	96.8	4	59	18	69	0.06	116	169
Libya	5.4	3.1	4.4	3.5	43	8	6.4	63	84	1,760	1	8	0.4	13	3.46	1,237	2,590
Lithuania	3.7	57	0.9	0	15	10	1.8	72	70	65.2	35	17	28	18	4.16	138	188
Luxembourg	0.4	158	0.7	1.8	12	11	1.7	75	88	2.6	...	...	...	...	14	20,288	15,693
Macedonia	2.2	85	1.6	1.4	17	7	1.9	70	59	24.9	16	26	37	8	0.98	566	498
Madagascar	15.2	26	2.7	6.3	45	13	6.1	56	25	582	5	58	27	75	0.04	33	19
Malawi	9.8	104	3.2	3.4	55	19	7.2	49	12	94.1	18	20	36	72	0.04	60	35
Malaysia	20.2	61	2.4	2.4	28	5	3.6	71	51	329	15	0	59	30	1.8	2,397	2,474
Mali	10.7	8.8	2.3	5.6	51	19	7.1	46	25	1,220	2	25	6	79	0.02	43	31
Malta	0.4	1,146	1.1	0.8	13	9	2.1	74	88	0.32	41	0	0	4	2	6,017	3,747
Mauritania	2.3	2.2	2.4	2.3	46	18	5.4	48	50	1,025	0	38	4	63	0.62	114	224
Mexico	93.3	49	2.9	1.6	27	5	3.2	70	74	1,909	13	39	21	28	1.89	853	654
Moldova	4.4	134	1.1	0.3	18	9	2.1	69	49	33.7	68	12	...	36	1.69	42	40
Mongolia	2.4	1.5	2.8	1.9	34	8	3.6	64	59	1,567	1	80	9	28	1.58	345	247
Morocco	26.9	60	2.4	1.4	33	8	3.8	63	47	446	22	47	18	34	0.41	275	131
Mozambique	17.8	23	2.6	4.6	44	17	6.5	49	30	784	4	56	18	81	0.03	61	8
Namibia	1.6	2	2.5	2.3	42	11	5.3	59	34	823	1	46	22	33	...	729	778
Nepal	22	160	2.6	2.8	36	13	5.4	54	12	137	17	15	39	91	...	42	19
Netherlands	15.5	457	0.8	0.7	13	9	1.6	78	89	33.9	27	31	10	3	7.12	7,951	8,578
New Zealand	3.6	13	1	1	16	8	2.2	76	86	268	2	51	28	9	5.94	2,785	3,045
Nicaragua	4.5	38	3	3.3	39	7	5	66	62	119	11	46	27	35	0.42	216	53
Niger	9.1	7.2	3	3.4	51	19	7.4	47	16	1,267	3	7	1	86	0.06	43	38
Nigeria	108.4	119	2.2	0	47	14	6.5	53	37	911	36	44	12	64	0.21	82	115
Norway	4.4	14	0.5	0.7	13	11	1.9	78	73	307	3	0.4	27	5	6.71	5,543	7,373
Pakistan	143.6	186	2.6	5.1	42	11	6.2	59	33	771	27	6	5	48	0.3	77	54
Panama	2.6	35	2.5	1.7	25	5	2.9	73	52	74.4	9	20	43	23	0.86	851	198
Papua New Guinea	4.3	9.5	2.5	2.1	33	11	5.1	56	15	453	1	0.2	84	64	0.28	314	634
Paraguay	5	13	3	3.1	33	6	4.3	67	51	397	6	55	32	46	0.33	315	146
Peru	23.6	18	2.7	1.1	29	8	3.4	65	71	1,280	3	21	53	33	0.48	215	154
Philippines	67.2	225	2.6	1.5	30	7	3.9	65	51	298	31	4	34	45	0.4	263	197
Poland	38.6	127	0.9	0.1	15	10	1.9	72	63	304	48	13	29	19	3.48	490	368
Portugal	10.6	115	0.8	0.6	13	10	1.6	74	34	92	35	9	36	14	2.11	2,461	1,556
Puerto Rico	3.7	416	1.7	1.2	18	8	2.3	76	77	8.86	14	38	20	3	2.27	3,200	3,700
Romania	22.9	99	0.9	-0.3	15	11	1.5	72	54	230	43	21	29	18	2.7	277	264
Russia	148.4	8.7	0.6	0	15	10	1.5	69	75	16,996	8	6	45	14	7.36	261	427
Rwanda	7.9	320	3.3	1.9	50	16	6.6	51	6	24.7	47	18	22	91	0.03	39	9
Saudi Arabia	18.4	8.6	5	5.4	42	7	6.4	66	78	2,150	2	56	1	37	6.1	1,649	2,987
Senegal	8.3	43	2.9	2.5	44	16	6.1	49	41	193	12	16	54	78	0.15	172	99
Sierra Leone	4.5	62	2.1	1.5	48	22	6.5	43	34	71.6	8	31	28	60	0.04	34	28
Singapore	3	4,902	1	2.1	16	6	1.7	75	100	0.61	2	0	5	1	8.5	29,697	25,787
Slovak Rep.	5.4	110	1.7	0.4	14	10	1.9	71	57	48.1	34	17	41	14	4.25	1,225	1,230
Slovenia	2	99	0.9	0.3	13	10	1.3	74	50	20.3	12	32	50	13	1.88	3,736	3,515
Somalia	9.2	15	3.8	1.1	47	18	7	47	25	627	2	69	14	68	0.05	16	13

Wealth							Social Indicators							Aid	
GNP 1993	GNP per capita 1993	Annual rate of change GNP per capita 1985-93	GDP share agriculture	GDP share industry	GDP share services	Real GDP per capita 1992	Human Development Index 1992	Food Intake	Population per doctor 1988-91	% of GNP spent on health 1991	% of GNP spent on education 1991	% of GNP spent on military 1992	Adult Illiteracy 1992	given (*) and received per capita 1993	
million US $	US $	%	%	%	%	US $		calories per day	persons	%	%	%	%	US $	
136,991	730	4.8	19	40	42	2,950	0.637	2,752	7,143	0.7	2.2	1.4	17	10.6	Indonesia
300,000	4,750	3	21	36	43	5,420	0.77	2,860	3,300	1.5	4.1	7.1	35	2.2	Iran
38,000	2,000	...	20	42	38	3,413	0.617	2,121	1,667	...	5.1	21.1	45	8.7	Iraq
44,906	12,580	4.8	8	10	82	12,830	0.915	3,847	633	8	5.9	1.2	1	22.8*	Ireland
72,662	13,760	2.3	7	93	0	14,700	0.907	3,050	300	4.2	6	11.1	5	243	Israel
1,134,980	19,620	1.9	3	32	65	18,090	0.912	3,561	210	8.3	4.1	2	3	53.3*	Italy
8,397	630	-5.2	37	24	39	1,710	0.369	2,491	11,111	1.7	7.2	0.8	63	63.1	Ivory Coast
3,362	1,390	3.1	8	41	51	3,200	0.721	2,607	7,143	...	6.1	0.7	16	46	Jamaica
3,926,668	31,450	3.6	2	41	57	20,520	0.937	2,903	600	6.8	5	1	1	90.3*	Japan
4,893	1,190	-5.9	8	26	66	4,270	0.758	3,022	649	1.8	5.9	11.2	16	64.2	Jordan
26,490	1,540	-4.6	29	41	30	4,270	0.798	...	250	4.4	...	3.8	2	...	Kazakhstan
6,743	270	0.3	29	17	54	1,400	0.481	2,075	10,000	2.7	6.8	2.8	25	35.2	Kenya
25,000	1,000	-8	...	...	...	3,026	0.733	2,833	400	...	3.7	25.7	5	0.7	Korea, North
338,062	7,670	8.1	7	44	50	9,250	0.882	3,285	1,205	2.7	3.6	3.8	3	0.8	Korea, South
3,752	830	-2.1	44	35	21	2,850	0.717	...	300	5	...	0.7	3	...	Kyrgyzstan
1,295	290	2.1	51	18	31	1,760	0.42	2,259	4,545	1	1.1	6.1	46	43	Laos
5,257	2,030	-4.5	15	32	54	6,060	0.857	...	200	6.1	...	0.5	1	...	Latvia
6,100	1,750	4.2	10	21	69	2,500	0.675	3,317	413	...	2	5	9	47	Lebanon
1,254	660	0.8	10	47	43	1,060	0.473	2,201	25,000	11.5	3.8	5.3	31	67.9	Lesotho
2,300	800	1.5	37	28	35	1,045	0.325	1,640	9,250	5.1	5.7	4.8	65	42.5	Liberia
32,000	6,500	1	6	50	44	9,782	0.768	3,308	962	2.7	9.6	6.3	28	1.2	Libya
4,891	1,310	-6.4	21	41	38	3,700	0.769	...	230	3.6	..	0.7	2	...	Lithuania
14,233	35,850	2.7	1	34	65	21,520	0.893	...	500	6.6	5.8	1.2	1	125.0*	Luxembourg
1,709	780	-15	17	60	23	...	...	...	425	...	...	...	10	...	Macedonia
3,039	240	-1.7	34	14	52	710	0.432	2,135	8,333	1.3	1.5	1.1	19	26.6	Madagascar
2,034	220	0.4	39	18	43	820	0.33	1,825	45,740	2.9	3.4	1.4	46	47.9	Malawi
60,061	3,160	5.7	19	35	46	7,790	0.822	2,888	2,564	1.3	6.9	4.8	18	5.2	Malaysia
2,744	300	-4.3	42	15	42	550	0.222	2,278	20,000	2.8	3.2	2.9	73	35.7	Mali
2,500	6,800	4.5	3	35	62	8,281	0.88	3,486	750	7.4	4.4	1.1	13	...	Malta
1,087	510	-0.1	27	30	42	1,650	0.359	2,685	16,667	...	4.7	3.1	64	153.2	Mauritania
324,951	3,750	0.9	8	28	63	7,300	0.842	3,146	621	1.6	4.1	0.5	13	4.4	Mexico
5,160	1,180	-5.4	35	48	18	3,670	0.757	...	250	3.9	26	2.1	4	...	Moldova
943	400	-0.3	21	47	33	2,389	0.604	1,899	389	...	8.5	5.9	19	48.3	Mongolia
27,645	1,030	0.9	14	32	53	3,370	0.554	2,984	4,500	0.9	5.5	4	59	23.3	Morocco
1,375	80	1.9	33	12	55	380	0.246	1,680	33,333	4.4	6.3	10.2	63	76.5	Mozambique
2,594	1,660	2.3	10	27	63	4,020	0.611	2,134	4,545	9.7	4.7	2.9	60	113.6	Namibia
3,174	160	1.8	43	21	36	1,170	0.343	1,957	16,667	2.2	2	1.1	74	17.3	Nepal
316,404	20,710	2	4	28	68	17,780	0.936	3,222	398	8.7	5.8	2.4	1	165.1*	Netherlands
44,674	12,900	0.2	7	26	67	14,990	0.919	3,669	521	7.7	5.8	1.6	1	28.3*	New Zealand
1,421	360	-6.2	30	20	50	2,790	0.611	2,293	2,000	6.7	4.1	10.9	35	81.9	Nicaragua
2,313	270	-2.1	39	18	44	820	0.207	2,257	34,850	3.4	3.1	1	88	39.1	Niger
32,988	310	3.2	33	43	24	1,560	0.406	2,124	5,882	1.2	1.7	0.7	47		Nigeria
113,527	26,340	0.5	3	35	62	18,580	0.932	3,244	309	8.4	7.6	3.3	1	239.2*	Norway
53,250	430	1.5	25	25	50	2,890	0.483	2,315	2,000	1.8	3.4	7.7	64	8	Pakistan
6,621	2,580	-0.7	10	18	72	5,600	0.856	2,242	562	21.8	5.5	1.2	10	31.1	Panama
4,637	1,120	1.1	26	43	31	2,410	0.508	2,613	12,500	2.8	4.7	1.8	30	87.3	Papua New Guinea
6,995	1,500	1.3	26	21	53	3,390	0.723	2,670	1,587	1.2	1.9	2	9	28.3	Paraguay
34,030	1,490	-3.5	11	43	46	3,300	0.709	1,882	1,031	1.9	1.5	3.8	13	24.5	Peru
54,609	830	1.6	22	33	45	2,550	0.677	2,257	8,333	1	2.9	2.2	6	22.9	Philippines
87,315	2,270	-1.8	6	39	55	4,830	0.855	3,301	467	5.1	4.9	2.3	1	...	Poland
77,749	7,890	4.7	6	38	56	9,850	0.874	3,634	352	6.2	5.5	2.9	14	24.9*	Portugal
25,317	7,020	1.8	1	41	58	6,500	...	...	350	10.7	8.2	...	11	...	Puerto Rico
25,427	1,120	-6.5	21	40	40	2,840	0.703	3,051	552	3.9	3.1	2.9	3	...	Romania
348,413	2,350	-5	12	48	40	6,140	0.849	...	210	3	8.2	...	1	...	Russia
1,499	200	-3.5	41	22	38	710	0.332	1,821	40,610	1.9	4.2	6.8	43	52.2	Rwanda
131,000	8,000	-0.9	6	50	43	9,880	0.762	2,735	704	3.1	6.2	11.8	39	1.8	Saudi Arabia
5,867	730	-0.3	19	19	61	1,750	0.34	2,262	16,667	2.3	3.7	2.1	69	62.8	Senegal
647	140	-0.6	38	16	46	880	0.221	1,694	12,500	1.7	1.4	2.3	71	44.7	Sierra Leone
55,372	19,310	6.1	0	36	64	18,330	0.878	...	725	1.1	3.4	5.4	10	8.2	Singapore
10,145	1,900	-2.6	6	44	50	6,690	0.872	...	275	...	7	...	1	...	Slovak Rep.
12,566	6,310	-1	8	61	31	6,500	...	...	500	...	5.7	...	1	...	Slovenia
3,400	500	-2.3	65	9	26	1,001	0.246	1,499	14,000	0.9	0.4	3.2	73	98.4	Somalia

	Population									Land and Agriculture					Energy	Trade	
	Population Total 1995	Population Density 1995	Average annual change 1970-80	Average annual change 1990-95	Birth Rate average 1990-95	Death Rate average 1990-95	Fertility Rate 1992	Life Expectancy average 1990-95	Urban Population 1992	Land area	Arable and Permanent Crops	Permanent grassland	Forest	Agricultural Population 1993	Consumption per capita 1992	Imports per capita	Exports per capita
	millions	persons per km²	%	%	births per thousand population	deaths per thousand population	children	years	%	thousand km²	% of land area	% of land area	% of land area	% of active pop.	tonnes of coal	US $	US $
South Africa	44	36	2.3	3	31	9	4.1	63	50	1,221	11	67	4	13	2.49	556	595
Spain	39.7	79	1.1	0.2	13	9	1.2	77	76	499	40	21	32	9	3.11	2,095	1,609
Sri Lanka	18.4	284	1.7	1.3	21	6	2.5	72	22	64.6	29	7	32	51	0.15	212	158
Sudan	30	13	3	3.5	43	14	5.7	52	23	2376	14	46	19	57	0.06	44	21
Surinam	0.4	2.7	-0.6	0.8	25	6	2.7	70	49	156	6	0.1	95	15	1.79	1,180	1,180
Swaziland	0.8	49	3	2	47	11	4.9	58	29	17.2	11	62	7	64	...	835	700
Sweden	8.9	22	0.3	1	13	12	2.1	78	83	412	12	1	68	3	6.94	4,879	5,699
Switzerland	7.3	184	0.2	1.9	12	10	1.6	78	60	39.6	12	28	32	4	4.88	8,173	8,457
Syria	14.6	80	3.5	3.1	43	6	5.9	67	51	184	32	44	4	23	1.29	311	229
Taiwan	21.1	586	2	0.7	17	5	1.7	75	75	36	26	11	52	20	...	3,670	4,044
Tajikistan	6.1	43	3	2.8	37	6	4.9	70	32	143	19	77	...	43	0.001	57	62
Tanzania	29.7	34	3.4	3	50	13	5.9	56	22	884	4	40	46	79	0.04	40	12
Thailand	58.4	114	2.7	0.4	20	7	2.1	67	19	511	39	2	26	62	0.89	786	635
Togo	4.1	76	2.6	3.2	45	13	6.6	55	30	54.4	12	33	27	69	0.08	122	70
Trinidad & Tobago	1.3	252	1.1	0.2	23	6	2.4	72	70	5.1	24	2	42	7	8.42	1,149	1,279
Tunisia	8.9	57	2.2	2	27	6	3.2	68	56	155	31	26	4	21	0.73	725	444
Turkey	61.3	80	2.3	0.9	27	8	3.4	66	64	770	36	16	26	46	1.05	485	257
Turkmenistan	4.1	8.4	2.7	2.3	33	7	4	67	45	488	3	96	...	43	4.13	128	268
Uganda	21.5	108	3	4.1	52	14	7.3	53	12	200	34	9	28	79	0.03	42	19
Ukraine	52	90	0.6	0.1	13	12	1.6	71	69	604	56	12	14	19	6	192	187
United Kingdom	58.3	241	0.1	0.4	14	12	1.8	76	89	242	27	46	10	2	5.4	3,562	3,135
United States	263.6	28	1.1	1.1	14	9	2.1	76	76	9,573	20	25	30	2	10.74	2,644	1,967
Uruguay	3.2	18	0.4	0.6	17	10	2.3	73	90	175	7	77	4	13	0.83	738	522
Uzbekistan	22.8	51	2.9	2.2	32	6	3.9	70	41	425	10	53	4	29	3.22	50	45
Venezuela	21.8	25	3.5	2	28	5	3.3	70	91	882	4	20	34	10	3.21	530	694
Vietnam	74.6	229	2.3	2.3	30	8	3.9	64	20	325	21	1	30	59	0.12	28	29
Yemen	14.6	28	1.9	5.3	51	14	7.6	52	31	528	3	30	4	54	0.33	136	10
Yugoslavia	10.9	107	1	1.1	15	9	2.1	71	52	102	36	21	30	5	1.6	1,134	917
Zaïre	44.5	20	2.9	4.6	45	13	6.7	54	29	2,267	3	7	77	64	0.06	9	9
Zambia	9.5	13	3.2	3.3	50	12	6	55	42	743	7	40	39	68	0.2	102	122
Zimbabwe	11.5	30	3.1	4.1	40	9	5	61	30	387	7	13	49	67	0.72	211	137

Many figures for Luxembourg are included in those for Belgium.

For energy the figures for South Africa include those for Botswana, Lesotho, Swaziland and Namibia.

The sign ... means that figures are not available.

Population Total. This is an estimate for the mid-year, 1995.

Population Density. This is the total population divided by the land area, both quoted in the table.

Population Change. This shows the average annual percentage change for the two periods 1970-80 and 1990-95.

Birth and Death Rates and Life Expectancy. These are UN estimates. The Birth and Death rates are the number of those occurrences per year, per thousand population. Life Expectancy is the number of years that a child born today can expect to live if the levels of mortality of today last throughout its life. The figure is the average of that for men and women.

Fertility Rate. This is the average number of children born to a woman in her lifetime.

Urban Population. This is the percentage of the total population living in urban areas. The definition of urban is that of the individual nations and often includes quite small towns.

Land Area. This is the total area of the country less the area covered by major lakes and rivers.

Arable Land and Permanent Crops This excludes fallow land but includes temporary pasture.

Forest and Woodland. This includes natural and planted woodland and land recently cleared of timber which will be replanted.

Agricultural Population. This is the percentage of the economically active population working in agriculture. It includes those working in forestry, hunting and fishing.

Energy. All forms of energy have been expressed in an approximate equivalent of tonnes of coal per person.

Trade. The trade figures are for 1993 or 1994. In a few cases the figure is older than this but is the latest available. The total Import and Export figures have been divided by the population to give a figure in US $ per capita.

Gross National Product (GNP). This figure is an estimate of the value of a country's production and the average production per person for 1993, in US $. The GNP measures the value of goods and services produced in a country, plus the balance, positive or negative, of income from abroad, for example, from investments, interest on capital, money returned from workers abroad, etc. The average annual rate of change is for the GNP per capita during the period 1985–93. The Gross Domestic Product (GDP), is the GNP less the foreign balances. The adjoining three columns show the percentage contribution to the GDP made by the agricultural, mining and manufacturing and service sectors of the economy.

Real GDP per capita. Using exchange rates to convert national currencies into US $ makes no attempt to reflect the varying domestic purchasing powers of the local currency. The UN has made these estimates of Real GDP taking into account these local purchasing values.

Human Development Index. This is a calculation made by the UN Development Programme using 1992 data and takes into account not only national income, but also life expectancy, adult literacy and the years in education. It is a measure of national human progress. The wealthy developed countries have an index approaching 1, and the figures range down to some of the poorer with an index of less than 0.1.

Food Intake. The figures are the average intake of calories per person per day.

Adult Illiteracy. This is the percentage of the population aged 15 and over who cannot read or write a simple sentence.

Aid. The bulk of the table is concerned with aid received but aid given is shown by an asterisk.

To convert square kilometres to square miles multiply by 0.39.

Wealth GNP 1993	GNP per capita 1993	Annual rate of change GNP per capita 1985-93	GDP share agriculture	GDP share industry	GDP share services	Real GDP per capita 1992	Social Indicators Human Development Index 1992	Food Intake	Population per doctor 1988-91	% of GNP spent on health 1991	% of GNP spent on education 1991	% of GNP spent on military 1992	Adult Illiteracy 1992	Aid given (*) and received per capita 1993	
million US $	US $	%	%	%	%	US $		calories per day	persons	%	%	%	%	US $	
118,057	2,900	-1.5	4	40	56	3,799	0.705	2,695	1,750	3.2	3.8	3	19	4.9	South Africa
533,986	13,650	3.1	5	35	61	13,400	0.93	3,708	262	6.5	5.6	1.7	2	31.0*	Spain
10,658	600	2.6	25	26	50	2,850	0.704	2,273	7,143	1.8	2.7	4.9	11	30.9	Sri Lanka
21,500	750	-0.2	34	17	49	1,620	0.379	2,202	10,000	0.5	4.8	15.8	57	18.2	Sudan
488	1,210	2.2	22	24	54	3,730	0.762	2,547	1,200	3.7	8.3	3.4	8	198.1	Surinam
933	1,050	3.8	12	39	50	1,700	0.522	2,706	9,091	5.9	6.4	1.4	26	69.2	Swaziland
216,294	24,830	0.1	2	31	67	18,320	0.929	2,972	395	8.8	6.5	2.5	1	202.2*	Sweden
254,066	36,410	0.7	4	36	61	22,580	0.925	3,379	585	8	5.4	1.6	1	114.3*	Switzerland
81,700	5,700	-2.1	30	22	48	4,960	0.761	3,175	1,220	0.4	4.1	16.6	32	12.3	Syria
225,000	11,000	7	4	41	56	12,000	...	3,048	900	...	3.6	5.2	7	...	Taiwan
2,686	470	-7.8	33	33	33	1,740	0.643	...	430	6	...	3.7	3	...	Tajikistan
2,521	100	1.4	56	14	30	620	0.364	2,018	22,000	3.2	5.8	3.6	36	34.9	Tanzania
120,235	2,040	8.4	10	39	51	5,950	0.827	2,432	4,762	1.1	3.8	2.7	6	10.7	Thailand
1,325	330	-3.4	49	18	34	1,220	0.409	2,242	11,111	2.5	5.7	3.1	52	32.2	Togo
4,776	3,730	-2.7	3	43	55	9,760	0.872	2,585	1,370	...	4.1	1.3	3	5.5	Trinidad & Tobago
15,332	1,780	2.2	18	31	51	5,160	0.763	3,330	1,852	3.3	6.1	3.3	37	27.5	Tunisia
126,330	2,120	3	15	30	55	5,230	0.792	3,429	1,176	1.5	4	4.7	19	7.7	Turkey
5,400	1,400	-1.6	31	31	38	3,400	0.731	...	375	5	...	4.8	2	...	Turkmenistan
3,486	190	1.9	53	12	35	860	0.329	2,159	25,000	1.6	2.9	2.9	41	35.5	Uganda
99,677	1,910	-3.9	35	47	18	5,010	0.842	...	259	3.3	...	3.8	5	...	Ukraine
1,042,700	17,970	1.3	2	33	65	17,160	0.916	3,317	300	6.6	5.3	4	1	50.0*	United Kingdom
6,387,686	24,750	1.2	2	29	69	23,760	0.937	3,732	420	13.3	7	5.3	1	37.7*	United States
12,314	3,910	3	9	27	64	6,070	0.881	2,750	500	2.5	3.1	2.7	3	38.4	Uruguay
21,100	960	-1.6	23	36	41	2,650	0.706	...	280	5.9	...	...	3	...	Uzbekistan
58,916	2,840	1	5	42	53	8,520	0.859	2,618	620	2	4.1	3.6	10	2.3	Venezuela
11,997	170	4.8	30	28	42	1,010	0.539	2,250	247	1.1	3	11	8	4.5	Vietnam
9,000	800	3.1	21	24	55	2,410	0.424	2,203	4,348	1.5	4.6	9.3	59	25.5	Yemen
10,000	1,000	1.8	18	52	30	4,000	...	...	250	...	6.1	...	11	...	Yugoslavia
21,000	500	-6	30	33	36	523	0.384	2,060	14,286	0.8	0.9	2.9	26	4.6	Zaïre
3,152	370	1.8	34	36	30	1,230	0.425	1,931	11,111	2.2	2.9	2.6	25	90.8	Zambia
5,756	540	-1.1	15	36	48	1,970	0.539	1,985	7,692	3.2	10.6	4.3	17	39.9	Zimbabwe

	Land Area thousand km²	Population 1995 thousands
American Samoa	0.20	58
Andorra	0.45	65
Anguilla	0.10	8.3
Antigua & Barbuda	0.44	67
Aruba	0.19	71
Ascension I.	0.09	1.1
Bahrain	0.68	558
Belize	22.8	216
Bermuda	0.05	64
Bhutan	47.0	1,639
Brit. Virgin Is.	0.15	20
Brunei	5.27	284
Cape Verde Is.	4.03	386
Cayman Is.	0.26	31
Cocos Is.	0.01	1.0
Comoros	2.23	654
Cook Is.	0.23	19
Djibouti	23.2	603
Dominica	0.75	89
Equatorial Guinea	28.1	400
Eritrea	117	3,850
Falkland Is.	12.2	2.0
Faroe Is.	1.40	47
Fiji	18.3	773
French Guiana	88.2	154

	Land Area thousand km²	Population 1995 thousands
French Polynesia	3.66	217
Gaza Strip	0.38	770
Gibraltar	0.01	28
Greenland	342	59
Grenada	0.34	94
Guadeloupe	1.69	443
Guam	0.55	155
Kiribati	0.73	80
Kuwait	17.8	1,668
Liechtenstein	0.16	31
Macau	0.02	490
Maldives	0.30	254
Marshall Is.	0.18	55
Martinique	1.06	384
Mauritius	1.90	1,100
Micronesia	0.71	125
Monaco	0.002	32
Montserrat	0.10	11
Nauru	0.02	12
Netherlands Antilles	0.80	199
New Caledonia	18.3	181
Niue	0.26	1.8
Norfolk I.	0.04	2.0
Northern Mariania Is.	0.48	49
Oman	306	2,120

	Land Area thousand km²	Population 1995 thousands
Palau	0.46	16
Qatar	11.0	594
Réunion	2.50	655
St Christopher-Nevis	0.36	45
St Helena	0.12	6.3
St Lucia	0.61	147
St Pierre & Miquelon	0.23	6.0
St Vincent & the Grenadines	0.39	111
San Marino	0.06	26
São Tomé & Principe	0.96	133
Seychelles	0.45	75
Solomon Is.	28.0	378
Svalbard	62.0	4.0
Tokelau	0.01	2.0
Tonga	0.72	107
Tristan da Cunha	0.10	0.3
Turks & Caicos Is.	0.43	15
Tuvalu	0.03	10
United Arab Emirates	83.6	2,800
US Virgin Is.	0.34	105
Vanuatu	12.2	167
Vatican City	0.0004	1.0
Wallis & Futuna	0.20	13
Western Sahara	267	220
Western Samoa	2.83	169

This list shows the principal cities with more than 500,000 inhabitants (for Brazil, Canada, China, India, Iran, Japan and USA only cities with more than 1 million are included). The figures are taken from the most recent census or estimate available, and as far as possible are the population of the metropolitan area, e.g. greater New York, Mexico or London. All the figures are in thousands. The top 20 world cities are indicated with their rank in brackets following the name.

	Population *Thousands*
Afghanistan	
Kābul	1,424
Algeria	
Algiers	1,722
Oran	664
Angola	
Luanda	1,544
Argentina	
Buenos Aires [6]	11,256
Córdoba	1,198
La Plata	640
Mar del Plata	520
Mendoza	775
Rosario	1,096
San Miguel de Tucumán	622
Armenia	
Yerevan	1,254
Australia	
Adelaide	1,070
Brisbane	777
Melbourne	3,081
Perth	1,193
Sydney	3,657
Austria	
Vienna	1,560
Azerbaijan	
Baku	1,149
Bangladesh	
Chittagong	2,041
Dacca	6,105
Khulna	877
Rajshahi	517
Belarus	
Gomel	506
Minsk	1,613
Belgium	
Brussels	952
Benin	
Cotonou	537
Bolivia	
La Paz	1,126
Santa Cruz	695
Bosnia-Herzegovina	
Sarajevo	526
Brazil	
Belém	1,246
Belo Horizonte	2,049
Brasília	1,596
Curitiba	1,290
Fortaleza	1,758
Manaus	1,011
Nova Iguaçu	1,286
Pôrto Alegre	1,263
Recife	1,290
Rio de Janeiro	5,336
Salvador	2,056
São Paulo [9]	9,480
Bulgaria	
Sofia	1,221
Burkina Faso	
Ouagadougou	634
Burma (Myanmar)	
Mandalay	533
Rangoon	2,513
Cambodia	
Phnom Penh	900
Cameroon	
Douala	884
Yaoundé	750
Canada	
Montréal	3,127
Toronto	3,893
Vancouver	1,603
Central African Rep.	
Bangui	597
Chad	
Ndjamena	530
Chile	
Santiago	5,343
China	
Anshan	1,204
Beijing [18]	6,690
Changchun	2,470
Changsha	1,510
Chengdu	2,760
Chongqing	3,870
Dalian	2,400
Fushun	1,202
Fuzhou, Fujian	1,380
Guangzhou	3,750
Guiyang	1,080
Hangzhou	1,790
Harbin	3,120
Hefei	1,110
Jilin	1,037
Jinan	2,150
Kunming	1,500
Lanzhou	1,340
Linhai	1,012
Macheng	1,010
Nanchang	1,440
Nanjing	2,490
Ningbo	1,100
Qingdao	2,300
Qiqihar	1,070
Shanghai [12]	8,930
Shenyang	4,050
Shijiazhuang	1,610
Taiyuan	1,720
Tangshan	1,044
Tianjin	5,000
Ürümqi	1,130
Wuhan	3,870
Xi'an	2,410
Zhengzhou	1,690
Zibo	2,400
Colombia	
Barranquilla	1,049
Bogotá	5,132
Cali	1,687
Cartagena	726
Medellín	1,608
Congo	
Brazzaville	938
Pointe-Noire	576
Croatia	
Zagreb	931
Cuba	
Havana	2,119
Czech Republic	
Prague	1,216
Denmark	
Copenhagen	1,337
Dominican Rep.	
Santo Domingo	2,200
Ecuador	
Guayaquil	1,508
Quito	1,101
Egypt	
Alexandria	3,380
Cairo [16]	6,800
El Gîza	2,144
Shubra el Kheima	834
El Salvador	
San Salvador	1,522
Ethiopia	
Addis Ababa	2,213
Finland	
Helsinki	516
France	
Bordeaux	696
Lille	959
Lyons	1,262
Marseilles	1,087
Nice	516
Paris [10]	9,319
Toulouse	650
Georgia	
Tbilisi	1,279
Germany	
Berlin	3,475
Bremen	552
Cologne	693
Dortmund	602
Düsseldorf	575
Duisburg	537
Essen	622
Frankfurt	660
Hamburg	1,703
Hannover	525
Munich	1,256
Stuttgart	594
Ghana	
Accra	965
Greece	
Athens	3,097
Guatemala	
Guatemala	2,000
Guinea	
Conakry	810
Haiti	
Port-au-Prince	1,402
Honduras	
Tegucigalpa	679
Hong Kong	
Hong Kong	6,149
Hungary	
Budapest	2,009
India	
Ahmadabad	3,298
Bangalore	4,087
Bhopal	1,064
Bombay [4]	12,572
Calcutta [7]	10,916
Coimbatore	1,136
Delhi [15]	7,207
Hyderabad	4,280
Indore	1,104
Jaipur	1,514
Kanpur	2,111
Lucknow	1,642
Ludhiana	1,012
Madras	5,361
Madurai	1,094
Nagpur	1,661
Patna	1,099
Pune	2,485
Surat	1,517
Vadodara	1,115
Varanasi	1,026
Vishakhapatnam	1,052
Indonesia	
Bandung	2,027
Jakarta [14]	8,259
Malang	650
Medan	1,686
Palembang	1,084
Semarang	1,005
Surabaya	2,421
Surakarta	504
Ujung Pandang	913
Iran	
Esfahan	1,127
Mashhad	1,759
Tabriz	1,089
Tehran	6,476
Iraq	
Al Mawşil	664
Arbil	770
As Sulaymaniyah	952
Baghdad	3,841
Diyala	961
Kadhimain	521
Ireland	
Dublin	1,024
Israel	
Jerusalem	544
Italy	
Genoa	668
Milan	1,359
Naples	1,072
Palermo	697
Rome	2,723
Turin	953
Ivory Coast	
Abidjan	1,929
Jamaica	
Kingston	644
Japan	
Fukuoka	1,269
Hiroshima	1,102
Kawasaki	1,200
Kitakyushu	1,020
Kobe	1,509
Kyoto	1,452
Nagoya	2,159
Osaka	2,589
Sapporo	1,732
Tokyo [5]	11,927
Yokohama	3,288
Jordan	
Amman	1,272
Az-Zarqā	605
Kazakhstan	
Alma-Ata	1,147
Karaganda	613
Kenya	
Nairobi	1,429
Korea, North	
Chinnampo	691
Chŏngjin	754
Hamhung	775
Pyŏngyang	2,639
Sinŭiju	500
Korea, South	
Chŏnju	517
Inchon	1,818
Kwangju	1,145
Puch'on	668
Pusan	3,798
Seoul [8]	10,628
Sŏngnam	541
Suwŏn	645
Taegu	2,229
Taejŏn	1,062
Ulsan	683
Kyrgyzstan	
Bishkek	628
Latvia	
Riga	840
Lebanon	
Beirut	1,500
Tripoli	500
Libya	
Tripoli	990
Lithuania	
Vilnius	576
Macedonia	
Skopje	563
Madagascar	
Antananarivo	1,053
Malaysia	
Kuala Lumpur	1,145
Mali	
Bamako	746
Mauritania	
Nouakchott	600
Mexico	
Acapulco de Juárez	592
Aguascalientés	506
Chihuahua	530
Ciudad Juárez	798
Culiacán Rosales	602
Guadalajara	2,847
León	872
Mérida	557
Mexicali	602
Mexico City [2]	15,048
Monterrey	2,522
Puebla	1,055
San Luis Potosí	526
Tijuana	743
Moldova	
Kishinev	667
Mongolia	
Ulan Bator	601
Morocco	
Casablanca	3,079
Fès	735
Marrakesh	665
Oujda	661
Rabat-Salé	1,344
Mozambique	
Maputo	1,070
Netherlands	
Amsterdam	1,091
Rotterdam	1,069
The Hague	694
Utrecht	543
New Zealand	
Auckland	896
Nicaragua	
Managua	974
Nigeria	
Ibadan	1,295
Kano	700
Lagos	1,347
Ogbomosho	661
Norway	
Oslo	714
Pakistan	
Faisalabad	1,104
Gujranwala	659
Hyderabad	752
Karachi	5,181
Lahore	2,953
Multan	722
Peshawar	556
Rawalpindi	795
Panama	
Panama	584
Paraguay	
Asunción	945
Peru	
Arequipa	620
Lima-Callao [20]	6,601
Trujillo	509
Philippines	
Caloocan	629
Cebu	641
Davao	868
Manila [17]	6,720
Quezon City	1,667
Poland	
Kraków	751
Łódź	847
Poznań	590
Warsaw	1,655
Wrocław	643
Portugal	
Lisbon	2,561
Oporto	1,174
Puerto Rico	
San Juan	1,816
Romania	
Bucharest	2,067
Russia	
Astrakhan	512
Barnaul	665
Chelyabinsk	1,170
Irkutsk	644
Izhevsk	651
Kazan	1,107
Kemerovo	559
Khabarovsk	626
Krasnodar	751
Krasnoyarsk	925
Lipetsk	504
Moscow [11]	8,957
Naberezhnyye-Chelny	517
Nizhniy Novgorod	1,451
Novokuznetsk	614
Novosibirsk	1,472
Omsk	1,193
Orenburg	574
Penza	553
Perm	1,108
Rostov	1,027
Ryazan	533
St Petersburg	5,004
Samara	1,271
Saratov	916
Simbirsk	638
Togliatti	677
Tula	591
Tomsk	506
Tyumen	550
Ufa	1,100
Vladivostok	675
Volgograd	1,031
Voronezh	958
Yaroslav	637
Yekaterinburg	1,413
Saudi Arabia	
Jedda	1,400
Mecca	618
Medina	500
Riyadh	2,000
Senegal	
Dakar	1,730
Sierra Leone	
Freetown	505
Singapore	
Singapore	2,874
Somalia	
Mogadishu	1,000
South Africa	
Cape Town	1,912
Durban	1,137
East Rand	1,379
Johannesburg	1,196
Port Elizabeth	853
Pretoria	1,080
Sasolburg	540
Soweto	597
Vanderbijlpark-Vereeniging	774
West Rand	870
Spain	
Barcelona	1,631
Madrid	3,041
Málaga	531
Sevilla	714
Valencia	764
Zaragoza	607
Sri Lanka	
Colombo	1,863
Sudan	
Khartoum	561
Omdurman	526
Sweden	
Gothenburg	783
Stockholm	1,539
Switzerland	
Zürich	840
Syria	
Aleppo	1,445
Damascus	1,451
Homs	518
Taiwan	
Kaohsiung	1,405
Panch'iao	544
T'aichung	817
T'ainan	700
T'aipei	2,653
Tajikistan	
Dushanbe	602
Tanzania	
Dar-es-Salaam	1,361
Thailand	
Bangkok	5,876
Togo	
Lomé	590
Tunisia	
Tunis	1,395
Turkey	
Adana	916
Ankara	2,559
Bursa	835
Gaziantep	603
Istanbul [19]	6,620
Izmir	1,757
Konya	513
Uganda	
Kampala	773
Ukraine	
Dnepropetrovsk	1,190
Donetsk	1,121
Kharkov	1,622
Kiev	2,643
Krivoy Rog	729
Lvov	807
Mariupol	523
Nikolayev	515
Odessa	1,096
Zaporozhye	898
United Kingdom	
Birmingham	1,400
Glasgow	730
Liverpool	1,060
London	6,378
Manchester	1,669
Newcastle	617
United States	
Atlanta	3,143
Baltimore	2,434
Boston	5,439
Buffalo	1,194
Charlotte	1,212
Chicago [13]	8,410
Cincinnati	1,865
Cleveland	2,890
Columbus	1,394
Dallas	4,215
Denver	2,089
Detroit	5,246
Hartford	1,156
Houston	3,962
Indianapolis	1,424
Kansas City	1,617
Los Angeles [2]	15,048
Miami	3,309
Milwaukee	1,629
Minneapolis–SP.	2,618
New Orleans	1,303
New York [1]	19,670
Norfolk	1,497
Philadelphia	5,939
Phoenix	2,330
Pittsburgh	2,406
Portland	1,897
St Louis	2,519
Sacramento	1,563
Salt Lake City	1,128
San Antonio	1,379
San Diego	2,601
San Francisco	6,410
Seattle	3,131
Tampa	2,107
Washington, DC	4,360
Uruguay	
Montevideo	1,384
Uzbekistan	
Tashkent	2,094
Venezuela	
Barquisimento	745
Caracas	2,784
Ciudad Guayana	524
Maracaibo	1,364
Maracay	800
Valencia	1,032
Vietnam	
Haiphong	1,448
Hanoi	3,056
Ho Chi Minh City	3,924
Yugoslavia (Serbia and Montenegro)	
Belgrade	1,137
Zaïre	
Kinshasa	3,804
Kolwezi	544
Lubumbashi	739
Mbuji-Mayi	613
Zambia	
Lusaka	982
Zimbabwe	
Bulawayo	622
Harare	1,189

INDEX TO
WORLD MAPS

The index contains the names of all the principal places and features shown on the World Maps. Each name is followed by an additional entry in italics giving the country or region within which it is located. The alphabetical order of names composed of two or more words is governed primarily by the first word and then by the second. This is an example of the rule:

New South Wales □, *Australia*.. **34 G8** 33 0S 146 0E
New York □, *U.S.A.* **43 D10** 42 40N 76 0W
New York City, *U.S.A.* **43 E11** 40 45N 74 0W
New Zealand ■, *Oceania*............ **35 J13** 40 0S 176 0E
Newark, *U.S.A.* **43 F10** 39 42N 75 45W

Physical features composed of a proper name (Erie) and a description (Lake) are positioned alphabetically by the proper name. The description is positioned after the proper name and is usually abbreviated:

Erie, L., *N. Amer.* **42 D7** 42 15N 81 0W

Where a description forms part of a settlement or administrative name, however, it is always written in full and put in its true alphabetical position:

Mount Isa, *Australia*...................... **34 E6** 20 42S 139 26E

Names beginning with M' and Mc are indexed as if they were spelt Mac. Names beginning St. are alphabetized under Saint, but Santa and San are all spelt in full and are alphabetized accordingly. If the same placename occurs two or more times in the index and all are in the same country, each is followed by the name of the administrative subdivision in which it is located. The names are placed in the alphabetical order of the subdivision. For example:

Columbus, Ga., *U.S.A.* **41 D10** 32 30N 84 58W
Columbus, Ind., *U.S.A.* **42 F5** 39 14N 85 55W
Columbus, Ohio, *U.S.A.* **42 F6** 39 57N 83 1W

The number in bold type which follows each name in the index refers to the number of the map page where that feature or place will be found. This is usually the largest scale at which the place or feature appears.

The letter and figure which are in bold type immediately after the page number give the grid square on the map page, within which the feature is situated. The letter represents the latitude and the figure the longitude. In some cases the feature itself may fall within the specified square, while the name is outside.

For a more precise location, the geographical co-ordinates which follow the letter-figure references give the latitude and the longitude of each place. The first set of figures represent the latitude, which is the distance north or south of the Equator measured as an angle at the centre of the Earth. The Equator is latitude 0°, the North Pole is 90°N, and the South Pole 90°S.

The second set of figures represent the longitude, which is the distance east or west of the prime meridian, which runs through Greenwich, England. Longitude is also measured as an angle at the centre of the Earth and is given east or west of the prime meridian, from 0° to 180° in either direction.

The unit of measurement for latitude and longitude is the degree, which is subdivided into 60 minutes. Each index entry states the position of a place in degrees and minutes, a space being left between the degrees and the minutes. The latitude is followed by N(orth) or S(outh) and the longitude by E(ast) or W(est).

Rivers are indexed to their mouths or confluences, and carry the symbol ➝ after their names. A solid square ■ follows the name of a country, while an open square □ refers to a first order administrative area.

ABBREVIATIONS USED IN THE INDEX

Afghan. – Afghanistan
Ala. – Alabama
Alta. – Alberta
Amer. – America(n)
Arch. – Archipelago
Ariz. – Arizona
Ark. – Arkansas
Atl. Oc. – Atlantic Ocean
B. – Baie, Bahia, Bay, Bucht, Bugt
B.C. – British Columbia
Bangla. – Bangladesh
C. – Cabo, Cap, Cape, Coast
C.A.R. – Central African Republic
C. Prov. – Cape Province
Calif. – California
Cent. – Central
Chan. – Channel
Colo. – Colorado

Conn. – Connecticut
Cord. – Cordillera
Cr. – Creek
D.C. – District of Columbia
Del. – Delaware
Domin. – Dominica
Dom. Rep. – Dominican Republic
E. – East
El Salv. – El Salvador
Eq. Guin. – Equatorial Guinea
Fla. – Florida
Falk. Is. – Falkland Is.
G. – Golfe, Golfo, Gulf
Ga. – Georgia
Guinea–Biss. – Guinea-Bissau
Hd. – Head
Hts. – Heights
I.(s). – Ile, Ilha, Insel,

Isla, Island, Isle(s)
Ill. – Illinois
Ind. – Indiana
Ind. Oc. – Indian Ocean
Ivory C. – Ivory Coast
Kans. – Kansas
Ky. – Kentucky
L. – Lac, Lacul, Lago, Lagoa, Lake, Limni, Loch, Lough
La. – Louisiana
Lux. – Luxembourg
Madag. – Madagascar
Man. – Manitoba
Mass.– Massachusetts
Md. – Maryland
Me. – Maine
Medit. S. – Mediterranean Sea
Mich. – Michigan
Minn. – Minnesota
Miss. – Mississippi

Mo. – Missouri
Mont. – Montana
Mozam.– Mozambique
Mt.(s).– Mont, Monte, Monti, Montaña, Mountain
N. – Nord, Norte, North, Northern
N.B. – New Brunswick
N.C. – North Carolina
N. Cal. – New Caledonia
N. Dak. – North Dakota
N.H. – New Hampshire
N.J. – New Jersey
N. Mex. – New Mexico
N.S. – Nova Scotia
N.S.W. – New South Wales
N.W.T. – North West Territory
N.Y. – New York
N.Z. – New Zealand

Nebr. – Nebraska
Neths. – Netherlands
Nev. – Nevada
Nfld. – Newfoundland
Nic. – Nicaragua

Okla. – Oklahoma
Ont. – Ontario
Oreg. – Oregon
P.E.I. – Prince Edward Island
Pa. – Pennsylvania
Pac. Oc. – Pacific Ocean
Papua N.G. – Papua New Guinea
Pen. – Peninsula, Peninsule
Phil. – Philippines
Pk. – Park, Peak
Plat. – Plateau
Prov. – Province,

Provincial
Pt. – Point
Pta. – Ponta, Punta
Pte. – Pointe
Qué. – Québec
Queens. – Queensland
R. – Rio, River
R.I. – Rhode Island
Ra.(s). – Range(s)
Reg. – Region
Rep. – Republic
Res. – Reserve, Reservoir
S. – San, South
Si. Arabia – Saudi Arabia
S.C. – South Carolina
S. Dak. – South Dakota
S. Leone – Sierra Leone
Sa. – Serra, Sierra
Sask. – Saskatchewan
Scot. – Scotland
Sd. – Sound

Sib. – Siberia
St. – Saint, Sankt, Sint
Str. – Strait, Stretto
Switz. – Switzerland
Tas. – Tasmania
Tenn. – Tennessee
Tex. – Texas
Trin. & Tob. – Trinidad & Tobago
U.A.E. – United Arab Emirates
U.K. – United Kingdom
U.S.A. – United States of America
Va. – Virginia
Vic. – Victoria
Vol. – Volcano
Vt. – Vermont
W. – West
W. Va. – West Virginia
Wash. – Washington
Wis. – Wisconsin

A

Aachen, *Germany* **10 C4** 50 45N 6 6 E
Aalborg, *Denmark* **6 G9** 57 2N 9 54 E
Aarau, *Switz.* **10 E5** 47 23N 8 4 E
Aare —►, *Switz.* **10 E5** 47 33N 8 14 E
Aarhus, *Denmark* **6 G10** 56 8N 10 11 E
Abadan, *Iran* **24 B3** 30 22N 48 20 E
Abbeville, *France* **8 A4** 50 6N 1 49 E
Abéché, *Chad* **29 F9** 13 50N 20 35 E
Abeokuta, *Nigeria* **30 C2** 7 3N 3 19 E
Aberdeen, *U.K.* **7 C5** 57 9N 2 5W
Abidjan, *Ivory C.* **28 G4** 5 26N 3 58W
Abitibi L., *Canada* **42 A8** 48 40N 79 40W
Abkhazia □, *Georgia* **15 F7** 43 12N 41 5 E
Abohar, *India* **23 D5** 30 10N 74 10 E
Abu Dhabi, *U.A.E.* **24 C4** 24 28N 54 22 E
Abuja, *Nigeria* **30 C3** 9 16N 7 2 E
Acapulco, *Mexico* **44 D5** 16 51N 99 56W
Accomac, *U.S.A.* **43 G10** 37 43N 75 40W
Accra, *Ghana* **30 C1** 5 35N 0 6W
Acklins I., *Bahamas* **45 C10** 22 30N 74 0W
Aconcagua, *Argentina* **47 F3** 32 39S 70 0W
Acre □, *Brazil* **46 C2** 9 1S 71 0W
Adamawa Highlands, *Cameroon* **29 G7** 7 20N 12 20 E
Adana, *Turkey* **15 G6** 37 0N 35 16 E
Adapazarı, *Turkey* **15 F5** 40 48N 30 25 E
Addis Ababa, *Ethiopia* **29 G12** 9 2N 38 42 E
Adelaide, *Australia* **34 G6** 34 52S 138 30 E
Adelaide, *S. Africa* **31 C4** 32 42S 26 20 E
Aden, *Yemen* **24 D3** 12 45N 45 0 E
Aden, G. of, *Asia* **24 D3** 12 30N 47 30 E
Adirondack Mts., *U.S.A.* **43 D10** 44 0N 74 0W
Admiralty Is., *Papua N. G.* **36 H6** 2 0S 147 0 E
Ado-Ekiti, *Nigeria* **30 C3** 7 38N 5 12 E
Adoni, *India* **25 D6** 15 33N 77 18 E
Adour —►, *France* **8 E3** 43 32N 1 32W
Adrar, *Algeria* **28 C4** 27 51N 0 11W
Adrian, *U.S.A.* **42 E5** 41 54N 84 2W
Adriatic Sea, *Medit. S.* **12 C6** 43 0N 16 0 E
Ægean Sea, *Medit. S.* **13 E11** 38 30N 25 0 E
Afghanistan ■, *Asia* **24 B5** 33 0N 65 0 E
'Afif, *Si. Arabia* **24 C3** 23 53N 42 56 E
Agadès, *Niger* **30 A3** 16 58N 7 59 E
Agadir, *Morocco* **28 B3** 30 28N 9 55W
Agartala, *India* **23 H13** 23 50N 91 23 E
Agen, *France* **8 D4** 44 12N 0 38 E
Agra, *India* **23 F6** 27 17N 77 58 E
Agrigento, *Italy* **12 F5** 37 19N 13 34 E
Aguascalientes, *Mexico* **44 C4** 21 53N 102 12W
Agulhas, C., *S. Africa* **31 C3** 34 52S 20 0 E
Ahmadabad, *India* **23 H4** 23 0N 72 40 E
Ahmadnagar, *India* **25 D6** 19 7N 74 46 E
Ahmadpur, *Pakistan* **23 E3** 29 12N 71 10 E
Ahvaz, *Iran* **24 B3** 31 20N 48 40 E
Ahvenanmaa Is., *Finland* **6 F11** 60 15N 20 0 E
Aïr, *Niger* **28 E6** 18 30N 8 0 E
Aisne —►, *France* **8 B5** 49 26N 2 50 E
Aix-en-Provence, *France* **8 E6** 43 32N 5 27 E
Aix-les-Bains, *France* **8 D6** 45 41N 5 53 E
Ajaccio, *France* **8 F8** 41 55N 8 40 E
Ajanta Ra., *India* **23 J5** 20 28N 75 50 E
Ajaria □, *Georgia* **15 F7** 41 30N 42 0 E
Ajmer, *India* **23 F5** 26 28N 74 37 E
Akashi, *Japan* **19 B4** 34 45N 134 58 E
Akita, *Japan* **19 A7** 39 45N 140 7 E
Akola, *India* **23 J6** 20 42N 77 2 E
Akranes, *Iceland* **6 B2** 64 19N 22 5W
Akron, *U.S.A.* **42 E7** 41 5N 81 31W
Aktyubinsk, *Kazakhstan* **15 D10** 50 17N 57 10 E
Akure, *Nigeria* **30 C3** 7 15N 5 5 E
Akureyri, *Iceland* **6 B4** 65 40N 18 6W
Al Ḥudaydah, *Yemen* **24 D3** 14 50N 43 0 E
Al Hufūf, *Si. Arabia* **24 C3** 25 25N 49 45 E
Al Jawf, *Si. Arabia* **24 C2** 29 55N 39 40 E
Al Kut, *Iraq* **24 B3** 32 30N 46 0 E
Al Qatif, *Si. Arabia* **24 C3** 26 35N 50 0 E
Al 'Ula, *Si. Arabia* **24 C2** 26 35N 38 0 E
Alabama □, *U.S.A.* **41 D9** 33 0N 87 0W
Aland Is. = Ahvenanmaa Is., *Finland* **6 F11** 60 15N 20 0 E
Alaska □, *U.S.A.* **38 B5** 64 0N 154 0W
Alaska, G. of, *Pac. Oc.* **38 C5** 58 0N 145 0W
Alaska Peninsula, *U.S.A.* **38 C4** 56 0N 159 0W
Alaska Range, *U.S.A.* **38 B4** 62 50N 151 0W
Alba-Iulia, *Romania* **11 E12** 46 8N 23 39 E
Albacete, *Spain* **9 C5** 39 0N 1 50W
Albania ■, *Europe* **13 D9** 41 0N 20 0 E
Albany, *Australia* **34 H2** 35 1S 117 58 E
Albany, *Ga., U.S.A.* **41 D10** 31 35N 84 10W
Albany, *N.Y., U.S.A.* **43 D11** 42 39N 73 45W
Albany —►, *Canada* **39 C11** 52 17N 81 31W
Albert L., *Africa* **32 D6** 1 30N 31 0 E
Alberta □, *Canada* **38 C8** 54 40N 115 0W
Albertville, *France* **8 D7** 45 40N 6 22 E
Albi, *France* **8 E5** 43 56N 2 9 E
Albion, *U.S.A.* **42 D5** 42 15N 84 45W
Albuquerque, *U.S.A.* **40 C5** 35 5N 106 39W
Albury, *Australia* **34 H8** 36 3S 146 56 E
Alcalá de Henares, *Spain* **9 B4** 40 28N 3 22W
Aldabra Is., *Seychelles* **27 G8** 9 22S 46 28 E
Aldan —►, *Russia* **18 C14** 63 28N 129 35 E
Aleksandrovsk-Sakhalinskiy, *Russia* **18 D16** 50 50N 142 20 E
Alençon, *France* **8 B4** 48 27N 0 4 E
Alès, *France* **8 D6** 44 9N 4 5 E
Alessándria, *Italy* **12 B3** 44 54N 8 37 E
Ålesund, *Norway* **6 F9** 62 28N 6 12 E
Aleutian Is., *Pac. Oc.* **36 B10** 52 0N 175 0W
Alexander Arch., *U.S.A.* **38 C6** 56 0N 136 0W
Alexandria, *Egypt* **29 B10** 31 13N 29 58 E
Alexandria, *La., U.S.A.* **41 D8** 31 18N 92 27W
Alexandria, *Va., U.S.A.* **42 F9** 38 48N 77 3W
Algarve, *Portugal* **9 D1** 36 58N 8 20W
Algeciras, *Spain* **9 D3** 36 9N 5 28W
Algeria ■, *Africa* **28 C5** 28 30N 2 0 E
Algiers, *Algeria* **28 A5** 36 42N 3 8 E
Alicante, *Spain* **9 C5** 38 23N 0 30W
Alice Springs, *Australia* **34 E5** 23 40S 133 50 E
Aligarh, *India* **23 F7** 27 55N 78 10 E
Alipur Duar, *India* **23 F12** 26 30N 89 35 E
Aliquippa, *U.S.A.* **42 E7** 40 37N 80 15W
Aliwal North, *S. Africa* **31 C4** 30 45S 26 45 E
Alkmaar, *Neths.* **10 B3** 52 37N 4 45 E
Allahabad, *India* **23 G8** 25 25N 81 58 E
Allegan, *U.S.A.* **42 D5** 42 32N 85 51W
Allegheny —►, *U.S.A.* **42 E8** 40 27N 80 1W
Allegheny Plateau, *U.S.A.* **42 G7** 38 0N 80 0W
Allentown, *U.S.A.* **43 E10** 40 37N 75 29W
Alleppey, *India* **25 E6** 9 30N 76 28 E
Allier —►, *France* **8 C5** 46 57N 3 4 E
Alma, *U.S.A.* **42 D5** 43 23N 84 39W
Almaty, *Kazakhstan* **18 E9** 43 15N 76 57 E
Almelo, *Neths.* **10 B4** 52 22N 6 42 E
Almería, *Spain* **9 D4** 36 52N 2 27W
Alor, *Indonesia* **22 D4** 8 15S 124 30 E
Alpena, *U.S.A.* **42 C6** 45 4N 83 27W
Alps, *Europe* **10 E5** 46 30N 9 30 E
Alsace, *France* **8 B7** 48 15N 7 25 E
Altai, *Mongolia* **20 B4** 46 40N 92 45 E
Altay, *China* **20 B3** 47 48N 88 10 E
Altoona, *U.S.A.* **42 E8** 40 31N 78 24W
Altun Shan, *China* **20 C3** 38 30N 88 0 E
Alwar, *India* **23 F6** 27 38N 76 34 E
Amadjuak L., *Canada* **39 B12** 65 0N 71 8W
Amagasaki, *Japan* **19 B4** 34 42N 135 20 E
Amarillo, *U.S.A.* **40 C6** 35 13N 101 50W
Amazon —►, *S. Amer.* **46 C4** 0 5S 50 0W
Ambala, *India* **23 D6** 30 23N 76 56 E
Ambikapur, *India* **23 H9** 23 15N 83 15 E
Ambon, *Indonesia* **22 D4** 3 35S 128 20 E
American Samoa ■, *Pac. Oc.* **35 C17** 14 20S 170 40W
Amiens, *France* **8 B5** 49 54N 2 16 E
Amman, *Jordan* **24 B2** 31 57N 35 52 E
Amos, *Canada* **42 A8** 48 35N 78 5W
Amravati, *India* **23 J6** 20 55N 77 45 E
Amreli, *India* **23 J3** 21 35N 71 17 E
Amritsar, *India* **23 D5** 31 35N 74 57 E
Amroha, *India* **23 E7** 28 53N 78 30 E
Amsterdam, *Neths.* **10 B3** 52 23N 4 54 E
Amsterdam, *U.S.A.* **43 D10** 42 56N 74 11W
Amudarya —►, *Uzbekistan* **18 E7** 43 58N 59 34 E
Amundsen Gulf, *Canada* **38 A7** 71 0N 124 0W
Amundsen Sea, *Antarctica* **48 E1** 72 0S 115 0W
Amur —►, *Russia* **18 D16** 52 56N 141 10 E
An Najaf, *Iraq* **24 B3** 32 3N 44 15 E
An Nasiriyah, *Iraq* **24 B3** 31 0N 46 15 E
An Nhon, *Vietnam* **22 B2** 13 55N 109 7 E
Anadyr, *Russia* **18 C19** 64 35N 177 20 E
Anadyr, G. of, *Russia* **18 C20** 64 0N 180 0 E
Anaheim, *U.S.A.* **40 D3** 33 50N 117 55W
Anambas Is., *Indonesia* **22 C2** 3 20N 106 30 E
Anantnag, *India* **23 C5** 33 45N 75 10 E
Anar, *Iran* **24 B4** 30 55N 55 13 E
Anatolia, *Turkey* **15 G5** 39 0N 30 0 E
Anchorage, *U.S.A.* **38 B5** 61 13N 149 54W
Ancona, *Italy* **12 C5** 43 38N 13 30 E
Anda, *China* **21 B7** 46 24N 125 19 E
Andalucía □, *Spain* **9 D3** 37 35N 5 0W
Andaman Is., *Ind. Oc.* **25 D8** 12 30N 92 30 E
Anderson, *U.S.A.* **42 E5** 40 10N 85 41W
Andes, *S. Amer.* **46 E3** 20 0S 68 0W
Andhra Pradesh □, *India* **25 D6** 18 0N 79 0 E
Andorra ■, *Europe* **9 A6** 42 30N 1 30 E
Andreanof Is., *U.S.A.* **38 C2** 52 0N 178 0W
Ándria, *Italy* **12 D7** 41 13N 16 17 E
Andros I., *Bahamas* **45 C9** 24 30N 78 0W
Angara —►, *Russia* **18 D11** 58 5N 94 20 E
Ånge, *Sweden* **6 F11** 62 31N 15 35 E
Angel Falls, *Venezuela* **46 B3** 5 57N 62 30W
Angerman —►, *Sweden* **6 F11** 62 40N 18 0 E
Angers, *France* **8 C3** 47 30N 0 35W
Anglesey, *U.K.* **7 E4** 53 17N 4 20W
Angola ■, *Africa* **33 G3** 12 0S 18 0 E
Angoulême, *France* **8 D4** 45 39N 0 10 E
Angoumois, *France* **8 D3** 45 50N 0 25 E
Anguilla ■, *W. Indies* **44 J18** 18 14N 63 5W
Anhui □, *China* **21 C6** 32 0N 117 0 E
Anjou, *France* **8 C3** 47 20N 0 15W
Ankara, *Turkey* **15 G5** 39 57N 32 54 E
Ann, C., *U.S.A.* **43 D12** 42 38N 70 35W
Ann Arbor, *U.S.A.* **42 D6** 42 17N 83 45W
Annaba, *Algeria* **28 A6** 36 50N 7 46 E
Annapolis, *U.S.A.* **42 F9** 38 59N 76 30W
Annecy, *France* **8 D7** 45 55N 6 8 E
Annobón, *Atl. Oc.* **27 G4** 1 25S 5 36 E
Anshun, *China* **20 D5** 26 18N 105 57 E
Antalya, *Turkey* **15 G5** 36 52N 30 45 E
Antananarivo, *Madag.* **33 H9** 18 55S 47 31 E
Antarctic Pen., *Antarctica* **48 D4** 67 0S 60 0W
Antibes, *France* **8 E7** 43 34N 7 6 E
Anticosti I., *Canada* **43 A16** 49 30N 63 0W
Antigua & Barbuda ■, *W. Indies* **44 K20** 17 20N 61 48W
Antofagasta, *Chile* **47 E2** 23 50S 70 30W
Antsiranana, *Madag.* **33 G9** 12 25S 49 20 E
Antwerp, *Belgium* **10 C3** 51 13N 4 25 E
Anyang, *China* **21 C6** 36 5N 114 21 E
Aomori, *Japan* **19 F12** 40 45N 140 45 E
Aparri, *Phil.* **22 B4** 18 22N 121 38 E
Apeldoorn, *Neths.* **10 B3** 52 13N 5 57 E
Apennines, *Italy* **12 B4** 44 0N 10 0 E
Apia, *W. Samoa* **35 C16** 13 50S 171 50W
Appalachian Mts., *U.S.A.* **42 G7** 38 0N 80 0W
Appleton, *U.S.A.* **42 C3** 44 16N 88 25W
Aqmola, *Kazakhstan* **18 D9** 51 10N 71 30 E
Ar Ramadi, *Iraq* **24 B3** 33 25N 43 20 E
Arabian Desert, *Egypt* **29 C11** 27 30N 32 30 E
Arabian Gulf = Gulf, The, *Asia* **24 C4** 27 0N 50 0 E
Arabian Sea, *Ind. Oc.* **24 D5** 16 0N 65 0 E
Aracaju, *Brazil* **46 D6** 10 55S 37 4W
Arad, *Romania* **11 E11** 46 10N 21 20 E
Arafura Sea, *E. Indies* **22 D5** 9 0S 135 0 E
Aragón □, *Spain* **9 B5** 41 25N 0 40W
Araguaia —►, *Brazil* **46 C5** 5 21S 48 41W
Arak, *Iran* **24 B3** 34 0N 49 40 E
Arakan Yoma, *Burma* **25 C8** 20 0N 94 40 E
Aral, *Kazakhstan* **18 E8** 46 41N 61 45 E
Aral Sea , *Asia* **18 E8** 44 30N 60 0 E
Arcachon, *France* **8 D3** 44 40N 1 10W
Arctic Ocean, *Arctic* **48 B17** 78 0N 160 0W
Arctic Red River, *Canada* **38 B6** 67 15N 134 0W
Ardabil, *Iran* **24 B3** 38 15N 48 18 E
Ardennes, *Belgium* **10 D3** 49 50N 5 5 E
Arendal, *Norway* **6 G9** 58 28N 8 46 E
Arequipa, *Peru* **46 D2** 16 20S 71 30W
Argentan, *France* **8 B3** 48 45N 0 1W
Argentina ■, *S. Amer.* **47 F3** 35 0S 66 0W
Arima, *Trin. & Tob.* **44 S20** 10 38N 61 17W
Arizona □, *U.S.A.* **40 D4** 34 0N 112 0W
Arkansas □, *U.S.A.* **41 D8** 35 0N 92 30W
Arkansas —►, *U.S.A.* **41 D8** 33 47N 91 4W
Arkhangelsk, *Russia* **14 B7** 64 38N 40 36 E
Arles, *France* **8 E6** 43 41N 4 40 E
Arlington, *U.S.A.* **42 F9** 38 53N 77 7W
Arlon, *Belgium* **10 D3** 49 42N 5 49 E
Armenia ■, *Asia* **15 F7** 40 20N 45 0 E
Arnhem, *Neths.* **10 C3** 51 58N 5 55 E
Arnhem Land, *Australia* **34 C5** 13 10S 134 30 E
Arnprior, *Canada* **42 C9** 45 26N 76 21W
Arrah, *India* **23 G10** 25 35N 84 32 E
Arran, *U.K.* **7 D4** 55 34N 5 12W
Arras, *France* **8 A5** 50 17N 2 46 E
Artois, *France* **8 A5** 50 20N 2 30 E
Aru Is., *Indonesia* **22 D5** 6 0S 134 30 E
Arunachal Pradesh □, *India* **25 C8** 28 0N 95 0 E
Arusha, *Tanzania* **32 E7** 3 20S 36 40 E
Asab, *Namibia* **31 B2** 25 30S 18 0 E
Asahigawa, *Japan* **19 F12** 43 46N 142 22 E
Asansol, *India* **23 H11** 23 40N 87 1 E
Asbestos, *Canada* **43 C12** 45 47N 71 58W
Asbury Park, *U.S.A.* **43 E10** 40 13N 74 1W
Ascension I., *Atl. Oc.* **27 G2** 8 0S 14 15W
Ashkhabad, *Turkmenistan* **18 F7** 38 0N 57 50 E
Ashland, *Ky., U.S.A.* **42 F6** 38 28N 82 38W
Ashland, *Ohio, U.S.A.* **42 E6** 40 52N 82 19W
Ashtabula, *U.S.A.* **42 E7** 41 52N 80 47W
Asifabad, *India* **23 K7** 19 20N 79 24 E
Asir □, *Si. Arabia* **24 D3** 18 40N 42 30 E
Asmara, *Eritrea* **29 E12** 15 19N 38 55 E
Assam □, *India* **23 F13** 26 0N 93 0 E
Assen, *Neths.* **10 B4** 53 0N 6 35 E
Assisi, *Italy* **12 C5** 43 4N 12 37 E
Asti, *Italy* **12 B3** 44 54N 8 12 E
Astrakhan, *Russia* **15 E8** 46 25N 48 5 E
Asturias □, *Spain* **9 A3** 43 15N 6 0W
Asunción, *Paraguay* **47 E4** 25 10S 57 30W
Aswân, *Egypt* **29 D11** 24 4N 32 57 E
Atacama Desert, *Chile* **47 E3** 24 0S 69 20W
Atbara, *Sudan* **29 E11** 17 42N 33 59 E
Atbara —►, *Sudan* **29 E11** 17 40N 33 56 E
Athabasca —►, *Canada* **38 C8** 58 40N 110 50W
Athabasca, L., *Canada* **38 C9** 59 15N 109 15W
Athens, *Greece* **13 F10** 37 58N 23 46 E
Athens, *U.S.A.* **42 F6** 39 20N 82 6W
Atikokan, *Canada* **42 A2** 48 45N 91 37W
Atlanta, *U.S.A.* **41 D10** 33 45N 84 23W
Atlantic City, *U.S.A.* **43 F10** 39 21N 74 27W
Atlantic Ocean **2 E9** 0 0 20 0W
Atyraū, *Kazakhstan* **18 E7** 47 5N 52 0 E
Au Sable —►, *U.S.A.* **42 C6** 44 25N 83 20W
Aube —►, *France* **8 B5** 48 34N 3 43 E
Auburn, *Ind., U.S.A.* **42 E5** 41 22N 85 4W
Auburn, *N.Y., U.S.A.* **42 D9** 42 56N 76 34W
Aubusson, *France* **8 D5** 45 57N 2 11 E
Auch, *France* **8 E4** 43 39N 0 36 E
Auckland, *N.Z.* **35 H13** 36 52S 174 46 E
Aude —►, *France* **8 E5** 43 13N 3 14 E
Augrabies Falls, *S. Africa* **31 B3** 28 35S 20 20 E
Augsburg, *Germany* **10 D6** 48 25N 10 52 E
Augusta, *Ga., U.S.A.* **41 D10** 33 28N 81 58W
Augusta, *Maine, U.S.A.* **43 C13** 44 19N 69 47W
Aunis, *France* **8 C3** 46 5N 0 50W
Aurangabad, *Bihar, India* **23 G10** 24 45N 84 18 E
Aurangabad, *Maharashtra, India* **23 K5** 19 50N 75 23 E
Aurillac, *France* **8 D5** 44 55N 2 26 E
Aurora, *U.S.A.* **42 E3** 41 45N 88 19W
Austin, *U.S.A.* **40 D7** 30 17N 97 45W
Australia ■, *Oceania* **34 E5** 23 0S 135 0 E
Australian Alps, *Australia* **34 H8** 36 30S 148 30 E
Australian Capital Territory □, *Australia* **34 H8** 35 30S 149 0 E
Austria ■, *Europe* **10 E8** 47 0N 14 0 E
Autun, *France* **8 C6** 46 58N 4 17 E
Auvergne, *France* **8 D5** 45 20N 3 15 E
Auxerre, *France* **8 C5** 47 48N 3 32 E
Avallon, *France* **8 C5** 47 30N 3 53 E
Avellino, *Italy* **12 D6** 40 54N 14 47 E
Avignon, *France* **8 E6** 43 57N 4 50 E
Ávila, *Spain* **9 B3** 40 39N 4 43W
Avranches, *France* **8 B3** 48 40N 1 20W
Axiós —►, *Greece* **13 D10** 40 57N 22 35 E
Ayers Rock, *Australia* **34 F5** 25 23S 131 5 E
Ayr, *U.K.* **7 D4** 55 28N 4 38W
Azamgarh, *India* **23 F9** 26 5N 83 13 E
Azerbaijan ■, *Asia* **15 F8** 40 20N 48 0 E
Azores, *Atl. Oc.* **2 C8** 38 44N 29 0W
Azov, Sea of, *Europe* **15 E6** 46 0N 36 30 E
Azuero Pen., *Panama* **45 F8** 7 30N 80 30W

B

Babol, *Iran* **24 B4** 36 40N 52 50 E
Babuyan Chan., *Phil.* **22 B4** 18 40N 121 30 E
Bacău, *Romania* **11 E14** 46 35N 26 55 E
Bacolod, *Phil.* **22 B4** 10 40N 122 57 E
Bad Axe, *U.S.A.* **42 D6** 43 48N 83 0W
Badajoz, *Spain* **9 C2** 38 50N 6 59W
Badalona, *Spain* **9 B7** 41 26N 2 15 E
Baden-Württemberg □, *Germany* **10 D5** 48 20N 8 40 E
Baffin I., *Canada* **39 B12** 68 0N 75 0W
Baghdad, *Iraq* **24 B3** 33 20N 44 30 E
Baguio, *Phil.* **22 B4** 16 26N 120 34 E
Bahamas ■, *N. Amer.* **45 C10** 24 0N 75 0W
Baharampur, *India* **23 G12** 24 2N 88 27 E
Bahawalpur, *Pakistan* **23 E3** 29 24N 71 40 E
Bahía = Salvador, *Brazil* **46 D6** 13 0S 38 30W
Bahía □, *Brazil* **46 D5** 12 0S 42 0W
Bahía Blanca, *Argentina* **47 F3** 38 35S 62 13W
Bahraich, *India* **23 F8** 27 38N 81 37 E
Bahrain ■, *Asia* **24 C4** 26 0N 50 35 E
Baia Mare, *Romania* **11 E12** 47 40N 23 35 E
Baie-St-Paul, *Canada* **43 B12** 47 28N 70 32W
Baikal, L., *Russia* **18 D12** 53 0N 108 0 E
Baja California, *Mexico* **44 B2** 31 10N 115 12W
Bakersfield, *U.S.A.* **40 C3** 35 23N 119 1W
Bakhtaran, *Iran* **24 B3** 34 23N 47 0 E
Baku, *Azerbaijan* **15 F8** 40 29N 49 56 E
Balabac Str., *E. Indies* **22 C3** 7 53N 117 5 E
Balaghat, *India* **23 J8** 21 49N 80 12 E
Balaton, *Hungary* **11 E9** 46 50N 17 40 E
Balboa, *Panama* **44 H14** 8 57N 79 34W
Baldwin, *U.S.A.* **42 D5** 43 54N 85 51W
Balearic Is., *Spain* **9 C7** 39 30N 3 0 E
Baleshwar, *India* **23 J11** 21 35N 87 3 E
Bali, *Indonesia* **22 D3** 8 20S 115 0 E
Balikeşir, *Turkey* **13 E12** 39 35N 27 58 E
Balikpapan, *Indonesia* **22 D3** 1 10S 116 55 E
Balkan Mts., *Bulgaria* **13 C10** 43 15N 23 0 E
Balkhash, *Kazakhstan* **18 E9** 46 50N 74 50 E
Balkhash, L., *Kazakhstan* **18 E9** 46 0N 74 50 E
Ballarat, *Australia* **34 H7** 37 33S 143 50 E
Balrampur, *India* **23 F9** 27 30N 82 20 E
Balsas —►, *Mexico* **44 D4** 17 55N 102 10W
Baltic Sea, *Europe* **6 G11** 57 0N 19 0 E
Baltimore, *U.S.A.* **42 F9** 39 17N 76 37W
Bam, *Iran* **24 C4** 29 7N 58 14 E
Bamako, *Mali* **28 F3** 12 34N 7 55W
Bamberg, *Germany* **10 D6** 49 54N 10 54 E
Bamenda, *Cameroon* **30 C4** 5 57N 10 11 E
Bancroft, *Canada* **42 C9** 45 3N 77 51W

Banda Brunei 107

Banda, India 23 G8 25 30N 80 26 E
Banda Aceh, Indonesia 22 C1 5 35N 95 20 E
Banda Is., Indonesia 22 D4 4 37S 129 50 E
Banda Sea, Indonesia 22 D4 6 0S 130 0 E
Bandar Abbas, Iran 24 C4 27 15N 56 15 E
Bandar Khomeyni, Iran 24 B3 30 30N 49 5 E
Bandar Seri Begawan, Brunei 22 C3 4 52N 115 0 E
Bandundu, Zaïre 32 E3 3 15S 17 22 E
Bandung, Indonesia 22 D2 6 54S 107 36 E
Bangalore, India 25 D6 12 59N 77 40 E
Banggai Arch., Indonesia 22 D4 1 40S 123 30 E
Bangka, Indonesia 22 D2 2 0S 105 50 E
Bangka Str., Indonesia 22 D2 2 30S 105 30 E
Bangkok, Thailand 22 B2 13 45N 100 35 E
Bangladesh ■, Asia 23 H13 24 0N 90 0 E
Bangor, U.S.A. 43 C13 44 48N 68 46W
Bangui, C.A.R. 32 D3 4 23N 18 35 E
Bangweulu, L., Zambia 32 G6 11 0S 30 0 E
Banja Luka, Bos.-H. 12 B7 44 49N 17 11 E
Banjarmasin, Indonesia 22 D3 3 20S 114 35 E
Banjul, Gambia 28 F1 13 28N 16 40W
Banks I., Canada 38 A7 73 15N 121 30W
Bankura, India 23 H11 23 11N 87 18 E
Bannu, Pakistan 23 C3 33 0N 70 18 E
Banská Bystrica, Slovak Rep. 11 D10 48 46N 19 14 E
Banyak Is., Indonesia 22 C1 2 10N 97 10 E
Baoding, China 21 C6 38 50N 115 28 E
Baoji, China 20 C5 34 20N 107 5 E
Baotou, China 21 B6 40 32N 110 2 E
Bar Harbor, U.S.A. 43 C13 44 23N 68 13W
Bar-le-Duc, France 8 B6 48 47N 5 10 E
Baracaldo, Spain 9 A4 43 18N 2 59W
Baramula, India 23 B5 34 15N 74 20 E
Baran, India 23 G6 25 9N 76 40 E
Baranovichi, Belarus 11 B14 53 10N 26 0 E
Barbados ■, W. Indies 44 P22 13 10N 59 30W
Barberton, S. Africa 31 B5 25 42S 31 2 E
Barberton, U.S.A. 42 E7 41 0N 81 39W
Barcelona, Spain 9 B7 41 21N 2 10 E
Barddhaman, India 23 H11 23 14N 87 39 E
Bardstown, U.S.A. 42 G5 37 49N 85 28W
Bareilly, India 23 E7 28 22N 79 27 E
Barents Sea, Arctic 48 B8 73 0N 39 0 E
Barhi, India 23 G10 24 15N 85 25 E
Bari, Italy 12 D7 41 8N 16 51 E
Bari Doab, Pakistan 23 D4 30 20N 73 0 E
Barisal, Bangla. 23 H13 22 45N 90 20 E
Barito →, Indonesia 22 D3 4 0S 114 50 E
Barkly Tableland, Australia 34 D6 17 50S 136 40 E
Barkly West, S. Africa 31 B3 28 5S 24 31 E
Barletta, Italy 12 D7 41 19N 16 17 E
Barmer, India 23 G3 25 45N 71 20 E
Barnaul, Russia 18 D10 53 20N 83 40 E
Barques, Pt. Aux, U.S.A. 42 C6 44 4N 82 58W
Barquísimeto, Venezuela 46 A3 10 4N 69 19W
Barrancabermeja, Colombia 46 B2 7 0N 73 50W
Barranquilla, Colombia 46 A2 11 0N 74 50W
Barre, U.S.A. 43 C11 44 12N 72 30W
Barrie, Canada 42 C8 44 24N 79 40W
Barry's Bay, Canada 42 C9 45 29N 77 41W
Bashkortostan □, Russia 14 D10 54 0N 57 0 E
Basilan, Phil. 22 C4 6 35N 122 0 E
Baskatong, Rés., Canada 43 B10 46 46N 75 50W
Basle, Switz. 10 E4 47 35N 7 35 E
Basque Provinces □ = País Vasco □, Spain 9 A4 42 50N 2 45W
Basra, Iraq 24 B3 30 30N 47 50 E
Bass Str., Australia 34 H8 39 15S 146 30 E
Basse-Terre, Guadeloupe 44 M20 16 0N 61 44W
Bassein, Burma 25 D8 16 45N 94 30 E
Basseterre, St. Christopher-Nevis 44 K19 17 17N 62 43W
Basti, India 23 F9 26 52N 82 55 E
Bastia, France 8 E8 42 40N 9 30 E
Bata, Eq. Guin. 32 D1 1 57N 9 50 E
Batangas, Phil. 22 B4 13 35N 121 10 E
Batavia, U.S.A. 42 D8 43 0N 78 11W
Bath, U.K. 7 F5 51 23N 2 22W
Bath, Maine, U.S.A. 43 D13 43 55N 69 49W
Bath, N.Y., U.S.A. 42 D9 42 20N 77 19W
Bathurst, Australia 34 G8 33 25S 149 31 E
Bathurst, Canada 43 B15 47 37N 65 43W
Batna, Algeria 28 A6 35 34N 6 15 E
Baton Rouge, U.S.A. 41 D8 30 27N 91 11W
Battambang, Cambodia 22 B2 13 7N 103 12 E
Batticaloa, Sri Lanka 25 E7 7 43N 81 45 E
Battle Creek, U.S.A. 42 D5 42 19N 85 11W
Batu Is., Indonesia 22 D1 0 30S 98 25 E
Batu Pahat, Malaysia 22 C2 1 50N 102 56 E
Batumi, Georgia 15 F7 41 39N 41 44 E
Bavaria □ = Bayern □, Germany 10 D6 48 50N 12 0 E
Bawean, Indonesia 22 D3 5 46S 112 35 E
Bay City, U.S.A. 42 D6 43 36N 83 54W
Bayamo, Cuba 45 C9 20 20N 76 40W
Bayan Har Shan, China 20 C4 34 0N 98 0 E
Bayern □, Germany 10 D6 48 50N 12 0 E
Bayeux, France 8 B3 49 17N 0 42W
Bayonne, France 8 E3 43 30N 1 28W
Bayrūt, Lebanon 24 B2 33 53N 35 31 E
Beacon, U.S.A. 43 E11 41 30N 73 58W
Beagle, Canal, S. Amer. 47 H3 55 0S 68 30W
Béarn, France 8 E3 43 20N 0 30W
Beauce, Plaine de la, France 8 B4 48 10N 1 45 E
Beaufort Sea, Arctic 48 B18 72 0N 140 0W
Beaufort West, S. Africa 31 C3 32 18S 22 36 E
Beauharnois, Canada 43 C11 45 20N 73 52W
Beaumont, U.S.A. 41 D8 30 5N 94 6W
Beaune, France 8 C6 47 2N 4 50 E
Beauvais, France 8 B5 49 25N 2 8 E
Beaver Falls, U.S.A. 42 E7 40 46N 80 20W
Beaver I., U.S.A. 42 C5 45 40N 85 33W
Beawar, India 23 F5 26 3N 74 18 E
Béchar, Algeria 28 B4 31 38N 2 18W
Beckley, U.S.A. 42 G7 37 47N 81 11W
Bedford, Ind., U.S.A. 42 F4 38 52N 86 29W
Bedford, Va., U.S.A. 42 G8 37 20N 79 31W
Bei'an, China 21 B7 48 10N 126 20 E
Beijing, China 21 C6 39 55N 116 20 E
Beira, Mozam. 33 H6 19 50S 34 52 E
Békéscsaba, Hungary 11 E11 46 40N 21 5 E
Bela, Pakistan 23 F1 26 12N 66 20 E
Belarus ■, Europe 11 B14 53 30N 27 0 E
Belau ■, Pac. Oc. 36 G5 7 30N 134 30 E
Belaya Tserkov, Ukraine 11 D16 49 45N 30 10 E
Belcher Is., Canada 39 C12 56 15N 78 45W
Belém, Brazil 46 C5 1 20S 48 30W
Belfast, S. Africa 31 B5 25 42S 30 2 E
Belfast, U.K. 7 D4 54 37N 5 56W
Belfast, U.S.A. 43 C13 44 26N 69 1W
Belfort, France 8 C7 47 38N 6 50 E
Belgaum, India 25 D6 15 55N 74 35 E
Belgium ■, Europe 10 C3 50 30N 5 0 E
Belgorod, Russia 15 D6 50 35N 36 35 E
Belgrade, Serbia, Yug. 13 B9 44 50N 20 37 E
Beliton Is., Indonesia 22 D2 3 10S 107 50 E
Belize ■, Cent. Amer. 44 D7 17 0N 88 30W
Belize City, Belize 44 D7 17 25N 88 0W
Bellaire, U.S.A. 42 E7 40 1N 80 45W
Bellary, India 25 D6 15 10N 76 56 E
Belle-Ile, France 8 C2 47 20N 3 10W
Belle Isle, Str. of, Canada 39 C14 51 30N 56 30W
Bellefontaine, U.S.A. 42 E6 40 22N 83 46W
Belleville, Canada 42 C9 44 10N 77 23W
Bellingshausen Sea, Antarctica 48 D3 66 0S 80 0W
Bellinzona, Switz. 10 E5 46 11N 9 1 E
Belmopan, Belize 44 D7 17 18N 88 30W
Belo Horizonte, Brazil 46 D5 19 55S 43 56W
Belonia, India 23 H13 23 15N 91 30 E
Belorussia ■ = Belarus ■, Europe 11 B14 53 30N 27 0 E
Beltsy, Moldova 11 E14 47 48N 28 0 E
Belukha, Russia 18 E10 49 50N 86 50 E
Ben Nevis, U.K. 7 C4 56 48N 5 1W
Benares = Varanasi, India 23 G9 25 22N 83 0 E
Bendigo, Australia 34 H7 36 40S 144 15 E
Benevento, Italy 12 D6 41 8N 14 45 E
Bengal, Bay of, Ind. Oc. 23 K12 15 0N 90 0 E
Bengbu, China 21 C6 32 58N 117 20 E
Benghazi, Libya 29 B9 32 11N 20 3 E
Bengkulu, Indonesia 22 D2 3 50S 102 12 E
Beni Suef, Egypt 29 C11 29 5N 31 6 E
Benidorm, Spain 9 C5 38 33N 0 9W
Benin ■, Africa 30 C2 10 0N 2 0 E
Benin, Bight of, W. Afr. 30 C2 5 0N 3 0 E
Benin City, Nigeria 30 C3 6 20N 5 31 E
Benoni, S. Africa 31 B4 26 11S 28 18 E
Benton Harbor, U.S.A. 42 D4 42 6N 86 27W
Benue →, Nigeria 30 C3 7 48N 6 46 E
Benxi, China 21 B7 41 20N 123 48 E
Berbérati, C.A.R. 32 D3 4 15N 15 40 E
Berea, U.S.A. 42 G5 37 34N 84 17W
Bérgamo, Italy 12 B3 45 41N 9 43 E
Bergen, Norway 6 F9 60 20N 5 20 E
Bergerac, France 8 D4 44 51N 0 30 E
Berhala Str., Indonesia 22 D2 1 0S 104 15 E
Berhampur, India 23 K10 19 15N 84 54 E
Bering Sea, Pac. Oc. 36 B9 58 0N 171 0 E
Bering Strait, U.S.A. 38 B3 65 30N 169 0W
Berlin, Germany 10 B7 52 30N 13 25 E
Berlin, U.S.A. 43 C12 44 28N 71 11W
Bermuda ■, Atl. Oc. 45 A12 32 45N 65 0W
Berne, Switz. 10 E4 46 57N 7 28 E
Berry, France 8 C5 46 50N 2 0 E
Berwick, U.S.A. 42 E9 41 3N 76 14W
Berwick-upon-Tweed, U.K. 7 D5 55 46N 2 0W
Besançon, France 8 C7 47 15N 6 2 E
Bethal, S. Africa 31 B4 26 27S 29 28 E
Bethlehem, S. Africa 31 B4 28 14S 28 18 E
Bethlehem, U.S.A. 43 E10 40 37N 75 23W
Béthune, France 8 A5 50 30N 2 38 E
Bettiah, India 23 F10 26 48N 84 33 E
Betul, India 23 J6 21 58N 77 59 E
Béziers, France 8 E5 43 20N 3 12 E
Bhagalpur, India 23 G11 25 10N 87 0 E
Bhandara, India 23 J7 21 5N 79 42 E
Bhanrer Ra., India 23 H7 23 40N 79 45 E
Bharatpur, India 23 F6 27 15N 77 30 E
Bhatinda, India 23 D5 30 15N 74 57 E
Bhatpara, India 23 H12 22 50N 88 25 E
Bhavnagar, India 23 J4 21 45N 72 10 E
Bhilwara, India 23 G5 25 25N 74 38 E
Bhima →, India 25 D6 16 25N 77 17 E
Bhiwani, India 23 E6 28 50N 76 9 E
Bhopal, India 23 H6 23 20N 77 30 E
Bhubaneshwar, India 23 J10 20 15N 85 50 E
Bhuj, India 23 H2 23 15N 69 49 E
Bhusaval, India 23 J5 21 3N 75 46 E
Bhutan ■, Asia 23 F13 27 25N 90 30 E
Biafra, B. of, Africa 26 F4 3 30N 9 20 E
Biała Podlaska, Poland 11 B12 52 4N 23 6 E
Białystok, Poland 11 B12 53 10N 23 10 E
Biarritz, France 8 E3 43 29N 1 33W
Biddeford, U.S.A. 43 D12 43 30N 70 28W
Bié Plateau, Angola 33 G3 12 0S 16 0 E
Biel, Switz. 10 E4 47 8N 7 14 E
Bielefeld, Germany 10 B5 52 1N 8 33 E
Bielsko-Biała, Poland 11 D10 49 50N 19 2 E
Bien Hoa, Vietnam 22 B2 10 57N 106 49 E
Big Rapids, U.S.A. 42 D5 43 42N 85 29W
Bighorn Mts., U.S.A. 40 B5 44 30N 107 30W
Bihar, India 23 G10 25 5N 85 40 E
Bihar □, India 23 G10 25 0N 86 0 E
Bikaner, India 23 E4 28 2N 73 18 E
Bikini Atoll, Pac. Oc. 36 F8 12 0N 167 30 E
Bilaspur, India 23 H9 22 2N 82 15 E
Bilbao, Spain 9 A4 43 16N 2 56W
Billings, U.S.A. 40 A5 45 47N 108 30W
Bina-Etawah, India 23 G7 24 13N 78 14 E
Binghamton, U.S.A. 43 D10 42 6N 75 55W
Binjai, Indonesia 22 C1 3 20N 98 30 E
Bioko, Eq. Guin. 30 D3 3 30N 8 40 E
Birmingham, U.K. 7 E6 52 29N 1 52W
Birmingham, U.S.A. 41 D9 33 31N 86 48W
Biscay, B. of, Atl. Oc. 8 D1 45 0N 2 0W
Bishkek, Kyrgyzstan 18 E9 42 54N 74 46 E
Bisho, S. Africa 31 C4 32 50S 27 23 E
Biskra, Algeria 28 B6 34 50N 5 44 E
Bismarck Arch., Papua N. G. 34 A9 2 30S 150 0 E
Bissau, Guinea-Biss. 28 F1 11 45N 15 45W
Bitolj, Macedonia 13 D9 41 5N 21 10 E
Bitterfontein, S. Africa 31 C2 31 1S 18 32 E
Biwa-Ko, Japan 19 B5 35 15N 136 10 E
Biysk, Russia 18 D10 52 40N 85 0 E
Black Forest = Schwarzwald, Germany 10 D5 48 30N 8 20 E
Black Sea, Eurasia 15 F6 43 30N 35 0 E
Black Volta →, Africa 30 C1 8 41N 1 33W
Blackburn, U.K. 7 E5 53 45N 2 29W
Blackpool, U.K. 7 E5 53 49N 3 3W
Blacksburg, U.S.A. 42 G7 37 14N 80 25W
Blagoveshchensk, Russia 18 D14 50 20N 127 30 E
Blanc, Mont, Alps 8 D7 45 48N 6 50 E
Blantyre, Malawi 33 H6 15 45S 35 0 E
Blenheim, N.Z. 35 J13 41 38S 173 57 E
Blitar, Indonesia 22 D3 8 5S 112 11 E
Bloemfontein, S. Africa 31 B4 29 6S 26 7 E
Bloemhof, S. Africa 31 B4 27 38S 25 32 E
Blois, France 8 C4 47 35N 1 20 E
Bloomington, U.S.A. 42 F4 39 10N 86 32W
Bloomsburg, U.S.A. 42 E9 41 0N 76 27W
Blue Mts., Oreg., U.S.A. 40 A3 45 15N 119 0W
Blue Mts., Pa., U.S.A. 42 E9 40 30N 76 30W
Blue Nile →, Sudan 29 E11 15 38N 32 31 E
Blue Ridge Mts., U.S.A. 41 C10 36 30N 80 15W
Bluefield, U.S.A. 42 G7 37 15N 81 17W
Bobcaygeon, Canada 42 C8 44 33N 78 33W
Bobo-Dioulasso, Burkina Faso 28 F4 11 8N 4 13W
Bóbr →, Poland 10 B8 52 4N 15 4 E
Bobruysk, Belarus 11 B15 53 10N 29 15 E
Bochum, Germany 10 C4 51 28N 7 13 E
Boden, Sweden 6 E12 65 50N 21 42 E
Bodø, Norway 6 E10 67 17N 14 24 E
Bodrog →, Hungary 11 D11 48 11N 21 22 E
Bogor, Indonesia 22 D2 6 36S 106 48 E
Bogotá, Colombia 46 B2 4 34N 74 0W
Bogra, Bangla. 23 G12 24 51N 89 22 E
Bohemian Forest = Böhmerwald, Germany 10 D7 49 8N 13 14 E
Böhmerwald, Germany 10 D7 49 8N 13 14 E
Bohol, Phil. 22 C4 9 50N 124 10 E
Bohol Sea, Phil. 22 C4 9 0N 124 0 E
Boise, U.S.A. 40 B3 43 37N 116 13W
Bolgatanga, Ghana 30 B1 10 44N 0 53W
Bolivia ■, S. Amer. 46 D3 17 6S 64 0W
Bolivian Plateau, S. Amer. 46 D3 20 0S 67 30W
Bologna, Italy 12 B4 44 29N 11 20 E
Bolshevik I., Russia 18 B12 78 30N 102 0 E
Bolton, U.K. 7 E5 53 35N 2 26W
Bolzano, Italy 12 A4 46 31N 11 22 E
Boma, Zaïre 32 F2 5 50S 13 4 E
Bonifacio, France 8 F8 41 24N 9 10 E
Bonn, Germany 10 C4 50 46N 7 6 E
Boonville, U.S.A. 42 F4 38 3N 87 16W
Boothia, Gulf of, Canada 39 A11 71 0N 90 0W
Boothia Pen., Canada 38 A10 71 0N 94 0W
Borås, Sweden 6 G10 57 43N 12 56 E
Bordeaux, France 8 D3 44 50N 0 36W
Borisov, Belarus 11 A15 54 17N 28 28 E
Borneo, E. Indies 22 C3 1 0N 115 0 E
Bornholm, Denmark 6 G11 55 10N 15 0 E
Bosnia-Herzegovina ■, Europe 12 B7 44 0N 17 0 E
Bosporus, Turkey 13 D13 41 10N 29 10 E
Boston, U.S.A. 43 D12 42 22N 71 4W
Bothnia, G. of, Europe 6 F12 63 0N 20 15 E
Botletle →, Botswana 31 A3 20 10S 23 15 E
Botoşani, Romania 11 E14 47 42N 26 41 E
Botswana ■, Africa 31 A3 22 0S 24 0 E
Bouaké, Ivory C. 28 G3 7 40N 5 2W
Bouar, C.A.R. 32 C3 6 0N 15 40 E
Boulogne-sur-Mer, France 8 A4 50 42N 1 36 E
Bourbonnais, France 8 C5 46 28N 3 0 E
Bourg-en-Bresse, France 8 C6 46 13N 5 12 E
Bourges, France 8 C5 47 9N 2 25 E
Bourgogne, France 8 C6 47 0N 4 50 E
Bourke, Australia 34 G8 30 8S 145 55 E
Bournemouth, U.K. 7 F6 50 43N 1 52W
Bowling Green, Ky., U.S.A. 42 G4 36 59N 86 27W
Bowling Green, Ohio, U.S.A. 42 E6 41 23N 83 39W
Bracebridge, Canada 42 C8 45 2N 79 19W
Bräcke, Sweden 6 F11 62 45N 15 26 E
Bradford, U.K. 7 E6 53 47N 1 45W
Bradford, U.S.A. 42 E8 41 58N 78 38W
Braga, Portugal 9 B1 41 35N 8 25W
Brahmanbaria, Bangla. 23 H13 23 58N 91 15 E
Brahmani →, India 23 J11 20 39N 86 46 E
Brahmaputra →, India 23 H12 23 58N 89 50 E
Brăila, Romania 11 F14 45 19N 27 59 E
Brampton, Canada 42 D8 43 45N 79 45W
Brandenburg, Germany 10 B7 52 25N 12 33 E
Brandenburg □, Germany 10 B6 52 50N 13 0 E
Brandon, Canada 38 D10 49 50N 99 57W
Brandvlei, S. Africa 31 C3 30 25S 20 30 E
Brantford, Canada 42 D7 43 10N 80 15W
Bras d'Or, L., Canada 43 C17 45 50N 60 50W
Brasília, Brazil 46 D5 15 47S 47 55W
Braşov, Romania 11 F13 45 38N 25 35 E
Brassey Ra., Malaysia 22 C3 5 0N 117 15 E
Bratislava, Slovak Rep. 11 D9 48 10N 17 7 E
Brattleboro, U.S.A. 43 D11 42 51N 72 34W
Brazil, U.S.A. 42 F4 39 32N 87 8W
Brazil ■, S. Amer. 46 D5 12 0S 50 0W
Brazzaville, Congo 32 E3 4 9S 15 12 E
Breda, Neths. 10 C3 51 35N 4 45 E
Bredasdorp, S. Africa 31 C3 34 33S 20 2 E
Bregenz, Austria 10 E5 47 30N 9 45 E
Breiðafjörður, Iceland 6 B2 65 15N 23 15W
Bremen, Germany 10 B5 53 4N 8 47 E
Bremerhaven, Germany 10 B5 53 33N 8 36 E
Brenner P., Austria 10 E6 47 2N 11 30 E
Bréscia, Italy 12 B4 45 33N 10 15 E
Brest, Belarus 11 B12 52 10N 23 40 E
Brest, France 8 B1 48 24N 4 31W
Bretagne, France 8 B2 48 10N 3 0W
Brewer, U.S.A. 43 C13 44 48N 68 46W
Breyten, S. Africa 31 B4 26 16S 30 0 E
Briançon, France 8 D7 44 54N 6 39 E
Bridgeport, U.S.A. 43 E11 41 11N 73 12W
Bridgeton, U.S.A. 43 F10 39 26N 75 14W
Bridgetown, Barbados 44 P22 13 5N 59 30W
Bridgewater, Canada 43 C15 44 25N 64 31W
Brighton, U.K. 7 F6 50 49N 0 7W
Bríndisi, Italy 13 D7 40 39N 17 55 E
Brisbane, Australia 34 F9 27 25S 153 2 E
Bristol, U.K. 7 F5 51 26N 2 35W
Bristol Channel, U.K. 7 F4 51 18N 4 30W
British Columbia □, Canada 38 C7 55 0N 125 15W
British Isles, Europe 4 E5 54 0N 4 0W
Brits, S. Africa 31 B4 25 37S 27 48 E
Britstown, S. Africa 31 C3 30 37S 23 30 E
Brittany = Bretagne, France 8 B2 48 10N 3 0W
Brive-la-Gaillarde, France 8 D4 45 10N 1 32 E
Brno, Czech. 11 D9 49 10N 16 35 E
Brocken, Germany 10 C6 51 47N 10 37 E
Brockville, Canada 43 C10 44 35N 75 41W
Broken Hill, Australia 34 G7 31 58S 141 29 E
Brooks Ra., U.S.A. 38 B5 68 40N 147 0W
Bruay-en-Artois, France 8 A5 50 29N 2 33 E
Bruce, Mt., Australia 34 E2 22 37S 118 8 E
Brugge, Belgium 10 C2 51 13N 3 13 E
Brunei ■, Asia 22 C3 4 50N 115 0 E

Brunswick, *Germany* **10 B6** 52 15N 10 31 E
Brunswick, *U.S.A.* **43 D13** 43 55N 69 58W
Brussels, *Belgium* **10 C3** 50 51N 4 21 E
Bryan, *U.S.A.* **42 E5** 41 28N 84 33W
Bryansk, *Russia* **14 D5** 53 13N 34 25 E
Bucaramanga, *Colombia* **46 B2** 7 0N 73 0W
Bucharest, *Romania* **11 F14** 44 27N 26 10 E
Buckhannon, *U.S.A.* **42 F7** 39 0N 80 8W
Buckingham, *Canada* **43 C10** 45 37N 75 24W
Bucyrus, *U.S.A.* **42 E6** 40 48N 82 59W
Budapest, *Hungary* **11 E10** 47 29N 19 5 E
Buena Vista, *U.S.A.* **42 G8** 37 44N 79 21W
Buenos Aires, *Argentina* **47 F4** 34 30S 58 20W
Buffalo, *U.S.A.* **42 D8** 42 53N 78 53W
Bug —►, *Poland* **11 B11** 52 31N 21 5 E
Buh —►, *Ukraine* **15 E5** 46 59N 31 58 E
Bujumbura, *Burundi* **32 E5** 3 16S 29 18 E
Bukavu, *Zaïre* **32 E5** 2 20S 28 52 E
Bukittinggi, *Indonesia* **22 D2** 0 20S 100 20 E
Bulandshahr, *India* **23 E6** 28 28N 77 51 E
Bulawayo, *Zimbabwe* **33 J5** 20 7S 28 32 E
Bulgaria ■, *Europe* **13 C11** 42 35N 25 30 E
Bunbury, *Australia* **34 G2** 33 20S 115 35 E
Bundaberg, *Australia* **34 E9** 24 54S 152 22 E
Bundi, *India* **23 G5** 25 30N 75 35 E
Buraydah, *Si. Arabia* **24 C3** 26 20N 44 8 E
Burgas, *Bulgaria* **13 C12** 42 33N 27 29 E
Burgersdorp, *S. Africa* **31 C4** 31 0S 26 20 E
Burgos, *Spain* **9 A4** 42 21N 3 41W
Burgundy = Bourgogne, *France* **8 C6** 47 0N 4 50 E
Burkina Faso ■, *Africa* **30 B1** 12 0N 1 0W
Burlington, *Vt., U.S.A.* **43 C11** 44 29N 73 12W
Burlington, *Wis., U.S.A.* **42 D3** 42 41N 88 17W
Burlyu-Tyube, *Kazakhstan* **18 E9** 46 30N 79 10 E
Burma ■, *Asia* **25 C8** 21 0N 96 30 E
Burnie, *Australia* **34 J8** 41 4S 145 56 E
Bursa, *Turkey* **13 D13** 40 15N 29 5 E
Buru, *Indonesia* **22 D4** 3 30S 126 30 E
Burundi ■, *Africa* **32 E5** 3 15S 30 0 E
Bushehr, *Iran* **24 C4** 28 55N 50 55 E
Butler, *U.S.A.* **42 E8** 40 52N 79 54W
Buton, *Indonesia* **22 D4** 5 0S 122 45 E
Butterworth, *Malaysia* **22 C2** 5 24N 100 23 E
Butuan, *Phil.* **22 C4** 8 57N 125 33 E
Buzău, *Romania* **11 F14** 45 10N 26 50 E
Bydgoszcz, *Poland* **11 B9** 53 10N 18 0 E
Byelorussia = Belarus ■, *Europe* **11 B14** 53 30N 27 0 E
Bytom, *Poland* **11 C10** 50 25N 18 54 E

C

Cabinda □, *Angola* **32 F2** 5 0S 12 30 E
Cabonga, Réservoir, *Canada* **42 B9** 47 20N 76 40W
Čačak, *Serbia, Yug.* **13 C9** 43 54N 20 20 E
Cáceres, *Spain* **9 C2** 39 26N 6 23W
Cadillac, *U.S.A.* **42 C5** 44 15N 85 24W
Cádiz, *Spain* **9 D2** 36 30N 6 20W
Caen, *France* **8 B3** 49 10N 0 22W
Cagayan de Oro, *Phil.* **22 C4** 8 30N 124 40 E
Cágliari, *Italy* **12 E3** 39 13N 9 7 E
Cahors, *France* **8 D4** 44 27N 1 27 E
Caicos Is., *W. Indies* **45 C10** 21 40N 71 40W
Cairns, *Australia* **34 D8** 16 57S 145 45 E
Cairo, *Egypt* **29 B11** 30 1N 31 14 E
Calabar, *Nigeria* **30 D3** 4 57N 8 20 E
Calábria □, *Italy* **12 E7** 39 0N 16 30 E
Calais, *France* **8 A4** 50 57N 1 56 E
Calais, *U.S.A.* **43 C14** 45 11N 67 17W
Calamian Group, *Phil.* **22 B3** 11 50N 119 55 E
Calapan, *Phil.* **22 B4** 13 25N 121 7 E
Calcutta, *India* **23 H12** 22 36N 88 24 E
Caledon, *S. Africa* **31 C2** 34 14S 19 26 E
Caledon —►, *S. Africa* **31 C4** 30 31S 26 5 E
Calgary, *Canada* **38 C8** 51 0N 114 10W
Cali, *Colombia* **46 B2** 3 25N 76 35W
Calicut, *India* **25 D6** 11 15N 75 43 E
California □, *U.S.A.* **40 C2** 37 30N 119 30W
California, G. of, *Mexico* **44 B2** 27 0N 111 0W
Calitzdorp, *S. Africa* **31 C3** 33 33S 21 42 E
Callao, *Peru* **46 D2** 12 0S 77 0W
Caltanissetta, *Italy* **12 F6** 37 29N 14 4 E
Calvi, *France* **8 E8** 42 34N 8 45 E
Calvinia, *S. Africa* **31 C2** 31 28S 19 45 E
Camagüey, *Cuba* **45 C9** 21 20N 78 0W
Camargue, *France* **8 E6** 43 34N 4 34 E
Cambay, G. of, *India* **23 J4** 20 45N 72 30 E
Cambodia ■, *Asia* **22 B2** 12 15N 105 0 E
Cambrai, *France* **8 A5** 50 11N 3 14 E
Cambrian Mts., *U.K.* **7 E5** 52 3N 3 57W
Cambridge, *U.K.* **7 E7** 52 12N 0 8 E
Cambridge, *Mass., U.S.A.* **43 D12** 42 22N 71 6W
Cambridge, *Md., U.S.A.* **43 F9** 38 34N 76 5W
Cambridge, *Ohio, U.S.A.* **42 E7** 40 2N 81 35W
Cambridge Bay, *Canada* **38 B9** 69 10N 105 0W
Camden, *U.S.A.* **43 F10** 39 56N 75 7W
Cameroon ■, *Africa* **30 C4** 6 0N 12 30 E
Cameroun, Mt., *Cameroon* **30 D3** 4 13N 9 10 E
Campánia □, *Italy* **12 D6** 41 0N 14 30 E
Campbellsville, *U.S.A.* **42 G5** 37 21N 85 20W
Campbellton, *Canada* **43 B14** 47 57N 66 43W
Campeche, *Mexico* **44 D6** 19 50N 90 32W
Campeche, G. of, *Mexico* **44 D6** 19 30N 93 0W
Campina Grande, *Brazil* **46 C6** 7 20S 35 47W
Campinas, *Brazil* **47 E5** 22 50S 47 0W
Campo Grande, *Brazil* **46 E4** 20 25S 54 40W
Campos, *Brazil* **46 E5** 21 50S 41 20W
Camrose, *Canada* **38 C8** 53 0N 112 50W
Can Tho, *Vietnam* **22 B2** 10 2N 105 46 E
Canada ■, *N. Amer.* **38 C10** 60 0N 100 0W
Canadian Shield, *Canada* **39 C10** 53 0N 75 0W
Canandaigua, *U.S.A.* **42 D9** 42 54N 77 17W
Canary Is., *Atl. Oc.* **28 C1** 28 30N 16 0W
Canaveral, C., *U.S.A.* **41 E10** 28 27N 80 32W
Canberra, *Australia* **34 H8** 35 15S 149 8 E
Cannes, *France* **8 E7** 43 32N 7 1 E
Canso, *Canada* **43 C17** 45 20N 61 0W
Cantabria □, *Spain* **9 A4** 43 10N 4 0W
Cantabrian Mts., *Spain* **9 A3** 43 0N 5 10W
Canterbury, *U.K.* **7 F7** 51 16N 1 6 E
Canton, *N.Y., U.S.A.* **43 C10** 44 36N 75 10W
Canton, *Ohio, U.S.A.* **42 E7** 40 48N 81 23W
Cap-Chat, *Canada* **43 A14** 49 6N 66 40W
Cap-de-la-Madeleine, *Canada* **43 B11** 46 22N 72 31W
Cape Breton I., *Canada* **43 B17** 46 0N 60 30W
Cape Charles, *U.S.A.* **43 G10** 37 16N 76 1W
Cape Coast, *Ghana* **30 C1** 5 5N 1 15W
Cape May, *U.S.A.* **43 F10** 38 56N 74 56W
Cape Town, *S. Africa* **31 C2** 33 55S 18 22 E
Cape Verde Is. ■, *Atl. Oc.* **27 E1** 17 10N 25 20W
Cape York Peninsula, *Australia* **34 C7** 12 0S 142 30 E
Capreol, *Canada* **42 B7** 46 43N 80 56W
Capri, *Italy* **12 D6** 40 33N 14 14 E
Caracas, *Venezuela* **46 A3** 10 30N 66 55W
Carbondale, *U.S.A.* **43 E10** 41 35N 75 30W
Carcassonne, *France* **8 E5** 43 13N 2 20 E
Cardiff, *U.K.* **7 F5** 51 29N 3 10W
Caribbean Sea, *W. Indies* **45 E10** 15 0N 75 0W
Caribou, *U.S.A.* **43 B13** 46 52N 68 1W
Carleton Place, *Canada* **43 C9** 45 8N 76 9W
Carletonville, *S. Africa* **31 B4** 26 23S 27 22 E
Carlisle, *U.S.A.* **42 E9** 40 12N 77 12W
Carmaux, *France* **8 D5** 44 3N 2 10 E
Carmi, *U.S.A.* **42 F3** 38 5N 88 10W
Carnarvon, *Australia* **34 E1** 24 51S 113 42 E
Carnarvon, *S. Africa* **31 C3** 30 56S 22 8 E
Carnegie, L., *Australia* **34 F3** 26 5S 122 30 E
Caro, *U.S.A.* **42 D6** 43 29N 83 24W
Carolina, *S. Africa* **31 B5** 26 5S 30 6 E
Caroline Is., *Pac. Oc.* **36 G6** 8 0N 150 0 E
Carpathians, *Europe* **11 D11** 49 30N 21 0 E
Carpentaria, G. of, *Australia* **34 C6** 14 0S 139 0 E
Carpentras, *France* **8 D6** 44 3N 5 2 E
Cartagena, *Colombia* **46 A2** 10 25N 75 33W
Cartagena, *Spain* **9 D5** 37 38N 0 59W
Casablanca, *Morocco* **28 B3** 33 36N 7 36W
Cascade Ra., *U.S.A.* **40 A2** 47 0N 121 30W
Casper, *U.S.A.* **40 B5** 42 51N 106 19W
Caspian Sea, *Eurasia* **15 F9** 43 0N 50 0 E
Cass City, *U.S.A.* **42 D6** 43 36N 83 11W
Castellón de la Plana, *Spain* **9 C5** 39 58N 0 3W
Castelsarrasin, *France* **8 E4** 44 2N 1 7 E
Castilla La Mancha □, *Spain* **9 C4** 39 30N 3 30W
Castilla y Leon □, *Spain* **9 B3** 42 0N 5 0W
Castres, *France* **8 E5** 43 37N 2 13 E
Castries, *St. Lucia* **44 N21** 14 2N 60 58W
Cataluña □, *Spain* **9 B6** 41 40N 1 15 E
Catanduanes, *Phil.* **22 B4** 13 50N 124 20 E
Catánia, *Italy* **12 F6** 37 30N 15 6 E
Catanzaro, *Italy* **12 E7** 38 54N 16 35 E
Catskill, *U.S.A.* **43 D11** 42 14N 73 52W
Catskill Mts., *U.S.A.* **43 D10** 42 10N 74 25W
Caucasus Mountains, *Eurasia* **15 F7** 42 50N 44 0 E
Caxias do Sul, *Brazil* **47 E4** 29 10S 51 10W
Cayenne, *Fr. Guiana* **46 B4** 5 5N 52 18W
Cayuga L., *U.S.A.* **42 D9** 42 41N 76 41W
Cedar Rapids, *U.S.A.* **41 B8** 41 59N 91 40W
Cegléd, *Hungary* **11 E10** 47 11N 19 47 E
Celebes Sea, *Indonesia* **22 C4** 3 0N 123 0 E
Celina, *U.S.A.* **42 E5** 40 33N 84 35W
Central African Rep. ■, *Africa* **32 C4** 7 0N 20 0 E
Central Makran Range, *Pakistan* **24 C5** 26 30N 64 15 E
Cephalonia = Kefallinía, *Greece* **13 E9** 38 20N 20 30 E
Ceram, *Indonesia* **22 D4** 3 10S 129 0 E
Ceram Sea, *Indonesia* **22 D4** 2 30S 128 30 E
Ceres, *S. Africa* **31 C2** 33 21S 19 18 E
Cerignola, *Italy* **12 D6** 41 17N 15 53 E
České Budějovice, *Czech.* **10 D8** 48 55N 14 25 E
Ceuta, *N. Afr.* **9 E3** 35 52N 5 18W
Cévennes, *France* **8 D5** 44 10N 3 50 E
Chad ■, *Africa* **29 E8** 15 0N 17 15 E
Chakradharpur, *India* **23 H10** 22 45N 85 40 E
Chaleur B., *Canada* **43 B15** 47 55N 65 30W
Chalisgaon, *India* **23 J5** 20 30N 75 10 E
Chalon-sur-Saône, *France* **8 C6** 46 48N 4 50 E
Châlons-en-Champagne, *France* **8 B6** 48 58N 4 20 E
Chamba, *India* **23 C6** 32 35N 76 10 E
Chambal —►, *India* **23 F7** 26 29N 79 15 E
Chambersburg, *U.S.A.* **42 F9** 39 56N 77 40W
Chambéry, *France* **8 D6** 45 34N 5 55 E
Champagne, *France* **8 B6** 48 40N 4 20 E
Champaign, *U.S.A.* **42 E3** 40 7N 88 15W
Champlain, L., *U.S.A.* **43 C11** 44 40N 73 20W
Chandigarh, *India* **23 D6** 30 43N 76 47 E
Chandpur, *Bangla.* **23 H13** 23 8N 90 45 E
Changchun, *China* **21 B7** 43 57N 125 17 E
Changde, *China* **21 D6** 29 4N 111 35 E
Changsha, *China* **21 D6** 28 12N 113 0 E
Changzhou, *China* **21 C6** 31 47N 119 58 E
Chanthaburi, *Thailand* **22 B2** 12 38N 102 12 E
Chapleau, *Canada* **42 B6** 47 50N 83 24W
Chapra, *India* **23 G10** 25 48N 84 44 E
Chardzhou, *Turkmenistan* **18 F8** 39 6N 63 34 E
Chārīkār, *Afghan.* **23 B2** 35 0N 69 10 E
Charleroi, *Belgium* **10 C3** 50 24N 4 27 E
Charles, C., *U.S.A.* **43 G10** 37 7N 75 58W
Charleston, *Ill., U.S.A.* **42 F3** 39 30N 88 10W
Charleston, *S.C., U.S.A.* **41 D11** 32 46N 79 56W
Charleston, *W. Va., U.S.A.* **42 F7** 38 21N 81 38W
Charleville, *Australia* **34 F8** 26 24S 146 15 E
Charleville-Mézières, *France* **8 B6** 49 44N 4 40 E
Charlevoix, *U.S.A.* **42 C5** 45 19N 85 16W
Charlotte, *Mich., U.S.A.* **42 D5** 42 34N 84 50W
Charlotte, *N.C., U.S.A.* **41 C10** 35 13N 80 51W
Charlottesville, *U.S.A.* **42 F8** 38 2N 78 30W
Charlottetown, *Canada* **43 B16** 46 14N 63 8W
Charolles, *France* **8 C6** 46 27N 4 16 E
Charters Towers, *Australia* **34 E8** 20 5S 146 13 E
Chartres, *France* **8 B4** 48 29N 1 30 E
Châteaubriant, *France* **8 C3** 47 43N 1 23W
Châteaulin, *France* **8 B1** 48 11N 4 8W
Châteauroux, *France* **8 C4** 46 50N 1 40 E
Châtellerault, *France* **8 C4** 46 50N 0 30 E
Chatham, *N.B., Canada* **43 B15** 47 2N 65 28W
Chatham, *Ont., Canada* **42 D6** 42 24N 82 11W
Chattanooga, *U.S.A.* **41 C9** 35 3N 85 19W
Chaumont, *France* **8 B6** 48 7N 5 8 E
Cheb, *Czech.* **10 C7** 50 9N 12 28 E
Cheboksary, *Russia* **14 C8** 56 8N 47 12 E
Cheboygan, *U.S.A.* **42 C5** 45 39N 84 29W
Chechenia □, *Russia* **15 F8** 43 30N 45 29 E
Chedabucto B., *Canada* **43 C17** 45 25N 61 8W
Chełm, *Poland* **11 C12** 51 8N 23 30 E
Chelyabinsk, *Russia* **18 D8** 55 10N 61 24 E
Chelyuskin, C., *Russia* **18 B12** 77 30N 103 0 E
Chemnitz, *Germany* **10 C7** 50 51N 12 54 E
Chenab —►, *Pakistan* **23 D3** 30 23N 71 2 E
Chengdu, *China* **20 C5** 30 38N 104 2 E
Cher —►, *France* **8 C4** 47 21N 0 29 E
Cherbourg, *France* **8 B3** 49 39N 1 40W
Cheremkhovo, *Russia* **18 D12** 53 8N 103 1 E
Cherepovets, *Russia* **14 C6** 59 5N 37 55 E
Cherkassy, *Ukraine* **15 E5** 49 27N 32 4 E
Chernigov, *Ukraine* **14 D5** 51 28N 31 20 E
Chernobyl, *Ukraine* **11 C16** 51 20N 30 15 E
Chernovtsy, *Ukraine* **11 D13** 48 15N 25 52 E
Cherski Ra., *Russia* **18 C16** 65 0N 143 0 E
Chesapeake B., *U.S.A.* **42 F9** 38 0N 76 10W
Chester, *U.S.A.* **43 F10** 39 51N 75 22W
Chesterfield Inlet, *Canada* **38 B10** 63 30N 90 45W
Chesuncook L., *U.S.A.* **43 B13** 46 0N 69 21W
Chhatarpur, *India* **23 G7** 24 55N 79 35 E
Chiai, *Taiwan* **21 D7** 23 29N 120 25 E
Chiba, *Japan* **19 B7** 35 30N 140 7 E
Chibougamau, *Canada* **43 A10** 49 56N 74 24W
Chibougamau L., *Canada* **43 A10** 49 50N 74 20W
Chicago, *U.S.A.* **42 E4** 41 53N 87 38W
Chiclayo, *Peru* **46 C2** 6 42S 79 50W
Chicopee, *U.S.A.* **43 D11** 42 9N 72 37W
Chicoutimi, *Canada* **43 A12** 48 28N 71 5W
Chidley, C., *Canada* **39 B13** 60 23N 64 26W
Chieti, *Italy* **12 C6** 42 21N 14 10 E
Chihli, G. of, *China* **21 C6** 39 0N 119 0 E
Chihuahua, *Mexico* **44 B3** 28 40N 106 3W
Chile ■, *S. Amer.* **47 F2** 35 0S 72 0W
Chilka L., *India* **23 K10** 19 40N 85 25 E
Chillán, *Chile* **47 F2** 36 40S 72 10W
Chillicothe, *U.S.A.* **42 F6** 39 20N 82 59W
Chilpancingo, *Mexico* **44 D5** 17 30N 99 30W
Chilton, *U.S.A.* **42 C3** 44 2N 88 10W
Chilung, *Taiwan* **21 D7** 25 3N 121 45 E
Chimborazo, *Ecuador* **46 C2** 1 29S 78 55W
Chimbote, *Peru* **46 C2** 9 0S 78 35W
Chimkent, *Kazakhstan* **18 E8** 42 18N 69 36 E
China ■, *Asia* **21 C6** 30 0N 110 0 E
Chindwin —►, *Burma* **25 C8** 21 26N 95 15 E
Chingola, *Zambia* **33 G5** 12 31S 27 53 E
Chinon, *France* **8 C4** 47 10N 0 15 E
Chíos, *Greece* **13 E12** 38 27N 26 9 E
Chipata, *Zambia* **33 G6** 13 38S 32 28 E
Chipman, *Canada* **43 B15** 46 6N 65 53W
Chita, *Russia* **18 D13** 52 0N 113 35 E
Chitral, *Pakistan* **23 B3** 35 50N 71 56 E
Chittagong, *Bangla.* **23 H13** 22 19N 91 48 E
Cholet, *France* **8 C3** 47 4N 0 52W
Chŏngjin, *N. Korea* **21 B7** 41 47N 129 50 E
Chongqing, *China* **20 D5** 29 35N 106 25 E
Chorzów, *Poland* **11 C10** 50 18N 18 57 E
Choybalsan, *Mongolia* **21 B6** 48 4N 114 30 E
Christchurch, *N.Z.* **35 J13** 43 33S 172 47 E
Christiana, *S. Africa* **31 B4** 27 52S 25 8 E
Chukot Ra., *Russia* **18 C19** 68 0N 175 0 E
Chumphon, *Thailand* **22 B1** 10 35N 99 14 E
Chur, *Switz.* **10 E5** 46 52N 9 32 E
Churchill —►, *Man., Canada* **38 C10** 58 47N 94 12W
Churchill —►, *Nfld., Canada* **39 C13** 53 19N 60 10W
Churu, *India* **23 E5** 28 20N 74 50 E
Chushal, *India* **23 C7** 33 40N 78 40 E
Chuvashia □, *Russia* **14 C8** 55 30N 47 0 E
Cicero, *U.S.A.* **42 E4** 41 48N 87 48W
Ciechanów, *Poland* **11 B11** 52 52N 20 38 E
Ciénaga, *Colombia* **46 A2** 11 1N 74 15W
Cienfuegos, *Cuba* **45 C8** 22 10N 80 30W
Cincinnati, *U.S.A.* **42 F5** 39 6N 84 31W
Cinto, Mte., *France* **8 E8** 42 24N 8 54 E
Circleville, *U.S.A.* **42 F6** 39 36N 82 57W
Cirebon, *Indonesia* **22 D2** 6 45S 108 32 E
Citlaltépetl, *Mexico* **44 D5** 19 0N 97 20W
Ciudad Bolívar, *Venezuela* **46 B3** 8 5N 63 36W
Ciudad Guayana, *Venezuela* **46 B3** 8 0N 62 30W
Ciudad Juárez, *Mexico* **44 A3** 31 40N 106 28W
Ciudad Madero, *Mexico* **44 C5** 22 19N 97 50W
Ciudad Obregón, *Mexico* **44 B3** 27 28N 109 59W
Ciudad Real, *Spain* **9 C4** 38 59N 3 55W
Ciudad Victoria, *Mexico* **44 C5** 23 41N 99 9W
Clanwilliam, *S. Africa* **31 C2** 32 11S 18 52 E
Claremont, *U.S.A.* **43 D11** 43 23N 72 20W
Clarksburg, *U.S.A.* **42 F7** 39 17N 80 30W
Clarksville, *U.S.A.* **41 C9** 36 32N 87 21W
Clearfield, *U.S.A.* **42 E8** 41 2N 78 27W
Clermont-Ferrand, *France* **8 D5** 45 46N 3 4 E
Cleveland, *U.S.A.* **42 E7** 41 30N 81 42W
Clifton Forge, *U.S.A.* **42 G8** 37 49N 79 50W
Cluj-Napoca, *Romania* **11 E12** 46 47N 23 38 E
Clyde —►, *U.K.* **7 D4** 55 55N 4 30W
Coast Mts., *Canada* **38 C7** 55 0N 129 20W
Coast Ranges, *U.S.A.* **40 B2** 39 0N 123 0W
Coaticook, *Canada* **43 C12** 45 10N 71 46W
Coatzacoalcos, *Mexico* **44 D6** 18 7N 94 25W
Cobourg, *Canada* **42 D8** 43 58N 78 10W
Cochabamba, *Bolivia* **46 D3** 17 26S 66 10W
Cochin, *India* **25 E6** 9 59N 76 22 E
Cochrane, *Canada* **42 A7** 49 0N 81 0W
Cockburn I., *Canada* **42 C6** 45 55N 83 22W
Cod, C., *U.S.A.* **41 B13** 42 5N 70 10W
Cognac, *France* **8 D3** 45 41N 0 20W
Coimbatore, *India* **25 D6** 11 2N 76 59 E
Coimbra, *Portugal* **9 B1** 40 15N 8 27W
Colebrook, *U.S.A.* **43 C12** 44 54N 71 30W
Colesberg, *S. Africa* **31 C4** 30 45S 25 5 E
Colima, *Mexico* **44 D4** 19 14N 103 43W
Collingwood, *Canada* **42 C7** 44 29N 80 13W
Colmar, *France* **8 B7** 48 5N 7 20 E
Cologne, *Germany* **10 C4** 50 56N 6 57 E
Colombia ■, *S. Amer.* **46 B2** 3 45N 73 0W
Colombo, *Sri Lanka* **25 E6** 6 56N 79 58 E
Colón, *Panama* **44 H14** 9 20N 79 54W
Colonial Heights, *U.S.A.* **42 G9** 37 15N 77 25W
Colorado □, *U.S.A.* **40 C5** 39 30N 105 30W
Colorado —►, *N. Amer.* **40 D4** 31 45N 114 40W
Colorado —►, *U.S.A.* **41 E7** 28 36N 95 59W
Colorado Plateau, *U.S.A.* **40 C4** 37 0N 111 0W
Colorado Springs, *U.S.A.* **40 C6** 38 50N 104 49W
Columbia, *U.S.A.* **41 D10** 34 0N 81 2W
Columbia —►, *U.S.A.* **40 A2** 46 15N 124 5W
Columbia, District of □, *U.S.A.* **42 F9** 38 55N 77 0W
Columbus, *Ga., U.S.A.* **41 D10** 32 28N 84 59W
Columbus, *Ind., U.S.A.* **42 F5** 39 13N 85 55W
Columbus, *Ohio, U.S.A.* **42 F6** 39 58N 83 0W
Comilla, *Bangla.* **23 H13** 23 28N 91 10 E
Communism Pk., *Tajikistan* **18 F9** 39 0N 72 2 E

Como   **Erie, L.**

Eritrea   **Greenville**

111

Greenville — Jahrom

Greenville, *Ohio, U.S.A.* **42 E5** 40 6N 84 38W
Grenada ■, *W. Indies* **44 Q20** 12 10N 61 40W
Grenoble, *France* **8 D6** 45 12N 5 42 E
Grey Ra., *Australia* **34 F7** 27 0S 143 30 E
Greymouth, *N.Z.* **35 J13** 42 29S 171 13 E
Greytown, *S. Africa* **31 B5** 29 1S 30 36 E
Gris-Nez, C., *France* **8 A4** 50 52N 1 35 E
Grodno, *Belarus* **11 B12** 53 42N 23 52 E
Groningen, *Neths.* **10 B4** 53 15N 6 35 E
Groot —►, *S. Africa* **31 C3** 33 45S 24 36 E
Groot Vis —►, *S. Africa* **31 C4** 33 28S 27 5 E
Gross Glockner, *Austria* **10 E7** 47 5N 12 40 E
Groundhog —►, *Canada* **42 A6** 48 45N 82 58W
Groznyy, *Russia* **15 F8** 43 20N 45 45 E
Grudziądz, *Poland* **11 B10** 53 30N 18 47 E
Guadalajara, *Mexico* **44 C4** 20 40N 103 20W
Guadalajara, *Spain* **9 B4** 40 37N 3 12W
Guadalete —►, *Spain* **9 D2** 36 35N 6 13W
Guadalquivir —►, *Spain* **9 D2** 36 47N 6 22W
Guadarrama, Sierra de, *Spain* **9 B4** 41 0N 4 0W
Guadeloupe ■, *W. Indies* **44 L20** 16 20N 61 40W
Guadiana —►, *Portugal* **9 D2** 37 14N 7 22W
Guadix, *Spain* **9 D4** 37 18N 3 11W
Guam ■, *Pac. Oc.* **36 F6** 13 27N 144 45 E
Guangdong □, *China* **21 D6** 23 0N 113 0 E
Guangxi Zhuangzu Zizhiqu □, *China* **21 D5** 24 0N 109 0 E
Guangzhou, *China* **21 D6** 23 5N 113 10 E
Guantánamo, *Cuba* **45 C9** 20 10N 75 14W
Guaporé —►, *Brazil* **46 D3** 11 55S 65 4W
Guatemala, *Guatemala* **44 E6** 14 40N 90 22W
Guatemala ■, *Cent. Amer.* **44 D6** 15 40N 90 30W
Guayaquil, *Ecuador* **46 C2** 2 15S 79 52W
Guaymas, *Mexico* **44 B2** 27 59N 110 54W
Guelph, *Canada* **42 D7** 43 35N 80 20W
Guéret, *France* **8 C4** 46 11N 1 51 E
Guilin, *China* **21 D6** 25 18N 110 15 E
Guinea ■, *W. Afr.* **28 F2** 10 20N 11 30W
Guinea, Gulf of, *Atl. Oc.* **26 F3** 3 0N 2 30 E
Guinea-Bissau ■, *Africa* **28 F2** 12 0N 15 0W
Guingamp, *France* **8 B2** 48 34N 3 10W
Guiyang, *China* **20 D5** 26 32N 106 40 E
Guizhou □, *China* **20 D5** 27 0N 107 0 E
Gujarat □, *India* **23 H3** 23 20N 71 0 E
Gujranwala, *Pakistan* **23 C5** 32 10N 74 12 E
Gujrat, *Pakistan* **23 C5** 32 40N 74 2 E
Gulbarga, *India* **25 D6** 17 20N 76 50 E
Gulf, The, *Asia* **24 C4** 27 0N 50 0 E
Guna, *India* **23 G6** 24 40N 77 19 E
Guntur, *India* **25 D7** 16 23N 80 30 E
Gurgaon, *India* **23 E6** 28 27N 77 1 E
Gurkha, *Nepal* **23 E10** 28 5N 84 40 E
Guyana ■, *S. Amer.* **46 B4** 5 0N 59 0W
Guyenne, *France* **8 D4** 44 30N 0 40 E
Gwadar, *Pakistan* **24 C5** 25 10N 62 18 E
Gwalior, *India* **23 F7** 26 12N 78 10 E
Gweru, *Zimbabwe* **33 H5** 19 28S 29 45 E
Gyandzha, *Azerbaijan* **15 F8** 40 45N 46 20 E
Gympie, *Australia* **34 F9** 26 11S 152 38 E
Györ, *Hungary* **11 E9** 47 41N 17 40 E
Gyumri, *Armenia* **15 F7** 40 47N 43 50 E

H

Haarlem, *Neths.* **10 B3** 52 23N 4 39 E
Hachinohe, *Japan* **19 F12** 40 30N 141 29 E
Hadd, Ras al, *Oman* **24 C4** 22 35N 59 50 E
Haeju, *N. Korea* **21 C7** 38 3N 125 45 E
Hafizabad, *Pakistan* **23 C4** 32 5N 73 40 E
Hafnarfjörður, *Iceland* **6 B3** 64 4N 21 57W
Hagen, *Germany* **10 C4** 51 21N 7 27 E
Hagerstown, *U.S.A.* **42 F9** 39 39N 77 43W
Hague, C. de la, *France* **8 B3** 49 44N 1 56W
Haguenau, *France* **8 B7** 48 49N 7 47 E
Haifa, *Israel* **24 B2** 32 46N 35 0 E
Haikou, *China* **21 D6** 20 1N 110 16 E
Hail, *Si. Arabia* **24 C3** 27 28N 41 45 E
Hailar, *China* **21 B6** 49 10N 119 38 E
Haileybury, *Canada* **42 B8** 47 30N 79 38W
Hainan □, *China* **21 E5** 19 0N 109 30 E
Haiphong, *Vietnam* **20 D5** 20 47N 106 41 E
Haiti ■, *W. Indies* **45 D10** 19 0N 72 30W
Hakodate, *Japan* **19 F12** 41 45N 140 44 E
Ḥalab, *Syria* **24 B2** 36 10N 37 15 E
Halberstadt, *Germany* **10 C6** 51 54N 11 3 E
Halden, *Norway* **6 G10** 59 9N 11 23 E
Haldwani, *India* **23 E7** 29 31N 79 30 E
Halifax, *Canada* **43 C16** 44 38N 63 35W
Halle, *Germany* **10 C6** 51 30N 11 56 E
Halmahera, *Indonesia* **22 C4** 0 40N 128 0 E
Halmstad, *Sweden* **6 G10** 56 41N 12 52 E
Hama, *Syria* **24 B2** 35 5N 36 40 E
Hamadan, *Iran* **24 B3** 34 52N 48 32 E
Hamamatsu, *Japan* **19 B5** 34 45N 137 45 E
Hamar, *Norway* **6 F10** 60 48N 11 7 E
Hamburg, *Germany* **10 B5** 53 33N 9 59 E
Hämeenlinna, *Finland* **6 F12** 61 0N 24 28 E
Hameln, *Germany* **10 B5** 52 6N 9 21 E
Hamersley Ra., *Australia* **34 E2** 22 0S 117 45 E
Hamilton, *Bermuda* **45 A12** 32 15N 64 45W
Hamilton, *Canada* **42 D8** 43 15N 79 50W
Hamilton, *N.Z.* **35 H14** 37 47S 175 19 E
Hamilton, *U.S.A.* **42 F5** 39 24N 84 34W
Hamm, *Germany* **10 C4** 51 40N 7 50 E
Hammerfest, *Norway* **6 D12** 70 39N 23 41 E
Hammond, *U.S.A.* **42 E4** 41 38N 87 30W
Hammonton, *U.S.A.* **43 F10** 39 39N 74 48W
Hancock, *U.S.A.* **42 B3** 47 8N 88 35W
Hangzhou, *China* **21 C7** 30 18N 120 11 E
Hannover, *Germany* **10 B5** 52 22N 9 46 E
Hanoi, *Vietnam* **20 D5** 21 5N 105 55 E
Hanover, *U.S.A.* **42 F9** 39 48N 76 59W
Haora, *India* **23 H12** 22 37N 88 20 E
Haparanda, *Sweden* **6 E12** 65 52N 24 8 E
Happy Valley-Goose Bay, *Canada* **39 C13** 53 15N 60 20W
Hapur, *India* **23 E6** 28 45N 77 45 E
Harare, *Zimbabwe* **33 H6** 17 43S 31 2 E
Harbin, *China* **21 B7** 45 48N 126 40 E
Harbor Beach, *U.S.A.* **42 D6** 43 51N 82 39W
Hardanger Fjord, *Norway* **6 F9** 60 5N 6 0 E
Harding, *S. Africa* **31 C4** 30 35S 29 55 E
Hari —►, *Indonesia* **22 D2** 1 16S 104 5 E
Haridwar, *India* **23 E7** 29 58N 78 9 E
Haringhata —►, *Bangla.* **23 J12** 22 0N 89 58 E
Härnösand, *Sweden* **6 F11** 62 38N 17 55 E
Harrisburg, *U.S.A.* **42 E9** 40 16N 76 53W
Harrismith, *S. Africa* **31 B4** 28 15S 29 8 E
Harrisonburg, *U.S.A.* **42 F8** 38 27N 78 52W
Harrisville, *U.S.A.* **42 C6** 44 39N 83 17W
Hart, *U.S.A.* **42 D4** 43 42N 86 22W
Hartford, *Conn., U.S.A.* **43 E11** 41 46N 72 41W
Hartford, *Ky., U.S.A.* **42 G4** 37 27N 86 55W
Harts —►, *S. Africa* **31 B3** 28 24S 24 17 E
Harvey, *U.S.A.* **42 E4** 41 36N 87 50W
Haryana □, *India* **23 E6** 29 0N 76 10 E
Harz, *Germany* **10 C6** 51 38N 10 44 E
Hasa, *Si. Arabia* **24 C3** 26 0N 49 0 E
Hastings, *U.S.A.* **42 D5** 42 39N 85 17W
Hathras, *India* **23 F7** 27 36N 78 6 E
Hatteras, C., *U.S.A.* **41 C11** 35 14N 75 32W
Haugesund, *Norway* **6 G9** 59 23N 5 13 E
Havana, *Cuba* **45 C8** 23 8N 82 22W
Havel —►, *Germany* **10 B7** 52 50N 12 3 E
Haverhill, *U.S.A.* **43 D12** 42 47N 71 5W
Hawaiian Is., *Pac. Oc.* **40 H17** 20 30N 156 0W
Hawkesbury, *Canada* **43 C10** 45 37N 74 37W
Hay River, *Canada* **38 B8** 60 51N 115 44W
Hazard, *U.S.A.* **42 G6** 37 15N 83 12W
Hazaribag, *India* **23 H10** 23 58N 85 26 E
Hazleton, *U.S.A.* **42 E10** 40 57N 75 59W
Hearst, *Canada* **42 A6** 49 40N 83 41W
Heath Pt., *Canada* **43 A17** 49 8N 61 40W
Hebei □, *China* **21 C6** 39 0N 116 0 E
Hechuan, *China* **20 C5** 30 2N 106 12 E
Heerlen, *Neths.* **10 C3** 50 55N 5 58 E
Hefei, *China* **21 C6** 31 52N 117 18 E
Hegang, *China* **21 B8** 47 20N 130 19 E
Heidelberg, *Germany* **10 D5** 49 24N 8 42 E
Heilbron, *S. Africa* **31 B4** 27 16S 27 59 E
Heilbronn, *Germany* **10 D5** 49 9N 9 13 E
Heilongjiang □, *China* **21 B7** 48 0N 126 0 E
Hejaz, *Si. Arabia* **24 C2** 26 0N 37 30 E
Helgoland, *Germany* **10 A4** 54 10N 7 53 E
Helmand —►, *Afghan.* **24 B5** 31 12N 61 34 E
Helsingborg, *Sweden* **6 G10** 56 3N 12 42 E
Helsinki, *Finland* **6 F13** 60 15N 25 3 E
Henan □, *China* **21 C6** 34 0N 114 0 E
Henderson, *U.S.A.* **42 G4** 37 50N 87 35W
Hengyang, *China* **21 D6** 26 52N 112 33 E
Henlopen, C., *U.S.A.* **43 F10** 38 48N 75 6W
Herat, *Afghan.* **24 B5** 34 20N 62 7 E
Herford, *Germany* **10 B5** 52 7N 8 39 E
Hermanus, *S. Africa* **31 C2** 34 27S 19 12 E
Hermosillo, *Mexico* **44 B2** 29 10N 111 0W
Hernád —►, *Hungary* **11 D11** 47 56N 21 8 E
's-Hertogenbosch, *Neths.* **10 C3** 51 42N 5 17 E
Hessen □, *Germany* **10 C5** 50 30N 9 0 E
High Atlas, *Morocco* **28 B3** 32 30N 5 0W
Hildesheim, *Germany* **10 B5** 52 9N 9 56 E
Hillsdale, *U.S.A.* **42 E5** 41 56N 84 38W
Hilo, *U.S.A.* **40 J17** 19 44N 155 5W
Hilversum, *Neths.* **10 B3** 52 14N 5 10 E
Himachal Pradesh □, *India* **23 D6** 31 30N 77 0 E
Himalaya, *Asia* **23 E10** 29 0N 84 0 E
Himeji, *Japan* **19 B4** 34 50N 134 40 E
Hindu Kush, *Asia* **23 B2** 36 0N 71 0 E
Hingoli, *India* **23 K6** 19 41N 77 15 E
Hinton, *U.S.A.* **42 G7** 37 40N 80 54W
Hiroshima, *Japan* **19 B3** 34 24N 132 30 E
Hisar, *India* **23 E5** 29 12N 75 45 E
Hispaniola, *W. Indies* **45 D10** 19 0N 71 0W
Hjälmaren, *Sweden* **6 G11** 59 18N 15 40 E
Ho Chi Minh City, *Vietnam* **22 B2** 10 58N 106 40 E
Hobart, *Australia* **34 J8** 42 50S 147 21 E
Hódmezövásárhely, *Hungary* **11 E11** 46 28N 20 22 E
Hoggar, *Algeria* **28 D6** 23 0N 6 30 E
Hohhot, *China* **21 B6** 40 52N 111 40 E
Hokkaidō □, *Japan* **19 F12** 43 30N 143 0 E
Holguín, *Cuba* **45 C9** 20 50N 76 20W
Hollams Bird I., *Namibia* **31 A1** 24 40S 14 30 E
Holland, *U.S.A.* **42 D4** 42 47N 86 7W
Homs, *Syria* **24 B2** 34 40N 36 45 E
Honduras ■, *Cent. Amer.* **44 E7** 14 40N 86 30W
Honduras, G. de, *Caribbean* **44 D7** 16 50N 87 0W
Hong Kong ■, *Asia* **21 D6** 22 11N 114 14 E
Hongha —►, *Vietnam* **20 D5** 22 0N 104 0 E
Honiara, *Solomon Is.* **35 B10** 9 27S 159 57 E
Honolulu, *U.S.A.* **40 H16** 21 19N 157 52W
Honshū, *Japan* **19 B6** 36 0N 138 0 E
Hooghly —►, *India* **23 J12** 21 56N 88 4 E
Hoopeston, *U.S.A.* **42 E4** 40 28N 87 40W
Hoorn, *Neths.* **10 B3** 52 38N 5 4 E
Hopetown, *S. Africa* **31 B3** 29 34S 24 3 E
Hopkinsville, *U.S.A.* **42 G4** 36 52N 87 29W
Hormuz, Str. of, *The Gulf* **24 C4** 26 30N 56 30 E
Horn, C., *Chile* **47 H3** 55 50S 67 30W
Hornavan, *Sweden* **6 E11** 66 15N 17 30 E
Hornell, *U.S.A.* **42 D9** 42 20N 77 40W
Hornepayne, *Canada* **42 A5** 49 14N 84 48W
Horsham, *Australia* **34 H7** 36 44S 142 13 E
Hospitalet de Llobregat, *Spain* **9 B7** 41 21N 2 6 E
Hotan, *China* **20 C2** 37 25N 79 55 E
Houghton, *U.S.A.* **42 B3** 47 7N 88 34W
Houghton L., *U.S.A.* **42 C5** 44 21N 84 44W
Houlton, *U.S.A.* **43 B14** 46 8N 67 51W
Houston, *U.S.A.* **41 E7** 29 46N 95 22W
Hovd, *Mongolia* **20 B4** 48 2N 91 37 E
Hövsgöl Nuur, *Mongolia* **20 A5** 51 0N 100 30 E
Howell, *U.S.A.* **42 D6** 42 36N 83 56W
Howick, *S. Africa* **31 B5** 29 28S 30 14 E
Howrah = Haora, *India* **23 H12** 22 37N 88 20 E
Høyanger, *Norway* **6 F9** 61 13N 6 4 E
Hradec Králové, *Czech.* **10 C8** 50 15N 15 50 E
Hron —►, *Slovak Rep.* **11 E10** 47 49N 18 45 E
Huainan, *China* **21 C6** 32 38N 116 58 E
Huambo, *Angola* **33 G3** 12 42S 15 54 E
Huancayo, *Peru* **46 D2** 12 5S 75 12W
Huangshi, *China* **21 C6** 30 10N 115 3 E
Hubei □, *China* **21 C6** 31 0N 112 0 E
Hudiksvall, *Sweden* **6 F11** 61 43N 17 10 E
Hudson —►, *U.S.A.* **43 E10** 40 42N 74 2W
Hudson Bay, *Canada* **39 C11** 60 0N 86 0W
Hudson Falls, *U.S.A.* **43 D11** 43 18N 73 35W
Hudson Str., *Canada* **39 B13** 62 0N 70 0W
Hue, *Vietnam* **22 B2** 16 30N 107 35 E
Huelva, *Spain* **9 D2** 37 18N 6 57W
Huesca, *Spain* **9 A5** 42 8N 0 25W
Hughenden, *Australia* **34 E7** 20 52S 144 10 E
Hull = Kingston upon Hull, *U.K.* **7 E6** 53 45N 0 21W
Hull, *Canada* **43 C10** 45 25N 75 44W
Humboldt —►, *U.S.A.* **40 B3** 39 59N 118 36W
Húnaflói, *Iceland* **6 B3** 65 50N 20 50W
Hunan □, *China* **21 D6** 27 30N 112 0 E
Hungary ■, *Europe* **11 E10** 47 20N 19 20 E
Hungnam, *N. Korea* **21 C7** 39 49N 127 45 E
Hunsrück, *Germany* **10 D4** 49 56N 7 27 E
Huntington, *Ind., U.S.A.* **42 E5** 40 53N 85 30W
Huntington, *W. Va., U.S.A.* **42 F6** 38 25N 82 27W
Huntsville, *Canada* **42 C8** 45 20N 79 14W
Huntsville, *U.S.A.* **41 D9** 34 44N 86 35W
Huron, L., *U.S.A.* **42 C6** 44 30N 82 40W
Húsavík, *Iceland* **6 A5** 66 3N 17 21W
Hwang-ho —►, *China* **21 C6** 37 55N 118 50 E
Hyderabad, *India* **25 D6** 17 22N 78 29 E
Hyderabad, *Pakistan* **23 G2** 25 23N 68 24 E
Hyères, *France* **8 E7** 43 8N 6 9 E
Hyères, Is. d', *France* **8 E7** 43 0N 6 20 E

I

Ialomița —►, *Romania* **11 F14** 44 42N 27 51 E
Iași, *Romania* **11 E14** 47 10N 27 40 E
Ibadan, *Nigeria* **30 C2** 7 22N 3 58 E
Ibagué, *Colombia* **46 B2** 4 20N 75 20W
Iberian Peninsula, *Europe* **4 H5** 40 0N 5 0W
Ibiza, *Spain* **9 C6** 38 54N 1 26 E
Iceland ■, *Europe* **6 B4** 64 45N 19 0W
Ichinomiya, *Japan* **19 B5** 35 18N 136 48 E
Idaho □, *U.S.A.* **40 B4** 45 0N 115 0W
Idar-Oberstein, *Germany* **10 D4** 49 43N 7 16 E
Ife, *Nigeria* **30 C2** 7 30N 4 31 E
Iglésias, *Italy* **12 E3** 39 19N 8 32 E
Ignace, *Canada* **42 A2** 49 30N 91 40W
Iguaçu Falls, *Brazil* **47 E4** 25 41S 54 26W
Iisalmi, *Finland* **6 F13** 63 32N 27 10 E
IJsselmeer, *Neths.* **10 B3** 52 45N 5 20 E
Ikerre-Ekiti, *Nigeria* **30 C3** 7 25N 5 19 E
Ila, *Nigeria* **30 C2** 8 0N 4 39 E
Île-de-France, *France* **8 B5** 49 0N 2 20 E
Ilesha, *Nigeria* **30 C2** 7 37N 4 40 E
Ilhéus, *Brazil* **46 D6** 14 49S 39 2W
Ili —►, *Kazakhstan* **18 E9** 45 53N 77 10 E
Iller —►, *Germany* **10 D6** 48 23N 9 58 E
Illinois □, *U.S.A.* **41 C9** 40 15N 89 30W
Iloilo, *Phil.* **22 B4** 10 45N 122 33 E
Ilorin, *Nigeria* **30 C2** 8 30N 4 35 E
Imperatriz, *Brazil* **46 C5** 5 30S 47 29W
Imphal, *India* **25 C8** 24 48N 93 56 E
Inari, L., *Finland* **6 E13** 69 0N 28 0 E
Inchon, *S. Korea* **21 C7** 37 27N 126 40 E
Incomáti —►, *Mozam.* **31 B5** 25 46S 32 43 E
Indals —►, *Sweden* **6 F11** 62 36N 17 30 E
India ■, *Asia* **23 K7** 20 0N 78 0 E
Indiana, *U.S.A.* **42 E8** 40 37N 79 9W
Indiana □, *U.S.A.* **42 E4** 40 0N 86 0W
Indianapolis, *U.S.A.* **42 F4** 39 46N 86 9W
Indigirka —►, *Russia* **18 B16** 70 48N 148 54 E
Indonesia ■, *Asia* **22 D3** 5 0S 115 0 E
Indore, *India* **23 H5** 22 42N 75 53 E
Indre —►, *France* **8 C4** 47 16N 0 11 E
Indus —►, *Pakistan* **23 G1** 24 20N 67 47 E
Ingolstadt, *Germany* **10 D6** 48 46N 11 26 E
Inn —►, *Austria* **10 D7** 48 35N 13 28 E
Inner Mongolia □, *China* **21 B6** 42 0N 112 0 E
Innsbruck, *Austria* **10 E6** 47 16N 11 23 E
Inowrocław, *Poland* **11 B10** 52 50N 18 12 E
Insein, *Burma* **25 D8** 16 50N 96 5 E
Interlaken, *Switz.* **10 E4** 46 41N 7 50 E
Inuvik, *Canada* **38 B6** 68 16N 133 40W
Invercargill, *N.Z.* **35 K12** 46 24S 168 24 E
Inverness, *U.K.* **7 C4** 57 29N 4 13W
Ionia, *U.S.A.* **42 D5** 42 59N 85 4W
Ionian Is., *Greece* **13 E9** 38 40N 20 0 E
Ionian Sea, *Medit. S.* **13 E7** 37 30N 17 30 E
Iowa □, *U.S.A.* **41 B8** 42 18N 93 30W
Iowa City, *U.S.A.* **41 B8** 41 40N 91 32W
Ipoh, *Malaysia* **22 C2** 4 35N 101 5 E
Ipswich, *U.K.* **7 E7** 52 4N 1 10 E
Iquique, *Chile* **46 E2** 20 19S 70 5W
Iquitos, *Peru* **46 C2** 3 45S 73 10W
Iráklion, *Greece* **13 G11** 35 20N 25 12 E
Iran ■, *Asia* **24 B4** 33 0N 53 0 E
Iran Ra., *Malaysia* **22 C3** 2 20N 114 50 E
Irapuato, *Mexico* **44 C4** 20 40N 101 30W
Iraq ■, *Asia* **24 B3** 33 0N 44 0 E
Ireland ■, *Europe* **7 E2** 53 50N 7 52W
Irian Jaya □, *Indonesia* **22 D5** 4 0S 137 0 E
Iringa, *Tanzania* **32 F7** 7 48S 35 43 E
Irish Sea, *U.K.* **7 E4** 53 38N 4 48W
Irkutsk, *Russia* **18 D12** 52 18N 104 20 E
Iron Gate, *Europe* **11 F12** 44 42N 22 30 E
Iron Mountain, *U.S.A.* **42 C3** 45 49N 88 4W
Ironton, *U.S.A.* **42 F6** 38 32N 82 41W
Irrawaddy —►, *Burma* **25 D8** 15 50N 95 6 E
Irtysh —►, *Russia* **18 C8** 61 4N 68 52 E
Ísafjörður, *Iceland* **6 A2** 66 5N 23 9W
Isar —►, *Germany* **10 D7** 48 48N 12 57 E
Isère —►, *France* **8 D6** 44 59N 4 51 E
Iseyin, *Nigeria* **30 C2** 8 0N 3 36 E
Ishpeming, *U.S.A.* **42 B4** 46 29N 87 40W
Iskenderun, *Turkey* **15 G6** 36 32N 36 10 E
Islamabad, *Pakistan* **23 C4** 33 40N 73 10 E
Island Pond, *U.S.A.* **43 C12** 44 49N 71 53W
Ismâ'ilîya, *Egypt* **29 B11** 30 37N 32 18 E
Israel ■, *Asia* **24 B2** 32 0N 34 50 E
Issoire, *France* **8 D5** 45 32N 3 15 E
İstanbul, *Turkey* **13 D13** 41 0N 29 0 E
Istres, *France* **8 E6** 43 31N 4 59 E
Istria, *Croatia* **10 F7** 45 10N 14 0 E
Itaipu Dam, *Brazil* **47 E4** 25 30S 54 30W
Italy ■, *Europe* **12 C5** 42 0N 13 0 E
Ithaca, *U.S.A.* **42 D9** 42 27N 76 30W
Ivanava, *Belarus* **11 B13** 52 7N 25 29 E
Ivano-Frankovsk, *Ukraine* **11 D13** 48 40N 24 40 E
Ivanovo, *Russia* **14 C7** 57 5N 41 0 E
Ivory Coast ■, *Africa* **28 G3** 7 30N 5 0W
Ivujivik, *Canada* **39 B12** 62 24N 77 55W
Iwaki, *Japan* **19 A7** 37 3N 140 55 E
Iwo, *Nigeria* **30 C2** 7 39N 4 9 E
Ixopo, *S. Africa* **31 C5** 30 11S 30 5 E
Izhevsk, *Russia* **14 C9** 56 51N 53 14 E
İzmir, *Turkey* **13 E12** 38 25N 27 8 E

J

Jabalpur, *India* **23 H7** 23 9N 79 58 E
Jackson, *Ky., U.S.A.* **42 G6** 37 33N 83 23W
Jackson, *Mich., U.S.A.* **42 D5** 42 15N 84 24W
Jackson, *Miss., U.S.A.* **41 D8** 32 18N 90 12W
Jacksonville, *U.S.A.* **41 D10** 30 20N 81 39W
Jacobabad, *Pakistan* **23 E2** 28 20N 68 29 E
Jaén, *Spain* **9 D4** 37 44N 3 43W
Jaffna, *Sri Lanka* **25 E7** 9 45N 80 2 E
Jagersfontein, *S. Africa* **31 B4** 29 44S 25 27 E
Jahrom, *Iran* **24 C4** 28 30N 53 31 E

Jaipur, *India* **23 F5** 27 0N 75 50 E
Jakarta, *Indonesia* **22 D2** 6 9S 106 49 E
Jalalabad, *Afghan.* **23 B3** 34 30N 70 29 E
Jalgaon, *India* **23 J5** 21 0N 75 42 E
Jalna, *India* **23 K5** 19 48N 75 38 E
Jalpaiguri, *India* **23 F12** 26 32N 88 46 E
Jamaica ■, *W. Indies* **44 J16** 18 10N 77 30W
Jamalpur, *Bangla.* **23 G12** 24 52N 89 56 E
Jamalpur, *India* **23 G11** 25 18N 86 28 E
Jambi, *Indonesia* **22 D2** 1 38S 103 30 E
James B., *Canada* **39 C11** 51 30N 80 0W
Jamestown, *Ky., U.S.A.* **42 G5** 36 59N 85 4W
Jamestown, *N.Y., U.S.A.* **42 D8** 42 6N 79 14W
Jammu, *India* **23 C5** 32 43N 74 54 E
Jammu & Kashmir □, *India* **23 B6** 34 25N 77 0 E
Jamnagar, *India* **23 H3** 22 30N 70 6 E
Jamshedpur, *India* **23 H11** 22 44N 86 12 E
Jaora, *India* **23 H5** 23 40N 75 10 E
Japan ■, *Asia* **19 G11** 36 0N 136 0 E
Japan, Sea of, *Asia* **19 G11** 40 0N 135 0 E
Japurá →, *Brazil* **46 C3** 3 8S 65 46W
Jask, *Iran* **24 C4** 25 38N 57 45 E
Jaunpur, *India* **23 G9** 25 46N 82 44 E
Java, *Indonesia* **22 D3** 7 0S 110 0 E
Java Sea, *Indonesia* **22 D2** 4 35S 107 15 E
Jedda, *Si. Arabia* **24 C2** 21 29N 39 10 E
Jeffersonville, *U.S.A.* **42 F5** 38 17N 85 44W
Jelenia Góra, *Poland* **10 C8** 50 50N 15 45 E
Jena, *Germany* **10 C6** 50 54N 11 35 E
Jerez de la Frontera, *Spain* **9 D2** 36 41N 6 7W
Jersey City, *U.S.A.* **43 E10** 40 44N 74 4W
Jerusalem, *Israel* **24 B2** 31 47N 35 10 E
Jessore, *Bangla.* **23 H12** 23 10N 89 10 E
Jhang Maghiana, *Pakistan* **23 D4** 31 15N 72 22 E
Jhansi, *India* **23 G7** 25 30N 78 36 E
Jhelum, *Pakistan* **23 C4** 33 0N 73 45 E
Jhelum →, *Pakistan* **23 D4** 31 20N 72 10 E
Jiamusi, *China* **21 B8** 46 40N 130 26 E
Jian, *China* **21 D6** 27 6N 114 59 E
Jiangsu □, *China* **21 C7** 33 0N 120 0 E
Jiangxi □, *China* **21 D6** 27 30N 116 0 E
Jihlava →, *Czech.* **11 D9** 48 55N 16 36 E
Jilin, *China* **21 B7** 43 44N 126 30 E
Jilin □, *China* **21 B7** 44 0N 127 0 E
Jima, *Ethiopia* **29 G12** 7 40N 36 47 E
Jinan, *China* **21 C6** 36 38N 117 1 E
Jinja, *Uganda* **32 D6** 0 25N 33 12 E
Jinzhou, *China* **21 B7** 41 5N 121 3 E
Jixi, *China* **21 B8** 45 20N 130 50 E
João Pessoa, *Brazil* **46 C6** 7 10S 34 52W
Jodhpur, *India* **23 F4** 26 23N 73 8 E
Johannesburg, *S. Africa* **31 B4** 26 10S 28 2 E
Johnson City, *U.S.A.* **43 D10** 42 7N 75 58W
Johnstown, *U.S.A.* **42 E8** 40 20N 78 55W
Johor Baharu, *Malaysia* **22 C2** 1 28N 103 46 E
Joliet, *U.S.A.* **42 E3** 41 32N 88 5W
Joliette, *Canada* **43 B11** 46 3N 73 24W
Jolo, *Phil.* **22 C4** 6 0N 121 0 E
Jönköping, *Sweden* **6 G10** 57 45N 14 10 E
Jonquière, *Canada* **43 A12** 48 27N 71 14W
Jordan ■, *Asia* **24 B2** 31 0N 36 0 E
Jos, *Nigeria* **30 C3** 9 53N 8 51 E
Juan de Fuca Str., *Canada* **40 A2** 48 15N 124 0W
Juiz de Fora, *Brazil* **46 E5** 21 43S 43 19W
Jullundur, *India* **23 D5** 31 20N 75 40 E
Junagadh, *India* **23 J3** 21 30N 70 30 E
Juneau, *U.S.A.* **38 C6** 58 18N 134 25W
Junggar Pendi, *China* **20 B3** 44 30N 86 0 E
Jupiter →, *Canada* **43 A16** 49 29N 63 37W
Jura, *Europe* **8 C7** 46 40N 6 5 E
Jutland, *Denmark* **6 G9** 56 25N 9 30 E
Jyväskylä, *Finland* **6 F13** 62 14N 25 50 E

K

K2, *Pakistan* **23 B6** 35 58N 76 32 E
Kabardino Balkaria □, *Russia* **15 F7** 43 30N 43 30 E
Kābul, *Afghan.* **23 B2** 34 28N 69 11 E
Kabwe, *Zambia* **33 G5** 14 30S 28 29 E
Kachin □, *Burma* **25 C8** 26 0N 97 30 E
Kaduna, *Nigeria* **30 B3** 10 30N 7 21 E
Kaesong, *N. Korea* **21 C7** 37 58N 126 35 E
Kagoshima, *Japan* **19 D2** 31 35N 130 33 E
Kai Is., *Indonesia* **22 D5** 5 55S 132 45 E
Kaifeng, *China* **21 C6** 34 48N 114 21 E
Kaiserslautern, *Germany* **10 D4** 49 26N 7 45 E
Kaitaia, *N.Z.* **35 H13** 35 8S 173 17 E
Kajaani, *Finland* **6 F13** 64 17N 27 46 E
Kakinada, *India* **25 D7** 16 57N 82 11 E
Kalahari, *Africa* **31 A3** 24 0S 21 30 E
Kalamazoo, *U.S.A.* **42 D5** 42 17N 85 35W
Kalamazoo →, *U.S.A.* **42 D4** 42 40N 86 10W
Kalemie, *Zaïre* **32 F5** 5 55S 29 9 E
Kalgoorlie-Boulder, *Australia* **34 G3** 30 40S 121 22 E
Kalimantan, *Indonesia* **22 D3** 0 0 114 0 E
Kaliningrad, *Russia* **14 D3** 54 42N 20 32 E
Kalisz, *Poland* **11 C10** 51 45N 18 8 E
Kalkaska, *U.S.A.* **42 C5** 44 44N 85 11W
Kalmar, *Sweden* **6 G11** 56 40N 16 20 E
Kalmykia □, *Russia* **15 E8** 46 5N 46 1 E
Kaluga, *Russia* **14 D6** 54 35N 36 10 E
Kama →, *Russia* **14 C9** 55 45N 52 0 E
Kamchatka, *Russia* **18 D18** 57 0N 160 0 E
Kamina, *Zaïre* **32 F5** 8 45S 25 0 E
Kamloops, *Canada* **38 C7** 50 40N 120 20W
Kampala, *Uganda* **32 D6** 0 20N 32 30 E
Kampuchea ■ = Cambodia ■, *Asia* **22 B2** 12 15N 105 0 E
Kamyanets-Podilskyy, *Ukraine* **11 D14** 48 45N 26 40 E
Kananga, *Zaïre* **32 F4** 5 55S 22 18 E
Kanawha →, *U.S.A.* **42 F6** 38 50N 82 9W
Kanazawa, *Japan* **19 A5** 36 30N 136 38 E
Kanchenjunga, *Nepal* **23 F12** 27 50N 88 10 E
Kanchipuram, *India* **25 D6** 12 52N 79 45 E
Kandy, *Sri Lanka* **25 E7** 7 18N 80 43 E
Kane, *U.S.A.* **42 E8** 41 40N 78 49W
Kangean Is., *Indonesia* **22 D3** 6 55S 115 23 E
Kanin Pen., *Russia* **14 A8** 68 0N 45 0 E
Kankakee, *U.S.A.* **42 E4** 41 7N 87 52W
Kankakee →, *U.S.A.* **42 E3** 41 23N 88 15W
Kankan, *Guinea* **28 F3** 10 23N 9 15W
Kano, *Nigeria* **30 B3** 12 2N 8 30 E
Kanpur, *India* **23 F8** 26 28N 80 20 E
Kansas □, *U.S.A.* **40 C7** 38 30N 99 0W
Kansas City, *Kans., U.S.A.* **41 C8** 39 7N 94 38W
Kansas City, *Mo., U.S.A.* **41 C8** 39 6N 94 35W
Kanye, *Botswana* **31 A4** 24 55S 25 28 E
Kaohsiung, *Taiwan* **21 D7** 22 35N 120 16 E
Kaolack, *Senegal* **28 F1** 14 5N 16 8W
Kaposvár, *Hungary* **11 E9** 46 25N 17 47 E
Kapuas →, *Indonesia* **22 D2** 0 25S 109 20 E
Kapuas Hulu Ra., *Malaysia* **22 C3** 1 30N 113 30 E
Kapuskasing, *Canada* **42 A6** 49 25N 82 30W
Kara Bogaz Gol, *Turkmenistan* **15 F9** 41 0N 53 30 E
Kara Kum, *Turkmenistan* **18 F8** 39 30N 60 0 E
Kara Sea, *Russia* **18 B8** 75 0N 70 0 E
Karachi, *Pakistan* **23 G1** 24 53N 67 0 E
Karaganda, *Kazakhstan* **18 E9** 49 50N 73 10 E
Karakoram Ra., *Pakistan* **23 B6** 35 30N 77 0 E
Karasburg, *Namibia* **31 B2** 28 0S 18 44 E
Karbala, *Iraq* **24 B3** 32 36N 44 3 E
Karelia □, *Russia* **14 A5** 65 30N 32 30 E
Karimata Is., *Indonesia* **22 D2** 1 25S 109 0 E
Karimunjawa Is., *Indonesia* **22 D3** 5 50S 110 30 E
Karlskrona, *Sweden* **6 G11** 56 10N 15 35 E
Karlsruhe, *Germany* **10 D5** 49 0N 8 23 E
Karlstad, *Sweden* **6 G10** 59 23N 13 30 E
Karnal, *India* **23 E6** 29 42N 77 2 E
Karnataka □, *India* **25 D6** 13 15N 77 0 E
Kärnten □, *Austria* **10 E8** 46 52N 13 30 E
Karsakpay, *Kazakhstan* **18 E8** 47 55N 66 40 E
Kasai →, *Zaïre* **32 E3** 3 30S 16 10 E
Kashan, *Iran* **24 B4** 34 5N 51 30 E
Kashi, *China* **20 C2** 39 30N 76 2 E
Kassalâ, *Sudan* **29 E12** 15 30N 36 0 E
Kassel, *Germany* **10 C5** 51 18N 9 26 E
Kasur, *Pakistan* **23 D5** 31 5N 74 25 E
Katha, *Burma* **25 C8** 24 10N 96 30 E
Katihar, *India* **23 G11** 25 34N 87 36 E
Katmandu, *Nepal* **23 F10** 27 45N 85 20 E
Katowice, *Poland* **11 C10** 50 17N 19 5 E
Katsina, *Nigeria* **30 B3** 13 0N 7 32 E
Kattegat, *Denmark* **6 G10** 57 0N 11 20 E
Kauai, *U.S.A.* **40 H15** 22 3N 159 30W
Kaukauna, *U.S.A.* **42 C3** 44 17N 88 17W
Kaunas, *Lithuania* **14 D3** 54 54N 23 54 E
Kavála, *Greece* **13 D11** 40 57N 24 28 E
Kawagoe, *Japan* **19 B6** 35 55N 139 29 E
Kawardha, *India* **23 J8** 22 0N 81 17 E
Kawasaki, *Japan* **19 B6** 35 35N 139 42 E
Kayes, *Mali* **28 F2** 14 25N 11 30W
Kayseri, *Turkey* **15 G6** 38 45N 35 30 E
Kazakhstan ■, *Asia* **18 E9** 50 0N 70 0 E
Kazan, *Russia* **14 C8** 55 50N 49 10 E
Kazerun, *Iran* **24 C4** 29 38N 51 40 E
Kebnekaise, *Sweden* **6 E11** 67 53N 18 33 E
Kecskemét, *Hungary* **11 E10** 46 57N 19 42 E
Kediri, *Indonesia* **22 D3** 7 51S 112 1 E
Keene, *U.S.A.* **43 D11** 42 56N 72 17W
Keetmanshoop, *Namibia* **31 B2** 26 35S 18 8 E
Kefallinía, *Greece* **13 E9** 38 20N 20 30 E
Keflavík, *Iceland* **6 B2** 64 2N 22 35W
Kelang, *Malaysia* **22 C2** 3 2N 101 26 E
Kelowna, *Canada* **38 D8** 49 50N 119 25W
Kemerovo, *Russia* **18 D10** 55 20N 86 5 E
Kemi, *Finland* **6 E12** 65 44N 24 34 E
Kemi →, *Finland* **6 E12** 65 47N 24 32 E
Kendari, *Indonesia* **22 D4** 3 50S 122 30 E
Kenhardt, *S. Africa* **31 B3** 29 19S 21 12 E
Kenitra, *Morocco* **28 B3** 34 15N 6 40W
Kenosha, *U.S.A.* **42 D4** 42 35N 87 49W
Kent, *U.S.A.* **42 E7** 41 9N 81 22W
Kenton, *U.S.A.* **42 E6** 40 39N 83 37W
Kentucky □, *U.S.A.* **42 G5** 37 0N 84 0W
Kentucky →, *U.S.A.* **42 F5** 38 41N 85 11W
Kentville, *Canada* **43 C15** 45 6N 64 29W
Kenya ■, *Africa* **32 D7** 1 0N 38 0 E
Kenya, Mt., *Kenya* **32 E7** 0 10S 37 18 E
Kerala □, *India* **25 D6** 11 0N 76 15 E
Kerch, *Ukraine* **15 E6** 45 20N 36 20 E
Kerinci, *Indonesia* **22 D2** 1 40S 101 15 E
Kermadec Trench, *Pac. Oc.* **35 G15** 30 30S 176 0W
Kerman, *Iran* **24 B4** 30 15N 57 1 E
Kestell, *S. Africa* **31 B4** 28 17S 28 42 E
Ketchikan, *U.S.A.* **38 C6** 55 21N 131 39W
Kewaunee, *U.S.A.* **42 C4** 44 27N 87 31W
Keweenaw B., *U.S.A.* **42 B3** 47 0N 88 15W
Keweenaw Pen., *U.S.A.* **42 B3** 47 30N 88 0W
Keweenaw Pt., *U.S.A.* **42 B4** 47 25N 87 43W
Key West, *U.S.A.* **41 F10** 24 33N 81 48W
Keyser, *U.S.A.* **42 F8** 39 26N 78 59W
Khabarovsk, *Russia* **18 E15** 48 30N 135 5 E
Khairpur, *Pakistan* **23 F2** 27 32N 68 49 E
Khamas Country, *Botswana* **31 A4** 21 45S 26 30 E
Khandwa, *India* **23 J6** 21 49N 76 22 E
Khanewal, *Pakistan* **23 D3** 30 20N 71 55 E
Khaniá, *Greece* **13 G11** 35 30N 24 4 E
Kharagpur, *India* **23 H11** 22 20N 87 25 E
Khargon, *India* **23 J5** 21 45N 75 40 E
Kharkov, *Ukraine* **15 E6** 49 58N 36 20 E
Khartoum, *Sudan* **29 E11** 15 31N 32 35 E
Khaskovo, *Bulgaria* **13 D11** 41 56N 25 30 E
Khatanga, *Russia* **18 B12** 72 0N 102 20 E
Kherson, *Ukraine* **15 E5** 46 35N 32 35 E
Khmelnitskiy, *Ukraine* **11 D14** 49 23N 27 0 E
Khorixas, *Namibia* **31 A1** 20 16S 14 59 E
Khorramshahr, *Iran* **24 B3** 30 29N 48 15 E
Khouribga, *Morocco* **28 B3** 32 58N 6 57W
Khulna, *Bangla.* **23 H12** 22 45N 89 34 E
Khulna □, *Bangla.* **23 H12** 22 25N 89 35 E
Khumago, *Botswana* **31 A3** 20 26S 24 32 E
Khushab, *Pakistan* **23 C4** 32 20N 72 20 E
Khuzdar, *Pakistan* **23 F1** 27 52N 66 30 E
Kicking Horse Pass, *Canada* **38 C8** 51 28N 116 16W
Kiel, *Germany* **10 A6** 54 19N 10 8 E
Kiel Canal → = Nord-Ostsee-Kanal →, *Germany* **10 A5** 54 12N 9 32 E
Kielce, *Poland* **11 C11** 50 52N 20 42 E
Kieler Bucht, *Germany* **10 A6** 54 35N 10 25 E
Kiev, *Ukraine* **11 C16** 50 30N 30 28 E
Kigali, *Rwanda* **32 E6** 1 59S 30 4 E
Kigoma-Ujiji, *Tanzania* **32 E5** 4 55S 29 36 E
Kikwit, *Zaïre* **32 E3** 5 0S 18 45 E
Kilimanjaro, *Tanzania* **32 E7** 3 7S 37 20 E
Kimberley, *S. Africa* **31 B3** 28 43S 24 46 E
Kimberley Plateau, *Australia* **34 D4** 16 20S 127 0 E
Kincardine, *Canada* **42 C7** 44 10N 81 40W
Kindu, *Zaïre* **32 E5** 2 55S 25 50 E
King William's Town, *S. Africa* **31 C4** 32 51S 27 22 E
Kingston, *Canada* **42 C9** 44 14N 76 30W
Kingston, *Jamaica* **44 K17** 18 0N 76 50W
Kingston, *N.Y., U.S.A.* **43 E10** 41 56N 73 59W
Kingston, *Pa., U.S.A.* **43 E10** 41 16N 75 54W
Kingston upon Hull, *U.K.* **7 E6** 53 45N 0 21W
Kingstown, *St. Vincent* **44 P20** 13 10N 61 10W
Kinshasa, *Zaïre* **32 E3** 4 20S 15 15 E
Kirensk, *Russia* **18 D12** 57 50N 107 55 E
Kirgiz Steppe, *Eurasia* **15 D10** 50 0N 55 0 E
Kiribati ■, *Pac. Oc.* **36 H10** 5 0S 180 0 E
Kirkenes, *Norway* **6 E14** 69 40N 30 5 E
Kirkland Lake, *Canada* **42 A7** 48 9N 80 2W
Kirkuk, *Iraq* **24 B3** 35 30N 44 21 E
Kirkwood, *S. Africa* **31 C4** 33 22S 25 15 E
Kirov, *Russia* **14 C8** 58 35N 49 40 E
Kirovograd, *Ukraine* **15 E5** 48 35N 32 20 E
Kirthar Range, *Pakistan* **23 F1** 27 0N 67 0 E
Kiruna, *Sweden* **6 E12** 67 52N 20 15 E
Kisangani, *Zaïre* **32 D5** 0 35N 25 15 E
Kishanganj, *India* **23 F12** 26 3N 88 14 E
Kishinev, *Moldova* **11 E15** 47 0N 28 50 E
Kisumu, *Kenya* **32 E6** 0 3S 34 45 E
Kitakyūshū, *Japan* **19 C2** 33 50N 130 50 E
Kitchener, *Canada* **42 D7** 43 27N 80 29W
Kíthira, *Greece* **13 F10** 36 8N 23 0 E
Kitikmeot □, *Canada* **38 A9** 70 0N 110 0W
Kitimat, *Canada* **38 C7** 54 3N 128 38W
Kittanning, *U.S.A.* **42 E8** 40 49N 79 31W
Kitwe, *Zambia* **33 G5** 12 54S 28 13 E
Kivu, L., *Zaïre* **32 E5** 1 48S 29 0 E
Kladno, *Czech.* **10 C8** 50 10N 14 7 E
Klagenfurt, *Austria* **10 E8** 46 38N 14 20 E
Klar →, *Sweden* **6 G10** 59 23N 13 32 E
Klawer, *S. Africa* **31 C2** 31 44S 18 36 E
Klerksdorp, *S. Africa* **31 B4** 26 53S 26 38 E
Klipplaat, *S. Africa* **31 C3** 33 1S 24 22 E
Klondike, *Canada* **38 B6** 64 0N 139 26W
Klyuchevsk Vol., *Russia* **18 D18** 55 50N 160 30 E
Knossós, *Greece* **13 G11** 35 16N 25 10 E
Knoxville, *U.S.A.* **41 C10** 35 58N 83 55W
Knysna, *S. Africa* **31 C3** 34 2S 23 2 E
Kōbe, *Japan* **19 B4** 34 45N 135 10 E
Koblenz, *Germany* **10 C4** 50 21N 7 36 E
Kobroor, *Indonesia* **22 D5** 6 10S 134 30 E
Koch Bihar, *India* **23 F12** 26 22N 89 29 E
Kodiak I., *U.S.A.* **38 C4** 57 30N 152 45W
Koffiefontein, *S. Africa* **31 B4** 29 30S 25 0 E
Koforidua, *Ghana* **30 C1** 6 3N 0 17W
Koh-i-Bābā, *Afghan.* **23 B1** 34 30N 67 0 E
Kohat, *Pakistan* **23 C3** 33 40N 71 29 E
Kokchetav, *Kazakhstan* **18 D8** 53 20N 69 25 E
Kokomo, *U.S.A.* **42 E4** 40 29N 86 8W
Kokstad, *S. Africa* **31 C4** 30 32S 29 29 E
Kola Pen., *Russia* **14 A6** 67 30N 38 0 E
Kolar, *India* **25 D6** 13 12N 78 15 E
Kolguyev I., *Russia* **14 A8** 69 20N 48 30 E
Kolhapur, *India* **25 D6** 16 43N 74 15 E
Kolomna, *Russia* **14 C6** 55 8N 38 45 E
Kolwezi, *Zaïre* **32 G5** 10 40S 25 25 E
Kolyma →, *Russia* **18 C18** 69 30N 161 0 E
Kolyma Ra., *Russia* **18 C17** 63 0N 157 0 E
Komandorskiye Is., *Russia* **18 D18** 55 0N 167 0 E
Komatipoort, *S. Africa* **31 B5** 25 25S 31 55 E
Komi □, *Russia* **14 B10** 64 0N 55 0 E
Kompong Cham, *Cambodia* **22 B2** 12 0N 105 30 E
Kompong Chhnang, *Cambodia* **22 B2** 12 20N 104 35 E
Kompong Som, *Cambodia* **22 B2** 10 38N 103 30 E
Komsomolets I., *Russia* **18 A11** 80 30N 95 0 E
Komsomolsk, *Russia* **18 D15** 50 30N 137 0 E
Konin, *Poland* **11 B10** 52 12N 18 15 E
Konya, *Turkey* **15 G5** 37 52N 32 35 E
Korce, *Albania* **13 D9** 40 37N 20 50 E
Korea, North ■, *Asia* **21 C7** 40 0N 127 0 E
Korea, South ■, *Asia* **21 C7** 36 0N 128 0 E
Korea Strait, *Asia* **21 C7** 34 0N 129 30 E
Kōriyama, *Japan* **19 A7** 37 24N 140 23 E
Korla, *China* **20 B3** 41 45N 86 4 E
Körös →, *Hungary* **11 E11** 46 43N 20 12 E
Kortrijk, *Belgium* **10 C2** 50 50N 3 17 E
Kos, *Greece* **13 F12** 36 50N 27 15 E
Košice, *Slovak Rep.* **11 D11** 48 42N 21 15 E
Kosovo □, *Serbia, Yug.* **13 C9** 42 30N 21 0 E
Kosti, *Sudan* **29 F11** 13 8N 32 43 E
Kostroma, *Russia* **14 C7** 57 50N 40 58 E
Koszalin, *Poland* **10 A9** 54 11N 16 8 E
Kota, *India* **23 G5** 25 14N 75 49 E
Kota Baharu, *Malaysia* **22 C2** 6 7N 102 14 E
Kota Kinabalu, *Malaysia* **22 C3** 6 0N 116 4 E
Kotka, *Finland* **6 F13** 60 28N 26 58 E
Kotri, *Pakistan* **23 G2** 25 22N 68 22 E
Kotuy →, *Russia* **18 B12** 71 54N 102 6 E
Kounradskiy, *Kazakhstan* **18 E9** 46 59N 75 0 E
Kra, Isthmus of, *Thailand* **22 B1** 10 15N 99 30 E
Kragujevac, *Serbia, Yug.* **13 B9** 44 2N 20 56 E
Krajina, *Bos.-H.* **12 B7** 44 45N 16 35 E
Kraków, *Poland* **11 C10** 50 4N 19 57 E
Krasnodar, *Russia* **15 E6** 45 5N 39 0 E
Krasnoturinsk, *Russia* **14 C11** 59 46N 60 12 E
Krasnovodsk, *Turkmenistan* **15 F9** 40 5N 53 5 E
Krasnoyarsk, *Russia* **18 D11** 56 8N 93 0 E
Kratie, *Cambodia* **22 B2** 12 32N 106 10 E
Krefeld, *Germany* **10 C4** 51 20N 6 33 E
Kremenchug, *Ukraine* **15 E5** 49 5N 33 25 E
Krishna →, *India* **25 D7** 15 57N 80 59 E
Krishnanagar, *India* **23 H12** 23 24N 88 33 E
Kristiansand, *Norway* **6 G9** 58 8N 8 1 E
Kristiansund, *Norway* **6 F9** 63 7N 7 45 E
Krivoy Rog, *Ukraine* **15 E5** 47 51N 33 20 E
Kroonstad, *S. Africa* **31 B4** 27 43S 27 19 E
Krosno, *Poland* **11 D11** 49 42N 21 46 E
Kruger Nat. Park, *S. Africa* **31 A5** 23 30S 31 40 E
Krugersdorp, *S. Africa* **31 B4** 26 5S 27 46 E
Kruisfontein, *S. Africa* **31 C3** 33 59S 24 43 E
Kruševac, *Serbia, Yug.* **13 C9** 43 35N 21 28 E
Kuala Lumpur, *Malaysia* **22 C2** 3 9N 101 41 E
Kuala Terengganu, *Malaysia* **22 C2** 5 20N 103 8 E
Kualakapuas, *Indonesia* **22 D3** 2 55S 114 20 E
Kucing, *Malaysia* **22 C3** 1 33N 110 25 E
Kudat, *Malaysia* **22 C3** 6 55N 116 55 E
Kumanovo, *Macedonia* **13 C9** 42 9N 21 42 E
Kumasi, *Ghana* **30 C1** 6 41N 1 38W
Kumayri = Gyumri, *Armenia* **15 F7** 40 47N 43 50 E
Kumbakonam, *India* **25 D6** 10 58N 79 25 E
Kunlun Shan, *Asia* **20 C3** 36 0N 86 30 E
Kunming, *China* **20 D5** 25 1N 102 41 E
Kuopio, *Finland* **6 F13** 62 53N 27 35 E
Kupang, *Indonesia* **22 E4** 10 19S 123 39 E
Kür →, *Azerbaijan* **15 G8** 39 29N 49 15 E
Kurashiki, *Japan* **19 B3** 34 40N 133 50 E
Kurdistan, *Asia* **24 B3** 37 20N 43 30 E
Kure, *Japan* **19 B3** 34 14N 132 32 E

Queenstown   Saskatchewan

119
Tabas Vännäs

T

Tabas, *Iran* 24 B4 33 35N 56 55 E
Tablas, *Phil.* 22 B4 12 25N 122 2 E
Table Mt., *S. Africa* 31 C2 34 0S 18 22 E
Tabora, *Tanzania* 32 F6 5 2S 32 50 E
Tabriz, *Iran* 24 B3 38 7N 46 20 E
Tacloban, *Phil.* 22 B4 11 15N 124 58 E
Tacna, *Peru* 46 D2 18 0S 70 20W
Tacoma, *U.S.A.* 40 A2 47 14N 122 26W
Tacuarembó, *Uruguay* 47 F4 31 45S 56 0W
Tadzhikistan ■ = Tajikistan ■, *Asia* 18 F8 38 30N 70 0 E
Taegu, *S. Korea* 21 C7 35 50N 128 37 E
Taejon, *S. Korea* 21 C7 36 20N 127 28 E
Taganrog, *Russia* 15 E6 47 12N 38 50 E
Tagus →, *Europe* 9 C1 38 40N 9 24W
Tahiti, *Pac. Oc.* 37 J13 17 37S 149 27W
Taibei, *Taiwan* 21 D7 25 4N 121 29 E
Taichung, *Taiwan* 21 D7 24 12N 120 35 E
Taimyr Peninsula, *Russia* 18 B11 75 0N 100 0 E
Tainan, *Taiwan* 21 D7 23 17N 120 18 E
Taiping, *Malaysia* 22 C2 4 51N 100 44 E
Taiwan ■, *Asia* 21 D7 23 30N 121 0 E
Taiyuan, *China* 21 C6 37 52N 112 33 E
Ta'izz, *Yemen* 24 D3 13 35N 44 2 E
Tajikistan ■, *Asia* 18 F8 38 30N 70 0 E
Tak, *Thailand* 22 B1 16 52N 99 8 E
Takamatsu, *Japan* 19 B4 34 20N 134 5 E
Takaoka, *Japan* 19 A5 36 47N 137 0 E
Takasaki, *Japan* 19 A6 36 20N 139 0 E
Takla Makan, *China* 20 C3 38 0N 83 0 E
Talaud Is., *Indonesia* 22 C4 4 30N 127 10 E
Talca, *Chile* 47 F2 35 28S 71 40W
Talcahuano, *Chile* 47 F2 36 40S 73 10W
Tallahassee, *U.S.A.* 41 D10 30 27N 84 17W
Tallinn, *Estonia* 14 C3 59 22N 24 48 E
Tamale, *Ghana* 30 C1 9 22N 0 50W
Tambov, *Russia* 14 D7 52 45N 41 28 E
Tamil Nadu □, *India* 25 D6 11 0N 77 0 E
Tamo Abu Ra., *Malaysia* 22 C3 3 10N 115 5 E
Tampa, *U.S.A.* 41 E10 27 57N 82 27W
Tampere, *Finland* 6 F12 61 30N 23 50 E
Tampico, *Mexico* 44 C5 22 20N 97 50W
Tamworth, *Australia* 34 G9 31 7S 150 58 E
Tana →, *Norway* 6 D13 70 30N 28 14 E
Tana, L., *Ethiopia* 29 F12 13 5N 37 30 E
Tanami Desert, *Australia* 34 D5 18 50S 132 0 E
Tananarive = Antananarivo, *Madag.* 33 H9 18 55S 47 31 E
Tando Adam, *Pakistan* 23 G2 25 45N 68 40 E
Tanga, *Tanzania* 32 F7 5 5S 39 2 E
Tanganyika, L., *Africa* 32 F6 6 40S 30 0 E
Tangier, *Morocco* 28 A3 35 50N 5 49W
Tangshan, *China* 21 C6 39 38N 118 10 E
Tanimbar Is., *Indonesia* 22 D5 7 30S 131 30 E
Tanjungbalai, *Indonesia* 22 C1 2 55N 99 44 E
Tanzania ■, *Africa* 32 F6 6 0S 34 0 E
Tapajós →, *Brazil* 46 C4 2 24S 54 41W
Tapi →, *India* 23 J4 21 8N 72 41 E
Tappahannock, *U.S.A.* 42 G9 37 56N 76 52W
Tarābulus, *Lebanon* 24 B2 34 31N 35 50 E
Tarābulus, *Libya* 29 B7 32 49N 13 7 E
Tarakan, *Indonesia* 22 C3 3 20N 117 35 E
Táranto, *Italy* 12 D7 40 28N 17 14 E
Táranto, G. di, *Italy* 12 D7 40 8N 17 20 E
Tarbagatai Ra., *Kazakhstan* 18 E10 48 0N 83 0 E
Tarbes, *France* 8 E4 43 15N 0 3 E
Tarim Basin, *China* 20 B3 40 0N 84 0 E
Tarkastad, *S. Africa* 31 C4 32 0S 26 16 E
Tarn →, *France* 8 E4 44 5N 1 6 E
Tarnów, *Poland* 11 C11 50 3N 21 0 E
Tarragona, *Spain* 9 B6 41 5N 1 17 E
Tarrasa, *Spain* 9 B7 41 34N 2 1 E
Tashkent, *Uzbekistan* 18 E8 41 20N 69 10 E
Tasman Sea, *Pac. Oc.* 36 L8 36 0S 160 0 E
Tasmania □, *Australia* 34 J8 42 0S 146 30 E
Tatarsk, *Russia* 18 D9 55 14N 76 0 E
Tatarstan □, *Russia* 14 C9 55 30N 51 30 E
Tatra, *Slovak Rep.* 11 D11 49 20N 20 0 E
Tatta, *Pakistan* 23 G1 24 42N 67 55 E
Tauern, *Austria* 10 E7 47 15N 12 40 E
Taung, *S. Africa* 31 B3 27 33S 24 47 E
Taunton, *U.S.A.* 43 E12 41 54N 71 6W
Taunus, *Germany* 10 C5 50 13N 8 34 E
Taurus Mts., *Turkey* 15 G5 37 0N 32 30 E
Tawas City, *U.S.A.* 42 C6 44 16N 83 31W
Tawau, *Malaysia* 22 C3 4 20N 117 55 E
Tbilisi, *Georgia* 15 F7 41 43N 44 50 E
Tchad, L., *Chad* 29 F7 13 30N 14 30 E
Tebingtinggi, *Indonesia* 22 C1 3 20N 99 9 E
Tegal, *Indonesia* 22 D2 6 52S 109 8 E
Tegucigalpa, *Honduras* 44 E7 14 5N 87 14W
Tehran, *Iran* 24 B4 35 44N 51 30 E
Tehuantepec, Gulf of, *Mexico* 44 D5 15 50N 95 12W
Tehuantepec, Isthmus of, *Mexico* 44 D6 17 0N 94 30W
Tel Aviv-Jaffa, *Israel* 24 B2 32 4N 34 48 E
Tell City, *U.S.A.* 42 G4 37 57N 86 46W
Telukbutun, *Indonesia* 22 C2 4 13N 108 12 E
Tema, *Ghana* 30 C2 5 41N 0 0 E
Temba, *S. Africa* 31 B4 25 20S 28 17 E
Témiscaming, *Canada* 42 B8 46 44N 79 5W
Tenerife, *Canary Is.* 28 C1 28 15N 16 35W
Tennessee □, *U.S.A.* 41 C9 36 0N 86 30W
Tennessee →, *U.S.A.* 41 C9 37 4N 88 34W
Tepic, *Mexico* 44 C4 21 30N 104 54W
Téramo, *Italy* 12 C5 42 39N 13 42 E
Teresina, *Brazil* 46 C5 5 9S 42 45W
Ternate, *Indonesia* 22 C4 0 45N 127 25 E
Terni, *Italy* 12 C5 42 34N 12 37 E
Ternopol, *Ukraine* 11 D13 49 30N 25 40 E
Terre Haute, *U.S.A.* 42 F4 39 28N 87 25W
Teruel, *Spain* 9 B5 40 22N 1 8W
Tetouan, *Morocco* 28 A3 35 35N 5 21W
Tetovo, *Macedonia* 13 C9 42 1N 21 2 E
Teutoburger Wald, *Germany* 10 B5 52 5N 8 22 E
Texas □, *U.S.A.* 40 D7 31 40N 98 30W
Texel, *Neths.* 10 B3 53 5N 4 50 E
Tezpur, *India* 23 F14 26 40N 92 45 E
Thabana Ntlenyana, *Lesotho* 31 B4 29 30S 29 16 E
Thabazimbi, *S. Africa* 31 A4 24 40S 27 21 E
Thailand ■, *Asia* 22 B2 16 0N 102 0 E
Thailand, G. of, *Asia* 22 B2 11 30N 101 0 E
Thal, *Pakistan* 23 C3 33 28N 70 33 E
Thal Desert, *Pakistan* 23 D3 31 10N 71 30 E
Thames →, *Canada* 42 D6 42 20N 82 25W
Thames →, *U.K.* 7 F7 51 29N 0 34 E
Thane, *India* 23 K4 19 12N 72 59 E
Thar Desert, *India* 23 E4 28 0N 72 0 E
The Hague, *Neths.* 10 B3 52 7N 4 17 E
The Pas, *Canada* 38 C9 53 45N 101 15W
Thessalon, *Canada* 42 B6 46 20N 83 30W
Thessaloníki, *Greece* 13 D10 40 38N 22 58 E
Thessaloníki, Gulf of, *Greece* 13 D10 40 15N 22 45 E
Thetford Mines, *Canada* 43 B12 46 8N 71 18W
Thiers, *France* 8 D5 45 52N 3 33 E
Thies, *Senegal* 28 F1 14 50N 16 51W
Thimphu, *Bhutan* 23 F12 27 31N 89 45 E
Thionville, *France* 8 B7 49 20N 6 10 E
Thunder B., *U.S.A.* 42 C6 45 0N 83 20W
Thunder Bay, *Canada* 42 A3 48 20N 89 15W
Thüringer Wald, *Germany* 10 C6 50 35N 11 0 E
Tian Shan, *China* 20 B3 43 0N 84 0 E
Tianjin, *China* 21 C6 39 8N 117 10 E
Tianshui, *China* 20 C5 34 32N 105 40 E
Tiber →, *Italy* 12 D5 41 44N 12 14 E
Tibesti, *Chad* 29 D8 21 0N 17 30 E
Tibet □, *China* 20 C3 32 0N 88 0 E
Ticino →, *Italy* 12 B3 45 9N 9 14 E
Ticonderoga, *U.S.A.* 43 D11 43 51N 73 26W
Tierra del Fuego, *Argentina* 47 H3 54 0S 69 0W
Tiffin, *U.S.A.* 42 E6 41 7N 83 11W
Tignish, *Canada* 43 B15 46 58N 64 2W
Tigris →, *Asia* 24 B3 31 0N 47 25 E
Tijuana, *Mexico* 44 A1 32 30N 117 10W
Tiksi, *Russia* 18 B14 71 40N 128 45 E
Tilburg, *Neths.* 10 C3 51 31N 5 6 E
Timaru, *N.Z.* 35 J13 44 23S 171 14 E
Timişoara, *Romania* 11 F11 45 43N 21 15 E
Timmins, *Canada* 42 A7 48 28N 81 25W
Timor, *Indonesia* 22 D4 9 0S 125 0 E
Tinaca Pt., *Phil.* 22 C4 5 30N 125 25 E
Tirana, *Albania* 13 D8 41 18N 19 49 E
Tiraspol, *Moldova* 11 E15 46 55N 29 35 E
Tîrgovişte, *Romania* 11 F13 44 55N 25 27 E
Tîrgu-Jiu, *Romania* 11 F12 45 5N 23 19 E
Tîrgu Mureş, *Romania* 11 E13 46 31N 24 38 E
Tirich Mir, *Pakistan* 23 A3 36 15N 71 55 E
Tirol □, *Austria* 10 E6 47 3N 10 43 E
Tiruchchirappalli, *India* 25 D6 10 45N 78 45 E
Tirunelveli, *India* 25 E6 8 45N 77 45 E
Tisa →, *Serbia, Yug.* 13 B9 45 15N 20 17 E
Titicaca, L., *S. Amer.* 46 D3 15 30S 69 30W
Titusville, *U.S.A.* 42 E8 41 38N 79 41W
Tizi-Ouzou, *Algeria* 28 A5 36 42N 4 3 E
Toamasina, *Madag.* 33 H9 18 10S 49 25 E
Toba Kakar, *Pakistan* 23 D2 31 30N 69 0 E
Tobago, *W. Indies* 44 R21 11 10N 60 30W
Tobermory, *Canada* 42 C7 45 12N 81 40W
Tocantins →, *Brazil* 46 C5 1 45S 49 10W
Togliatti, *Russia* 14 D8 53 32N 49 24 E
Togo ■, *W. Afr.* 30 C2 8 30N 1 35 E
Tokelau Is., *Pac. Oc.* 35 B16 9 0S 171 45W
Tōkyō, *Japan* 19 B6 35 45N 139 45 E
Toledo, *Spain* 9 C3 39 50N 4 2W
Toledo, *U.S.A.* 42 E6 41 39N 83 33W
Toliara, *Madag.* 33 J8 23 21S 43 40 E
Toluca, *Mexico* 44 D5 19 20N 99 40W
Tomaszów Mazowiecki, *Poland* 11 C10 51 30N 19 57 E
Tombouctou, *Mali* 30 A1 16 50N 3 0W
Tomini, G. of, *Indonesia* 22 D4 0 10S 122 0 E
Tomsk, *Russia* 18 D10 56 30N 85 5 E
Tonga ■, *Pac. Oc.* 35 D16 19 50S 174 30W
Tonga Trench, *Pac. Oc.* 35 E16 18 0S 173 0W
Tongaat, *S. Africa* 31 B5 29 33S 31 9 E
Tongking, G. of, *Asia* 20 E5 20 0N 108 0 E
Tonk, *India* 23 F5 26 6N 75 54 E
Tonlé Sap, *Cambodia* 22 B2 13 0N 104 0 E
Toowoomba, *Australia* 34 F9 27 32S 151 56 E
Topeka, *U.S.A.* 41 C7 39 3N 95 40W
Torne →, *Sweden* 6 E12 65 50N 24 12 E
Torne, L., *Sweden* 6 E11 68 24N 19 15 E
Tornio, *Finland* 6 E12 65 50N 24 12 E
Toronto, *Canada* 42 D8 43 39N 79 20W
Torre del Greco, *Italy* 12 D6 40 47N 14 22 E
Torreón, *Mexico* 44 B4 25 33N 103 26W
Tortosa, *Spain* 9 B6 40 49N 0 31 E
Toruń, *Poland* 11 B10 53 2N 18 39 E
Toscana □, *Italy* 12 C4 43 25N 11 0 E
Toteng, *Botswana* 31 A3 20 22S 22 58 E
Toul, *France* 8 B6 48 40N 5 53 E
Toulon, *France* 8 E6 43 10N 5 55 E
Toulouse, *France* 8 E4 43 37N 1 27 E
Touraine, *France* 8 C4 47 20N 0 30 E
Tournai, *Belgium* 10 C2 50 35N 3 25 E
Tournon, *France* 8 D6 45 4N 4 50 E
Tours, *France* 8 C4 47 22N 0 40 E
Touwsrivier, *S. Africa* 31 C3 33 20S 20 2 E
Towanda, *U.S.A.* 42 E9 41 46N 76 27W
Townsville, *Australia* 34 D8 19 15S 146 45 E
Towson, *U.S.A.* 42 F9 39 24N 76 36W
Toyama, *Japan* 19 A5 36 40N 137 15 E
Toyohashi, *Japan* 19 B5 34 45N 137 25 E
Trabzon, *Turkey* 15 F6 41 0N 39 45 E
Trafalgar, C., *Spain* 9 D2 36 10N 6 2W
Trail, *Canada* 38 D8 49 5N 117 40W
Trang, *Thailand* 22 C1 7 33N 99 38 E
Trangan, *Indonesia* 22 D5 6 40S 134 20 E
Transantarctic Mts., *Antarctica* 48 F16 85 0S 170 0W
Transylvania, *Romania* 11 E12 45 19N 25 0 E
Transylvanian Alps, *Romania* 11 F13 45 30N 25 0 E
Trápani, *Italy* 12 E5 38 1N 12 29 E
Traverse City, *U.S.A.* 42 C5 44 46N 85 38W
Trento, *Italy* 12 A4 46 4N 11 8 E
Trenton, *Canada* 42 C9 44 10N 77 34W
Trenton, *U.S.A.* 43 E10 40 14N 74 46W
Trier, *Germany* 10 D4 49 45N 6 38 E
Trieste, *Italy* 12 B5 45 40N 13 46 E
Trincomalee, *Sri Lanka* 25 E7 8 38N 81 15 E
Trinidad & Tobago ■, *W. Indies* 44 S20 10 30N 61 20W
Tripura □, *India* 23 H13 24 0N 92 0 E
Trivandrum, *India* 25 E6 8 41N 77 0 E
Trnava, *Slovak Rep.* 11 D9 48 23N 17 35 E
Trois-Rivières, *Canada* 43 B11 46 25N 72 34W
Trollhättan, *Sweden* 6 G10 58 17N 12 20 E
Trondheim, *Norway* 6 F10 63 36N 10 25 E
Trondheim Fjord, *Norway* 6 F10 63 35N 10 30 E
Troy, *N.Y., U.S.A.* 43 D11 42 44N 73 41W
Troy, *Ohio, U.S.A.* 42 E5 40 2N 84 12W
Troyes, *France* 8 B6 48 19N 4 3 E
Trujillo, *Peru* 46 C2 8 6S 79 0W
Truk, *Pac. Oc.* 36 G7 7 25N 151 46 E
Truro, *Canada* 43 C16 45 21N 63 14W
Tsau, *Botswana* 31 A3 20 8S 22 22 E
Tshabong, *Botswana* 31 B3 26 2S 22 29 E
Tshane, *Botswana* 31 A3 24 5S 21 54 E
Tshwane, *Botswana* 31 A3 22 24S 22 1 E
Tsimlyansk Res., *Russia* 15 E7 48 0N 43 0 E
Tsu, *Japan* 19 B5 34 45N 136 25 E
Tsumis, *Namibia* 31 A2 23 39S 17 29 E
Tuamotu Arch., *Pac. Oc.* 37 J13 17 0S 144 0W
Tubuai Is., *Pac. Oc.* 37 K12 25 0S 150 0W
Tucson, *U.S.A.* 40 D4 32 13N 110 58W
Tugela →, *S. Africa* 31 B5 29 14S 31 30 E
Tula, *Russia* 14 D6 54 13N 37 38 E
Tulcea, *Romania* 11 F15 45 13N 28 46 E
Tulle, *France* 8 D4 45 16N 1 46 E
Tulsa, *U.S.A.* 41 C7 36 10N 95 55W
Tunis, *Tunisia* 28 A7 36 50N 10 11 E
Tunisia ■, *Africa* 28 B6 33 30N 9 10 E
Tunja, *Colombia* 46 B2 5 33N 73 25W
Tura, *India* 23 G13 25 30N 90 16 E
Turabah, *Si. Arabia* 24 C3 28 20N 43 15 E
Turin, *Italy* 12 B2 45 3N 7 40 E
Turkana, L., *Africa* 32 D7 3 30N 36 5 E
Turkey ■, *Eurasia* 15 G6 39 0N 36 0 E
Turkmenistan ■, *Asia* 18 F7 39 0N 59 0 E
Turks & Caicos Is. ■, *W. Indies* 45 C10 21 20N 71 20W
Turku, *Finland* 6 F12 60 30N 22 19 E
Tuscany = Toscana □, *Italy* 12 C4 43 25N 11 0 E
Tuticorin, *India* 25 E6 8 50N 78 12 E
Tuvalu ■, *Pac. Oc.* 35 B14 8 0S 178 0 E
Tuxtla Gutiérrez, *Mexico* 44 D6 16 50N 93 10W
Tuz Gölü, *Turkey* 15 G5 38 42N 33 18 E
Tuzla, *Bos.-H.* 13 B8 44 34N 18 41 E
Tver, *Russia* 14 C6 56 55N 35 55 E
Two Rivers, *U.S.A.* 42 C4 44 9N 87 34W
Tychy, *Poland* 11 C10 50 9N 18 59 E
Tyrol □ = Tirol □, *Austria* 10 E6 47 3N 10 43 E
Tyrrhenian Sea, *Medit. S.* 12 E5 40 0N 12 30 E
Tyumen, *Russia* 18 D8 57 11N 65 29 E
Tzaneen, *S. Africa* 31 A5 23 47S 30 9 E

U

U.S.A. ■ = United States of America ■, *N. Amer.* 40 C7 37 0N 96 0W
Ubangi → = Oubangi →, *Zaïre* 32 E3 0 30S 17 50 E
Ube, *Japan* 19 C2 33 56N 131 15 E
Uberaba, *Brazil* 46 D5 19 50S 47 55W
Uberlândia, *Brazil* 46 D5 19 0S 48 20W
Ucayali →, *Peru* 46 C2 4 30S 73 30W
Udaipur, *India* 23 G4 24 36N 73 44 E
Udaipur Garhi, *Nepal* 23 F11 27 0N 86 35 E
Údine, *Italy* 12 A5 46 3N 13 14 E
Udmurtia □, *Russia* 14 C9 57 30N 52 30 E
Udon Thani, *Thailand* 22 B2 17 29N 102 46 E
Ufa, *Russia* 14 D10 54 45N 55 55 E
Uganda ■, *Africa* 32 D6 2 0N 32 0 E
Uitenhage, *S. Africa* 31 C4 33 40S 25 28 E
Ujjain, *India* 23 H5 23 9N 75 43 E
Ujung Pandang, *Indonesia* 22 D3 5 10S 119 20 E
Ukraine ■, *Europe* 15 E5 49 0N 32 0 E
Ulan Bator, *Mongolia* 20 B5 47 55N 106 53 E
Ulan Ude, *Russia* 18 D12 51 45N 107 40 E
Ulhasnagar, *India* 23 K4 19 15N 73 10 E
Ulm, *Germany* 10 D5 48 23N 9 58 E
Ulyasutay, *Mongolia* 20 B4 47 56N 97 28 E
Ume →, *Sweden* 6 F12 63 45N 20 20 E
Umeå, *Sweden* 6 F12 63 45N 20 20 E
Umtata, *S. Africa* 31 C4 31 36S 28 49 E
Umzimvubu, *S. Africa* 31 C4 31 38S 29 33 E
Umzinto, *S. Africa* 31 C5 30 15S 30 45 E
Ungava B., *Canada* 39 C13 59 30N 67 30W
Ungava Pen., *Canada* 39 C12 60 0N 74 0W
Uniontown, *U.S.A.* 42 F8 39 54N 79 44W
United Arab Emirates ■, *Asia* 24 C4 23 50N 54 0 E
United Kingdom ■, *Europe* 7 E6 53 0N 2 0W
United States of America ■, *N. Amer.* 40 C7 37 0N 96 0W
Upington, *S. Africa* 31 B3 28 25S 21 15 E
Uppsala, *Sweden* 6 G11 59 53N 17 38 E
Ural →, *Kazakhstan* 15 E9 47 0N 51 48 E
Ural Mts., *Eurasia* 14 C10 60 0N 59 0 E
Uralsk, *Kazakhstan* 14 D9 51 20N 51 20 E
Uranium City, *Canada* 38 C9 59 34N 108 37W
Urbana, *Ill., U.S.A.* 42 E3 40 7N 88 12W
Urbana, *Ohio, U.S.A.* 42 E6 40 7N 83 45W
Urmia, L., *Iran* 24 B3 37 50N 45 30 E
Uruguay ■, *S. Amer.* 47 F4 32 30S 56 30W
Uruguay →, *S. Amer.* 47 F4 34 12S 58 18W
Ürümqi, *China* 20 B3 43 45N 87 45 E
Usakos, *Namibia* 31 A2 21 54S 15 31 E
Ushant, *France* 8 B1 48 28N 5 6W
Ust Urt Plateau, *Asia* 18 E7 44 0N 55 0 E
Ústí nad Labem, *Czech.* 10 C8 50 41N 14 3 E
Utah □, *U.S.A.* 40 C4 39 20N 111 30W
Utica, *U.S.A.* 43 D10 43 6N 75 14W
Utrecht, *Neths.* 10 B3 52 5N 5 8 E
Utsunomiya, *Japan* 19 A6 36 30N 139 50 E
Uttar Pradesh □, *India* 23 F8 27 0N 80 0 E
Uttaradit, *Thailand* 22 B2 17 36N 100 5 E
Uusikaupunki, *Finland* 6 F12 60 47N 21 25 E
Uzbekistan ■, *Asia* 18 E8 41 30N 65 0 E
Uzhhorod, *Ukraine* 11 D12 48 36N 22 18 E

V

Vaal →, *S. Africa* 31 B3 29 4S 23 38 E
Vaal Dam, *S. Africa* 31 B4 27 0S 28 14 E
Vaasa, *Finland* 6 F12 63 6N 21 38 E
Vadodara, *India* 23 H4 22 20N 73 10 E
Vadsø, *Norway* 6 D13 70 3N 29 50 E
Vaduz, *Liech.* 10 E5 47 8N 9 31 E
Váh →, *Slovak Rep.* 11 D9 47 43N 18 7 E
Val d'Or, *Canada* 42 A9 48 7N 77 47W
Valahia, *Romania* 11 F13 44 35N 25 0 E
Valdés, Pen., *Argentina* 47 E3 42 30S 63 45W
Valdez, *U.S.A.* 38 B5 61 7N 146 16W
Valdivia, *Chile* 47 F2 39 50S 73 14W
Valence, *France* 8 D6 44 57N 4 54 E
Valencia, *Spain* 9 C5 39 27N 0 23W
Valencia, *Venezuela* 46 A3 10 11N 68 0W
Valenciennes, *France* 8 A5 50 20N 3 34 E
Valladolid, *Spain* 9 B3 41 38N 4 43W
Valletta, *Malta* 12 G6 35 54N 14 31 E
Valparaíso, *Chile* 47 F2 33 2S 71 40W
Van, L., *Turkey* 15 G7 38 30N 43 0 E
Van Buren, *U.S.A.* 43 B13 47 10N 67 58W
Van Wert, *U.S.A.* 42 E5 40 52N 84 35W
Vancouver, *Canada* 38 D7 49 15N 123 10W
Vancouver I., *Canada* 38 D7 49 50N 126 0W
Vanderbijlpark, *S. Africa* 31 B4 26 42S 27 54 E
Vanderkloof Dam, *S. Africa* 31 C3 30 4S 24 40 E
Vänern, *Sweden* 6 G10 58 47N 13 30 E
Vännäs, *Sweden* 6 F11 63 58N 19 48 E

Vannes